NOT
WITHOUT
HONOR

NOT
WITHOUT
HONOR

*The History of
American
Anticommunism*

RICHARD GID POWERS

THE FREE PRESS

New York   London   Toronto   Sydney   Tokyo   Singapore

The Free Press
A Division of Simon & Schuster Inc.
1230 Avenue of the Americas
New York, NY 10020

Printed in the United States of America

printing number
2 3 4 5 6 7 8 9 10

Library of Congress Cataloging-in-Publication Data

Powers, Richard Gid
  Not without honor: the history of American anticommunism /
Richard Gid Powers.
      p.   cm.
  Includes bibliographical references (p.   ) and index.
    ISBN 0–684–82427–2
    1. United States —Politics and government—20th century.   2. Anti-communist movements—United States—History—20th century.
I. Title
E743.5P65   1995
335.4'0973—dc20   94–45953
                                                                                      CIP

For
Erwin Glikes

And they were offended in him. But Jesus said unto them,
"A prophet is not without honor,
save in his own country, and in his own house."

—Matt. 13:57

CONTENTS

PROLOGUE

On June 12, 1987, Ronald Reagan traveled to Berlin and, in a rare display of anger, shouted "Mr. Gorbachev, tear down this wall." More than a few Americans questioned whether their President was sounding an old and outmoded war cry inappropriate in the late twentieth century when relations with the Soviet Union had never been better, hopes for limits on nuclear weapons never brighter. But here was the President of the United States, an unrelenting anticommunist, stirring up hatreds best forgotten, provoking the Soviets with talk of Evil Empires and Star Wars.

To what purpose? To strike a dramatic pose for television news back home, to wrap himself in nostalgic memories of the Berlin Airlift and JFK's "Ich bin ein Berliner"? To distract the public from his arms-for-hostages deals with Iran and the illegal diversion of funds to his rag-tag anticommunist army in Nicaragua? Those alarmed by Reagan's anticommunist rhetoric had been appalled by the spectacle of the bemedaled Marine Colonel Oliver North facing down congressmen with attacks on their patriotism and by CIA director William Casey violating the law to pursue Reagan's crusade against communism in Central America. They viewed the President as a vestige of the anticommunist extremists who had been blocking peaceful relations with the Communist world since the beginning of the cold war; extremists like John Foster Dulles with his nerve-wracking strategy of brinkmanship, Barry Goldwater and his notion that extremism in pursuit of liberty was no vice, and General Curtis LeMay who threatened to bomb Communists back into the stone age. He was seen as part of a chain that stretched back to JFK and the Bay of

Pigs, the CIA's assassination plots against Castro, and ultimately, to Vietnam itself. Reagan's dramatic demand at the Berlin Wall rankled those who had written off anticommunism as the bitter heritage of earlier generations of anticommunists: Joe McCarthy's charges of treason against General George C. Marshall and spurious lists of spies and traitors, the John Birch Society's insane theory that President Eisenhower was a Communist, cars plastered with "Better Dead Than Red" bumper stickers, Red Scares, inquisitions, FBI files, and Hollywood blacklists. Reagan's challenge to the Soviets revived all those disturbing images. Many Americans feared his combative rhetoric threatened all that had been achieved to keep the peace in a world permanently divided between the Communist East and the noncommunist West.

Reagan's own image of himself stood in marked contrast to that drawn by his critics. He meant what he said when, shortly before leaving the White House, he declared: "I am proud to say I am still an anticommunist." From the beginning of his career in the 1940s, Reagan had self-consciously counted himself a member of an anticommunist movement, and his beliefs had drawn upon a well-defined tradition of American anticommunist doctrine. In his speech that called the Soviet Union an Evil Empire, he invoked the writings of Whittaker Chambers and the sentiments of thousands like Chambers who believed that the cold war was a moral struggle between good and evil.

At the Berlin Wall, Reagan was reaffirming his solidarity with a long line of anticommunists that stretched back to the earliest days of opposition to the Russian Revolution, men and women who had seen resistance to communism as a moral duty, and who felt obliged to oppose communism, halt its spread, liberate those living under it, and ultimately, destroy it. Although most Americans instinctively rejected communism, they did not feel compelled to actively struggle against it. Only a few Americans throughout the century felt the need, the passion, and the will to dedicate themselves totally to the fight against communism. Reagan was one of them.

By the late 1980s the convictions that had brought Reagan to the Berlin Wall were known to few except the anticommunists themselves, their original force tarnished and obscured by bitter memories of Joe McCarthy, the John Birch Society, and now Oliver North. To recover this anticommunist tradition we must peel away the accretions of time to encounter the first Americans drawn into that century-long struggle.

NOT
WITHOUT
HONOR

Chapter 1

LENIN AND WILSON

"*Sub specie aeternitatis* . . . It is certain that mankind must make up
its mind either for Wilson or for Lenin."
— Hermann Kesser, 1918[1]

November 7, 1917. From Petrograd, Russia, the news reached America
that an unheard-of group called "Bolsheviks" under Vladimir Lenin had
wrested power from the Social Democrats who had themselves toppled
the Tsar in March. In days, Americans were staggered by news that Russia's new rulers were breaking their military alliance with the United
States, taking Russia out of the war America had entered just that April.
The Communist era in world history had begun, and with it the history
of American anticommunism.

For as long as communism would survive, it would be a challenge to
America so profound as to force the nation repeatedly to recover, reevaluate, and sometimes even to reject the values that formed the core of
its character.

So it was at the beginning. Only after the war would the set of convictions called anticommunism begin to emerge, the belief that Americans had a moral duty to fight what Lenin had brought into the world.
But the immediate shock of the Communist Revolution compelled
other Americans to redefine their world views in response to this blow
to the ideas that had from time immemorial governed the lives of men
and nations.

President Wilson had to state in specific terms the kind of world he
hoped to create after the war. From this effort emerged the ideas of liberal internationalism that would direct America's approach to the world
to the present day. And far outside the circles of power, a segment of the
American left would redefine itself in terms of solidarity with Lenin's

1

revolution, drawing down on it the wrath of a public that regarded any questioning of the war effort as tantamount to treason.

Throughout the rest of its history, American anticommunism would have to contend with these two rivals to shape America's response to a world in which communism was a massive and, it seemed, permanent challenge to American values and to American power. And so in the immediate aftermath of Lenin's November revolution, even before anticommunism would organize itself into coherent form, the forces began to gather strength that would shape and challenge it for the rest of the century.

For three demoralizing years the exhausted troops of Britain, France, Italy, and Russia had been advancing and retreating, pounding away at the equally exhausted armies of the Central Powers—Germany, the Austro-Hungarian Empire, and Turkey. In November American troops had just arrived at the front lines in France, and at home the national mood rose and fell with each day's dispatches. In recent weeks the news had not been good. Over the summer the Austrians had broken through Allied lines into Italy. German U-boats were taking a heavy toll on Allied shipping, and the Eastern front had begun to crumble with the collapse of the Russian summer offensive.

In Russia, the provisional government had been losing strength since taking power in March. Its armies on the front were disintegrating, refusing to fight, and deserting in droves. In the capital of Petrograd, Premier Alexander Kerensky's government had been ceding authority to the workers' councils, the Soviets, dominated by the Bolshevik faction of antiwar revolutionary socialists. By then Kerensky's government actually governed little more than a few offices in the Winter Palace where he and his ministers went through the motions of drafting proclamations and issuing orders that no one obeyed. But Russia was still vital to American military strategy. Despite the weakness of the Russian army, it was still tying down 147 German divisions on the Eastern front. America's hopes of victory and the safety of its troops depended on Russia's holding the line.

Then, on November 7, 1917, the Bolshevik leader Vladimir Lenin, realizing that all power would fall to whichever political faction struck hardest, fastest, and most ruthlessly, sent his Red Guards to storm the

Winter Palace. The next day, November 8, Kerensky fled. The city and the government were in the hands of the Bolshevik Communists.

Peace for Russia, land for the peasants, and power to the Soviets— this had been the Bolsheviks' formula for victory. The day after their coup, their "Decree on Peace" declared the war to be a conspiracy by the international ruling class against the workers of the world. They demanded a "just and democratic" end to the war. Workers and soldiers of both sides should declare a cease fire and should insist on a new revolutionary international order that would put the means of production and the instruments of power in the hands of the working class. Lenin ordered Russian generals in the field to meet with the Germans to discuss the terms of an armistice.[2]

Though it would not be immediately apparent, Lenin's revolution— the next year the Bolsheviks would officially adopt the name of Communists—would reshape American politics. In the weeks that followed Lenin's seizure of power, however, Americans had no clear idea of the forces at work in Russia. The nature of the Communist Revolution, the political and economic ideas of the Communists, and Lenin's dreams of world revolution were of remote concern to Americans in November 1917. What mattered was whether the Bolsheviks would actually take Russia out of the war as they promised, and what would happen to American troops in France when Germany redeployed its armies from the Eastern front to the West.

Over the next few weeks American newspapers were filled with hopeful rumors that the Bolsheviks' days were numbered. According to these accounts, Kerensky was on his way back to Petrograd and Lenin's hold on power was slipping. By the end of November, however, members of the German general staff were negotiating an armistice with Bolshevik representatives at the front, while Trotsky humiliated the Allies by publishing their secret agreements to divide Germany and Austria after the war. Americans were now getting reports that the Russian infantry was abandoning the trenches. On December 2 Germany announced it had reached an agreement with Russia on terms for an armistice. Americans had to face the bitter truth: Russia was really out of the war, and its defection had eliminated Germany's second front. The Bolsheviks' seizure of power had given the Germans a strategic victory that might decide the war.

Americans felt a particular sense of betrayal over Russia's defection because they might never have entered the war had it not been for Russia. By the end of 1916 President Wilson had become convinced that Germany was on the verge of a victory that would threaten America's security and prosperity, but he had hesitated to join an alliance that included Tsar Nicholas II, the most autocratic ruler in Europe. After the first Russian revolution of March 1917 had toppled the Tsar and installed a liberal democratic government in Petrograd, however, Wilson could finally tell Americans they would be fighting to make the world safe for democracy. All the allies, Wilson could say, Russia no less than the rest, were fit partners for a "League of Honor." Now, by defecting from the Alliance, Russia had become "the Judas of the nations." The Bolsheviks were "escaped murderers . . . hysterical, criminal, and impatient socialist fanatics."[3]

Communism, which America would battle for the rest of the century, had crashed into the national consciousness like the crack of doom. Whether Lenin and the Bolsheviks were the German agents they were labeled by the Allied press (and they were not), Americans' first impression of communism was that it had sold out the Allies to the Germans. The Communist Revolution had put America in danger at a moment when the nation's very survival hung in the balance, and when any shift in the military situation might mean sudden and final disaster. Without yet knowing anything about communism or the character of the Russian Communists, America's immediate and visceral reaction against communism was the spontaneous response of a people suddenly forced to look into the abyss of military defeat and national ruin.

It was President Wilson who first had to cope with the immediate consequences of Russia's defection and Lenin's challenge to Wilson's moral justification for the war. Out of his attempts to impose order on the chaos into which Lenin's revolution had thrown his war strategy would emerge the broad outlines of American foreign policy for the rest of the century.

Wilson had to act immediately to deal with the Bolshevik Revolution's very real impact on his military strategy. He had to rush more men and supplies to France to prepare for the enemy offensive that could be expected once Germany shifted troops from the Russian front. He had to evaluate pleas from Britain and France to join a military effort to topple the Bolsheviks and drag Russia back into the alliance. Just as urgently, he had to arrive at a principled and convincing response to the Bolsheviks' challenge to his ideological and moral rationale for continuing the war.

The Bolsheviks' Decree on Peace forced Wilson to set down in concrete terms the goals of the American war effort. This he did in his Fourteen Points address of January 8, 1918, directed to the war-wearied peoples of the world who might be swayed by the Bolshevik leader's call for a new revolutionary world order to eliminate the causes of imperialist conflagrations like the great war.[4]

In the Fourteen Points, Wilson asked the Russian people, whose Bolshevik leaders were even then negotiating peace terms with the Germans at Brest-Litovsk, to compare Germany's territorial demands with the Fourteen Points' "principle of justice to all peoples and nationalities, and their right to live on equal terms of liberty and safety with one another, whether they be strong or weak." He told Russia that its hopes for "liberty and ordered peace" could be fulfilled only if the Allies won the war; only then "the world [would] be made fit and safe . . . for every peace-loving nation which . . . wishes to live its own life, determine its own institutions, be assured of justice and fair dealing by the other peoples of the world as against force and selfish aggression."[5]

Wilson's response to the immediate challenge of Lenin's Decree on Peace transcended the international situation of January 1918 to formulate the goals pursued by American leaders for the rest of the century: a world order governed by "the reign of law, based upon the consent of the governed and sustained by the organized opinion of mankind."[6] This doctrine, liberal internationalism, was defined in response to the Communist challenge, but it was not simply a response to that challenge. Wilson's internationalism projected American values onto the world, and in his mind, what could have been more natural, more appropriate? As America was being drawn irresistibly into the international arena, what should guide it except American values? Communism was simply an impediment, although at the moment a mortally dangerous impediment, to the realization of the Wilsonian dream. While anticommunists would focus their attention, sometimes obsessively, on the evils of communism and its threat to America and the world, Wilson and all later internationalists would keep their eye on their goal of a liberal world order, not on obstacles like communism that temporarily blocked the path toward a destiny they believed was foreordained and inevitable.

Wilson's liberal internationalists believed that America's experience in organizing "diverse sections and a hundred million people into a federal system" would one day "provide a structure for a world organization," a goal that could be realized only through American leadership and idealism. All nations, Wilson said, "should with one accord adopt the doctrine of President Monroe as the doctrine of the world. . . . These are American principles, American policies. We could stand for no others. And they are also the principles and policies of forward looking men and women everywhere, of every modern nation, of every enlightened community. They are the principles of mankind and must prevail."[7]

Wilsonian internationalism was formulated in response to communism, but it was not simply anticommunism.[8] It was that optimistic strain of American idealism so characteristic of the culturally dominant Protestant professional upper-middle class, who, like Wilson, merged their religious faith and their patriotism into a confident Americanism that did not doubt that in the long run an idealized version of American values would prevail over doomed alternatives like communism. This was eloquently stated by Wilson in his League of Nations proposal to the Senate: "The stage is set, the destiny disclosed. It has come about by no plan of our conceiving, but by the hand of God who led us into this way. We cannot turn back. We can only go forward, with lifted eyes and freshened spirit, to follow the vision. It was of this that we dreamed at our birth. America shall in truth show the way. The light streams upon the path ahead, and nowhere else."[9]

American radicalism, too, was profoundly changed by the news from Petrograd. Prewar American radicalism had been forged in the bitter industrial conflicts of the late nineteenth and early twentieth century when industrialists adamantly refused to recognize the right of their workers to organize, and the government and the courts conspired with management to frustrate efforts to secure workers' rights. To make matters worse, the craft unions of the conservative American Federation of Labor, the only successful labor organization, had abandoned the mass of unskilled laborers, opening the door to radical unions like the Industrial Workers of the World (IWW), seen by middle-class Americans as the flag-bearers of revolution.[10]

The prewar radical community included middle-class reformers, pacifists, socialists, anarchists, and violent revolutionaries pulled together into an unstable coalition by the labor wars of the previous three decades. The heroes of the radical movement—Eugene Debs, Big Bill Haywood, Alexander Berkman, and Emma Goldman—had become legends as fearless defenders of labor in the face of ruthless repression.

At the center of the American radical movement was the Socialist Party. Founded in 1901 by rail unionist Eugene V. Debs and by Morris Hillquit, a veteran of Daniel De Leon's older Socialist Labor Party, it provided a common meeting ground for reformers and revolutionaries otherwise divided by fundamental disagreements about the nature of American society and the best strategy for fighting injustices.[11] Gathered around the Socialist Party, if not within it, were Socialist-minded Protestant ministers, radical rabbis, and Catholic priests trying to apply the church's teachings on social justice. The radical movement included progressive Republicans like Senator Robert La Follette of Wisconsin and Socialists like Kate Richards O'Hare, William Bross Lloyd, and William English Walling. The Socialist Party provided lines of communication between them and revolutionaries like Emma Goldman, Alexander Berkman, and the Wobblies of the IWW. These revolutionaries in turn had ties to violent bands of Italian anarchists who preached the "propaganda of the deed" (dynamite). All these radicals were given moral and sometimes financial support by establishment progressives who shared their commitment to the labor union movement, if not their revolutionary ideology. After the European war broke out in 1914, these radicals were a valued part of an antiwar movement that included reformers, socialists, progressives—even Woodrow Wilson himself, who ran for reelection in 1916 on the slogan, "He kept us out of war."

But entry into the war cut American radicals off from the political mainstream. The American Socialist Party had condemned the European conflict as a private feud between international capitalists, imperialists, and militarists. The day after America joined the war, while a wave of patriotic war enthusiasm was sweeping the country, the Socialist Party assembled in St. Louis to brand the war "a crime against the people of the United States and against the nations of the world."[12] This split the party, and drove many "War Socialists" out to join the war effort.

With the nation at war and public opinion mobilized against the enemy, the radicals' stand against the war isolated them. Their former allies in the reform movement now used every legal weapon—which now included new wartime loyalty laws—to punish their former comrades.

Radicals were called slackers, traitors, and pro-German, and were overwhelmed by an unprecedented wave of popular hatred and government persecution. Soon the most famous radicals in the country were on their way to prison.

Then came the news out of Russia, sending an electrifying shock of hope through radical America. While the rest of the country raged against the Bolsheviks for leaving the Alliance, radicals hailed Lenin's Decree on Peace. American radicals saw in Bolshevik Russia a powerful ally that might shift the balance of power in the war against the ruling class. In their enthusiasm for the Bolsheviks, native-born American radicals were joined by immigrants from Eastern Europe—Russians, Poles, Finns, and Latvians—some of whom had joined the Socialist Party's Language Federations. To these refugees from the Tsar's empire, the Bolshevik Revolution looked like the beginning of socialist democracy in their old homeland.

It was among all these battered survivors of the radical movement, furious over Wilson's betrayal of his promise to keep America out of war, convinced that only revolution could gain justice for the American working class, and hated by other Americans for their opposition to the war, that the roots of American communism would take hold during the dark days of the war.

While the rest of the country was raging at Russia, American radicals could not contain their joy. When he got word of the Bolsheviks' success, Socialist Eugene Debs declared his solidarity with the Bolsheviks: "from the crown of my head to the soles of my feet I am a Bolshevik, and proud of it." He endorsed Lenin's Decree on Peace, agreeing that only a worldwide revolution could end the war. Big Bill Haywood of the IWW was in jail in November 1917, awaiting trial for interfering with the war effort. He wrote, "We have lived to see the breaking of the glorious Red Dawn. . . . The world revolution is born, the change is here." He called the Russian revolution "the greatest event of our lives. It represents all that we have been dreaming of and fighting for all our lives. It's the dawn of freedom and industrial democracy." Anarchist Emma Goldman had been sent to jail in July 1917 for urging resistance to the draft. She was free on appeal when she got word of the November Revolution. She spent her last months of freedom defending the Bolsheviks on the lecture circuit, and back in jail, wrote that she had "set my face toward the red glow on the social horizon; after all that is the only real and worthwhile love."[13]

John Reed and his wife, Louise Bryant, were in Petrograd when the Bolsheviks seized power. He returned to New York in April 1918 to spread the good news, and reported that his audiences would "weep with joy to know that there is something like dreams-come-true in Russia." Large, enthusiastic crowds came to hear Bryant on a publicity tour for her *Six Months in Red Russia*. "It is wonderful," she said. "All this new awakening—all over the earth . . . I can hear the feet of that great army across the world." Reed's classic eyewitness account of the Bolshevik uprising, *Ten Days That Shook the World*, appeared in March 1919. It gave generations of American radicals dreams of shaking the world themselves.[14]

The antiwar clergy shared the radicals' enthusiasm for Lenin's revolution. Congregationalist A. J. Muste's Fellowship of Reconciliation was the leading Christian antiwar organization, and its denunciation of the war echoed Lenin: "The blame for such criminal warfare rested with greedy business interests in their rivalry for raw materials and markets. This in turn could be traced to the very nature of the capitalist system." The Fellowship's journal editorialized that "only those who have felt something of the passion for social justice and industrial democracy can realize how truly revolutionary Russia, with all its faults and excesses, is the promised land, the father land of the spirit to multitudes of radical workers throughout the world."[15]

During the war, solidarity with the Bolsheviks was all that sustained antiwar radicals. Powerless at home, the American radical left was intoxicated with the sense of being part of an international movement that had won the revolution's first victory over the forces of capitalism, militarism, and imperialism. The Bolsheviks gave the American left hope during its darkest days. As a result, the Bolshevik Revolution and the Communist Party of the Soviet Union would forever after dwell in the imagination of the revolutionary left in America. The Bolshevik Revolution pushed an already alienated radical community far outside the mainstream of American politics so that, in its imagination, America's radical left now inhabited a different world than the rest of the nation: its heart was in another country—Russia—and in another time—the future, after the Revolution.[16]

Finally, joining liberal internationalism and the revolutionary—or what would be called the "progressive"—left, were the first stirrings of

American anticommunism. The radicals' enthusiasm for the Bolshevik revolution attracted the attention of Americans already on the alert for evidence of disloyalty and less than ardent enthusiasm for things American. The war had produced a network of patriotic organizations dedicated to rooting out any disloyalty that might subvert the war effort. These "countersubversives" now cast a cold and suspicious eye on Americans who supported the Bolsheviks' decision to leave the war. The country's first anticommunists would come out of these countersubversive groups—governmental, civic, business, labor, and religious—who had appointed themselves guardians of the home front.

At the center of this network was the Justice Department, which in 1917 faced the monumental task of registering 480,000 German "alien enemies." At the end of the year, the declaration of war against Austria-Hungary added four million more to the alien enemy list. This job belonged to the Alien Enemy Bureau of the Justice Department, where one of the clerks was the twenty-two-year-old J. Edgar Hoover, who was assigned to investigate the political beliefs or associations of the aliens—generally membership in the IWW or the Socialist Party—that might make them ineligible for parole. The Department also worried about other immigrants hostile to the allies, especially Irish and Indian nationalists opposed to the British empire. President Wilson himself believed that immigrants "poured the poison of disloyalty into the very arteries of our national life. . . . America never witnessed anything like this before. . . . Such creatures of passion, disloyalty, and anarchy must be crushed out."[17]

But the Justice Department could not do the job by itself. Its detective agency, the Bureau of Investigation (it was not the Federal Bureau of Investigation until 1935), was so small, with only three hundred agents at the beginning of the war, and had so many tasks—dealing with alien enemies and enforcing the wartime espionage and sedition laws—that it had to delegate most of its investigations to volunteer civilian groups. The largest of these countersubversive organizations was the American Protective League. Founded in March 1917, by the end of the war it had over 1,200 branches with 250,000 members busily investigating rumors of disloyalty, rounding up draft evaders, disrupting Socialist functions, even serving as strikebreakers. Many of the country's first anticommunists gained their first experience as countersubversives during the war, expertise they would later bring to bear on American communism.[18]

Other patriotic groups cooperated and sometimes competed with the APL during the war, among them the National Security League, the American Defense Society, and the National Civic Federation, which was perhaps the most important. Founded in 1900 to foster the peaceful resolution of labor–management conflicts (Mark Hanna and Samuel Gompers were both on its board), the NCF, chaired by Ralph M. Easley, redirected its energies during the war to investigating German espionage and searching for disloyalty. By the end of the war, antiradicalism had eclipsed labor mediation as the primary aim of the Federation.[19]

State and local governmental agencies also joined the loyalty crusade. New York City, with the nation's largest concentration of alien enemies, had its Mayor's Committee on Aliens. Its chairman, Archibald E. Stevenson, another future anticommunist, worked for the Justice Department as a special agent investigating enemy propaganda.

Long before World War I, conservative business organizations like the National Association of Manufacturers, the Chamber of Commerce, and the network of employers' groups and trade associations had been fighting the IWW and the radical left.[20] These antilabor groups needed no urging to support the government's campaign against their old enemies in the radical labor movement, now suspected of impeding the war effort.

The American Federation of Labor also threw itself into the wartime drive against disloyalty. The AFL subscribed to the same patriotic values and free enterprise ideology as the business community, and had long been battling radicals inside the labor movement. During the war, AFL president Samuel Gompers joined the government's American Alliance for Labor and Democracy, part of George Creel's Committee on Public Information that worked to maintain public support for the war. Even before the Bolshevik Revolution, Gompers and the AFL were attacking Socialists and Wobblies for lacking patriotism. After November 1917, the AFL used radicals' support for the Russian Revolution to deny that radical unions could be authentic representatives of the interests of American workers.[21]

Organized religion also joined the countersubversives' attack on wartime radicalism. All American faiths, particularly the major Protestant denominations, regarded religious obervance as the foundation of national values. Since prewar radicalism was outspokenly antireligious, mainstream religious groups—Protestant, Catholic, and Jewish—

tended to trace radicalism's lack of patriotism to its hostility to religion, which now seemed close to treason. During the war religious leaders took advantage of the situation to settle scores with the Christian Socialist ministers who had scandalized conservative Protestants by abandoning the clergy's traditional wartime role of praising God and passing the ammunition.

The priests and rabbis who led the immigrant Catholic and Jewish communities also despised radicals for their hostility toward religion. The Catholic Church's antiradical tradition went well back into the nineteenth century and the early papal social encyclicals against socialism. Cardinal William O'Connell of Boston warned his flock that "there cannot be a Catholic socialist." Since the vast majority of Catholics were workers, the Church also feared that radical unions might destroy the faith of their flocks, so the bishops created the American Federation of Catholic Societies to fight the "destructive propaganda of Socialism."[22]

Even before the Communist revolution, the countersubversive patriots who led the wartime loyalty drives had come to associate radicalism with disloyalty. But after the Bolsheviks took Russia out of the war to the applause of American radicals, the left's sympathy for communism itself was regarded as an act of disloyalty and as evidence of disloyalty. Those suspicions remained as strong as ever at war's end.

In 1917, of the Americans transfixed by the events in Russia, only Wilson's liberal internationalists were in a position to act on their beliefs. Radicals could only excitedly discuss the prospect of joining forces with their Russian comrades. Countersubversives could only denounce radicals for their disloyalty and demand that the government use the wartime sedition laws against Russian Bolshevism's American allies.

But while Wilson and the liberal internationalists were just as disgusted as the countersubversives at the radicals' sympathy for the "pro-German" Russian communists, they had to do more than harass radicals for disloyalty. They had to take concrete measures to repair the damage done the alliance by Lenin's revolution. The policies Wilson pursued toward Bolshevik Russia would provide the first indication of one of the most important facts in the history of anticommunism: although in 1917 Wilson was as angry at the Communists as any anticommunist would later be, there was an important difference between the hostility to communism felt by liberal internationalists and by those anticommunists who would oppose communism out of hatred for the thing itself, and this difference would have enormous consequences in the history of American anticommunism.

The difference was that in theory, internationalists could imagine a situation in which communism and their proposed world order could coexist. Wilson argued that "if this Bolshevism remains within its own frontiers this is no business of ours."[23] Liberal internationalism could accommodate revolutionary regimes, although Wilson was troubled by the violence of the Bolsheviks' revolution. He believed almost as strongly as the radicals that the status of workers in industrialized societies was so unjust that it might indeed take radical change, even revolution, to achieve social justice. In any case, if revolutionary regimes respected national sovereignty and abided by international law, he could envision admitting them into the community of states and the new League of Nations.

This possibility of accord between liberal internationalists and Communists seemed remote, of course, in the wake of the Bolshevik Revolution. After Russia's withdrawal from the war, the French and British pressed Wilson to help the anti-Bolshevik "White" armies bring Russia back into the alliance by defeating the Red Army Trotsky had mobilized. When the Allies insisted Wilson do something to prevent Allied war materials sent to Russia from falling into the hands of the Germans and to protect a Czech legion isolated in Russia by the Brest-Litovsk treaty, Wilson contributed troops to an Allied expeditionary force to northern Russia and to Siberia.[24]

For European anticommunists like British Secretary of State for War Winston Churchill, the leading British advocate of intervention, the scarcely concealed motive of the expedition was to have forces on hand to support the anti-Bolshevik White Armies in Siberia, the Crimea, and in the Baltic States in a coordinated drive on Moscow and Petrograd. For the anticommunist Churchill, protecting war materials and the Czech legion was only a pretext for the British and French. For the internationalist Wilson this was the real justification for the expedition. He joined the intervention, in fact, partly to be able to prevent his allies from escalating the mission's objectives.[25]

The American military expedition to Northern Russia eventually involved five thousand troops in Northern Russia, and lasted from May 1918 until July 1919 (suffering some five hundred casualties). Wilson also sent nine thousand troops to Siberia between August 1918 and April 1919. But despite Allied entreaties, Wilson refused to let the expeditionary force take part in the Russian civil war. Wilson considered intervention legitimate only when dictated by military strategy against Germany. He vetoed the Allies' plans for a military operation aimed at destroying the Bolsheviks.

Wilson's Fourteen Points principle of national self-determination was reason enough for his refusal, but history had also taught him that foreign intervention in civil wars was invariably counterproductive. Intervention, he argued, would generate a "hot resentment in Russia" that would rally patriotic sentiments behind the Communists. Drawing on the analogy with the foreign intervention that had mobilized France behind its revolution and Napoleon, he feared that attempts to suppress the Russian revolution would only delay Russia's progress toward democracy. He had learned the same lesson from his own disastrous intervention in Mexico just before the war, when he had General Pershing chase Pancho Villa for almost a year, accomplishing nothing except to create more anti-Americanism and an undeserved reputation for Villa as a Mexican Robin Hood. Moreover, Wilson and other liberal internationalists believed that *some* kind of revolution in Russia was necessary. "The Government of the United States," he said, "entertains the greatest sympathy [for the Russian Revolution], in spite of all the unhappiness and misfortune which has for the time being sprung out of it." For Wilson, revolutions were painful but often necessary steps on the path to liberal democracy.[26]

Wilson's realization that no matter how limited the American intervention in Russia was, it still violated liberal internationalist principles, made him receptive to spurious reports that the Bolsheviks were in reality nothing but German agents. It was to provide a liberal internationalist justification for the intervention that Wilson embarrassed himself by releasing papers [the "Sisson documents"], later proven to be forgeries, that supposedly revealed that Lenin had been installed in power by the German general staff, and remained subject to their orders. Wilson's credulity stemmed from his eagerness for proof that Lenin was a German agent to justify military action against the Bolsheviks as part of the war effort against Germany.[27]

Liberal internationalism's willingness to contemplate coexistence with communism had limits. Wilson would not endorse normal relations with a regime that was trying to stir up insurrection around the world. Until the Soviets stopped violating the principle of self-determination themselves, liberal internationalists would not let them enter the world order. In the long run, Wilsonians believed the Communists would have to liberalize—that is, give up communism—because they would not be able to survive without the economic and political resources available only in the international community of free-market liberal democracies. In the short run, communism would have to be contained.

Most Americans emerged from the war with a general, unfocused hostility toward the Russian revolution for damaging the war effort, but there were now broadly divergent views of communism held by three groups with deeply felt reactions toward what was happening in Russia. There were liberal internationalists who had defined their goals in foreign policy as a response to Lenin's challenge to their dream of a new international order, and who saw communism as a serious, but not insurmountable, obstacle to their goals. There was now a radical left that identified its hopes for power and influence in America with the Bolsheviks' dream of a world revolution. Finally, there were the veterans of the patriotic countersubversive network, full of fury at the radical left for its disloyalty and for defending Lenin's defection from the war.

Of all those Americans—liberal internationalists, radicals, and countersubversives—stirred to outrage or enthusiasm by the Bolshevik Revolution, countersubversives knew the least about communism, its ideas, its tactics, and its goals, but the war left them in position to lead America's first drive against communism.

What they did have—perhaps to excess—was a passionate belief they had learned during the war that communism was thoroughly alien to American values, and so was to be resisted with all their considerable energy. That moral conviction would serve America well over the years, but only when guided by real knowledge of the enemy and moderated by wisdom about the ways of man. At the end of the war, however, when revolution overseas and political violence at home created politically irresistible demands to take action against a Communist movement that seemed on the verge of bringing America to the same state of chaos as Europe, real knowledge about communism was not yet to be had, and wisdom was, as is often the case, in short supply.

Chapter 2

RED YEARS AND RED SCARES

The Movement advances at such dizzy speed that it may be said with confidence: Within a year we will already begin to forget there was a struggle for communism in Europe, because within a year all Europe will be Communist.
—Gregory Zinoviev, head of the Communist International, March 1919[1]

At the end of the war, liberal internationalists, the revolutionary left, and America's first anticommunists were poised for a clash that would define the lines of battle between them for the rest of the century. By the time it was over, all three would bear lasting scars, and one of the most durable figures in the history of American anticommunism, J. Edgar Hoover, would have taken his place on the national scene. Largely because of Hoover's actions during these years, there would persist forever after a stereotype of anticommunism as a right-wing conspiracy against the civil liberties of the left, an image that was not far from the mark in describing some of the noisiest and most reckless anticommunists over the years, but it was also one that could be manipulated to frustrate responsible anticommunists in their efforts to expose the grim reality behind the glorious ideals professed by Communists both in America and abroad.

The armistice of November 11, 1918, began what the Italians called the *biennio rosso*, the "Red Years," when communism and its enemies struggled for power from one end of Europe to the other. Order across Europe had broken down after the Armistice, leaving the European working class resentful and mutinous. There was no central authority in Russia or the rest of the old tsarist empire (Finland, Latvia, Estonia, Lithuania, Poland). There was no real government in the wreck of the Austro-Hungarian empire (Austria, Hungary, modern-day Czechoslovakia, and Yugoslavia). Anarchy ruled in the German states that had been united in the Kaiser's Reich, while the Ottoman empire in the Balkans and the Middle East lay in ruins.

The Bolsheviks believed that their own revolution was doomed unless it spread across Europe, particularly to Germany, which Bolshevik leader Leon Trotsky declared would be the real center of the revolution.[2] Trotsky predicted a Communist Latvia, Poland and Lithuania, Finland, and Ukraine would soon link Soviet Russia to a future Soviet Germany and Austria-Hungary, and that did not seem farfetched in 1918 and 1919. There were pro-Bolshevik mutinies in the German fleet, and Communist insurrections in Kiel, Hanover, and Bremen. Four days before the Armistice there was an uprising in Munich. The German Spartacists (the future Communist Party of Germany), led by Rosa Luxemburg and Karl Liebknecht, laid plans to seize power in Berlin. More Bolshevik uprisings broke out in Hungary, Austria, and Bulgaria. And from their European base, the Bolsheviks hoped to "set the East ablaze," to communize Asia and the Middle East, to forge bonds with the revolutionary government in Mexico, and—at last—join forces with the revolutionary movement in America.

On August 20, 1918, Lenin wrote his first "Letter to American Workers," calling on the American working class to revolt against its rulers elite.[3] As if in answer, there was a surge of strike activity after the Armistice. Labor stoppages had been outlawed during the war, and so the industrial unrest of the winter of 1918–1919 seemed seditious, although the strikes were a predictable response to postwar pay cuts during a period of mounting inflation. Those susceptible to alarm, however, thought the European war between capital and labor had spread to America.

In January 1919, Lenin appealed once again to American workers: "We see a whole series of communist proletarian parties, not only in the border areas of the former tsarist empire . . . we see the powerful 'Soviet' movement . . . in Western European countries and in the neutral countries [Switzerland, Holland, and Norway]. . . . The revolution in Germany . . . which is particularly important and characteristic as one of the most advanced capitalist countries . . . [has taken] on 'Soviet' forms." He begged American workers to join the revolution.[4]

The strikes of 1919 were accompanied by a fiery revolutionary rhetoric America had not heard before. As if scripted by Lenin, the Industrial Workers of the World announced that "every strike is a small revolution and a dress rehearsal for the big one." On January 21, 1919, that "big one" seemed at hand. In the Pacific Northwest, where the IWW was strongest, 35,000 Seattle shipyard workers walked off the job. A few days later the Seattle Central Labor Council voted to support the shipyard workers. On February 6, 60,000 more workers joined the walkout, closing schools, public transportation, businesses, and stores.[5]

Press headlines—"REDS DIRECTING SEATTLE STRIKE—TO TEST CHANCE FOR REVOLUTION"—warned that the strike was the beginning of a Bolshevik revolution in America. Samuel Gompers's American Federation of Labor feared a public backlash against all unions, so it joined in the attack on the Seattle strikers. Seattle Mayor Ole Hanson called the strike an act of class war led by radicals who "want to take possession of our American Government and try to duplicate the anarchy of Russia." Riding in a flag-draped car, Hanson led federal troops from a nearby army base into the city where he ordered strikers to go back to work or lose their jobs. The AFL denounced the strikers for abandoning traditional unionism. They were playing, Gompers said, into the hands of anti-labor employers and politicians. After four days the workers gave up.[6]

Meanwhile, pressure mounted on Washington to do something about the labor unrest. Aliens, who did not enjoy constitutional protection from arrests, jailing, and deportation, became the target of convenience. Attorney General Thomas W. Gregory announced he was going to deport seven or eight thousand "alien anarchists and trouble makers."[7] The Immigration Bureau of the Labor Department loaded thirty-six alien Seattle Wobblies onto a train on February 6 and dispatched it to Ellis Island. The papers called it the "Red Special," and immigration officials promised it would be the first of many.[8] After the Seattle strike, every picket sign looked like a red flag to alarmists, and picket signs were everywhere. Major strikes broke out in Lawrence, Massachusetts and Butte, Montana in February, and there were 175 more strikes across the country in March, 248 in April, 388 in May, 303 in June, 360 in July, and 373 in August.

This wave of unrest in America, together with the spread of revolutionary insurrections across Europe and the spectacular achievements of the revolution in Russia were now to profoundly reshape the American left. The Bolsheviks' most enthusiastic supporters in America raced to ally the American movement to the center of the revolution in Moscow, and so the "Left Wing" of the American Socialist Party established a Communist Propaganda League in November 1918. In January 1919 they were excitedly planning affiliation with the Bolsheviks when the Russians invited all revolutionaries to a Moscow conference of what the Russians called the "now well-defined and existing revolutionary International." The Moscow meeting would discuss the "tremendously swift pace of world revolution" and how to defend it from the counter-revolutionary capitalist cabal with the "hypocritical title of 'League of Nations.' "[9]

It was this flurry of activity of the left that began to transform the veterans of the wartime countersubversive movement into anticommunists. North Carolina's Senator Lee Slater Overman's Judiciary Committee had begun scrutinizing the predominantly German brewing industry in 1918. It had expanded its inquiry to the general phenomenon of "pro-Germanism," but Overman's investigation would seem to have been rendered pointless by the Armistice. One of their witnesses, however, explained to the Senators that Bolshevism was "the result of German propaganda." Archibald E. Stevenson of the New York City Mayor's Committee on Aliens claimed that German socialism was "the father of the Bolsheviki movement in Russia" and so "the radical movement which we have in this country today has its origin in Germany."[10] That sent the Overman committee back to the Senate to request and receive permission to investigate that radical movement. During the winter of 1918–1919 the committee heard a parade of Russian emigrés and Americans back from Russia recite hair-raising tales of Bolshevik outrages against private property, churches, the family, and everything sacred. Some of the accounts of atrocities seemed so exaggerated in their descriptions of violence that they seemed to discredit the disturbing reports of mass murder in Russia. Tragically, many of them later turned out to have been, if anything, understated.

Meanwhile, on March 4, 1919, Communists from all over the world met in Russia to found the Third Communist International (the "Comintern"). Its manifesto announced that "the Third International is the international of open mass action of revolutionary realization. Socialist criticism has sufficiently stigmatized the bourgeois world order. The aim of the International Communist Party is to overthrow it and raise in its place the structure of the socialist order."[11]

Russian and foreign Communists were so confident that the world was on the brink of revolution that at the Comintern's closing session they boasted that "the Movement advances at such dizzy speed that it may be said with confidence: Within a year we will already begin to forget there was a struggle for communism in Europe, because within a year all Europe will be Communist."[12] Two weeks later, Bela Kun's Communists established a Soviet Republic in Hungary.

President Wilson and his liberal internationalist advisors were in Paris in March 1919 negotiating the peace treaty. When Lenin and Trotsky created the Comintern as the revolutionary alternative to the League of Nations, Wilson ordered Herbert Hoover, head of the Allied relief efforts, to withhold food supplies to pressure Eastern European governments to suppress their Communist movements. The Allies were sending twelve trainloads of food each day to Austria, and they stipulated that this aid was contingent on the authorities' keeping their Communists under control. Hungary was warned that there would be no relief supplies as long as it had a Communist government.[13]

For Wilson, Bolshevism now seemed a greater threat to the new world order than the old imperialist system. He began to draw closer to the unabashedly imperialist leaders of England and France who were terrified that communism would spread from Russia. Wilson insisted that the conference act quickly to organize a League of Nations, now with the aim of stopping the spread of revolution. Despite pleas from his doctors, he refused to rest from the debilitating pace of the negotiations: "Give me time," he told them. "We are running a race with Bolshevism and the world is on fire."[14]

The League began to lose support among progressives as it came to resemble an international alliance against Bolshevism. There were only a few internationalists who still clung to the original Wilsonian vision of a liberal world order open to all nations and hostile to none. When the President got home from Paris on July 8, treaty in hand, leaflets were passed out to the crowd at the dock: "Everybody's business: To stand by our government. To help the soldier get a job. To help crush bolshevism."[15]

Up to now, the veteran countersubversives from the wartime loyalty groups had done little except denounce postwar radicalism, upbraid the

Bolsheviks, and deport hapless alien radicals. Nothing had galvanized them into action until April 1919, when bombs began to explode across America.

On April 28, 1919, an explosive package was discovered (and dismantled) at the home of Seattle Mayor Ole Hanson. The next day an explosion at the Atlanta home of former Senator Thomas Hardwick tore the hands off Hardwick's maid. Thirty-four more bombs were intercepted before reaching their targets. They were addressed to public figures like Frederick Howe (the commissioner of immigration at Ellis Island), Senator Lee Overman, Supreme Court Associate Justice Oliver Wendell Holmes, Jr., Postmaster General Albert Burlson, and Judge Kenesaw Mountain Landis (who had sentenced Socialist Victor Berger and the IWW's Big Bill Haywood to jail). Others went to the new Attorney General A. Mitchell Palmer, Secretary of Labor William Wilson, John D. Rockefeller, and J. P. Morgan.[16] It seemed a premature and unusually violent celebration of May Day, which would be marked that year in scores of American cities by Red Flag parades and retaliatory mob attacks on local Socialist headquarters.

A month later, on June 2, the violence reached a climax when a bomb destroyed the entrance to the home of Attorney General Palmer in Washington, D.C., though it failed to injure Palmer or his family. When, along with the grisly debris of the bomber's body, police found fragments of a leaflet signed "the Anarchist Fighters" and filled with threats against the "capitalist class," Palmer concluded the bomber was part of a well-coordinated campaign of terror by radicals against the government.

Although it would be American Communists who would suffer the consequences of the June 2 bombing, the bomber was in all probability not a Communist at all. He was almost certainly Carlo Valdinoci, publisher of *Cronaca Sovversiva*, the journal of a small group of followers of the Italian anarchist Luigi Galliani. Valdinoci's anarchist cell was probably the Gallianist "Gruppo Autonomo" of East Boston, about fifty strong, which had among its members the soon-to-be-famous Nicola Sacco and Bartolomeo Vanzetti, who had themselves probably helped plan the June bombing. The same group, seeking revenge for the government's jailing of Italian anarchists during the war, may well have been responsible for all the bombings of 1919 and 1920.[17]

Warning that radicals were planning "to rise up and destroy the government at one fell swoop," Palmer got an appropriation from Congress to investigate and suppress the radical movement in America by rounding up and deporting alien radicals. Palmer reached deep into the ranks of Justice Department lawyers to head a newly formed "Radical Division" of the Justice Department. His choice was the twenty-four-year-old J. Edgar Hoover.[18]

Hoover had what was the typical background of the countersubversive anticommunists, who tended to come from the same white Protestant middle class as the liberal internationalists, though from its less secure lower ranks. Internationalists were confident that American values were the goals of all mankind, and so were destined to be someday accepted the world over. Countersubversives like Hoover saw American values as fragile, vulnerable to alien influences, and so liable to be croded by immigrants infected with the virus of foreign radicalism that seemed at war with religion, private property, and individual liberty.

During the summer of 1919 Hoover immersed himself in a study of communism at the moment it was moving briskly towards affiliation with the Comintern. He collected, read, and transcribed hair-raising passages from Communist publications that gave him an impression he would never lose, one of the Communist movement as a confident, expansive force sure of success, a movement that saw America as the most formidable obstacle to its success. He came to see communism as the antithesis of Americanism. An active supporter of the Presbyterian church, he was shocked by attacks on religion by radicals like Emma Goldman, who wrote that "religion . . . [is] a nightmare that oppresses the human soul and holds the mind in bondage."[19] He was angered by communism's repudiation of private property, and most of all, he was appalled by communism's repudiation of patriotism, because love of country was the highest of the values that made up Hoover's personal code.[20]

By November Hoover's Radical Division had completed a classification of over 60,000 "radically inclined" individuals in the "ultraradical movement." His Publications Section was scanning 625 papers for information on the radical movement, and it had created a card catalog of 200,000 entries on "various subjects or individuals."[21] Hoover had turned himself into the government's first resident authority on communism, a reputation he jealously guarded for the rest of his long life.

While Hoover's immediate goal was a mass deportation of radical aliens, his ultimate objective was to secure a peacetime sedition law that would give the government the same authority over radical citizens it had over aliens.[22] Late in 1919 such a bill was introduced into the House by Martin Davey of Ohio. Hoover hoped the 1919–1920 campaign against aliens would build support for that bill, which would allow him to move against all revolutionaries, citizens as well as aliens.

When Hoover began his research into communism, there was as yet no single revolutionary organization large enough to be a plausible target for the roundup of alien radicals he was planning. That would change at the end of the summer when American radicals organized their own branch of the Bolshevik movement.

The Socialist Party's Left Wing had hoped to carry the entire Socialist Party into the Comintern, but the Socialists' national leaders feared that Comintern affiliation would make them all vulnerable to prosecution under the threatened peacetime sedition law, so they expelled two-thirds of the more radical members for trying to bolshevize the party. When the main body of the Socialist Party remained non-revolutionary under the leadership of Eugene Debs and Morris Hillquit, the Left Wing formally seceded from the party on August 31, 1919. The next day, the foreign-language groups of the Left Wing formed a "Communist Party of America" under Louis Fraina, Nicholas Hourwich, and Charles Ruthenberg. The Left Wing's English-speaking members then constituted themselves as the "Communist Labor Party," led by John Reed, Benjamin Gitlow, and William Bross Lloyd. There were now two Communist parties in the United States with a claimed combined membership of between forty and seventy thousand, and with party platforms openly calling for the violent overthrow of the government. About 90 percent of these Communists were aliens. They were exactly what Hoover had been looking for.[23]

When the Comintern had summoned the world's Communists to battle in March 1919, the triumph of the revolution seemed to be imminent and inevitable. But as the year wore on, the revolution's fortunes were more in doubt. In April Eugene Levine, one of Rosa Luxemburg and Karl Liebknecht's Spartacists, had proclaimed a Bavarian Soviet with its capital in Munich. The next month a legion of German war veterans called the Freikorps recaptured Munich and executed Levine. In August Bela Kun's Communist regime that had ruled Hungary since March fell to anticommunists led by Admiral Miklos Horthy, followed by the slaughter of all the Communists Horthy could lay hands on.[24] Within Russia, however, Bolshevism was still gaining strength. In June Trotsky's Red Army defeated the White armies advancing on Moscow. In September the Allies evacuated their troops from Archangel and Murmansk. Over the next two months Trotsky smashed the White forces in Siberia and the Baltic region. Only in the southwest around the Black and Azov Seas did General Denikin and Baron Wrangel, who had been recognized by the Paris Peace Conference as the legitimate rulers of Russia, still lead serious White resistance to the Communists.

By the fall of 1919, events had moved Wilson's liberal internationalists and Hoover's countersubversives into a temporary alliance of convenience. Wilson was touring America, more convinced than ever that only the League of Nations could stop the advance of bolshevism, and that the Bolsheviks and their supporters were the greatest threat to achieving his dream of a League.[25] On September 12 Wilson warned an enthusiastic crowd in Coeur d'Alene, Idaho, that the Germans were meeting with the Bolsheviks to lay new plans for aggression. "Germany wants us to stay out of this treaty. . . . It was America that saved the world, and those who oppose the treaty propose that after having redeemed the world we should desert the world."[26]

While Wilson was promoting the treaty as the world's best defense against bolshevism, countersubversives in Congress were demanding a more direct action. On October 14 the Senate unanimously passed a resolution[27] requiring Palmer to report his progress against the Spring bomb plots and the status of his other radical investigations. That spurred Hoover and Palmer into action. On November 7, the second anniversary of the Bolshevik revolution, Hoover sent local police and Bureau of Investigation agents to break into the meeting halls of the Union of Russian Workers in twelve cities. This organization, formally dedicated to the anarchist goals of the overthrow of all governments, was in actuality a haven for homesick Russian immigrants, few of whom had any knowledge of the organization's fiery goals. The police and Justice Department agents ransacked the union's offices and carried away anything that looked like evidence. They arrested several thousand of the union's members, releasing most after questioning.[28]

The next day, New York State and City police under the direction of Clayton Lusk's State Assembly antiradical investigating committee raided seventy-three radical centers in New York and made five hundred arrests. Across the country local red squads carried out similar raids, all coordinated by the Justice Department. In Centralia, Washington, a battle broke out between the IWW and the American Legion. One Wobbly, a World War I veteran, was murdered.[29]

The raids had the effect Hoover desired. On December 3 the *New York Times* endorsed a peacetime sedition bill. Letters of congratulations flooded the Justice Department. There were calls for similar action against the IWW, the Communist Party, and even the American Federation of Labor. There was also a letter from the National Civil Liberties Union charging that the prisoners taken at the Russian People's House in New York had been beaten by the raiders, but the Justice Department was so euphoric over the success of the November raids that it paid no attention to its few critics.[30]

Hoover needed alien radicals with names known to the public to lend a fearsome face to the anonymous rabble he was billing as the red menace, and so it was inevitable that his eyes would fall on Emma Goldman and her close associate and sometime lover, Alexander Berkman, who had served fourteen years for trying to kill Henry Clay Frick during the 1892 Homestead steel strike. Hoover conferred with the Immigration Bureau and confirmed that both were deportable: Berkman as an alien, and Goldman because of a technically defective naturalization.

Hoover requisitioned the transport *U.S.S. Buford* from the War Department to carry the radicals to Russia and on December 21, the ship cast off from New York with a cargo of 249 aliens that included Goldman and Berkman. This was only the beginning. Hoover announced, "The Department of Justice is not through yet, by any means. Other 'soviet arks' will sail for Europe, just as often as it is necessary to rid the country of dangerous radicals." Bureau of Investigation Director William J. Flynn said that the country had rid itself of "the brains of the ultra-radical movement."[31]

Meanwhile, Hoover put the finishing touches on his plans against the two new Communist parties. To secure a ruling that their alien members were deportable he wrote briefs on both parties. He added a third brief urging the deportation of the unaccredited representative of the Soviet government, Ludwig C. A. K. Martens. Hoover would later refer to these products of his youth as the beginning of the "nation's response to communism."[32]

On Christmas Eve of 1919 the Labor Department reviewed Hoover's request for 2,768 warrants, along with his arguments that the two Communist parties fell within the provisions of the 1918 Immigration Law.[33] That night Secretary of Labor William B. Wilson approved the arrests of members of both parties. Hoover notified the Bureau of Investigation to prepare to round up Communists.[34]

On January 2, 1920, while Hoover stayed in touch by telephone from the Bureau offices in the Justice Department, teams led by his agents broke into Communist meeting halls in twenty-three states (the Bureau had urged its informants to schedule meetings and other gatherings that evening). They herded more than four thousand radicals into detention centers where more agents waited with warrants Hoover had obtained from the Labor Department.

Hoover had wanted all this to have the greatest possible impact on public opinion and radical morale, and he wanted to strike before Communist leaders could destroy the records he would need for mass deportations, so he acted quickly, and the size and speed of the raids made any effective control over the raiders impossible. The Bureau had only 579 agents, so Hoover had to recruit help from local police and volunteers from anticommunist organizations like the American Legion and veterans of the recently disbanded American Protective League. That the aliens would be mistreated should have been obvious—and they *were* mistreated, enduring manhandling, humiliation, imprisonment in wretched conditions, deprived of communication with friends, family, or legal counsel.[35]

Hoover's January raids were so bold that for a time opposition was stunned into silence. For the time being, he could bask in a triumph even greater than that following the November raids and the *Buford*. Newspapers cheered the Justice Department with headlines like "ALL ABOARD FOR THE NEXT SOVIET ARK."[36] He began to dream regal dreams about how the raids would propel his career toward greatness, and he decorated his Washington office with mementos from Communist offices. He wrote the U. S. Attorney in New Jersey that he was "endeavoring to place upon the walls of my office here a representative collection of Communists, and if you could forward to me some of the larger photographs of the world-wide Communist movement, I would greatly appreciate it."[37] Hoover may have contemplated a roundup of the radicals' wealthy supporters, the so-called parlor Bolsheviki. He asked the Post Office's radical section to send him any list they had of "certain wealthy women who are giving financial aid to various radical publications."[38]

To sustain his drive's momentum, Hoover now had to show how his raids fitted into the larger plan of a national campaign against radicalism. He released his briefs on the two Communist parties to demonstrate that "both the Communist Party and the Communist Labor Party had as their aim the destruction of the American Government and supplanting it with Soviet control."[39]

Publishing these briefs was intended to build public support for Hoover's policies. He wanted to turn his Radical Division into the core of a national anticommunist movement, and so out of his office poured a flood of publications and press releases encouraging organizations and individuals to join him. In January he began a newsletter called the *Bureau of Investigation General Intelligence Bulletin*,[40] filled with of items he thought might encourage the anticommunist community, applauding patriotic groups that assisted the Justice Department, among them the Knights of Columbus, the Masons, and the Fraternal Order of Eagles. The American Legion was one of Hoover's strongest allies during the antiradical campaign. The Legion was founded on May 5, 1919, by American officers in Paris who had watched thousands of French veterans carrying the red flag of revolution in that year's May Day parade. The founders included Theodore Roosevelt, Jr. and William Donovan of the Fighting Sixty-ninth of New York (and future leader of the Office of Strategic Services in World War II). They feared bolshevism might infect demobilized American soldiers, and they had in mind as a model the German antiradical veterans' organization, the Freikorps, which had recently put down the Spartacist uprising in Berlin.[41]

Another of Hoover's publications was a pamphlet called *The Red Radical Movement* with an introduction signed by Palmer, but written in Hoover's flamboyant style. It appealed for the support of "all elements of good citizenship," explaining that the Justice Department's "legal prosecutions of sedition" could not succeed "unless those prosecutions are backed by the systematic and hearty efforts" of the public. "There is a menace in this country" though "it may not be the menace of immediate revolution." The pamphlets called for the public to acquaint itself with "the real menace of evil-thinking which is the foundation of the red movement," specifically, "the destruction of all ownership in property, the destruction of all religion and belief in God. It is a movement organized against Democracy, and in favor of the power of the few built by force. Bolshevism, syndicalism, the Soviet Government, sabotage, etc., are only names for old theories of violence and criminality."[42]

Shortly after the Second Congress of the Communist International met in Amsterdam in February 1920, Hoover released his "popular survey" of radicalism titled *The Revolution in Action*. It described a world with armed Communists poised in every country and colony waiting for Moscow's command to attack. In America, the "protagonists and helpers of the international revolutionary scheme, the I. W. W., the communists, the Communist Labor party, the anarchists, the radical associations of rebellious schools, and unaffiliated Reds, and parlor Bolsheviks, fired by the enthusiasm thrown across the seas by flaming Russia and the glowing torch of the third international" had begun " 'to beat anvil blows,' the revolutionary poets would say, for an actual revolutionary uprising in the United States." According to Hoover, all the disturbances of 1919, the general strikes in Winnipeg and Seattle, the coal strike, and the bomb plots, were part of this Moscow-coordinated revolutionary upheaval, because the Bolsheviks believed that the revolution could not survive unless it succeeded everywhere.[43] What it all meant, Hoover wrote, was that "civilization faces its most terrible menace of danger since the barbarian hordes overran West Europe and opened the dark ages."[44]

While Hoover continued to raise the alarm against the spectre of revolution, around the country doubts were beginning to surface. The menace Hoover warned against was vague, conjectural. Only his words connected the bombings and the upheaval in Europe to the thousands of miserable aliens now awaiting an uncertain fate in unheated holding pens across a wintry continent. Their sufferings, on the other hand, were very real. By February of 1920, a storm of criticism was swirling about the Justice Department. Hoover's raids were so outrageous by any standards of decency and legality that they mobilized lawyers, clergymen, and civil libertarians to demand a halt to the antiradical campaign. Hoover was beginning to sense the changed political realities. He announced he was going to delay plans for the department's drive against the alien Wobblies, explaining that since "the deportation policy must be supported solely by public opinion, I feel that a dragnet raid would be detrimental.[45]

The Labor Department, which had until March supported and encouraged Hoover to round up alien radicals, decided to take a second look. Louis Post, a veteran assistant secretary of labor just assigned to reviewing deportation cases, rejected Hoover's theory that a membership card or a name on a membership roll should be enough to deport an alien.[46] On March 5 Post decided that each individual case had to be scrutinized to make sure that when the alien had become a member of the Communist Party he understood what he was doing. Post had learned that many of the "Communists" had been automatically transferred from the Socialist Party's foreign language groups to the Communist Party's rolls when their leaders had joined the new party, so many individuals did not know that they had become Communists.[47]

Enraged by Post's ruling, Hoover was provoked to a rash decision that would cast a long shadow over American anticommunism. His original assignment had been to bring to justice those responsible for the spring bombings of 1919. Instead of restricting his investigation to those elusive criminals, whose identities were probably known to him within a matter of weeks, he broadened it to target the entire radical movement. But in actuality a "radical movement" existed only in the hopes of the radicals and the fears of the countersubversives. It was—literally—a myth, a pattern constructed out of the emotional need of humans to see an order and a direction in the chaos of passing events.

Hoover now had thousands of alien Communists in jail, without a shred of evidence to connect them to the bombings that had so alarmed the public earlier in the year. He was discussing plans to round up alien Wobblies next, and then radical American citizens.

As protests mounted from humanitarians, civil libertarians, and concerned members of the public appalled at what was happening, Hoover took the fateful step of making his critics the targets of his anger against radicals. His publications began to denounce civil libertarians and liberals as supporters of the Bolsheviks, perhaps Bolsheviks themselves, and he began referring to them as "parlor pinks." His *General Intelligence Bulletin* denounced "leading radicals," a category broad enough to include Socialist Morris Hillquit, civil libertarians John Haynes Holmes and Roger Baldwin and the liberal Catholic priest John A. Ryan. He railed against critics of the anticommunist drive like Louis Post, federal judge George Anderson, and editor and columnist Walter Lippmann.[48]

Hoover did not content himself with denouncing his enemies. He went to his supporters in Congress and persuaded the House Rules Committee to consider impeaching Louis Post. That turned out to be one of the major disasters in the history of American anticommunism.

During these hearings which began on April 27, Post managed to turn the tables and transform them into an examination of misdeeds by Hoover and Palmer. Staggered by Post's testimony, the Committee suspended all further action, and canceled further consideration of Hoover's peacetime Sedition Act.[49]

On May 5 Hoover was stunned again when Secretary of Labor Wilson ruled that membership in the Communist Labor Party was not a deportable offense because members had not been required to read the Party's constitution. The three hundred members of that party who had been rounded up in the dragnet were freed.[50]

In May Hoover suffered another blow. Hoover's Radical Division took Lenin's prediction of a worldwide soviet state by the summer of 1920 seriously, and spewed out warnings that there would be a wave of assassinations, general strikes, and bombings that May Day, and in cities like New York and Boston, the police went on alert. Nothing happened. The radicals had never been quieter. The Red Scare was beginning to look ridiculous.[51]

Finally, on June 23, Judge George Anderson of the Boston Federal Court issued a ruling drafted by Harvard law professor and future Supreme Court justice Felix Frankfurter. Anderson ruled that *neither* Communist Party *nor* Communist Labor Party membership made aliens subject to deportation. The holding pens were emptied. Hoover's crusade against communism had collapsed.[52]

Hoover's attack on Post would be a watershed in the history of American anticommunism. In trying to destroy Post by claiming that he was a "Bolshevik" himself, Hoover tried to exploit the stereotype of a unified radical movement run by American Communists for the benefit of Moscow. His use of that powerful, but false and dangerous, stereotype would not only be ineffective, but would have the unforeseen and catastrophic consequence of providing the left with a far more useful counterstereotype of the anticommunist as the sworn enemy, not of communism, but of civil liberties. It was an image that obviously contained more than a little truth. Like all stereotypes, however, it was a gross oversimplification, and over the years it would persuade many

Americans to disregard what was true and vitally important in what anticommunists were saying about communism at home and abroad, and instead to pay attention only to the sufferings of those who suffered when communism came under attack.

This stereotype took concrete form when Post's lawyer persuaded the National Popular Government League, aided by the National Civil Liberties Bureau (later the ACLU) to investigate Palmer and the Justice Department. The twelve prominent lawyers who looked into Post's allegations against Palmer were a formidable and prestigious group that included some of the most distinguished members of the American bar: Zechariah Chafee, Jr., Ernst Freund, Francis Fisher Kane, Roscoe Pound, and Felix Frankfurter, along with two dependable supporters of radical causes, Frank P. Walsh and Swinburne Hale, and Post's lawyer, Jackson Ralston.[53]

They published their findings in late May as the *Report Upon the Illegal Practices of the United States Department of Justice.*[54] The sixty-seven-page *Lawyers' Report* charged the Justice Department with inflicting cruel and unusual punishments, making arrests without warrant, performing unreasonable searches and seizures, using agents provocateurs, and forcing witnesses to incriminate themselves. The Department was also accused of conducting a propaganda campaign without congressional authorization: "The legal functions of the Attorney General," the lawyers charged, "are: to advise the Government on questions of law, and to prosecute persons who have violated federal statutes. For the Attorney General to go into the field of propaganda against radicals is a deliberate misuse of his office and a deliberate squandering of funds entrusted to him by Congress." This was the most serious charge against Palmer, because it constituted an impeachable offense (misusing appropriations).

The indictment continued: The Justice Department, charged with guarding the Constitution and enforcing the laws, had engaged in "the continued violation of that Constitution and breaking of those Laws under the guise of a campaign for the suppression of radical activities." The real crisis of 1920, concluded the lawyers, was "no question of a vague and threatened menace" like the supposed Communist threat, "but a present assault upon the most sacred principles of our Constitutional liberty."[55]

The *Lawyers' Report* went far beyond the issue at hand, and its consequences were still being felt three quarters of a century later. What the *Report* tried to do—and did, for the left and much of the public influenced by the left—was to shift the Communist controversy from communism to the excesses of anticommunism. According to the *Report*, the issue was not communism at all, not the beliefs, associations, or even the activities of Communists. The real issue was anticommunism, which was defined simply as a false and dangerous attack on the civil liberties of all reformers and all Americans. Under the guise of fighting communism, anticommunists were really trying to stamp out the civil liberties of anyone who disturbed the secure slumbers of the rich and powerful. Building on the undeniable fact that the Justice Department had engaged in illegal and unethical activities during the raids the lawyers charged that, under the "guise" of an antiradical campaign, anticommunists had conspired in an "assault" on the Constitution.

With the 1920 *Lawyers' Report*, the foundation had been laid for the mythic history of anticommunism that would be written by its enemies, and that would be for many Americans to the present day, *the* history of anticommunism. It was one that—like most conspiracy theories—declared that there was a *real* and dangerous purpose (discernible only to the initiated) beneath the stated goals of anticommunists like Hoover. But in fact, while the Justice Department had undeniably played fast and loose with due process, there is no evidence that Hoover's motives were any different than advertised. He really did believe that the government had the responsibility of protecting the country against the threat of political violence. He really did believe that the 1919 bombings proved there was a clear and present danger to the country, posed by radicals in America tied to the Communist International.

The Red Scare raids had now given American politics two new and complementary conspiracy theories. Some anticommunists, Hoover among them, believed there existed a radical conspiracy organized and coordinated by Communists linked to the Soviet Union, and that this conspiracy was responsible for much of what was wrong with American society. The left now had a countermyth that held anticommunism was simply a conspiracy by the government and conservatives to stamp out the civil liberties of dissenters, a conspiracy disguised as a campaign to defend the country against revolution. The *Lawyers' Report* had given the left an enduring image of itself as the eternal victims of the anticommunist conspiracy led by an arch-conspirator, J. Edgar Hoover, and his omnipresent and all-powerful Bureau. That stereotype would do more to shape many Americans' images of anticommunism than anything the anticommunists themselves would ever say or do.

Another ironic result of Hoover's anticommunist campaigns of 1919 and 1920 was that by creating a coalition of Wilsonian progressives, socialists, and radicals to defend the civil liberties of Hoover's victims, the raids had created a reasonable facsimile of the radical movement that would inhabit the nightmares of anticommunist conspiracy theorists for years to come. In their minds, this took tangible shape and form in the American Civil Liberties Union, organized by radicals, liberals, and civil libertarians in 1920 to protect the victims of the Red Scare raids.

The ACLU was an offshoot of the American Union Against Militarism, founded in 1915 by Paul Kellogg, editor of a journal for social workers (*Survey*), along with Jane Addams of Hull House, and Lillian Wald of the Henry Street Settlement House.[56] Roger Baldwin, who would lead the ACLU for the rest of his long life, joined the AUAM in 1917 and organized within it a Bureau for Conscientious Objection. Baldwin's Bureau split from the AUAM to become the National Civil Liberties Bureau on October 1, 1918, and it took the name of American Civil Liberties Union on January 20, 1920.

The ACLU of these years fit the countersubversives' stereotype of the radical movement because Baldwin and the early leaders of the ACLU saw themselves as activists in the American class struggle. In 1919 Baldwin said that he was "going to do what a so-called intellectual can do in the labor movement and aid in the struggle of the workers to control society in the interests of the mass." Baldwin began his letters to Communists and anarchists with "Dear Brother" and "Dear Comrade," and assured them that "we are frankly partisans of labor in the present struggle." He looked for members among "(1) Those directly engaged in the labor struggle . . . (2) those who by their writing and speaking are close to labor problems, and (3) those who stand on general principles for freedom of expression."[57]

The board of directors of the ACLU looked like the broad-based radical coalition of Communists, Socialists, labor unionists, liberal intellectuals, social concerned clergymen, and parlor pinks (wealthy supporters of radical causes) that Hoover had denounced in *The Red Radical Movement*. There were Duncan McDonald, head of the United

Mine Workers, pacifist Jeannette Rankin, Norman Thomas, Crystal Eastman, John Haynes Holmes, Judah Magnes, Joseph Cannon, Elizabeth Gurley Flynn, William Z. Foster, Felix Frankfurter, Helen Keller, Scott Nearing, and Oswald Garrison Villard. The ACLU's first annual report called for a "union of organized labor, the farmers, radical and liberal movements." It seemed exactly like the kind of radical conspiracy Hoover feared the Communists were organizing, although the names of such establishment stalwarts as Robert Morss Lovett ought to have reassured the less easily frightened.[58]

The founding chairman of the ACLU's board of directors was the Methodist minister Harry F. Ward. Ward was the epitome of what countersubversives like Hoover called the fellow traveler, that is, the noncommunist radical who embraced the Communist movement. Ward's wartime experience had taught him that only a unified left could protect a radical against repression by the government and employers, particularly a radical as alienated as Ward from the American mainstream. For a leftist like Harry Ward, the sense of community he gained from solidarity with the left was as important as any of their common goals, and so Ward treated any attack on any member of the left as an attack on all.

After the Bolshevik Revolution, Ward was a reliable apologist for Soviet communism. "In all Revolutions," he explained, "extremists have mistreated enemies. The American revolution was no exception. . . . Those who contrived to undermine the new government in the USSR and to restore private enterprise were executed. Considering all this, it was not equivalent . . . to the mass killings of the disarmed and innocent in major wars or the perpetual slow killings of the people of a nation by exploitation and induced famine in British India. As for atheism, the government had to uphold the principle of separation of church and state."[59] He said he would be willing to condemn atrocities committed by the Bolsheviks, if any could be proven, which he refused to admit, but he insisted that the fundamental principle of the Bolshevik Revolution was correct: the abolition of the sin of private profit.[60]

For Ward, all anticommunists were equally vile. Ward's son recalled that Ward "considered red baiters to be intellectually and morally dishonest cowards. Fears of becoming identified with professional red baiters and their shadow-box controllers influenced his writings a great deal."[61]

The presence of fellow travelers like Ward on the ACLU Board led countersubversive anticommunists to the dangerously false suspicion that the ACLU was the center of a secret network of Communists and fellow travelers.[62] And the ACLU, by treating any attack on Communists as an assault on the Bill of Rights, sometimes wittingly, sometimes not, did help promote the stereotype of anticommunism as the enemy of civil liberties.

By early 1920, the government's campaign against communism was losing momentum, largely because the international situation was far less frightening. The Bolsheviks were consolidating their power in Russia, but outside the borders of the Soviet state the revolution was ebbing. In America the strikes and political violence that had been so alarming early in 1919 no longer seemed so clearly to be part of a revolutionary march against America.

In Russia, resistance to the Bolsheviks was ebbing. In 1919 Admiral Kolchak had been the self-proclaimed Supreme Ruler of the White Forces and had controlled all of eastern Russia and Siberia from his capital in Omsk, with the exception of two enclaves dominated by the Japanese. On January 15, 1920, Kolchak was captured by the Bolsheviks, and a few weeks later he was shot and his body disposed of under the ice of the river Angara. Bolshevik patrols and the frigid winter finished off the rest of the anticommunist opposition in Siberia, and when spring arrived in 1920, the Soviets were in control of Russia's vast eastern reaches, except for a few Japanese strongholds that were not fully evacuated until October 25, 1922.[63]

The remaining White resistance was also collapsing before the Red Army's advance. In the fall of 1919 General Anton Denikin's Volunteer Army and General Nikolai Yudenitch's western White Army in the Baltic region were within 250 miles of Moscow and on the outskirts of Petrograd, respectively.[64]

But that was as far as they got. On October 23 the White advance against Petrograd was stopped by Trotsky's forces, and had to retreat. By mid-November Yudenitch's army had been driven from Russia into Estonia. The Reds went on the offensive against Denikin, and drove him back to his last stronghold in the Crimea.

The final threat to the Bolsheviks came from Poland. On April 25, 1920, Polish forces invaded the Ukraine, with the goal of detaching the Ukraine, Georgia, Armenia, and Azerbaijan from Russia and perhaps also the Cossack regions on the Don and Kuban. Poland's Marshal Joseph Pilsudsky thought that his country would be able to dominate this cordon of anticommunist states. The Poles quickly captured Kiev, the capital of Ukraine, but on June 12 a Soviet counterattack under the twenty-seven-year-old Russian General Mikhail Tukhachevsky recaptured the city. On August 1 the Red Army, was on the outskirts of Warsaw. Polish Communists were raising red flags to welcome the advancing Red Army into the city.[65]

Communists from around the world were in Moscow for the Second Congress of the Comintern, and excitedly awaited news of the proclamation of a Polish Soviet republic. The ground lost to counterrevolution in 1919 was about to be reclaimed, and more, since Poland would be a new beachhead for an advance on Western Europe. Eugene Lyons, then in Italy writing for radical papers, recalled that "every advance of the Soviet forces into Poland was a personal triumph."

But it was not to be. The commander of the Polish forces, Marshal Pilsudsky, with the help of the French General Maxime Weygand, spotted a fatal error in the disposition of Tukhachevsky's troops around Warsaw. Plunging through an undefended gap in the Russian lines on August 17, the Poles outflanked and scattered the Russians. Lyons recalled that "the bottom seemed to drop out of my own life" that day.[66] By the end of September Poland had regained all its lost territory, and after two months of inconclusive engagements, an armistice was signed on October 12.

The battle of Warsaw doomed any efforts to export the Revolution from Russia; it also doomed the last surviving White forces in Russia. Trotsky now unleashed all his forces against Denikin's Volunteer Army in the Southwest, now commanded by Baron Wrangel. In November 1920 Wrangel and his surviving soldiers were evacuated by the French from the Crimea to Turkey.

The Bolsheviks were now forced to concede the Revolution's failure outside Russia were daunted by the enormous task of communizing their own vast country. Lenin denounced conspiratorial activity in *Left Wing Communism, An Infantile Disorder*, calling it dangerous romantic escapism that avoided the long struggle communism faced before its eventual triumph, and he told Western Communists to enter into parliamentary politics. In July 1921, during the Third Congress of the Comintern, Trotsky admitted that "now we see and we feel that we are not so near the goal of the conquest of power, of the world revolution.

We formerly believed, in 1919, that it was only a question of months and now we say that it is perhaps a question of years."[67]

Despite the obvious decline of international communism, Attorney General Palmer made a last desperate effort to rescue his anticommunist campaign. He demanded a hearing before the House Rules Committee to deny the charges in the *Lawyers' Report*. Hoover spent late May coaching Palmer for his testimony, and when the hearing began on June 1, Hoover sat by Palmer's side. But Palmer could not refute the overwhelming evidence Post and his supporters had collected on the Justice Department's offenses.

Hoover tried to put the best face on the situation and described Palmer's appearance before the House Committee as another Justice Department triumph. He sent Congress transcripts of Palmer's testimony, along with copies of the Radical Division's newest publication, a *Photographic History of the Bolshevik Atrocities*, which showed "the acts indulged in by the present authorities of Soviet Russia."[68]

Despite Hoover's best efforts, Congress concluded the Red Scare was a dead issue. The Rules Committee decided to halt all further investigations without censuring anyone. Hoover's only solace was to paste in his scrapbook of souvenirs a typescript poem enclosed in a hand-colored red crayon frame, next to a newspaper photo of Post, likewise hand-colored in red. Hoover may have been the artist, even the poet.

THE BULLY BOLSHEVIKI

Disrespectfully dedicated to "Comrade" Louie Post

So then all hail, dear Comrade Post!
With all his ways so tricky
And ponder well, that it was only he
Who saved the "Bullsheviki"[69]

In America, the Red Scare and the Red Years ended with all involved —radicals, internationalists, and anticommunists—battered and wounded. The left had been devastated by the raids. At the beginning of 1919 there had been a Socialist Party in America with 109,000 members, the institutional base of American radicalism. By the end of 1920

that Party had been split into the Communist Party, the Communist Labor Party, and the much diminished Socialist Party, and all together they
totaled only 36,000. The split with the Communists had destroyed the
once-great Socialist Party as a real factor in American politics.

The Communists themselves declined to 5,700 members in December 1920, and were left with a Party subject to Moscow's will and whim.[70]
Shifts in the party line made it so important for a Communist to keep
aligned to Russian developments that his thinking inevitably acquired
(or never lost) a foreign accent. Between "the government's harass-
ments" and "the furious inner squabbles of the Communist sects," wrote
an historian of the young Party, "mass arrests, underground existence,
and the sustained sectarianism had completed their isolation from
American life and turned the entire movement into an arena for political cannibalism."[71]

Communists now thought of themselves as underground revolutionaries, which blocked all efforts to rebuild the prewar coalition of the left.
They blamed their Socialist rivals for the failure of the international
revolution, and showered abuse on their erstwhile comrades that soon
turned American Socialists into the hardest of hard-line anticommunists.

Liberal internationalism was also badly weakened by the Red Years.
With America's failure to join the League of Nations, crusading internationalism of the Wilsonian variety was no longer politically viable.
Foreign policy continued to be directed by internationalists like Charles
Evans Hughes (Harding's secretary of state) and Herbert Hoover (his
secretary of commerce), but they set themselves the more modest goals
of regional agreements and arms limitation. Internationalists continued
to shape American policy toward Soviet Russia. Since the Soviets continued to flout international law, and refused to settle their debts with
American creditors, internationalists refused to grant diplomatic recognition to the Soviet regime.

The fledgling anticommunist movement was in the sorriest state of
all—politically debilitated and morally discredited. During the 1920
election, the Democratic presidential nominee, James M. Cox, repudiated the antiradical drive, and when Congress reconvened for a lame-
duck session after the election, Senator Thomas Walsh demanded

another investigation of Palmer. From January 19 to March 3, 1921, Palmer and Hoover were grilled by Walsh, who exercised a senator's prerogative to harangue his witnesses while they had to sit and take it. The transcript of the hearings was a stinging indictment of the Justice Department management of the Red Scare raids. Two years later Walsh published a last blast against Hoover and Palmer's antiradical campaign in the *Congressional Record*.[72]

Measured against the ambitions of Hoover and Palmer, the antiradical campaign was a failure. Palmer, the Justice Department, and, to a certain extent, Hoover were discredited. The drive for a peacetime sedition law collapsed. The fact that they had all but obliterated the revolutionary left dissipated any sentiment for continuing the campaign. The Justice Department had demonstrated it was dangerous to belong to Communist organizations. Communist Labor Party organizer Benjamin Gitlow bravely asserted that "the raids helped the communist party separate the wheat from the chaff," but those few diehards who stayed in the party now belonged body and soul to Moscow. And so even if the political conditions had permitted a continuation of the 1919–1920 drive, by late 1920 there was hardly anything left for the Justice Department to move against.

Hoover was left with no doubts that his raids really had prevented the spread of bolshevism to America. In a report Hoover almost surely drafted for Palmer, the Department of Justice claimed that "the result of the arrests of January 2, 1920, was that there was a marked cessation of radical activities in the United States. For many weeks following the arrests the radical press had nearly gone out of existence in so far as its communistic tendencies were concerned. Meetings were not held of the organizations and an examination of their subsequent literature shows that they had been completely broken by the activities of the Department of Justice."[73]

Hoover's own anticommunism would forever be shaped by his memory of those frenzied days when communism poured out of Russia and seemed on the verge of painting the entire globe in the deepest shade of red. But in the public memory, the political and historical context of Hoover's antiradical campaign was forgotten, while only his abuse of civil liberties was remembered. And so the left's conspiracy theory of anticommunism now had become part of the national consciousness. And in official accounts of the raids later approved by Hoover, he all but conceded that he had lost the historical battle to convince the public that he had been right in 1919, and so he did his best to minimize his role in the raids. Only when he was with anticommunist audiences would Hoover proudly point to the deportation of Goldman, Berkman, and Martens, and the briefs on the two Communist parties as proof that he had been the first to raise the alarm about communism.

The Red Years were over. At the beginning of 1919 no one knew how far the Bolshevik Revolution would spread outside Russia. After 1920 it was clear now that communism was going to be confined within Russia's borders for the foreseeable future. The emergency was clearly over, and there was no public support for further emergency measures.

But these years had left a permanent imprint on American politics. Anticommunism now had an institutional base in the General Intelligence Division of the Justice Department, and an ambitious and wily leader in J. Edgar Hoover, biding his time for another chance to resume his war against the hated enemy. Anticommunists had begun to acquire a body of knowledge about international and domestic communism, but, unfortunately, much of what they had learned—the delusion that the entire left was somehow part of a Communist plot to subvert the country—was simply not true.

In the long run, the most important consequence of Hoover's anticommunist campaign was to create that malevolent stereotype of anticommunism as an unconstitutional conspiracy against the left. After 1920, the history of American anticommunism was being written by its enemies, and myths about anticommunism were overshadowing the reality.

But while there is no doubt that Hoover exaggerated the extent of the Communist movement in 1919, in almost everything he had said there was also a grain of truth. There *was* now an international revolutionary force with a secure base in Russia capable of projecting its ambitions into every country of the world. The country did need to know the truth about the relationship between American radical groups and this new Communist movement.

But Americans needed the truth, and not the fantasies of the countersubversive right. And fantasies were what Hoover—sometimes directly, sometimes by publicizing the irresponsible charges of groups like the American Legion and the National Civic Federation—had promoted in 1919 and 1920. Although Hoover, more than almost anyone in the country in those years, knew the facts about the radical movement and knew the difference between the facts and the fantasies of conspiracy theory, not for the first time, political expediency and the attraction of power won out over the truth.

The country would pay a high price for Hoover's and Palmer's failure to tell the unembellished truth about the links being forged between domestic radicalism and international communism, because the countersubversives' exaggerations, lies, and ruthless disregard for the rights of individuals had made it possible for an ideology and a movement that deserved the closest scrutiny to hide behind the claim that it was the innocent victim of anticommunist persecution. With anticommunism so discredited, it was now possible to ignore the unsettling facts about communism that lay behind the lies of the countersubversives.

Chapter 3

A NEW BREED

Russia has at present less freedom that it had in the earliest days of
Romanov rule. . . . The world has never yet seen such a despotism.
—Socialist Abraham Cahan, after a trip to Russia in 1923

With the collapse of the Red Scare, a new breed of anticommunist began to appear. Countersubversive anticommunists from the old-stock
middle class like Hoover continued to view ethnic and working class
America as a spawning ground for communism, anarchism, and revolution. Since they had so little real experience of life outside the secure
precincts of respectable, middle-class America, they were drawn irresistibly to conspiracy theories that blamed communism for everything
they hated about an America that was changing with bewildering speed,
and their suspicions increasingly frightened them, and invariably were
directed at immigrants, labor unions and the left, both revolutionary
and democratic.

But these very groups—the targets of the countersubversives' red-
baiting conspiracy theories—now began to produce their own anticommunists during the twenties. Unlike the old-stock countersubversives,
the social background of the new anticommunists made them immune
from the nativist delusions of the countersubversives, and so they were
able to give the country witheringly accurate assessments of what Communists were doing in an America and a world that was unknown to the
countersubversives.

These were days when it was difficult for anyone to focus on the Soviets' abuses of human rights because of a famine throughout Russia that
had the regime appealing for relief and blaming all their problems on
natural calamities. Though the real situation in Russia was known to
only a few foreigners, Lenin, until his death in January 1924, and then

43

Stalin were establishing the most total system of state control over society in history, a network of party commissars in every branch of government and division of the armed forces that delivered the party's
orders to the bureaucrats formally in charge, a system that subjected
every segment of civil society to state control, or, as some would have
it, eliminated civil society altogether. The Soviet Communist Party had
become a "conspiracy in power," operating behind the administrative
mechanism of the state, maintaining its authority through an official
policy of "Red Terror" that had been in effect since October 1918, when
Lenin had given his secret police, the Cheka, "unlimited power above
all law." The terror placed all Russian social classes except workers and
poor peasants outside the new economic system, to be dispossessed, pau-
perized, and left adrift without the means of survival and subject to harsh
laws against vagrancy. And so while the American Communist Party
was small and ineffective in the early twenties, it was, like Communist
parties everywhere, devoted to the interests of the most absolute system
of tyranny the world had ever seen.[1]

During the 1920s American anticommunism began to take on the ethnically diverse character of the country as a whole. Jewish anticommunists would be a formidable presence in American anticommunism
throughout the history of the movement, a reflection of the peculiar importance of the Communist controversy within that community.

Jewish communism and anticommunism were both shaped by the
politics of that immigrant group in the decade before the Bolshevik
Revolution. Many of the Russian Jewish immigrants later prominent
in American radicalism had belonged to the most powerful political
organization in the Jewish community in Russia, the strongly socialist
Jewish Bund (General Jewish Workers Union), founded in Vilna in
1897. The Bund early established a foothold in America, so immigrant
Bundists like future garment workers' union leaders David Dubinsky
and Sidney Hillman could find an hospitable political environment as
soon as they arrived. The Bundists who emigrated to America in large
numbers after the abortive revolution in 1905 brought their Socialist
sympathies with them. For them an interest in Russian and Socialist
politics was as natural as the interest of New York's Irish in Irish nationalism.[2]

Their Russian Socialist background drew large numbers of Jewish immigrants into the American Socialist Party. One of them, Morris Hillquit, was a co-founder of that party in 1901, along with Eugene Debs.[3] A Jewish Socialist Federation within the Socialist Party was founded in 1912. The leading role of Jewish Socialists gave a strongly Socialist character to the Jewish union movement, the most important secular force in the Jewish community. The same was true for the Workmen's Circle, the leading Jewish fraternal order, and *The Forward*, the most influential Jewish newspaper, which was edited by Socialist Abraham Cahan.

When the American Socialist Party took its position against World War I in April 1917, Morris Hillquit's part in writing the St. Louis Declaration that announced its antiwar decision stirred up anti-Semitic attacks. There was more anti-Semitism when Hillquit ran for mayor of New York City in 1917, a campaign that mobilized Lower East Side Jews behind their favorite son, while the more assimilated German Jews worried that Hillquit's antiwar position would cast into doubt the loyalty of the entire community. If Jews voted for Hillquit, one leader warned, Jews "shall be charged by the American people . . . with virtual treason and sedition."[4]

Many Russian Jews believed that *any* political change in Russia could only help their relatives and friends still in the old country, so there was general joy in the American-Jewish community over the fall of the Tsar. Many American Jews, particularly Jewish Socialists, became obsessed with Russian politics, especially after the November Revolution. Lenin had belonged to the same Russian Social Democratic Labor Party as many American Jewish radicals, before it split into Bolshevik and Menshevik factions in 1903, which was another factor creating sympathy for the Revolution among Jews. When the Communist Revolution captured the attention of the entire American radical movement, Jews' familiarity with Russian politics gave them enormous prestige in American radical circles. That also meant, however, that anti-Semitic countersubversives would single out Jews as the symbols of radicals' disloyalty during the war.[5]

When the Bolshevik Revolution split the American Communist parties from the Socialist Party late in 1919, there was a parallel split in the Jewish Socialist Federation into "warring camps which refuse[d] to listen to or understand one another." Some Federation members, led by

Alexander Bittleman, left for the Communist Party. Others founded the Jewish Socialist Farband, which tried to steer a middle way between the Socialists and Communists, but by 1923 Communist attacks on the Farband had made it strongly anticommunist. Some of the Socialists who stayed in the Jewish Socialist Federation after the split tried to reunite with the Communists in December 1921 by joining the Workers Party, the Communists' "legal" adjunct to their underground organization. The Socialists soon found, however, that the Communists' rule-or-ruin tactics made common cause with them impossible. With Jewish Socialists now disillusioned with their former comrades in the Communist Party, the Jewish Socialist Federation soon dissolved.[6]

Communism's influence among the poorer Jewish immigrants from Eastern Europe alarmed the wealthier, more established German Jewish community. Their instrument for fighting Jewish communism was the American Jewish Committee, founded in 1909 in large part to check the spread of radicalism among poorer Jews.[7] The AJC was pushed further in the direction of anticommunism by its efforts to defend the Jewish community against the dangerous stereotype of the Jew as Communist.

At the time of the Russian Revolution, the AJC was still led by one of its founders, Louis Marshall, a New York corporation lawyer at the center of an influential group of Jewish businessmen and financiers that included Jacob Schiff, Julius Rosenwald, and Felix Warburg that dominated the major Jewish organizations until the mid-twenties. Marshall was also president of the most influential temple in the country, New York's Emanu-El, and the leading fund-raiser for the American Jewish Relief Committee.[8]

Soon after the November Revolution, Marshall realized that anti-Semitic anticommunists were blaming the Bolshevik Revolution on Jews by making Leon Trotsky the symbol of the entire Revolution. Arkady Sack, director of the anticommunist Russian Information Bureau, warned Marshall that Jews could expect a rise in anti-Semitism because of Jewish participation in the Communist movement, and so Marshall joined the board of Sack's Bureau, and financed its efforts to distribute propaganda against the Bolshevik regime.

On October 20, 1918, Marshall sent an AJC statement through the State Department to all American ambassadors: "The American Jewish Committee deem it a duty to . . . express their horror and detestation of the mob tyranny incompatible with the ideas of a republican democracy which is now exercised by the Bolshevik government as being destructive of life, property and the political and personal rights of the individual. . . . The Lenin-Trotsky Cabinet has several members of Jewish ancestry . . . which led to the erroneous assumption that the Jews of Russia were identified with this bloodthirsty and irresponsible group. The Jews of Russia in overwhelming proportion are not in sympathy with the doctrines and much less with the methods of the Bolsheviki."[9]

Marshall had to confront the Jewish-Bolshevik stereotype again in February 1919, when the Overman Committee that was investigating Bolshevism was told by a Methodist minister that nineteen out of twenty Communists were Jews and that he had "no doubt that the predominant element in this Bolsheviki movement in America is, you may call it, the Yiddish of the East Side." In rebuttal, Marshall told the Committee that "everything that real Bolshevism stands for is to the Jew detestable."[10]

Marshall's anticommunism provoked a backlash among Communist sympathizers in the Jewish community. Rabbi Judah Magnes, head of the Kehillah, a New York conference to promote Jewish interests, resigned from the AJC to protest its anticommunism. The Bolsheviks were an improvement over the Tsar, said Magnes, and in any case a Jewish organization ought not to be attacking other Jews. At this early stage, the split between Socialists and Communists did not yet seem irreparable, and Magnes opposed anything that might widen the breach.

Defending against the stereotype of the Jewish Bolshevik would become nearly a full-time job for Marshall. There was, for instance, a Brooklyn magazine called the *Anti-Bolshevist,* "Devoted to the Defense of American Institutions Against the Jewish Bolshevist Doctrine of Morris Hillquit and Leon Trotsky." The stereotype was also being promoted by anti-Semitic anticommunists in American Polish organizations, in Rotary Clubs, and even in the widely read *McClure's Magazine.*

Marshall was joined in his war against the Jewish-Bolshevik stereotype by the Anti-Defamation League, which sent a collection of essays (compiled by Isaac Don Levine) on Russian Jewish opposition to Communism to five hundred newspapers. Defending against the Jewish-Bolshevik stereotype was also the motive behind the establishment of a national Hebrew war veterans organization to "furnish living testimonials to the fact that the Jews of our country are not irreconcilable extremists, sanguinary Reds or ravaging anarchists."[11]

Contributing to this new wave of anti-Semitism was the startling ap-

pearance in America of the *Protocols of the Elders of Zion*. Fabricated by
the tsarist secret service, the *Protocols* had then traveled to England, and
were finally turned over to the director of American Army Intelligence
in New York.

The *Protocols* purported to be the secret minutes of Theodor Herzl's
first Zionist Congress, held in Basel in August 1897. They described a
Jewish plot to take over the world, and were punctuated with sneering
gibes at gentiles rendered helpless by the power and stratagems of the
Jewish cabal. In February 1920, the *Protocols* were published in the London *Morning Post*, then collected as a book with the title, *The Cause of
World Unrest*. A year later, the *Times* of London investigated the *Protocols* and concluded that they were a forgery.[12]

When the *Protocols* appeared in America, they were adapted to im-
plicate well-known American Jews as leaders of the plot. Cyrus Adler,
one of the founders of the American Jewish Committee, was alarmed
to note that, according to the *Protocols*, "Mr. Marshall was supposed to
be the head of [the plot]. . . . His principal lieutenants were Brandeis
and Frankfurter; that the Warburgs managed the international and
banking end; that the department stores had a combined system
whereby they controlled credits; that [Horace] Kallen was the head of
our secret service and that I [Adler] was the propagandist among the intellectuals."[13]

It was a staggering blow to an American Jewish community already
traumatized by these attacks when auto magnate Henry Ford began to
blame international Jewish financiers for the world's economic ills.
Since Ford was the foremost symbol of American enterprise, his sudden
conversion to anti-Semitism in 1920 terrified the Jewish community, especially when he proceeded to publish the *Protocols* in his Dearborn *Independent*. Beginning in May 1920, the paper devoted ninety-one issues
to "The International Jew," each installment based on a section of the
Protocols, each blaming yet another social evil on the Jews.[14]

Louis Marshall took charge of the campaign to defend American Jews
from what was perhaps the most dangerous threat to their security in
American Jewish history.[15] He organized a protest against the *Independent* by a hundred non-Jews, including Woodrow Wilson and William
Howard Taft, and he was able to have the Federal Council of Churches
denounce Ford. Perhaps because of this protest campaign, or perhaps
because Ford was worried that the controversy was interfering with his

proposals to reform the country's monetary system, he halted the "International Jew" series in January 1922, only to revive it a few years later in the *Independent*.[16] This time Marshall underwrote the costs of a libel lawsuit against Ford by a Jewish resident of Detroit. Facing court proceedings, Ford unexpectedly capitulated, apologized, paid costs, and signed a statement, drafted by Marshall, in which he admitted that the *Protocols* were a forgery. But even that was not the end of it, as ten million copies of *The International Jew* were published in a reprint of the *Independent* series compiled by the *Independent*'s editor, William J. Cameron.

In Marshall's experiences could be seen the predicament of the Jewish anticommunist. When he spoke out against communism, particularly Jewish communism, he was attacked by Jews for giving comfort to anti-Semites. When he defended the community against anti-Semitic anticommunists like Henry Ford, he found himself confirming the anti-Semitic stereotype of the Jew as the protector of Communists, the persecutor of anticommunists.

Jewish anticommunists also had to worry about the effect of their activities on Jews still in Soviet Russia, where the Jewish middle class had been turned into paupers by the abolition of free enterprise and private property. Their situation was even more hopeless because it was almost impossible to leave Russia because of newly restrictive American immigration laws and the difficulty of immigrating to Palestine.

In 1924, Marshall tried to negotiate an agreement with the Soviets for American Jews to finance Russian Jewish settlements in agricultural communities in the Crimea and the Ukraine. The project was a miserable failure, and Marshall blamed the Soviet Communists, calling communism "a tyranny of absolutism . . . bent on destroying all religions except their own insane fetish. They are as abhorrent to me as Tsarism." He was particularly furious at Jewish Communists in Russia, charging that "they would stop at nothing. . . . They have no consciences." He called them "our greatest enemies in Russia. They are infinitely more virulent than the non-Jewish Bolsheviks. This is by no means a novel phenomenon."[17]

The most important Jewish anticommunist of the twenties was Abraham Cahan, founder and editor of the *Forward*, which he had turned into the greatest foreign-language paper in America, the unrivaled voice of the immigrant Jewish community.

Cahan was born in Russia in 1860, and was a Socialist before he came to the United States in 1882. He became active in Jewish and Socialist politics in New York, and founded the *Forward* in 1897. At first Cahan was an enthusiastic supporter of the Bolshevik Revolution, and as late as 1922 he was still trying to bring about a reconciliation between the Socialists and the Communists. He defended the Bolsheviks even when their regime was clearly indefensible according to democratic Socialist principles. When the Communists were accused of stifling civil liberties in Russia, Cahan wrote that "the fruit of the whole revolution would be . . . swept away if [the Bolsheviks] were to allow political freedom."[18]

Cahan's defense of Soviet atrocities began to anger other Jewish Socialists, who denounced him for abandoning the principles of democratic socialism out of sympathy for the Bolshevik dictatorship. Vladimir Medem, author of an influential Socialist critique of bolshevism, listed the Bolsheviks' violation of human rights and told Cahan that "if a reversion to the Spanish Inquisition is necessary for the realization of socialism, then we can do without such a socialism."[19]

Menem's words made Cahan take a fresh look at what the Soviets were doing to socialism, and he began to print stories about the Bolsheviks' persecution of their Socialist rivals. After a trip to Europe in Autumn 1923, he fully shifted position on communism, and wrote, "Russia has at present less freedom than it had in the earliest days of Romanov rule. . . . The world has never yet seen such a despotism."[20]

Cahan's conversion to anticommunism was a blow to the Communists' position in the Jewish community, and their Yiddish *Morgen Freiheit* was filled with assaults on the *Forward* editor.[21] By the end of 1923 Cahan was so deeply anticommunist that he was furnishing the anticommunist National Civic Federation with information on Communist fronts like the Friends of the Soviet Union, although, given the Federation's anti-labor reputation, he could not afford to let this become known.[22]

And so by the early twenties, while the Communists were working hard to gain influence in the Jewish community, there were influential voices like Marshall's and Cahan's to point out the gap between the Communists' glorious ideals and their sorry record in the Soviet Union. Other Jewish anticommunists would soon join them, and for much the same reason: Their experience with communism in the Jewish community had convinced them that the Communists' contempt for democratic procedures and individual freedom was bad for everyone, and particularly bad for Jews.

The American Roman Catholic church would be the backbone of American anticommunism for most of the movement's history. It could trace its anticommunism back to the mid-nineteenth century encyclicals like Pius IX's *Syllabus of Errors* (1864), Leo XIII's *Rerum Novarum* (1891), and Pius XI's *Quadragesimo Anno* (1931). These popes had all declared that secularism and Marxism were opposed to Catholicism, and that communism was "the great enemy of Catholicism, the ultimate expression of modern man's revolt against God, the Church, and civilization."[23]

American Catholics' anticommunism was so strong as to be a cause of friction between them and other American religious communities. Many Catholics believed that non-Catholics cherished a secret—and sometimes not so secret—sympathy for revolutionary socialism simply because the radicals attacked a religious institution non-Catholics hated. The anti-Catholic and anticlerical 1911 Mexican Revolution confirmed Catholics in this belief. American Catholics appealed in vain to other American denominations to help the beleaguered Mexican Catholic Church, but many American Protestants and Jews had bitter memories of their treatment at the hands of the Church in Mexico and other Catholic countries, and they did not want to stir up trouble for Protestants and Jews by angering the revolutionary authorities. A Catholic editor lamented, "Again the Mexican question. And what of the Catholic Church in that land! The Church has been seized, robbed, beaten and left lying on the ground helpless. . . . Our American press, the slave of invisible powers, is keeping silent. It can go into spasms over a young woman who shoots her worthless husband, but it cannot say a single word about the oppression of millions of people or of their oppressors."[24]

The Mexican Revolution left a deep scar in the American Catholic community. Catholics thought they saw history repeating itself in Russia. It had been the Mexican Revolution that converted William F. Buckley, Jr.'s family to anticommunism even before the Bolshevik Revolution. Buckley's father was an oilman in Mexico at the time of that Revolution, and he witnessed churches and convents being sacked, priests and nuns tortured and killed, all in the name of the Revolution. The senior Buckley hid Mexican priests from the authorities and helped them out of the country. In 1921 he participated in a failed plot to overthrow the revolutionary government, and was deported and his property expropriated.

For the rest of the decade, Mexico and Russia were much the same to Catholics. The elder Buckley denounced the "Bolshevik" character of the Mexican regime in a 1923 issue of the Knights of Columbus magazine, and he demanded that the United States refuse to recognize the Mexican revolutionary regime until religious liberty was guaranteed.[25] During the twenties, Catholic journalists made a point of reporting friendly contacts between the Mexican government and the Russian Revolution, although these expressions of revolutionary solidarity had to do more with traditional Mexican anti-Americanism than any real allegiance to Moscow.

Catholics' intimate awareness of the Church's plight in revolutionary Mexico and Russia made their anticommunists warn that all religions could expect the same treatment wherever Communists gained power. This was the message of the most influential Catholic anticommunist in the country, Dean of Georgetown University and founder (in 1919) of its Foreign Service School, Jesuit Edmund A. Walsh.

Walsh's academic training was in Russian history, which brought him to the attention of the Pope in 1922 when he needed a director for the Papal famine relief mission to Russia. Walsh, who also carried credentials as the Pope's confidential envoy, was directed to do what he could to protect the interests of the Roman Catholic Church in Russia. Walsh attended political trials of priests and bishops on charges of conspiring against the regime. He was at the notorious trials of Archbishop Cieplak and Monsignor Budkiewicz where he saw verdicts rendered in courtrooms filled with armed soldiers, the priests deprived of attorneys and due process, some of them tortured into confessing outlandish crimes. Walsh had always been a passionate defender of the Pope and the rights of the Church. His experience in Russia turned him into an anticommunist activist for the rest of his life.

Upon returning to the United States in 1924, Walsh devoted himself to raising Americans' consciousness about the human rights situation that he had found in Russia, particularly the Communists' persecution of religion. This he could do to great effect, because as head

of Georgetown's Foreign Service School, he was regularly invited to address distinguished audiences in Washington and across the country.
Through his widely read books on Russian history, he was able to make
his views known to an even larger audience that extended beyond the
Catholic community.

Walsh also became a leading opponent of diplomatic recognition for
the Soviet regime. He helped organize an anti-recognition coalition
that brought countersubversives like the National Civic Federation's
Ralph Easley together with business leaders who wanted their Russian
debts repaid and with labor unionists who wanted freedom for the Russian union movement and an end to Communist infiltration of their
own unions.[26]

There were also many Catholic anticommunists less well-motivated
than Walsh. While he based his anticommunism on Church doctrine
and on his first-hand experience with the persecution of the Church under revolutionary regimes, many Catholics' anticommunism could be
traced to their conflicts with other ethnic groups, and their outrage at
the anti-Catholicism characteristic of much of the left, Socialists and
Communists alike. Their anger was reinforced by a Catholic press that
made a point of reprinting and denouncing radicals' libels against the
Church. Catholic groups like the Knights of Columbus published tracts
that contained the worst of the revolutionary left's abuse of Catholicism, and racks in the rear of churches were filled with pamphlets on
topics like "The Socialist Conspiracy Against Religion," many filled
with antireligious passages from the classics of European and Mexican
socialism.

Catholic antiradical pamphleteers also searched the writings of
American radicals for insults against the Church. Particularly reliable
sources of such material were Protestant ministers in the Christian Socialist movement with their ancestral memories of the St. Bar-
tholomew's Day Massacre, the Inquisition, and *Pilgrim's Progress's* twin
villains of Pope and Pagan. Catholics were also appalled by advertisements in Socialist magazines for the old classics of anti-Catholicism:
Confessions of a Nun, *Merry Tales of the Monks*, *Sins of My Lady Peni-
tents*, and *Secrets of Black Nunnery*. Catholics learned from their newspapers that Socialists published stories for children that taught
"Christmas is a fib, Christmas is a fraud." They learned there was a Socialist catechism that gave insultingly atheistic answers to the questions

Catholic grammar school children studied in their religion classes. A self-styled "atheist minister" from Plymouth, Massachusetts, Reverend William T. Brown seemed to take an especially unholy delight in lambasting Catholics with offensive insults.

The Church could point to the anti-Catholicism of American radicals when it taught that "a religious or Christian Socialist is a contradiction in terms," and that Socialists hated "this glorious institution, founded by Almighty God Himself" because the Church "prevents the spread of their revolutionary doctrines by teaching respect for law, order and authority, and by exposing to all the world the deceptions, frauds and empty promises of the conspirators against religion."[27]

In America, unlike Europe, Catholic workers still strongly identified with the Church, and the Church did not want to lose them. The Church also feared that it was in competition with communism for the loyalty of the Catholic working class. Catholic unionists in the American Federation of Labor preached working-class anticommunism to Catholic workers and the rest of the union movement. One of the most vigorous of these early Catholic labor union anticommunists was Peter W. Collins, president of the Boston Labor Council, secretary of the Brotherhood of Electrical Workers and editor of its paper. Collins described himself as a Catholic "expert on Socialism, Bolshevism, and Radicalism" when he testified in 1920 before the New York State Assembly. He appeared on the lecture platform under the auspices of the Knights of Columbus, and the Knights distributed Collins's anticommunist pamphlets that carried such titles as "Twelve Reasons Why a Christian Cannot be a Socialist." In "Socialist Opportunism and the Bolshevik Mind," which appeared first in the *New York World* and then in the *Literary Digest*, Collins called on "the labor organizations of this country [to unite] . . . in a fight against Bolshevism and all that it represents [and] . . . to conduct a vigorous campaign among the workers of the nation to stifle the menace of Bolshevism." He would remind his Catholic audiences of the "savage attacks upon the Catholic Church, which these Socialists look upon as their greatest enemy—Victor Berger says the great conflict of the future will be between the 'black international' (the Catholic Church) and the 'red international' (Socialism)."[28]

While WASP countersubversives like J. Edgar Hoover and Ralph Easley catered to the in-house anxieties of the Protestant middle-class by denouncing "parlor pinks" as traitors to traditional Protestant val-

ues, Collins tailored his anticommunist appeals to suit Catholic workers' class resentments, mocking revolutionary intellectuals ("university
graduates like Marx [and] Engels") who passed themselves off as spokesmen for the working class. In his "Red Glow of Bolshevism in America," Collins charged that "the damage to our cause by the soap-boxer
among the working men was much less than the pink-tea philosopher
type in his circle and the circles to which his way was unbarred." Collins
reminded working-class audiences that workers had been unfailingly patriotic during the war, while it had been the upper class—particularly
upper-class radicals—who had held back. Socialism, he said, is "not a
working class doctrine or philosophy, but is the greatest enemy of the
working class not only as a class, but as an integral and most important
part of society."[29]

Patrick Scanlan, managing editor of the *Brooklyn Tablet*, official paper of the Brooklyn Catholic diocese, emerged in the twenties as the
leading spokesman for an especially pugnacious brand of militant
Catholic anticommunism, that of Irish Americans who, after suffering
from a hundred years of anti-Catholic prejudice in America, reacted to
any criticism of the Church as a bigoted attack on their own hard-won
status in American society. A fervent Irish nationalist and battler for
Catholic interests, Scanlan became managing editor of the *Tablet* in
1917, where he used his editorials to insist that all America pay heed to
Catholic sensitivities on the issue of communism.

Scanlan turned his "Managing Editor's Desk" column in the *Tablet*
into a weekly diatribe against the enemies of the Church—often defined as enemies of Ireland, whether the traditional Anglo-Saxon enemies of the Irish, or the equally touchy Jewish community that lived
across the street or down the hall. He combined a vivid writing style,
filled with Menckenesque invective, with an unbridled love of controversy. Under Scanlan the *Tablet* became the national voice of Irish
Catholic anticommunism—and a thorn in the side of New York's
Protestants and Jews.[30]

Scanlan's anticommunism was steeped in the ethnically sensitive values of New York politics, and he was quick to see anti-Catholicism as
the real motive for Communist activities. Never very bashful in his anti-
Semitism, he suspected Jews of an enthusiasm for anything—like communism—that hurt the Church or the Irish. He also resented Jews'
ability to gain public sympathy for their causes. "To the man on the side-
lines," he wrote, "one of the seven wonders of the age is the respect the

daily press has for everything connected with Judaism." Scanlan complained that "in the Mexican muddle when hundreds were murdered for their faith, you could hardly find an editorial protest even with a search warrant." He recalled that "when an anti-socialist speaker made disparaging remarks in regard to Judaism, he was promptly brought to court, the Mayor of the city demanded an example be made of him, and a magistrate with an Irish name (and with one eye on a future appointment) sentenced the young man to the penitentiary. . . . Meanwhile an individual, by the name of Moskowitz, has . . . [been] in Madison Square for two years and insists on insulting everything Catholic, down to the beads. He is unmolested."[31]

Scanlan also regarded all Protestants as incorrigible anti-Catholics, and he treated crusades like Prohibition as direct attacks on the Irish, and, by inference, an attack on the Church. Though he was as anticommunist as J. Edgar Hoover himself, he suspected that the Justice Department's anticommunist drive was at bottom a nativist plot against immigrants.[32] He denounced Protestants who felt entitled to criticize the patriotism of lesser breeds. "Up to several years ago," he wrote, "there was a mistaken theory among a certain class of people in this country, a breed of super-patriots, that unless a person's ancestors came over on the Mayflower one could not be a good American." The patriotism of immigrants during the war, he said, "made this theory look foolish. Now, however, . . . the press acts as the hurdy-gurdy for Palmer and his aides with their discord of 'reds,' 'radicals,' 'revolutionist.' "[33]

Scanlan had a hard time believing anyone except a Catholic could be a real anticommunist. For him, communism was a form of secularism, and he saw secularism in almost everything non-Catholic: Communism, Socialism also, and even Protestantism. "We think with the Bishops," he wrote, "that secularism is the root of all unrest and that religion is the only force that can bring the world back to a stable basis." The answer to communism was religion and since Catholicism was the only true faith, the only true anticommunism was Catholicism. "Here is the test for any country, 'is it a nation under God?' If not, it does not, it cannot, survive. There is the test. The nation that is not under God cannot survive, it is not a democracy." That brought him back to Mexico and Russia: "In Mexico we have a nation which we helped to make Godless, in it ruin, riot, rebellion and revolution reign. Rats that gnaw and squeal are tearing down the rotting body they infest. In Russia we have a new form of humbug, they call it Bolshevikism. We wonder if it is pro or anti-American. Why not apply the test? The Bolsheviki have passed anti-religious laws, they have confiscated private property, they have violated decency and democracy, they have desecrated the laws of justice and honesty. They do not favor a nation under God, they will fall."[34]

Scanlan enjoyed exposing the disloyalty of the upper-class WASPs who suspected the Irish of treason since the days of the antidraft riots of the Civil War. Scanlan hooted when the historian Charles Beard was forced to resign from Columbia University during World War I for uttering "blasphemies against patriotism."[35]

Even though he railed against radicals and their revolution, Scanlan was no blind defender of the economic status quo. He applauded the American bishops for criticizing laissez-faire capitalism in their pastoral letter of 1919. He demanded the government establish a welfare state that gave workers a share of decision making and profits.[36] Scanlan, like the bishops, strongly endorsed labor unions, as long as they were not radical or Socialist. He nearly worshipped Samuel Gompers, and generally endorsed Gompers's positions on social issues. Scanlan agreed with Gompers that the American economic system, though it needed reform, offered more opportunity to workers than any other in history. Any political ideology that threatened that economic system would be a disaster for workers. For both Scanlan and Gompers, Communists were therefore the true enemies of the working class.[37]

Scanlan's habit of expressing his anticommunism in ethnic terms was incendiary in the combustible atmosphere of urban America. Predisposed to think the worst of rival ethnic communities, Scanlan could not help pointing out the racial and religious backgrounds of the Communists he attacked. From there it was only a short step to libeling whole groups for the beliefs of a few. The ethnic rage that fueled the anticommunism of Scanlan and other Catholics would make Catholics all but immune to the attractions of communism, but it would also make Catholic anticommunists vulnerable to the appeals of anti-Semites and other bigots who offered them the chance to score off their ethnic rivals under the guise of fighting communism.

It was also in the early twenties that America saw the beginnings of anticommunism in the black community, even though communism, for all its high hopes, made little headway in recruiting blacks. Communists believed that racial conflicts were a product of the class struggle, and that with the victory of the working class the problems of blacks would be solved. "The Negro problem is a political and economic problem," was the original party line. "The racial oppression of the Negro is simply the expression of his economic bondage and oppression, each intensifying the other." Since this hardly accorded with blacks' perception that race was a greater problem than class, blacks felt little attraction to the Communist movement. There were, for instance, probably no blacks at the 1919 Chicago meetings that founded the two American Communist parties, and initially neither Communists nor Socialists believed they needed to tailor their program to the interests of black Americans.[38]

Nevertheless, there were a few blacks in the Socialist Party, and they had their own specific consciousness as black Socialists. When the Communists and Socialists split apart, the division between blacks tended to separate American from West Indian Socialists. Most black American Socialists, including the most influential, A. Philip Randolph, stayed in the Socialist Party when the Communists defected. For the most part the black Socialists who organized the African Blood Brotherhood, the black adjunct to the Communist Party, were immigrants from the West Indies like Richard Moore, Cyril V. Briggs, and Otto Huiswoud.[39]

In 1922 the Communist party changed its line on the race question. The Fourth Congress of the Comintern established a "Special Commission on the Negro Question" with Otto Huiswoud as the representative of American blacks. The Commission's report, "Theses on the Negro Question," now interpreted the plight of blacks in America in the light of international colonialism, and cast American blacks in the role of "the vanguard of the African struggle against oppression."[40] With American blacks destined to play such an important part in the worldwide revolution, Moscow ordered American Communists to intensify efforts bring them into the Party.

The African Blood Brotherhood was given the job of developing programs to attract the black masses, but instead became entangled in bitter disputes with Marcus Garvey's Universal Negro Improvement Association, clashes that had more to do with West Indian politics than with Communist doctrine or Comintern policies.[41]

Moscow was no more successful when its Red International of Labor

Unions (Profintern) ordered its American affiliate, William Z. Foster's Trade Union Educational League, to recruit black workers. Because there was too much racial prejudice against blacks in the unions the TUEL was trying to infiltrate. The Party also tried and failed to infiltrate the National Association for the Advancement of Colored People and the National Urban League.[42]

The career of George S. Schuyler, the most important black in the history of American anticommunism, emerged out of these battles between black Socialists and Communists, and between American and West Indian black radicals. Schuyler was working on the staff of A. Philip Randolph's Socialist newspaper, the *Messenger*, in June 1923 when Randolph chose Schuyler to defend Socialism in a debate against the African Blood Brotherhood's Otto Huiswoud. In his speech at New York City's 135th Street Public Library, Schuyler took the position "that the Negro had difficulties enough being black without becoming Red." He charged that Huiswoud and the Communists were trying "to make a dupe out of the Negro which could only end in race war and his extermination; that this could benefit only the Kremlin cabal, not the white laboring classes who would be as enslaved as the Russian people."

Schuyler later wrote that communism posed a particular threat to black security because "we had just experienced a spate of race riots all over the country, the Ku Klux Klan was mobilizing and marching everywhere, and the government had just recently scraped together a shipload of the most obnoxious extremists and shipped them to Russia on the U. S. transport *Buford*. With Communism bringing only misery to white people, what could it offer non-whites?"[43]

Schuyler went on to become Harlem editor of the *Pittsburgh Courier*. This was one of the country's leading black newspapers, and as its most popular columnist, he used his position to torment the Party for its frequent twists and turns on race policy. He also made sure that everyone, but particularly race-baiting whites, understood how few blacks were attracted to the Party: only about 150 in 1925. "In the mid-Twenties" Schuyler wrote, "there was then nothing the Communists were doing which was the least attractive to Negroes of high or low estate, what with attacks on the Negro churches and established race organizations. Their tactics repelled possible recruits who had always been suspicious and distrustful of poor whites pretending to 'save' them."[44]

Schuyler's militant anticommunism was unusual, even unique,

among American blacks, but most blacks and black organizations quietly came to the same conclusion as he, that communism would be even more of a disaster for blacks than for the rest of America. And in fact, Communist campaigns to infiltrate black organizations continued to be notably unsuccessful, and did little except raise the suspicions of countersubversives like J. Edgar Hoover, who kept the NAACP and other black organizations under continuous surveillance to see if the Communists were making any headway. Knowing that they were under such close scrutiny gave the NAACP even more reason to be resolutely anticommunist, which was not hard since so many of its leaders were ministers angered by radicals' attacks on religion, and so opposed to communism as a matter of principle.

Most black anticommunism was of this defensive variety, but not George Schuyler's. He ripped into Communists for their racism, their cynical manipulation of black concerns, and their contempt for democracy, and for decades forcefully defended his position that no matter how badly white noncommunists treated blacks, Communists would treat them even worse.

Important as Catholic, Jewish, and black anticommunism would be in the history of the movement, by far the most important development during the twenties was the addition of large numbers of embittered and determined recruits from the very left the Communists were trying to dominate.

The anticommunism of the democratic left was the direct result of their bitter experience in trying to recapture the solidarity that had made radicalism a force to be reckoned with before the war. The Socialist Party still had the potential to again serve as an umbrella for such a movement. Eugene Debs, campaigning from prison, got his largest vote ever in 1920 (917,799 out of 26 million votes cast). But unless the left included the Communists with their vital link to the Soviet Union, no left coalition could any longer claim to be in the vanguard of the revolution. Moreover, now that the Bolsheviks seemed to have created a workers' state in Russia, the entire American left yearned to be part of this revolutionary movement that had succeeded where all before had failed.

There were also practical reasons for the left to try to recapture its lost solidarity. The plight of workers in the twenties was so desperate that labor unions, particularly the militant railroad brotherhoods, believed that they would have to go into politics to defend their wartime gains against management's antiunion offensives by pushing the "Plumb Plan" through Congress. This was their proposal to expand the concept of the wartime public management of the railroads to the rest of the economy by nationalizing basic industries, expanding the public ownership of national resources, and establishing a new public banking system, all under the banner of the "cooperative commonwealth" of "production for use, not profit."[45]

But the democratic left found that unity with Communists—though logical and essential—was more easily imagined than accomplished. Debs and the other Socialist Party leaders sang the praises of the Bolshevik Revolution at the beginning of the decade—"the most inspiring work in the history of the human race"—but the Communist Party line as dictated by Moscow made unity impossible except on terms of unconditional surrender.[46]

Since Moscow had decided by the end of 1920 that a general European revolution was not in the offing, the Russians began to plan for an indefinite period of socialism in one country, and so they tightened their control over the foreign parties. They made clear their preference for docile, even if ineffective, puppets over strong and independent foreign Communist movements that might put their own national interests over those of the Soviet Union. At the Second Congress of the Comintern in August 1920 Lenin decreed that the foreign parties, to gain or retain membership in the Comintern, had to reorganize themselves after the Russian Bolshevik model, and had to submit unquestioningly to the dictates of the Comintern. These conditions were spelled out in the Comintern's famous twenty-one theses.[47]

Democratic Socialists everywhere rejected the twenty-one theses as wrong and fatal to the political prospects of any party operating in a democracy. The noncommunist Socialist parties met in Berne later that year to denounce the Communists for attempting to "abolish the autonomy of the different socialistic parties." They warned that Moscow was trying to "shatter all socialist parties which do not unhesitatingly submit to its dictation." The Communists retaliated by accusing Socialists who refused to submit to Moscow's authority of being traitors to the working class, more treacherous than capitalists themselves.

American Socialists soon began to learn for themselves the harsh realities of trying to cooperate with Communists. During the 1920 Debs campaign, Communists disrupted Socialist rallies, denouncing New York City's Morris Hillquit as "a second Kerensky."[48]

Nevertheless, Socialists continued to chase the dream of a unified left. During the 1920 election the idea of a new third party that could gather together all the scattered parties of the left began to take hold of the imagination of many radicals. In the old Northwest and the Midwest a Farmer-Labor Party had made a respectable showing, but after the election it collapsed everywhere except in Washington State and Illinois, where an alliance was worked out between the new Farmer-Labor organization and the old Socialist Party.

This caught the attention of the railroad unions, who organized a Conference for Progressive Political Action (CPPA) in Chicago in February 1922, a coalition of sixteen railroad unions, the United Mine Workers, the Amalgamated Clothing Workers, the Socialist Party, and the Farmer-Labor Party. To many in the left (and to some of their enemies), the CPPA seemed the first move toward the goal of the entire left, an American Labor Party.[49]

Most of the founders of the Conference, however, wanted it to limit its direct involvement in elections to endorsing sympathetic candidates in the two major parties. It had some success with this strategy in the 1922 elections. The Chicago Farmer-Labor Party, however, had wanted the CPPA to be a true third party, so they announced they would host a convention in July 1923 to set up a new political coalition modeled after the British Labour party and they invited everyone on the left to join them.

A shift in the Party line had put American Communists in a position to accept. Moscow had merged the American Communist Labor and Communist parties into a single Communist Party of America in the spring of 1921. There were in all about 5,700 members.[50] This new Communist Party, still fearful of government repression, continued to operate as an underground organization, so it established a "Workers Party" in December 1921 as its legal adjunct. In April 1923 the Communist International ordered the underground arm liquidated, and told American Communists that the Workers Party would now be their official organization. The new party was ordered to work through William Z. Foster's Trade Union Educational League to form alliances with other leftist groups. The ultimate goal of the Communists would be to con-trol this new united party of the left.[51]

When the Chicago Farmer-Labor Party issued its call for a general convocation of the left, the Socialists declined, preferring to work with the CPPA and to maintain their ties with the major AFL unions who were opposed to direct political action. The Communists, however, op-erating through their new Workers Party, accepted. They showed up in force, took over the convention, and dominated the vote for establish-ing a new Federated Farmer Labor Party. Reacting to the Communist take-over now in charge, most of the original Farmer-Labor Party mem-bers bolted, leaving the Communists in possession of little more than the name of what many had hoped would be a new and independent third party, but was now simply a party front. A labor newspaper com-mented that the "Workers' Party Captures Itself and Adopts a New Name."[52]

The democratic radicals and labor unionists who had gone to Chicago with high hopes for left unity were now furious at the Com-munists for having destroyed the new party "at the very time the na-tional movement for a farmer-labor party was gaining momentum." The Chicago Federation of Labor was so bitter it discontinued any further moves toward a labor party and gave further vent to its anger by voting to oppose diplomatic recognition of Soviet Russia.[53]

The Communists destroyed still another fledgling third party move-ment later in 1923. Minnesota's Farmer-Labor Party had managed to elect a United States Senator in 1922 and another in 1923, which en-couraged the Minnesotans to think about expanding into a national Farmer-Labor Party for the 1924 elections. In November 1923 they hosted a successful organizational meeting that attracted progressives from across the country, including representatives from several AFL unions. Their goal was to persuade the progressive Republican senator from Wisconsin, Robert La Follette, to accept their nomination for pres-ident in 1924. Meanwhile, the CPPA, still opposed to a third party, had decided that it would endorse the more progressive of the two major party candidates, probably the Democrat William G. McAdoo.

Hopes ran high throughout the left that a unified radical party was finally at hand, and at first the new Farmer-Labor Party welcomed par-ticipation by both the Communists' Workers Party and their puppet Federated Farmer Labor Party. The Communists' characteristic energy and organizational skills at first impressed Farmer-Labor leaders who remarked that the Communists were the "dynamos of the movement." The Communists' real purpose in entering the Farmer-Labor organization, however, was to take it over and then to persuade the CPPA to swallow its anti-third-party scruples and throw its weight behind Robert La Follette, thus putting the Communists in a position to dominate the La Follette campaign.[54]

But it was not to play out as scripted. La Follette refused to break with the Republican party until after their June convention, hoping that he might capture that nomination. Furthermore, the Conference for Progressive Political Action and the railway unions continued to oppose the third-party strategy. They hoped that the Democrats would nominate William McAdoo or that the Republicans would nominate La Follette so that they could endorse a sympathetic major party candidate.

The AFL unions were led in their opposition to third parties by Samuel Gompers, who had built his powerful and successful movement on the principle of pure and simple unionism, rejecting any direct participation in the electoral system. This time he had another objection. He warned trade unionists and their congressional allies that "the Communists controlled the Farmer-Labor movement" and that unless the Farmer-Labor senators and congressmen (from Minnesota) rejected Communist support, they would be defeated and "we will be set back a decade." He insisted that any labor cooperation with this particular third-party effort would "play into the hands of Moscow." The word of Gompers, as always, carried great weight, and a Minnesota delegate said, after hearing Gompers, that "we have to do everything to purge ourselves, to disavow any connection with Communists."[55]

The McAdoo candidacy supported by many unionists collapsed after revelations that he had accepted contributions from oil companies. Then it became all but certain that the union-hating Coolidge would get the Republican nomination. Sentiment mounted within all reform groups to fall into line behind an independent bid for the presidency by La Follette, and the obvious vehicle seemed the Farmer-Labor Party, Communist-dominated or not. Just before the planned June 17 convention of the Farmer-Labor Party, however, La Follette shattered these hopes. He said that the Farmer-Labor Party had made the "fatal error" of permitting Communists to work within the coalition, and that the Communists' goal was "a soviet form of government and the dictatorship of the proletariat" subject to "orders from the Communist International in Moscow." Communists, he said, were "antagonistic to the progressive cause and their only purpose in joining such a movement is to disrupt it," so that to "pretend that the Communists can work with the progressives is deliberately to deceive the public."[56] He would, in short, not accept the Farmer-Labor nomination, and would not join any coalition that included Communists.

When the Farmer-Labor convention met in St. Paul, La Follette's defection kept it far smaller than the Communists had hoped, but they proceeded with their plan by nominating a noncommunist candidate who welcomed the support of the Communists, Duncan MacDonald. A few weeks later the Conference for Progressive Political Action met in Cleveland and endorsed La Follette's independent bid for the presidency running on the Progressive ticket, with Burton K. Wheeler as his running mate.

Now it was the turn of remaining noncommunists in the Farmer-Labor Party to learn the hazards of trying to cooperate with Communists. The Communist Party leaders had begun to worry that they might be violating a Comintern ban on formal, top-down alliances with noncommunist parties. (The Comintern formula was a "united front from the bottom," which meant infiltrating rival groups to take them away from their noncommunist leaders.) The Party sent William Z. Foster to Moscow to ask for advice, and he returned with orders from Moscow to revoke its endorsement of the noncommunist MacDonald. The Communist-dominated executive committee of the Farmer-Labor Party dutifully took back its nomination of MacDonald and handed it to Foster, naming Benjamin Gitlow as his running mate.

That set the stage for a bitter battle between the democratic and the Communist left during the campaign, and a heartbreaking defeat, which the Socialists and the labor unions blamed on Communist treachery. The La Follette-Wheeler campaign captured the enthusiasm of all noncommunist reformers, and Debs and Hillquit put the Socialist Party at the disposal of La Follette's organization, which was also supported by the unions. But the Communists, with Foster and Gitlow running on both the Workers Party and Farmer-Labor Party tickets, spent their time denouncing La Follette and smearing Debs for supporting him. Furious at the Communists for once again splitting the left, Debs replied, "You may be right in your criticism of my position and I may be wrong, as I have often been before. Having no Vatican in Moscow to guide me I must follow the light I have."[57] La Follette and Wheeler did manage to win almost five million votes (compared to sixteen million for Coolidge and eight million for the Democrat John W. Davis). In the opinion of the noncommunist left, however, the Communists had destroyed La Follette's campaign and had cost reformers a real chance to create a true party of the left.

The La Follette campaign was a watershed in the formation of an anticommunist, democratic left. It convinced the AFL, the Socialists, and the Farmer Labor groups that cooperation with Communists was doomed and suicidal. Nearly every democratic group on the left that had had any dealings with the Communists had now been turned into adamant anticommunists.[58] The labor union movement and the democratic left were becoming fortresses of dedicated, knowledgeable, principled anticommunism.

By the early twenties, a new anticommunism was now taking shape, produced by the internal dynamics of the Catholic, Jewish, and black communities, and by the democratic left's searing contacts with Communists during their attempts to reunify the American left. American anticommunism, that is to say, was now being augmented by those who were the targets of Communist propaganda and recruitment. With these new additions, American anticommunism began to reflect the same tensions, conflicts, and forces that were operating in the rest of American society.

Each of these groups would develop its own variation on the anticommunist theme, each shaped by its own special concerns and experiences. There were now Catholics like Patrick Scanlan, whose anticommunism seethed with ethnic jealousy of Jews and Protestants, other Catholics like Edmund Walsh whose anticommunism was informed by a wealth of information about religious and political persecution in Russia. There were Jewish anticommunists like Abraham Cahan, who saw communism as a betrayal of the Socialist ideal, and like Louis Marshall, who saw in Jewish communism fuel for anti-Semitic conspiracy theorists like Henry Ford. There were blacks like George Schuyler who feared communism as a mischievous and self-destructive distraction from the real problems of black America. There were anticommunist Socialists, labor unionists, and democratic radicals.

The Red Scare had left America with the image of anticommunism as a repressive force contemptuous of civil liberties and hostile to workers and ethnic minorities. There would be many countersubversive anticommunists—even those like J. Edgar Hoover, who knew better—who continued to fit the stereotype of the anticommunist painted by Felix Frankfurter's *Lawyers' Report* on the Red Scare, as they chased chimerical conspiracies though paranoid labyrinths. They thought they knew everything about American communism, and knew next to nothing.

But there was now emerging a new breed of anticommunist, whose hatred of communism was based on hard-won knowledge of what communism really was doing. Their anticommunism was rooted in their commitment to democracy and their loyalty to their own communities. Already, the reality of American anticommunism was too complex— and too human—to be captured by stereotypes.

Chapter 4

TANGLED IN RED WEBS

The people of the United States, their government and their Presidents, since the war "to make the world safe for democracy" was fought, have been deliberately and unconscionably tricked by the mob-minded apostles of that very "democracy," aided, abetted, goaded and, in some instances, financed by the red oligarchy of Moscow and its American addicts and dupes.
— Blair Coan, *The Red Web*, 1925[1]

There was now a realistic American anticommunism based on real knowledge about communism, but countersubversives, still in the grip of fantastic conspiracy theories, continued to search for the Moscow gold they were sure was behind the country's social unrest. They recklessly red-smeared even the democratic left that was fighting communism far more effectively than they. At a time when the famine and terror in Russia should have made the case against communism clear to all, countersubversive anticommunists instead quivered in fear of Red Napoleons in the Kremlin whose machinations controlled events in faraway Massachusetts, Kentucky, and North Carolina. At a time when American Communists were actually destroying the unity of the left, reducing a once great Socialist Party to shambles during the La Follette campaign, countersubversives became entangled in the delusion that a revolutionary left directed by Moscow's agents was on the verge of overthrowing the government. The anticommunist movement would barely survive these countersubversives who would reduce the cause to a travesty by the beginning of the thirties.

The Harding administration was antiunion to a degree unusual even when viewed against the historic American alliance of government and

69

industry against labor. That administration's political scandals and its attempts to blame its troubles on the reds encouraged countersubversives to launch wrong-headed and self-destructive attacks on red plots that existed nowhere except in their own feverish imaginations.

Warren G. Harding's attorney general, Harry Daugherty, and his Bureau of Investigation director, William Burns, were in the habit of redbaiting anyone who challenged the economic status quo, labor unions in particular. During the nationwide railroad strike of 1922, Daugherty obtained an injunction that was so unfair to labor that both Secretary of Commerce Herbert Hoover and Secretary of State Charles Evans Hughes contemplated resigning.

Before taking over at the Bureau of Investigation, Burns had been director of a private detective agency that provided employers with intelligence on radical union activism. As director of the Bureau of Investigation, Burns swore to Congress that radicals controlled by Moscow were behind the labor disturbances of the early twenties.[2] He also had J. Edgar Hoover provide the State Department with information on Moscow-backed agitation in the United States to block diplomatic recognition of the Soviet regime.

It was that anti-labor bias in the Justice Department that led Samuel Gompers to charge in October 1922 that there was a "conspiracy against labor" in the Justice Department "inspired and in all probability more or less actively directed from a central point." The result, Gompers said, was that the early twenties had witnessed "the mightiest onslaught of reaction through which our nation ever passed."[3]

When scandals began to break out during the Harding administration, the left took advantage of the administration's woes to attack a Justice Department that had been turned into a strikebreaking service for reactionary employers. For its part, the administration said it was under attack by an unholy conspiracy of radicals furious over the government's efforts to protect the country from revolution.

The scandals that destroyed the Harding administration began in the Veterans Bureau and the Interior Department. They culminated in the Teapot Dome scandal in which Interior Secretary Albert Fall was sent to prison for having accepted bribes from oilman Harry Sinclair for oil from the Teapot Dome Naval Oil Reserve (near Casper, Wyoming). Attorney General Daugherty was forced to resign for having conspired to cover up the scandals. Progressives like senators Robert La Follette,

William Borah, Tom Walsh, and Burton K. Wheeler were able to use Daugherty's disgrace to dismantle his labor-baiting Justice Department.

True to form, Daugherty unleashed the Bureau of Investigation against the administration's critics, and obtained an indictment of Senator Wheeler for representing a private client before a federal agency, a charge generally seen as a frame-up. This was also the view of the jury, which acquitted Wheeler in a trial that proved Daugherty had used the Justice Department and the Bureau of Investigation to try to discredit Wheeler's exposure of administration corruption.

Countersubversives watching their hero's disgrace were as convinced as Daugherty that Teapot Dome was a radical plot whose goal all along was to destroy an effective enemy of the Communist conspiracy. Their suspicions seemed confirmed when the Teapot Dome scandals led to the left's achieving one of its most cherished political goals: stopping the Bureau of Investigation from spying on labor and harassing the left.

After Harding's death and the forced resignation of Daugherty, the new Coolidge administration was desperate to get the Teapot Dome scandal behind it and saw it could mollify leftist opposition by removing the one provocation that unified all radicals against the government—J. Edgar Hoover's anti-radical General Intelligence Division in the Justice Department. Coolidge's new attorney general, future Supreme Court Justice Harlan Stone, was impressed enough by Hoover's bureaucratic skills to keep him on as the new director of the Bureau, but only on condition that Hoover halt all future "general intelligence" investigations and confine his operations to investigations of federal crimes.

Daugherty and his countersubversive anticommunist defenders charged that this had been the real motive all along for the Teapot Dome investigation. The ACLU had led the crusade against the Justice Department's surveillance of radicals, so countersubversives were now more convinced than ever that the Civil Liberties Union was part of the Communist conspiracy. Countersubversives also charged the opposition to Daugherty in the Senate meant that the red network had established a dangerous presence within the government itself.[4]

It became an article of faith among countersubversives that Teapot Dome had been a Communist plot. Harry Daugherty devoted the rest of his life to promoting this theory and in 1931 he made it the thesis of his *Inside Story of the Harding Tragedy*. Explaining his refusal to turn over his files to the Senate committee investigating the Justice Department, he claimed that doing so would have compromised national security because two of the committee's members (Wheeler and Smith W. Brookhart) were "Bolsheviks" who were "received in the inner Soviet circles as comrades."[5]

In 1925 a book appeared that pulled together all the tattered countersubversive themes of Communist infiltration and wove them into a semicoherent explanation of American politics since the end of the war. This was Blair Coan's *Red Web*, whose title may well serve to identify the entire class of durable and mischievous delusions that mesmerized so many anticommunists from the beginning to the end of the Communist era. Coan was a former operative in the Daugherty Justice Department who had been involved in the efforts to frame its critics during Teapot Dome. Coan claimed that the full extent of the Communist conspiracy had been revealed to him during a 1922 trip to Tampico, Mexico, to represent Hollywood's Essanay Film Company. There he met an American Comintern agent who told him that the Communists had complete control over that Mexican city. The agent bragged that "it's only a question of time, and maybe the time is not so remote, either, when we'll have the same control, in effect, across the Rio Grande. We're going into the elections this year in the United States for all we're worth. . . . Our campaign is in the Western states . . . Montana is an especially promising state." (Montana was the home of Daugherty's nemesis, Burton Wheeler.) According to Coan, he learned that there already were a number of men in the American Congress favorable to "the cause" and that "the cause" was being carried into the American labor organizations, the pacifist groups, the universities, the women's clubs, the churches, and the schools. Coan was told that Russian money was available for the promotion of "the revolution" among the youth of America; and that "the program of operation was of Russian origin and that the financial support for it came in no small measure from Moscow."[6]

His Comintern source told Coan that the political upheaval that surged across Europe and into America in 1919 and 1920 was caused and coordinated by the Russian Bolsheviks. As the "revolution swept eastward and southward into farther Russia and Asia, [it] sank Hungary in the slough, grasped Italy in its tentacles, struck at Poland, sought Germany, aimed at France and England, and reached out toward America."

The revolution made its first appearance in North America, Coan learned, with "the attempt to overthrow civil government in Seattle." The "outlaw" railroad strike, the coal strike, the steel strike, the dynamiting of Palmer's home were all parts of the plot, as was "the constant demand for higher wages among highly-paid employees . . . [and] the fostering of class spirit, particularly of the obstructionist or destructionist kind."[7]

According to Coan's informant, that revolutionary movement was able to make such rapid progress because it had been relatively fragmented in the past, but it now had a secure base in Russia. Before 1917, the working class had won no victories because "in each country [it] fought isolatedly" but now "the international working class fighting against the world bourgeoisie" had "a *base*," to serve as "a sort of revolutionary rear."[8]

Coan's informant confirmed that the plot against Daugherty was part of the master plan. Just as Daugherty had suspected, the Comintern agent revealed that the radical movement had been enraged by Daugherty's investigation of Russian famine relief, and by his injunctions against the railroad strike of 1922. Moscow had ordered the American Communists to work toward the "violent destruction of the entire legal machinery," which meant eliminating Hoover and Daugherty.[9]

Coan claimed he had learned that Robert La Follette's personal political organization, the People's Legislative Service, was "the direct link of the radical 'coalition' of the reds and the pinks with the Legislative branches of the United States Government, the Senate and the House of Representatives." The Communist Party itself was far less dangerous than this "pink radicalism" that extended Moscow's influence to the farthest reaches of the red web. The United States was "peculiarly fortified against red radicalism," Coan explained, but "pinks" like La Follette and Wheeler and Brookhart were "dangerous to ordered government, for without them and their following the more extremely radical elements are but a puny minority all dressed up, but with no place to go." Throughout history he claimed, it had been men like La Follette, Borah, Wheeler and Walsh, "whose tongues stir mobs and kindle hatreds," who had blazed the path for "the Dantons, the Robespierres, the Lenins and the Zinovievs [to] ride roughshod to power."[10]

Coan was so convinced that the radical movement was on the verge of seizing power that he waved away inconvenient evidence like La Follette's loss in 1924, and his rejection of Communist support, and the shift of so many in the democratic left into the anticommunist camp. The La Follette–Wheeler presidential campaign of 1924, Coan claimed, had been designed to lure radicals into this revolutionary coalition, and he claimed it had been a great success.

The split between the "reds" and the "pinks," Coan explained, was simply a stratagem to permit "pinks" like La Follette and Wheeler to pose as the safer alternative to the more violent revolutionaries. The "reds" and "pinks," he claimed, were in complete agreement as to their ultimate goals: "to overthrow American capitalism, bolshevize American industry and do away with the republican form of government provided for in the American Constitution." The 1924 election was merely one of the "preliminary skirmishes" of a revolution that would destroy the country unless Americans heeded Coan's call to arms. Countersubversives like Coan were so caught up in the intricacies of red web theories that nothing—not facts, not logic, not even common sense—would be able to stop them from pursuing the elusive proof that they were convinced was buried someplace, somewhere.[11]

The red web primarily meant the radical political coalition that was giving countersubversives nightmares. But they also saw a threat in what looked like growing radical control over cultural institutions. In the proliferation of leftist groups organized for charitable, cultural, and other civic purposes, they thought they saw a red web network of radical organizations spreading across American society—seemingly independent but actually controlled by the Party—a powerful adjunct to the radical political coalition.

The oldest of these Communist "fronts" was the Society for Technical Aid to Soviet Russia, which Ludwig Martens had set up in 1919. There was the National Defense Committee, later the Labor Defense Council organized to defend Communists arrested in the Palmer Raids. After 1921 there were the Workers Unemployment Councils to mobilize the out-of-work. Another durable Communist front was the Friends of Soviet Russia, which went back to the international drive to collect money for Russian famine relief. Others included the Women's Bureau, headed by the mother of Communist leader Benjamin Gitlow; the National Council for the Protection of the Foreign Born; and the Anti-Fascist Alliance of North America.[12]

The godfather of this burgeoning network was one of the most re-markable figures in the history of world communism, Willi Muenzen-berg, based until Hitler's rise in Berlin, thereafter in Paris. Muenzenberg began his empire building as president of the Communist Youth International founded in 1919, when this leader of youthful radicalism was thirty-two. During the Russian famine he organized a relief agency with the writer Maxim Gorki as its spokesman. From there he went on to create the International Workers' Aid Committee with American branches, and the League Against Imperialism. He founded a Communist publishing empire in Berlin that put out daily newspapers and weekly magazines which were amazingly successful. He sponsored the Left Book Club in England. In Japan he had a periodical network of nineteen magazines and a film distribution company. Muenzenberg called the fronts his "Innocents Clubs."[13]

As these fronts multiplied, so did the suspicions of anticommunist conspiracy theorists. The American Defense Society distributed a "Spider Web chart" that traced the supposed connections between scores of radical organizations to demonstrate that "pacifism and the Socialist movements were part of the same radical conspiracy." At the top of this "Socialist–pacifist" plot the chart showed twenty-one "radicals" led by Mrs. Maud Wood Park of the League of Women Voters and Mrs. Frederick J. Libby, the head of the National Council for the Prevention of War. Mrs. Libby's group was supposedly the "holding company for all of the peace societies in the United States." The common doctrine subscribed to by all of them, from pink to red, was "to hell with the government, to hell with the law, and to hell with the right of any person to be possessed of any property."[14] The Spider Web chart was the brainchild of newspaperman Richard Whitney, the head of the American Defense Society. In 1924 Whitney wrote *Reds in America* based on Communist documents seized in one of the Bureau of Investigation's most spectacular coups in its long war with American communism, its raid on the Communist Party's national meeting at Bridgman, Michigan, in the summer of 1922.

The agent in charge of the raid was himself to have a long career as a countersubversive anticommunist. This was the Russian-born Jacob Spolansky. Just two years before he had hidden under a leaf pile to monitor an outdoor meeting of the Party at which Communist officials had organized their underground apparatus.

In August 1922 Spolansky heard that the Communists were going to meet somewhere near St. Joseph, Michigan. He discovered that a farm in the vicinity had been hired by eighty-six members of a "singing society." From a hidden vantage point he satisfied himself that the singing society was in fact the national executive council of the Communist Party.

Before Spolansky could move in with his agents, he was spotted by Communist leader William Z. Foster, who sounded the alarm. The Communists hid their papers and fled. But Spolansky had another undercover agent at the meeting who led him to where the Party records had been buried in some potato barrels. The documents were turned over to the Michigan authorities, who used them to try the Party's leadership on charges of sedition.[15]

After the trial, J. Edgar Hoover gave the Bridgman documents to Whitney, who used them in *Reds in America* to describe how the red web was constructed through "interlocking directorates." If Communist officials appeared on the managing board of one organization, and any of the members of this board—even noncommunist members—served as directors of a second, then Whitney would claim the second organization was also tied into the Communist web. By a similar chain of associations, Whitney could tie almost every reform or radical group in America into a mammoth conspiracy to subvert American institutions and bring the country under the control of the international Communist movement.

In *Reds in America* Whitney took his readers on a tour through the major institutions of American education, publishing, labor unions, and entertainment. He produced evidence from the Bridgman meeting to show that the Communists had targeted all of them for agitation and propaganda, which was enough for Whitney to tie them into his red network.

Since Whitney had learned a good deal about Communist front activities from Hoover and from his own research, much of this was accurate. He correctly identified front organizations like the Worker's Party, William Z. Foster's Trade Union Educational League, the Friends of Soviet Russia, the Young Workers' League, and the American Committee for Russian Famine Relief as propaganda, recruiting, or fundraising puppets for the Communists. His book is still useful—if handled with care—as a guide to what the Communist Party was doing during the early twenties. But the pattern he thought he saw behind all this— a red web that coordinated the efforts of all the radical groups in America into one irresistible force—was an illusion. A few fellow travelers *were* ubiquitous presences in a host of leftist groups. The Communists *were* creating deceptive organizations that attracted noncommunists whose prestige the party then exploited. But most of the fronts were mere "letterhead" organizations that existed only on official stationery, and just because leaders of noncommunist organizations lent their names to Communist fronts did not mean that the members of these noncommunist organizations were thereby delivered into the clutches of the Communists. Hoover had used that same faulty logic during the Red Scare when he tried to deport members of the Socialist foreign language federations whose leaders joined the Communist movement, but this reasoning had been rejected by Louis Post and anyone else who took the trouble to examine the facts.

Whitney proposed as a defense against the red web a peacetime sedition law like those that had died after the collapse of Palmer's antiradical drive. He thought a strong argument in favor of such a law was that its opponents were the same ACLU lawyers who had defended Louis Post. The goal of the ACLU, Whitney claimed, was "to create in the minds of the ill-informed people the impression that it is un-American to interfere with the activities of those who seek to destroy American institutions." He used chains of associations to show that the ACLU "is definitely linked with Communism through the system of interlocking directorates, so successfully used by the Communist Party of America with a view to getting control so that when the time comes for the great general strike, which, they believe and hope, will lead to the overthrow of the United States government by violence, they will already have these bodies definitely aligned with them."[16]

Much of the information about Communist activities in *Reds in America* was true—but, in a larger sense, none of it was true. Whitney saw a pink tree here, a pink shrub there, and imagined he was seeing a radical forest draped in the deepest hues of red. For countersubversives like Whitney, Communist hopes of controlling the American left were the same as deeds. If Communists bragged that they were going to capture Robert La Follette's political movement, Whitney leaped to the conclusion that La Follette was theirs, thereby smearing an anticommunist who had done all he could to keep the American reform movement out of Communist hands. What Whitney saw as a left coalescing into a formidable radical movement was in reality just the opposite: a left splitting permanently into two warring factions, with a larger democratic wing adamantly anticommunist, and a smaller one tied to a Soviet Russia that regarded all Communist parties as mere adjuncts to Soviet foreign policy.

The same suspicion of conspiracies Whitney displayed in *Reds in America* would repeatedly lead countersubversive anticommunists to self-destructive attacks on imaginary enemies, with collateral damage to hosts of innocent bystanders, honest anticommunists taking as many casualties as anyone else. Countersubversives like Whitney and Coan began their investigations sure they had all the answers, and so they tended to leap to the most extreme conclusions when they thought they had evidence that seemed to prove their point. More often than not, they would find themselves tripped up in mistakes and lies that discredited the entire anticommunist movement, their misfortunes only confirming them in the belief that their tormentors were part of the conspiracy.

Conspiracy theorists' allegiance to views of reality rejected by most of the world drew conspiracy theorists to one another. That may have been why in the preface to *Reds in America*, Whitney let slip the name of Nesta Webster. Whitney was merely one of the first of many American countersubversive anticommunists who fell under the spell of the charismatic Miss Webster, a comfortably born Englishwoman who lived from 1876 to 1950 and who had worked out a master conspiracy theory that all of world history since the revolutions of the eighteenth century had been masterminded by secret societies, with the Bolsheviks only the most recent. The conspiratorial thread ran from the Masons to the Jews, the Jesuits, and the Illuminati, and finally to the Communists. A frightening trip to Russia just after the November Revolution had started Webster on the trail of the Communist conspiracy, though she also traced her hatred of revolution to her belief that in a previous life she had been guillotined during the French Terror of 1793.[17]

Webster documented her theory in maddening and digressive detail in five weirdly fascinating volumes written between 1919 and 1931, *The French Revolution*, *The Socialist Network*, *The World Revolution*, *Secret Societies and Subversive Movements*, and *The Surrender of an Empire*. They were a madhouse collection of legends, lies, and scraps of fact all woven together and illustrated with diagrams that showed how secret societies begat other and even more secret societies that generated revolutionary movements directed by all-powerful conspirators. Her mind could seize on the most (seemingly) unrelated historical events and make them part of a cohesive plot whose outrageous irrationality seemed to countersubversives a wisdom that surpassed the understanding of more conventional intellects. Even today she is held in reverence in conspiracy theory circles, and the John Birch Society still reprints her work as one of those adepts who had gazed most deeply into the truths that rule the world.[18]

In Webster's books, the Russian Communists were the heirs of all the ancient conspiracies against religion and civilization. She illustrated that lineage in charts that rivaled in their intricacy the blueprints of a major city's underground utility system. For her the founder of modern conspiracies was a Jesuit-trained Bavarian born in 1748 named Adam Weishaupt, who had founded an "Order of the Illuminati" in 1776, dedicated to the universal reign of reason. The Illuminati instigated the French Revolution, as well as the revolutions of 1848, 1871, 1905, and 1917. The Illuminati, she taught, were also behind the IWW, the Irish Republicans, the British Labour party, the German General Staff, the Carbonari, the Polish Secret Society, the Nihilists, and the Fabians, and hundreds of other "secret societies" whose subtleties were displayed in her chart of the "Socialist Network" that had interlocking links bonding all the radical groups of the twenties into an incomprehensibly complex web of subversion. The permanent goal of this enduring conspiracy was the destruction of Christianity and the creation of a world state.

Webster's books were catnip to American countersubversives who had abandoned the world of commonplace appearances to delve into an occult world of hidden motives, causes, and processes. Securing proof for this underlying conspiracy became an obsession for some countersubversives, launching them on searches for "Moscow gold," proof that the Soviets were bankrolling the American revolution.

Believing that this evidence, if they could lay their hands on it, would destroy radicalism once and for all, they were soft touches for confidence men who beguiled them with promises that they could supply—for a price—the proof that American radicals had taken the Kremlin's rubles.

Fear of these "red webs" on the left drove countersubversives to set up organizations like the American Coalition of Patriotic Societies dedicated to exposing them. The Coalition had evolved out of an earlier "coalition" of civic organizations formed in 1924 to restrict immigration. One of the leaders of this original nativist coalition, John B. Trevor of New York, turned it into an umbrella organization of patriotic and genealogical societies (Sons and Daughters of the American Revolution, Daughters of the Confederacy, and the like) that tried to persuade the government to deport alien radicals and investigate the Communist Party. Trevor intended his organization to be a patriotic version of the red network whose tendrils he was convinced were slyly wrapping themselves around the country's most intimate cultural organs.[19]

The National Republic Organization, founded in 1924 by Walter S. Steele, was another nativist countersubversive group dedicated to tearing up the red web. He also edited its *National Republic* magazine, which furnished countersubversives with an arsenal of alarmist reports on the subversive activities of the left. In 1932 Steele began compiling a card index based on press clippings of individuals who belonged to groups associated with the Communist Party. Eventually he had filed more than forty thousand entries. Karl Baarslag, the American Legion's expert on communism after World War II, recalled that the FBI, the Civil Service Commission, and the American Legion all copied Steele's material and incorporated its information and misinformation into their own files.[20]

The American Legion, which in these early days considered radicalism the result, for the most part, of foreign birth or exotic faiths like Catholicism or Judaism, was one of the most active—and sometimes the most irresponsible—of the countersubversive anticommunist groups. Local Legion posts' activities got out of hand so often that the Legion headquarter's Americanism Commission (its antiradical division) complained to the national commanders that if "we undertake to name members of various organizations [as Communists] . . . we are going to get in a hell of a jam." The Legion denounced some of the local posts' more extreme "red-baiters," a term it used itself for extremist countersubversives like Harry Jung of the American Vigilant Association and Fred Marvin of the Key Men of America. The Americanism Commission complained that red-baiters were people "utterly devoid of reason and principle" who refused to concede that not all who associated with Communists were themselves Communists, but only "sheep . . . that were merely dissatisfied with their lot and ready to follow any medicine man that whooped up a panacea." (For his troubles, the head of the Americanism Commission found himself labeled a Communist by red-baiters.[21])

Despite these scruples, the Legion itself produced one of the most widely circulated of the "red web" diagrams of the left. The same head of the Americanism Commission who had warned against red-baiting boasted in 1925 that he was subsidizing a network of informants in "Communist organizations." The Legion's *National Legionnaire* kept members informed on radical activities and on the Legion's counter-measures, and it also put out a "Bi-weekly Report on Radicalism."[22] The Legion also maintained a blacklist of radical speakers (as did the Daughters of the American Revolution) it used to alert members when radicals were scheduled to speak in their area.

The Legion's national headquarters tried to be responsible (but still aggressive) in exposing and opposing communism, but it had little control over individual members or the local posts. The posts did what they liked, and often what they liked was to demonstrate their patriotism by wreaking real or verbal violence on radicals. The Legion headquarters itself was involved in a serious violation of civil liberties in 1928 when it harassed pacifist Sherwood Eddy on his national speaking tour. In 1929 the Legion embarrassed itself by calling on Congress to investigate the radical activities of the National Council of Churches, which called down on it the wrath of the Protestant clergy.[23]

The Legion's antiradicalism kept alive suspicions about the radical threat to American institutions throughout the twenties. When radicalism surged once again in the thirties, the Legion's "red web" charts fueled new fears that the government itself had fallen under the power of the Communists, when many of the reformers whose names figured in the red web charts moved into the government.[24]

By far, the most active countersubversives group was Ralph M. Easley's National Civic Federation. During the twenties the NCF completely abandoned its prewar function of mediating industrial disputes, and went full time into red-hunting. During the war Easley had developed a taste for tracking down the disloyal, and now he turned the NCF's "Department on the Study of Revolutionary Movement" into a coordinating committee to lead a grass-roots anticommunist movement against the left.[25] His Revolution Department, as he labeled his anti-radical unit, was managed by Conde B. Pallen, editor of the *Catholic Encyclopedia*. They set up committees on labor, the churches, the colleges, the schools, the armed forces, charities, agriculture, the press, foreign groups, women's organizations, government employees, and blacks.[26] Of the Revolutionary Department's seventy members the most influential was Matthew Woll, president of the Photoengravers Union, for decades the most active anticommunist in the AFL's ruling circles.

Easley himself took charge of the Revolutionary Department's Committee on the Study of Socialism in the Churches. This was his special fixation, and one of the mind-clouding obsessions of WASP countersubversives who felt personally betrayed by Protestant ministers who suported American radicals, and who could introduce those radicals into some of the wealthiest and most powerful circles in American society. He had undercover operatives interview leading liberal clergymen, and he circulated the transcripts among the corporate elite to discredit Protestant social action groups like the interdenominational community center movement and the social service commissions of the major Protestant churches.

Easley, like all of the early countersubversives, was terrified at the thought of a radicalized labor movement. He made the NCF's files available to Samuel Gompers in his battles against Communist efforts to infiltrate AFL unions.

Easley also cast a suspicious eye on members of the cultural and social elite who returned from quick tours of Russia proclaiming that they had been over into the future, and that it worked. When pioneer fellow travelers Lincoln Steffens, Raymond Robins, and William B. Thompson[27] managed to persuade midwestern progressive senators Hiram Johnson and William Borah to support American recognition of the Bolshevik regime, Easley came to suspect the entire progressive bloc of midwestern isolationists of Bolshevik tendencies.[28]

In 1924, Borah convened a Senate Foreign Relations Committee hearing on recognition of the Soviet Union. Easley helped organize a group of anti-Bolshevik Russian experts led by Samuel N. Harper of the University of Chicago to fight the proposal.[29] A parade of anticommunist officials and public leaders testified against recognition. The State Department asked the Department of Justice to prepare a report on Russian agitation in the United States. J. Edgar Hoover submitted a "brief" of more than four hundred pages documenting Soviet activities in the United States, his last intensive investigation of communism until the prohibition against his gathering "general intelligence" was lifted in the mid-thirties.[30]

Easley considered himself one of the most informed and responsible students of American radicalism. He even warned Samuel Gompers to steer clear of antiradical groups (other than Easley's own) because "most of them are fakes to get money out of scared employers and capitalists."[31] And yet it was Easley who turned the red web fantasy of Moscow gold into one of the worst disasters in the history of American anticommunism.

Like all countersubversives, Easley was convinced that there must exist somewhere documentary proof of the Communist conspiracy that would bring the nation to its senses about the danger of revolution. Easley thought he had finally found what he was looking for in 1928. Documents surfaced that seemed to prove that several senators, among them William Borah, Burton Wheeler, and George Norris, had taken money from the Soviets to promote recognition of the Soviet Union. Wheeler had been suspect to conspiracy hunters ever since he had pushed the investigation of Teapot Dome and had run for vice president with La Follette in 1924. Borah, chairman of the Senate Foreign Relations Committee, had outraged countersubversives by annually introducing resolutions in the Senate calling for diplomatic relations with Russia. Since Easley was already convinced these senators were traitors, when he saw photocopies of receipts for payments to the senators from Amtorg, the Soviet trading company in New York, the evidence seemed overwhelming. Easley released them to the press, which dubbed them the "Amtorg papers."[32]

Anyone with a reasonable degree of skepticism should have been wary of this type of sensational material, because there had been several widely publicized recent cases of forged documents about Communist plots. There had been the so-called "Zinoviev note" in 1924 that revealed a plot to sow sedition in the British army. It had caused a scandal that brought down the British Labour government before being exposed as an anti-Soviet forgery. Another counterfeit document had seemed to prove that the Soviets were responsible for a cathedral bombing in Sofia, Bulgaria, that killed many government officials. This forgery, too, had been traced to anti-Soviet sources.

Earlier in 1928, Borah and Norris themselves had been the target of another set of forged documents published by the Hearst newspaper chain. They supposedly revealed bribes to Borah and Norris from the Mexican government to obtain favorable treatment in disputes with Washington over nationalization of American oil holdings and the persecution of the Catholic Church. A Senate investigation produced convincing evidence that the "Hearst documents" were forgeries.[33]

The Hearst fiasco should have given Easley pause, but he recklessly pressed ahead, even when Borah denounced the papers as forgeries and demanded an official investigation of their origins. Eight weeks after Easley released the Amtorg papers, H. R. Knickerbocker of the *New York Post* reported that he had been offered incriminating documents concerning Borah that seemed suspiciously similar to the Amtorg material. Knickerbocker suspected that all of them were the work of a well-known forgery ring in Berlin, so he turned them over to the German authorities. They arrested the counterfeiters, anti-Soviet Russians who confessed to "wholesale frauds over a five-year period" that included the Zinoviev note. The *Post* boasted that its reporting had shut down a prosperous document-counterfeiting factory which had "waxed fat upon the credulity of muck-raking publicists, ax-grinding politicians and information-hungry embassies."[34]

Even though Easley had been burned by the Amtorg documents, he remained convinced that the revelations in the documents were accurate. Reassured himself by means of a theory popular in countersubversive circles that these forgeries were produced by the Communists themselves to embarrass anticommunists and throw the red-hunters off the trail. The idea was that when Communists feared their activities were on the verge of being exposed, they created spurious documents revealing what they had been doing. These documents were then placed in the hands of anticommunists. When the anticommunists released them, the Communists would expose them as forgeries, or else tip off "independent" investigators to expose them. The anticommunists would be discredited for having foisted fraudulent documents on the public, and the public would conclude that since the documents were not on the level, the information in the documents about Communist activities was also false. Countersubversives called forgeries created for this purpose "disinfection materials."

This "disinfection" theory made Easley incapable of skepticism about documents that exposed the Bolshevik underground, so he rose to the bait again when he was told he could get his hands on documentary proof that the Soviets were responsible for the political strikes and demonstrations of the late twenties.

On March 13, 1929, an informant approached Easley with exciting news. The Trotskyite wing of the American Communist Party had spirited away eight trunks filled with documents on Amtorg's (and the Soviets') role in fomenting American labor unrest. Easley's man said that he knew where these documents were, but the Soviet secret police were hot on the trail of the trunks, and unless Easley moved fast, the documents would be lost forever.

The mysterious figure who spun this exciting yarn for Easley was actually Gaston Means, one of the most notorious (and thoroughly discredited) confidence men in American history. Means had already had quite a career. He had in all likelihood murdered his wife for her money. He had worked for both American and German intelligence during the war, and after the war had sold information from Bureau of Investigation files to criminals when he worked there under William Burns. When J. Edgar Hoover took over the Bureau in 1924, firing Means had been a symbol of his "housecleaning." Means would be exposed again as a rogue when he collaborated with May Dixon Thacker (sister of Thomas Dixon, author of *The Klansman* of "Birth of a Nation" fame) on a book claiming that President Harding had been poisoned by the first lady. A year afterward, Mrs. Thacker repudiated their book, *The Strange Death of President Harding,* and accused Means of having dreamed up the whole story, a charge Means genially admitted.[35]

Means now claimed to Easley that his past dishonesty was reason for believing him now. By helping expose the Communists, Means told Easley, he hoped to redeem himself in the eyes of his new wife and child. Easley swallowed the bait, gave Means money, and begged him to get on the track of the trunks and the documents they held.[36]

Means set off on a cross-country chase, reporting back to Easley that a "Soviet agent, Nels Jorgenson [a fictitious character, invented by Means], moved the trunks from Bethesda, Maryland, to Chicago, from Chicago to Windsor, Canada, from Windsor, Canada back to Chicago, from there up to Vancouver, British Columbia and down to Los Angeles, then into Mexico and finally back to Maryland." At each stop, Means would report that he had just missed capturing the trunks, getting more of Easley's money each time. Before long Easley had handed over his life savings and his wife's, had mortgaged his house, and had borrowed heavily from his rich friends in the National Civic Federation.

Easley was convinced he would soon have proof that Moscow was behind every radical strike in the country. He wrote to the owner of a textile mill in Gastonia, North Carolina, where Communist union leaders were on trial for murdering a police chief during a Communist-led strike:

> We have, for over a year, been studying the extended menace of the Red program in this country and are soon going to make a report. Confidentially, I will say to you that as bad as the Daily Worker, Labor Defense Council, Trade Union Education League and other Bolshevik programs are, they are all in the open and they make no attempt at concealment, but the dangerous thing in this country—not that they are not dangerous—and more so because the public pays no attention, is the underground movement, and the leader of that movement is directing the activities in the South and especially Gastonia, right now.
>
> As you doubtless know, the Bureau of Investigation in the Department of Justice has its hands completely tied by the fact that the Communists went there three years ago and challenged their right to use Federal money in these Bolshevik movements because they came under the State anti-syndicalist laws. For that reason, J. E. Hoover, head of that bureau, had to discharge all of his under-cover men and today, they not only can do nothing but they do not know anything over there. The State Department head of the Secret Service depended entirely upon the Department of Justice for information on domestic matters, and when the Department of Justice fell down, they, of course, went with them, so far as domestic information is concerned. The Army and Navy, in peacetime, can do nothing while the Treasury Department is only confined to domestic matters, so there we are today, a hundred and twenty million people perfectly helpless.[37]

Now Easley received an amazing letter from a California detective named Lucien C. Wheeler, who claimed he had "definite and conclusive facts and can fix the responsibility on secret Communist agents directly sent from Russia to the South for the specific purpose of fomenting and inciting labor disturbances and committing sabotage." Wheeler had "a definite and positive plan that should crush the conditions that are prevailing in other sections of the United States as a result of the Soviet Governments activities, and bring about the exposure and arrest of their agents and associates of their agents in this country."[38]

Wheeler was a confederate of Means's, working to provide Easley with seemingly independent confirmation that the Soviet documents existed and were what Means claimed. The scheme worked better than Means and Wheeler could have imagined. Easley hired Wheeler to help

Means and wrote him that "I can see that you are the very man with whom our Department on Subversive Activities will want to connect up, on the Pacific Coast; and, further, to confer with you on your plan suggested for meeting the Red situation all over the United States."[39]

Convinced by now that he was on the verge of a sensational coup, Easley wrote a Gastonia mill owner: "IN STRICT CONFIDENCE, . . . I hope to give you the whole Communist plan of underground operations in the cotton industry in the South, together with suggestions looking to the capture of the heads of that movement. As I told you, this will not cost you any money. You can reciprocate by hanging this bunch on behalf of the country at large!"[40]

Easley's friends warned him, "How do you know the documents are not forgeries? Don't forget that Mr. Hearst put it all over the United States with forged documents and that there are Bureaus in Europe, if not in this country, which subsist upon the furnishing of forged documents to fit any and all occasions." Easley joked about this to Means, laughing at the notion that he was being swindled, though he confessed that "the Hearst stuff was very vivid in my mind because I 'fell' for it, myself." Means offered Easley more bait. He told Easley he had learned that along with the documents, there was a million dollars in the trunks, the legendary "Bolshevik gold," and that the money would be Easley's once the trunks were secured.

So far, the only real impact of the swindle had been on Easley's rapidly shrinking bank balance. But now Easley dragged one of the nation's leading anticommunists into the hoax, and all would have a catastrophic impact on the anticommunist movement.

Word must have been circulating that Easley would believe anything. Early in 1930, while he was still financing Means's nationwide hunt for the elusive trunks, Easley was given papers, probably by Russian emigrés in New York, that seemed to reveal Amtorg's plans for a revolutionary uprising in New York on May Day of that year.

Easley passed these papers along to Representative Hamilton Fish of New York and to New York City Police Commissioner Grover Whalen. Fish rose in Congress, brandished Easley's documents, and demanded the House authorize a special investigation of Communist activities. Relying on Fish's characterization of the sensational contents of the documents, the House gave Fish his committee. For years countersubversives had been clamoring for an official investigation of radicalism, and now they had gotten what they wanted. This would be the first federal inquiry into Communist activities since the Overman hearings of 1918–1919. (There *had* been state investigations in New York and elsewhere.)[41]

Congressman Hamilton Fish was a man sure of himself and his beliefs, which centered around patriotism and football. (He was one of the greatest football players in Harvard history, tackle on Walter Camp's All-Time All-American team.) He had commanded a black regiment during World War I, and came out of the war an extreme isolationist, combining an almost pacifist opposition to any further wars in Europe with a readiness to go to almost any lengths to protect American interests in the Western hemisphere.[42]

He was, of course, no Socialist, but he had no objections to Socialists participating in the political process if they were content to pursue their goals democratically. He could even tolerate radicals if they went to Harvard, and years later he still valued his friendship with John Reed. (He got Reed his position as cheerleader for the Harvard football team and he placed flowers on Reed's grave in Moscow.) The only bad thing he could say about Socialist Norman Thomas was that he had gone to Princeton. Thomas was "a wonderful man," Fish said, "because he was a socialist, and socialists are never for war, always for peace. Communists are for war." In debates with Thomas he used to invite him to join the Republican party where he could have some real influence on American politics.[43]

Fish had been one of the founders of the American Legion, and had written the statement of patriotic principles that still serves as the preface to the Legion's constitution. An anticommunist from the start, he went to Russia with a congressional delegation in the early twenties, where he met many who had been persecuted, imprisoned, and tortured by the Bolsheviks. He witnessed the misery the Revolution was causing throughout Russian society, and, incidentally, managed to buy a fine collection of art and jewelry at distress prices.

The hearings on Communist investigations he chaired in 1930 and 1931 made Fish the best-known anticommunist in the country. He and his committee *were* anticommunism as far as the American public was concerned, for better or for worse. For many, it was for the worse, because no sooner had the Whalen papers gotten Fish his committee than they were exposed as the latest addition to what was becoming an extensive collection of forgeries.

Fish was no genius, but he had been smart enough not to let anyone see the documents Easley had given him. New York City's Police Commissioner Whalen was less discreet and released them to the press after May Day so he could take credit for having prevented the Communists from carrying out the May Day uprising the documents described.

When reporters saw what became known as the "Whalen papers," they were suspicious, and within a few days reporter John Spivak, who wrote for the *Daily Worker* and the *New Masses*, had located a Lower East Side printer who had produced the letterhead paper used for the documents. The evidence pointed to a forgery by local anticommunist Russian emigrés.

Congressman Fiorello La Guardia, a political foe of Whalen and Whalen's boss, Mayor Jimmy Walker, went on the floor of the House to show that the "Whalen papers" were a forgery. Fish and Whalen were now being ridiculed, not just in the left-wing press, but even in conservative and anticommunist papers. It was too late to rescind the vote authorizing Fish's committee, which had already started its investigations, but the Whalen papers scandal ensured that the Fish Committee was discredited before it began.

The Fish committee held hearings in a dozen cities during the summer of 1930. Real or self-styled experts on Russian and American communism were invited to testify. Appearing were Ralph Easley, Edmund Walsh, the chairman of the Americanism Commission of the American Legion, the heads of patriotic organizations like the Daughters of the American Revolution and the American Coalition, as well as Communist chief William Z. Foster.

Fish thought the most important testimony was Foster's. Asked where his loyalty lay, Foster said he would fight for the red flag of communism against the "Red, White, and Blue." Fish said, "That was all I needed to hear, and so I went everywhere to tell the country that these fellows were unpatriotic."[44]

Meanwhile, Fish was getting excited calls from Easley that he was on the verge of acquiring new and even more astounding evidence of Bolshevik subversion. These were, of course, the papers that Means had been chasing, documents that would prove, Easley now believed, that the Whalen papers had been not forgeries at all but a clever "disinfection" plot to discredit the anticommunist movement. Finally Easley got word from Means that the documents were in a Baltimore produce warehouse. Easley telegrammed Fish to join him. When Fish arrived, they rounded up some police officers, and raided the warehouse.

Reporters heard that something sensational was in the works and rushed to join in the fun. When they got there, Easley and Fish were nowhere to be seen. The sidewalk was strewn with broken vegetable crates and loose heads of lettuce. The *Daily Worker* wrote, "All we can say is that the lettuce should have been cabbage heads. Cabbage is much more attractive to the ordinary jackass. But then, Mr. Fish is an extraordinary jackass." The mainstream press was not much kinder.[45]

This could not have happened at a worse time for Fish. When Fish published his committee's report, he staged a giant rally at Madison Square Garden, with representatives from three hundred anticommunist organizations. He announced he was setting up an "American Alliance," widely believed to be the launching pad for his presidential campaign. At Carnegie Hall on January 10, 1931, Fish denounced the Communist movement, as well as "pink intellectuals and sobbing Socialists" who were "more to be despised than real revolutionists." He called for new immigration laws to allow deportation of alien Communists, and authority for the Bureau of Investigation to investigate Communist activities. Edmund Walsh spoke, as did Matthew Woll of the AFL. Out of the meeting emerged a Committee to Combat Communism, which sponsored anticommunist events for the next few years.[46] Fish had dreamed that his investigations would propel him onto the national scene as a serious presidential candidate. The cabbage caper dashed those hopes. Fish's reputation as a serious anticommunist—or a serious anything else—was ruined.

For the next two years Easley stubbornly insisted that the trunks would yet turn up, but even he had to admit he was hoodwinked when Means was arrested in 1932 for bilking Washington socialite Evalyn McLean out of $100,000 to help recover the Lindbergh baby. At Means's court hearing, Easley was astounded to see in Means's company a man Means had introduced to Easley as one of the Bolshevik agents he was supposedly pursuing; shortly thereafter, Means had told Easley that the agent had been murdered by a rival faction of Bolsheviks. Now Easley could gaze upon the resurrected agent in handcuffs with Means as a co-conspirator in the Lindbergh fraud.

These blunders not only finished off Easley's money and his last shreds of credibility, but ended the effectiveness of the National Civil Federation. Between them, Easley and Fish had so discredited investigations of communism as to render them suspect for years after.

Remarkably, this was not the last time Easley would lure Fish into his calamitous enterprises. In 1932 Easley persuaded Fish and other countersubversive anticommunists to endorse a translation of Adolph Ehrte's *Communism in Germany*, an anti-Semitic tract that claimed Jews were responsible for German communism, and that Hitler had been Germany's only means of avoiding a Jewish-Communist takeover. A Jewish member of the National Civic Federation's board of directors, anticommunist labor lawyer Louis Waldman, demanded that Easley and the NCF disavow the book. Fish begged Easley to get his name off the list of endorsers and Easley had to retreat in a trail of excuses and apologies.

Easley's misadventures were not the only setbacks for anticommunism at the beginning of the depression. Herbert Hoover tried to blame the 1932 Veterans's Bonus March on the Communists. His charges were false and his red-smear attack on the veterans was condemned as dishonest and cowardly. The depression itself cut into the discretionary cash that allowed wealthy countersubversives to pursue their hobby. On July 1, 1932, Francis Ralston Welsh of Philadelphia, who maintained an extensive card file on the radical movement, announced to his friends that he would have to give up his anticommunist activities.[47]

Anticommunism had been badly wounded by the spectacular blunder of countersubversives like Easley and Fish, whose antics generated far more publicity than the testimony of responsible anticommunists who knew what they were talking about. Throughout the twenties and early thirties, countersubversives' fantasies exposed the entire anticommunist cause to ridicule. Communists and their sympathizers were coming to be protected by the general belief that they were victims, not villains, more sinned against than sinning. Communism's bleak record in Russia could hide behind a smokescreen of lies that was largely the creation of the anticommunists themselves, countersubversives like Nesta Webster, Blair Coan, Richard Whitney, Ralph Easley, and Hamilton Fish. They made it hard for anyone to believe that the danger of communism was anything except a figment of the paranoid imagination, and that anticommunism was anything more than a delusion about an illusion.

Chapter 5

A SCHOOL FOR ANTICOMMUNISTS

"all right, then, we are two nations"
—John Dos Passos (*The Big Money*)

While anticommunists were discrediting their cause with nonsensical red web theories and fiascoes like Hamilton Fish's cabbage caper, Communists were using sensational trials and strikes to draw political activists and intellectuals into the Party's sphere of influence. Communists were winning a reputation as the oppressed's most courageous defenders. Anticommunists were living up to the stereotype of being agents of repression.

But by drawing liberals and democratic radicals into close contact with the Party, communism would disillusion many of its most idealistic recruits. Communist public relations might succeed in hiding the brutal reality of life in Stalin's Russia from most of the left, but that reality was devastatingly revealed to those drawn most deeply into the Party orbit.[1] The American Communist Party and its fronts became schools for anticommunists whose graduates would add their bitter experience in the Communist movement to the well-informed and articulate anticommunism that was already a powerful force in the Catholic, Jewish, and black communities, within the labor movement, and throughout the democratic left.[2]

The first of communism's public relations triumphs was the Sacco-Vanzetti case, which the Party turned into a sensational dramatization of the class war and one of the defining experiences in the history of the American left.[3]

Nicola Sacco and Bartolomeo Vanzetti had been languishing on the back pages since their murder convictions in 1921 on charges stemming from a 1920 payroll robbery in Braintree, Massachusetts. From 1921 to 1925, the case and the appeal of their conviction had been rather ineffectually managed by the American section of Sacco and Vanzetti's Italian anarchist organization. As their appeal moved slowly through the court system, their defense was no more than a local cause in Boston for well-to-do reformers. An out-of-town reporter told his editor that he had wasted his trip to Boston: just "two wops in a jam."

All that changed in 1925 when Willi Muenzenberg's European propaganda machine began to churn out publicity and the American branch of his International Labor Defense organization (Red Aid) took charge of the case. Left-leaning intellectuals led by Anatole France, Romain Rolland, and Henri Barbusse took up the cause. *The Nation* magazine published Anatole France's plea: "Listen to the appeal of an old man of the old world. . . . Do not let this most iniquitous sentence be carried out. The death of Sacco and Vanzetti will make martyrs of them and cover you with shame. . . . Save Sacco and Vanzetti." There were demonstrations for Sacco and Vanzetti in Italy, France, Switzerland, Belgium, Spain, and Portugal, as well as in Scandinavia and throughout South America.[4]

Felix Frankfurter had turned victims of the Red Scare raids into martyrs for civil liberties. Now he transformed Sacco and Vanzetti into martyrs of the class struggle. First he collaborated in a motion for a new trial. When that was turned down on October 22, 1926, he persuaded the *Boston Herald* to take up the case, starting with an editorial he "coached." From the headquarters of Red Aid in Berlin there poured a torrent of propaganda: Sacco-Vanzetti buttons, posters, pamphlets.[5]

In March 1927 Frankfurter's explosive essay, the "Case of Sacco and Vanzetti," appeared in the *Atlantic Monthly*, challenging the fairness of the trial, the ethics of the prosecution, and the impartiality of the judge. Frankfurter's article, quickly issued as a book, was one of the transformative events in the history of American radicalism. It turned the two anarchists into symbols of the wretched of the earth ground down by wealth concealed behind the law. Other intellectuals lit their own torches from Frankfurter's flame, and spread the blaze of protest across the artistic and intellectual world. In England H. G. Wells read Frankfurter's article and published his own manifesto on June 5, 1927, in the *London Sunday Express*, to summon his countrymen to the cause.[6]

In Communist propaganda the Sacco-Vanzetti case was a microcosm of the class struggle, so the intensity of intellectuals' identification with the case established a moral bond between them and the Party. As the execution grew near, the case dramatized in the starkest terms the confrontation between the powerless and the powerful, the poor and the rich, the obscure and the famous, and the wretched against the respectable. The Sacco-Vanzetti case seemed to validate the Communist proposition that the history of the world was the history of class struggle.[7]

Books, poems, and essays on Sacco and Vanzetti were appearing everywhere—something on the case seemed obligatory from any writer with progressive convictions. Walter Lippmann, Heywood Broun, John Dewey, Norman Thomas, Jane Addams, Robert La Follette, Sherwood Eddy, H. L. Mencken, John Dos Passos all enlisted in the defense. Radicals and intellectuals demonstrated on Boston Common. Katherine Anne Porter joined the Communist pickets.[8] Upton Sinclair wrote his two-volume novel *Boston* about the case, although he privately became convinced of Sacco's guilt while researching the book. Maxwell Anderson's *Winterset* was based on the case. John Haynes Holmes of the ACLU compared *The Letters of Sacco and Vanzetti*, co-edited by Frankfurter's wife, to Plato's *Apology*. Communist novelist Howard Fast said that the case was "your passion and mine. . . . It is the passion of the Son of God who was a carpenter." Ben Shahn's Sacco-Vanzetti mosaic expressed his conviction that "this was a crucifixion itself—right in front of my own eyes." When Sacco and Vanzetti were executed at midnight on August 23, 1927, Paris's Communist newspaper *L'Humanité* headlined its story "*ASSASSINES.*" There were riots in Paris, Geneva, Berlin, Bremen, Hamburg, and Stuttgart.

John Dos Passos remembered that at the moment of the execution, it "was as if, by some fairy-tale spell, all the different kinds of Americans, eminent and obscure, had suddenly, in a short burst of intensified life, been compelled to reveal their true characters in a heightened exaggerated form."[9] He made the night of the execution the climax of his great *USA* trilogy, and his "all right, then, we are two nations" was as much the epigraph for the generation of the thirties as Gertrude Stein's "you are all a lost generation" was for the twenties. And the American Communist Party was very much part of the "nation" that was born in the protest against the outrage of the Sacco and Vanzetti executions.

Although it looked as if the Party had led the crusade to save Sacco and Vanzetti, in fact the Communists had merely put themselves in a position to take advantage of the left's need to feel part of a force powerful enough to confront the brutality of the ruling class. But the case became a cause for the intellectual and academic left that shaped their political attitudes for the rest of their lives. The Communist Party could take credit for having given intellectuals, "in their postwar sense of isolation and alienation, . . . a community of spirit, the pentecostal feeling of belonging. . . . Their indignation was itself liberating, a catharsis of the emotions, a commitment of faith where the need to believe became the will to believe and finally became belief itself."[10] A generation of radicals and liberals would never lose its sense of comradeship with all who had acted out their rage against the execution. The case had created an emotional tie between the Party and democratic radicals and liberals that nothing would be able to break, not evidence of Sacco and Vanzetti's guilt or revelation of the Party's treachery or Soviet duplicity. It was an emotional bond that the Party would be able to exploit for decades.

Before World War I the left's unity had been based on solidarity with workers in their battles with American capital. During the twenties and thirties Communists were able to draw on those memories as they thrust themselves into the most dangerous labor conflicts of the era, turning textile and mine strikes into political pageantry dramatizing the class war. One of their propaganda successes was that 1929 Communist National Textile Workers Union's strike against the Loray Mills of Gastonia, North Carolina into which Ralph M. Easley had so ludicrously thrust himself. The strike escalated into an armed battle between the strikers and the National Guard and police. A chief of police was killed and a strike leader, song writer Ella Mae Wiggins, was murdered. A few years later, Communist organizers led strikes in the textile mills of Lawrence, Massachusetts. Communists' leading role in the labor war gave the party an even more powerful hold on the radical imagination, although the AFL was winning more real, though undramatic, gains for workers.[11]

The Communist National Miners Union's strikes in West Virginia, Pennsylvania, and Harlan County, Kentucky, in the early thirties were as successful as the Sacco-Vanzetti protests in attracting intellectuals to the Party. The Communists' National Committee for the Defense of Political Prisoners sent celebrities like Theodore Dreiser to Kentucky to propagandize for the strikers and the Party.[12]

The Communists were also winning a reputation as the most courageous defenders of black civil rights. In 1931 nine young blacks were accused of raping two white women while they were all hitching a ride in a freight boxcar near Scottsboro, Alabama. They were swiftly tried and convicted. A lynching seemed likely, execution certain. A Party organizer, summoned to the scene by a local Party member, notified the national headquarters that Scottsboro could be another Sacco-Vanzetti case. Brushing aside the NAACP, the Party seized control of the Scottsboro defense and organized a National Scottsboro Action Committee under its own direction. Noncommunists attracted to the Committee included Roger Baldwin, J. B. Matthews, Adam Clayton Powell, Heywood Broun, and A. J. Muste.[13]

With blacks across the country passionately identifying with the Scottsboro defendants, the case opened doors into the black community that had always been closed to the Party. Communists were invited to speak at black churches, and were praised by formerly anticommunist black newspapers. A Party-organized All-Southern United Front Scottsboro Defense conference in Chattanooga was joined by Theodore Dreiser and his Committee for Defense of Political Prisoners. Blacks flocked to Party meetings to find out what they could do, while the Communists used the case to denounce anticommunists in black organizations.[14]

The Angelo Herndon case in 1931 forged another link between the Party and the civil rights movement. Herndon, a black Communist organizer arrested while leading a biracial demonstration protesting unemployment in Atlanta, was sentenced to twenty years on the chain gang for "inciting to insurrection."[15] The Party's Angelo Herndon defense committees pulled black and white civil rights workers into an alliance with the Party, and allowed the Party to argue that anticommunism was the real motive for legal lynchings like Herndon's.

As the country sank deeper into the depression after 1929, Communist-organized street demonstrations on behalf of the unemployed provoked well-publicized clashes with authorities, dramatizing the Party's role as the champion of the poor. A Communist protest over the killing of a demonstrator by city police led to a melee in New York's City Hall Park in 1930. An International Unemployment Day rally in New York on March 6, 1930, exploded into a battle between the police and Communist-led demonstrators, some of whom seemed transported back to the country of their dreams as they shouted curses at the "murderous Cossacks" of the police department. Across the country that day, over a million unemployed listened to Communist speakers linking the depression to the class struggle.[16]

By 1932 many intellectuals had come to believe that neither the Republicans nor the Democrats could repair an economy too broken to be fixed. Some intellectuals, responding to the Communists' militancy, supported the Party's nominee, William Z. Foster, for President. The Communists' League of Professional Groups persuaded many of America's leading writers and artists to sign petitions for Foster.

The Party used all these causes to add to its roll call of Communist fronts—many of them branches of Willi Muenzenberg's European network. In 1931 the Communists formed a National Student League that cooperated with the Young Socialist League for Industrial Democracy, which let the Party appeal to youthful radicals. Though its membership never exceeded a thousand students, it included some young people who were beginning remarkable careers, including Joseph Lash, a friend and future biographer of Eleanor Roosevelt, and Molly Yard, who would head the National Organization of Women in the 1980s. There were the John Reed clubs that brought Richard Wright and other authors into the Party orbit. By 1932, the Communist Party had more than restored its former image as the most militant and charismatic force on the left, with an influence that far exceeded the weight of its still small number of enrolled members.

The payoff to the Party from these forays onto American political battlefields was enormous. To a great extent, once again there was a left community based on shared attitudes of revulsion against a system so skewed against the poor and on a common sense of alienation from the smug self-satisfaction of the economically secure.

But in the end the Party's cynical strategies and brutal political tactics destroyed almost every cause it touched, scarring for life reformers caught in the Party's embrace. The Party's attempts to form coalitions with other leftists turned many of the Communists' closest political allies into anticommunists. Group after group learned that it was almost always a fatal mistake to try to cooperate with Communists.

In the Sacco-Vanzetti movement, for example, there were idealists who met Communists who openly admitted that Sacco and Vanzetti would do more good for the Party dead than alive. Some noncommunists in the Sacco-Vanzetti protest were convinced that "the martyrdom of these two men had been used more to emphasize the Communist attitude towards the American Government than to save their lives."[17] Future anticommunist Isaac Don Levine set up a Citizens National Committee for Sacco and Vanzetti in Boston for the Party on the eve of the executions, and his experience there was one of the factors that eventually turned him against the Party and toward a career exposing the KGB's espionage activities in America and Europe.[18]

Bertram Wolfe was another radical attracted to the Party by causes like Sacco-Vanzetti. He came to Boston to represent the Party's national headquarters on Sacco and Vanzetti's defense committee, and he coordinated appeals to individual Supreme Court justices for a stay of execution. Later expelled from the Party in a clash with the Stalinist leadership, Wolfe became the anticommunist movement's leading expert on Soviet communism.

Eugene Lyons was born in Russia in 1898 and came to America when he was nine. He learned his socialism at the Jewish Workmen's Circle's Sunday classes, then joined the Young People's Socialist League. He became a reporter and covered the 1919–1920 revolutions in Italy. Back in the United States, he edited *Soviet Russia Pictorial* (1922), published by the front group, Friends of Soviet Russia. Lyons was TASS's American assistant director, and he managed publicity for the defense committee. His *Life and Death of Sacco and Vanzetti* (1927) made him a hero to the left. Like Upton Sinclair, however, Lyons's research into the case convinced him that Sacco was guilty. (He based his conclusion on information obtained from anarchist Carlo Tresca and defense attorney Fred Moore.) After a reporting assignment in Russia revealed the truth to him about Stalin's terror, Lyons would turn decisively against communism.

Ironically, the Party's success in appealing to intellectuals was one reason it failed to attract any significant numbers of workers. The Sacco-Vanzetti protest exposed a class war within the class war when it mobilized radicals and intellectuals, but not workers or the poor. Resentment against the high-toned elite character of the protest movement in New England produced lower-middle-class demands that the execution proceed on schedule to show that the Massachusetts government was not controlled by Harvard or New York. The radical movement associated with the Party was so militantly antibourgeois and so hostile to the values of the upwardly striving working class as to provoke anti-elitist reactions from workers and the poor. They resented intellectuals' pretensions to represent a working class whose social and religious values the radicals despised. Communist critic Granville Hicks had to concede sadly that in the Sacco-Vanzetti affair, the real class war was "between the intellectuals and everybody else."[19]

Even the Scottsboro case, which gave the Party such a reputation for civil rights activism, eventually hurt the Party within the black community when it began to appear that the Party actually welcomed legal defeat to demonstrate the injustices of the capitalist system, and that the defendants' interests were being sacrificed for "larger concerns," the interests of the Party and the Soviet Union. To focus the Scottsboro efforts squarely on saving the defendants, attorney Samuel Leibowitz, the lead lawyer, had to remove Communists from the defense team in 1934, and separate his team from the International Labor Defense, which had financed the costs of the appeals. In retaliation the Party attacked Leibowitz as a "politician and a careerist."[20]

When the Scottsboro case broke, George S. Schuyler was on Fernando Po Island off the coast of Nigeria gathering materials for a book on the revival of slavery (*Slavery Today!*). He hurried home to write about the affair, and soon he was charging that the Communist Party had stolen the case "from the NAACP by legal trickery." Blacks who accepted help from the Party were being fooled, Schuyler wrote, and he warned his readers that he "recognized all the earmarks of a Communist plot" in the Scottsboro defense.[21]

Until Scottsboro, Schuyler had believed that the Party had no chance in the black community. The doctrine of "the right of self-determination of the Negro in the black belt" upon which the Party based its appeal to blacks, Schuyler said, was regarded by them as "the sheerest lunacy." But now, he wrote, blacks were in danger of being "won over because they did not see that the speakers sent to their churches were Communists bent on destroying a way of life of which they approved, but saw them simply as advocates of justice for nine black boys caught in the toils of Southern justice."[22] Schuyler made it his business to disabuse them. He reported that the black leaders of the Scottsboro drive had been trained at the Lenin School in Moscow, and were using the Scottsboro case as a cover to raise funds for the general welfare of the Communist Party. Schuyler learned from Samuel Leibowitz that the Communists had raised $250,000 for the case and had spent a mere $12,000 on the two appeals. A Communist official admitted that "we don't give a darn about the Scottsboro boys. If they burn it doesn't make any difference. We are only interested in one thing, how we can use the Scottsboro case to bring the Communist movement to the people and win them over to Communism."[23]

Schuyler's anticommunism provoked angry retaliation from the Communists. The *Daily Worker* called him a "vicious pen prostitute," a "police agent," and an "assistant lyncher," and the Party tried to have him fired from the *Courier*. Twenty-four black intellectuals, including Langston Hughes and Benjamin J. Davis, Jr., signed a petition demanding Schuyler's dismissal. Schuyler later wrote that the case made it "abundantly clear to me that I must devote all of my energies to fighting this conspiracy to destroy the Negro population to ensure a Communist victory. . . . Knowing what I did about the Communist world conspiracy against civilization, it would be criminal not to expose to the world, and especially to the Negroes, what was behind the machinations of this Kremlin criminal cabal." When his anticommunist columns were criticized by William N. Jones, the fellow-traveling managing editor of the *Afro-American* of Baltimore, Schuyler replied that Communists "make the Negro problem worse instead of better by their insane tactics. They give the murderous Southern Neanderthals the very opportunity and excuse they are looking for to commit additional homicide." He quoted the pacifist Fellowship of Reconciliation's A. J. Muste, who had once been a close ally of the Party: "The Communist Party in the United States today suffers from a mechanical dictation from the outside which severely handicaps it in dealing with the American situation. It does not have its roots primarily in the American soil. It has pursued a divisive and sectarian policy in the trade unions. It has abandoned an honest effort to build a mass labor policy. It talks a fantastic and doctrinaire language which American workers do not understand."[24]

Schuyler kept, in his words, "relentlessly harrying the Red brethren

and the increasing number of black mouthpieces they were corralling."
But while Schuyler enjoyed the give and take of political debate, he
pointed out that the violence of the Communists' rhetoric made the
civil exchange of ideas vital to democracy almost impossible:

> It is impossible to differ with our American Communists or take them to
> task for obvious tactical errors without being immediately labeled as an
> agent of J. P. Morgan and the National City Bank. They have quite the
> same sort of grooved mentalities as Ku Kluxers, Garveyites and other race
> fanatics, black and white. The course they tentatively pursue is held the
> only true one and whoever takes exception is denounced as an enemy of
> humanity, even though they may have to change that course in a few
> months. Like the Garveyites, and professional Anglo-Saxons, these quaint
> folk are devoid of a sense of humor. Their claptrap is unbelievably weari-
> some to anybody with adult mentality, and in their effort to appear revo-
> lutionary they often succeed merely in becoming ridiculous. No wonder
> they have driven the most intelligent comrades from their party.[25]

On the occasion of a Communist "hunger march" on Washington,
Schuyler mocked the Party's hopes for a revolution in America:

> Because the Communists were exceedingly lucky in Russia, they imagine
> that they will have the same luck elsewhere. They confuse the American
> capitalists with the decadent Russian nobility. Capitalism here is sick, but
> it is far from being dead. If it were supported only by those who squeeze
> great profits from it there might be a chance for a revolution in the near
> future, but capitalism in the United States is supported by the vast ma-
> jority of the American people who will fight and die for it to the last ditch
> because they believe in it. What the obtuse communists fail to realize is
> that the Americans are much more inclined to the Anarchist theory of
> great individualism and mutual aid with a minimum of government than
> they are to an all-embracing collectivism enforced at the point of a bayo-
> net by a small minority of revolutionists who have substituted Marx for
> Jesus.[26]

In 1932 an ambitious Communist effort to make a film on the American race problem provided Schuyler with more ammunition against the
Party. The Communists had encouraged Langston Hughes and some two
dozen other black artists to work on *Black and White*, but at the last
minute the Party line changed. The Communists canceled their fund-

ing and halted the production. Schuyler interviewed cast and crew members who claimed that the fiasco was due to Stalin's desire "to curry favor with the United States, with an eye to eventual diplomatic recognition, the great desideratum." When the Communists claimed that the picture had simply been postponed for a year because of "necessary changes in the scenario," Schuyler pointed out that in Hollywood such changes could be made in a "few days or weeks. Why is it necessary to wait eight or nine months in Russia? Is socialism less efficient than capitalism? Are we to believe that the land of Stalin trails the land of Ford?"[27] For years after, Schuyler would recall this episode for his readers as a classic example of what awaited blacks who placed their faith in communism or its American disciples.

Schuyler made black Communist intellectuals a persistent target of his columns. Communism was attractive to intellectuals, he sneered, because they could then write for Party publications, which printed manuscripts that would never be accepted elsewhere. "This was called proletarian literature," he wrote, "and did not belie the name. To the delight of the newly recognized authors, the editors paid for it, too, and touted them to the skies." Schuyler explained to his readers that Willi Munzenberg had perfected this technique for attracting writers to communism, and that Communists were using it all over the world to capture "colored and white petit bourgeoisie and aspiring intellectuals." But such beguilements worked only on intellectuals of modest talents, Schuyler cheerfully reported, and Communist efforts to attract the black working class into the Party "died aborning."[28]

Schuyler was the most prominent black anticommunist, but he was joined by others, particularly Socialists like Frank Crosswaith, head of the Harlem Labor Committee, who published a 1930 series on "The Negro and Communism" in the Negro World. Socialists were particularly effective in exposing the Communists' readiness to jettison their commitment to blacks whenever required by the goals of Soviet foreign policy.[29]

The greater the Party's success in pulling intellectuals into its front network, however, the greater the number who recoiled violently from their initiation into the Party and its tactics. The Party created the League of Professional Groups to draw intellectuals into William Z. Foster's presidential campaign in 1932. It produced no significant number of votes for the Communists, but so many of the League's intellectuals left for careers as anticommunists (among them Sidney Hook, Elliott Cohen, and James Rorty) that an historian of American communism dubbed the League "a school for anticommunism."[30]

In fact, the man who did more than any other American to put together the country's front movement himself became an anticommunist, devoted to exposing and fighting fronts as an expert on the payroll of government committees. This was J. B. Matthews, who was the very archetype of the fellow traveler in the twenties. (He titled his memoirs *The Odyssey of a Fellow Traveler*.) Beginning as a Christian pacifist and a Methodist missionary in Burma, Matthews joined the left during the 1924 La Follette campaign. He moved on to the Socialist Party and then to A. J. Muste's Fellowship of Reconciliation.

By then Matthews was obsessed with the idea of reviving the united left of prewar years. He turned himself into a one-man front coalition, a microcosmic red network. He was simultaneously a functionary in the Lovestoneite anti-Stalinist faction of the American Communist Party and a member of the revolutionary Norman Thomas wing of the Socialist Party, all the while serving as executive secretary of the Fellowship of Reconciliation. He joined party fronts like the Friends of Soviet Russia as fast as he could sign his name. Though he claimed never to have actually joined the Party, he worked within circles controlled by the Party, and was rewarded with trips to the Soviet Union every year from 1927 to 1932. He said that communism appealed to him because "the Communist Party alone was energetically working for the united front. . . . Its united front activities seemed to be the place to spend my own efforts to help the pitifully weak leftist groups to combine their resources in order to make a real Marxist impression upon the American scene."[31]

In the six months between January and June 1933, Matthews joined fifteen Communist front organizations, and served as the national chairman of the most important of all the thirties' fronts, the United States Congress Against War, later the League Against War and Fascism, with Matthews still chairman. The fervently anticommunist Socialist Party expelled him when he made a party-line speech defending the Soviet Union without mentioning the Socialist prisoners Stalin was holding in his jails.

The final result of Matthews' experiences with the Communist Party, however, was to convince him that Communists were inveterate plotters who, far from working to produce a united left, were themselves the reason why the left could not regain its lost unity. After he broke with the Party he became so disgusted with leftists who continued to place their faith in the Communists that in the end he repudiated the left altogether.

As a school for anticommunists, the front movement was rivaled only by the Communist Party as it tied itself into knots in the late twenties trying to follow Stalin's maneuvers to eliminate his rivals—first Trotsky, then Bukharin—until he himself finally emerged as the absolute leader of world communism. Each tactical shift by Stalin was followed by shifts in the top leadership of the American Party, as the supporters of each of Stalin's hapless colleagues were ritually denounced, degraded, and expelled. Each successive stage in the process of Stalinizing the Party would produce a new crop of ex-Communists—expellees, defectors, and other casualties—and out of them would emerge a new contingent of anticommunists who would play influential roles in the history of American anticommunism.

Many of these new anticommunists came out of the top ranks of the American Communist Party. After Lenin's death in 1924, Stalin allied himself with Comintern chief Nikolai Bukharin against Trotsky. This was the cue for a faction of American Communists led by Jay Lovestone to side with Bukharin against Trotsky's American disciples, led by James Cannon. When Cannon was expelled, about one hundred Trotskyists followed him out of the Party to found the "Communist League of America (Opposition)," where many future anticommunists paused for breath before taking the last step.

Once Stalin had eliminated Trotsky and his supporters, he turned against Bukharin. The leaders of the American Party—Jay Lovestone, Ben Gitlow, and Bertram Wolfe[32]—were in Moscow when they got caught on the wrong side of the new split. Stalin ordered them to submit in advance to any Comintern decrees concerning the American Party. They protested they needed to exercise their own judgment as to revolutionary strategy for the United States. Gitlow told Stalin to his face, "Not only do I vote against the decision, but when I get back to the United States, I will *fight* against it." Stalin shouted back, "Who do you think you are? Trotsky has defied me. Where is he? Zinoviev defied me. Where is he? Bukharin defied me. Where is he? And you! Who are you? Yes, you will get back to America [the three must have breathed a sigh of relief]. But when you get there, nobody will be with you except your wives."[33]

He was right. When Gitlow and his comrades got back to New York, they were promptly expelled from the Party, along with New York secretary Ben Mandel, who eventually joined Matthews on the research staff of the House Un-American Activities Committee. Lovestone and two hundred of his followers formed their own party, the "Communist Party (Majority Group)," and began their own long march toward anticommunism. After World War II, Lovestone would become the resident expert on communism for the AFL-CIO and a major force in American labor's cold war. The purges of Bukharinites and Trotskyists would produce anticommunists whose firsthand experience with Stalin—which had earlier given them immense authority in Communist councils—would later give them even more prestige in the anticommunist movement.[34]

But nothing was more important to the Party than its efforts to gain influence in the American labor movement. Everything else was peripheral to this central concern. It was here that the Party expended most of its time, money, and energy, and it was here that Party efforts produced the greatest gains for anticommunism.

The Party's most dramatic failure was in New York City's Jewish needle trades unions. The largest of these was the International Ladies Garment Workers Union, headed by Morris Sigman, who at first tried to cooperate with his union's Communists. By 1925, however, he was locked in a bitter struggle with Foster's Trade Union Educational League for control of his own union. When the Communists managed to capture three locals, Sigman suspended their leaders. He regained control of two of the locals, but the third remained in the hands of Communists who used it as a base for a campaign to take over the whole union. By early 1926 the Communists were on the verge of controlling the entire ILGWU.[35]

Their gains were short-lived. On July 1, 1926, the Communists called a general strike against the garment manufacturers, and won a favorable settlement from the employers. Because of a power struggle within the

Party leadership, however, the strike leaders could not get the Party to approve the terms of the agreement, and so the strike dragged on, prolonged only by Communist Party politics. The strikers' suffering finally reached the point where the union's international leaders had to step in, suspend the Communists, and settle the strike on December 13, 1926. For Communists in the major Jewish garment unions, their moment had passed. Their irresponsibility had left the union's anticommunist Socialist leaders in firm control of the ILGWU and more bitterly anticommunist than ever. The strike made ILGWU chief David Dubinsky one of the most powerful figures in the American union movement, and set him on the course that would make him the most committed anticommunist in American labor.[36]

Not all of the garment workers' union leaders came out of the 1926 experience as anticommunist as Dubinsky, however. The Amalgamated Garment Workers Union's Sidney Hillman reached an accommodation with his Communist members by supporting a pro-Soviet line on foreign policy, while keeping the Communists out of any real power in the union's labor relations efforts. A third Jewish union, the Furriers, under Communists Ben Gold and Aaron Gross, remained one of communism's strongholds in the Jewish community.[37]

The Communist-Socialist clash in the Jewish labor unions spilled over into the principal workers' fraternal order, the Jewish Workmen's Circle. The Circle's Communist members bolted in 1929 to set up a rival International Workers Order. Only a few members followed the Communists out of the Circle, however, and the split made the Circle as anticommunist as the ILGWU, a defeat that cost the Communists much of their influence in the Jewish community."[38] All told, the only lasting impact of the Communists' effort to gain control of the Jewish labor union movement was to give anticommunism a militant base within Jewish unionism.

The Communist Party's position within the Jewish community was also undercut by the Party's line on issues important to American Jews. In 1929, Arabs massacred Jewish settlers in Palestine (the "mullah riots"). Following the Party line, Jewish Communists praised the Arabs as "fighters for national liberation," infuriating almost all American Jews. Religious Jews were also scandalized by the antireligious rhetoric of Jewish Communists, which sometimes verged on blasphemy and anti-Semitism. Some Jewish Communists held mock seders on Passover, dances on Rosh Hashanah, and lectures on Yom Kippur to demonstrate their liberation from "tribal superstitions." "The yearly anti-religious demonstration organized by the Jewish Bureau of the Communist Party on Kol Nidre night," boasted the Communist paper *Freiheit*, "has become a recognized institution among revolutionary Jewish workers who fight darkness and religious poison."[39]

Before 1930, the Party's efforts had done little but strengthen the hands of union anticommunists. In 1929 a change in its line plunged the Communists into another confrontation with the mainstream unions, with the same result as before—an even greater degree of anticommunism in the American union movement. That year, Stalin announced his "Third Period" theory of revolution. The first period, 1917–1921, was one of world revolutionary crisis. The second, from 1921 to 1927, had seen the destabilization of capitalism. The third and ultimate stage of the revolution had begun in 1928, and would produce the internal disintegration of capitalism. To ensure that the Communists would be poised to seize power when capitalism collapsed, he ordered each national party to crush nonrevolutionary groups on the left.[40] In keeping with this "Left Turn," the Comintern now denounced Foster's TUEL for the "boring from within" strategy he had adopted in obedience to earlier Moscow directives. The Party was now to organize its own unions in competition with the AFL's. To prepare Russia for the final crisis, Stalin launched the forced collectivization of Soviet agriculture, and instituted the first five-year plan of industrial mobilization.

The new Party line made the Communists "dual unionists" in the eyes of the AFL membership and leadership alike—the unpardonable sin—and so made the Communists anathema, helping the AFL unions repel the challenge. By 1932 the Party's policy was an obvious failure, although it conjured up visions of a Communist-controlled union movement that terrified countersubversives, when, in fact, the union movement was becoming more militantly anticommunist with each passing year.

Unlike other communities prominent in the anticommunist movement, American Catholics were not spurred toward anticommunism by

Communist inroads in their ranks. American Catholics' solidarity with Catholic suffering under revolutionary regimes and the teachings of the popes kept Catholics from forgetting the issue of communism, however, so American Catholicism remained an anticommunist fortress. Catholics tried to counter Communist propaganda by publicizing the facts about persecution of religion in the Soviet Union. Edmund Walsh remained in his post as head of the School of Foreign Service at Georgetown, where he assembled a notable archival collection on Russian communism. He taught a course at Georgetown on "Russia in Revolution" and in 1924 began an annual course of lectures at the Smithsonian which were so well subscribed that they had to be moved to the much larger Constitution Hall for the next eighteen years.[41] Walsh also taught courses on communism at officer training schools, at the Command and General Staff School at Fort Leavenworth, and at the Judge Advocate General School at the University of Michigan. His scholarly works on Russia contributed to his reputation as one of the country's real experts on Soviet communism. His *Fall of the Russian Empire* provided a detailed analysis of how the Bolsheviks managed to seize power in Russia. This was followed by an impressive study of Stalin's economic policies, *The Last Stand—An Interpretation of the Soviet Five Year Plan.*

Walsh's anticommunism kept him at the head of the opposition to diplomatic recognition of the Soviet Union. Each year the final installment of his lecture series at Constitution Hall was "The Recognition of Russia by the United States," in which he enumerated the arguments against diplomatic relations. The communists recognized they had a dangerous enemy in Walsh. When Walsh presented evidence in 1930 that six thousand Orthodox priests had been executed by the Soviets, young Communists picketed Walsh's lecture hall, accusing Walsh of trying to start a war with Russia "under the guise of [opposing] religious persecution."[42]

American Catholics' hatred of all revolutions as a matter of doctrine and faith created a gulf between them and even some anticommunists who opposed the Church's alliance with the most reactionary elements in many repressive regimes. When the Mexican government executed Father Miguel Pro in 1927 on charges of plotting to assassinate the head of state, the Knights of Columbus organized a protest campaign that equated support for the Mexican revolution with anti-Catholicism.[43] Father John Ryan, head of the Social Action Department of the National Catholic Welfare Conference and the American Church's most prominent liberal, resigned from the ACLU when Norman Thomas and Roger Baldwin made excuses for the Mexican regime's persecution of the Church. Thomas, an ordained Presbyterian minister, offended Ryan by saying he was "amused" to be lectured by a Catholic priest on the subject of religious liberty.[44]

While many liberals and democratic radicals strained to find positive elements in the Soviet experiment, Catholics persisted in judging the Communist regime by how it treated religion, and particularly how it acted toward the Church. The Vatican made sure that American Catholics never forgot this issue. In March 1930, the Pope ordered American Catholics to pray each Sunday for the reconversion of Russia, and until the 1960s such prayers would be the routine conclusion at every Catholic Mass. In his sermon announcing the new prayers, the Bishop of Baltimore told his diocese:

> The eyes of the whole world just now are turned towards Soviet Russia in sad contemplation of a condition of suffering heretofore unprecedented in the history of mankind. The Communistic principles of Karl Marx, who died in 1883, are being driven by the new Russian Government to their grim logical conclusions. Lenin, now dead, and Trotsky, exiled by his radical brethren, visualized not only Russia, but the world, as their theater of war against Capital and God. That war planned soon after the close of the world conflict is now at its height under Stalin, the present leader of Bolshevism, in the land of the Czars.

Catholics should remember in their prayers, the Bishop reminded them,

> the unspeakable agonies of millions of believers—Catholic, Protestant and Jewish—in the far-flung Russian area. A Godless nation is aborning. Atheism is the recognized State Religion. Only Atheism has full freedom to carry on its propaganda. The Government had its officially formed "Society of the Godless," subsidized to snatch from the heart of Russia's millions the very idea of a God. Nine universities were established by the Soviet powers within the past year to teach Atheism. Blasphemous and revolting caricatures of God and Christ are scattered in millions of copies and posters throughout the land. Churches, temples and monasteries have been razed or, if left standing, have been handed over by the Government to Communistic uses and in cases employed for pornographic purposes.

Mass executions have been the order of the day in Soviet Russia. Force, intensified daily, is fundamental to Communism. It has resulted in death and exile worse than death to countless numbers of the Faithful, their priests and bishops. No religion is spared. Only the negation of Atheism may flourish. We can scarcely visualize the moral conditions consequent on such a war against God.[45]

To deliver the sermon at the Baltimore Cathedral that inaugurated the prayers for "bleeding Russia" on March 19, 1930, the Baltimore bishop chose Edmund Walsh.

Catholic anticommunists like Edmund Walsh were quick to rebut favorable reports on communism in Russia. In 1931 there was a sharp exchange between Walsh and George Bernard Shaw, just back from a ten-day tour of Russia and at the height of his enthusiasm for the Soviet experiment. CBS gave Shaw a chance to ridicule American "boobs" for being unable to appreciate the Russian miracle. Perhaps feeling that the reputation of Catholics in America had been sullied by pro-Communist sentiments from an Irishman—even one of Protestant background—Walsh demanded and was given time to reply over the same network.[46]

In a creditable imitation of Shaw's sarcastic style, Walsh jeered at the dramatist's "important" discoveries about Russia:

Within the brief compass of ten days, spent in observing the selected facts and Potemkin villages arranged by those skilled window-dressers in the Political Bureau of the Communist party, that venerable comedian was enabled to compare the entire Russian achievement with conditions in the United States—which he has never visited for so much as one day. There's a lightning calculator for you! Addressing his American hearers as "boobs," and stooping down to accommodate his tone and language to their illiteracy, he urged the American people to scrap their Constitution and the political experience of a hundred and fifty years in favor of the better plan which he found in Moscow. Now, Mr. Shaw is, of course, the acknowledged Playboy of the Western World. He is the licensed charlatan of English letters. . . . But even a favorite court jester must keep his pranks within his privilege and not don caps and bells at every turn.

The situation in Russia was too terrible to be served by the talents of a comedian, Walsh complained. Shaw had descended from "jibes and insults" to outright lies when he claimed that "Mr. Stalin's craft" was the only ship of state still afloat during the depression. The direction a ship was sailing, Walsh said, was more important than its speed, and the Soviets had steered a starving Russia into the grip of the most tyrannical regime the world had ever seen. Communism had given Russia

> a military dictatorship of one percent over the remaining ninety-nine and cynically sustaining it through a terrorism that is matter of public record. The published and solemn protests of socialists, anarchists, and sincere liberals the world over place this fact above and beyond charges of partisanship. There is no more impressive indictment of this enslavement than the indignant protests of Albert Einstein, George Brandes, Sinclair Lewis, Maurice Maeterlinck, Knut Hamsun, H. G. Wells, Israel Zangwill and Bertrand Russell registered in the preface of that Macedonian cry for help, "Letters from a Russian Prison."[47]

Many Americans, Walsh knew, even anticommunists, had a patriotic reverence for the word "revolution." But he argued that when the Bolsheviks dispersed the Constituent Assembly on January 19, 1919, they had betrayed Russia's democratic revolution and ushered in terrorist counterrevolution:

> Instead of the factories to the proletariat, it is the proletariat to the factories and the mines under the lash of the Five Year plan, there to toil as serfs or convicts, and be paid, if paid at all, in depreciating currency by the sole owner of the factory, the State itself. . . . [S]hould the victims murmur or protest, they are executed without trial as "counter-revolutionaries."
>
> There have been thirteen unbroken years of Soviet terrorism, summary requisitions, domiciliary visits, and wholesale executions without trial before hidden tribunals. It is over this, the most hideous of Soviet iniquities, that Mr. Shaw makes most unnatural merriment.
>
> And you tell us that capital punishment has been abolished. Acceptance of that patent falsehood is plain intellectual suicide. Not to mention the mass murders during the terror, the number of executions has steadily mounted since the inception of the Five Year Plan in 1928. . . . These are facts of public record.

Knowing now what history has revealed about the reality of Stalin's Russia, facts readily available to Shaw himself if he had wanted to face them, it would be hard to deny that Walsh got the better of the exchange.[48]

Although there was little that countersubversives and the realistic anticommunists could agree on, they did have one thing in common—opposition to diplomatic recognition of the Soviet Union.

During Roosevelt's first year in office, anticommunists were alarmed by reports that the President was planning to establish diplomatic relations with the Soviets. Edmund Walsh organized an anti-recognition committee to answer the arguments of an administration-backed pro-recognition committee.[49] The National Civic Federation, under Acting President Matthew Woll of the AFL, collected the signatures of six hundred civic leaders opposed to recognition.

Nevertheless, Roosevelt announced in October 1933 that he had invited the Soviets to send a representative to Washington. On the day of the announcement he called Father Walsh to the White House as a gesture to quiet the predictable outrage of the Catholic community. Walsh was politician enough to see that the issue was settled and that there was no use arguing with the President. Walsh confined his remarks to warning Roosevelt that he would find the Soviets very difficult to work with. Roosevelt replied, in an offhand way, "Leave it to me, Father; I am a good horse trader." Out of politeness, the President asked Walsh for a report on religious freedom in Russia and another on the personality of Soviet negotiator Maxim Litvinov. Walsh refrained from discussing religious liberty for Catholics in Russia, perhaps because he knew that a Protestant President might have replied with questions about religious liberty for Protestants and Jews in Catholic countries.[50]

In a dramatic demonstration of anticommunism's political impotence in the early thirties, Roosevelt's executive order of November 16, 1933, extending diplomatic recognition to the Communist government in Russia, contained not a phrase that recognized the warnings and the opposition of anticommunists. This was an enormous foreign policy triumph for the Soviets that ended their isolation from the world community. It also indirectly legitimized the American Communist Party by legitimizing its Soviet patrons.

As part of the agreement to extend recognition, Roosevelt had gotten the Russians to make a meaningless promise to halt the American

Party's subversive activities and its revolutionary propaganda, a promise that was promptly ignored. The Soviets had also agreed to let Americans in Russia practice their religion. This hardly consoled Catholics, who felt betrayed by a President they ardently supported on domestic issues. The *Brooklyn Tablet* protested that "twenty million Catholics will look upon this step as treason not only to them and to every liberty-loving citizen of our glorious country but every man and woman who has suffered or died for it since the Republic's birth in 1776."[51]

The decision to recognize the Soviet regime revealed once again the difference between anticommunism and liberal internationalism. Liberal internationalists had felt at the time of the Versailles Conference that the world order depended on excluding such a disruptive element as the Soviets. Conditions had now changed. Liberals now believed that there were more disruptive forces than the Soviets at large in the world—Mussolini, Hitler, and the Japanese. International security now needed to be buttressed by a Soviet counterforce to the fascist powers openly aiming at overturning the international order. Roosevelt hoped too that the Soviets would work with him to block Japanese expansion on the Asian mainland, and that trade with the Soviet Union would stimulate the American economy.[52]

There was nothing that a group as removed as anticommunists from the inner circles could have done to keep Roosevelt from recognizing Russia. But the anticommunists had themselves to blame in part for their irrelevance. Fish and Easley had reduced anticommunism to a joke, making it easy for Roosevelt to ignore anticommunists and their ideas.

American anticommunism in the early thirties wore a face of futility. The Communist regime in Russia had now entered the community of nations. American Communists, despite the Soviets' promises, were still infiltrating American institutions and serving Soviet interests. The Justice Department was still prohibited from investigating American radicalism. Congressional investigation of communism had been discredited.

And yet, the Communists' apparent successes were misleading. Judged by their ability to garner publicity out of the Sacco-Vanzetti and Scottsboro cases, and by the burgeoning number of front groups—the Communists were gaining a foothold in American politics and increasing their influence in American life. But while thousands of Americans passed through the Party and these fronts, many becoming lifelong sympathizers, the Party's increased visibility and activity was having the perverse effect of making Communist ideas and behavior known to increasing numbers of Americans, an exposure that turned a good proportion of them into aggressive anticommunists. The merciless power struggles within the American Party, aggravated by Moscow-dictated shifts in the Party line, also sent a steady stream of ex-Communists into the ranks of the anticommunist movement.

And so communism's successes, such as they were during the twenties and early thirties, were deceptive. Countersubversives' conspiracy theories would continue to shape the public's image of anticommunism. That stereotype would make it easy for Communists to turn anticommunists' criticisms back against them. Communists in America could point to the increasing prestige of Stalin and the Soviet Union during the depression as reason for taking them and their programs seriously, and they found an increasingly receptive audience for their efforts to move into the mainstream of American reform.

But the paradoxical nature of communism's successes was becoming a major factor in the history of both communism and anticommunism. If there is any truth in that old merchandising maxim that the best way to kill a bad product is with good advertising, the Communists' formidable public relations skills were killing communism. The more the Communists succeeded in attracting Americans to join their political and cultural campaigns, the more these erstwhile Communists and fellow travelers violently recoiled from them, bringing their experience to the anticommunist movement. Anticommunism, while it still labored under the know-nothing stereotype created by countersubversives like Easley and Fish, was fast becoming a repository for one of the most vital truths of the twentieth century, the truth about communism.

And yet, in the months ahead, there would be another truth over which many anticommunists would stumble—the truth about Hitler.

Chapter 6

THE RED DECADE

> Books and articles attacking native and foreign purveyors of Stalin's special brand of totalitarianism . . . are condemned automatically by a portion of the American public as "red-baiting." . . . It is a neatly contrived device of heading off free and uninhibited discussion of such little things as man-made famines, horrifying blood purges, forced labor on a gigantic scale—if they happen to occur in Russia. It is no less useful in preventing or discrediting in advance all exposures of Stalinist activities directed against the institutions or even against the life of non-Soviet nations.
>
> —Eugene Lyons, *The Red Decade* (1941)[1]

On February 1, 1933, Adolf Hitler became chancellor of Germany. Anticommunists now had to adjust to a world in which there was a far more urgent and dangerous threat to mankind than communism—the moral, political, and military challenge of aggressive fascism.

Moreover, anticommunists during the thirties had to cope with a transformed political landscape in which communism managed to redefine itself as antifascism, so that anticommunists had to feel their way through a bewildering moral labyrinth to oppose communism without seeming to support Hitler and without weakening the antifascist coalition against his aggression.

What America needed from anticommunism in the thirties was a principled defense of democracy against both communism and insurgent fascism. Unfortunately some anticommunists failed that test and became what Communists were calling them: nothing but fascists, who used their anticommunism as a weapon against Jews and political enemies. But there were also clear-headed and courageous anticommunists,

117

who bore witness to the truth about communism in the thirties under the most daunting conditions and in the face of the most withering opposition, and who exposed the almost unbelievable brutality of Stalin's regime and the monumental dishonesty of his Western apologists.

The need to resist Hitler made it almost impossible for anticommunism to survive the thirties at all. Yet not only did it survive, but American anticommunists provided the country with a devastatingly detailed assessment of communism as fascism's totalitarian brother under the skin, and of Stalin as a ruthless dictator who, given the proper inducements, would be far more likely to find common cause with Hitler than to oppose him—a prediction that events at the end of the decade would prove to have been uncannily accurate.

On February 27, 1933, the Reichstag building burst into flames, giving Hitler a pretext to move against the left. The fire was the start of a Communist revolution, he said, and the Nazis would rescue Germany. They arrested four thousand Communists, among them the Party's deputies in the Reichstag, and suspended civil liberties. On March 21, 1933, Hitler proclaimed the Third Reich, and assumed absolute power. By mid-1933 the first anti-Jewish laws were in place, and refugees had begun to stream out of Germany (Einstein arrived October 17, 1933). Independent labor unions were abolished. In July the Nazis were declared the only legal political party. In late 1933 Hitler took Germany out of the League of Nations. The courts went under Nazi control in 1934, and Hitler renounced foreign debts. Then in 1935 Italy, fascist since 1922, invaded Ethiopia. Who could doubt that Hitler would soon follow his anticommunist propaganda with a military move against the Soviet Union?

Stalin had to bear part of the blame for Hitler's rise to power. He had thought Hitler represented a strategic opportunity for communism to position itself to seize power in Germany after so many failures. The Comintern ordered German Communists to refuse to cooperate with the democratic left against Hitler. Even though Hitler's police were rounding up Communists, charging them with planning a coup, the Comintern ordered German Communists to avoid clashes with the Nazis. Let Hitler take power. His murderous regime would soon discredit itself and deliver Germany into the hands of the German Communists. "After Hitler, us," was their slogan.

The Party line to all this was to label anticommunism—or anything short of unconditional support of the Soviet Union—as fascism. This strategy began to emerge in the immediate aftermath of the Reichstag fire. Hitler tried to frame the leaders of the German Communist Party and the European branch of the Comintern for the Reichstag fire, but Willi Muenzenberg brilliantly turned Hitler's theory of a Communist plot back against him. Muenzenberg's countertheory was that the Nazis themselves had started the fire to precipitate a crisis that would destroy German communism. Muenzenberg laid this out in his quickly produced *First and Second Brown Books of the Hitler Terror and the Burning of the Reichstag Fire,*[2] published just a few weeks before the Leipzig trial of the Communist defendants. He also staged a "counter-trial" in London in September 1933 to try the Nazis in absentia for starting the fire. The London tribunal was carefully stage-managed by Muenzenberg to look like an independent investigation. H. G. Wells, Sir Stafford Cripps, and ACLU board member Arthur Garfield Hayes took part, and they rendered their decision against the Nazis the day before the Leipzig trial began. When the Communist defendants in Leipzig were acquitted by a not-yet-fully-corrupted German court, Muenzenberg's propaganda could now point to the Reichstag fire to argue that any criticism of the Soviet Union or of communism was the same sort of fraudulent fascist plot.[3]

As the Nazi threat grew more menacing, Stalin began to look for a way out of isolation. While Roosevelt was immobilized by American isolationist sentiment, Stalin put communism at the front of the international drive to stop Hitler. In September 1934 the USSR joined the League of Nations, which it had always regarded as the imperialist rival to the Comintern. In May 1935 Stalin negotiated mutual assistance pacts with France and Czechoslovakia.

Roosevelt and most other internationalists also recognized the immediate danger of Hitler and that America, too, needed to look to collective security to defend itself. But there were limits to what could be done, because liberal internationalism had been under isolationist attack since 1919. This backlash against internationalism culminated in Senator Gerald Nye's Munitions Committee hearings in 1934 and 1935 to promote the theory that America had been maneuvered into World War I by Wall Street to protect its loans to Great Britain. Isolationist sentiment in America would produce the first neutrality acts in 1935, hobbling Roosevelt's search for collective security against Hitler.[4]

Stalin now gave world Communists the job of defending the Soviet Union by finding it allies against Hitler. He ordered them to cease revolutionary agitation and appeal to their governments to establish ties with the Soviet Union in a united front against fascism. Accordingly, in August 1933, Willi Muenzenberg organized a meeting in Amsterdam under the sponsorship of French writers Romain Rolland and Henri Barbusse. Rolland announced the meeting with a radical call to arms against fascism: "The Fatherland is in danger! Our international Fatherland . . . the USSR is threatened." The Amsterdam meeting was endorsed by Albert Einstein, John Dos Passos, Upton Sinclair, George Bernard Shaw, H. G. Wells, and Theodore Dreiser. Sherwood Anderson sat on the speakers' platform. The American committee included Roger Baldwin, Malcolm Cowley, Dreiser, Dos Passos, Michael Gold, and Sinclair.

In June 1933 Muenzenberg organized another antifascist gathering of intellectuals, the European Anti-Fascist Congress at the Salle Pleyel in Paris. Ten days later the Pleyel and Amsterdam groups merged to form the Committee of Struggle Against War and Fascism.[5]

Muenzenberg's mobilization of intellectuals against fascism came to America when the American League Against War and Fascism (at first called the American Committee for Struggle Against War) held its first meeting in September 1933, largely attended by Communists and leaders of front organizations. Though it later claimed to be an independent antifascist group, until 1934 it was quite openly a Communist organization. But by exploiting the growing antifascist sentiment, such Communist fronts became remarkably successful in pulling American students, artists, intellectuals, and government employees into the Party orbit.

Front groups like the American Youth Congress and the League for Peace and Democracy were taken very seriously by anticommunists and Communists alike, but they were far less representative of public opinion than they claimed. They computed their impressive membership figures—four and a half million in the case of the Youth Congress—by adding up the memberships of the groups that had affiliated with them. These groups had often simply given perfunctory approval to a member to attend the front organization's meetings. For publicity purposes the entire membership of the organization was added to the progressive masses the front claimed to represent. Such sleight of hand made it appear that the Party had a real grip on American intellectual opinion.[6]

In 1935 a change in the Communist Party line put Communists in a position to work effectively with noncommunist organizations' real goal of discrediting their leaders and taking them over. To promote the new goal of supporting the Soviet Union against Hitler, the Seventh Congress of the Comintern on July 25, 1935, ordered Communists everywhere to cooperate with all antifascist groups. In a phrase that would become part of anticommunist lore, Comintern chief Georgi Dimitrov told the delegates that they should use mass organizations as "Trojan Horses" to "penetrate the very heart of the enemy's camp."[7]

This change in the Party line was one of the factors that made it possible for Communists finally to begin to make inroads in the American labor union movement in the late thirties. Even more important to the Communists' success was the National Labor Relations Act (the Wagner Act) of 1935, which recognized labor's right to organize and gave federal protection to workers exercising that right. For the first time in American history, the power and prestige of the federal government had been placed on the side of workers. There was now a real possibility of unionizing the mass of the country's unorganized industrial workers, long shunned by the AFL's craft unions. When the AFL rejected once again the idea of industrywide organization of unskilled workers—"industrial unionism" with its associations of radicalism and of loss of craft status—John L. Lewis, the powerful (and anticommunist) leader of the United Mine Workers, organized a Committee for Industrial Organization to "promote organization of workers in the mass production and unorganized industries of the nation."

A half year before, the Communists had scuttled their own rival to the AFL (Foster's TUEL) to concentrate on gaining influence in the AFL unions. At the end of 1934 they could claim to control 135 AFL locals and two central labor councils, and they had organized caucuses in five hundred locals. There were sixty Communists on New York's Central Trades and Labor Council, and the Communist-controlled Fur Workers Union had rejoined the AFL. The CIO presented an historic opportunity to American Communists, but also a risk to their newly won foothold in the AFL unions, because the AFL voted in 1936 to suspend any unions that joined the CIO. Thus, affiliation with the CIO would cost Communist unions their AFL affiliation. They were also seeking out as allies union leaders who were hardly naive about Communists' motives or goals. Lewis, Dubinsky, Hillman, and the other anticommunist organizers of the CIO might be willing to use Communist organizational talents, but they also knew that Communists were unreliable and treacherous allies.[8]

The CIO needed labor organizers, however, and the Communists had organizers with good contacts in the very industries targeted by John L. Lewis, and so he welcomed them—warily—into his new movement. When the CIO began chartering its own unions in 1937, the Communist-dominated Fur Workers', Longshoremen's, and Transport Workers' unions left the AFL. In addition, about 40 percent of the CIO's noncommunist member unions eventually fell under the influence of the Communists. The CIO's national publicity director, Len De Caux, and the general counsel, Lee Pressman, were both Communists. Communists did most of the work of organizing the CIO Steelworkers Union and they were in the forefront of the dangerous sit-down strikes that organized Detroit for the United Auto Workers. By 1937 the Party's position in the CIO was so solid that the Party ordered the Communist-dominated unions still in the AFL that wanted to secede to stay in the AFL so the Party could retain some influence in the older organization.[9]

While Communists did not completely control the CIO, never had an institution this vital to the functioning of American society been so strongly influenced by the Party. But since most liberals in the labor movement in the thirties shared the Communists' antifascist goals and respected their organizational talents, the issue of Communist infiltration lay dormant. Communist organizers were secretive about their Party affiliation and the CIO had a "don't ask, don't pursue" policy regarding local officers (though there was usually no doubt about which ones were Communists). Anticommunists in the unions and in government, in management, and in anticommunist organizations suspected—correctly—that Communists were working to make labor an adjunct to the goals of the Party—that is, to the foreign policy of the Soviet Union, but that did not become an issue until the beginning of the cold war.[10]

The Communists' success in the CIO, however, meant that non-communist union leaders needed help from assistants experienced in dealing with Communists, and this created opportunities for hard-line anticommunists to move into positions of influence in the union movement. Homer Martin of the United Auto Workers brought Jay Lovestone into his union in 1937 to help purge Communists from his executive board. Martin lost that battle (and his board membership), but Lovestone continued to work for anticommunist union leaders, defending them against Communist efforts to drive them from office.[11]

In the long run, however, the Party's success in building the CIO doomed its dream of radicalizing the American worker. Before the CIO, the state of labor was so desperate, and the alliance between government and management so powerful, that it was hard not to agree with the Communists that the class war between worker and capitalist could not be resolved within the system, that only by abolishing capitalism would workers gain justice, and that peaceful means would not be enough. After 1935, however, while industrial conflicts might still be bitter and violent, there were remedies for workers within the structure of American institutions. In creating the CIO the Communists had helped eliminate the conditions that had given the Party whatever small appeal it had ever had for American workers.

In the mid-thirties the role of Communists in the CIO caused the Catholic Church to worry that communism might win the working class from the Church in the United States, as it had in France and Italy. In November 1935 the Jesuits opened a School of Social Sciences at Philadelphia's St. Joseph's College. There the Church trained more than a thousand Catholics a year for labor union activism, specifically anticommunist activism. St. Joseph's was the model for more Catholic labor schools throughout the country. The Church also founded the Association of Catholic Trade Unionists in 1937 to demonstrate that the Church was as interested as the Communists in the welfare of the working class, and to compete with Communists for union leadership. The ACTU created a generation of Catholic anticommunists with detailed knowledge about Communist networks in the union movement. In turn, the Catholic anticommunist unionists provided their bishops with detailed and accurate intelligence about Communist activity in the labor movement. Despite their concern over Communist infiltration in the unions, liberal Catholics defended John L. Lewis and the

CIO against Catholic anticommunists who condemned the entire movement because of its Communist elements. When Father Coughlin told Catholics they could not join the CIO because of its Communist leadership, Archbishop Mooney of Detroit countered that every worker had a moral responsibility to become an active member of his union.[12]

What appeared to be an alliance between the New Deal and the revolutionary left in the union movement and in the united front against Hitler naturally drew the fire of countersubversive anticommunists, joined by enemies of the New Deal and of the union movement who used the Communist issue to attack New Deal policies they opposed. During Roosevelt's second term, these rabidly anti-Roosevelt countersubversive anticommunists managed to create an institutional stronghold within the legislative branch of government. This was the House Un-American Activities Committee.

The Committee originated in efforts to investigate links between German Nazism and American anti-Semitic fascist groups. In January 1934, New York Congressman Samuel Dickstein requested a new investigation of "un-American" activities. What Dickstein had in mind was German-Americans' enthusiasm for the new Germany of Adolf Hitler. Dickstein represented the Lower East Side of New York, where Jews were also becoming uncomfortably aware that local anti-Semites—many of them Catholics gripped by the venerable Jewish-Bolshevik stereotype—were also being encouraged in their bigotry by the success of the Nazi movement in Germany. A special investigatory committee was established under the nominal chairmanship of John McCormick of Massachusetts, but it was Vice-Chairman Dickstein who directed the investigation of what became known as the "Dickstein Committee." This committee published its findings in February 1935. Two years later, Nazi propaganda having shown no signs of diminishing, Dickstein appealed for a new and even more expansive probe into fascist movements. To attract support for a more ambitious investigation, Dickstein proposed that the new committee target all "un-American" activities. The committee would investigate, in Dickstein's words, "everybody."

Dickstein's resolution was tabled, but a resolution along the same lines was introduced by Martin Dies of Texas with Dickstein's support.

Dickstein's original idea had been to investigate the Nazi-controlled German-American Bund movement that seemed to be gaining influence in New York City's German neighborhoods. Dies, who had entered Congress as a New Dealer representing the oil and cotton regions of East Texas, had joined the Southern Democratic caucus in attacking the administration over civil rights, the CIO, and the WPA. Dies wanted to dig into Communist infiltration of the CIO and the New Deal programs he hated. An investigation of extremists of both left and right appealed to just about everybody. Dies's motion was approved on May 26, 1938, establishing the House Un-American Activities Committee (HUAC), which would be the nerve center of countersubversive anticommunism for the next quarter century.

Dies's committee consisted of two liberal Democrats, two conservative Democrats, and two right-wing Republicans. Dies got most of the publicity from the hearings he chaired over the next six years, but the Committee was actually steered by the head of its research unit, J. B. Matthews, whom Dies hired on August 20, 1938, on the recommendation of anticommunist columnist George Sokolsky.[13]

Matthews, after a career as the most notable fellow traveler of the early thirties, had just broken with the left during a Communist-led strike at Consumers' Research, the product testing organization he directed. Matthews believed that the real purpose of the strike was to capture Consumers' Research for the Party. During the course of the strike, the Party held a "public trial" of Matthews at New York City's Town Hall chaired by Heywood Broun and Vito Marcantonio. This was the final straw, and Matthews resolved, he later said, to fight "the drift of the age toward statism, or government interventionism, or collectivistic regimentation, or whatever it should be called, that plagues the nations of our time. . . . Communism, whether judged by spiritual, or intellectual, or economic tests, is, I am convinced, the most complete illusion ever born in the human brain.[14]

In 1938 Matthews published his memoirs of his days in the left, *Odyssey of a Fellow Traveler*. The book was highly emotional and alarmist, but citizens far more temperate than Matthews were becoming alarmed at the reality he was describing: A vast array of seemingly independent groups catering to every conceivable purpose, producing an illusion of an aroused public opinion in support of Communist objectives. These groups seemed to be controlled by their noncommunist members, but in reality, he wrote, quoting Communist Party chief Earl Browder, "the conscious moving and directive force of the united front movement in all its phases . . . [was] the Communist party."[15]

Matthews was denounced as a red-baiter for his exposé of the Party's domination of the front movement, for the most part he simply related the historical facts of how the front movement was created and operated. And, as he himself pointed out, the Party's attacks on him really proved his point—that to the Communists and their supporters, "any criticism of communists is, per se, red-baiting. . . . When it comes to carefully planned campaigns of abusiveness, ridicule, and mendacity, communists are the world's best baiters. They bait most successfully when they accuse their best-informed critics of baiting."[16]

With Matthews as a guide, on August 12, 1938, Dies and his committee began with hearings on the German-American Bund, although the Roosevelt administration tried to hobble their efforts by denying Dies the use of FBI agents as investigators, even though the pro-Roosevelt La Follette Civil Liberties Committee had been given Bureau assistance. The next day, the topic was Communist infiltration of the CIO. John P. Frey, president of the Metal Trades Department of the AFL charged that Communist organizers dominated the new industrial unions, had infiltrated the Democratic party, and had established themselves in positions throughout the Roosevelt administration. Frey also charged that the La Follette Civil Liberties Committee, which was highly critical of the Dies Committee, was controlled by Communist staffers, and in fact La Follette himself later had to purge Communists from his staff. Walter Steele, head of the American Coalition, an umbrella that united 114 patriotic organizations, testified for two days on the Communist front movement. He exposed the committee to ridicule, not for the first time, when he seemed to suggest that there was reason to suspect the loyalty of the Camp Fire Girls.

The next target of the Committee was the Works Progress Administration, the New Deal's relief agency. This was an irresistible target, since its Federal Theater Project had attracted many actors, directors, and writers infatuated with communism and the Party's concept of art as agitprop. The Committee's J. Parnell Thomas charged that "practically every play presented under the auspices of the Project is sheer propaganda for Communism or the New Deal." The director of the theater project hardly helped her cause when she claimed that only 10 percent of the productions had social themes, and in fact there was no denying the radical thrust of WPA theater. By loading up the theater staff with their comrades and fellow travelers, the Communists had made it even more vulnerable. The Dies hearings embarrassed the administration enough for it to jettison the Theater Project in June 1939. But the Committee also took some hits from the administration. When Dies compared Secretary of the Interior Harold Ickes to Browder and Stalin, Ickes called Dies "the outstanding zany in our political history."[17]

The Committee also went after Secretary of Labor Frances Perkins for not deporting Harry Bridges of the Longshoremen's Union. The FBI and HUAC said Bridges was a Communist, which, in fact, he was. The Labor Department said it could not find enough evidence to make the charges stick. There the matter rested, inconclusively, for decades.

Just before the 1938 elections, the Committee heard testimony from a California American Legion official that the state's Democratic candidates for governor, lieutenant governor, and the Senate were linked to the Communist Party. Another witness claimed that the Minnesota Farmer-Labor Party was a front for the Party. Another charged Michigan Governor Frank Murphy had coddled Communist sit-down strikers at General Motors in 1937. Roosevelt was so outraged at the attack on Murphy that he called the hearings "a flagrantly unfair and un-American attempt to influence an election." Murphy lost, and it did not escape politicians' notice that it could be costly to be attacked by the Committee.[18]

In 1939 the Committee probed communism in the labor movement—focusing on Joseph Curran's Maritime Workers. Curran's union was dominated by Communists, but Curran insisted that he was in charge, and that he tolerated the Communists only because they were valuable organizers. And in 1945, when the Communists' usefulness was at an end, Curran did expel them.[19]

In 1939 Dies also investigated the American Youth Congress, a Communist-dominated umbrella organization with seventy-nine mostly noncommunist constituent member groups that included the Boy and Girl Scouts. During the Committee's sessions on the American Student Union, a Party-dominated front headed by Joseph Lash, who at this time was closely associated with the Young Communist League and the Party itself, Eleanor Roosevelt sat with the students, conspicuously laughing with them while the congressmen were questioning witnesses. Pictures and accounts of these sessions circulated in countersubversive circles for years, supposedly demonstrating the Roosevelt White House's tender sentiments toward the Party. New Deal–hating anticommunists paid less attention when Mrs. Roosevelt ended her ties to these groups because—obeying the Party line after the Hitler-Stalin pact—they were trying to block FDR's preparedness programs, the draft, aid to England, and Lend-Lease.[20]

Although Dies's hearings themselves often degenerated into countersubversive circuses, the Committee's report for 1939 was an evenhanded summary of Communist and fascist activities during a period when both groups were making prodigious efforts to affect American public opinion. The Committee accurately reported that ten or twelve CIO unions were "more than tinged" with Communism, but that "most of its largest organizations are free of Communist control, domination, or even serious influences." It listed only eleven organizations as fronts, and warned against red-smearing. The *New York Times* called it "an astonishingly able and balanced document." According to rumors, Dies decided not to release his staff's report on Communist activity in Hollywood after meeting with Hollywood stars who asked the star-struck Texan to go easy on the industry.[21]

But the most enduring result of the 1939 hearings was a bonanza Matthews handed to the left when he exhibited—as evidence of Communist influence in the movie industry—a letter of "hearty greetings" to the French Communist newspaper *Ce Soir* signed by Clark Gable, Robert Taylor, James Cagney, and Shirley Temple. The Committee's enemies, led by the President himself, could now jeer that "attempts to identify the New Deal . . . with Communism . . . were on a par with accusing Shirley Temple of being a Communist."[22] Forever after, Martin Dies—and American anticommunism—had to bear the burden of "having called Shirley Temple a Communist." And the left never let anyone forget it.

The information the Committee collected in the thirties still forms the foundation for much of what we know today about communism in that decade. But the Committee really was not all that interested in simply collecting and publishing facts on the Communist Party and its activities. It was far more intent on using that information as ammunition for red-smearing attacks on the administration, attacks on the union movement, and attacks on unpopular opinions and associations.

On balance, the Dies Committee hurt anticommunism more than it did communism. While the Committee did little damage to the Party, it helped reinforce again the image of the left as the innocent victim of government repression. The excesses of countersubversive anticommunism had again made civil liberties seem the real issue in the controversy over communism. Countersubversives had made all anticommunists appear to be clowns who thought that Hollywood child stars were part of the Kremlin's plot to subvert the Republic. And even though the Committee's reports on Communist activities were for the most part accurate, they had the unfortunate result of stoking the paranoia of the countersubversive anticommunist community by giving them facts, true but misleading, they could embroider into their conspiracy theories.

While Martin Dies was wildly irresponsible and did lasting damage to the cause of responsible anticommunism, he was not particularly malicious. The same could not be said of a bizarre figure who made herself the center of a tiny, but noisy, group of wildly irresponsible, anti-Semitic countersubversives on the lunatic right during the thirties. This was Elizabeth Dilling.

Dilling was a University of Chicago educated, conservatory trained concert harpist married to a Chicago attorney who enthusiastically supported her red-hunting extravaganzas. She became converted to anticommunism, she said, during a trip to Russia in 1931 when she was shocked by the anti-Christian propaganda she saw in Russian cathedrals converted to museums of atheism. When she returned home she gave up her concert career and threw herself into the fight against communism. "The Russian trip ended a musical career," she wrote, "and a 'nice' suburban existence." She was supported, she claimed, by Henry Ford, "who never changed his mind about the role of Jewry."[23]

Elizabeth Dilling's magnum opus was *The Red Network* (1934)—still read and revered today in countersubversive circles. Relying on her own clipping files and those of other countersubversive red webbers like Richard Whitney, Walter Steele, and Francis Ralston Welsh, and drawing on the printed reports of the Lusk and Fish committees, Dilling twisted the history of the left and of the American reform movement into a bizarre and breathless melodrama. Secretary of Labor Frances Perkins, Roosevelt brain trusters Rexford Guy Tugwell and Paul Douglas, University of Chicago President Robert M. Hutchins, even New York's Senator Robert Wagner were all part of of a red-directed conclave that controlled the New Deal. To prove that individuals belonged to this plot, she cited—as the case might be—their support for Russian recognition, stipends from the left-oriented Garland fund, or bylines in magazines like the *Nation*. She drew on a sixth sense to discover Communist sympathies in unlikely quarters, so it was impossible to predict where her suspicions might point next. She charged that Father Coughlin's "radio propaganda" was "deeply appreciated by radicals," and claimed that Father John A. Ryan was a Coughlin supporter, at a time when Ryan was well known to be leading the Catholic opposition to Coughlin.[24]

In September 1936, Dilling self-published her second book, *The Roosevelt Red Record and Its Background*, which provided 428 pages of text, facsimiles of agit-prop posters for WPA plays, and letterheads listing New Deal officials in red fronts, all intended to demonstrate the New Deal's fully reciprocated passion for Stalin and Stalin's American disciples.

Her proof consisted of slush piles of misleading or misinterpreted facts—Eleanor Roosevelt's encouragement of liberal and radical groups supporting the New Deal programs; Jane Addams's ubiquitous presence throughout the world of leftist organizations; grants from liberal foundations like the Garland and Twentieth Century funds (and some, like the Rockefeller Foundation, not so liberal). So many connections between so many people, she insisted, added up to conspiracy. Ironically, the left would be able to use her ubiquitous presence in nearly every anticommunist group or gathering to prove—as her anti-Semitic tendencies became more pronounced—that there was an anti-Semitic thread that tied anticommunist groups from left to right into a vast anti-Semitic fascist plot—and that the thread was Dilling herself.

Like Richard Whitney or Blair Coan, Dilling was blithely undisturbed by facts that controverted her theories. Describing the Communist Party's efforts to control the 1924 La Follette movement, she conceded that La Follette ended the campaign a bitter enemy of the Communists, but she simply remarked that if the Party failed with La Follette, it succeeded with Roosevelt.[25] At the end of her account of the fraudulent documents that showed progressive senators had been bribed by the Mexican government to win support for the Mexican Revolution, she added, as though of no consequence, that the documents were discredited and the senators cleared of all charges.

In her alphabetical index of reds in the Roosevelt administration, she put the name of pacifist Representative Jeannette Rankin next to that of ultraconservative and wildly anticommunist Representative John Rankin of Mississippi, who was a socialist in her eyes because he supported the Tennessee Valley Authority project. She listed Father John A. Ryan as a Communist sympathizer because of his membership in the ACLU although he was leading the Catholic campaign against communism in the labor unions.

Dilling was easily distracted from the hunt for the red menace when her indignation was aroused by women who violated her decidedly rigid sense of feminine respectability. She despised professional women who failed to use their married names, so she always placed ironic quotation marks around the "Miss" before the names of Frances Perkins and journalist Dorothy Thompson. It irked her that Jane Addams, supposedly a leader of the red network, was a member of the Daughters of the American Revolution, while she was not. Dilling adored the DAR, and haunted its meetings, though she could not meet the ancestry requirements for membership. Addams, perhaps aware of Dilling's feelings on the subject, once cruelly invited Dilling to pose with her for a picture to demonstrate the political diversity of the Daughters. Dilling had to admit, in some embarrassment, that she was not a member.[26] She was congenitally unable to resist weird digressions. She worried that "Miss" Frances Perkins's criticism of women's hat styles meant that the New Deal was plotting to require government-dictated fashions for American women in the Soviet mode, which Dilling described as "the available rag for the head and the meal-sack-like dress." She herself, she vowed,

> would resist dictation and limitation to a specified number of hat and dress models standardized and authorized by the Department of Labor. (Heaven forbid!) Many, who, like myself, are fond of sewing, would probably delight in making "bootleg" styles. Nor would we forego without a struggle the joys of window shopping past the lovely displays at moderate prices which fill American shop windows. No picture gallery is more diverting than the artistic designs and displays American designers and window dressers conceive. Must we kill that instinct too?[27]

Dilling's dark musings, while laughable to anyone who did not share her obsessions, had a major impact on the lunatic fringe of obsessive countersubversives. Her books, with their glossaries and indexes, were relied on as the conspiracy theorists' Who's Who in the Communist Conspiracy. The uninformed on the far right were now also misinformed. Even worse, they were all misinformed with the same misinformation, which they recited like in an infernal chorus that sometimes drowned out the words of knowledgeable anticommunists who were trying to acquaint the public with the facts about Russia and American communism. Eventually, Dilling's maniacal commingling of fact and fancy produced the effect of absolving from suspicion real Communists and fellow travelers, in what might be called innocence by association. Since she was wrong about most of her so-called reds, she must be wrong about all. And, by an illogical, but understandable inference, if her *Red Network* was a tissue of malicious lies, then so must be all other books on American communism, even those written with scrupulous regard for the facts.

Crackpots like Elizabeth Dilling, who had little influence outside their own tiny circles, were not the worst blights on anticommunism during the thirties. There was another form of irresponsible and dangerous anticommunism that was—if not followed—at least listened to by millions of Americans. This was the anti-Semitic demagoguery of Father Charles E. Coughlin, the radio priest from Royal Oak, Michigan.

Father Coughlin's weekly radio broadcasts in the thirties reached all the major metropolitan centers in the Midwest and East, with at least ten million listeners.[28] In 1933 he sold nearly a million copies of an edition of his sermons. In the minds of millions, friends and foes alike, he made anticommunism simply the latest guise worn by the oldest hatred of all—anti-Semitism.

Coughlin's rise was the almost predictable result of the Roman Catholic Church's willingness in the thirties to tolerate anyone—even Hitler—who could present himself as an effective fighter against communism. During those years, many Catholics believed that Hitler's claim to be an anticommunist put him on the same side of the barricades as the Pope, who also claimed to be defending Western civilization against the Bolshevik onslaught.

In 1933 rumors spread that the Pope was contemplating proclaiming a "war on communism" in cooperation with Hitler and Mussolini, although nothing came of it. In 1936, Pope Pius XI compared communism to the Ottoman Moslem invasion of Europe two centuries before.[29]

Hitler seemed to be competing for the leadership of world anticommunism with the Pope when Hitler, who had put an exhibit on the horrors of communism on tour throughout Europe, denounced the Pope for trying to usurp his "historic" position as the champion of Europe against communism.[30]

The question of the Vatican's complicity with fascism is debatable, but certainly the Pope was not antifascist in the thirties. Italian priests had discovered some similarity between fascism's rejection of class conflict and the Catholic vision of a social unity between the classes. Mussolini worked hard in the twenties to win the approval of Catholic leaders. He legitimized his marriage and had his children baptized. In 1929, Pius XI and Mussolini signed the Lateran Treaty, regularizing diplomatic relations between the Vatican and the Italian government, and making Catholicism the state religion.

Nor did the Church's fondness for fascism halt at the borders of Italy. The Pope's influential secretary of state, Eugenio Cardinal Pacelli, believed that "Marxism was the greatest danger of all time to the Church" and that only authoritarian governments could hold out against revolution. As the Pope's ambassador to Germany in the twenties, Pacelli, who would become Pope Pius XII in 1939, had come to regard Germany as Christianity's bulwark against communism.

Despite their shared anticommunism, however, the Vatican and the fascist dictators were scarcely political allies. In 1931, Pacelli had his secretary, Monsignor (and future Cardinal) Francis Spellman smuggle an encyclical[31] out of Italy that denounced fascist persecution of the church there and condemned "pagan worship of the State."[32] Pius XI finally turned against Hitler over Nazi persecution of the Church in Germany, and in 1937 the Vatican condemned German Nazism in the encyclical *Mit brennender Sorge* (*With Burning Sorrow*). The Pope's differences with Hitler and Mussolini did not, however, diminish his hostility to communism, or his conviction that Stalin was the greater of the twin enemies of the Church.

While other Americans were waking up to the threat of aggressive fascism, American Catholics were answering the Pope's summons to battle with communism. The Catholic War Veterans, with the approval of the Pope, launched their own drive against communism in 1935. That same year Father Coughlin started his "Father Pro Clubs," calling Father Pro, a Mexican priest killed by revolutionaries in 1926, in Guadalajara, Mexico, the "first martyr killed by Communists in America." The Passionist Fathers distributed a "Catechism on Communism for Catholic High School Students."[33]

Although Catholics supported Roosevelt's domestic programs, they were angered by his foreign policies. Granting diplomatic recognition to the Soviet Union had appalled them. The Spanish Civil War—which began July 17, 1936—deepened the gulf between the New Dealers and American Catholics. Non-Catholics tended to understand the battle between the Popular Front government of the Spanish Republic—a coalition of liberals, anarchists, Socialists, and Communists elected in 1936—and Franco's insurrection—backed by the upper classes and by Spanish fascists supported by their allies in Germany and Italy, and by the Catholic Church—as part of the struggle between democracy and fascism. Catholic papers, however, insisted that the real issue was the persecution of the Spanish church by a government controlled by Communists. The *Brooklyn Tablet's* Patrick Scanlan was such a faithful supporter of Franco that after the war Franco's government gave him a medal.[34]

To rally support for Franco, in December 1936 the Pope announced a worldwide anticommunist campaign. Catholics established anticommunist "Pro Deo" leagues in every country, and were told by the Pope that the Soviet Union's admission to the League of Nations, Communist propaganda in the French elections, and the Spanish Civil War all showed the growing strength of the Communist movement. In his Christmas address for 1936 the Pope called communism "the enemy" and said that Spain revealed the fate being prepared for the rest of Europe. And just a few days after he issued the anti-Nazi *Mit brennender Sorge* in 1937, the Pope released another encyclical, *Divini Redemptoris* (*On Atheistic Communism*), to set "clearly before the world the primacy of the red menace in the eyes of the Church."[35]

American Catholics tried in vain to persuade the rest of the country that communism, not fascism, was the real issue in Spain. Early in 1937 the Knights of Columbus launched a National Drive Against Communism, Atheism, and Home Destruction and appealed to Protestants to join them. The Knights distributed twenty thousand copies of the Spanish Bishops' *Joint Pastoral Letter to the Whole World* that called on all Catholics to support Franco. In 1938 the Knights sponsored a series of lectures on the "Peril of Communism" by George Hermann Derry in which Russia was blamed for the war against the Church in Spain and Mexico. In Wilkes-Barre, Pennsylvania, the Knights halted the showing of the pro-Republican film *Defense of Madrid* and stopped Communist Robert Minor's speeches defending the Republic. When Eleanor Roosevelt endorsed a program to bring five hundred Basque refugee children to the United States, Catholics denounced it as a propaganda ploy to create sympathy for the Spanish Republic, and Edmund Walsh claimed the administration was pressuring government employees to support the Spanish Republican cause. The Catholic Bishops organized a "Crusade for Christian Democracy" to fortify Catholic children against "the spread of subversive teachings" in Communist front organizations appealing to the young.[36]

The Catholics' pro-Franco efforts reinforced suspicions among non-Catholics that the Church was hostile to democracy and sympathetic to fascism. A Socialist group in Milwaukee told the Knights of Columbus they had no moral right to raise the alarm against communism because, unlike the Socialists, they offered no real alternative to the unjust status quo.[37]

It was this heritage of uncritical anticommunism that made American Catholicism receptive to a demogogue like Coughlin. He started as an enthusiastic supporter of the New Deal and in 1933 popularized the slogan "Roosevelt or Ruin." By 1934 Coughlin began to sour on the New Deal. Roosevelt had rejected Coughlin's overtures to be included among the administration's policymakers because he did not trust Coughlin, and Secretary of the Treasury Henry Morgenthau attacked the priest by releasing a list of silver investors who had been pressuring the President to remonetize silver, and the list included the name of Coughlin's private secretary who had been speculating with Coughlin's funds.

In November 1934 Coughlin moved into politics by organizing the National Union for Social Justice. Evidently he hoped this would evolve into a third party to challenge the President. He also began to make anti-Semitic attacks on the Roosevelt administration. In a January 1935 sermon Coughlin accused the administration of plotting to sacrifice American independence to the World Court. The administration's ultimate objective, he charged, was to deliver the country into the hands of international financiers—and most of those he named were Jewish. Coughlin's organization was turning into one of the most dangerous anti-Semitic movements in American history.[38]

But Roosevelt could be a dangerous enemy, and the President moved to destroy Coughlin's support. By 1935 so many doors in Washington had been closed to Coughlin that he shut down his lobbying office in the capital.

Coughlin counterattacked by trying to expand his power base in the heartland. He allied himself with union organizers in Detroit's auto industry, and searched for allies among politicians disaffected from the New Deal. He found one in Louisiana's Huey Long. After Long's assassination in September 1935, Coughlin joined forces with Long's assistant, Gerald L. K. Smith, and what was left of Long's organization. He allied his forces to Dr. Francis E. Townsend and Townsend's nationwide lobby for a national old age pension system, and placed the entire movement behind North Dakota Congressman William Lemke's run for the presidency on the makeshift Union Party ticket. Coughlin promised that as he was "instrumental in removing Herbert Hoover from the White House, so help me God, I will be instrumental in taking a Communist out of the chair once occupied by Washington." Roosevelt himself was worried enough by the red-baiting charges leveled at him by the likes of Coughlin, Smith, and Elizabeth Dilling that he formally denounced communism and Marxism in a Syracuse speech on September 29, 1936.[39]

But while Coughlin's brand of anti-Semitic anticommunism did find supporters among conspiracy-minded Catholics, most Catholic priests and laymen were disturbed and offended by Coughlin's red-baiting. The bishop of Omaha angrily denounced Coughlin's smears: "there is not one shred of evidence, direct or indirect, to connect the name of President Roosevelt with Communism, its principles, and its propaganda." Moreover, Coughlin's attacks on Roosevelt cost him the support of many Catholics, and liberal priests like the influential Father John Ryan of the Theology Department of Catholic University, the director of the Bishops National Catholic Welfare Conference, denounced Coughlin as a false and dangerous guide for Catholics.[40] And despite fears that Coughlin's anti-Semitic anticommunism might mobilize an anticommunist coalition against Roosevelt, the Lemke ticket received less than 2 percent of the vote in 1936.[41]

Coughlin's career in electoral politics was over, but he still had a rabid following that terrified Jews in cities like Boston and Brooklyn with a large Irish community. After 1936, Coughlin's politics grew more reactionary, his anti-Semitism more fanatical. His newspaper, *Social Justice*, began to reprint the *Protocols of the Learned Elders of Zion*, and he preached that communism was a Jewish conspiracy. After *Social Justice* borrowed phrases from a speech by Goebbels, many of his radio outlets canceled his Sunday sermons, and he lost all his stations in New York City. Within the Church, liberal priests attacked Coughlin and the Catholic Worker movement organized a group specifically to fight Coughlin's anti-Semitism.[42]

But Coughlin had revealed an ugly anti-Semitic streak in American Catholicism. Patrick Scanlan's *Brooklyn Tablet* printed Coughlin's sermons on its front page after Coughlin was banished from the New York airwaves. Coughlin's supporters organized a frighteningly militant and anti-Semitic "Christian Front" with his encouragement. The group's name was meant to suggest that the Communist "Popular Front" was Jewish. In Brooklyn the Christian Front was led by Father Edward Lodge Curran, who led his own anti-Semitic International Truth Society, through which he distributed pamphlets blaming communism on Jews.

There had always been a self-defensive strain of Jewish anticommunism that tried to protect Jews against anti-Semites using the Jewish-Bolshevik stereotype to smear the entire Jewish community. Frightened by the increasingly militant anti-Semitism of Catholic anticommunists, in October 1938 some New York City members of the American Jewish Veterans of the World War, supported and led by the Modell family of Brooklyn, owners of a chain of sporting goods stores, organized an American Jewish Federation to Combat Communism and Fascism. The Federation's stated goal was to "controvert the false propaganda that 'all Jews are Communists' " and to convince Catholics that the vast majority of Jews were anticommunist by maintaining that "only a small minority—less than 1%—of the Jews of the United States are Communists."

Since its target audience was the Catholic community, the Federation advertised its activities in Catholic newspapers, booked Knights of Columbus halls for its rallies, and invited prominent Catholics to speak on radio broadcasts that it sponsored. The Federation appealed to Jews to combat "Communist and Fascist influences carried on among the Jewish youth of the nation in schools, colleges and other educational institutions," and stated that its own goal was to "create a solid mass of Jewish public opinion opposed to doctrines of government contrary to the eternal principles of religious liberty and freedom of speech and press, and the adoption of which would destroy Judaism and which aim equally to destroy the foundations of all religious beliefs." The goal of all this was admittedly communal self-defense: "to give continued unanswerable proof of the loyalty and patriotism of American Jews and their love of flag and country." The National Chaplain of the Catholic War Veterans responded by reminding Catholics that the Jewish War Veterans had protested the persecution of Catholics in Mexico, and that "Catholic War Veterans know and believe that no religious Jew can be a Communist or a Fascist."[43]

The Federation tried hard to persuade Catholics that Coughlin's anticommunism was simply a disguised form of anti-Semitism. "Many of the organizations in the United States," the Federation argued, "claiming to be motivated by purely patriotic purposes and which oppose Nazism or Fascism only, or which oppose Communism only, have an anti-Semitic background, which is only too apparent, and are not genuinely American in their objectives or in the methods they use to reach these objectives. Much of the propaganda flooding the country in the names of these organizations is intended to breed religious and racial hatred and is, of course, wholly un-American." There were, the Federation reported, more than eight hundred anti-Semitic patriotic organizations in the United States. These groups were preaching hatred of Jews by "linking them as a body with the Communists." The Federation warned that "this line of attack was so successful in Nazi Germany as an entering wedge against all the principles of democratic government and the enslavement of minorities, [and] the same tactics are being employed here."[44]

The Federation even made overtures to Coughlin himself, and it tried to have Coughlin's *Social Justice* carry articles on its anticommunist activities. They gave up when it became apparent that Coughlin was too caught up in his anti-Semitic obsessions for there to be any hope of dialogue. By June 1939 the Federation was calling him an American Hitler, and had also given up on Patrick Scanlan's *Brooklyn Tablet*, which it had also been wooing with letters and advertising.[45]

Self-defensive anticommunism like that of the Jewish Federation was really a peripheral aspect of Jewish anticommunism. The Jewish anticommunism that would have the greatest impact came out of the experiences of Jewish Socialists, ex-Communists, and ex-fellow travelers who had discovered the shocking gap between the Communists' self-proclaimed goals and the brutal reality of Communist behavior when they had power in Russia, in Spain, and in the American Communist Party.

The disproportionate number of Jews in the first generation of American Communists meant that there was also a disproportionate number of Jews among the embittered ex-Communists and former fellow travelers who moved on to the anticommunist movement after the Trotskyist and Bukharinist splits from the Party. So, too, a great number of the Socialists who became anticommunist activists were Jewish. Likewise, among the intellectuals whose brush with the Party had turned them into enemies of communism, the most prominent were Jewish. But while the background of so many of these anticommunists of the left was Jewish, theirs was an anticommunism that transcended its origins to ground itself in universalist values—democracy, social justice, intellectual honesty, and cultural freedom.

The most formidable of the Jewish anticommunist intellectuals was the philosopher Sidney Hook. A disciple of Bertrand Russell and John Dewey, Hook was already one of the country's best known academic philosophers by the early thirties, having written the first major American study of Marxism. Until 1932 Hook was a fellow traveler because, he said, he was ignorant of what was really happening in the Soviet Union, even though he had visited the country in 1929. He had been attracted to communism out of his hatred of war, because he thought that the First World War had been the inevitable consequence of capitalism, and that only the abolition of capitalism could end war. The rise of Nazism in Germany had given him an even stronger reason to embrace the Party, since he thought that only the Soviet Union could stop Hitler.

But when Hitler came to power with no interference from the German Communists, and then the Communists did not try to overthrow him, Hook began to doubt their sincerity. Then he read William Z. Foster's *Toward a Soviet America* in 1932, which boasted that a victorious American Party would do away with competing bourgeois social and intellectual institutions. Hook recalled this as the "horrifying and embarrassing discovery" that the American Communist Party he had been supporting had been completely Stalinized despite its democratic pretenses. He concluded that the Party was undemocratic to the core, that the Communists had been lying to him, that they knew they were lying, and had lied to him nonetheless. Their lies, he said, had openly revealed "the true face of Communism." To someone as fervently devoted to the truth and to logical consistency as Hook, such dishonesty was unforgivable.

Hook devoted the rest of his life to combating communism's seduction of the Western intellectual. "Although Communism," he wrote,

> as a world movement dominated and controlled by the Kremlin, was a danger *to* America rather than *in* America, the agents and partisans of that movement, who had infiltrated strategic positions in government, trade unions, educational establishments, and centers for influencing public opinion, had to be exposed and opposed. After all, the leaders of the Communist Party had publicly proclaimed that in the event of war between the United States and the Soviet Union, they would not support the United States. This gave rise to legitimate fears concerning the loyalty of those who knowingly followed the Communist party line in other fields of social and cultural activity.[46]

During the thirties, Hook believed that his best chance to open the eyes of Western intellectuals to the totalitarian nature of Soviet communism was to expose the terrible truth behind the fantastic purge trials that consumed almost the entire leadership of the Soviet Union between 1935 and 1938, something so unbelievable that most of the left refused to believe it, and, having deluded themselves about this, went on to delude themselves about the rest of the reality of communism. The reality was that Stalin, having turned the Soviet Union into a vast prison camp, was now sending millions to the execution chamber, among them the heroes of the Bolshevik Revolution. To hide the truth about this mass slaughter Stalin had spun one of history's most preposterous—and sinister—conspiracy theories, a wild fantasy that was soberly reported as a serious possibility by left-leaning Western reporters in Moscow and subscribed to as gospel by the American Party and its fellow travelers.[47]

Stalin's "Great Terror" began on December 1, 1934, with the murder of Leningrad Communist Party chief, Sergei Kirov. The Kirov murder, which many then and now believe Stalin had engineered, touched off a fantastic wave of retribution that eventually totaled eight million arrests, a million executions, and seven million deaths from starvation and disease in the forced labor camps of the Gulag between 1937 and 1938. A plausible estimate is that some twenty million Soviets eventually lost their lives under Stalin in execution chambers and labor camps, in addition to those who died in politically decreed famines.[48]

During the first purge (which began on January 15, 1935) Stalin's prosecutors blamed a "Moscow Center" of plotters for the Kirov assassination, and charged that the defendants, including "Old Bolsheviks" like Grigori Zinoviev and Lev Kamenev, had planned to kill Stalin and his top lieutenants. An even more amazing trial of "Zinovievites and Trotskyites" began on August 8, 1936, during which the defendants confessed to membership in a worldwide Trotsky network that prosecutors diagramed in spider web charts worthy of Richard Whitney or Nesta Webster. In his summation, the head prosecutor shouted that "these mad dogs of capitalism tried to tear limb from limb the best of the best of our Soviet land. . . . I demand that these dogs gone mad should be shot—every one of them." And they were, under streamlined procedures that permitted their immediate execution after conviction. (Stalin's laws permitted the arrest and execution of the friends, relatives, and even children of enemies of the state.)[49]

At a third show trial on January 23, 1937, Stalin's prosecutors claimed that an "anti-Soviet Trotskyite Center" in Moscow had conspired with Hitler to deliver Russia to the Nazis. The negotiations had supposedly taken place in Norway between Hitler's deputy, Rudolf Hess, and the exiled Trotsky. "This is the abyss of degradation!" shouted prosecutor Andrei Vyshinsky. "This is the limit, the last boundary of moral and political decay! This is the diabolical infinitude of crime!" According to the Soviet line, dutifully repeated by Communists the world over, Trotsky had become "the central rallying point of all the forces hostile to socialism." Trotskyists were a "gang of mere bandits, spies and murderers who placed themselves entirely at the disposal of foreign secret services, became finally and irrevocably transformed into lackeys of capitalism, into restorers of capitalism in our country."[50]

Another wave of executions eliminated the high command of the Red Army after a trial that began on June 12, 1937. Finally, on March 2, 1938, in the so-called "Great Trial," what was left of the Party leadership went on trial, including Genrikh Yagoda, the Secret Police chief, who had carried out the earlier trials and purges. They, too, were quickly executed.[51]

Liberal and Socialist anticommunists had long been telling the radical community about Lenin's and Stalin's persecution of dissidents, pointing to earlier political show trials—in 1922, 1928, 1930, 1931, and 1933—as proof that the Soviet Union had abolished liberty, human rights, and law. Anticommunists on the left thought that this last orgy of butchery would finally break the Soviet Union's enduring spell over the radical imagination.

The non-Stalinist left now turned Stalin's charges against Trotsky into a test case to expose the fraudulent nature of Stalinism itself in its claim to represent the revolutionary heritage of the left. From Norway, Trotsky denied all charges. To force Stalin to produce his "evidence" in open court, he demanded that the Soviets initiate extradition proceedings against him. Bowing to Soviet pressure, however, Norway deported him without any formalities.

Recalling the left's tradition of organizing defense committees for dissidents persecuted by repressive regimes, Hook organized an American defense committee for Trotsky, appealing to civil libertarians and progressives who had come to the aid of Tom Mooney, Sacco and Vanzetti, the Scottsboro boys, and Angelo Herndon to rally to the defense of this victim of the latest form of tyranny. Hook's first goal was to find a country to give Trotsky asylum after he left Norway. Once Mexico had taken him in, Hook changed the name of the Committee to the "Commission of Inquiry into the Truth of the Moscow Trials."

To emphasize the seriousness of this enterprise, Hook persuaded John Dewey, America's most distinguished philosopher, to chair the Commission. Dewey, seventy-eight years old in 1937, had at first been reluctant to make the trip to Mexico to interrogate Trotsky, but when the Communists tried to intimidate him into not going, Dewey agreed to what would have been arduous for a much younger man, and set off for Mexico City. During the hearings in Mexico City, which followed strict legal procedures, Trotsky refuted Stalin's preposterous charges brilliantly and convincingly, to all who were open to persuasion.[52]

Like many anticommunists before and after, Hook fondly believed that the truth about communism would open the eyes of those who had been beguiled by its lofty goals, and so he had high hopes that the transcripts of the inquiry, published in two volumes in 1937 and 1938, would finally break the hold of communism on the imagination of American intellectuals:

> Had most of the architects of "the great experiment"—which still enjoyed great prestige in the West, partly because of ignorance of the terrible events

of the famine years, but mainly because of the domestic effects of the depression—been agents of the Western secret police? The notion was inherently incredible. If bizarre court proceedings were a rigmarole played out for some dark punitive purpose of Stalin and his regime, then the promise of socialism was revealed as a mockery of the great humanist ideals—as culminating in the reality of a hell on earth.[53]

But far from convincing the friends of the Soviet Union that Stalin had betrayed their hopes by turning the workers' democracy into a Kafkaesque nightmare, Hook and Dewey found themselves subjected to the standard charge leveled at all anticommunists in the thirties. Since communism was the highest form of antifascism, by attacking Stalin, they were helping Hitler. Henry Roth, author of the depression classic, *Call It Sleep*, wrote that there was "only one way of accomplishing . . . the united front against fascism and that was to support the verdict of the Moscow Trials and to destroy Trotskyism." Even liberals were reluctant to doubt the word of the Kremlin's great antifascist. The *New Republic* said the evidence seemed to support Stalin's position, and there was "no evidence that civil liberties were so certainly violated in this case as to make a protest on this ground necessary and we see no reason . . . to take the trial at other than its face value."[54] Dewey resigned from the *New Republic*'s editorial board in protest.

The entire front movement massed to attack Hook and Dewey. Corliss Lamont and eighty-seven other fellow travelers signed an "Open Letter to American Liberals" that insisted there was no cause for an inquiry because "impartial observers present at the trials have reported that the trials were properly conducted" and that "the demand for an investigation of trials carried on under the legally constituted judicial system of the Soviet Government can only be interpreted as political intervention in the affairs of the Soviet Union with hostile intent."[55]

The fellow-traveling left's rejection of the Dewey Commission's findings illustrated just how ingrained it had become among liberals and on the left to reject anything that originated from anticommunist sources. And anticommunists, in some sense, had themselves to blame. Countersubversive anticommunists had departed from the facts on so many occasions that many liberals had formed the habit of dismissing anything anticommunists had to say about communism or the Soviet Union, even if—like Hook and Dewey—they were reporting nothing but the truth.[56]

Appalled at the ability of the front network to persuade intellectuals to defend, in the name of intellectual freedom, a regime that had abolished all freedom, Hook now founded the most important institution of the thirties for anticommunist intellectuals, the American Committee for Cultural Freedom (CCF). This originated in a meeting on May 15, 1939 between Hook, John Dewey, Frank Trager (a Socialist Party member then on the staff of the American Jewish Committee), and Ferdinand Lundberg (author of the famous analysis of the concentration of America's wealth and power, *America's Sixty Families* [1937]). Hook wanted to create a force that would be able to counter the American League for Peace and Democracy, the League of American Writers, the American Artists Congress, the American Committee for Democracy and Intellectual Freedom, and the other Communist fronts that claimed to speak for intellectuals. Hook felt that the Communist Party front organizations "dominated the cultural, literary, and in part the academic landscape," and so he was determined "to challenge this massive phenomenon that was corrupting the springs of liberal opinion and indeed making a mockery of common sense."[57]

Hook's group drew up a Declaration of Principles and released it to the press over the names of ninety-six signers. The manifesto of the American Committee for Cultural Freedom was written by Eugene Lyons. It was a frontal assault on the Popular Front's claim that communism was the most effective force in the fight against fascism and so was vital to an effective left. The Committee insisted that, on the contrary, communism and fascism were morally equivalent. Both were varieties of totalitarianism.

> Under varying labels and colors, but with an unvarying hatred for the free mind, the totalitarian idea is already enthroned in Germany, Italy, Russia, Japan, and Spain. There, intellectual and creative independence is suppressed and punished as a form of treason. . . . Literally thousands of German, Italian, Russian and other victims of cultural dictatorships have been silenced, imprisoned, tortured or hounded into exile.
>
> We therefore call for the formation of a COMMITTEE FOR CULTURAL FREEDOM, an organization independent of control, whether open or secret, by any political group, pledged to expose repression of intellectual freedom under whatever pretext, to defend individuals and groups victimized by totalitarian practices anywhere, to propagate courageously the ideal of untrammeled intellectual activity.[58]

The original signers of the CCF's manifesto would for decades provide the brains (and to a great extent the backbone) of the anticommunist movement, not only during the late thirties, but during anticommunism's surge to power after World War II, and even during the bleak Vietnam years when the country made anticommunism the scapegoat for the Southeast Asian disaster.[59]

Naturally, Hook's Committee was attacked by the fellow-traveling left. Freda Kirchwey of the *Nation* claimed that since American Communists supported the New Deal, it would be "a counsel of disruption" to expose the fronts. But not all of its critics were fellow-travelers. The League for Cultural Freedom and Socialism, a group of anticommunist Socialists including F. W. Dupee, J. T. Farrell, James Burnham, William Phillips, and Philip Rahv, insisted that only democratic socialism—not capitalism—could guarantee real cultural freedom.[60]

To counter the propaganda of the fellow-traveling left, the CCF published a *Bulletin* and sponsored public lectures on the Communist issue. On October 13, 1939, it presented a panel on "Cultural Freedom and the World Crisis" that featured KGB defector Walter Krivitsky, together with speeches by Harry Gideonse, president of Brooklyn College, George Hartmann of the Columbia Teachers College, and Willi Schlamm from Germany. The Committee also sponsored monthly radio broadcasts in New York.

The Committee was concerned that it would be discredited by the antics of countersubversive red-hunters like the Dies Committee, so the Committee's bylaws stated that respect for civil liberties must take precedence even over the fight against totalitarianism. The CCF would support freedom of speech for everyone, even Communists and fascists. The Committee was "vehemently" opposed to any cooperation with the Dies Committee. In April 1940 the Committee issued its own authoritative *Report* (drawn up by Frank Trager) on the Communist front movement, to serve as an authoritative alternative to the Dies reports, which few liberals would touch, let alone use.

Eugene Lyons was another of the important Jewish anticommunists from the left who fought communism's influence during the thirties. His *Red Decade: The Stalinist Penetration of America* (1941) became anticommunism's definitive characterization of the thirties' romance with communism.

After writing *The Life and Death of Sacco and Vanzetti* (1927), which made him a revered figure on the left, Lyons went to the Soviet Union as a reporter from 1927 to 1933. Upon his return, his first report on his Russian experiences, *Moscow Carousel*, still sought to balance the benefits against the costs of Stalin's regime. Soon afterward, however, he concluded that nothing could justify those costs. In June 1935, his "To Tell or Not to Tell" in *Harper's Monthly* revealed that he had fully lost whatever faith in communism he ever had. He published the full account of his disillusion in *Assignment in Utopia* (1937). This made him a pariah to his old friends on the left, but established Lyons as one of the most knowledgeable and literate of the former fellow-travelers turned anticommunists.[61]

"We had gone to Europe," Lyons wrote in *Assignment in Utopia*, "believing there were good dictatorships and bad. We left convinced that defending one dictatorship is in fact defending the principle of tyranny." Reversing the theme of Soviet propaganda, he charged that a defense of one form of tyranny, communism, was a defense of all, a defense, even, of fascism. "As long as the Rollands and G. B. Shaws and Barbusses condoned political murder and mass exile and the crushing of human decencies in one place and for one cause, they were supporting those methods in all places and for all causes." Lyons now believed that Nazism and communism were identical in their contempt for the individual human being. They represented a "moral collapse of Europe . . . far more terrible than its economic collapse." The struggle was "not between communism and fascism," he wrote. "It is the struggle for the moral and ethical ideals which have been renounced by both those movements."[62]

The Great Depression had destroyed the faith of many intellectuals in American institutions and had set them to searching for an alternative, like communism, to liberal democracy. But Lyons insisted that even at its worst, even admitting "the racketeering profit system, its political corruptions, its pious hypocrisies, its shrieking contrasts of wealth and poverty," Americans should feel grateful that they had been spared "the tensions of authoritarian Europe." To anyone who had experienced the soul-chilling political systems of Germany and the Soviet Union, "the commonplace freedoms of press, speech and assembly" no longer seemed so commonplace: "These liberties, for all their limitations and blemishes, were wrenched from unwilling masters and are treasures to be guarded." Only someone like himself who had been to Russia and returned, he said, could appreciate "the elation of political freedom" he had felt during the 1936 election when he campaigned for Roosevelt.[63]

Lyons lashed out at American radicals who refused to see what had happened to the revolution in Russia, and who called anyone who told the truth a red-baiter. His critics on the left, he charged, rather than challenging his evidence or his logic, attacked his character: "Intellectuals who had bartered logic and their entire heritage of libertarian and humanistic ideals for a solid faith backed up by a Red Army and a G.P.U." had libeled him as a red-baiter, a "shameless vandal" for undermining their illusions about Russia in which "so many weary or bored or panicky Americans had made their spiritual homes."[64]

Lyons insisted that his rejection of communism had not turned him into a reactionary, but had made him proud and protective of democracy. "In the knowledge of the Russian experiment I am able once more to affirm without shame the value of such things as justice, humaneness, truth, liberty, intellectual integrity and human dignity. From the Russian mistakes I have drawn the strength to assert that without these things social systems can only be variations on the old injustice."[65]

As someone who had once suffered from the same delusion, he called on the American defenders of the Soviet regime to reexamine their faith in the light of facts that should have been clear to all:

> I, too, was infected by that disease. I was ready to liquidate classes, purge millions, sacrifice freedoms and elementary decencies, arm self-appointed dictators with a flaming sword—all for the cause. It was a species of revenge rationalized as social engineering. Then I saw these things in full swing and discovered that the revenge was being wreaked on the very masses who were to be saved by that cause.[66]

Others on the left besides Lyons had reached the same conclusion, that Stalin could not be relied on as an ally against Hitler. John Haynes Holmes congratulated Lyons for having written "a great book." Anticommunist Socialist Abraham Cahan of the *Jewish Forward* wrote to thank Lyons "for having produced this wonderful fountain head of truth about Soviet Russia. From thousands of reports I know that the book is doing marvelous proselytic work, opening eyes that have been closed to Russian realities by communist propaganda and by an idiotic vogue that had a grip on the American intelligentsia for so many years." Anticommunist journalist William Henry Chamberlin wrote that "I may be too optimistic, but I think the heyday of fraudulent misrepresentation about the USSR is over. The facts of life there are now a bit too overwhelming for all but inimitable specimens like Mike Gold or Walter Duranty."[67]

Most gratifying of all to Lyons must have been a long letter from London, where Emma Goldman was representing the Spanish anarchists: "I had waited seventeen years for just such a story as yours to come out of Russia, [so] you will realize how enthralled I was. . . . How well I understand the struggle you made, your inner conflict whether 'to tell or not to tell.' " But she complained that he had not gone far enough in his denunciation of the Soviet system.

> There is also this unfortunate mistake which you seem to have made, namely that the horrors in Soviet Russia are due entirely to Stalin, whereas the foundation for all the subsequent things that happened in Russia was laid by Lenin and his group of comrades. Stalin merely built the terrifying citadel on the foundation of his comrade and teacher.

Goldman told Lyons not to be discouraged by "the howl of the pack of hounds that went up when your book appeared." When she wrote her *My Disillusionment in Russia*, she recalled, "I was paid greater honour— I was burned in effigy and the person who called for that demonstration was none other than Rose Pastor Stokes, once a friend of mine." Lyons should bear up under Communist attacks with humor and contempt, since

> the tragedy of Russia is too far-reaching and too deep to care much about one's own personal wrongs. . . . As you know yourself, a lie perpetuates itself much longer than the truth. It will take many years before the masses and the intellectuals will penetrate the colossal humbug of the Soviet regime as the articulator of the Russian Revolution. Meanwhile, the Bolshevik myth has infiltrated itself in all sorts of places, has corrupted the entire Labour Movement in the world, has destroyed the integrity and decency as well as the mutual confidence that existed before."[68]

But there were those on the left who refused to concede the anticommunist case against Stalin might have some merit. Freda Kirchwey of the *Nation* wrote Lyons that she would not print an excerpt from *Assignment* because "factional bitterness and inter-factional warfare are among the most dangerous forms in which the weakness of the left shows itself . . . the world is in too desperate straits for liberals or radicals to use their power and fighting spirit for mutual destruction; and I don't want *The Nation* to contribute to any such cause."[69]

Isaac Don Levine, who was responsible for some of the thirties' most sensational exposés of the activities of the Soviet underground apparatus in the West, was another of the Jewish anticommunists who emerged out of the left, though he began his move away from communism earlier than the rest. Levine was born in Russia in 1892, and came to America in 1911. Initially sympathetic to the Communist revolution, he went back to Russia as a reporter in 1919. On his return he lectured—apparently, according to FBI informants, impartially—on Russian conditions. Lenin's 1922 purge of the Russian Social Revolutionaries began to move him in the direction of anticommunism. Levine represented the Hearst syndicate in Berlin in the early twenties, and during the thirties he wrote a column on international affairs for Hearst's *New York Evening Journal American*.

Around the beginning of 1939, a fantastic publishing scoop landed in his lap. A veteran secret agent of the Comintern, Walter Krivitsky, had defected from the Soviet underground and needed a professional writer to ready his story for publication in English. He came to Levine, and Levine got out his typewriter.

Walter Krivitsky left the Comintern's secret service at the end of 1937 when Stalin's assassins murdered Ignaz Reiss, Krivitsky's boyhood friend, for defecting from the Soviet underground. Before that, Krivitsky had led a life of high drama. He could tell Levine hair-raising stories of life in the Kremlin during Stalin's terror, as well as suspenseful tales of the shadow world of spies and revolutionaries in the European political underground. Levine took some license with the record to dramatize Krivitsky. He promoted him from his probable rank of lieutenant colonel to general, and from Comintern resident agent in Hague to the chief of the Comintern underground for all Europe. Likewise, Levine made Krivitsky the hero of all the book's adventures, whether they had actually involved Krivitsky or some other agent.

The articles Levine ghosted for Krivitsky were a sensation when they appeared in the *Saturday Evening Post* during 1939, among them "Stalin's Hands in Spain," "Why Did They Confess?" "My Flight from Stalin," and "The Red Army Auxiliary of Germany's Military Might."

The collected stories appeared at the end of 1939 as a book, *In Stalin's Secret Service*, and became a best-seller. Levine fully expected that the book would once and for all open the eyes of the fellow-traveling left to Stalin's betrayal of the Socialist ideal, and at least in the case of fellow-traveling literary critic Malcolm Cowley, he was right. Cowley wrote that Krivitsky's book was one of "a series of writings and events that caused me to change my judgment of Soviet Russia."[70] But Levine, like Hook, was to be disappointed at how few fellow travelers reacted to the book in that manner. It had been hopes, not facts, that had attracted them to communism, and facts were not going to tear them loose.

In Stalin's Secret Service was more than a cloak and dagger adventure. Krivitsky had turned his life into a demonstration of how Stalin had corrupted and betrayed the ideals that had persuaded millions like him to devote their lives to the revolution. "What hero or heroine of our revolution has not been broken and destroyed?" Krivitsky asked.

> I could think of but few. All those whose personal integrity was absolutely above question had gone down as "traitors" and "spies" or common criminals. . . . And then the great purge—sweeping all before it, destroying those who had labored hardest to build a state in which man should no longer exploit his fellow man.[71]

In agonizing detail Krivitsky's pages gave a vivid picture of the corrupt and luxurious life-styles of high Party officials, and of the contrast with the millions of starving kulaks Stalin had uprooted like cattle to the slaughterhouse, driven by the "hard faced militiamen of the OGPU."

Much of the book was devoted to explaining why and when he had broken with Stalin. He had devoted his entire life to the Bolshevik cause, he explained, but his faith had been destroyed by the Stalinist purge of the Republicans in Spain, the show trials and executions in Russia, and the purge of the Red Army's heroes.

Worst of all had been Stalin's betrayal of antifascism. It was "pure myth," Krivitsky said, that Stalin and Hitler were mortal enemies. "Stalin was the suitor. There was enmity on Hitler's part. On Stalin's there was fear." The final break came when Krivitsky was ordered to deliver one of his friends to be executed in the purges. "I forced my mind to know that, whether there was any other hope in the world or not, I was serving a totalitarian despot who differed from Hitler only in the socialist phrases, the relic of his Marxist training—socialist phrases to which he hypocritically clung."[72]

And just as he had finally faced the fact that the Bolshevik dream was dead, he called on the others whom Stalin had betrayed to do the same. It had been intellectuals who had given Stalin a veneer of respectability, Krivitsky said. It was time for them to face the truth and start telling the truth.

> Now that it has become painfully clear that the worst way of fighting Hitler is to mitigate the crimes of Stalin, all those who were maneuvered into that folly ought to speak. If these last tragic years have taught us anything, it is that the march of totalitarian barbarism cannot be halted by strategic retreats to positions of half-truth and falsehood. While no one can dictate the method by which civilized Europe will restore to man his dignity and worth, I think that all those not destined for the camp of Hitler and Stalin, will agree that truth must be the first weapon, and murder must be called by its real name.[73]

One of Krivitsky's *Saturday Evening Post* stories predicted Stalin's rapprochement with Hitler well before the Hitler-Stalin pact. He had written that if Hitler would give Stalin peace, Stalin would give the Nazis whatever they wanted. For this Krivitsky was mocked as a pathological liar, a ludicrous example of how far anticommunists would go to defame Stalin and the Soviet Union.

Far from being persuaded, the fellow-traveling press urged the administration to deport Krivitsky as an undesirable alien, and the Immigration Service actually had begun to bow to the pressure when Socialist labor lawyer Louis Waldman intervened to halt the proceedings.

Krivitsky now began to search out other forums to tell his story. In October 1939 he appeared before the Dies Committee. He was disappointed at the primitive level of the knowledge of communism and espionage displayed by the Committee, and he was amused that they seemed more concerned with having themselves photographed with him for campaign publicity than with making use of the information he had given them. In January 1940 he went to England where he furnished British intelligence with the names of scores of Russian operatives in that country.

Not long afterwards, Krivitsky's anticommunist career came to a violent end. He was found dead in a Washington hotel room, killed by a bullet to the head from his own pistol. His death could have been a suicide, but there were suspicions it was one of the many political murders carried out in the thirties and forties by Stalin's far-flung assassination teams.

Late in 1939 Levine began to work with a second defector from the Soviet secret service. This was Richard Krebs, alias Jan Valtin. His first story appeared in *American Mercury*'s November 1939 issue under the title "Communist Agent."[74] His book, *Out of the Night*, appeared in 1941 and was a Book-of-the-Month Club selection and one of the year's best sellers.

Valtin, the son of a seaman, grew up in Hamburg, Germany. As a young radical, he took part in the 1919 Spartacist uprising in Germany, and when that was suppressed, he went to Russia, where he was educated as a special agent of the Comintern at a training school in Leningrad's old Duma building. He was arrested in the United States while on an undercover assignment and spent three years in San Quentin. After his release, he served as political chief of the Comintern's Marine Section, headquartered in Hamburg. After that he was the Comintern inspector general for England, reporting back to Moscow on the British party.

Through Valtin, Levine was able to reveal for the first time the full story of Stalin's betrayal of the antifascist front in Germany, and of his complicity in Hitler's rise to power. Valtin revealed that German Communists had been ordered to ignore the Nazis and to concentrate on destroying the Social Democrats to remove them as rivals to the Communists within the left, even though it meant sabotaging any chance for the democratic left to stop the Nazis in 1932.

Soon after the Reichstag fire, Valtin was captured by the Gestapo. His description of his months in a Nazi cell was shaped by Levine into a classic of prison literature, a sickening ordeal of torture at the hands of sadistic Nazi guards. He was released when the Comintern ordered him to feign defection to the Gestapo, but on the outside he found himself marked for extermination during Stalin's purges and so, like Krivitsky, he broke with the Party.

All his sacrifices, Valtin saw, had been for nothing. His comrades in the Comintern who died serving Stalin "did not die for the world revolution; they only thought they did; they died to gratify the lust for power of the Stalin clique; they died because they had been made to believe that it was more honorable to be a stinking corpse than a living thing outside the party."[75]

He fled to America to escape Stalin's death squads, but his picture had been printed on the front page of every Communist paper in the world, with the caption, "On the Watch! Gestapo!" By framing him as a Nazi agent, he said, the Communists were trying "to make the police departments of all countries do the work of the GPU—to track me down and to deliver me to Germany, the Gestapo, and death."[76]

Through Krivitsky's and Valtin's stories, Isaac Don Levine gave the American public for the first time an inside look at the worldwide web of subversion and espionage woven by the Soviet secret services. He let Americans experience the terror of being on the run from Stalin's agents, or of being held in Stalin's prison cells to be processed by the torturers and executioners who now ruled Russia. Through Krivitsky and Valtin, Levine was able to explain to the general public how Willi Muenzenberg had created the Communists' international propaganda empire, and how that propaganda had been able to extend communism's influence throughout American cultural life. It was not simply the intrinsic drama of the stories nor Levine's writing skills that made so many readers find these two books so compelling. It was the moral passion he brought to his tasks, the outraged morality of an anticommunist whose own dreams had been betrayed by those who had betrayed Krivitsky and Valtin.

Anticommunists like Sidney Hook, Eugene Lyons, and Isaac Don Levine had, against all odds, set before Americans the facts of what Stalin had done to a Bolshevik Revolution that had once raised the hopes of the left around the world, and the damage Communists had done to the dream of a unified left in America. They had rallied the democratic left against what American fellow travelers were doing to put American culture at the service of a regime that had eliminated cultural freedom and personal liberty.

And yet, the Stalinist penetration of American cultural institutions and of the American labor movement proceeded apace, unmolested by the enormity of the case anticommunists could lay against them. The issue of the thirties was Hitler and how to stop him, and, as long as Stalin could claim to lead the international resistance to Hitler, his supporters could maintain that an attack on communism was an attack on antifascism, and they were able to point to Martin Dies, Charles Coughlin, and Elizabeth Dilling to prove that anticommunism and fascism were one and the same.

As long as the Soviet Union seemed to be in the forefront of the fight against fascism, and as long as the American Communists could claim to be America's most militant enemies of Hitler, nothing anticommunists said about the reality of communism dented the Communists' impregnable defense of being the shock troops of antifascism. Not even the revelation that the Kremlin had refused to join with the democratic left to stop Hitler when he might have been stopped weakened the left's gratitude for Stalin's leadership against fascism. Not even a liberal with the impeccable credentials of John Dewey escaped the charge that by exposing the crimes of Stalin he was helping Hitler.

Then came the bombshell of August 24, 1939. For a decade the Soviets had claimed to be leaders of the antifascist resistance. Now came news that the German and Soviet foreign ministers—Ribbentrop and Molotov—had signed a treaty of peace and friendship, the Hitler-Stalin Pact. With a stroke of a pen Stalin had eliminated the antifascist shield that had protected the Communists and their fellow travelers from the truth. Throughout the thirties anticommunists had been arguing without effect that communism and fascism were twin forms of totalitarianism, and that free societies had to reject both. What they had been straining to prove had now been proven by Stalin himself. *Quid erat demonstrandum, demonstratum est.* The case against communism was closed. Or was it?

Chapter 7

DANCING WITH THE DEVIL

The Alliance with Stalin

They are a danger. They are a menace. They are not loyal. They
are not faithful. They have their feet on our ground, on our soil,
but their hearts belong elsewhere. Beware of them!
    —David Dubinsky on American Communists, 1944[1]

The Hitler-Stalin Pact, far from clinching the case against communism,
inaugurated one of the most trying periods in the history of anticommunism. Recovering quickly from the disgrace of Stalin's alliance with
Hitler, by the end of the world war American Communists would have
managed to represent themselves as the most loyal and enthusiastic supporters of the war effort, while anticommunists, for doubting the long-
term value of the America's wartime alliance with the Soviets, would
open themselves to the charge of being unenthusiastic about the war,
even of sympathizing with the enemy.

    The history of American anticommunism after the Hitler-Stalin Pact
and during World War II falls into three distinct phases. Until the German invasion of the Soviet Union on June 22, 1941, the Party line made
American Communists the noisiest opponents of President Roosevelt's
efforts to save England from the German blitz. But after the invasion of
the Soviet Union, the Communists threw their support to Roosevelt,
clamoring for the United States to help the Soviets and all the other
forces fighting Hitler. After Pearl Harbor, Communists were advocates
of an all-out war effort, demanding an immediate second front in Europe. Anticommunism emerged after each of these changes in the Party
line in a weakened position until, at the end of the war, it was suspected

155

of having opposed, or at best having given only grudging assent, to a war whole-heartedly supported by almost all Americans. By the end of the war, anticommunism had the appearance of disloyalty. Communism, by contrast, seemed almost respectable.[2]

The Hitler-Stalin Pact had made fascism, according to Molotov, "a matter of taste." A week later, Hitler drove into Poland to claim his spoils and Britain and France declared war. According to the pact, Poland was to be divided; Stalin would get Finland, Estonia, and Latvia; and Germany Lithuania. On September 16, with Warsaw about to fall to German troops, Stalin sent in his army to take possession of his half of Poland.

The Hitler-Stalin Pact left the Party reeling, the Popular Front in a shambles. Anticommunists seemingly had only to point silently at the headlines to prove that they had been right in calling communism and fascism twin forms of totalitarianism. In America, the pact caused thousands of quiet defections from the Party and from front organizations. But despite the crushing blow of the pact, the Party was not crushed. Despite the Communists' abandonment of the antifascism that had attracted so many to the Party, the Party was not abandoned by the left it betrayed.

There were some notable public exits from the Popular Front. Civil libertarian John Haynes Holmes wrote:

> If we liberals were right on certain single aspects of the Russian Revolution, we were wrong, disgracefully wrong, on the question as a whole. We were wrong because, in our enthusiasm over Russia's liberation from the Czar, our hope for the further liberation of the Russian people from economic as well as political serfdom and our vision of a new world springing from the womb of this Russian experiment, we permitted ourselves to condone wrongs that we knew must be wrongs. We consented to violations of principle that we knew to be fatal to the moral integrity of mankind.
>
> We defended, or at least apologized for, evils in the case of Russia which horrified us wherever else they appeared, and by whomsoever else they were done.[3]

Within the black community, according to an historian of black communism, the pact made "militant anticommunism emerge as a powerful Harlem intellectual current for the first time."[4] George Schuyler had spent the thirties pointing out how the Communist Party had sacrificed the interests of black Communists to the goals of the Soviet Union.

Black Communists had felt betrayed when the Soviets, still hoping for good relations with Mussolini, refused to support Ethiopia when it was invaded by Italy, and former Communists Ira Kemp and Arthur Reid demonstrated in front of Italian-owned stores. Schuyler wrote contentedly that the few blacks who had been attracted to communism were losing interest because of the "botching" of the Scottsboro case, Ethiopia, the "Black and White" film fiasco, and the Party's abandonment of the race issue when the Party line shifted to the United Front against Hitler. "Saving the Jews in Germany became suddenly more important than saving the Negroes in Mississippi." He had celebrated April Fool's Day, 1938, by mocking the contortions of American Communists trying to justify the Moscow Purge trials, writing that "there seems to be a complete unanimity among thinking Negroes as to the effectiveness of communist work among Negroes. It is nil. Being a canny fellow, the Negro is militant when there is hope of success. It's trouble enough being black without going red." And Schuyler reported that the Communist Party line on blacks—"self-determination of the Negro in a black belt" in the deep South—continued to alienate black America. "Negroes do not want a black belt," Schuyler declared. "Their efforts are toward eliminating black belts. Race is far more important than class as the cause of the Negroes' problems."[5]

Black leaders like Walter White of the NAACP and Frank Crosswaith of the Harlem Labor Council had attacked the Party's civil rights front, the National Negro Congress. They feared that it would destroy black organizations more truly representative of black interests. The failure of Communist-dominated labor unions to accept blacks members produced more black anticommunists, and so did the Party's refusal to give blacks non-menial jobs in those garment trade unions that they dominated. In New York City, Harlemites had been angered by discrimination against blacks in labor contracts negotiated by the Communist Transport Workers Union.[6] After the Hitler-Stalin Pact, black leaders like A. Philip Randolph, Frank Crosswaith, and Layle Lane tried to drive Communists out of civil rights campaigns, and they made plans to end the influence the Party had won during the Scottsboro and Herndon struggles.[7]

It did not take long, however, for the remnants of the fellow-traveling left to regroup and recapture their old sense of being victimized by an anticommunist conspiracy. Anticommunists themselves helped revive the spirits of the Communists and their allies by backing them into a corner after the pact, and kicking them when they were down.

It would have taken an angelic strain of mercy for anticommunists like those in Hook's Committee for Cultural Freedom not to show their joy over the shame and confusion of the fellow-traveling left. But Hook's group did not simply point out the mistakes of the Popular Front, or invite the sinners back into the fold. Instead they seemed to take pleasure in humiliating communism's former apologists.

Just before the pact, a so-called Committee of Four Hundred—sharing the headquarters of Corliss Lamont's American Soviet Friendship Committee—had been formed for the express purpose of attacking the CCF. Lamont's group charged that "Fascists and their allies" (meaning the CCF) were trying to destroy the unity of the progressive left: By "sowing suspicion between the Soviet Union and other nations interested in maintaining peace" and by trying to "pervert American antifascist sentiment to their own ends . . . they have encouraged the fantastic falsehood that the USSR and the totalitarian states are basically alike." The truth, according to the Lamont group, was that "Soviet Socialism differs fundamentally from totalitarian fascism."[8]

Hook, Lyons, and their friends could now jeer at Lamont and his fellow travelers as the clowns of the "last loony scene" of the Red Decade. They taunted them about their role in "a goofy epoch [that] had exploded in farce. And in the tragedy of war."[9] It was not enough for fellow travelers like Vincent Sheean, Maurice Hindus, Granville Hicks, Heywood Broun, and Louis Fischer to turn against communism after the pact. Sidney Hook demanded that fellow travelers admit that they had always been wrong, the anticommunists always right. "Although the Nazi-Soviet Pact and the succession of shocking events in its train must have brought some of the signers to reconsider the contents of the letter [attacking the CCF]," Hook wrote, "none made any public acknowledgment of it, or a public apology to the CCF. Not even Granville Hicks and Vincent Sheean, who were soon to repudiate the Communist Party and its policies, made formal amends." John Dewey wrote to each member of Lamont's group, demanding to know how, in the light of the Hitler-Stalin Pact, they could any longer deny the validity of the CCF's categorization of Nazism and Stalinism as being equally objectionable forms of totalitarianism. Hook said he was appalled that Dewey received "not a single reply."

Hook should have tried to use the pact to form alliances with former fellow travelers, rather than use it to further humiliate men and women whom Stalin had already humiliated past endurance.[10] Anticommunist attacks on the fellow-traveling left were so violent that some on the left even began to make excuses for the Communists, who had been so ill-served by Stalin. The *Nation* refused to bow to Hook's demands that the left banish Communists from the left community: "To advocate a policy of 'clearest differentiation' on the left is a counsel of disruption. With all their faults, the Communists perform necessary functions in the confused struggle of our time. They have helped to build up and to run a string of organizations known as 'fronts' by their opponents—which clearly serve the cause not of 'totalitarian doctrine' but of a more workable democracy. And the value of these organizations lies largely in the energy and discipline and zeal of their Communist elements."[11] The Comminists defended Stalin's invasion of "fascist" Poland as a contribution to "the cause of world peace," repulsing all but the truest of believers. The Party claimed "the war that has broken out in Europe is the Second Imperialist War. The ruling capitalist and landlord classes of all the belligerent countries are equally guilty for this war. . . . It is a war between rival imperialisms for world domination. The workers must be against this war."[12]

The front movement had obviously been badly wounded by the pact. It was all but demolished organizationally. Communist-controlled organizations lost almost all their noncommunist members. The American Civil Liberties Union, which had long welcomed Communists, decided in February 1940 to ban anyone from the ACLU board who belonged to "any political organization which supports totalitarian dictatorships in any country, or who by his public declarations and connections indicates his support for such principles."[13] That led to the resignation of Harry F. Ward, chair of the ACLU's Board of Directors. On May 7 the directors voted to remove Communist Elizabeth Gurley Flynn from the board.

The unity of the radical left had always depended on the left's shared sense of victimization. The pact splintered the radical left, but the war emergency, by reviving the government surveillance and repression of radicalism suspended after the Red Scare raids and Teapot Dome, once again gave them the sense of being persecuted by a government conspiracy. When Roosevelt proclaimed a state of national emergency at the outbreak of the European war, he ordered J. Edgar Hoover once again to take charge of government measures against sabotage, espionage, and subversion.

The entire left was outraged when the FBI, at the direction of the Justice Department, raided the headquarters of the veterans of the Abraham Lincoln Brigade for having violated laws against recruiting soldiers for foreign armies during the Spanish Civil War.[14] It sounded like new Red Scare raids were being planned, and the FBI was back in business as the unifying demon in left mythology.

The arrests served to rally the left around one of the still-pristine symbols of those days when the Soviet Union and the Popular Front were leading the antifascist movement. The arrests had a bracing effect on the demoralized fellow-traveling left. The liberal and radical press raked Hoover and the Justice Department over the coals. The administration bowed to the pressure and dismissed the charges as meaningless, since the war in Spain was over.[15]

The Abraham Lincoln Brigade arrests made the left take a fresh look at what "G-man Hoover" and Roosevelt had been doing on the internal security front—which Hoover would call the "FBI Front" during the war. Hoover's testimony before Congress in November 1939 revealed that he had revived the old General Intelligence Division of the Palmer days. On January 5, 1940, he told the Appropriations Committee that he had created an "index" of persons to be taken into custody in an emergency.[16] Everyone who had ever been associated with the Party could feel at risk, which allowed the Communists to find refuge once again within a new sense of solidarity on the left. Liberals who had learned to tolerate the "new" Hoover, the popular hero who had gotten Dillinger and Pretty Boy Floyd in the mid-thirties, now remembered the "old" Hoover of the Palmer-Daugherty years.

Hoover fought back by claiming he was the victim of a Communist "smear" plot—which was not far from the truth. Meanwhile, he was giving Roosevelt reports on the Communist affiliations of the opponents of the President's preparedness programs.

The Dies Committee also did its share to reunite the left by persuading it to rally to the defense of victimized Communists and fellow travelers. The Committee spent the spring of 1940 raiding Communist headquarters and photostating their membership records, staying two steps ahead of the law. In Philadelphia the law caught up with Dies, and two of the Committee's investigators were jailed for an illegal search. Dies obtained contempt dictations against five Party functionaries for refusing to give up their membership lists. Dies also took credit for the Senate's passage of the Smith Act in 1940, which made it illegal to establish or belong to organizations that would "teach and advocate the overthrow of the United States government by force and violence."[17] The peacetime sedition law Hoover and Palmer had yearned for in 1919 was now on the books, and a shiver went down the spine of the entire left.

The Committee's hearings on the Popular Front were so obviously intended to red-smear all reformers that they also helped restore the solidarity of the left. On October 23, 1939, the Committee grilled Rev. Harry F. Ward, chairman of the American League Against War and Fascism. With J. B. Matthews leading the questioning, the Committee brought out that the League was a creature of the Communist Party, and that the credulous Ward had been a puppet hardly aware of the strings that made him dance to Moscow's tune.

But Dies was not satisfied with making the facts known. He wanted to smear, he wanted to punish, and two days later he released the membership roll of the League's Washington, D.C. chapter. The list had the names of 563 federal employees, and Dies wanted to drive them from their jobs. When the two liberals on the Committee protested that it had no way of knowing if the list was accurate, Dies insultingly said that any inaccuracies in the Committee's list were the League's fault for not maintaining its membership rolls properly. The radical press reacted with headlines like "FASCISM HITS WASHINGTON."[18]

Smeared by Dies, the left smeared back. Early in 1940, the *Nation* obtained documents that showed close ties between Dies and William Dudley Pelley, head of the anti-Semitic American fascist Silver Shirts. The *Nation* claimed these proved Dies had a secret understanding with Pelley to block Committee investigations of anti-Semites and Nazi sympathizers like Pelley and Charles Coughlin. During a congressional debate over whether to continue the Dies Committee, Congressman Frank E. Hook of Michigan used the *Nation's* story to argue that the Committee should be abolished.

But the Dies documents were a forgery. It came out that a lobbyist for

Labor's Non-Partisan League, a political action committe backed by the CIO, had gone to a Pelley associate to see if he had anything that would incriminate Dies. Pelley's staffer obligingly forged some letters and turned them over, and then notified the Dies Committee of the plot. After the left had gone public with the papers, the Dies Committee sprung the trap. Congressman Hook was embarrassed and outraged. He apologized and withdrew the letters from the *Congressional Record*. Now it was the *Nation* that adopted the countersubversives' "disinfection" theory, arguing that fascists had created the forgeries to allow Dies to deny the truth—that he was a fascist.[19]

The Committee performed its work in a smog of character assassination and guilt by association, and it was no excuse that the Committee's critics often used the same smear tactics. The Committee came to be regarded as so untrustworthy by the liberal and moderate press that even when it furnished accurate information about Communist activities it was not believed. By sheer dint of repeating stories of the Committee's outrages, its enemies perpetuated the belief that Dies and American fascists were linked by the same sort of chain of association the crazier countersubversives used to construct red webs. For example, one of the Committee's investigators once shared an office with James True, notorious in counter-anti-Semitic circles as the inventor of a billy club known as the "Kike Killer." Seldom was there a story about Dies in the leftist press that did not remind readers of this interesting fact.

During the two years between the pact and Pearl Harbor, anticommunism was battered in one of the most bitter melees in American political history. On one side were the interventionists, led by the Committee to Defend America by Aiding the Allies, who wanted to assist Great Britain by measures up to and (for some) including war. On the other were the isolationists, who—for a variety of reasons—opposed American participation in any more European wars. The chief isolationist organization was the America First Committee. Both sides attracted swarms of like-minded groups and individuals, some responsible, others not. Even if the Dies Committee had not continued to discredit honest anticommunism during the post-pact period when the case against the Party should have been all but unanswerable, anticommunists would still have found themselves besieged and beleaguered during this debate.

With the Nazis in control of all of Europe, and England standing alone as the last obstacle to Hitler's ambitions, interventionists foresaw the doom of Western civilization if the United States did not come to the aid of Great Britain. Isolationists saw a plot to sacrifice once again American lives in the interests of European powers who had been quarreling since the dawn of history. Some isolationists saw another of the Wall Street plots they blamed for World War I. Others saw a Communist conspiracy aimed at eliminating the world's most fierce anticommunist, Adolf Hitler.

In this fight, nothing was held back. Isolationist Senator Burton K. Wheeler called FDR's Lend-Lease program to provide warships to Britain a program to "plow under every fourth American boy." Interventionists' most effective way of discrediting their enemies was to link them to anti-Semites and pro-Nazis (who were, of course, against helping Britain against Hitler) so that they could claim that isolationism was a Nazi fifth column in America. The same countersubversive extremists who had discredited anticommunism for twenty years—the Fishes and the Dillings and the Coughlins—now became the focus of attack for the interventionists' assault against the isolationists.

This technique of "brown smearing"—discrediting conservatives by linking them with the brown-shirted Nazi movement—was so prevalent during the debate over intervention and afterwards that these years until the end of World War II and the breakdown of the Soviet-American alliance have been called the American Brown Scare.[20]

Although the interventionists' aim was to discredit isolationism, through a natural process of association anticommunism was brownsmeared as well, since so many of the most prominent isolationists were well known as anticommunists. Those same countersubversive anticommunists were now linked to Berlin-directed anti-Semitic American fascism. All anticommunists were again discredited by the countersubversive fringe, even though most responsible anticommunists supported intervention. Most of them had held all along that Hitler was a greater threat than Stalin, even while they insisted that Stalin was not a reliable ally against Hitler, and that communism was as much an enemy to freedom as fascism. Ironically, anticommunists first suffered from this brown-smear abuse at a time when the Communists themselves were opposing aid to England, and so, by any objective analysis, were helping Hitler.

American isolationism began to organize itself into a political force in the spring of 1940. A group of Yale Law School students, among them future President Gerald Ford and future Supreme Court Justice Potter Stewart, decided that an organization was needed to oppose the interventionist Committee to Defend America by Aiding the Allies led by Kansas editor William Allen White. The result in September 1940 was the America First Committee, with Sears president Robert E. Wood as its national chairman, and Oswald Garrison Villard, Henry Ford, Chester Bowles, Burton K. Wheeler, and Hamilton Fish among its more prominent members. Although most union leaders backed intervention, John L. Lewis of the United Mine Workers threw his support to America First; his daughter represented him at its deliberations. For a brief time the young John F. Kennedy, following the lead of his isolationist father, was also an America Firster. America First's most famous (and eventually, most disastrous) spokesman was the aviator Charles Lindbergh. Norman Thomas, head of his own "Keep America Out of the War Committee," also appeared at America First rallies, but Thomas was almost alone among the Socialists in opposing Roosevelt's defense policies. At its peak before Pearl Harbor the AFC had grown to 450 chapters nationwide, with at least 250,000 members.[21]

Lined up against the isolationists were liberal internationalists like Roosevelt who clearly saw that Hitler was the immediate threat to the world order. Most of the non-fellow-traveling left—because of its profound antifascism and detestation of Hitler—also wanted to help the Allies. The Communists themselves, however, were the most intransigent of isolationists, right up to the moment on June 22, 1941, when Hitler invaded the Soviet Union.

Contrary to the brown-smear stereotype, almost all prominent anticommunists favored aid to England up to, and in some cases including, military intervention. Almost all liberal anticommunists (including many liberal Catholics), as well as radical, Socialist, and Jewish anticommunists, were interventionists. But even though most anticommunists favored intervention, the prominent role of countersubversive anticommunists in the isolationist camp allowed all anticommunists to be brown-smeared when these countersubversives were accused of being Nazis and anti-Semites. And, in fact, some of the countersubversives swarming about the isolationist movement *were* noisy and unabashed pro-Nazis and anti-Semites, to the chagrin of the America First Committee's respectable national leadership.

As the battle over intervention intensified during the fall of 1939, nearly twenty years of antiwar propaganda had put interventionists at a disadvantage. Public opinion, in fact, remained predominantly isolationist until Pearl Harbor. But organized isolationism was glaringly vulnerable because of its extremist hangers-on, and so they became the targets of the interventionists' heaviest guns.

The work of turning the fascist and anti-Semitic isolationists into dramatic symbols of the entire isolationist camp was done by militant interventionist "attack" groups. These included generally responsible groups like the Institute for Propaganda Analysis, Raymond Graham Swing's Council for Democracy, and the Fight for Freedom Committee (which became Freedom House in 1942), as well as others, like Leon M. Birkhead's Friends of Democracy, that used shameless brown-smear tactics.[22] All of them ferreted out the anti-Semites and the pro-Nazis within the isolationist movement, and used them to argue that the power behind isolationism was American fascism, in conscious alliance with Hitler.

The Institute for Propaganda Analysis, founded in October 1937 by Edward Filene of the Garland Foundation (through his Good Will Fund), worked energetically to expose the activities of native fascists in the isolationist movement. The Institute established a network of discussion groups across the country, and provided chapter leaders with reading materials and guidance in running discussions to clarify current issues by identifying groups and interests that were trying behind the scenes to bend public opinion in their direction.[23]

Nazi propaganda became the standard by which the Institute judged all attempts to manipulate public opinion. Its standard approach entailed identifying similarities between the public relations methods of American political groups and those of the Nazis. If there was any similarity, then the American group was judged to have failed to conform to "to American principles of democracy."

While not explicitly characterizing all isolationists as Nazi propagandists in Uncle Sam suits, month after month the Institute slashed away at the Coughlins, Gerald Winrods, and other Nazi-tinged isolationists. The impression emerged that these were the only isolationists that mattered. Furthermore, the bibliographies it distributed did recommend brown-smearing works like William Gellerman's *American Legion as Educator*, which called the Legion "potentially fascist" and linked it to native Nazi groups.[24]

The January 1940 issue of the Institute's monthly attacked right-wing isolationists William Dudley Pelley, George W. Christians, Gerald Winrod, George Deatherage, and Father Coughlin. The Institute argued that Coughlin's Christian Front was "an organization in the cities of the industrial East, which can only be described as fascist—an organization whose members talk of killing the Jews and blasting their way to power with guns and dynamite."[25] The Institute held the Christian Front to be a potential brown network linking the Amerika-deutscher Volksbund, Allen Zoll's American Patriots, Inc., and Merwin K. Hart's New York State Economic Council to mainstream conservative politicians like George U. Harvey, borough president of Queens. While the Institute was more careful with its facts then were Elizabeth Dilling or Richard Whitney, the approach was the same: the most tenuous associations were used to tie into a conspiracy individuals whose inability to get along with each other was precisely what kept them on the powerless fringe of American politics.

Harold Lavine, the Institute's director, used the Institute's research to write *The Fifth Column in America* (1940). Here he asserted that the far right had evolved into a Nazi underground. Almost all the individuals and groups he implicated in this underground were active in the isolationist movement, so other interventionists cited the Institute when they blasted the isolationist movement for being Nazi-controlled. George Seldes' *Witch Hunt: The Technique and Profits of Red-Baiting* (1940) went even further, explicitly making anticommunism an infallible indicator of Nazi sympathies.[26]

White's Committee to Defend America by Aiding the Allies used the same line of attack in its publicity. On June 10, 1940, it ran full-page advertisements proclaiming that "The Fifth Column is led in this as in other countries by Nazis and Communists and their fellow travelers. . . . Their object is to destroy national unity . . . sabotaging all aid to the Allies."[27] Now Roosevelt began to call enemies of his preparedness programs a Fifth Column (and worse). "If I should die tomorrow, I want you to know this," he told Treasury Secretary Morgenthau, "I am convinced that Lindbergh is a Nazi."[28]

A group that raised brown-smearing to something of a fine art was Unitarian Minister Leon M. Birkhead's Friends of Democracy. Birkhead founded the FOD in 1937 to combat Gerald Winrod's native fascist movement. The group's advisory panel included mystery writer Rex

Stout, who was its president after 1942. Friends of Democracy had a file of eight hundred pro-Nazi groups by 1939, and it insisted that sympathy for the Nazi cause was the real motive behind isolationism. A typical Friends of Democracy pamphlet for March 1941 called the America First Committee a "Nazi front."[29]

The administration was just as brutal in brown-smearing the isolationists. Roosevelt himself called America First the "unwitting aides of the agents of Nazism." Walter Winchell, strongly supporting Roosevelt on intervention, labeled America First the "Hitler First–America Last" Committee.[30]

No smear is effective unless it contains at least a grain of truth. The America First Committee and Norman Thomas's group tried to maintain their distance from anti-Semites and fascists, but the lunatic fringe of countersubversives was drawn irresistibly to them, wild for the possibility of becoming part of a powerful mainstream political movement. Gerald L. K. Smith, Elizabeth Dilling, Gerald B. Winrod, William Dudley Pelley, Charles Coughlin, Laura Ingalls, and all of the country's other notorious anti-Semitic anticommunist crackpots joyously raised the temperature of the debate by attacking defense preparations as Jewish inspired and Communist directed. Even though the national America First Committee did its best to exclude the anti-Semitic extremists, they simply joined America First's local affiliates. Laura Ingalls, later indicted as a German agent, appeared before a southern California chapter to urge isolationists to adopt a left-hand version of the Nazi salute.[31] In New York the anti-Semitic Christian Front proclaimed its unwelcome support for America First, and the Nazi propaganda network also embarrassed America First with an unsolicited endorsement. The head of Huey Long's organization, the rabble-rousing Gerald L. K. Smith, formed a "Committee of One Million" to make the support he offered America First seem more impressive.

Smith also organized a National League of Mothers to oppose intervention, and that sparked a brood of imitation "mothers movements" across the country. In Chicago there was "We, the Mothers, Mobilize for America." The irrepressible Elizabeth Dilling put together her own "Mothers" group and in February 1941 led them to Washington where they joined forces with the other mothers' groups to lobby the halls of Congress, shouting anti-Semitic slogans at pro-intervention senators and congressmen. When they mobbed the office of Senator Carter Glass of Virginia, he quipped: "I believe it would be pertinent to inquire whether they are mothers. For the sake of the race, I devoutly hope not."[32]

Charles Coughlin had now taken off the wraps that had concealed his anti-Semitism. Although his tirades were muffled by a nearly total radio blackout, he lashed out against Great Britain, praised Hitler, and blamed the Jews for moving the country toward war. He paraded his pro-Nazi affinities, saying that "had we Christians enforced the discipline and produced the good accomplished by the Nazis for a good end, we would not be weeping at the wailing wall."[33]

Hamilton Fish, who had done so much to discredit anticommunism in 1930, now did more than anyone else to establish the association between anticommunism and the American Nazi Fifth Column. Fish—one of the bitterest enemies of Roosevelt and the New Deal—was still seen as one of the country's leading anticommunists, though in a somewhat farcical light. He was one of the America First Committee's most prominent supporters and spokesmen, and so it was devastating to the image of isolationism and anticommunism alike when Fish's secretary, who served as chief of his Washington staff, was exposed as having turned Fish's congressional office into a distribution center for isolationist propaganda furnished by German agents and then mailed under the congressional frank of Fish and other isolationist congressmen. Fish's secretary went to jail, and Fish himself narrowly escaped indictment.[34]

On June 22, 1941, Hitler stunned the world—Stalin most of all—with an all-out attack against the Soviet Union along a front that stretched from the Black Sea to the Baltic. In the first few days much of the Soviet air force was destroyed. The Wehrmacht—three million soldiers, 3,300 tanks, 2,770 aircraft—was driving irresistibly through Russia toward Moscow. Stalin, who had refused to credit intelligence reports that the Germans were massing on his borders, was stunned that his faith in his fellow dictator had been so brutally betrayed.

Winston Churchill, though as anticommunist as ever, declared immediately that he would send all possible aid to help Russia hold out against Germany. Two days later Roosevelt announced that the United States, too, would give Russia anything that could help it against Hitler.

Presidential Assistant Harry Hopkins spent July 1941 in Moscow extending Lead-Lease aid to Russia and making preparations for a working relationship between Roosevelt and Stalin.[35]

While American Communists howled for the United States to rescue the Soviet Union, the administration reversed its attitude toward the Communist state. The American ambassador to the Soviet Union, Joseph Davies, spent the summer of 1941 writing his pro-Soviet memoir, *Mission to Moscow* to create support for the Soviets. Though written well before Pearl Harbor, Davies referred to the Soviets as "our allies" and said that they were "fighting our fight."[36]

The administration passed word discouraging criticism of the Soviet Union. According to the *New York Times*'s Arthur Krock, uncritical praise of the Soviets became "so much the fashion that even to point out [flaws in Soviet-American relations] was to bring down the charge of sympathy with 'fascism.' " Krock remembered that this "terror of offending Russia" became so extreme "that at the request of the State Department the publishers of Leon Trotsky's biography of Stalin suppressed the book and recalled reviewers' copies which had been sent out."[37]

American Communists, released from their Hitler-Stalin Pact disgrace, reasserted their former status as leaders of the antifascist left. Where before their slavish obedience to the Soviet Union had always kept them from being taken seriously, that close relationship with the Soviet Union gave Communists prestige with the public they had never before enjoyed. If it was now almost un-American to attack the Soviet Union, it also seemed almost unpatriotic to attack the Soviet Union's American comrades.

Earlier in 1941 Eugene Lyons's *Red Decade* had won him new popularity. But now he nervously contacted the FBI in New York City. He was worried that the changed political climate might encourage the Communists and fellow travelers he attacked in *The Red Decade* to sue him for libel, and he wondered if the Bureau might have corroborating evidence on those he had named in the book. Hoover's aides told him that Lyons had endeavored "to expose with little regard for his ability to substantiate the exposés." Hoover replied that he "would be inclined to help in this if we had something that was not strictly secret. Lyons has done a noble job and of course now will be 'smeared.' "[38]

Isolationist anticommunists were now more vulnerable than ever. On July 25, Secretary of War Henry L. Stimson charged that Senator

Burton Wheeler, leader of the Senate's isolationists, was "coming very close to the line of subversive activities against the United States, if not treason." Wheeler protested that "if a man was noninterventionist, he was ipso facto considered a reactionary, and probably pro-Hitler as well."[39]

The heaviest attacks on the America First Committee were now being concentrated on the Committee's most famous spokesman, the aviator Charles Lindbergh. Lindbergh's hatred of war and his belief that the American air force would be overwhelmed by a vastly superior German military machine made him an outspoken isolationist. He had accepted a military medal from Goering, which made him vulnerable to accusations of being a Nazi sympathizer. Roosevelt called him "a copperhead" and a "modern Vallandigham," a reference to an Ohio congressman banished during the Civil War for treasonous speeches. In mid-July 1941 Interior Secretary Harold Ickes called Lindbergh "a Nazi mouthpiece." Leon M. Birkhead's Friends of Democracy released a pamphlet, "Is Lindbergh a Nazi?" Finally, in Des Moines on September 11, 1941, Lindbergh, provoked to recklessness, accused "the British, the Jewish, and the Roosevelt administration" of pushing the nation into war.[40]

The Des Moines speech gave interventionists all they needed to brand the America First Committee and the entire isolationist movement anti-Semites and Nazis. No longer was the issue isolation versus intervention, but democracy versus fascism. Isolationism was mortally wounded. Pearl Harbor would provide the coup de grace. Since most isolationists were also anticommunists, anticommunism had been disgraced as well.

During the thirties the Soviets succeeded in establishing espionage rings in the federal bureaucracy. Rumors of these rings had long been used to smear liberal and radical New Dealers, but the administration and the press had learned to judge these spy stories by their sources, unreliable countersubversives like Fish, Dies, and Dilling.

After the Hitler-Stalin Pact more reliable information about Soviet spy networks began to surface. Between 1932 and 1938, Communist Whittaker Chambers had acted as liaison between Soviet military intelligence and Communist espionage rings in the federal government.

By the time of the Hitler-Stalin Pact, he had already broken from the Party and was living in fear of Stalin's deadly reprisal. The Pact encouraged Chambers to think that he could safely surface and pass along his information about Soviet espionage in Washington. He contacted Isaac Don Levine, who was currently in the news for helping Walter Krivitsky and Jan Valtin publish their own exposés of Soviet intelligence.

Like Levine, Chambers believed that a convincing exposé of the Soviet Union and its intrigues, put into the right words by the right man, would be all it would take to destroy the hold of communism on Western fellow travelers. The experiences of other defectors—he was particularly moved by Vladimir Tchernavin's *I Speak for the Silent*, about life in the Siberian slave labor camps—had helped Chambers decide to break with the Party.[41]

Levine brought Chambers to Assistant Secretary of State Adolph Berle, who handled internal security for the Department, on September 2, 1939. Chambers told Berle what he knew—and it was a great deal—about Communist cells in the Agriculture Department, the National Labor Relations Board, Army weapons laboratories, the State Department, the Securities and Exchange Commission, and the Treasury Department. He provided specific details on the espionage activities of Donald and Alger Hiss and Alger Hiss's wife Priscilla. Levine and Chambers hoped their report would unleash a government crackdown on Soviet espionage.[42]

Nothing happened. Berle went to Roosevelt, who dismissed the allegations. When Berle persisted, FDR told him, in words that Chambers said it was "necessary to paraphrase," that Berle should "go jump in a lake."[43]

Out of his profound disappointment, Chambers theorized that liberals were in such agreement with Communists on shifting power from business to government that "every move against the Communists was felt by the liberals as a move against themselves." All Communists had to do, he said, was "to shout their innocence and cry: 'Witch hunt!' for the liberals to rally in all innocence to their defense."[44]

The cry of "witch-hunt" was so effective precisely because there had been so many anti–New Deal witch-hunts by anticommunists like Martin Dies and Elizabeth Dilling. Some of the same men named by Chambers—Alger Hiss and Lee Pressman—had been listed in Elizabeth

Dilling's *The Roosevelt Red Record and Its Background*, along with Felix Frankfurter, Robert La Follette, Harold Ickes, and almost anyone else in the administration who had annoyed the far right by working for social or economic reform. The administration could assume that Chambers's accusations were no more worthy of notice.

The Roosevelt administration had further reason to overlook reports of Soviet espionage. Anticommunists longed to prove that the Soviets had violated the agreements they had made to obtain diplomatic recognition from Washington, and one of the points of that agreement had been to cease using American Communists for agitation and espionage. An exposé of Soviet espionage would have given anticommunists more ammunition to use to force the administration to end diplomatic relations with the Soviets.[45]

But the most important reason Roosevelt refused to pay attention to warnings about Communist espionage was certainly that anything that diverted Americans' attention away from the Nazi threat would have made Roosevelt's task of building an anti-Nazi coalition more difficult, and once Hitler attacked Stalin, FDR could not afford to let anything block aid to Russia. A probe of Communist espionage could only strengthen opposition to that policy.

After Pearl Harbor, Roosevelt's war strategy required him to constantly reassure Stalin about America's good intentions, since Stalin was doing the brunt of the fighting, taking most of the casualties, while destroying most of Hitler's armies. Since the United States would not give Stalin an early second front, Roosevelt indicated his good faith to Stalin in other ways. Roosevelt kept J. Edgar Hoover from investigating Soviet espionage during the war, he released Earl Browder from jail (he had been convicted of passport fraud), and intervened to prevent the deportation of Browder's wife, an illegal alien. The administration also encouraged pro-Soviet propaganda such as Davies' *Mission to Moscow* and the movie based on it, both to build public support for the Soviet alliance and also to reassure Stalin that the alliance was secure.

Anticommunists could expect to be denounced by the administration as obstructionists during the war if they criticized Stalin, the American Communist Party, or its fronts. Martin Dies was attacked when he published his *Trojan Horse in America* (ghostwritten by J. B. Matthews) in 1942. Westbrook Pegler was branded a Nazi sympathizer when he let loose a blast at Russia in December 1942. When Elmer Davis of the Office of War Information mocked the Nazis for portraying themselves as crusaders against communism, he seemed to be suggesting that American anticommunists were part of the Nazi propaganda machine.[46]

Ignoring Chambers's revelations of Communist espionage rings, therefore, made good sense during the war. Indeed, any other policy might have been disastrous, but after the war, when the espionage rings of the thirties came to the surface, countersubversive anticommunists would charge that Roosevelt, for reasons that seemed less persuasive once Stalin had replaced Hitler as the nation's enemy, had neglected the country's security by shutting his eyes to credible reports of Soviet infiltration and espionage.

Anticommunists were among the most persistent critics of Roosevelt's grand strategy for winning the war, which did not make them popular with the administration or its supporters. Many anticommunists, particularly those who had been isolationists before the war, argued that a Europe First policy would benefit Stalin more than the United States. They demanded that America concentrate first on defeating Japan, and only after that turn its attention to Germany. Catholic anticommunists were particularly well represented among these "Asia Firsters." A Milwaukee diocesan paper insisted that "our first duty is to this country and its own fronts, to Guadalcanal before Stalingrad." Another Catholic paper complained that if supplies sent to England under Lend-Lease had been shipped to the Pacific they might have prevented American defeats. Still other Catholics suspected that the Europe First strategy amounted to a betrayal of the anticommunist Chiang Kai-shek, forcing him to fight both the Japanese and the Red Chinese without sufficient American aid or reinforcements.[47]

Because of their visceral anticommunism, and because of their concern for the Catholic populations of Eastern Europe, especially Poland and Lithuania, American Catholics were the most outspoken critics of the American-Soviet alliance. The bishops and the Catholic press would not fall in line with the administration's policy of praising Stalin for the duration, although the Catholic hierarchy did bend to pressure from the administration to silence Father Coughlin. In May 1942 Coughlin withdrew from politics, and confined himself to his duties as a parish priest. They insisted on calling attention to evidence of Stalin's duplicity in Eastern Europe, particularly in Poland. They insisted that the triumph of the Red Army in Eastern Europe would doom those largely Catholic countries to the misery of antireligious Communist regimes controlled by Moscow.

In February 1944 Catholic papers were outraged when *Izvestia*, citing the Vatican's 1929 Concordat with Mussolini, charged that the Vatican had supported Italian and German fascism. The Kremlin continued to attack the Pope for the rest of the war, and the *Brooklyn Tablet* held that Communist attacks on Catholicism "make ridiculous all the pious hopes of the star-gazers who think Russia has changed." Although the Vatican's record of appeasing fascist dictators gave American Catholics the same problem the Hitler-Stalin Pact gave Communists and fellow-travelers before June 1941, American Catholics argued that Stalin's attacks on the Pope only proved that the Communists recognized the Church as the chief obstacle to their plans to dominate postwar Europe.[48]

In the spring of 1944, a priest from Springfield, Massachusetts, spent four hours with Stalin discussing the situation in Poland. The priest said that Stalin promised he would do "all in his power to cooperate with the Church so that there will be no persecution" in Poland after the war. Catholics were furious that a priest had been foolish enough to believe Stalin and he was denounced as a traitor and a "fellow traveler." He was disavowed by the Church, suspended from his duties, and forced to apologize to his bishop. The *Nation*—ever ready to criticize the Church—said that American Catholics had delivered a "slap in the face of Joseph Stalin at the very moment when . . . he is showing himself particularly kindly disposed toward the Catholic and other religious faiths."[49]

Catholics were revolted when the administration treated the Soviet Union as one of the "democracies." Catholic papers insisted that Nazism and communism were essentially identical: "Nazism is brown fascism; communism is red fascism. Both destroy liberty, peace and religion." The *Michigan Catholic* blamed communism for the rise of German and Italian fascism, claiming that communism was the "fascism of the Left which sometimes brings on fascism of the Right."[50]

At a time when it was politic to overlook disturbing features of Stalin's regime, Catholics kept raising the issue of religious freedom in the Soviet Union. They were not impressed when Stalin allowed the Russian Orthodox church to resume its traditional role in society.

"What were his first words?" Bishop Fulton J. Sheen's asked about the Orthodox Church's primate's reaction. "Thanks to God? No, he asked for a second front."[51]

Catholic papers denounced the administration's efforts to create sympathy for Russia. James Gillis of the *Catholic World* said it was "a religious and patriotic duty" for Catholics "to remind their countrymen that the Soviet Union was only a limited military partner, not a genuine friend of the United States." They criticized the famous March 1943 issue of *Life* that glorified Russia, its people, and its leaders. Catholics were provoked by Joseph Davies' pro-Soviet *Mission to Moscow* and the movie based on it. The Catholic Legion of Decency condemned the movie (which made it off limits to faithful Catholics), labeling it "pictorial propaganda," and suggesting that its proper title should be "Submission to Moscow."[52]

The great issue of the war for Catholic anticommunists was the future of Poland. Catholics believed—correctly—that the Red Army was guilty of slaughtering the Polish officer corps in the Katyn forest, when many Americans were content to accept Stalin's assurances that the Nazis were responsible. Catholics denounced Stalin for allowing the Germans to put down the Warsaw uprising, letting the Germans slaughter the Polish patriots who had counted on Russian aid. Once again, Catholics refused to bow to the administration's policy of not annoying Stalin.[53]

Catholics made it clear that they would judge the success of the war by the fate of Catholic Poland and Lithuania. Buffalo's Bishop John Duffy declared that "the test is Poland." "If the Poles are forced to exist in misery and slavery then only a bitter, cruel world can be expected for all mankind." When the pro-administration Catholic *Commonweal* was rash enough to suggest that the most postwar Poland could hope for was membership in an Eastern European federation dominated by Russia, Gillis of *Catholic World* said that *Commonweal* had given him "a sinking at the pit of the stomach as if some tried and true companion in the effort to keep political thinking on a high plane had suddenly surrendered and gone over to the practitioners of moral mediocrity." Catholics knew that Catholic Poland's survival after the war depended on Roosevelt's forcing Stalin to abide by the Atlantic Charter's guarantee of national self-determination, and they doubted Roosevelt would do anything to thwart Stalin. Catholics denounced the Yalta conference as a sellout, a victory for Stalin, and a violation of the Atlantic Charter. Catholic papers had headlines like "President and Churchill throw 9,000,000 Catholic Poles to Reds." For not dropping the Polish issue, the Catholic press was called pro-fascist by the *New Republic* and the *Nation*.[54]

Catholics' fears about the fate of the Church in Eastern Europe were dismissed by the administration. Derided by the left as obstructionists who were soft on Hitler, Catholic anticommunists writhed in frustration when what they feared came to pass in Poland, unresisted by an administration that seemed willing to sacrifice millions of Catholics to a policy of appeasing Stalin.[55]

Labor anticommunists had to cope with a surge of Communist influence in the unions due to the Party's rehabilitation in left and liberal circles. But the wartime policies pursued by resurgent Communists in the unions so antagonized even sympathetic noncommunists that by the end of the war labor union anticommunism was more intense and powerful than ever.

The American Federation of Labor was anticommunist during the war, as it had been before. It was in the CIO (separated from the AFL since October 1937) that the Communists had made their greatest gains. By Pearl Harbor the Party dominated many CIO unions and had an influential, sometimes decisive voice in determining CIO policy.

That position was undermined and eventually destroyed by the Party's wartime labor policies, particularly in the CIO's largest union, the United Auto Workers. There the struggle between Communist and anticommunist unionists produced an anticommunist labor leader, Walter Reuther, who emerged after the war as the Communists' most determined foe in the CIO.[56]

Union Communists were determined to set an example of willingness to do anything to help the war effort. They demanded that American workers subscribe to a "no strike" pledge. Even more obnoxious to the rank and file, they urged workers to accept a performance-boosting piecework (incentive) pay system instead of hourly wage rates. The Communists—almost alone among unionists—endorsed FDR's request for legislation authorizing him to draft striking workers into the army.[57] So committed were Communists to increasing war production that theirs became company unions during the war. There were even reports that employers preferred their workers to join Communist unions since these unions were more cooperative than noncommunist shops that refused to surrender the rights they had won in the thirties.

The AFL, naturally, rejected piecework out of hand. The idea was so unpopular that the CIO's national leadership declared itself neutral, despite Communist pressure. In the CIO's United Auto Workers union, however, Walter Reuther, a Socialist and former fellow traveler, saw that piecework could be the issue that he could use to defeat his Communist rivals, since the rank and file hated piecework and considered it tantamount to slavery. He denounced the "crusade to put across incentive [piecework] pay" as something "cooked up jointly by the Communist Party and those employers who yearn for the 'good old days' of piecework and slave-driving." Earl Browder replied for the Party that anyone who was against piecework was simply "against the war, that's all." The Communists said that Reuther was trying to "spread the infections of disunity and defeatism." Reuther then charged that the Communists were backing piecework because "they think, mistakenly, that that is the best way to help Russia win the war and because they don't give a tinker's damn what happens to the American labor movement."[58]

At the UAW convention of October 1943, the Communists charged that Reuther and his anticommunist supporters were "trying to disguise their opposition to the anti-Axis struggle by an orgy of red-baiting in the well-known manner of Goebbels and Martin Dies." But the piecework fight convinced many leaders and rank and file members that "the ultimate commitment of domestic Communist leaders . . . was less to the defense of the American working class in its day-to-day struggles than to the political/military success of the Russian regime." Reuther won his campaign against piecework and was rewarded with the vice presidency of the union.[59]

John L. Lewis's anticommunism became even more pronounced during the war. He had taken his mine workers out of the CIO in October 1942, charging that it was Communist dominated. When Lewis's union went out on strike in 1943, Communists called him Hitler's "most effective ally." Lewis cast aside all restraints on his not-inconsiderable talent for invective, denouncing "bug-house Commie finks" who wanted to "hang on to the coattails of the Red Army and try to build an ideological bridge between our loyalty to Russia and their own pet scheme."[60]

The war—or more precisely the battle over intervention—gave Jay Lovestone further opportunities to enlarge his role as one of the most influential labor anticommunists. When the 1940 AFL convention voted to support help for Britain, David Dubinsky's ILGWU, which rejoined the AFL in June 1940, decided to hire a coordinator for labor's campaign for aid to England. Dubinsky chose Lovestone, who had been assisting anticommunist officials in the United Auto Workers union and the ILGWU. After Lovestone served Dubinsky with distinction in the campaign to help the Allies, Dubinsky made him the head of the ILGWU's International Relations Department, which soon became the command center of labor union anticommunism.

The AFL continued to stress its anticommunist convictions during the war. AFL President William Green and Teamster chief Dan Tobin prefaced any discussion of the alliance with Russia with the qualification that they were willing to work with Stalin not because "we hate Communism less, but because we hate Hitlerism more." Dubinsky warned against taking the Communists' newfound patriotism seriously. "They are a danger," he said in 1944. "They are a menace. They are not loyal. They are not faithful. They have their feet on our ground, on our soil, but their hearts belong elsewhere. Beware of them!" Matthew Woll, an AFL anticommunist from the Gompers days, declared that "the American Federation of Labor and its spokesmen have never made a secret of their opposition to Communism, its practices and policies."[61]

The AFL rejected out of hand an invitation from the British Trades Union Council to strengthen the British-American alliance with Russia by joining them in affiliating with the Soviet labor unions. Secretary-Treasurer George Meany explained that the AFL affiliated only with free labor unions, and "there were no [free] Russian trade unions." The AFL Carpenters Union's journal charged that "the so-called Trade Union movement of Russia is dominated, controlled, and directed by the Soviet Communist Government, and is, therefore, not a free Trade Union Movement [so] we cannot endorse or participate in any such procedure [of affiliation]. . . . The United Brotherhood of Carpenters and Joiners of America can in no way cooperate or collaborate with the Communist Trade Union Movement of Russia."[62] When the 1943 AFL convention decisively rejected proposals to explore cooperation with

Russian unions, the AFL's Socialist unionists were just as opposed as the conservatives.

Communists were strong enough in the CIO to carry that union into the World Federation of Labor with its Russian representatives. The Party applauded the CIO and charged the AFL with "defeatism" verging on treason for rejecting affiliation with the WFL. "They do not realize that in opposing labor unity," the Communists charged, that "they are following in the footsteps of the Munichers who are ready to sell our country to Hitler for fear of the Soviet Union. Such policies give grist to the mill of the defeatists and the Fifth Column, who play on outmoded fears and prejudices against the Soviet Union." In a speech before the New York Central Trades and Labor Council on April 5, 1945, George Meany responded to this Communist attack. "What common ground," he asked, "could we find in cooperation with those who pretend to speak for the workers but in reality represent the government? What could we talk about? The latest innovations being used by the secret police to ensnare those who think in opposition to the group in power? Or, perhaps, bigger and better concentration camps for political prisoners?"[63]

Union anticommunists echoed Catholics in warning about Soviet intentions in Eastern Europe. Matthew Woll said that Stalin had designs on the Balkans, and that America "might well lose the war after having achieved military victory in Europe." The AFL formed a committee that included Matthew Woll, David Dubinsky, and George Meany to define union policy toward postwar Europe. The staff was drawn largely from Dubinsky's anticommunist ILGWU staff. At a meeting of this committee in April 1945, Matthew Woll charged that "one of our allies on the continent is altering the face of Europe to suit itself, by its own means and to its own pleasure, without any relation to the principles accepted by all of the United Nations as the basis for the new world."[64]

The AFL set up a Free Trade Union Committee in 1944 to counter Soviet designs on Europe. Jay Lovestone was chosen by Dubinsky, Green, and Meany to serve as the committee's executive secretary. Lovestone's associate, Irving Brown, was made its European representative. The AFL supplied the FTUC with a million dollars to aid independent noncommunist unions in the liberated countries of Europe and in Latin America. The committee's mission was to combat "the growth of communism as a world force, . . . a new and alien element . . . [in] the international labor movement" and "to support a labor movement devoted to freedom and democracy."[65] The Lovestone-Brown combine would make the AFL the most effective American instrument after the war for promoting anticommunism in Europe and the rest of the world.

In the collective memory of each distinctive anticommunist community there was usually one particular trauma that seemed to them to epitomize all reasons for hating communism. The term ex-radicals used for the shock that turned them into anticommunists was "a Kronstadt experience," a reference to the revulsion so many radicals felt in March 1921 when Trotsky slaughtered the sailors at Petrograd's Kronstadt fortress who had mutinied against the Bolsheviks.

World War II provided American Socialists with a Kronstadt experience that made them even more ferociously anticommunist than before. This was Stalin's arrest of the leaders of the Jewish Bund of Poland, Henryk Erlich and Victor Alter, followed by their deaths at the hands of his secret police.

Erlich and Alter were very well known to American Jewish Socialists, many of whom had belonged to the Jewish Bund before coming to the United States. They knew that the two were unyielding antifascists who had urged Socialists to fight Hitler by joining the Comintern's Popular Front before the Hitler-Stalin pact, and had organized an underground resistance movement after Hitler's invasion of Poland. When Erlich and Alter fled to Eastern Poland to escape the Nazis, the Russians arrested them and kept them in prison until Germany invaded the Soviet Union on June 22, 1941. The Russians released the two Socialists so they could organize a Jewish Anti-Fascist Committee in Moscow to rally Polish Jews in Russia against the Nazi invaders. They were also named delegates to the Polish government in exile in London.

Before they could leave Russia in December 1941, however, they were again arrested. Alarm spread through the international Socialist and labor communities. Norman Thomas, Eleanor Roosevelt, Reinhold Niebuhr, and Albert Einstein all appealed for information about their location and safety. The Soviets offered no response. Finally, in March 1943, the Soviet ambassador to the United States notified the AFL's

William Green that the two had been executed in December 1942 for conspiring with the Nazis to surrender the Red Army to the Germans.

No Socialists believed the Russians. Socialists deduced that Stalin had begun to liquidate any alternatives on the left to Communist rule in postwar Poland. The democratic left took the murder of Alter and Erlich as proof of Stalin's barbarity and as demonstrating what communism had in store for them everywhere.

Sidney Hook recalled that the Erlich-Alter murders and the Katyn forest massacre were "two occasions on which we despairingly hoped that the American government and American public opinion would recognize the face of Stalinist terror behind the honeyed words of adulation" of fellow travelers. But once again the Roosevelt administration acted as though criticism of Stalin was a more serious offense than the substance of the criticism. It deflected all questions on the case, saying that to comment might "serve to harm the unity of the United Nations."[66] The fellow-traveling left offered the sickly defense that "all the chief United Nations have sins on their consciences like the Erlich-Alter case."

Socialists thereafter dedicated themselves to focusing Western attention on the murderous behavior of the Soviet regime, because they realized this scrutiny could be the difference between life and death for those in Stalin's grip. Socialists never forgot that under communism many lives—particularly of Socialist dissidents like themselves—were in mortal danger, and the world must not forget their plight.

Conservatives like the Catholics raised anticommunist objections to Roosevelt's military decisions. Senator Albert "Happy" Chandler was the leader of an Asia First bloc that believed the longer the American invasion of Europe was delayed the better. The longer the invasion was put off, the more losses Russia would suffer. They also feared that if the United States helped the Soviets defeat Germany before the war in the Pacific was over, the Soviet Union would be able to have its way with Europe while the United States would have to turn its attention to Japan. The United States should finish off Japan first, said Senator Burton Wheeler. Then "we would be in a much better position to deal with Russia when we came to the peace table, and to protect Poland."[67]

Asia First conservative anticommunists were outraged when the Soviet Union honored its April 1941 neutrality pact with Japan, and even more when Stalin negotiated a fishing treaty with the Japanese in April 1943. They suggested that Stalin might be passing American aid along to the Japanese. They worried that if the United States took too long in defeating Japan, the Russian-backed Chinese Communists would have a greater opportunity to communize China.[68]

Conservative anticommunists—like Catholic, labor union, and Socialist anticommunists—were convinced well before 1945 that Stalin's postwar goal was to dominate Eastern Europe. Poland was a central issue for conservative anticommunists, as it was for the Catholics, and Senator Styles Bridges of New Hampshire demanded that Roosevelt delay the invasion of Europe until the Polish question was settled. Hamilton Fish noted late in 1944 that the country "in whose behalf World War No. Two was started" was now "about to be turned over to the Communists in utter disregard of its terrible sacrifices in fighting the Nazis and the pledges given to the Polish people by the Allies."[69]

Anticommunists could see with a clarity denied their internationalist colleagues the nature of Stalin's plans for Eastern Europe. Anticommunists labeled the Yalta agreements a "direct violation of the spirit and the letter of the Atlantic Charter." In 1943 Hearst's *San Francisco Examiner* predicted that Stalin would "install in every country in Europe a Red Regime, which means more torture-chambers, concentration camps, massacres, atheism and continuous reign of terror." Hearst's *New York Daily Mirror* called Roosevelt's meeting with Stalin at Teheran a "Red Munich." George Sokolsky said that Yalta had ensured that the postwar era would be "the Era of Stalin." It would allow Stalin to unify "Europe under the rule of Moscow." Conservative anticommunists in Congress predicted that after the war, Americans were going to "suffer one of the worst disillusionments they have ever experienced."[70]

For these strikingly accurate predictions, the anticommunists were attacked as traitors by Communists and their supporters. Hearst was called "Hitler's helper." Westbrook Pegler was the "American Goebbels." Fellow traveler George Seldes called George Sokolsky an "agent" of "fascist" interests, Pegler a "mental hoodlum," and Hearst "America's No. 1 enemy." Joe and Cissy Patterson (owners of the *New York Daily News* and the *Washington Times-Herald*) were called "America's No. 1 and No. 2 exponents of the Nazi propaganda line." The *New*

Republic claimed that the *Daily News* could not have been more dangerous if it "were intentionally grinding out quotations for the Axis propaganda." The *New Republic* ominously called for the sedition laws to be used to silence the conservative press.[71]

The Roosevelt administration ignored, for reasons of state, the anticommunists' accurate analysis of Stalin's postwar intentions. But the anticommunists were not merely ignored. Roosevelt all but accused his anticommunist critics of treason, saying that the war "must not be impeded by a few bogus patriots who use the sacred freedom of the press to echo the sentiments of the propagandists in Tokyo and Berlin."[72] His anger toward his anticommunist critics finally led to a spasm of political repression as ill-conceived in its own way as the government persecution of the left in 1919 and 1920.

Even before Pearl Harbor, Roosevelt had been pressing the Justice Department to discredit the opponents of his preparedness policies by rounding up some of the more disreputable and putting them on trial. He seemed to have in mind a mass trial that would have congressional critics of his policies like Martin Dies, Burton Wheeler, and Hamilton Fish in the same dock as extremist Nazi sympathizers and anti-Semites.

Attorney General Francis Biddle finally gave in to the White House pressure and assigned Special Assistant William Power Maloney to unearth connections between the isolationists and German propaganda and intelligence networks. In 1942 Maloney leaked hints that he was going to indict isolationist Representatives Hamilton Fish and Clare Hoffman, though he failed to follow through. On July 21, 1942, Maloney finally announced that he had obtained indictments of twenty-eight extremist opponents of the war—countersubversive anticommunists, anti-Semites, extreme isolationists, native fascists—for conspiring to destroy morale in the armed forces.[73]

For the next two years the case languished, even though the fellow-traveling left kept urging the Justice Department to push the case to a trial that would give official endorsement to the radical left's claim that anticommunism constituted a fascist plot. The government realized that the jerrybuilt theory upon which the case rested—that American crackpots like Elizabeth Dilling were important cogs in an international Nazi conspiracy—might be difficult to sustain in court. What finally persuaded the government to go to trial in 1944 was a sensational exposé of the isolationist movement that topped the best-seller lists in 1944, given all the more urgency by the outrageous antics of one of America's most notorious anti-Semites, who had the effrontery to make a run for the presidency that same year.

The conspiracy theory the government used in the sedition trial of 1944 was almost identical to that set forth in *Undercover*, John Roy Carlson's report on the isolationist right, which appeared in magazines throughout 1943 and then sold briskly when it appeared as a book later that year. Carlson was a pseudonym for Avedis Derounian, who was supported by the Friends of Democracy and the Anti-Defamation League during his undercover investigation of anti-Semitic hate mongers in the isolationist movement.

Carlson skillfully exploited the undercover exposé formula that took press stories and spiced them up by interjecting the adventures of an intrepid undercover agent who had risked his life investigating violent conspirators. Passing himself off as a pro-fascist, anti-Semitic Italian, Carlson sidled up to far right isolationists of the pre-Pearl Harbor period. Along the way, he became friendly with eighteen of the defendants in the sedition trial: "it was a dirty job, but I felt that someone had to do it and live to tell about it."[74]

Carlson claimed that the book demonstrated the "tie-in" between far-right anti-Semitic pro-Nazis and a group of ten representatives (including Fish and Hoffmann) and fourteen senators (Wheeler, Nye, and Taft among them), and his technique was just like that of red web countersubversives like Richard Whitney, Elizabeth Dilling, and J. B. Matthews: interlocking letterheads and chains of associations (some of them requiring Carlson himself as an essential link) that tied together into an ominous conspiracy individuals who may have never met.[75]

Defendant Lawrence Dennis thought that Carlson's book encouraged the government to go to trial with the sedition case, and Burton Wheeler later demanded a Senate investigation of Carlson and his book. When the Senate refused in March 1945, America First veteran John T. Flynn went on the offensive, charging that Derounian had been the agent of a conspiracy against isolationists by the Friends of Democracy and the Anti-Defamation League, which he called "private gestapos." He claimed that they had invented a "new technique in character assassination" by linking men like himself, Wheeler, and Nye with Nazis and anti-Semites. He published these charges in a series of articles that ran in conservative newspapers, and then collected them in a pamphlet in 1947, *The Smear Terror*.[76]

Carlson's book was the top nonfiction bestseller of 1944. Its success was aided mightily by the activities of Gerald L. K. Smith, who continued his campaign against the international Jewish conspiracy during the war, and who warned that Roosevelt was plotting with Stalin to deliver the world to communism. In 1944 Smith, who had been effectively exiled from mainstream politics by the Brown Scare and by his own increasingly strident anti-Semitism, ran for president as candidate of the America First Party. His party platform denounced "the Jewish problem." The left wing press could now tie the defunct prewar America First Committee and all anticommunists to Smith's sordid little letterhead organization, even though by now Smith had been repudiated by most countersubversive anticommunists.[77]

By the time the case came to trial in Washington on April 17, 1944, there were thirty defendants. There were German propagandist George Sylvester Viereck and one of his associates; four leaders of the German-American Bund; American fascist intellectual Lawrence Dennis, and a collection of anti-Semitic extremist isolationists, including Gerald Winrod, William Pelley, Joseph McWilliams, George E. Deatherage, Robert E. Edmondson, James True, and Elizabeth Dilling. Two targets of the investigation, Father Coughlin and Gerald Smith, were not indicted for political reasons and lack of evidence, respectively.

By 1944 the passions of war had persuaded New Dealers that criticism of their policies amounted to treason, and that it was the work of a monstrous brown web conspiracy. The far left, of course, looked at the trial as an opportunity to permanently discredit its critics. It took real courage to point out that the trial was a farce based on a fantasy, and that the fantasy was being manipulated for political motives. New Dealer liberals and Communists and fellow travelers were conveniently hunting the same witches. When Representative Clare Hoffman protested that the defendants were "no more guilty of conspiracy than I am," the *Daily Worker* took it as a confession of Hoffman's own guilt, and demanded that he too go on trial. Civil libertarians were divided on the issue of the trial. ACLU chief counsel Morris Ernst argued that the defendants were guilty of treason in wartime, and deserved what they were getting, while most leaders of the ACLU denounced it as a legal travesty and a dangerous precedent.

The government proposed to prove that a dangerous international

Nazi conspiracy existed outside the imaginations of Hitler's propagandists in Germany and his adoring disciples in the German-American community. Prosecutor O. John Rogge read portions of *Mein Kampf* into the record and waved Nazi flags at the jury—inflammatory gestures in 1944. The prosecution was able to cite a few contacts between German propagandists and some of the defendants, and point to the membership of a few in the Bund, but the bulk of Rogge's case that the defendants were linked to Hitler mainly depended on similarities between Nazi propaganda and statements of the defendants.

The prosecution used a method for analyzing this propaganda developed by social psychologist Harold Lasswell for the Propaganda Analysis Section of the Federal Communications Commission. Fourteen themes of Nazi propaganda were listed, which were then looked for in the writings of the defendants, producing a numerical measure of the theoretical consistency between the two. But the Lasswell method was easily adjusted to ensure that the conclusions would be what the researchers were looking for. As defendant Dennis protested at the trial, the question was whether the test characteristics chosen were really the crucial, determinative characteristics of Nazi ideology, or whether they were selected because of the probability that they would turn up in the writings of the defendants. He argued that it would be easy to find fourteen characteristics of Islam that might be found in Christianity, and then conclude that the two religions were the same. It would also be possible to use another fourteen characteristics and determine that these two related religions had no connections whatever. Years later he made the further point that when the prosecutions at the Nuremberg trials listed the essential ideas of Nazism, they produced a completely different set of characteristics than the sedition trial prosecutors.[78]

In his book about the case, Lawrence Dennis claimed that the trial was an attempt to force the public to see all mankind as divided into two camps, fascists and antifascists, and to permit those in power to determine who would be included in each group. It was, he said, the same as the Communist practice of dividing "the world into Communist and anti-Communist. If you are anti-Communist then you are pro-fascist."[79]

The contrast between the prosecution's dire image of a Nazi plot to take over America and the preposterous personalities and behavior of the defendants also weakened the government's case. The defendants joked, postured, and misbehaved. Lawrence Dennis referred to prosecutor Rogge as "Vyshinsky Rogge," though he later claimed Vyshinsky was a lawyer of greater ability.[80] The prosecutors showed no more respect for due process. A mistrial was declared on December 7, 1944, when the trial judge died. The far left pressed for a retrial, but the changing political climate after the war made further proceedings pointless. The case was dropped for good in 1947.

The wartime Brown Scare made all criticism of Roosevelt's policies—especially his dealings with Stalin—seem sinisterly motivated by hatred of Jews and Nazi sympathies. As a sign of the times, Hamilton Fish (targeted by Jewish groups) was defeated in his 1944 reelection bid and Martin Dies (targeted by the CIO) decided not to seek reelection. But even while they were suffering this abuse, writes George Sirgiovanni in his history of wartime anticommunism, it was the anticommunists who

> understood—more clearly than did many of their countrymen—the self-serving and expedient nature of the alliance, as underscored by the Soviets' refusal to enter the war against Japan even as they demanded that America immediately open a second European front. Wartime congressional critics of the U.S.S.R. also correctly predicted that Stalin would dominate postwar Eastern Europe. . . . However limited one believes FDR's options to have been, the fact remains that he did not fulfill the promises of the Atlantic Charter, at least not in Eastern Europe. Those who suspected as much during the war were vindicated by history."[81]

In 1939 the American Communist Party had exposed itself as the puppet of a foreign power that had betrayed its allies for the second time in two decades. By the end of the war it could represent itself as the honest broker between the United States and its mighty Soviet ally.

Soaring on the winds of the American-Soviet alliance and the Brown Scare hysteria, the American Communist Party was prospering as never before. At the end of the war, the Party had 63,000 members, with another 10,000 in the armed forces. For the first time a significant number—ten percent—were black. The Party was publishing two million books and pamphlets a year. Its Sunday *Daily Worker* had a run of 65,000 copies, while on the West Coast the Party published the thriving *People's World*. The Communist Yiddish *Freiheit* had a run of 20,000. The Party's educational network included the Abraham Lincoln School in

Chicago, the San Francisco Labor School, the Walt Whitman School of Social Science in Newark, the Thomas Paine School in New Rochelle, the Samuel Adams School in Boston, and the Jefferson School of Social Science in New York. In the union movement, a quarter of the CIO unions were Communist dominated while many of the others were under Party influence. The CIO's general counsel and the editor of its newspaper were concealed Communists.

Earl Browder believed that the alliance had ushered in a new era for communism as an equal partner in building a postwar world. He called Stalin's meeting with Roosevelt at Teheran "the greatest, most important turning point in all history."[82] The Party envisioned itself moving into the mainstream of American politics. After Stalin dissolved the Comintern in 1943 as a gesture of good faith to the West, Browder said that Communists were "ready to cooperate in making this capitalism work effectively." In 1944 Browder renamed the Communist Party the Communist Political Association, and its headquarters was draped with banners of Roosevelt, Churchill, and Stalin.

There was good reason for Browder's rosy view of the Party's political future. In 1943 Communists took over New York's American Labor Party which had been dominated by David Dubinsky (whereupon Dubinsky abandoned it to found the Liberal Party). That gave the Party a puppet "left wing adjunct" to the Democratic party. In 1944 the Amalgamated's Sidney Hillman had let Communists into the CIO's Political Action Committee (CIO-PAC), which was one of the Democratic party's most important allies in the 1944 elections. The Communists had also established strong presences in the politics of California, Washington, and Minnesota. An historian of the Party wrote that "at the end of World War II popular hostility toward communism was . . . lower than it had been at any time since the Bolshevik Revolution."[83]

The Party could rely on liberals in the administration to join the progressive left in denouncing anticommunists for threatening the grand alliance that seemed, to most Americans, the only hope of a peaceful postwar world. When William L. White, son of the Kansas editor, published his critical *Report on the Russians* early in 1945, the fellow-traveling New York newspaper *PM* ran a roundup of reviews, commenting: "Several critics consider that the book should never have been published, since it is likely to hurt the feelings of our ally and thereby jeopardize the chances of future world peace. And almost all are agreed in deploring the tone in which the book is written." Peace was worth,

Communists and fellow travelers seemed to be saying, if not quite Paris, then at least a few Eastern European capitals.[84]

The war ended with a Communist Party on the ascendant, and a fellow-traveling left that had perfected the use of the brown smear against an embittered anticommunist community, eager to exact revenge on their enemies when they had the opportunity. Countersubversives who had been battered for their isolationism promised that the day would come when they could strike back at their tormentors. Burton Wheeler wrote to John T. Flynn in 1943 that the more he was attacked now, "the more it is going to react against them when this war is over."[85] These battle-scarred countersubversives longed for a chance to revenge themselves on their wartime tormentors.

But most anticommunists simply pointed out that Stalin was doing now just what they had been predicting throughout the war: turning Europe—now occupied by the Red Army and administered by local Communists—into his front yard. Whatever their motives, anticommunists were ready to offer their leadership to a nation that would soon need their insight and experience. They would not have long to wait.

Chapter 8

COLD WAR ANTICOMMUNISM

The experience with Communism has had one singularly healthy effect: it has made us reclaim democratic ideas which a decade ago we tended to regret and even to abandon. The defense of these ideas against both right and left will be a continuous and exacting commitment. But there lies in that commitment the possibility of recharging the faith in democracy with some of its old passion and principle.

—Arthur M. Schlesinger, Jr., *The Vital Center*, 1949.

Discredited, disgraced, and battered during the war, anticommunism erupted after 1945 and in less than five years moved from the margins to the center of American politics, as Joseph Stalin, refusing to be bound by the accommodating provisions of Yalta, extended his power across half of Europe.

American anticommunists during these early years of the cold war were able to support each other's objectives to an unprecedented degree despite their political differences. Liberal anticommunists located the moral foundation of American containment policies in the universal struggle between freedom and totalitarianism, demonstrating that if America were to remain true to its values it was obliged to resist communism. It was a belief given definitive expression in Paul Nitze's National Security Council Document 68, offered to President Truman as an authoritative statement of "our objectives in peace and war."

By placing containment on a firm foundation of morality, anticommunism during these days passed along a legacy that would sustain American resistance until that day when communism collapsed and the Soviet empire crumbled.

But there was a dark side to anticommunism's resurgence. Counter-

191

subversives were able to prove that American Communists had engaged in espionage for the Soviet Union during the depression and war and were able to obtain legal judgments that the Party was an illicit conspiracy. This encouraged wild-eyed red web conspiracy theorists once again to cast their nets in the direction of the left, blasting careers and reputations more recklessly than ever before.

By the end of the decade, liberals had laid the foundation for a worldwide military, political, and cultural bulwark against communism, but the stability of the anticommunist consensus of these years was precarious. Countersubversives were recklessly tearing away at those achievements, until the movement was vulnerable to be captured by the first demagogue able to cloak paranoid red web conspiracy theories in the mantle of major party respectability.

During the five critical years between the end of World War II and the Korean War,[1] anticommunists of all persuasions jostled for power: countersubversives, religious and ethnic anticommunists, liberals, and socialists. The anticommunist orthodoxy that emerged as the cold war consensus combined the objectives of the liberal internationalists who dominated the foreign policy establishment with the ideas and values of liberal and left anticommunists. Excluded from this consensus, however, were those unmollified isolationist anticommunists still furious over being brown-smeared during the war by liberals allied with the progressive left. During the late forties, these vengeful countersubversives were able to expand their base within the Republican party until, with the outbreak of the Korean war, they could push themselves to the center of American politics, to take revenge against the same liberal anticommunists who were the architects of the free world's defenses against communism.

American Catholics had seen Catholic Poland divided between Hitler and Stalin at the beginning of the war, then completely overrun by the Nazis, and finally captured in its entirety by the Red Army on its march towards Berlin. When the Soviets installed a Communist regime in Rumania, the omens for a free Poland were not good, and a Catholic paper warned, "As Poland goes, so goes the world."[2] The war ended with two groups of Polish leaders—one anticommunist, the other pro-

Soviet—vying for control. Roosevelt's Yalta agreements with Stalin favored the Communist government in Lublin over the anticommunists in exile in London. And it was clear by Roosevelt's death on April 12, 1945, that Stalin was not going to let Poland have the free elections promised at Yalta. When the Truman administration recognized the Communist government in Warsaw, the Polish American Congress called it a "tragic historical blunder," "appeasement," "paving the way for world chaos."[3] For American Catholics, Communist control of Poland was unthinkable. For the American government to tolerate it was an outrage against American Catholics and against the entire Church.

Poland woke up the liberal internationalists as well, who had been rather willing—for the sake of the wartime alliance and postwar peace—to let Stalin do as he pleased to his own people and to carve out a sphere of influence between Russia and Germany as long as he did not invade or subvert his neighbors. But they had not realized that "sphere of influence" for Stalin meant total control over some of the proudest and most historic nations of Europe, reducing them to colonies run by quisling dictatorships.

In September 1945 the Council of Foreign Ministers, created to adjudicate great power disputes in liberated Europe, broke up over the question of Soviet intentions in Bulgaria and Rumania.[4] To awaken the country to the gravity of the crisis, Truman invited Winston Churchill to speak at Westminster College in Fulton, Missouri on March 5, 1946. America's great wartime ally, who had rallied the democracies in the darkest hours of the war, told Americans that "from Stettin in the Baltic, to Trieste in the Adriatic, an iron curtain has descended across the continent allowing 'police governments' to rule Eastern Europe." Bulgaria, Rumania, and Albania were soon behind that "Iron Curtain."

A recent shift in the Kremlin's Party line for foreign Communists had just caught the attention of those who devoted themselves to deciphering such mysteries. In April 1945, Jacques Duclos, a French Communist official close to Stalin, denounced American Communist Party Chairman Earl Browder for collaborating with the United States's bourgeois leaders. Browder was duly replaced by the venerable Stalinist William Z. Foster in July. The Party discarded its *nom de guerre* of the "Communist Political Association," and once again became the Communist Party of the United States of America. It now resumed "third period" hard-line revolutionary propaganda and agitation. In February

1946 Stalin made a speech calling conflict between capitalism and communism inevitable. The international Communist movement was evidently putting on its ideological combat gear.[5]

J. Edgar Hoover believed all this meant that the world had entered a prewar crisis like that before the Nazi invasion of Poland, or the attack on Pearl Harbor. He was not going to ignore anything that might afterwards be interpreted as advance warning of an attack. Early in 1946 he began to bombard the White House with indications that the Soviets were planning war. In February 1946 he told Truman he had heard from American Communist sources that Communist uprisings were scheduled in France within six weeks, the start of an advance that would place "Soviet troops on the Atlantic Coast and on the Mediterranean."[6]

The same sense of impending doom filled the American Catholic community. Catholics were furious over Stalin's persecution of the Eastern European Church. In September 1946 Archbishop Stepinac, the prelate of the Yugoslav Church, was sentenced to sixteen years in prison for collaborating with the Germans, prompting Catholic protests across America. Forty thousand Catholics in Philadelphia massed to demand Stepinac's release. The crisis over the Church in Eastern Europe saw New York's Francis Cardinal Spellman emerge as the American Catholic spokesman against Communist persecution, while Monsignor Fulton J. Sheen's nationally broadcast sermons warned Catholics against "the fellow travelers in the United States and those whose hearts bleed for Red fascism."[7]

The Knights of Columbus and the Catholic War Veterans mobilized lay Catholic anticommunism. In 1946 the Knights, 600,000 strong, urged Americans to reject fellow travelers at the polls and to fight "the infiltration of atheistic Communism into our American life and economy." The Knights boycotted entertainment featuring Communists or fellow travelers. In 1947 they produced a six-part anticommunist radio series, *Safeguards for America*, aired on 226 stations. Catholic war veterans stopped the loading of Russian freighters bound for Soviet bloc regimes, and they picketed meetings of pro-Soviet groups. In New York they demanded the city purge Communists from the municipal work force and that it bar Communist front groups from public facilities.[8]

Just as the Bolshevik Revolution of 1917 had produced a backlash against its American supporters, the European crisis produced another wave of popular resentment against Stalin's American allies, which reached a fever pitch when evidence began to surface of Communist subversion during the years when Russia was supposed to be America's ally. Countersubversives had been claiming for years that the New Deal was infested with Communist spies and subversives, but these exaggerated and inaccurate charges had been repeatedly discredited. Now countersubversives produced facts to support their suspicions.

The first of the postwar spy scandals was the *Amerasia* case. On June 6, 1945, John Stewart Service, a State Department China expert, was arrested for passing hundreds of classified State Department documents to an American left-wing scholarly journal, *Amerasia*. This "espionage" could have been considered the sort of "document leak" that sustained the mainstream media, except that Philip Jaffe, the editor of *Amerasia*, was generally considered to be a Communist. The Justice Department charged Service, Jaffe, and four others with espionage, but when the case was found to have been tainted by illegal FBI and OSS searches of the magazine's offices, the government had to settle for fining Jaffe, and had to drop the charges against the others. At the very least, however, the *Amerasia* case demonstrated an all-too-cozy relationship between leftist officials in the administration and a fellow-traveling left that was now mobilizing against the administration's policy of containing Stalin.[9]

As the Soviet-American alliance crumbled, J. Edgar Hoover once again began sending the White House reports about undercover Communists in government. Hoover's suspicions centered on Assistant Secretary of the Treasury Harry Dexter White, Treasury Secretary Henry Morgenthau's right-hand man since 1934. Three different sources had named White as a Soviet agent: Whittaker Chambers, interviewed in depth by the Bureau on May 10, 1945; Igor Gouzenko, a Russian code clerk at the Soviet Embassy in Canada who defected in September 1945 and was questioned by the Canadian RCMP in October 1945; and Hoover's prize informant on Soviet espionage, the "blond spy queen" Elizabeth Bentley, who from 1938 to 1945 had been the courier between the spy network and her lover, Jacob Golos, Soviet espionage's chief operative in the United States.[10] But the administration's interest in discovering the truth about Communist infiltration had been dulled by years of false charges about the "Roosevelt Red Record" from the countersubversive right. The administration not only failed to heed Hoover's warnings, but promoted White, a blunder Truman later defended as a stratagem to keep White from suspecting he was under suspicion.[11]

Hoover's warnings about spies were circulated initially only within the highest levels of the executive branch. Soon they began to reach the public by way of a Baltimore priest with long experience in the fight against communism in the labor movement.[12] This was Father John F. Cronin.

Cronin had authored a four-part series, "Communism in Baltimore," in the *Catholic Review* in April 1944 that brought him to the attention of the Catholic bishops. In December he was directed to prepare a report on the Communist problem. Cronin already had amassed a wealth of information on Communist influence in the union movement. His friends in the FBI gave him Bureau reports, among them Hoover's memo to Truman based on Elizabeth Bentley's testimony about spy rings in the government.[13]

Cronin's report was distributed to the bishops on December 4, 1945. His approach was deliberately noninflammatory. Was communism a menace to America? If that meant "the danger of America's going Communist or the possibility that large numbers will be won over to intellectual acceptance of Communism or organizational adherence to the party," Cronin's answer was "an equivocal 'No.'"

The Communist problem, he argued, should be understood as the ability of the Party and the fellow-traveling left to soften American resistance toward Soviet expansion. "The question is not so much that of direct Communist control, but rather a question of pressure, confusion, deception, and general misleading of the public and public opinion. The agencies involved would be front groups, minority groups, and labor organizations." The issue was whether America's will to resist Communist expansion could be maintained in the face of pro-Soviet agitation aimed at persuading the public to "an acceptance of Soviet policies," and the evidence was discouraging. America's failure to defend Poland against Stalin, he argued, revealed the power of the front movement. If Roosevelt or Truman had publicly protested Stalin's actions, he said, "the whole pack of front groups would commence braying about American imperialism. Only a strong government, backed by united public opinion, would ignore such protests. It is probable that the Communist groups would create sufficient confusion to lead to a do-nothing policy."[14]

Cronin told the bishops that Soviet strategy was aimed at absorbing the Baltic republics, while setting up puppet governments in Poland,

Rumania, Bulgaria, Albania, and Yugoslavia. Meanwhile, the Soviets were infiltrating Czechoslovakia, Hungary, Austria, Finland, and East Germany, and gaining influence in Italy, France, possibly Belgium and the Netherlands, while trying to overthrow the governments of Spain and Portugal. They were gaining influence in Africa, the Dardanelles, and Iran, Outer Mongolia, and Manchuria. "The danger, accordingly, is primarily in the spread of world Communism, and this by the power of arms rather than by conviction. . . . Only a strong Anglo-American foreign policy can save China, India, and possibly Italy and France."[15]

Cronin recommended that the bishops educate the public about the danger and that they make a Catholic alternative to communism the centerpiece of their anticommunist programs. He warned against red-hunting and any alliances with countersubversives and their red web theories. He specifically criticized Walter Steele of the *New Republic,* saying that "a careless reader of his publications could easily confuse Communists and liberals, and communism and social reform. They are not recommended for use by any one but specialists in this subject. The *New Leader* is much more accurate."[16]

It was not long before Cronin's report reached the public. The United States Chamber of Commerce was looking for a way to take advantage of the alarm over the spread of European communism to warn the public about Communist influence in the labor union movement. Francis P. Matthews, the former head of the Knights of Columbus and chair of the Chamber's Committee on Socialism and Communism, hired Cronin to prepare a similar document for the Chamber, a forty-page pamphlet titled "Communist Infiltration in the United States" that was released on October 7, 1946. Four hundred thousand copies went out in time for the November elections, which the Republicans were billing as offering a choice between "Communism and Republicanism."[17]

Those elections gave Republicans control of the House and Senate for the first time in more than a decade, and President Truman suddenly realized that his political enemies had captured the most explosive political issue of the day. He announced his own plan for ridding the executive branch of Communists, Executive Order 9835, the "Truman Loyalty Program," on March 22, 1947, but it was too little, too late. The issue of Communist infiltration of the executive branch had given the Republicans a powerful weapon against the administration, and they were not going to let Truman off the hook.[18]

At the same time, American policy toward communism overseas had reached a critical divide. Great Britain had been helping the Greek and Turkish governments against Communist pressure. At the beginning of 1947, London notified Washington that it could continue that aid no longer. If communism was going to be stopped in Europe, the United States would have to do it. President Truman did not hesitate. His "Truman Doctrine" message to Congress of March 12, 1947, announced that America had become the free world's defender against communism.[19]

The Truman Doctrine added anticommunism to the liberal internationalism that had been since the Wilson years the basic principle of American foreign policy. Truman justified his aid to Greece and Turkey by arguing that the two countries were facing insurgencies or threats supported by a foreign power, which constituted aggression, and liberal internationalism required that aggression, whether Communist or not, had to be stopped by the world community.

What Truman had now added to liberal internationalism was the argument that the ideology of the foreign power that was disturbing the world order made it absolutely imperative for the United States to intervene. "Nearly every nation," he told Congress, "must choose between alternative ways of life." One was "based upon the will of the majority, and is distinguished by free institutions, representative government, free elections, guarantees of individual liberty, freedom of speech and religion, and freedom from political oppression. The second way of life is based upon the will of a minority forcibly imposed upon the majority. It relies upon terror and oppression, a controlled press and radio, fixed elections, and the suppression of personal freedoms."

The Truman Doctrine's synthesis of liberal internationalism and anticommunism was significantly influenced by the ideas of the State Department's leading expert on the Soviet Union, George Kennan, who would play a long and complex role in the evolution of American anticommunism. Kennan had been stationed in Moscow between 1944 and 1946, and had opposed Washington's uncritical embrace of Stalin and its naivete about the Soviets' aggressive designs. In his "Long Telegram" of February 22, 1946 and his landmark "Mr. X." article in the journal of the Council on Foreign Relations, *Foreign Affairs* (presented first as an address to the Council on January 7, 1947, and on January 24 to the War College), Kennan described Soviet communism as a tool for traditional Russian imperialism. It made possible the state's total control over society and gave it the ability to subvert the targets of its aggression. Stalin's immediate goal, he believed, was to restore the tsarist dimensions of the Russian empire.[20]

Communism gave Stalin a fifth column in every nation of the world, but in the long run that ideology would be a liability for the Soviet Union, since it produced economic failures that would destabilize the overextended Soviet empire. If America could contain Soviet expansion, the system would rot and self-destruct—Kennan thought in ten or fifteen years.

This "containment" policy, with which Kennan's name would forever be associated (despite his later efforts to repudiate it), was less anticommunist than it appeared. Kennan had no use for communism, but he regarded it less as an evil to be feared than a long-term weakness to be exploited, if it was denied easy and quick triumph. In the short run, however, Soviet aggression was a danger to world order because it would (to use Kennan's metaphor) flow like water to fill every cranny available to it.[21]

Notably lacking in Kennan's analysis of the Soviet Union was any of the anticommunists' sympathy for those suffering under Communist regimes. Kennan's containment was actually old-fashioned balance of power politics in the guise of liberal anticommunism, so it should have been no shock years later when Kennan began to denounce anticommunism and foreign policy based on it.

But Truman ignored these subtleties, and his synthesis of liberal internationalism and anticommunism patched together two divergent outlooks that had been at odds since 1917. Internationalism was guided by its impulse toward order, and was always willing to sacrifice moral concerns if that was necessary to maintain stability in world affairs, while anticommunism insisted on the primacy of morality over order, and so was willing at least to contemplate policies that might destabilize the precarious balance of power between the nations of the world.

Truman's synthesis of liberal internationalism and anticommunism was inherently unstable, made all the more fragile because anticommunism during the early cold war was itself an uneasy alliance between two mutually repellent forms of anticommunism, liberal anticommunism and countersubversive anticommunism.

Liberal anticommunism was the dominant form of cold war anticommunism. It defined itself during the Truman administration's battle against the fellow-traveling left in the early years of the cold war.

As soon as Truman announced his containment policy, American Communists and fellow travelers began to brown-smear all who opposed the Soviet Union's foreign policy, calling any criticism of Stalin "pro-fascist." John Spivak's *Pattern for American Fascism*, for example, made "fighting fascism" the litmus test for political virtue. For the Party-oriented left, "fascism" simply meant any deviation from the Party line, which naturally included the doctrine of liberal internationalism.[22] Communists and fellow travelers also began to look for an alternative to the Democratic party, and so they threw their support to an anti-cold war third party movement gathering behind Commerce Secretary Henry Wallace, fired by Truman in September 1946 for criticizing containment.

The coalition supporting Wallace was anchored by the Progressive Citizens of America (PCA), created in December 1946 through a merger of the National Citizens Political Action Committee (NC-PAC), a subsidiary of the CIO-PAC founded in 1944, and the Independent Citizens Committee of the Arts, Sciences and Professions (ICCASP). The PCA was supported by liberals and radicals who still insisted that the Communists were an essential part of any left worthy of the name, and who regarded it as red-baiting to object to Communists' goals or methods.[23]

Liberals who did object to Communists and their support for Soviet foreign policy threw their support to the Union for Democratic Action (UDA), founded in 1945 by liberals and internationalist Socialists opposed to Norman Thomas's isolationism. Chaired by Reinhold Niebuhr and supported by Eleanor Roosevelt, the UDA was run by New Dealer James Loeb. It specifically excluded Communists from membership.

When the progressive left, dominated by its Communists, tried to obstruct Truman's earliest moves to block Soviet expansion, the UDA's James Loeb wrote a long letter in May 1946 to the *New Republic* calling on liberals to demonstrate to the public the difference between liberalism and communism. During the congressional campaign of 1946, the UDA's Conference of Democratic Progressives denounced Communist infiltration of liberal organizations, and blamed the radical left for the Republican victories of 1946. The UDA warned that unless liberals disassociated themselves from Communists and fellow travelers, the achievements of the New Deal and Fair Deal would be at risk. The group also issued a "statement of principles" by Reinhold Niebuhr that called liberalism "a fighting faith," the democratic alternative to "fascist reaction and Communist totalitarianism."[24]

To counter the pro-Soviet agitation of the Progressive Citizens of America, the UDA organized the Americans for Democratic Action in January 1947 under the leadership of Eleanor Roosevelt, Hubert Humphrey, Walter Reuther, and David Dubinsky. The ADA was outspokenly anticommunist. It rejected "any association with Communists or sympathizers with Communism as completely as we reject any association with Fascists or their sympathizers. Both are hostile to the principles of freedom and democracy on which this Republic has grown great."[25] The founding of the ADA was, Arthur M. Schlesinger, Jr. later wrote, "the watershed at which American liberalism began to base itself once again on a solid conception of man and of history."[26]

Wallace announced his candidacy for president in December 1947, charging that Truman's Loyalty Program and containment policies were bringing fascism to America. The ADA became the administration's primary defender against attacks from the left, and went on the offensive to drive Communists from positions of influence in liberal and labor organizations. The ADA was, according to one of its leaders, "a leading factor in the rout of the U.S. Communist movement in the 1948 campaign. . . . Probably ADA did more than any other single agency to expose the frauds and the fallacies, the double think and double standards through which the Communists tried to entrap American liberals in the late 1940s as they had in the mid-1930s."[27]

The CIO also desperately wanted Truman to be reelected, hoping for protection against the anti-labor Republican Congress that had passed the Taft-Hartley Law on June 23, 1947, over President Truman's veto. Though all labor leaders, Communist and noncommunist alike, opposed Taft-Hartley, the law was especially hard on Communist unions, since it deprived unions whose leaders failed to sign an oath that they were not Communists of protection under the National Labor Relations Act. Not even the strongest unions could risk giving up their NLRA rights. When the administration made it clear that Communists who filed false anticommunist declarations would be prosecuted for perjury, CIO President Philip Murphy understood that the union movement's once-useful alliance with Communists was no longer viable. He began a purge of Communists from the CIO that would eliminate all of them from the union by 1950. In the key United Auto Workers Union, anticommunist Walter Reuther, who had captured the presidency in 1946, dislodged the remaining Communists from the executive board in November 1947.

In 1948 the CIO joined the ADA in working against Wallace and his third party movement. It expelled Wallace supporters from union leadership positions, so most Communist union leaders found themselves removed from power.[28] Lee Pressman, the CIO's Communist chief counsel, resigned in February to work for Wallace. The Communist head of New York's Transport Workers Union, Mike Quill, quit the Party himself and eliminated Communists from his union's leadership.

In Europe, Stalin was raising the stakes. Late in December 1947, Rumania's Communist leaders forced King Michael to abdicate. On February 25, 1948, a purge transformed Czechoslovakia into a Soviet satellite. (Wallace defended the Czech coup as defensive, necessary to forestall an *American* takeover.)[29] On April 1, the Soviets blocked Western land access to Berlin, so that the Americans and British had to airlift all supplies to West Berlin until September 30, 1949. Stalin continued to tighten his control over the international Communist movement, purging "Titoists" (that is, Communists who gave any indications of imitating Yugoslavia's Josip Tito in asserting their independence from Moscow) from national Communist parties, and reviving the Comintern, calling it the "Cominform."

In July 1948 Wallace's supporters met for their national convention, and the Communists were clearly in control. This was demonstrated by the fate of a "Vermont resolution" holding that criticism of American diplomacy did not mean the new party endorsed any other country's foreign policies. For the Communists in the Wallace movement, anything less than unequivocal support for Stalin was "red-baiting," and the Vermont resolution went down to overwhelming defeat.

The ADA and the CIO succeeded in turning the Wallace campaign into a referendum on the role of Communists and fellow travelers in American politics. Wallace received less than three percent of the vote. All that the Party had achieved since the 1930s—its network of social, cultural, and political associations, its influence in the labor movement and liberal left—it gambled and lost on Wallace. The Wallace campaign "broke the back of communism in America. . . . What followed was a long dying."[30]

After the election, the CIO punished its Communist-dominated unions for their support of Wallace, demolishing the Farm Equipment Workers Union, lifting the charter of the Communist-led New York CIO council, and forcing the United Electrical Workers, the largest Communist union, to secede. A year later the CIO expelled its last seven Communist unions.

Meanwhile the Communists were putting themselves through another of their periodic self-immolations. The Party expelled former leader Earl Browder and his supporters for the heresy of Titoism. It devastated itself further in a hunt for "white chauvinism," during which black comrades and their white allies grilled, punished, and even expelled their comrades for using tabooed racial terms.[31]

Between 1947 and 1949 the Truman administration was rebuilding American military strength and erecting a powerful web of alliances against Communist expansion in Europe: among these measures were the Marshall Plan to rebuild European economies and the National Security Act that established the Air Force and the CIA and combined the military branches in a new Defense Department (both in the summer of 1947); the NATO alliance was founded in April 1949.[32]

Meanwhile, liberal anticommunists laid out the principles that would guide American foreign policy in its struggle with the Soviet Union. The 1948 clash between liberal anticommunists and the progressives that demolished the fellow-traveling left also produced the classic manifesto of liberal anticommunism, Harvard historian Arthur M. Schlesinger's Jr.'s The Vital Center.

In The Vital Center Schlesinger carved out a position for anticommunist liberals between the fellow-traveling progressive left and the countersubversive anticommunist right. Schlesinger was a liberal writing for liberals defending a liberal administration, and he simply redefined anticommunism—realistic, effective anticommunism—as liberalism, liberalism rising to the challenge of protecting democracy from the threat of totalitarianism.

The cold war, Schlesinger argued, was the struggle between free society and totalitarianism around the world "for the souls and hearts of men." By reframing the conflict in this way, Schlesinger attacked the Communists' best argument, that they had always been the antifascists par excellence, and that they were being victimized for having been "premature antifascists." Schlesinger denied that fascism and communism were opposites at all. Rather, they were two extremes, equally distant from freedom, that should be visualized as the totalitarian south pole of a circle, while the north pole of that political circle represented the common ground where moderate liberalism and conservativism met at their point of agreement, the "vital center": respect for individual freedom and dignity, and a commitment to peaceful, democratic means for resolving political differences.

Schlesinger saw totalitarianism—whether communism or fascism—as a false refuge from anxieties over modernization's corrosion of traditional values. The realistic answer to communism, then, was not to repress it, but to attack the causes of totalitarianism, the vulnerability of the individual in modern society to giant forces outside his control. Liberal anticommunism, therefore, worked to remedy the conditions that produced communism through a program of social reform, while countersubversives made the situation worse by trying to restore laissez-faire capitalism with all its iniquities and by red-baiting reformers, liberals as well as communists, who were trying to deal with the psychological and material problems of modern society. Only liberals had a program of reform that could preserve individual freedom against the twin temptations of fascism and communism by alleviating the insecurities that tempted men to abandon freedom.

The cold war was rooted in the discontents of modernity, but it was no mere theoretical debate between philosophical systems. The Soviet Union was a clear and present danger to America and the West, Schlesinger wrote, because "nothing less than the entire world can in the end satisfy totalitarian imperialism." But a totalitarian state that relied on terror could not long sustain the high pitch of energy aggression required. Soviet policy, he explained, could be "roughly described as a policy of kicking at doors. If the doors fly open, the USSR moves in." If the doors were locked, the aggressor would move on looking for other doors. The United States had to work to stabilize the world order, which would open up fissures in the Communist world; "if the democratic world continues stable and prosperous, the disintegration of Soviet power will accelerate."[33]

Communism was dangerous, but Schlesinger insisted that it was primarily a threat *to*, not *in*, the United States. "The Soviet campaign against the United States . . . has two aspects: the pressures exerted in the traditional manner of power politics; and the pressures exerted through the network of Communist parties. . . . Given the nature of the Soviet drive against free society, given the frightful tyranny implicit in the principle cuius regio, eius religio, there is surely no alternative to paying exact and unfaltering attention to the Communists in our midst." And because Communist parties "are faithful in their essential mission, which is to run interference for Soviet foreign policy," the American Communist Party could not be treated like an ordinary political opposition during the present crisis. He thought that Elizabeth Bentley and other informers had "undoubtedly exaggerated" their exposés of Communist espionage networks, but he conceded that there could be "no serious question that an underground Communist apparatus attempted during the late thirties and during the war to penetrate the United States Government, to influence the formation of policy and even to collect intelligence for the Soviet Union." Almost as dangerous as the Party itself were its fellow-traveling allies. He called them "doughface progressives," a reference to the "northern men with southern principles" who had obstructed the Union's war effort during the Civil War. The fellow-traveling leftists, he charged, were "democratic men with totalitarian principles."[34]

But despite the success of Communist efforts at espionage and subversion, Schlesinger insisted there was no danger from domestic Communists that could not be handled by the constitutional methods of "debate, identification and exposure." To abridge civil liberties in an effort to fight communism was to betray the cause of freedom. Since the cold war was a battle between totalitarianism and freedom, the totalitarian tactics of countersubversives were unacceptable: "The performance of the House Committee on Un-American Activities . . . has shown clearly the dangers to civil freedom of a promiscuous and unprincipled attack on radicalism. The fact that late in 1948, after sowing confusion and slander for more than a decade, the Committee finally found some valuable information . . . should blind no one to the reckless accusations and appalling procedures which have characterized its career."[35]

Free society could survive, Schlesinger warned, only if democracy became a "fighting faith" people were willing to die for, and that would happen only with a program to "restore community to the social order."

Liberals must work to create an "individualism which does not wall man off from community" because "people deprived of any meaningful role in society, lacking even their own groups to give them a sense of belonging, become cannon fodder for totalitarianism."[36] The answer to communism was the reform program of the Democratic party in the New and Fair Deals to enlist all citizens in a creative effort to solve the problems of life in modern society. Schlesinger thought he saw signs that America was indeed rededicating itself to those democratic ideals in response to the Soviet challenge. The "experience with Communism," he wrote, "has had one singularly healthy effect: it has made us reclaim democratic ideals which a decade ago we tended to regret and even to abandon. . . . There lies in that commitment the possibility of recharging the faith in democracy with some of its old passion and principle."[37]

Schlesinger's belief that there was a universal human longing for freedom gave him hope that if America were faithful to its democratic traditions while patiently resisting Soviet aggression and subversion, communism would eventually collapse from within, destroyed by its attempt to resist the irresistible, man's desire for freedom. And yet he also warned against complacency, since the anxieties that were the modern condition could move individuals and nations to abandon freedom for the spurious security of totalitarianism. Schlesinger's pragmatic optimism mirrored that of the great revivalists he had studied in the age of Jackson, who believed that the triumph of good was preordained, but for it to occur in anything like the near future would take the best and most energetic efforts of the party of virtue.

Schlesinger's faith in democracy was a characteristic that distinguished liberals from the apocalyptic extremes of anticommunists like James Burnham. That former Communist was arguing in *The Struggle for the World* (1947) that the United States was already involved in a "third world war" against a Soviet communism bent on "the conquest of the world."[38] Burnham thought that the historic tides were running against freedom, so he denounced Truman's containment policies, and called on America to take the offensive against the Soviet Union while the United States still had a monopoly on nuclear weapons. Burnham urged Washington to outlaw the American Communist Party, form an anticommunist political federation with Great Britain and the rest of Europe, and encourage rebellion by anticommunist dissidents in Eastern Europe.[39]

Schlesinger, too, called on Americans to take the offensive against communism in Europe, but by using political and economic, not military, weapons. The key to fighting Communism in Europe was its "Non-Communist Left" (NCL), and he applauded the Truman administration for realizing that "socialists were 'among the strongest bulwarks in Europe against Communism.' " The Truman administration, he said, had taken the advice of liberal anticommunists and had organized a "winning coalition"—the CIO (purged of its Communists), the AFL, the ADA, and the supporters of the NCL in the State Department—all providing support for the European NCL's program of undercutting the appeal of communism through the reconstruction of the European economies.[40]

Liberal anticommunism's redefinition of the cold war as the defense of freedom against totalitarianism provided the theoretical basis for an effective counteroffensive against the revived European popular front of artists and intellectuals that was being organized to support the Soviet Union against American containment policies.

In October 1947, shortly after Stalin had unveiled the new Cominform to replace the Comintern he had dissolved in 1943, Soviet writers issued an "Open Letter to Writers and Men of Culture in the United States," inviting American intellectuals to join the fight against the "new threat of fascism"—that is, against the Truman Doctrine. The result was a "Cultural Conference for Peace" held in Breslau (now Wroclaw), Poland, from August 25 to 28, 1948, which attracted assorted veterans of the fellow-traveling left like painter William Gropper, film writer Donald Ogden Stewart, sculptor Jo Davidson, novelist Howard Fast, and Harlow Shapley, a Harvard scientist shortly to become a key organizer of the postwar American front movement.

This Soviet "Peace Offensive" was able to call on some of the world's most admired artists, intellectuals, and scientists, figures like Pablo Picasso (who contributed his famous Peace Dove symbol to the movement), Charlie Chaplin, and Albert Einstein, whose immense prestige made it seem as if the mind and soul of the West had risen up to condemn containment and the Marshall Plan, and to defend the Soviet Union as the victim of American aggression.

Sidney Hook's prewar Committee for Cultural Freedom had played a critical role in exposing the fronts of the thirties. He now wrote to the Americans at the Breslau meeting to protest "that the main interest of the conference was in furthering the foreign policy of the Soviet Union."[41] Hook denounced what he branded as a revival of the pre-Hitler-Stalin Pact "Russian *mythos*," the "liberal fifth column" with its "campaign of 'concealment, misrepresentation and deception' in the interests of the Soviet Union." The old popular front of Communists and fellow travelers had been bad enough, he warned, when it was defending a Communist state huddled behind its borders, fearful of the encircling capitalism world. It was a far worse danger to world peace now that the Soviet Union's powerful Red Army was setting up puppet regimes in states from the Baltic to the Balkans.[42]

Brushing off Hook's protests, the Americans at the Breslau Conference laid plans for an American "Cultural and Scientific Conference for World Peace" scheduled for March 1949 at New York's Waldorf Astoria Hotel. The organizers of the Waldorf Conference were veterans of the Independent Citizens Committee of the Arts, Sciences and Professions, the same progressive leftists who had supported Wallace in 1948. Among the more notable sponsors were Albert Einstein, Charlie Chaplain, Paul Robeson, and Leonard Bernstein.

Once again, Sidney Hook took the lead in organizing a protest of this new effort by Communists and their sympathizers to influence American intellectual opinion. Hook set up an "Ad Hoc Committee for Intellectual Freedom," soon renamed "Americans for Intellectual Freedom," with Dwight Macdonald, Mary McCarthy, Nicolas Nabokov (cousin of the novelist), and Arnold Beichman as some of its organizers. They attended the Waldorf Conference to pointedly question Soviet participants about intellectual freedom in the Eastern bloc. Their protest rally at Freedom House against the Waldorf Conference attracted such a large crowd that the overflow met at Bryant Park. But since Catholic and American Legion groups also picketed the Waldorf Conference, the progressive left claimed that "not Communism but Catholicism, not the Kremlin but the Vatican, threatened peace and freedom in the world."[43] A month after the Waldorf Conference, another even more spectacular group of pro-Soviet Western cultural luminaries gathered at the Paris "World Peace Congress." In the battle to influence public opinion in the West, the Soviets and their allies clearly were distancing their rivals.

The Bolshevik Revolution of November 7, 1917, and Lenin's call for the overthrow of the capitalist world order: the history of American anticommunism begins...

Responding to the Communist challenge, President Woodrow Wilson's Fourteen Points speech (top) calls for a world community of liberal, free market democracies united in a League of Nations. American radical John Reed (below, left) organizes an American Communist Party in solidarity with the Third Communist International (Comintern) that Lenin organizes in March 1919. A twenty-four-year-old lawyer in the Justice Department, J. Edgar Hoover (below, right), believing that Lenin's revolution is spreading to America, arrests thousands of alien radicals in 1919 and 1920.

Hoover's antiradical campaign devastates American communism, but makes martyrs out of radicals like Emma Goldman (above, right), deported by Hoover in 1919, and the Italian anarchists Sacco and Vanzetti (below), tried in 1921 for a 1920 payroll murder and executed in 1927. Harvard law professor and future Supreme Court Justice Felix Frankfurter (above, left) portrays the Red Scare raids and the Sacco-Vanzetti case as a right-wing conspiracy that uses fear of communism to attack the civil liberties of all who protest the status quo. It is a stereotype that would forever after haunt anticommunists.

Countersubversive anticommunists like Ralph M. Easley (above) of the National Civic Federation and New York Congressman Hamilton Fish (below, left) concoct their own conspiracy theory, the fantasy that the Communists have tied the entire American left into a plot to bring the revolution to America, as illustrated in this "red spider web" diagram (below, right) of the alleged conspiracy circulated by New York's antiradical Lusk Committee in 1923.

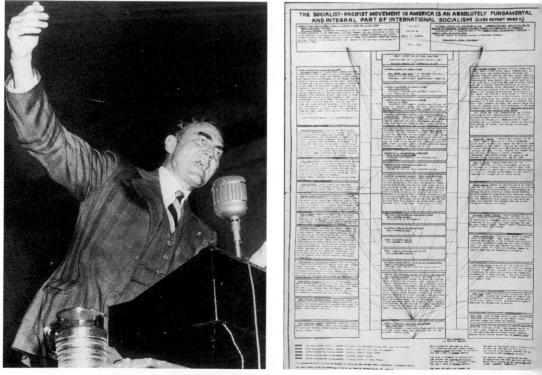

Ethnic America, suspected of revolutionary potential by nativist countersubversives and Communists alike, begins contributing knowledgeable and committed anticommunists to the movement. Patrick Scanlan (top) turns the *Brooklyn Tablet* into the militant voice of grassroots Irish Catholic anticommunism. Edmund Walsh, S. J. (bottom left, in Russia), founder of the Georgetown University School of Foreign Service and an expert on Tsarist and Revolutionary Russia, is director of Papal Relief in Russia during the famine of 1922, and uses his experience to reinforce the doctrinally based anticommunism of American Catholics.

Edmund A. Walsh, S. J., papers, Special Collections Division, Georgetown University

Communists' efforts to recruit blacks produce America's most militant and durable black anti-communist, George S. Schuyler, who begins his long career as an anticommunist debating black leaders of the Communist Party in the twenties, and continues this war against the Party as Harlem editor and columnist for the national black newspaper, the *Pittsburgh Courier*.

Communist inroads in the Jewish community rouse Jewish anticommunists to repel Communist efforts to infiltrate Jewish labor, social, and cultural institutions. Louis Marshall (above) of the American Jewish Committee defends Jews against anti-Semitic anticommunists like Henry Ford. Abraham Cahan (below), Socialist editor of the *Jewish Forward*, lashes out at Communists for betraying the Socialist ideal in Russia and for destroying the hope of a unified left in America.

Brown Brothers

The American labor union movement is led by committed anticommunists like the AFL's Samuel
Gompers (above), whose union is
from the beginning a bulwark of
the anticommunist movement.
Ex-Communist Jay Lovestone
(below), seen here speaking and
sharing the platform with the
anticommunist David Dubinsky of
the International Ladies Garment
Workers Union, moves out of the
Communist Party to direct American unionism's anticommunist
programs.

The Communist Party and the popular front of the thirties graduate anticommunists disenchanted with Stalin and the Party. In the late thirties philosopher Sidney Hook (above, left) recruits John Dewey to probe the truth of the purge trials and Stalin's charges against Trotsky, and organizes the America Committee for Cultural Freedom to counter the Party's influence among intellectuals. Eugene Lyons (below, center), who had helped turn Sacco and Vanzetti into Communist propaganda, returns from Russia in 1932 to expose Stalin's Russia in *Assignment in Utopia* and the American popular front in *The Red Decade*. Journalist Isaac Don Levine (above, right) introduces the American public to defectors from the Soviet underground Jan Valtin and Walter Krivitsky, and brings Whittaker Chambers to the State Department and the FBI after Chambers defects from the underground in 1949.

Knowledgeable anticommunists like Hook, Levine, and Lyons are overshadowed in the thirties by the outrageous activities of anticommunist conspiracy theorists who use the red smear against Jews, labor unions, and the New Deal, reinforcing the stereotype of the anticommunist as fascist. Elizabeth Dilling's (above, right) *Red Network* and *The Roosevelt Red Record* become the bibles of red web conspiracy theory. Father Charles Coughlin (below) blames Jews for communism and reprints the *Protocols of Zion* in his newspaper. Martin Dies (above, left) and his House Un-American Activities Committee red-bait the New Deal.

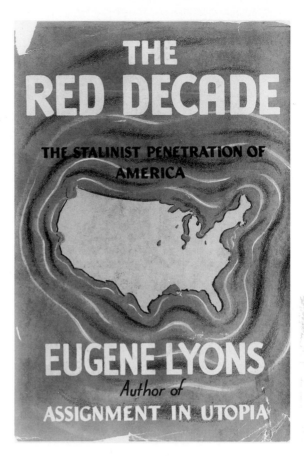

Eugene Lyons's *The Red Decade* demonstrates how Communists have used the Popular Front to create support for Stalin's Soviet Union in the thirties. Despite Stalin's 1939 pact with Hitler, which anticommunists predicted, exposés like John Roy Carlson's *Under Cover* discredit anticommunism by associating it with the anti-Semites and Nazi sympathizers of the isolationist movement. By the end of World War II, the prestige of America's Soviet ally has left anticommunism demoralized and discredited.

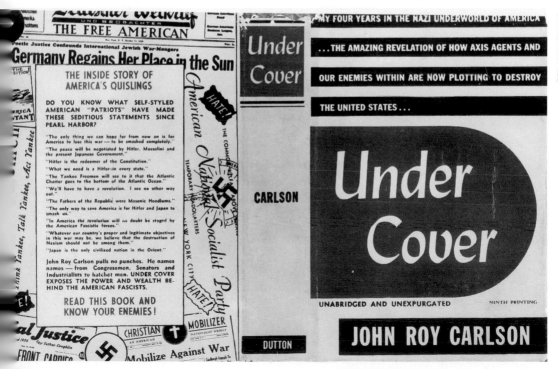

But even before the end of the war, American Catholics are warning of Stalin's designs on Catholic Eastern Europe. New York's Francis Cardinal Spellman (below, left) rallies the Catholic community against Soviet expansion. The trial and imprisonment of Hungary's Cardinal Mindszenty (top) mobilizes Catholics in rallies, marches, and prayer meetings. Baltimore labor priest John Cronin (below, right) produces reports on Communist influence for the Catholic bishops and the Chamber of Commerce that publicize FBI memos on Soviet espionage networks in Washington.

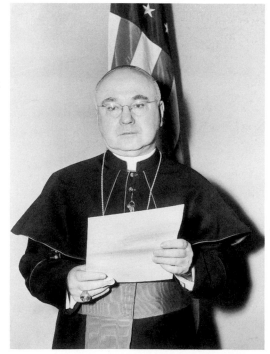

J. Edgar Hoover (top) warns the public about Communist espionage, subversion, and infiltration, and in 1947 allies the Bureau with the House Un-American Activities Committee to attack the Truman administration's loyalty program. Former Communist espionage agent Whittaker Chambers (center) testifies in 1948 that former State and Treasury Department official Alger Hiss (listening to Chambers, far left) had spied for the Soviet Union during the thirties. Hiss is convicted of perjury for denying Chambers's charges. Hoover's investigations help convict the leadership of the American Communist Party (bottom) in 1949 of organizing a conspiracy to overthrow the government.

Liberal anticommunists campaign against Henry Wallace's Communist-supported bid for the presidency in 1948. Harvard historian Arthur M. Schlesinger, Jr.'s (top) *Vital Center* defines communism and fascism as forms of totalitarianism, and declares that liberalism is the most effective form of anticommunism. Sidney Hook (center, lower right, listening to Arthur Koestler) leads the American delegation to Berlin in June 1950 to help found the Congress for Cultural Freedom, which will organize the noncommunist left against the Soviet-sponsored "Peace Offensive" against containment. Paul Nitze (bottom, at the head of the table, with the State Department's Policy Planning Staff) uses the ideas of liberal anticommunists to draft the most authoritative statement of America's cold war goals, NSC-68.

Labor unions and the entertainment industry respond to the international crisis, government pressure, and rising popular anticommunism by purging Communists from their institutions. Ronald Reagan, President of the Screen Actors Guild, appears in Washington in 1947 to announce cooperation with the House Un-American Activities Committee to eliminate Communists from Hollywood.

"You Mean I'm Supposed To Stand On That?"

Obsessed by red web conspiracy theories, Joe McCarthy charges that General George Marshall is a Communist, along with ever-changing numbers of government officials. Here he lectures a pained Army counsel Joseph Welch during the 1954 Army-McCarthy hearings that precede his censure and disgrace (top). McCarthy's false and irresponsible charges of widespread Communist infiltration pollute the political climate of the early fifties, and are a catastrophe for responsible anticommunism. Cartoonist Herbert Block coins the term McCarthyism in this cartoon, a term gradually enlarged to stigmatize all discussion or criticism of communism (*Herblock: A Cartoonist's Life* [Lisa Drew Book, Macmillan, 1993]).

Robert Welch (top) and his John Birch Society become the symbols of political "extremism" during the fifties and sixties, and, by extension, of anticommunism. In 1963 the AFL-CIO adapts the right's old red spider web charts (bottom) to tie right-wing anticommunism to the Birch Society.

HOW BIRCH SOCIETY LINKED WITH OTHER RIGHTIST GROUPS

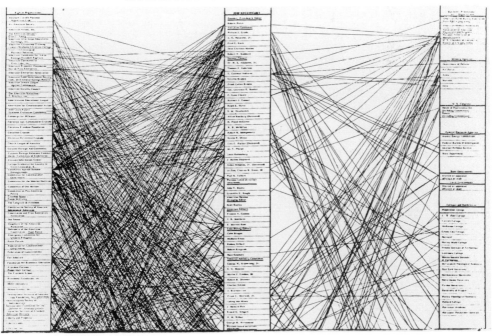

William F. Buckley, Jr. (top, at an editorial meeting with his sister Priscilla and editorial board member James Burnham), founds the *National Review* in 1955 to rebuild conservative anticommunism after the McCarthy debacle. Despite Buckley's best efforts, the association of anticommunism with extremism is fatal to Barry Goldwater's 1964 campaign for the presidency (bottom), when his opponents portray his anticommunism as evidence of extremist tendencies that might lead to fascism at home and nuclear war aboard.

The Vietnam War turns opponents of the war against the anticommunism they hold responsible for the disaster. Senator J. William Fulbright (top) denounces anticommunism as a dangerous myth that has led America to disaster. Daniel Ellsberg (center) calls the Vietnam War an anticommunist criminal conspiracy, and government efforts to block his release of the Pentagon papers convince many that he is right. J. Edgar Hoover comes to be viewed as a master conspirator against American liberties under the pretext of fighting communism, as illustrated in David Levine's caricature (bottom) (Reprinted with permission from *The New York Review of Books* © 1982, Nyrev, Inc.).

In the climax of the post-Vietnam reaction against anticommunism, President Jimmy Carter (center) announces at Notre Dame that America has freed itself from its "inordinate fear" of communism. William F. Buckley (bottom, also at Notre Dame) counters that there is nothing inordinate about fearing an ideology that is still denying hundreds of millions their freedom, still poses a military threat to the United States, and is still expanding throughout the world. Soviet dissidents like the exiled Russian novelist Alexander Solzhenitsyn (top, speaking at Harvard) demand that America return to its anticommunist principles.

Norman Podhoretz (top), editor of the American Jewish Committee's magazine *Commentary*, restates the intellectual case for anticommunism in the late 1970s and helps rebuild the anticommunist coalition. The Committee on the Present Danger, organized by Paul Nitze and Eugene Rostow (left and right of CPD member Ronald Reagan) and directed by Charles Tyroler, II (far right), leads a resurgence of anticommunism in Washington, attacking Carter's policy of detente and supplying presidential candidate Reagan with strategic expertise during his 1980 campaign.

Committee on the Present Danger.

Ronald Reagan enters the White House believing that "communism is another sad, bizarre chapter in human history whose last pages even now are being written." He makes anticommunism the basis of his foreign policy, challenges the Soviets to a new arms race, and harasses an overextended Soviet empire. He revives the anticommunist coalition in Europe to supply aid to Lech Walesa's Solidarity movement in Poland (below, right), a coalition now buttressed by the militant anticommunism of Pope John Paul II (above). Reagan's Director of Central Intelligence, William Casey (below, left), supplies military aid to anticommunist insurgencies in Latin America, Africa, and Central Asia. When it is discovered the administration has illegally supplied funds to the contra army in Nicaragua, the crisis threatens Reagan's anticommunist foreign policy and his presidency itself.

In June 1987 Reagan calls on Gorbachev to "tear down this wall." On November 11, 1989, after a year that has seen Lech Walesa's Solidarity win an election against Poland's Communist regime, followed by the collapse of Communist rule across the Soviet bloc, the Germans tear down the Berlin Wall, symbol of the Iron Curtain and the postwar division of Europe.

In August 1991, after an armed attempt by Communist hardliners to restore Party rule, communism falls in Russia itself, outlawed by Russian President Boris Yeltsin. Across Russia, statues of Vladimir Lenin topple, along with the revolution he had hoped would sweep the world. After seventy-four years, the era of communism has come to an end, and, with it, the history of American anticommunism.

At this time, the only well organized American opposition on the left against the Soviet Union cultural offensive was the group of anti-Stalinist socialists associated with Philip Rahv's *Partisan Review*. Hook's "Americans for Intellectual Freedom" seemed to hold the potential of forming the nucleus of a broader American anticommunist intellectual coalition to counter Communist penetration of Western culture.[44]

Anticommunist intellectuals in Europe were also beginning to organize to fight the increasingly pro-Soviet cast of European cultural life. Anticommunists like George Orwell, Arthur Koestler, and Hannah Arendt found it difficult or impossible to find publishers in Europe, particularly in France, where Sartre's famous dictum that "an anticommunist is a rat" was the conventional view of Paris intellectuals. And so in August 1949, three anticommunist intellectuals met in Frankfurt to plan a counteroffensive. They were Melvin J. Lasky, the American editor of Berlin's anticommunist monthly *Der Monat*, Ruth Fischer, anticommunist sister of Gerhard Eisler, the Comintern's former representative to the United States, and the ex-Communist German historian Franz Borkenau. Their idea was to hold an international conference of anticommunist intellectuals the next year in Berlin.[45]

Melvin J. Lasky was a Bronx-born Jew with long experience in the fellow-traveling left. He had broken with the Popular Front at the time of the Hitler-Stalin Pact and had gone to work for the Social Democrats' *New Leader*. During the war he served with the Seventh Army in France and Germany. He stayed in Berlin after his discharge from the Army, and he attracted the attention of the American and Soviet authorities with an outspokenly anticommunist speech at the 1947 German Writers' Conference in East Berlin. Over Soviet objections, the American military command helped Lasky found *Der Monat* in October 1948. He assembled a high-powered lineup of contributors including Bertrand Russell, Arthur Koestler, Arnold J. Toynbee, and George Orwell. Lasky was able to use *Der Monat* to issue the call for intellectuals to attend the "Congress for Cultural Freedom" he had planned with Fischer and Borkenau.

That June 1950 Berlin meeting of the new Congress for Cultural Freedom (CCF) signaled the emergence of an activist anticommunist movement within the leftist Western intellectual community.[46] There were a hundred invited participants. The Americans were led by Sidney Hook, James Burnham, novelist James T. Farrell, George Schuyler, black ex-

Communist Max Yergan, and film actor Robert Montgomery. James Burnham told the Congress that "so long as the Communist power threatens the world, genuine peace, or even the prospect of peace, will prove impossible. Through a moral, psychological, and political counter-offensive, through a worldwide anti-Communist Resistance, we can disintegrate the Communist power without the last desperate resort—which otherwise will surely come—to atomic bombs. Such a counteroffensive, driven forward by the resolute will of free men, is today the only road to peace."[47]

The best-known Europeans at the conference were Arthur Koestler and Ignazio Silone. The leading anticommunist intellectual in France, Raymond Aron, could not attend but sent a paper to be read in which he charged that "appeasement of the Soviets between 1944 and 1947 had increased the chances of war and that only the U.S. atomic weapons had saved the West; the choice now was between capitulation and active political resistance."

The most militant anticommunist at the Berlin Congress was Arthur Koestler, formerly a propagandist for Willi Muenzenberg, and author of the classic anticommunist novel (and play) *Darkness at Noon*. Koestler's violent rhetoric made him the particular target of the Communists' wrath. The French Communist paper *L'Humanité* printed a map of Paris with an arrow pointed at Koestler's house with the caption, "This is the headquarters of the Cold War. This is where Chip Bohlen, the American ambassador, trains his para-military Fascist militia."[48]

Each night Koestler, Hook, Burnham, Lasky, and Irving Brown (the AFL's European representative, the conduit for American aid to noncommunist European labor unions) met to plan the next day's political maneuvers against an opposition led by the British historian Hugh Trevor-Roper, who wanted to stake out a neutral ground between the warring behemoths of the Soviet Union and the United States.

In the end the Congress adopted Robert Montgomery's position that "there is no neutral corner in Freedom's room." But the conference rejected Arthur Koestler's harsh rhetoric, which had become an irritant to his fellow anticommunists, who used the verb "Koestlerize" to refer to an especially contemptuous attack on fellow travelers. The Congress strongly endorsed Schlesinger's NCL strategy and approved of the network set up to implement it, known as the "Lovestone Empire" after its coordinator, Jay Lovestone. Although some anticommunists, among them Koestler, Burnham, and Hook, distrusted the NCL because of its often anti-American rhetoric, it was precisely those demonstrations of its independence from American control that made the NCL so effective in its battles against the fellow-traveling left for the allegiance of noncommunist but anti-American nationalists in Europe and the Third World. This would not be the last time Americans would have trouble trusting the reliability of foreign anticommunists who displayed any skepticism about American leadership in the cold war.[49]

At its final meeting, the Berlin conference approved Lasky's recommendation to turn the Congress for Cultural Freedom into a permanent organization. They established an executive committee of Irving Brown, Arthur Koestler, Eugen Kogon, Denis de Rougemont, David Rousset, Ignazio Silone, and Stephen Spender. The alternates were Haakon Lie, Raymond Aron, Carlo Schmid, Georges Altmoa, Nicola Chiaromonte, T. R. Fyvel, Andre Philip, Malcolm Muggeridge, Melvin Lasky, Sidney Hook, and Manes Sperber.[50]

The CCF's executive committee appointed a Secretariat based in Paris to direct the affairs of the new organization. This was managed by Executive Director Michael Josselson, who ran the organization for the next seventeen years. Josselson was a naturalized American of Jewish-Estonian background who had been with the United States High Commission in Germany as a public affairs officer when he joined Melvin Lasky in protesting the American and British occupation authorities' appeasement of the Soviets in cultural matters. He was also, not without consequence for the later reputation of the CCF, an agent of the Central Intelligence Agency. Nicolas Nabokov represented the Congress at international meetings as secretary general. Nabokov, a cousin of the novelist, was a protegé of diplomat Charles Bohlen, who had placed him on the High Commission in Germany and then at the staff of the Voice of America before finally getting him his position with the CCF.[51]

In the early days the Congress's financial support came in large part from the CIA's International Organizations Division, headed by Thomas W. Braden. The CIA strongly endorsed the CCF's NCL strategy. Braden and Frank Wisner, director of CIA policy coordination, believed that "in much of Europe in the 1950s, socialist people who called themselves 'left' . . . were the only people who gave a damn about fighting Communism." Braden's assistant, Cord Meyer, who had organized the United World Federalists and had helped the liberal American Veterans Committee avoid a takeover by Communists after the war, also believed that "the real competition with the Communists for votes and influence [in Europe] was focused on the left side of the political spectrum, where the struggle for the allegiance of the European working class and the liberal intelligentsia would be decided." The CIA's funding for the CCF was ostensibly secret, but was well known to the Congress's friends and foes alike.[52]

Based at first in London, Paris, and Berlin, the Congress established national committees in nearly every country of the noncommunist world. It sponsored concerts, art exhibits, and symposiums of scholarly and intellectual interchange. It helped nourish a flourishing anticommunist cultural community that expressed its opposition to communism in journals sponsored by the Congress and in works like Richard Crossman's influential collection of essays by ex-Communists, *The God that Failed*.[53]

On January 31, 1950, President Truman asked his advisors to reexamine the country's objectives in the cold war. The result, transmitted to the President on April 7, 1950, was National Security Council Document 68 (NSC-68), prepared by Paul Nitze, then forty-three years old, head of the State Department's Policy Planning Staff. It was the most authoritative statement ever made of American cold war aims, and, to a remarkable degree in a document never intended for public view, and not declassified until February 1975, Nitze's group analyzed the fundamental issues of the cold war in the same terms as John Cronin, Arthur M. Schlesinger, Jr., and the liberal anticommunists of the CCF.[54]

In NSC-68, the underlying issue of the cold war was the moral clash between the values of freedom and totalitarianism. It pitted the "fundamental purpose" of the United States, "to assure the integrity and vitality of our free society, which is founded upon the dignity and worth of the individual," against that of the Soviet Communists, "to retain and solidify their absolute power, first in the Soviet Union and second, in the areas now under their control." To accomplish this, the Soviets were working towards "the complete subversion or forcible destruction of the machinery of government and structure of society in the countries of the non-Soviet world and their replacement by an apparatus and structure subservient to and controlled by the Kremlin."[55]

Nitze and his team did not believe that military conflict with the Soviet Union was likely in the near term. The Soviets' long-range goal was to dominate the Eurasian land mass so as to isolate the United States from its allies. The United States would then have to submit to Soviet dictates or fight from a position of weakness.

To avoid that, Nitze recommended the implementation of the containment policy Truman had already planned, a "rapid build-up of political, economic and military strength in the Free World." Like Schlesinger and Kennan, Nitze believed that if the Soviet Union were prevented from achieving its expansive goals, it would crumble, because "the Soviet monolith is held together by the iron curtain around it and the iron bars within it, not by any force of natural cohesion," and because "the idea of freedom" is "peculiarly and intolerably subversive of the idea of slavery."[56]

Nitze, like Schlesinger and Cronin, insisted that the threat to the United States was primarily external and military, not domestic, and yet he, like them, warned that the Soviets were trying, through "infiltration and intimidation," to turn "every institution of our society" against the policies necessary to preserve freedom at home and abroad. The institutions "that touch most closely our material and moral strength are obviously the prime targets, labor unions, civic enterprises, schools, churches, and all media for influencing opinion. The effort is not so much to make them serve obvious Soviet ends as to prevent them from serving our ends, and thus to make them sources of confusion in our economy, our culture and our body politic."[57]

To combat Communist subversion and to build public support for an anticommunist foreign policy, Nitze urged the government to utilize "the traditional democratic process." A free society, he said, must tolerate "those within it who would use their freedom to destroy it. . . . The free society does not fear, it welcomes, diversity."[58] Rather than a drive against domestic dissent, Nitze urged the administration to ensure that "sufficient information regarding the basic political, economic, and military elements of the present situation be made publicly available so that an intelligent popular opinion may be formed. Having achieved a comprehension of the issues now confronting this Republic, it will then be possible for the American people and the American government to arrive at a consensus."[59]

But even as Washington was arriving at a cold war consensus woven from the doctrines of liberal anticommunism, countersubversives were

214 Not Without Honor

embarking on their own crusade against domestic communism, a crusade that would not only threaten that fragile cold war consensus, but would turn the public's fears of communism against those same liberal anticommunists who were the architects of the military, political, and economic policies that were so effectively halting Soviet expansion around the world.

The key point of difference dividing liberals from countersubversive anticommunists was their attitude toward the American Communist Party. Liberal anticommunists regarded the Party as despicable and annoying, but as absolutely incapable of ever gaining any real power in the United States. Communists were dangerous only insofar as they made it more difficult to maintain public support for the policy of containing Soviet aggression overseas. Countersubversives, on the other hand, saw American Communists as dangerous in themselves—not only were they the agents of a hostile foreign power, but they were infecting the country with collectivist values incompatible with American traditions, with the goal of eventually imposing a Soviet-style system on the United States. Furthermore, some countersubversives saw liberals and Communists as equally destructive of the religious and patriotic values seen to be the basis of America's national identity.

Liberals and countersubversives also were in sharp disagreement as to the proper strategy to adopt against domestic Communism. While liberals believed that discussion and debate would be sufficient to expose the insincerity and disloyalty of the progressive left, countersubversives insisted that Communists and fellow travelers had to be exposed, denounced, and punished, and that the Party's covert activities made it necessary to employ the same law enforcement techniques as against any other criminal conspiracy. Liberals were only too aware that once the process of legal repression had begun, political partisanship would soon take over, and all New and Fair Deal liberals would be vulnerable to the assaults of investigators armed with countersubversive red web conspiracy theories.

The issue that led to war between liberal and countersubversive anticommunists was Communist infiltration of the government, and at the center of that clash was that countersubversive turned national hero, J. Edgar Hoover.

By 1946, the increasing tensions with Russia led Hoover to expect he would soon have to arrest or intern enemy sympathizers, just as he had in 1917 and 1941. He needed a workable "custodial detention program," and because of the ideological nature of the confrontation with Russia, enemy sympathizers this time would be distinguished by their political beliefs rather than nationality. This possibility posed complex and unprecedented problems for Hoover.[60]

Hoover remembered that the Palmer raids had been derailed because he had not worked out every detail of the dragnets ahead of time. He also recalled how attacks from liberals and civil libertarians like Louis Post, Judge George Anderson, and Tom Walsh had nearly destroyed him during the Palmer days. So he not only needed to develop procedures for rounding up detainees, but he also needed superiors and political allies who would defend him from the inevitable liberal counterattack. In February 1946 Hoover approved a recommendation from the Bureau executive conference that "an effort should be made now to prepare educational material which can be released through available channels so that in the event of an emergency we will have an informed public opinion" to be able to counter the "flood of propaganda . . . in the event of extensive arrests of Communists."[61]

This was the Bureau's "Mass Media Program," a coordinated effort by the Crime Records Division and the Bureau's top executives and field supervisors to shape public opinion to support the actions the FBI would have to take during an emergency. To mobilize public opinion against communism, the Bureau's presence in popular entertainment again reached the remarkable levels of the mid-thirties. FBI entertainment introduced America to the newest G-man hero, the undercover agent infiltrating the Communist Party on the radio, movie screen and, soon, television.[62]

In March 1946 Hoover advised Attorney General Tom Clark that he was going to "intensify [the Bureau's] investigation of Communist Party activities and Soviet espionage cases." He would compile a complete list of "all members of the Communist party and any others who would be dangerous in the event of a break in diplomatic relations with the Soviet Union, or any other serious crisis involving the United States and the U.S.S.R."[63]

But soon Hoover began to worry that he was not being given the support he needed from the Truman administration. He would be left in a politically exposed position, perhaps even set up as a scapegoat, if the public mood about communism changed, as it had changed several times before. By failing to support Hoover's plans for a custodial detention program, the Truman administration would be forcing him to round up Communists and fellow travelers without sufficient legal justification to protect him from retribution after the crisis had passed.

When President Truman, under pressure from the Republicans, finally announced his own program to purge Communists from the government, Hoover saw that the President had denied him the complete authority over internal security he needed if he were to succeed in this difficult task. The FBI was being forced to take part in an inherently faulty domestic security program, and Hoover knew he would take the blame when its failures became apparent. He was now convinced that the President was not truly serious about the issue of domestic communism.

From Wilson to Roosevelt, Hoover had been the obedient servant of presidents, ever willing to carry out their most confidential and sensitive assignments. Now he would turn against President Truman, and ally himself, his Bureau, and the vast numbers who worshiped him with the bitterest political enemies of the Truman administration.

Hoover signaled his break with the administration in a sensational appearance before the administration-hating, Republican-controlled House Un-American Activities Committee, on March 26, 1947. This was the old Dies Committee, now chaired by Republican J. Parnell Thomas of New Jersey.[64] Since HUAC was a symbol of right-wing opposition to the New Deal, Hoover's appearance was an open declaration of political war against a President too weak politically to retaliate against Hoover's disloyalty.

In his testimony before the Committee, Hoover endorsed HUAC's strategy of attacking subversives by means of "prescriptive publicity." The FBI and the Committee had the same goal, Hoover told the congressmen, but the FBI had to produce evidence acceptable in a court of law, while HUAC through its hearings could expose "the forces that menace America—Communist and Fascist. . . . This Committee renders a distinct service when it publicly reveals the diabolic machinations of sinister figures engaged in un-American activities."[65]

The most explosive portion of Hoover's testimony all but accused the administration of protecting Communists in government. HUAC's drive to keep "Communists and sympathizers out of government services," he said, was necessary because the administration had failed to take the Bureau's warnings seriously. Out of 6,193 cases the Bureau had investigated under the Hatch Act, there had been only 101 firings, 21 resignations, and 75 cases of administrative action.

It was up to HUAC, he said, to expose Communists wherever they might be found. "I feel that once public opinion is thoroughly aroused as it is today, the fight against Communism is well on it way. Victory will be assured once Communists are identified and exposed, because the public will take the first step of quarantining them so they can do no harm. Communism, in reality, is not a political party. It is a way of life—an evil and malignant way of life."

It was now to Hoover, not the administration, that the media turned for authoritative analysis of the problem of domestic communism. Hoover told *Newsweek* that the "slogan in the fight against Communism" should be "uncover, expose and spotlight their activities. Once this is done, the American people will do the rest—quarantine them from effectively weakening our country." And it was not only Communists who menaced the country. There were also "Communist sympathizers," "fellow-travelers," and "Communist stooges." It did not matter whether they were "innocent, gullible, or willful . . . because they further the cause of Communism and weaken our American democracy." The best defense against them all, Hoover said, was "our own American way of life." President Truman could use the presidency to define the foreign threat; he had lost the ability to control the domestic security agenda.[66]

While Hoover and HUAC were rallying countersubversives to battle against the progressive left, John Cronin produced two more reports on communism for the Chamber of Commerce. *Communists Within the Government*, published early in 1947, claimed there were about four hundred Communists in the federal government, with their own secret patronage system to protect their hiring and advancement. Cronin wrote this in collaboration with HUAC researcher Benjamin Mandel, who had also provided Cronin with HUAC materials for his 1945 report to the bishops.[67] Cronin's last report, also published early in 1947, was on *Communists Within the Labor Movement*.

HUAC, with the FBI director's blessing, now set out to expose Communist infiltration in the labor movement, cultural institutions, and the entertainment industry. And what better place to start than Hollywood? Why harass hapless government clerks, when they could be grilling movie stars?

Beginning in October 1947 a parade of screen personalities regaled the investigators with tales of Communist influence in the industry, while unfriendly witnesses responded with sullen silence or bellowed their defiance at the fascist witch-hunters. When a group of Communist screenwriters—the Hollywood Ten—took the Fifth Amendment when asked about their Party membership, the leading Hollywood producers met at New York's Waldorf-Astoria on November 24, 1947, and banned screenwriter John Howard Lawson, the most notorious Hollywood Communist, and the rest of the Hollywood Ten from employment in the industry. They extended the blacklist to include others known to be Communists, or anyone who refused to answer the Committee's questions. The producers begged the government to clarify the status of the Party as an outlaw organization, and they asked for legislation so that they could be sure of the blacklist's legal footing.[68]

Among the friendly witnesses from Hollywood who appeared before the Committee was one who would play an epochal role in the history of American anticommunism. This was Ronald Reagan.

Reagan became an anticommunist during the Hollywood labor wars in the forties between two AFL unions fighting to represent the film set workers, the anticommunist International Alliance of Theatrical Stage Employees (IATSE or IA) and the Communist-supported Conference of Studio Unions (CSU). Reagan became convinced that the ostensible jurisdictional differences between the two unions were only masks for the real issue, an effort by Hollywood Communists, supported by the Party itself, to gain control over one of America's key cultural institutions.

The fight between the two unions began before the war, when the IA was accused of being gangster dominated, and the CSU and its leader, Herb Sorrell, were charged with accepting support from Communist-dominated CIO unions. The charges stuck. The IA *was* mob connected, and Sorrell *was* enthusiastically supported by the Communists. Although he denied being a member of the Party, Sorrell did follow the Party line, from supporting the Popular Front and the "Yanks are Not Coming" slogans of the Hitler-Stalin Pact period to the pro-intervention and second front demands following Hitler's invasion of Russia.[69]

After the war, the Communist Party marshaled its forces to support the CSU against the IA. For its part, the IA asked for help from the anticommunist central offices of the AFL, which sent Roy Brewer to lead the fight against the CSU. Brewer made the CSU's Communist support the central issue, charging that behind the struggle between the IA and the CSU was "a long-range program instituted many years ago by a certain political party for one reason: to take over and control organized labor in the motion picture industry."[70]

Reagan was by now a major Hollywood star, a popular celebrity just a notch below the Gary Coopers, John Waynes, and Clark Gables. Within the Hollywood community, however, he was even more highly regarded as one of the most effective leaders of the actors' union, the Screen Actors Guild. He had been on the SAG board of directors since 1940. In 1946 Reagan was named president of SAG and served in that capacity until 1952 (he had another term as SAG president in 1959).

When Sorrell and the CSU continued to disrupt the film community, Reagan became as convinced as Brewer that communism was at the bottom of the industry's troubles. He put through a resolution that "no one shall be eligible for office in the organization unless he signs an affidavit stipulating that he is not a member of the party." Under Reagan SAG became a powerful anticommunist force in the industry and in California politics, and Reagan became the most prominent anticommunist in the industry.[71] He drew even closer to Brewer when they both joined the Motion Picture Alliance for the Preservation of American Ideals (the MPA) founded in 1944 by director Sam Wood, Walt Disney, Cecil B. DeMille, and Morrie Ryskind to fight communism in Hollywood. Roy Brewer eventually succeeded John Wayne as president of the MPA.

Reagan also became aware of Communist efforts to influence public opinion through noncommunist liberal political organizations, since he was active during this period in liberal Democratic politics in California. Reagan was a pro-Roosevelt New Deal liberal in the thirties and forties, and in 1947 joined the Hollywood Independent Citizens Committee of the Arts, Sciences and Professions (HICCASP), the local affiliate of the national ICCASP. HICCASP put Reagan on its board of directors to take advantage of Reagan's stature as a star and a power in SAG. He soon discovered that the HICCASP board was dominated by a group of secretly Communist actors and scriptwriters. Anticommunists like Reagan and fellow HICCASP directors James Roosevelt, Dore Schary, and Olivia de Havilland were suspicious about what was happening, but it was regarded as red-baiting to speculate openly about the subject of Party control.

Reagan later recalled that when his anticommunism became more obvious, there was a HICCASP meeting when everyone on his side of the table got up and moved to avoid sitting near him. On another occasion, his brother Neil told Reagan that HICCASP was Communist dominated, and the FBI warned him that the Communist directors were plotting against him. He and Olivia de Havilland resigned from HICCASP when the board rejected their resolution that communism was not "desirable for the United States."[72]

By now convinced that Communists were trying to take over the industry, Reagan threw the Screen Actors Guild into battle, and worked with the FBI to purge Communists from SAG. Warned that he was in danger of being physically attacked by the Communists, he began to carry a pistol for self-protection.[73]

When Reagan testified before HUAC in 1947, he told the Committee that it was up to the government to decide whether the Party should be outlawed. "As a citizen I would hesitate, or not like, to see any political party outlawed on the basis of its political ideology. We have spent 170 years in this country on the basis that democracy is strong enough to stand up and fight against the inroads of any ideology. However, if it is proven that an organization is an agent of a power, a foreign power, or in any way not a legitimate political party, and I think the Government is capable of proving that, if the proof is there, then that is another matter."[74]

Reagan helped Roy Brewer purge Communists from Hollywood and it was to Reagan, among others, that those named on the blacklist went to be cleared. He would tell them, he said, that "we can't clear you, but we can help you clear yourself," after which they were told to go the FBI and HUAC. Reagan even cleared his future wife, Nancy Davis, when she was accused of having Communist associations. He found that she had been confused with another Nancy Davis, and that "she had nothing to worry about." Reagan joined Brewer in founding the Labor League of Hollywood in 1948 to endorse anticommunist candidates for political office. In 1949 they formed the Motion Picture Industrial Council (MPIC) to convince the public that Hollywood really had purged itself of Communists.[75]

The 1940s turned Reagan into Hollywood's best known anticommunist activist. He had acquired "firsthand experience how Communists used lies, deceit, violence, or any other tactic that suited them to advance the cause of Soviet expansionism. I knew from the experience of hand-to-hand combat that America faced no more insidious or evil threat than that of Communism."[76]

Since 1917, countersubversives had been searching for the fabled Moscow Gold, the proof that the Soviet Union had extended its influence into the most powerful levels of the national government through the American radical movement. After twenty-five years of failure, countersubversives were finally able to prove one of their charges in a court of law. At last they had powerful support for their red web theories, and so a beleaguered President Truman, who had been regularly denying their charges as malicious fantasies, and who was already under attack from Hoover, HUAC, and the congressional Republicans, now faced the wrath of vengeful isolationist anticommunists bent on settling scores for what they had suffered during the wartime Brown Scare.

Alger Hiss, a political advisor in the State Department's Far Eastern Division from 1939 to 1944, was first named as a Soviet agent during Whittaker Chambers's meeting with Adolf Berle in 1939. In May 1942 Chambers told the Bureau that Hiss and his brother Donald had been undercover Communists when they were in the Agriculture Department together in the mid-thirties, but Hoover dismissed the eight-page memo as "either history, hypothesis or deduction."[77]

Chambers had his second interview with the FBI on May 10, 1945. This time Hoover took the twenty-two-page memo on the interview more seriously when the FBI got corroborating information in October 1945 from Elizabeth Bentley and from the Royal Canadian Mounted Police, who sent him a report on their interrogation of Soviet defector Igor Gouzenko. Hoover sent Truman his first memo on Hiss on November 27, 1945. This was the same report on "Soviet Espionage in the United States," largely based on the Bentley interviews, that John Cronin had used in his report to the bishops. In March 1946 Hoover recommended that the State Department ease Hiss out without bringing formal charges against him so as not to "alert him and ruin an important investigation." By the end of 1946 Hiss had learned of the probe into his loyalty, which may have encouraged him to leave the State Department on December 10 to head the Carnegie Endowment.[78]

On August 3, 1948, the Hiss-Chambers affair exploded into one of the great dramas in American political history. Chambers, now a *Time* magazine writer and editor, appeared before HUAC to tell the Committee that when he was a courier for Soviet intelligence he had known Hiss as a member of an underground Communist cell of government employees headed by Harold Ware, son of the Communist Party's famous "Mother" Bloor. Chambers claimed that the "purpose of the [Hiss-Ware] group at that time was not primarily espionage. Its original purpose was the Communist infiltration of the American government. But espionage was certainly one of its eventual objectives."[79] Reporters had their headlines when Chambers mentioned that Hiss had helped set up the Dumbarton Oaks conference that drew up plans for the United Nations and that he had organized that United Nations' first meeting at San Francisco. There were more headlines when they learned that Hiss had been with Roosevelt at Yalta, by now a symbol of appeasement to anticommunists.

It appeared, however, that Chambers's sensational charges were going to be discredited as completely and quickly as Grover Whalen's or poor Ralph Easley's or the preposterous Hamilton Fish's. Hiss appeared before HUAC on August 5, and said he had never been a Communist, had never been a member of a Communist front, had no friends who were Communists, and had never known Chambers. He seemed convincing even to the unfriendly Committee, and one HUAC member moaned "We've been had! We're ruined!"[80]

The administration also hoped the Committee had been "ruined." A reporter asked the President, "Do you think that the Capitol Hill spy scare is a red herring to divert the public's attention from inflation?" Truman answered that he did. The press, erroneously but understandably (and unforgettably), turned "red herring" into a presidential quote and headlined it across the country. Truman had bet his administration on Hiss's innocence.

With the survival of HUAC (and the Republican party's "Communists in government" issue) at stake, one member of the Committee realized that the Hiss-Chambers case was far from dead. Since Hiss and Chambers had contradicted one another, one of them must be lying, and he decided to have them confront one another, repeat their testimony, and then leave it to a grand jury to decide which of them—if not both—should be tried for perjury. The congressman was Richard M. Nixon, and it was the Hiss case that launched his career as a national politician.[81]

After his discharge from the Navy, Nixon had adopted the national Republican party's "Communists in government" issue in his 1946 campaign for Jerry Voorhis's Twelfth Congressional District east of Los Angeles. He charged that the CIO's Communist-infiltrated political action committee (CIO-PAC) had taken over the Democratic party, and that liberals like Voorhis, by protecting radicals in the government and the unions, were as dangerous as the Communists themselves.

Nixon came to Washington pledged to "smash the labor bosses . . . [and] to accept no dictation from the CIO-PAC." Once in Congress, he became aware of the broader domestic and international context of the Communist issue when he met John Cronin, who became a mentor, a confidant, and eventually a speech writer for Nixon's vice presidential campaigns. Nixon learned more about Communist subversion when he helped HUAC interrogate Gerhard Eisler, the Comintern representative to the American Party. When Eisler's sister, Ruth Fischer, told HUAC that Eisler was guilty of spying and murder, Nixon said it "brought home to me the character of the Communist Party and the threat which it presented to the country. . . . It was the beginning of my education in this field."

As Nixon's interest in foreign policy developed, his anticommunism was reinforced by his analysis of the Soviet Union's geopolitical challenge to American power and values. A trip to Europe in 1947 persuaded him that perilous economic conditions in France and Italy required immediate help from America, or "we will be faced with the almost certain prospect of a United States standing virtually alone," and he became one of the first Republicans to support the Marshall Plan. He debated the cold war with French and Italian Communist leaders and was appalled by their disloyalty to their countries. "Communists throughout the world," he said, "owe their loyalty not to the countries in which they live but to Russia."

Nixon's initial intention was simply to rescue HUAC from a public relations debacle by having one of the two men indicted for perjury. But on November 4 Chambers raised the ante by revealing that, far from trying to destroy Hiss as Hiss had charged, Chambers had been "shielding" him by not revealing that Hiss had been not only an "agent of influence" for the Soviets, but a spy. Chambers turned over to the Committee more than seventy official documents he said he had gotten from Hiss to be transmitted to his Soviet handlers.

And then there were the notorious "Pumpkin Papers." These were three undeveloped rolls and developed strips of microfilm Chambers had kept hidden for a short time in a hollowed out pumpkin on his farm in Westminster, Maryland. They contained information on suspected spy Harry Dexter White's recollections of foreign policy decisions in the Treasury Department, unclassified naval technical papers, and notes in Hiss's own handwriting from his days in the State Department. Chambers also turned over sixty-five more documents written on Hiss's own typewriter.

The Pumpkin Papers gave the case the element of the fantastic that turned it into one of the great popular culture extravaganzas in American history. The authenticity of the Pumpkin Papers now became the test of the countersubversives' entire case against the Communist underground, and Nixon's efforts to verify them produced one of the more melodramatic moments in the history of American anticommunism.

Nixon had sent the microfilm to Kodak in Rochester to see if the company could date the film stock used for the pictures. Chambers said he had taken the pictures in 1938, but from Kodak came the word that the film had been manufactured in 1945.

Nixon went into "complete shock." He could see his career crumbling before the eyes of the entire nation. He must have known all about the earlier countersubversives who had been duped with forged documents, and must have foreseen that his Pumpkin Papers would enter the annals with Hamilton Fish's cabbage caper, and the potato barrels that had held the Communists' hidden papers at Bridgman. Nixon and the Committee called a press conference. They were going to confess that "we were sold a bill of goods . . . that we were all wet."

The phone rang again. Kodak made a "little mistake." The film stock had been manufactured in 1938 as well, then discontinued until 1945. In the excitement, Nixon forgot to tell the good news to Chambers, who went out and bought cyanide to do away with himself.[82]

The statute of limitations on espionage committed in 1938 had expired by 1948, so Hiss could be indicted only on charges of having lied in denying he had known Chambers or passed him documents. Hiss's first trial ended in a hung jury, but on January 20, 1950, he was convicted on both counts of perjury.[83]

Never before had countersubversives been able to sustain their by now tired charges of treason in high places. Now they had their proof, and they could use Hiss's conviction to lend credibility to their most outlandish red web fantasies. Truman had lost his gamble that the Hiss case was a "red herring," and by losing he had handed to Nixon, to HUAC, to Hoover, and to the countersubversives the internal security issue that should have been his by right of office.

On January 26, 1950, a triumphant Nixon reported to Congress on the Hiss case. He insisted on sharing credit with the FBI but he pointedly did not thank Truman's Justice Department. The administration, he said, had "failed or refused to institute an investigation which would lead to prosecution and conviction of those involved." Above all, Nixon said, "we must give complete and unqualified support to the FBI and J. Edgar Hoover, its chief. Mr. Hoover recognized the Communist threat long before other top officials recognized its existence. The FBI in this trial did an amazingly effective job of running down trails over 10 years old and in developing the evidence which made the prosecution successful."[84]

The Hiss case was obviously a disaster for Truman and the liberal anticommunists who had minimized the threat of domestic communism. What was not so obvious was that it was a disaster as well for the whole anticommunist cause. It shifted the balance of power in the movement from the responsible liberal anticommunists who had built the awesome defensive alliances that were containing communism around the world, and had given new credibility to some of the most bizarre and irresponsible figures in American politics, the right-wing countersubversive anticommunists of the prewar isolationist movement. Truman's failure to control the politics of internal security had created a power vacuum. A host of ambitious politicians far more irresponsible than Nixon and Hoover quickly moved to take advantage of this volatile and dangerous situation.

Countersubversive anticommunists could also point to the trial of the high command of the American Communist Party, who were indicted on June 29, 1948, on charges of violating the Smith Act, which prohibited organizing or belonging to an organization dedicated to the overthrow of the government.

Like so many of the FBI's more controversial activities during these years, the Smith Act prosecution of the Party grew out of J. Edgar Hoover's need for a legal basis for a roundup of Communists in the event of a crisis with the Soviet Union. When the Justice Department rejected his request for new legislation authorizing detention of dangerous citizens during hostilities, Hoover asked the Department to prosecute a test case so that the Bureau could use the Smith Act as grounds in an emergency for arresting Communists as "substantive violators" of that law."[85]

Gil Green, one of the Smith Act trial defendants, later pointed out that the Bureau's strategy "was predicated on the inevitability of war, for [Hoover's memo] did not say 'should' hostilities break out but '*at the time*' they do." From Green's point of view this choice of words had sinister connotations, but a more persuasive reading is that Hoover and his aides really believed there was a likelihood of war between the United States and Russia.[86]

During the trial of the Communist leaders at New York's Foley Square federal courthouse the government was able to demoralize the defendants by producing Herbert Philbrick as a prosecution witness. Philbrick was a mid-level official of the Party who had been cooperating with the FBI since 1940. The Party was staggered to learn it had been so deeply penetrated and that its most confidential activities were well known to the Bureau. Another witness was Angela Calomaris, who had been active in the Party right up to the moment of her testimony.[87]

The most important of the ex-Communist witnesses at the Smith Act trial was Louis Francis Budenz, former managing editor of the *Daily Worker*, who had left the party in 1945. The government really wanted to establish the guilt of the Communist Party itself, not merely the defendants. For this the government relied on a massive "brief" Hoover had submitted to the Internal Security Section of the Justice Department that bulked to 1,350 pages with 546 exhibits. To explain how this arcana pertained to the overthrow of the government the prosecution relied on witnesses like Budenz. Budenz argued that "the Communist party of the United States is basically committed to the overthrow of the Government of the United States as set up by the Constitution of the United States." The Communists' denials of violent intent should

be rejected as "Aesopian language," "window dressing asserted for protective purposes."[88]

The jury found all the Communist defendants guilty and their convictions were upheld by the Supreme Court. Seven of the Communist
leaders reported to prison. The other five went underground to continue
their Party functions.

Over the next few months Hoover was able to round up the remaining members of the Communist Party hierarchy for the so-called "second echelon" trials. In the end 126 Communist leaders were indicted,
93 were convicted, and only 10 acquitted. The FBI's campaign to send
Communists to jail finally slowed after Hoover decided that having his
informants testify at their trials was harming "the highly essential intelligence coverage which this Bureau must maintain in the internal security field."[89]

The Smith Act convictions advanced Hoover's goal of "educating"
the public against communism. He was pleased, he said, that "a wider
public knowledge of the aims, plans, and purposes of the party has resulted from the continuing arrests and convictions of Communist leaders for conspiring to teach and advocate the violent overthrow of the
government; and an enlightened public is one of the most potent
weapons against the nation's internal enemies."[90]

All anticommunists agreed that Communists were disloyal, but liberals wanted the Party to be fought through the democratic process, to
let the public make up its own mind. Now countersubversives had made
communism a crime, to be dealt with through law enforcement, not political debate.

Overseas events were rushing to a climax that would sweep away the
counsels of reason, and overwhelm the liberal anticommunists trying to
hold the line against the countersubversive onslaught and continue the
calm and firm containment strategy of the Truman administration. The
arrest and show trial of Hungary's Joseph Cardinal Mindszenty in December 1948 drove Catholics into a frenzy. New York's Archbishop
Spellman and Mindszenty were friends, and Spellman proclaimed February 6, 1949, a day of prayer for Mindszenty's release from "Christ-
hating Communists." In Brooklyn twenty thousand Catholics gathered
at Ebbetts Field to pray for Mindszenty as a martyr for the Church

"against Red tyrants." Local priests organized anticommunist Mind-szenty Circles and Freedom Foundations for their parishioners.[91]

Over the past four years communism had spread across Eastern Europe. In the spring of 1949 China fell to the Communists, and Chiang Kai-shek's Nationalist Army was driven off the mainland of China to a refuge on the island of Formosa. The most populous nation on earth had been added to the Communist bloc. Catholics had long known through their missionaries in China that Mao was winning the civil war there, and had been begging the Truman administration for more aid to Chiang. Catholics had blamed Chinese Communist gains on the defeatism of Henry Wallace, and on the anti-Chiang biases of General Joseph W. Stilwell, and of pro-Communist advisors in the State Department, and "pink reporters" like Theodore White. While Americans were still absorbing the shocking news from China, the Soviet Union exploded its first nuclear bomb on August 28. Countersubversives charged that the loss of China and the Soviet bomb were both the results of Communist espionage and treachery at the highest levels in Washington.[92]

To defend itself, in 1949 the State Department released a 1,054-page White Paper that maintained that "the ominous result of the civil war in China was beyond the control of the government of the United States. Nothing that this country did or could have done within the reasonable limits of its capability could have changed that result. Nothing that was left undone by this country contributed to it. It was the product of internal Chinese forces, forces which this country tried to influence but could not. A decision was arrived at within China, if only a decision by default."

Republican and Catholic anticommunists who had opposed FDR's Europe-first war strategy all along now charged that there had been a plot by fellow travelers, Communists, and, significantly, liberals in the administration to deliver China to the Communists by blocking aid to Chiang.

This group of anticommunists was called the "China Lobby" by their enemies to create the impression that they were bought and paid agents of the Chinese nationalists. (They were also accused, equally falsely, of being supported by Chinese drug traffickers.) At the center of this group was a wealthy importer of Chinese handkerchiefs named Alfred Kohlberg, who had become convinced that the most important organization of Asian scholars, the Institute of Pacific Relations (IPR), was a

Communist front, and that its China experts—notably John Stewart Service and Owen Lattimore—were Communist agents who had maneuvered anticommunists out of the Asian section of the State Department. Kohlberg had founded the American China Policy Association in 1946 to counter the influence of the IPR.

The China Lobby's conspiratorial explanation for the loss of China would eventually evolve into one of the most malicious theories in the annals of American politics. This was the bizarre notion that the remarkably effective anticommunist containment policies of the Truman administration were actually a plot by the nation's highest leaders and military heroes to hand the world over to communism.

But although the final conclusions of the China Lobby were utterly maniacal, their initial premises were not so farfetched. Kohlberg pushed his case too far—Service and Lattimore were fellow travelers, not Soviet agents—but he was correct in holding that the Institute was hostile to anticommunist views on China. It did promote the idea that the Chinese might be better off under Mao than Chiang, and that in any case the Chinese Communists were no threat to the United States.[93]

The Hiss and Smith Act cases, the loss of China, and HUAC's exposés of Communist infiltration were for the first time giving conspiracy-minded countersubversives a significant public following. Countersubversives outside the government were now encouraged by the successes of HUAC and the FBI to conduct their own investigations of front groups and Communist influence in labor, the churches, the media, and the schools. Frederick Woltman of the *New York World Telegram* won a Pultizer for his articles on the fronts.[94]

There was a revival of self-defensive Jewish anticommunism. Rabbi Benjamin Schultz of Yonkers founded an "American Jewish League Against Communism" in 1948 to ferret out "all Communist activity in Jewish life, wherever it may be." Schultz's organizing committee included Alfred Kohlberg, Benjamin Gitlow, George Sokolsky, Eugene Lyons, and Isaac Don Levine. Schultz published a series of well-researched newspaper articles on Communist influence in the Protestant, Catholic, and Jewish clergy. Predictably, these groups reacted with outrage to Schultz's charges.[95]

The American Legion's All-American Conference continued to

bring together civic leaders to hear countersubversive reports on Communist subversion at home and abroad. Ominously, conspiracy-minded countersubversives were appearing in the same forums as realistic experts on Communism. In 1947 the Legion sponsored William Bullitt, George Sokolsky, Lowell Thomas, Ben Gitlow, Isaac Don Levine, Howard Rushmore, Suzanne La Follette, Ralph De Toledano, John F. Cronin, and Karl Baarslag. In February 1949 the Legion's Conference on Subversive Activities in New York invited Ben Gitlow, Eugene Lyons, Benjamin Schultz, George Schuyler, and Ben Mandel of HUAC to speak. Appearing with these responsible countersubversives, however, were J. B. Matthews, who by now was selling his files to red-baiting employers, Ted Kirkpatrick, publisher of the blacklisting journal *Counterattack*, and the by-now-unstable Elizabeth Bentley.[96]

The Chamber of Commerce and the Legion tried to present the more responsible of the countersubversives, but the arrests of spies and the convictions of Communist leaders opened the doors to red web countersubversives still smarting from the wartime brown smear who were looking for revenge. They were now Roosevelt-haters past the limits of reason. Many of them were anti-Semites as well, hoping to revive isolationism and anti-Semitism by proving that America's participation in the war, which had discredited isolationism and anti-Semitism and had restored the Soviet Union to the community of nations, had been a Communist plot hatched in the White House.[97]

At the center of this effort to prove that Roosevelt and his advisors had pulled the United States into the war to save the Soviet Union from Hitler was John T. Flynn, former head of America First, who was still trying to get even with old antagonists like the Friends of Democracy for having used the brown smear to ruin America First. Flynn's circle included former Nazi sympathizers, anti-Semites, and Roosevelt haters of the old 1936 Liberty Lobby variety. In 1945 Flynn tried to found a new anticommunist political party, American Action Inc., and discussed the project with the rabidly anti-Semitic Gerald L. K. Smith. Flynn's *Secret of Pearl Harbor* and *The Smear Terror* (an attack on the ADL) became holy writ to the countersubversives who were beginning to run wild in the late forties.[98]

One of the bizarre conspiracy theories that flourished in the late forties and early fifties was the Tyler Kent case. This was promoted by the former Christian Fronter and Coughlinite, Edward Lodge Curran, among others. Kent had been an employee of the American embassy in London who had leaked information to the isolationists about the Roosevelt administration's prewar assistance to Britain. Countersubversives claimed that by allowing the British to imprison Tyler Kent, the Roosevelt administration had kept from the public information that would have steeled it against the war. Hamilton Fish and Laura Ingalls (of sedition trial fame) had their own variations on the theory that World War II had been a Communist plot directed by traitors in Washington. Gerald L. K. Smith joined with Elizabeth Dilling to promote conspiracy theories involving Jewish Bolsheviks.[99]

J. B. Matthews was now selling his files on the fronts to anyone who would buy them. Around the country, countersubversives were harassing university faculties with information and misinformation from Matthews. Their charges were panicking university presidents and trustees into firing professors for refusing to answer questions about Party membership or associations. Those whose presidents refused to be browbeaten survived unscathed, but universities with presidents who bent to public pressure, or anticipated it, were terrorized.[100]

Until the late forties, conspiracy theorists like Coughlin, Dilling, and Smith had been relegated to the lunatic fringe, too removed from the mainstream to be truly dangerous. But some of these hate-mongers had once been responsible analysts of the front movement, like J. B. Matthews, or honest isolationists like John T. Flynn, who had become soured and scarred during the days of the brown smear. Their rage pushed them into the ranks of paranoid conspiracy theorists, where they joined forces with far more disreputable countersubversives, while still maintaining their earlier access to mainstream politicians and journalists.

Now, during the late forties, some still responsible countersubversive journalists began to act as mediators between the lunatic fringe and the political mainstream. Their dark suspicions about the New Deal's alliance with domestic and foreign Communists during the war began to infect the nation's political discourse. Popular journalists like George Sokolsky, Westbrook Pegler, and Upton Close provided publicity for countersubversives' red web fantasies, and sometimes retailed them themselves. George Sokolsky charged that Burton K. Wheeler had been defeated for reelection in 1944 by "a group of men in New York, terrifyingly financed, fanatical in their zeal, utterly ruthless in their methods, un-American in their concepts, honest in their purposes but immoral in their tactics, who have made a god of Hitler as some of the peoples of Asia worship the devil." He meant the ADL. In 1946 Sokolsky accused FDR of having pursued a dual policy: open support of Four Freedoms, secret appeasement of Stalin. Two years later Sokolsky was wondering why Adolf Berle and FDR had not paid attention to Chambers's accusations against Hiss before the war. He was charging that Truman's China policy had been a deliberate betrayal of Chiang.[101]

A new confidence that bordered on arrogance was running through the countersubversive anticommunist community at the end of the decade, as their ideas percolated into the nation's anticommunist consensus. George Sokolsky regularly published an honor roll of countersubversives who had warned the country about communism when to do so exposed them to the brown smear. In 1949 his list included himself, Westbrook Pegler, John Flynn, Fulton Lewis, Isaac Don Levine, J. B. Matthews, Eugene Lyons, and Ben Gitlow. This was a promiscuous mingling of realists and fantasists, but Sokolsky treated an attack on any one of them as an attack on all. Even responsible criticism of countersubversives he denounced as "new smears of anticommunists."[102]

By 1950 the countersubversives' self-confidence had become bravado. Sokolsky began proudly using the term "red-baiters" as an honorific, meaning an effective anticommunist, and began calling his friends the "Ancient Order of Red-Baiters." He rejected a senator's slighting reference to "professional anticommunists." The professional anticommunists had been proven right by history, he said, and then he listed some of those professionals: Max Eastman, David Dalin, William Henry Chamberlin, J. B. Matthews, Ted Kirkpatrick, Karl Baarslag, Father Walsh, Jay Lovestone, Ben Gitlow, Joe Sack, Louis Budenz, Eugene Lyons, Elizabeth Bentley, and Whittaker Chambers. "They are needed," he said, but some of them were once again indulging in the promiscuous red smearing that had so often discredited the anticommunist cause in the past.[103]

Some of the more responsible countersubversives realized what was happening. Isaac Don Levine was one. In June 1946, after a meeting John Cronin had set up between Alfred Kohlberg, HUAC research director Ben Mandel, and three ex-FBI agents, Kenneth Brierly, Theodore Kirkpatrick, and John Keenan at Levine's home in Norwalk, Connecticut, Kohlberg appointed Levine editor of a new anticommunist journal, *Plain Talk*. A few weeks later Levine found out that the ex-agents were selling their files to red-baiting groups and individuals. After he fired them, the three founded "American Business Consultants" in the spring of 1947 and published the blacklisting journal *Counterattack*, which pressured radio networks to blacklist Communist talent.[104]

Levine suspended *Plain Talk* in 1950 after an article he published denouncing anti-Semitic anticommunism drew attacks from anti-Semites who were now confident enough to insist that the anticommunist movement make room for their bigotry. He also learned that his longtime confidant, J. B. Matthews, was selling his files to anti-Semitic conspiracy theorists. Another anticommunist, Freda Utley, told her anticommunist friends she "knew JB when he was with the Dies Committee. He is not to be trusted. Always double-crossing his own friends. He is an uncontrollable drunkard. He is brilliant, unscrupulous, willful. But he is an alcoholic and that is what limits his effectiveness."[105]

Ironically, despite the truly frightening nature of the Soviet threat, the conspiracy theories of rabid right-wing countersubversives were gaining new credibility at the very moment when the strength and influence of the American Communist Party had never been weaker, and the influence of the fellow-traveling left had never been so low. The reality was that liberal anticommunists had arrayed against communism an international economic, military, and cultural alliance more powerful than anything the world had ever seen before.

But countersubversives were less than ever impressed by reality, less than ever bound by common sense or decency, when, on February 9, 1950, one of them rose to speak to a gathering of Republican women in Wheeling, West Virginia.

Chapter 9

McCARTHYISM

How can we account for our present situation unless we believe that men high in this Government are concerting to deliver us to disaster? This must be the product of a great conspiracy, a conspiracy on a scale so immense as to dwarf any previous such venture in the history of man.
—Senator Joseph R. McCarthy, speech to the Senate, June 14, 1951.

Senator Joseph R. McCarthy's speech at the 1950 Lincoln Day dinner in Wheeling, West Virginia, was, in retrospect, the greatest disaster in the disastrous history of American anticommunism. Anticommunism would never be the same after those instantly famous words: "While I cannot take the time to name all the men in the State Department who have been named as active members of the Communist party and members of a spy ring, I have here in my hand a list of 205—a list of names that were made known to the Secretary of State [Dean Acheson] as being members of the Communist party and who nevertheless are still working and shaping policy in the State Department." For many Americans, McCarthy made ludicrous the notion that anticommunism could be based on sound morality or a realistic view of the world. In the mouth of McCarthy, the truths of anticommunism would turn into evil, malicious lies.[1]

Within a matter of hours, McCarthy's was the most talked-about name in America, and his rabid charges that there were Communist traitors among the nation's most trusted leaders—the age-old fantasy of red web cultists—eclipsed the sober and truthful accounts of communism that anticommunists had provided over the past half decade, making anticommunism seem nothing more than the ravings of a dangerous madman.

235

For more than four years, from 1950 to 1954, radical countersubversives in McCarthy's wake would wreak havoc on American political civility. But countersubversive anticommunism's lunge for national power could not have occurred if the world had not been in a state of crisis. While McCarthy's first wild charges were being investigated by the Senate, the Communist North Koreans invaded South Korea, on June 25, 1950. Seoul was captured by the North Koreans on June 28, and on June 30, American troops, authorized by a United Nations resolution, landed on the Korean peninsula. On July 8 Douglas MacArthur took command.

While the country was reeling from the first engagements of what looked to be a prelude to a full-scale war with the Soviet Union, Julius Rosenberg was arrested for passing atom bomb secrets to the Russians on July 17, and his wife Ethel a few weeks later. The home front was looking for traitors to be blamed for the dangers faced by the troops. From the time of the Rosenbergs' arrests through the start of their trial on March 6, 1951, to their conviction on March 29 and the pronouncement of their death sentence on April 5, American troops advanced to the borders of Communist China, then had to retreat before a Red Chinese onslaught. All the while, there lurked the danger of war with Stalin's Soviet Union, armed with the atom bomb since September 1949.[2]

Over the next four years, before his career crashed in disgrace and alcoholic oblivion, McCarthy redefined anticommunism in his own image, and anticommunism would never fully recover its good reputation. McCarthy gave the enemies of anticommunism what they had been looking for since the beginning of the cold war: a contemporary name and face for their old stereotype of the anticommunist fascist. During the previous five years, the behavior of the Soviet and American Communists had proven that everything anticommunists had said against them was true. But now, because of McCarthy, anticommunism would be not the amply demonstrated truth about Stalin, his regime, and his threat to his neighbors, but a lie, that absurd red web conspiracy delusion that collapsed whenever it was exposed to the light of day.[3]

Up to a point, McCarthy's origins explain his anticommunism. McCarthy was born in 1908 in Grand Chute, Wisconsin, into a working-class Irish Catholic culture that had strongly supported Father Coughlin in the thirties. McCarthy would have heard many Sunday sermons on the evil of Russia. He would have heard the Church attack communism, socialism, and liberalism. And when he attended Milwaukee's Catholic Marquette University, he would have encountered anticommunism in courses on history and social issues.

Many Irish Catholics of McCarthy's humble background associated the word "liberal" with everything they hated and feared—a liberal elite bent on destroying the independence of the church that Catholics had sacrificed to build. By the late thirties, Catholic frustration, isolation, and alienation often shifted over into Roosevelt-hating. It was inevitable that somewhere in the United States some American Catholic, probably Irish, was primed and ready to explode into a Joe McCarthy once the cold war began.

When McCarthy ran for the Senate in 1946 after a tour in the Pacific with the Marines and a term as a district judge, the Communists-in-government issue was central to the Republicans' attacks on Truman. McCarthy's speeches lambasted the administration for its handling of the Soviets: "We retreated mentally and morally in Austria, in Poland, in the Baltic States, in the Balkans, in Manchuria, and today in Iran," he would say, "and there is no reason to believe that tomorrow we shall not do the same thing in Norway, Sweden, and Turkey, which apparently are next on the agenda." He denounced the Yalta division of Europe, and said that the election of the isolationist Robert La Follette, Jr., now running as a Republican, would mean catastrophe for "the future of human liberty if the Communists move in." He asked, "Does he care? Doesn't he realize what it would mean for the rank and file of the people of all the nations of Europe?" He accused La Follette of being "communistically inclined," and used *Daily Worker* endorsements of his opponents to label them fellow travelers and worse.[4] Newspapers reported McCarthy's charges, but gave only brief coverage to the rebuttals. Many anticommunists in the state supported McCarthy as a way of standing up against communism.

As a freshman senator, McCarthy opposed David Lilienthal's nomination to be chair of the Atomic Energy Commission, based on FBI suspicions. He appeared on the *Town Meeting of the Air* radio program to urge outlawing the Communist Party. He wanted the Taft-Hartley bill amended to permit workers to petition their employers to fire Communist fellow workers. On a nationwide radio broadcast he said, "We've been at war with Russia for some time now, and Russia has been winning this war at a faster rate than we were, during the last stages of the last war. Everyone is painfully aware of the fact that we are at war—and that we're losing it." He denounced the administration for failing to support Chiang Kai-shek.[5]

In Washington, McCarthy chose his friends from anticommunist circles. He was befriended by Joseph P. Kennedy and the entire Kennedy clan, all ardent anticommunists, and went to the racetrack with J. Edgar Hoover. Jean Kerr, McCarthy's secretary and future wife, was another ardent anticommunist. McCarthy often consulted the Georgetown Jesuits like Edmund Walsh who were bulwarks of Catholic anticommunism. On October 24, 1949, Charles H. Kraus, a professor of political science at Georgetown's Foreign Service School, joined McCarthy's staff. These Catholic anticommunists were infuriated by the Truman administration's failure to support Chiang, and they introduced McCarthy to the obsessions of the China Lobby anticommunists and to the fixations of embittered prewar isolationists like John T. Flynn.[6]

A one-hundred-page FBI report on Communist subversion completed McCarthy's conversion to countersubversive extremism, and he delivered a speech in Wisconsin on "Communism as a Threat to World Peace." On November 15, 1949, he attacked China hand John Stewart Service, charging that the State Department was run by Communists. He broadened his field of fire by accusing Leland Olds of the Federal Power Commission of being a Communist.[7]

McCarthy's anticommunism at this stage was the China Lobby variety, although the violence of his charges against leftist China experts Service and Owen Lattimore put him in its most conspiratorial wing. The recognized leader of this group was General Patrick Hurley, who had headed the American mission to China during the war. Hurley blamed the failure of his efforts to broker a coalition between the Communist and nationalist forces on "the professional foreign service men [who] sided with the Chinese Communist armed party and . . . openly advised the Communist armed party to decline unification of the Chinese Communist Army with the national Army unless the Chinese Communists were given control." In Hurley's view, this anti-Chiang contingent was led by John Stewart Service, John Paton Davies, John Carter Vincent, and the other "old China hands."[8]

McCarthy also became friendly with Alfred Kohlberg, who had al-

ity at first protected him. J. Edgar Hoover, Richard Nixon, Alfred Kohlberg, and J. B. Matthews all loaded him down with material to help him sustain his charges. The entire literature of conspiratorial anti-communism now lay about his office, and McCarthy was soon addicted to it, all skepticism blasted away by the sheer mass of details in the red web volumes that had been accumulating since 1920. He may have be-gun as a cynical politician toying with a new political tactic, but by the end of February 1950 he had become a true believer, a "zealot." Hearst sent J. B. Matthews to Washington to see if McCarthy was on the level, and when he was satisfied, Hearst began to have George Sokolsky and Westbrook Pegler slant their stories to support him.[12]

But the Democrats, who had been on the wrong side of the Communists-in-government issue, sensed that the Republicans had fi-nally gone too far. Senate Democrats convened a hearing chaired by Maryland's Senator Millard Tydings to investigate McCarthy's Wheel-ing charges. In a panic, McCarthy's staff, headed now by ex-FBI agent Donald A. Surine, began rounding up information from the right-wing network. They called on HUAC, the FBI, J. B. Matthews, Alfred Kohl-berg, attorney Robert Morris, ex-Communists Louis Budenz and Freda Utley, the Chicago Tribune's Willard Edwards and Walter Trohan, Fred-erick Woltman of the New York World Telegram and Hearst's George Sokolsky, Westbrook Pegler and Howard Rushmore.[13] J. B. Matthews's "Appendix Nine of the 1944 HUAC Report," a monumental accumu-lation of innuendo and hearsay, became McCarthy's reference source and bible.

With the Tydings Committee now scrutinizing McCarthy's "facts," the inaccuracy of the red web theorists began to destroy the credibility of the entire anticommunist movement. Even true believers had always known that the red web books were not reliable, but as long as they were circulated only to the already converted, their demonstrable errors had hardly mattered. J. Edgar Hoover had turned over material on the fronts and on fellow travelers to HUAC because he had recognized that this evidence was too shaky for him to use in court. Matthews himself cau-tioned his clients not to get in trouble by making statements based solely on "Appendix Nine." But now McCarthy was staking his own reputa-tion and that of the anticommunist cause on evidence that dissolved under the first skeptical examination.

The Tydings Committee began to investigate whether there were in fact 57 or 205 Communists in the State Department. McCarthy responded with another smokescreen of attacks and innuendo, among them a smear of Dean Acheson's wife, whose name had appeared in "Appendix Nine."[14] One by one McCarthy's "Communists" took the stand to deny and disprove his charges. When the press examined McCarthy's accusations, it found them not only false, but unbelievably wide of the mark. But McCarthy airily dismissed this as caviling because he now had the name of the "top Russian espionage agent in the country."

McCarthy's "top agent" was that old obsession of the China Lobby, Owen Lattimore, who was in Karachi, Pakistan, on a United Nations assignment. McCarthy said that the proof was in Lattimore's FBI file, and demanded that the administration hand it over. Instead, President Truman invited the Tydings Committee to the White House to review a summary of the file in the presence of Attorney General J. Howard McGrath and J. Edgar Hoover. They all agreed that there was nothing in the file that remotely suggested that Lattimore had been a Communist or a spy.[15]

McCarthy's face was becoming the sinister image of irresponsible, red-smearing. On March 29, 1950, a Herblock cartoon in the *Washington Post* showed the GOP elephant forced to balance on a barrel perched on buckets of steaming tar and wailing, "You mean I'm supposed to stand on that?" The barrel was labeled, "McCarthyism."[16]

McCarthy's staff finally managed to locate a witness, Louis Budenz, who would testify that Lattimore had been a member of the Communist Party, and even had a code name in the underground. After marathon sessions with his advisors to put together a case against Lattimore, on March 30 McCarthy claimed that Lattimore had dominated the Far Eastern Division of the State Department and the Voice of America. Dean Acheson was "the voice for the mind of Lattimore," said McCarthy. McCarthy claimed Ambassador at Large Philip Jessup had an "unusual affinity . . . for Communist causes." McCarthy had gotten all this from Kohlberg, who had been saying that the entire left-wing component of the State Department's Far Eastern group were traitors for so long that he had forgotten that outside China Lobby circles he would actually be expected to prove his charges.[17]

On vacation in Key West, President Truman told the press that McCarthy was the Kremlin's greatest asset in America. McCarthy's supporters rose to the bait and defended their champion against a thrust which was close to the truth.

When Lattimore appeared before the Tydings Committee on April 6 he easily refuted all of McCarthy's charges. He made the telling point that McCarthy's key accusations were merely charges Alfred Kohlberg had been peddling for years. "It is easy to understand the joy of Kohlberg and his associates," Lattimore gibed, "when they found the willing hands and innocent mind of Joseph McCarthy."[18]

McCarthy began to retreat from his original position that Lattimore, Service, and Jessup were actually Communists. The charge was now that they had merely followed the Party line, which he might have been able to sustain if he had started with it. His waffling did not go unnoticed, and his enemies taunted him for cowardice. The Tydings Committee called an ex-Communist witness, Bella V. Dodd, who denied that she had ever heard Lattimore mentioned as a Communist during her days in the Party. She had read Lattimore's books, she said, and they had not always followed the Communist line. She also derided Budenz's qualifications as an expert witness. Earl Browder, an ex-Communist himself now, against his will, also denied that Lattimore was a Communist. According to Browder, Lattimore was actually an anticommunist. Frederick Vanderbilt Field, the fellow-traveling financial angel of the Institute of Pacific Relations, also testified that Lattimore was not connected to the Party, but Browder's and Field's endorsements were probably not helpful to Lattimore. When the Tydings Committee released its report later that summer, Lattimore was cleared of all charges, and McCarthy was flayed for his recklessness and irresponsibility. For their part, the Republicans defended McCarthy, calling the report a partisan smear of a senator whose only offense had been to anger the administration.

McCarthy tried in vain after the Lattimore debacle to destigmatize his name. He sought to redefine "McCarthyism" as a synonym for Americanism, using it himself as the title of his book, *McCarthyism, The Fight for America*. He also claimed, falsely, that it had been Lattimore who had first used it as an epithet, and indeed Lattimore had used it with telling effect in his Senate testimony. But the damage was done. Previously, the idea that anticommunism was a fascist plot against all dissent had been confined to the far left and its liberal sympathizers. The counterattack against McCarthy had carried it into the political mainstream. The progressive left could now dispense with the old epithet of "fascism," which had been so misused and overused by the Party in smearing their enemies as to be almost useless. Now there was a far more devastating synonym for anticommunism: "This is McCarthyism.

This is the means by which a handful of men, disguised as hunters of subversion, cynically subvert the instruments of justice and hold up to contempt the government itself in order to help their own political fortunes."[19]

But McCarthy was impervious to insult, to humiliation—indeed, he had no shame. It was a quality that accounted for both his triumphs and his disasters. A year later, on June 14, 1951, on the floor of the Senate, totally unchastened by the Lattimore experience, McCarthy delivered the most astounding, the most irresponsible speech ever heard in that chamber. In a harangue that lasted almost three hours, McCarthy called General George C. Marshall—the supreme commander of the American military in World War II, the former secretary of state, the current secretary of defense—a traitor who had acted all his life in the service of the Soviet Union. This was the speech that McCarthy published soon afterward as *America's Retreat from Victory: The Story of George Catlett Marshall.* It was the red web thesis raised to the grandiose levels of cosmic madness.

In this speech, McCarthy made Marshall the villain in every area of American foreign policy since the beginning of World War II, which he also blamed on Marshall. Marshall had tried to send the United States into a premature invasion of Europe that might have lost the war, just to save Stalin a few divisions. Every American setback, every Communist success since the war had been the result of "a conspiracy on a scale so immense as to dwarf any previous such venture in the history of man." It was a conspiracy that had become all-powerful. The President was "their captive."

At the center of it all was "this grim and solitary man," George C. Marshall. "If Marshall were merely stupid," said McCarthy, "the laws of probability would have dictated that at least some of his decisions would have served this country's interest. . . . What is the objective of the conspiracy? I think it is clear from what has occurred and what is now occurring: to diminish the United States in world affairs, to weaken us militarily, to confuse or spirit with talk of surrender in the Far East and to impair our will to resist evil. To what end? To the end that we shall be contained and frustrated and finally fall victim to Soviet intrigue from within and Russian military might from without."[20]

It was an astounding performance, so outrageously filthy as almost to soil anyone who had to lower himself to answer it. And yet, in the intensely partisan atmosphere of 1951, even though the Republican right knew that McCarthy had taken leave of sanity and reality, they had to defend McCarthy again as they had before, or else make common cause with the Truman administration they detested.

McCarthy's attack on Marshall encouraged the most irresponsible countersubversives to try to force their brand of anticommunism on the country as a national orthodoxy. Governor Allen Shivers of Texas proposed that Texas make Party membership a capital offense, and he encouraged other states to enact similar legislation. Shivers told an Illinois audience that American adherents to the international Communist conspiracy were "traitors—period." Americans, he said, were either pro-Communist or anti-Communist. There was no room for a middle position.[21]

Local governments began to investigate schools and universities, and to impose noncommunist loyalty oaths as a condition of employment. The University of Washington led the way in 1948 by firing three professors who had either admitted that they were Communists or who had refused to answer questions from the state un-American activities committee. Between 1952 and 1954, after HUAC hearings and exposés by J. B. Matthews and his accomplices, about one hundred professors were fired for refusing to answer questions about their possible Communist affiliations.[22]

McCarthyism was anticommunism conducted on the level of symbolic politics. It turned individuals, whether actually Communists or not, into symbols of communism, denouncing, degrading, and, if possible, destroying them. It was in the world of entertainment, which also operated by turning individuals into symbols, that McCarthyite repression cut deepest.[23]

Blacklisting on the popular level was a product of Americans' tendency to act as though the fantasy universe created by entertainment was the real one. American political controversy, then and now, tended to shift from the political arena into sallies and parries in the make-believe world of the entertainment industry.

The Hollywood blacklist that began at the Waldorf Astoria meeting of producers in November 1947 was in full force by the beginning of the McCarthy period. That blacklist at first had contained only ten names:

Adrian Scott (a producer), Edward Dmytryk (a director), and writers Lester Cole, Ring Lardner, Jr., Dalton Trumbo, John Howard Lawson, Albert Maltz, Alvah Bessie, Samuel Ornitz, and Herbert Biberman. Nine others, including actor Larry Parks and screenwriter Waldo Salt, known to be prepared to refuse to answer but not called by HUAC, were on the "shadow" blacklist. The shadow blacklist also included those who signed the petitions of a Committee for the First Amendment that protested the HUAC hearings. Entertainment figures who supported an appeal to the Supreme Court protesting the Hollywood Ten's convictions for contempt of Congress also found themselves blacklisted. Between 1951 and 1954, 324 Hollywood personalities were named as Communists by HUAC, and so also were blacklisted.[24]

The blacklist was enforced by a host of grassroots pressure groups: the Wage Earners Committee picketed films with anyone named as a Communist. The Catholic War Veterans also enforced the blacklist, as did the American Legion. The American Legion signaled that it was going to support the blacklist when an article by J. B. Matthews appeared in the December 1951 issue of the Legion's magazine "Did the Movies Really Clean House?" Matthews charged that the studios had not gone far enough in ridding themselves of Communists. He named sixty-six Hollywood figures from lists of supporters of the Hollywood Ten or opponents of HUAC, or drawn from lists of front members in Appendix Nine, who were still working. The industry panicked, and asked the Legion to send them the names of objectionable employees. The Legion sent along some three hundred names.[25]

The Legion's headquarters were soon flooded with nervous inquiries asking how suspects could be "cleared." It was a process that entailed a visit to local Legion officials to explain suspect affiliations. Those who refused to state whether they were Communists or refused to disavow past Communist associations became unemployable. Those who satisfied this initial scrutiny were asked to "write the letter" requesting clearance. The industry and the Legion selected George Sokolsky as a kind of "pope" of the clearance process, to sit in judgment on the accuracy and sincerity of these letters. Sokolsky was generally (but by no means universally) liked and trusted by both sides, and had at his disposal J. B. Matthews's mammoth files of card entries. Sokolsky expressed some misgivings about "wrecking careers" but felt that since there was no government procedure for clearing suspects, it was up to private citizens like himself. When Roy Brewer was approached for clearances, he would turn an applicant over to an ex-Communist assistant on his staff named Howard Costigan, who would advise the blacklistee to give the FBI any information he had, and then volunteer to testify before HUAC. The clearance process often involved theatrical lawyer Martin Gang, whose specialty was obtaining clearances for blacklistees. He too had his clients see the FBI and agree to testify before HUAC.

So many of the blacklisted entertainers were Jewish that Arnold Forster of the Anti-Defamation League and other ADL officials would investigate the non-Communist bona fides of Jewish blacklistees, and try to get them cleared. One of the organizations that enforced black-lists, AWARE, led by Godfrey Schmidt, Cardinal Spellman's lawyer, published *The Road Back: Self-Clearance*, which suggested a "twelve-step" program for rehabilitation of ex-Communists.[26]

The broadcast industry's blacklist originated in April 1947, when the three ex-FBI agents who had started as researchers on the staff of Alfred Kohlberg's and Isaac Don Levine's *Plain Talk* set up American Business Consultants to publish a magazine (*Counterattack*) to report on the political backgrounds of entertainers. In June 1950 ABC produced *Red Channels*, a listing of the Popular Front and Party backgrounds of entertainers which quickly became the basic reference for broadcast industry blacklisting.[27] Persons named in *Red Channels* or its updates could not work until they had passed through the clearance system.

The man behind *Red Channels* and AWARE was a former Naval Intelligence officer, Vincent Hartnett. Hartnett was working for radio producer Phillips H. Lord's *Gangbusters* program when Lord began to face charges that his shows were employing Communists and discriminating against anticommunists. Hartnett began to specialize in helping producers choose politically correct casts for shows, and he wrote in Catholic magazines like *Sign* about Communists in show business. In 1950 Hartnett joined the *Counterattack* staff to work on *Red Channels*, which he referred afterwards to as "my" *Red Channels*. (Hartnett's later updates of *Red Channels* were called *File 13, Volume 1* and *File 13, Volume 2*.) He compiled his lists by checking names against reports of HUAC, the Senate Internal Security Subcommittee (SISS), the McCarthy Subcommittee, and Communist Party publications. Hartnett was one of the founders of AWARE in 1953, and served as its vice president. In 1951 Hartnett testified before SISS on "Subversive Infiltration of Radio, Television and the Entertainment Industry," and charged that Actors Equity between 1936 and 1950 had become dominated by Communists.[28]

By far the most important of the organizations enforcing the broadcast blacklist was the Veterans Action Committee of Syracuse Supermarkets, formed by the Syracuse Post #41 of the American Legion and Syracuse supermarket owner Laurence A. Johnson. Johnson's daughter, Eleanor Buchanan, an instructor at Vassar, was married to a Marine. Mrs. Buchanan was angered by the agitation against the war by the progressive left while her husband was fighting in Korea. She lined up the American Legion, the Rotarians, the Kiwanis, business leaders, and ordinary citizens of Syracuse to bring pressure on manufacturers sponsoring radio programs employing actors listed in *Red Channels*. The Syracuse American Legion post, to which her father belonged, began publishing a newsletter, *Spotlight*, which was eventually taken over by the Legion's national headquarters to report on efforts to enforce the blacklist. Johnson also had one of his employees head the Veterans Action Committee of Syracuse Supermarkets. Among their other projects, the Syracuse groups protested sales of records by the folk group the Weavers, and asked radio stations and juke box distributors to ban their records. (Pete Seeger of the Weavers was a Communist and was listed in *Red Channels*.)[29]

The American Legion's newsletter *Firing Line* also serviced the broadcast blacklist. Lee Pennington, who edited *Firing Line* in Washington, had served with the FBI for twenty-five years before resigning to take over the Legion's Americanism Commission in 1953. Pennington's sources included the Tenney Commission of California, the Broyles Committee of the Illinois legislature, and the transcripts of the old Fish Committee. He also possessed an index of all names in the *Daily Worker* since 1940. Pennington worked with James Francis O'Neil, director of the Legion's publications, to decide whether a listee had done enough to clear himself, often calling on his friend George Sokolsky for advice. There were also security officers at the major advertising agencies and the networks to enforce the broadcast blacklist. The most important was Jack Wren, security officer at Batten Barton Durstine and Osborne. At CBS Daniel T. O'Shea handled screening and clearances.[30]

In a media-obsessed culture like America, all parties in political disputes try to use popular entertainment to win symbolic victories. The manipulative use of celebrity names for political purposes was based on the same theory as commercial advertising: an imaginative association with a celebrity can persuade the consumer to adopt the same product or the same political views as the celebrity. Such endorsements create an aura of glamor around a product—or a political position. If the political left—which had no mass base, but had deeply penetrated the cultural elite—could use celebrity endorsements to promote leftist causes, then anticommunists would retaliate against those same celebrities.

The blacklist grew out of the unquestioned right to boycott, to refuse to patronize businesses associated with abhorrent political views. But the blacklisting system soon became a way for countersubversive anticommunists to browbeat their opponents into submission. In many cases personal hostilities or union conflicts determined whether a person was blacklisted. Instead of democratic debate, countersubversive anticommunists simply repressed entertainers they associated with dangerous opinions. But as with other extremist measures employed by countersubversives, the blacklist hurt anticommunism almost as much as its victims. The existence of the blacklist let the left shift attention from the communism for which the blacklisted were being persecuted to the fact of their persecution. Ronald Reagan's anticommunist mentor, Roy Brewer, complained that blacklisters like the California legislature's Tenney Committee were "about 90 percent correct on factual material—but Tenney's conclusions weren't correct," and that publications like *Red Channels* gave ammunition to "amateurs." Brewer moaned that "one of the by-products of this problem is that we make heroes out of guys who are not heroes, and enemies out of people who ought not to be enemies. People who have social consciences are penalized, and guys who never helped anybody are way out in front. It was only the people who were trying to help others who got involved. And they ought not to be punished."[31]

There was a still vital civic culture of anticommunism from the early days of the cold war that began to be eclipsed as McCarthy surged into the headlines. All strains of American anticommunism were represented in this grassroots movement: liberal intellectuals, labor unionists, religious leaders, conservatives, and countersubversives. The grassroots anticommunism in the McCarthy era reflected the great struggle of the American public to come to grips with the monumental challenge history had imposed on their generation—to lead the world against a militant and expansive Communist movement. The public's debate on the Communist issue was none too genteel—it was messy and sometimes frightening—but it was probably the only way a great, unsophisticated, none-too-educated democracy could ever grapple with such an awesomely complex issue.

The anticommunist consensus seemed solid at the beginning of the fifties. On January 25, 1951, the Women's Patriotic Conference on National Defense held its twenty-fifth meeting. Speakers included conservative ex-Communist Ben Gitlow, blacklister Vincent Hartnett, Joe McCarthy, Rabbi Benjamin Schultz, George Sokolsky, and *Washington Times Herald* editor Frank Waldrop. The coalition of liberals and countersubversives was becoming increasingly unstable however as McCarthyism moved toward undiscriminating attacks on the entire left, anticommunists as well as fellow travelers. For example, the Patriotic Conference also included General George Marshall and President Truman himself. Obviously, all these names would not be found on the same program after McCarthy's attack on Marshall a few months later.[32]

But to a great extent the grassroots movement continued its activities throughout the McCarthy era. The American Legion's All-American Conference provided an umbrella for all wings of the anticommunist movement. In 1950, for example, seventy-six major organizations met at the conference, with W. C. "Tom" Sawyer, head of Legion's Americanism Commission, presiding. Speakers included General Walter Bedell Smith, James B. Carey, Matthew Woll, Karl Mundt, Jack B. Tenney, George Sokolsky, Bishop Sheen, Reverend Daniel Poling, Rabbi Schultz, and Frank Gordon, the assistant prosecutor in the Foley Square trial. CIA Director Walter Bedell Smith told the Legion conference that the Communists had an active fifth column in America. George Sokolsky called for national unity, and denounced Communist attempts to smear business, the Catholic Church, and the Republican party. Monsignor Sheen described the Catholic Church's programs against communism. The Conference sponsored a "Know America" week, held in some 1,600 communities across the country, to promote patriotism with an anticommunist edge.[33]

Before the McCarthy hysteria took hold, there was a consensus among American leaders that the public, particularly students, should be educated about the nature of communism. The disagreement was on how this should be done. Conservatives believed that effective anti-communist education meant indoctrinating the public in the religious and philosophical underpinnings of American democracy. Liberals thought that an objective presentation of communism's record would be enough. In one of several youth forums on communism sponsored by the *New York Times*, Arthur Schlesinger, Jr., called on the schools to provide more information on communism and more instruction in the Russian language. "It is important that we know something about our enemies," said Schlesinger. "The teaching should be objective. Anyone who made an objective study of communism would come out very much opposed to it." J. Edgar Hoover spoke out throughout the fifties on the need for anticommunist education in the schools.[34]

All the major religious denominations had anticommunist educational programs. Catholics took particular pride in their church's uncompromising anticommunism. American Catholics were told that the world Church had turned to America to protect Catholicism from communism. New York City's Police Commissioner Thomas F. Murphy proudly stated that the Irish had led the fight against communism, and cited the Hiss trial witnesses to prove his point. "I can't even recall one Irish name among the many thousands that have been called before the House Committee on Un-American Activities," he said. "If there was, he probably changed his name." New York's Jesuit Fordham University hired ex-communist Louis Budenz to teach a course on Communist tactics.[35]

Baptist Daniel A. Poling and Catholic Edmund A. Walsh, who had sparred during the forties over the sincerity of Catholic protests against religious persecution in Russia, joined to warn that communism was out to capture the soul of mankind. Walsh called communism a challenge to the nation's basic and fundamental faith, "the faith of all men who believe in the sonship of all of us under the fatherhood of God."[36] But the old religious conflicts sometimes marred this new unity. In 1953 the Protestants and Other Americans United for Separation of Church and State (POAU) in Texas claimed that HUAC was dominated by Catholics out to rule America according to the Jesuits' secret plan, and Catholics protested that they should be praised, not attacked, for their efforts against communism. The Catholic *Sunday Messenger* complained once more that Protestant ministers were indifferent to Communist persecution of religion in Europe and China because the Catholic Church was the target. There was a dispute between a minister at New York City's Fifth Avenue Presbyterian Church and a Catholic priest who claimed that communism was an outgrowth of the Protestant reformation. Catholics created hostility by treating criticism of McCarthy as evidence of anti-Catholicism.[37] Within the Jewish community there were efforts to spread the word about anti-Semitism in the Soviet Union. Rabbi Schultz's Jewish anticommunist movement, however, was poorly received by most major Jewish organizations, which worried that such strident anticommunism might simply stir up more anti-Semitism.[38]

Popular anticommunism entered mass entertainment in the early fifties. An FBI undercover informant, Matt Cvetic, told his story, "I Posed as a Communist for the F.B.I." in the *Saturday Evening Post* in July 1950. This was turned into the movie, *I Was a Communist for the FBI* in 1951, and a syndicated radio show, beginning in 1952.[39] The film showed Matt Cvetic's brothers throwing him out of their house for being a "slimy Red." Cvetic's son tells him he would rather die than grow up a Communist like his father. In the end, the FBI lets Cvetic testify before Congress about the Party's espionage, sabotage, and subversion. With his proud family watching, he tells the congressmen that "Communism's only goal is to gain complete control over every human mind and body in the world." To the accompaniment of the National Anthem, he warns Communists that "You've got a lot of people like me in the party, but you don't know it."

My Son John (1952) was another film that identified anticommunist patriotism with family loyalties. Helen Hayes tells son Robert Walker that she has come to despise him for becoming a Communist, and his father orders him out of the house because he can't "love his Uncle Sammy." He is finally murdered by the Communists at the Lincoln Memorial, but only after making a tape recording of his reconversion to Americanism to be played at his college graduation. *New York Times* film critic Bosley Crowther thought *My Son John* was "so strongly dedicated to the purpose of the American anti-communist purge that it seethes with the sort of emotionalism and illogic that is characteristic of so much thinking these days." George Sokolsky, on the other hand, praised the film and complained that it was being smeared by leftist critics: *My Son John* was a picture that every American parent should take his children to, Sokolosky wrote, so "that they may learn to love and serve America."[40]

The movie *Walk East On Beacon* (1951) was based on J. Edgar Hoover's account of the atom spy case, "Crime of the Century," which had appeared in the *Reader's Digest.* The film opened by informing the audience that the "FBI's responsibility is to protect the American people against the communist world conspiracy which seeks to overthrow free government everywhere. Nothing is more important to the FBI's efforts than the support of alert Americans." Stock footage showed J. Edgar Hoover working in his office. Because the Rosenberg case was still in the courts, the script changed the espionage target from the atomic bomb to a secret computer. The hero of the film is the corporate FBI personified in J. Edgar Hoover himself. Hoover's photo decorates the agents' offices, and he personally oversees their work. Interestingly, the film makes use of a theory popular among liberal anticommunists that the absence of intellectual freedom under communism made real scientific achievement impossible. A kidnapped American scientist tells his Communist captors, "you have no men of genius. Their talents are in chains. Now you have to steal the creations of free men." Hoover warns at the end that "there are other hidden enemies and they can only be exposed by Americans armed with the Bureau's motto: Fidelity, Bravery, Integrity."[41]

Each of the 117 episodes of *I Led Three Lives* that ran on television from 1953 to 1956 began, "This is the story, the fantastically true story, of Herbert A. Philbrick, who for nine frightening years did lead three lives—average citizen, high-level member of the Communist Party, and counterspy for the Federal Bureau of Investigation." The show glamorized counterintelligence to the extent that government agencies used it for "indoctrination and enlistment" purposes. The show's producer remembered that he and the rest of the crew "felt that there was a genuine Communist threat to undermine the United States, perhaps to take over the United States. The FBI felt that they must have surveillance, and the public was entitled to know that that type of surveillance was going on. I feel that we rendered that service to the general public. You may or may not approve of that in today's times. At that time I felt that it rendered a proper service."[42]

The public even created its own anticommunist passion plays. In May

1950 the Wisconsin town of Mosinee staged a mock takeover by Communists, a pageant scripted and directed by the local American Legion, with ex-Communist Ben Gitlow retained as technical advisor. During the takeover, the mayor was "arrested" and the police chief "shot." Restaurants featured a Communist dining hall menu: black bread and potato soup. Clothing stores raised $42 suits to a revolutionary price of $252, while coffee sold at the Russian price of an astronomical $4.14 a pound. The pageant took a serious turn when the town's mayor died from a heart attack brought on by the strain of the ambitious project and the attention of the national media.[43]

No one did more to turn anticommunism into popular culture than J. Edgar Hoover himself, who gave speeches on an almost weekly basis, usually stressing religious reasons for fighting communism, which was, he said, the end result of the loss of religious faith. "The danger of Communism in America lies not in the fact that it is a political philosophy but in the awesome fact that it is a materialistic religion, inflaming in its adherents a destructive fanaticism. Communism is secularism on the march. It is a moral foe of Christianity. Either it will survive or Christianity will triumph because in this land of ours the two cannot live side by side."[44]

There had always been differences between conservative and liberal anticommunists, but they had been obscured by the urgency of supporting containment. They had agreed, at least, on the reality of the Soviet threat and on the need to oppose domestic Communists and fellow travelers. But now McCarthy and the countersubversive right were attacking not just the progressive left that defended the American Communists and the Soviet Union, but the anticommunist left as well.

The McCarthy period saw the differences between liberal and conservative anticommunists deepen to the point that a break was inevitable. Conservatives saw communism as an attack on *popular values*: religion, patriotism, the family, and local civic society. Liberal anticommunists saw communism as an assault on the elite values they held most dear: intellectual and academic freedom, freedom of artistic expression, and the constitutional guarantees of due process, limited government, and the freedom of the individual.

Sidney Hook defined anticommunism in terms of intellectual freedom. He wanted the schools to teach students to see communism as the denial of scientific inquiry and artistic expression. For Hook, therefore, conservatives' reliance on religion and tradition put them in the same camp—theoretically at least—with the Communists in their shared fear of cultural freedom.[45]

Conservative anticommunists, by contrast, insisted on traditional American values as the answer to communism. "Instead of having schools and colleges studying communism," they said, "let us see to it that the Bible is put in them on the basis that it covers every phase of life which no lesser textbook can possibly do." Senator Edward Martin of Pennsylvania told a YMCA convention that there should be an "American program to guard religious ideas of the country from 'godless forms of tyranny and dictatorship.' " Catholics were urged by their own anticommunist Christopher Society to ward off communism by reciting the words, "Savior of the world, save Russia."[46]

On a somewhat more philosophical level, historian Arnold Toynbee also saw the roots of communism in modern religious infidelity. He called communism a return to pre-Israelite as well as pre-Christian worship of collective human power, and called on students to develop an appreciation of the Christian spiritual values that had guided Western civilization before the wrong turn towards rationalism and skepticism. The West needed a new spiritual vision to replace the secular ideals that had misled it for 250 years.[47]

President Harry Truman was so baffled by McCarthyism that he too began to search through history and philosophy to understand what seemed to him a monumental onslaught of political insanity.

He commissioned an aide to produce a study that traced "hysteria and witch-hunting" in American history from the Salem witch trials to the Alien and Sedition Act, the anti-Masonic movement (Truman was a Mason), the Know-Nothings, the Ku Klux Klan, the Palmer Raids, Huey Long, and Father Coughlin, and finally to contemporary witch-hunting anticommunism.

The study concluded that there was a permanent undercurrent of "hate and intolerance" in America, that this periodically produced outbursts of intolerance against new victims of popular hysteria. Truman thought that the similarities between these earlier outbursts of intolerance and the current wave of McCarthyism were so evident that they discredited the new red scare by exposing it as nothing more than one of these recurrent bouts of irrationality. Truman was reassured that after each of these earlier episodes, "the common sense of the American people soon began to tire of the alarms" as they had "more serious things to think about."[48] After McCarthy's Wheeling speech, Truman pressed this study of witch-hunting on Sam Rayburn, the Voice of America, the Democratic National Committee, and congressmen, and sent it to liberal organizations across the country.[49]

It was not just President Truman who saw McCarthyism as an outbreak of dangerous political insanity. Many liberals found in German social scientist Theodore Adorno's 1950 *Authoritarian Personality* a persuasive explanation of McCarthyism. Adorno saw right-wing behavior in general and anti-Semitism in particular as the result of fascist tendencies (authoritarianism) in the democratic masses. Liberal interest in theories that analyzed countersubversive anticommunism as a psychological disorder also led readers to Harold Lasswell's *Personal Insecurity and World Politics*, which had been out of print 14 years.

The explanation of McCarthyism that gained the greatest currency among liberal intellectuals emerged from a Columbia faculty seminar on McCarthyism in 1954. Historian Richard Hofstadter claimed that McCarthyism was a projection onto society of the fears and anxieties of "pseudo-conservatives," a term he borrowed from Theodore Adorno. Hofstadter saw McCarthyism as "status politics," as opposed to "interest politics" that battled for shares of the national wealth. "Political life," wrote Hofstadter, "is not simply an arena in which the conflicting interests of various social groups in concrete material gains are fought out; it is also an arena into which status aspirations and frustrations are, as the psychologists would say, projected. It is at this point that the issues of politics, or the pretended issues of politics, become interwoven with and dependent upon the personal problems of individuals. We have, at all times, two kinds of processes going on in inextricable connection with each other: *interest politics*, the clash of material aims and needs among various groups and blocs; and *status politics*, the clash of various projective rationalizations arising from status aspirations and other personal motives."[50]

Hofstadter and social scientist Daniel Bell, editor of the collection of essays that emerged from the seminar, saw the internal security issue as the struggle of the "new, prosperity-created 'status groups' which, in their drive for recognition and respectability, have sought to impose older conformities on the American body politic." Bell was willing to concede that there was *some* "rational" basis for the Communist issue: the surprise attack in Korea, an emotional reaction against Chinese and Russian Communists, Whittaker Chambers's disclosures "of the infiltration of Communists into high posts in government and the existence of espionage rings, [which] produced a tremendous shock in a nation which hitherto had been unaware of such machinations." Nevertheless, he agreed with Hofstadter that the public's worries about communism were an irrational fear of an imaginary threat.[51]

The Adorno-Hofstadter-Bell theory that McCarthyism and popular anticommunism were fundamentally irrational had serious consequences, immediate and long-lasting. Once liberal intellectuals, liberal anticommunists included, had dismissed the public's ideas about communism as illusions, they could stop trying to understand them, and so the real history of popular anticommunism in America went unstudied. Had they based their ideas about anticommunism on historical evidence rather than off-the-shelf social science, they would have discovered that the public's anticommunism was, as much as the liberals', based on real knowledge of what communism was and what it was doing in the United States and abroad. They would have learned that extremist countersubversion like McCarthy's had long been present in America as a perversion of countersubversive anticommunism, that it had inherited a tradition of nonsense woven into a seemingly persuasive doctrine by generations of anticommunist conspiracy theorists, and that it was this literature, not psychological demons, that had swept over McCarthy's untutored and unresisting intellect like a tidal wave over a sand castle.

There were some external similarities between McCarthyism and earlier outbreaks of intolerance, but it could not be explained by resemblances to unrelated phenomena like the nineteenth-century anti-Masonic movement. McCarthyism was simply an adaptation to the cold war of the countersubversive anticommunist conspiracy theories that had been a fixture of American politics since 1919. McCarthyism was a particularly malignant form of a habitual intellectual error of countersubversive anticommunists which had little to do with the state of the economy or the relative fortunes of "status groups."

When a diverse democracy like America debates its fundamental values, it is unlikely that the proceedings will follow Robert's Rules of Order. The public will focus on personalities and will interpret issues in symbolic form. This gave the mudslinging style of countersubversives like McCarthy a powerful rhetorical advantage over liberals' realistic assessments of communism. In popular politics famous and powerful figures become symbols of political ideas. McCarthyites demonized Alger Hiss, Owen Lattimore, and even General Marshall—for the same reason the left had demonized Martin Dies, Father Coughlin, J. Edgar Hoover, and Joseph McCarthy—as shorthand for ideas they hated. Among both countersubversives and radicals there were conspiracy theories that aided such demonization, and in a mass democracy, negative campaigning works.

In a paradoxical sense, what was irrational about conspiracy-minded countersubversion was its *excess* of rationality. McCarthy insisted that political events revealed a rational pattern to those initiated into the mysteries of the conspiracy that was invisible to the casual observer. But when liberals dismissed McCarthyism and popular anticommunism as an irrational projection of social anxieties, they were dangerously close to denying the public the right to debate the great issues of the day, a debate that would inevitably lead to errors (like McCarthyism) as well as to insight. It was surely the insight the American public developed during the forties and fifties into the nature of communism's threat to freedom everywhere that explains the nation's amazing willingness to endure half a century of sacrifice to contain and defeat it. It was a sustained commitment to principle that no theorist of popular democracy could have imagined or expected.

The savagery of the McCarthyite attacks increased the desperation of anticommunist liberals. The Americans for Democratic Action, which had been founded to fight communism, bore the brunt of the attacks. Late in 1949 countersubversives John T. Flynn, Westbrook Pegler, and Homer Capehart charged that the ADA was not sincerely opposed to communism. Capehart raved that the ADA was involved in "an international conspiracy to socialize America." Throughout 1950 countersubversives used membership in the "Communist-infiltrated" ADA to red-smear Democratic candidates. The ADA replied that McCarthyites were aiding communism by opposing the sorts of programs that could halt its spread.[52]

In 1952 the ADA went on the offensive against McCarthy, calling for his expulsion from the Senate, and sponsoring campus lecture tours of anti-McCarthy speakers. It obtained and published a suppressed report by the Senate Subcommittee on Privileges and Elections on McCarthy's finances and challenged him to sue for libel. In a debate with McCarthy's chief counsel, Roy Cohn, the ADA's Joseph Rauh called McCarthy's investigation of espionage at the Signal Corps laboratories at Fort Monmouth, New Jersey, a hoax, and in June 1954 there was an ADA-sponsored forum on "The People vs. McCarthy" at New York's Hunter College.[53]

Attacking McCarthy gave liberal anticommunists in the Congress for Cultural Freedom a chance to refute charges that their anticommunism was simply American nationalism (or imperialism). But although almost all in the CCF had begun left of center in the political spectrum, some were already moving toward the right. The strain of McCarthyism hastened this split, when opposition to McCarthy became a test of good faith within the CCF. Mary McCarthy argued that a refusal to oppose McCarthy constituted a new *"trahison des clercs"* by "anti-anti-McCarthyites" in the CCF like James Burnham and George Schuyler who defended McCarthy against his critics.[54]

The CCF's first journal, *Preuves* (the title referred to its "proofs" of Soviet violations of human rights), was "Altanticist, pro-NATO and pro-American," but it emphatically tried to demonstrate that it did not approve of the faults of American society such as McCarthyism. *Preuves* was, of course, strongly anti-Stalinist and anti-Soviet. It endorsed Hannah Arendt's theory of totalitarianism, supported Soviet bloc dissidents and defectors like Czeslaw Milosz, and published essays by emigré Russians on the glories of pre-Soviet Russia. It demanded that intellectuals commit themselves to freedom or totalitarianism. While political neutrality between the superpower blocs was unacceptable, moral neutrality between "free thought and servitude" was not. That was a "lie against which we have to struggle."[55]

It was this general consensus within the CCF against McCarthyism that, in October 1953, made the first issue of the Congress's *Encounter* such a scandal. The magazine was edited in England by the American Irving Kristol and the English poet Stephen Spender. Their manifesto in that first issue, "The Battle for the Mind of Europe," promised that *Encounter* would welcome a diversity of opinions unified by "love of liberty" and "respect for culture." The free play of the intellect in a free culture would be the best argument against the stifling pressures of Communist rule.[56]

But a magazine cannot exist on pious intentions. It also needs the spice of controversy, and Kristol was a seasoned polemicist. In 1952, when he was still an assistant editor of *Commentary*, Kristol wrote an essay on McCarthyism for that magazine in which he blamed liberals for McCarthyism because they did not lead the attack on communism themselves during the thirties: "Did not the major segment of American liberalism, as a result of joining hands with the Communists in a popular front, go on record as denying the existence of Soviet concentration camps? Did it not give its blessing to the 'liquidation' of the kulaks? Did it not apologize for the mass purges of 1936–38, and did it not solemnly approve the grotesque trials of the old Bolsheviks? Did it not applaud the massacre of the non-Communist left, by the GPU during the Spanish Civil War?" Liberals had themselves to blame for McCarthy's rise: "For there is one thing that the American people know about Senator McCarthy: he, like them, is unequivocally anti-Communist. About the spokesmen for American liberalism, they feel they know no such thing. And with some justification."[57]

Kristol was looking for something to disturb the smug assurance of liberals who felt that theirs were the last words to be uttered on the subjects of communism, anticommunism, and McCarthyism. He found it in Leslie Fiedler's notorious "Postscript to the Rosenberg Case" essay, which Kristol ran in the first issue, four months after the execution of the atom spies.

While Fiedler condemned the death penalty and the execution in passing, he deliberately provoked liberals who balanced their opposition to communism against their compassion for the victims of McCarthyism. He denounced the Rosenbergs for pretending to be "innocent, patriotic, baseball loving Americans martyred by racists" when they had willingly let themselves be turned into symbols to advance the cause of the dehumanizing ideology of communism. Many of his readers had already moved to the position that all victims of McCarthyism must perforce be innocent victims, and Fiedler's insistence on the

Rosenbergs' moral as well as legal guilt was an outrage to these new pieties.[58]

The CCF's most important contribution to the intellectual debate over communism, the "end of ideology" theory, was developed at least in part as a way for liberal anticommunists to distance themselves from Mc-Carthyism. By September 1951 *Preuves* was working out a distinction between "dogmatic ideologies" like fascism and communism, and "living ideas," like liberalism. The West was moving, *Preuves* argued, into a "new age of reform without dogmas or totalist world views." This new age demanded the rejection of both communism *and* the anticommunism of the right, such as McCarthyism (or, for that matter, religious anticommunism). Liberal democracy was a neutral arena within which free citizens could work out their political differences and create economic arrangements that would provide economic security and political liberty in a free society. Edward Shils published an article in *Encounter* that used "The End of Ideology?" as a title, and Raymond Aron used it as a chapter title in *L'Opium des Intellectuels*, both of them placing a question mark after the phrase. The book by Daniel Bell that made it famous dropped the question mark from the title. "What Shils and Aron called 'the end of ideology,' " writes an historian of the Congress, "was in a sense the basis of almost all the Congress's activity. . . . Its mood was decidedly optimistic, emphasizing less 'the God that failed' than the liberation from dogma."[59] The Congress would condemn all ideology—right and left—while celebrating the vigor of free culture.

But there were some in the CCF, like Sidney Hook's American Committee for Cultural Freedom, who took issue with *Encounter*'s "end of ideology" for "being willing to compromise with an atmosphere far too tolerant of totalitarianism and hostile to America's role in the preservation of a free world."[60] No one was more devoted to the ideal of a free society than Hook, but he also believed that the free society depended on a theory of freedom, an ideology, as it were. Unless a free society had a clear understanding of how freedom worked, it was vulnerable to the twin threats of anarchy and totalitarianism. Hook was also coming to believe that the free world's survival depended on American military strength and moral resolve, and that these rested on citizens' loyalty to their society and their leaders. Hook was not alone in wondering whether the "end of ideology" would be enough to steel the free world's resolve for the long struggle ahead. And so, while conservative anticommunists continued the political philosopher's traditional task of working out a theory of the political and economic underpinnings of freedom, liberals decided that an ironic, skeptical attitude toward ideas was the mark of the free mind. Conservative and liberal anticommunists day by day were discovering that they had less in common than they had thought. Many Americans, even those devoted to cultural freedom, were beginning to regard any criticism of the United States from the allies as disloyalty. The end of ideology doctrine was also vulnerable to the criticism raised against the Hofstadter-Bell dismissal of popular anticommunism as irrational status politics. Whether liberals were analyzing popular anticommunism as irrationality or ideology, they were saying that legitimate anticommunism was something that could be properly understood only by the elite; the public should be encouraged to divert itself in other directions.

Liberals were not the only anticommunists who were beginning to worry about McCarthyism. The American Legion's *Firing Line* protested that nationally syndicated columnist Westbrook Pegler—whose anticommunism was becoming increasingly anti-Semitic—was red-baiting Irving Brown, the AFL's very effective European representative. McCarthy's success was encouraging anti-Semitic anticommunists to be bolder in equating Jews and communism. Isaac Don Levine suspended *Plain Talk* in May 1950 because the anti-Semitism of the magazine's readers was too much for him to bear. The anticommunist American Jewish Committee lashed out at Benjamin Schultz's American Jewish League Against Communism for promulgating conspiracy theories almost indistinguishable from those of anti-Semites when it questioned the patriotism of General Marshall and Admiral Nimitz.

Eugene Lyons, who had founded the American Committee for the Liberation of the Peoples of Russia, stepped down because of sniping by anti-Semitic Russian nationalists. Isaac Don Levine quit the group for the same reason. Arnold Forster of the ADL worried that while McCarthy himself might not be anti-Semitic, "there was scarcely a professional American anti-Semite who had not publicly endorsed the Senator."[61]

Republicans captured control of the Senate in the November 1952 elections, and McCarthy became chairman of the hitherto obscure Investigations Subcommittee of the Committee on Government Operations. He had shrewdly spotted that this subcommittee would give him the power to harass all agencies of the federal bureaucracy. On January 2, 1953, when McCarthy hired Roy M. Cohn as the chief counsel of his new committee, the saga of McCarthyism entered its final chapter.

The twenty-five-year-old lawyer, a veteran of the Smith Act, Rosenberg, and Lattimore cases, was introduced to McCarthy by George Sokolsky. Cohn was undeniably brilliant, and was determined to prove by his own anticommunist exploits that not all Jews were Communists. Cohn hired G. David Schine, a twenty-six-year-old Harvard graduate and hotel chain heir, to serve as his assistant.

Before 1953, McCarthy had been savaging a Democratic administration. Now it was the Republicans' turn. Armed with information from John T. Flynn, McCarthy attacked Eisenhower's nomination of Harvard President James B. Conant as high commissioner for Germany. He accused Conant of protecting Harlow Shipley, the fellow-traveling Harvard astronomer, and of backing the Morgenthau Plan of deindustrializing Germany, which many anticommunists saw as an invitation to Soviet aggression. He relented on Conant as a peace gesture to Eisenhower, but fought against Charles E. Bohlen's confirmation as ambassador to the Soviet Union because Bohlen had served on the American delegation at Yalta. A former FBI agent, Scott McLeod, serving as Assistant Secretary of State for Security Affairs, was feeding McCarthy information on Bohlen and other suspect nominees.

Eisenhower tried to maintain polite relations with McCarthy, but inwardly was seething. He told a friend that "nothing would please him [McCarthy] more than to get the publicity that would be generated by public repudiation by the President." He told his friend Emmett John Hughes, "I just will not—I refuse—to get into the gutter with that guy."[62]

Eisenhower's political instincts were impeccable. McCarthy's power came from the widespread perception that the executive branch of government—Democratic or Republican—was engaged in a whitewash of Communist subversion. Had Eisenhower publicly attacked McCarthy, he would have placed himself in the same light as Truman, an obstacle to presumably sincere efforts to rid the government of Communists. Let McCarthy keep on blasting away and eventually he might shoot himself. And indeed, right-wing anticommunist newspapers were beginning to complain that "there are times when Joe McCarthy makes it tough to play on his team."[63]

McCarthy set his sights next on the Voice of America. This was the successor agency of the wartime Office of War Information, long considered a den of leftists by the right. Meanwhile other Congressional McCarthyites roamed the land. While William Jenner's Senate Internal Security Subcommittee probed the United Nations and hunted Communists on the college campuses, Harold Velde's HUAC harried red actors and pink clergymen.

McCarthy was now accusing State Department officials of free love, atheism, even of staying away from church on Sundays. Anyone who criticized McCarthy risked being dragged before television cameras to be raked over the coals for schoolboy political associations. James Wechsler of the *New York Post* was examined for his Young Communist League membership in 1937 as a Columbia University student. McCarthy accused the staunchly anti-Communist liberal of having made a "phony" break with communism.[64] Then McCarthy went after European shipping companies that were handling trade with Red China. He negotiated with Greek owners to ban such shipments to Communist countries.

McCarthy began browbeating State Department officials over supposedly Communist-inclined books in the two hundred overseas Information Center libraries. He claimed that they had stocked thirty thousand volumes by 418 Communist writers (he was counting John Dewey, Arthur Schlesinger, Jr., Robert M. Hutchins, even Foster Rhea Dulles, John Foster's cousin, a diplomatic historian). The Department panicked and banned works by "Communists, fellow travelers, et cetera" from the libraries. McCarthy's enemies called it a Nazi book burning. Dulles said only eleven books were actually burned; probably there were many more.[65]

Cohn and Schine set out for Europe in April 1953 to see for themselves how well the American Information Center libraries had cleaned their shelves of suspect literature. Everywhere they went, in Bonn, Berlin, Munich, Vienna, Belgrade, Athens, Rome, and Paris, the local press headlined the bizarre antics of the pair.[66] The anti-American press said that McCarthy revealed the sinister nature of American imperialism, the fascist face of America. At the Dartmouth graduation exercises, Eisenhower denounced book burning in an oblique reference to Cohn and Schine.

Almost as soon as he entered office, President Eisenhower began to defang, domesticate, and finally eliminate the countersubversives who had been terrorizing Washington since 1950, even though he had pledged to carry out the countersubversive agenda. The 1952 Republican platform promised to "repudiate all commitments contained in secret understandings such as those of Yalta which aid Communist enslavements."[67] Once in power, however, the administration realized that any such "repudiation" of Yalta and Potsdam—neither of which actually contained any "secret" codicils—would destabilize the arrangements, like the occupation of Germany, that depended on them. The administration mollified anticommunists by proposing simply to condemn the Soviet Union for "perverting" those treaties by using them to enslave Eastern Europe. When Stalin died on March 5, 1953, just two months after Eisenhower took office, the whole matter of repudiating Yalta was shelved.[68] On April 16 the President responded to the Soviet "Peace Offensive" with a speech on "The Chance for Peace." On July 27 a truce was finally signed between the United Nations and North Korea, and so Eisenhower could begin his presidency during a palpable relaxation of cold war tensions.

During the international crises of Eisenhower's first year in office—the revolt in East Germany (June 17) and the start of American financial aid to the French in Vietnam—his winning personality and adroit political skills gave the country confidence that the international situation, if not quite getting better, was at least not getting worse. The biggest news event of Eisenhower's first year was not a cold war emergency but the spectacular June 2 coronation of Queen Elizabeth II.

Eisenhower moved quickly to defuse the Communists-in-government issue by outlining a new and more stringent loyalty program. The President mollified J. Edgar Hoover by assuring him that the FBI would have full control of internal security matters. Eisenhower also pacified the countersubversives, though at considerable cost to his reputation and sense of self-respect, when he refrained from directly criticizing McCarthy after McCarthy defamed Eisenhower's mentor and hero, General Marshall. The President had also allowed Attorney General Herbert Brownell to attack former President Truman for promoting Assistant Secretary Harry Dexter White to the World Monetary Fund while White was the subject of an FBI investigation as a Soviet spy. In sum, these actions deprived countersubversives of any reasons to continue to believe that Washington was still soft on communism. As a result, the public was losing interest in the Communist issue even as Joseph McCarthy was beginning his outrageous tenure as chairman of his own investigating committee.

A cold-blooded assessment might conclude that nothing Eisenhower did during his first year was more effective in laying the Communist issue to rest than execution of the Rosenbergs on June 19, 1953. Their significance as symbols of the cold war had been stressed by Judge Irving R. Kaufman in pronouncing sentence on them. "This country is engaged in a life and death struggle with a completely different system," he told them. "This struggle is not only manifested externally between these two forces but this case indicates quite clearly that it also involved the employment by the enemy of secret as well as overt outspoken forces among our own people. All our great democratic institutions are, therefore, directly involved in this great conflict." The Rosenbergs' crime was "worse than murder" because "conduct in putting into the hands of the Russians the A-bomb, years before our best scientists predicted Russia would perfect the bomb, had already caused, in my opinion, the Communist aggression in Korea, with the resultant casualties exceeding 50,000 and who knows but that millions more innocent people may pay the price of your treason."[69]

The situation called for a demonstration of strength, even brutality, to convince the public that the government shared its concerns and was determined to guard the nation's safety.[70] Clemency would have revived the countersubversive hysteria. The Rosenbergs' execution ritualistically bonded the country and government together in a pact of blood against the Communist foe. Eisenhower's refusal to grant clemency was meant to put the Soviets and potential spies on alert that espionage would be dealt with mercilessly in the future, but just as surely it sent a message to countersubversives that their services were no longer needed.

On June 18, 1953, McCarthy made the first of the blunders that would lead to his downfall. He hired the Dies Committee's venerable countersubversive, J. B. Matthews, as executive director of his Committee. Just before he joined the staff, Matthews's "Reds and Our Churches" appeared in the July issue of *American Mercury*. Its soon-to-be-famous lead paragraph began, "The largest single group supporting the Communist apparatus in the United States today is composed of Protestant clergymen."[71]

vestigation all meant the same thing. McCarthy was trying to give his speeches more punch by adding bogus specificity to the sweeping accusation countersubversives felt to be true in principle—that the State Department was dominated by Communists and traitors. At Wheeling, however, McCarthy violated precaution all previous countersubversive politicians had observed: Keep accusations vague to make them impossible to disprove.[11]

Before McCarthy, "names" had been "named" only in the subliterature of countersubversion written by characters like Elizabeth Dilling, and they were so far outside the pale that it had hardly been worth the trouble, though it would have been easy, to refute them. McCarthy's Wheeling speech belonged to the tradition of Elizabeth Dilling's *Red Network*, Richard Whitney's *Reds in America*, Blair Coan's *Red Web*, even Nesta Webster's *World Revolution*, but McCarthy was a United States senator and senators were presumed to have some facts to back up what they said.

McCarthy thought he was simply making a familiar story exciting for the Republican ladies of Wheeling by taking this well-worn countersubversive literature, loading it with numbers and names, specifying that the traitors were Communists (not merely fellow travelers) and claiming that he had proof. But he was actually putting himself on a treadmill where he—and later his defenders—had to keep providing new and more startling charges to save face each time the last outrageous charge was disproved. If Harry Truman's unfortunate "red herring" tag line had made the Hiss case the test of the Truman administration's anticommunist credentials, the Wheeling speech had made McCarthy's list of names the test of the countersubversive case—and by extension, the test of all anticommunism. And McCarthy's charges were so far from the truth that while it might take time to demonstrate that he was a fraud, the final outcome, to those who knew the facts, was never in doubt. Isaac Don Levine recalled that the moment he had heard what McCarthy had done in Wheeling, he had known the anticommunist cause was doomed.

But his names and numbers made McCarthy the most feared man in America. It was unbelievable to vast numbers of Americans that a United States senator could simply be lying, and so McCarthy's audac-

ready come to the same conclusion. His American China Policy Association, which included such notables as Clare Boothe Luce and the
right-wing New Hampshire newspaper publisher William Loeb, was
leading the attack against the China hands. Kohlberg also ran a Committee for Constitutional Government that distributed hundreds of
thousands of copies of pro-Chiang material by anticommunists like
Freda Utley and John T. Flynn. McCarthy seemed mesmerized by the
intricate detail of the China Lobby theories.[9]

McCarthy's Wheeling speech was assembled by *Washington Times-
Herald* reporters Ed Nellor and George Waters and *Chicago Tribune*
writer Willard Edwards out of HUAC reports, the press reports on the
Amerasia case, Edwards's exposés of John Stewart Service's career, a
Nixon speech on Alger Hiss, and FBI reports to the Senate Judiciary
Committee. The names McCarthy mentioned were standard in right-
wing conspiracy theories, but he had no "list of names that were made
known to the Secretary of State and who nevertheless are still working
and shaping policy in the State Department." There was no list of 205
names, nor of 57, nor of any number. The figure 205 was the result of
slightly faulty arithmetic. Secretary of State James Byrnes had written
Congressman Adolph Sabath that 285 security risks had been located
in the Department, and 79 had been fired. After subtraction, the remainder, 206, mistakenly became McCarthy's 205 in the speech.[10]

Since McCarthy had no list of 205 names, he thought he was safer
with the "57" when he put the speech in the *Congressional Record*. That
supposedly was the number of "card-carrying members or certainly loyal
to the Communist Party" in the State Department, which he claimed
was "thoroughly infested with Communists." This came from a report
by Robert E. Lee, the chief of staff of the House Appropriations Committee, that Willard Edwards had given McCarthy. Lee had complained
that 57 State Department employees out of an original list of 108 suspects he had reported to State were still on the government payroll in
March 1948. But of these 57, 35 had already been cleared by the FBI.

In any case, McCarthy did not have the actual names of anyone since
in the loyalty reports they were identified only by case numbers, and
even their original accusers had simply named them as suspects, not
known Communists or even fellow travelers. McCarthy did not have
the vaguest notion what he was talking about. To him one list was much
the same as another—security risks, Communists, and subjects of in-

McCarthy's enemies pounced. The "Clearing House," an anti-McCarthy task force of liberal Democrats operating out of the Democratic National Headquarters, quickly forwarded the article to the Democrats on McCarthy's Committee, who demanded that Matthews be fired. The administration, sensing that McCarthy was finally vulnerable, sent the article to leading churchmen for their predictable reaction. Deputy Attorney General William Rogers, speech writer Emmett John Hughes, and Vice President Nixon raced to put out a statement for Eisenhower to release just before Matthews resigned on July 9. The President attacked Matthews for "destroying trust in the leaders of Protestantism, Catholicism or Judaism by wholesale condemnation." Eisenhower said such attacks "weaken the greatest American bulwark against atheistic materialism and Communism."

Republican and Democratic leaders vied with each other in denouncing McCarthy. Senator Mike Monroney was attacking McCarthy on the Senate floor, deriding Cohn and Schine as Keystone Kops. McCarthy blustered that Monroney's was "the most flagrant, the most shameful example of anti-Semitism" he had ever seen. The President's brother Arthur called McCarthy "the most dangerous menace to America" and said "when I think of McCarthy, I automatically think of Hitler." With hardly concealed anti-Catholicism, he called McCarthy "a throwback to the Spanish Inquisition."[72]

McCarthy was now demanding to be allowed to investigate the CIA, armed with leaked information, according to one staff investigator, from former director Walter Bedell Smith. Eisenhower, backed by the National Security Council, refused to permit the investigation.

Blocked from looking into the CIA, McCarthy announced he was going to investigate the Army, and that he was going to demand that Army Secretary Robert T. Stevens appear before the Committee. McCarthy's expert witness, Louis Budenz, had claimed that the only explanation for a supposedly Communist-slanted Army textbook on Russia was a Communist concealed somewhere in the military. In addition, Roy Cohn thought he had caught the Army quashing a probe of espionage at the Signal Corps Center at Fort Monmouth, New Jersey. The Army hurried to conduct its own investigation and on November 13, Stevens announced that there were no spies, no cases of subversion. McCarthy exploded, and during his hearings on the Fort Monmouth situation, brutalized the Army witnesses.[73]

On January 21 William Rogers, Presidential Assistant Sherman Adams, and Senator Henry Cabot Lodge met in Attorney General Brownell's office, where they listened "in amazement" as the Army's Counsel John Adams described the pressure McCarthy and Roy Cohn had been putting on the Army to get preferential treatment for G. David Schine, who had been drafted in November and sent to Fort Dix in New Jersey for basic training. These were shrewd politicians, and they immediately recognized that the material on Schine, properly handled, could be explosive. They told Adams to keep a log of communications about Schine between the Army and the McCarthy staff, and to begin to leak it when it would do the most good. With McCarthy attacking generals as ferociously as he had Truman's officials, Eisenhower himself took command of the administration's campaign against McCarthy at the end of February 1954.[74]

McCarthy's attacks on the administration were forcing Republicans to choose between McCarthy and Eisenhower. Republican Senator Ralph Flanders of Vermont made a landmark speech against McCarthy, deriding investigations of obscure security risks like an Army dentist: "Whole countries are now being taken over by the Communists . . . the world seems to be mobilizing for the great battle of Armageddon. Now is a crisis in the age-long warfare between God and the Devil for the souls of men." In this crisis, said Flanders, McCarthy "dons his war paint. He goes into his war dance. He emits war whoops. He goes forth to battle and proudly returns with the scalp of a pink dentist."[75]

On March 9, 1954, CBS broadcast its classic Edward R. Murrow *See It Now* documentary on McCarthy. It offered a devastating view of McCarthy's recklessness and cruelty as he smeared Reed Harris of the Voice of America and Adlai Stevenson. Murrow's wrap-up was a call to arms: "This is no time for men who oppose Senator McCarthy's methods to keep silent. . . . We proclaim ourselves, as indeed we are, the defenders of freedom—what's left of it—but we cannot defend freedom by deserting it at home. The actions of the junior Senator from Wisconsin have caused alarm and dismay among our allies abroad and given considerable comfort to our enemies. . . . He didn't create this situation of fear. He merely exploited it, and rather successfully. . . . Good night— and good luck."[76]

Public opinion was turning against McCarthy. On March 22, *Time* ran a brutally critical cover story on Cohn and Schine. Bishop Bernard

J. Sheil of Chicago exposed the cracks in McCarthy's Catholic support, attacking him as a "man on horseback" who was a threat to democracy. "Anticommunism is a serious business," he said, and not "a game to be played so publicity-mad politicos can build fame for themselves."[77]

On May 11, with the opposition to McCarthy growing bolder by the day, the administration released the devastating chronology of Cohn's pressure on the army to get favors for Schine. The implication was that McCarthy had brought his charges that the Army had failed to investigate espionage in order to force the Army to give Schine special treatment. Don Whitehead, a reporter with excellent sources in the military and the intelligence establishment, wrote that "a good many people, including some of McCarthy's colleagues in the Senate, think the inquiry could be the crossroads of the McCarthy career." Ominously for McCarthy, of the large majority of the public who had an opinion on the hearings, 46 percent began by believing Army Secretary Stevens, only 23 percent siding with McCarthy.[78]

The hearings began on April 22 to review twenty-nine charges by the Army that McCarthy and Cohn had tried to win favors for David Schine by using the Fort Monmouth probe to force the Army to release Schine from the normal rigors of military discipline. The counsel for the Army, Boston lawyer Joseph N. Welch, skillfully turned side issues into major points of contention whenever they cast McCarthy in an unfavorable light. There was a picture of Schine and Army Secretary Stevens that turned out to have had two other men cropped to emphasize the affable relationship between the private and the Army secretary. Welch proclaimed this a "doctored photo." Even J. Edgar Hoover abandoned McCarthy. There was a letter McCarthy had introduced as evidence, supposedly from Hoover, that the Army had not acted on FBI warnings of espionage at Fort Monmouth. Hoover had written the memo quoted in the letter, but Hoover deposed that he had not actually written the letter itself. Without any further explanation, the clear implication was that McCarthy had made use of a forgery. In all of these instances Welch created the impression that he was merely scratching the surface of McCarthy's dishonesty.

The hearings seethed with hostility between McCarthy and Welch. Welch demanded to know if a "pixie" had produced the cropped photo. McCarthy requested that Welch favor them with his definition of a "pixie." His smile loaded with innuendo, Welch informed him that "a pixie is a close relative of a fairy . . . have I enlightened you?" Few failed to catch the reference to rumors spread by Las Vegas publisher Hank Greenspun and columnist Drew Pearson that McCarthy was a homosexual, or to the general assumption that Cohn and Schine were.

Comedians began to mimic and ridicule McCarthy's whining and petulant "point of order" interruptions of the proceedings. The Herblock-Murrow caricature of McCarthy was now what people saw. When he objected to the Army's taping his calls as "indecent and dishonest," the audience laughed at him. McCarthy's bullying style, his irritating voice, his heavy beard, all combined to create an overwhelming sense of sinister malice. Senator J. William Fulbright called the hearings "a painful thing and it sickens me, but it is essential to wake up the American people to the truth about the man."[79]

McCarthy would now learn what it was like to be red-smeared. One of his opponents stood in the Senate and said that McCarthy was doing the Communists' work for them. "One of the characteristic elements of Communist and fascist tyranny is at hand, as citizens are set to spy upon each other. Established and responsible government is besmirched. Religion is set against religion, race against race. Churches and parties are split asunder. All is division and confusion. Were the junior Senator from Wisconsin in the pay of the Communists, he could not have done a better job for them." McCarthy was being treated to a full dose of McCarthyism himself.

Finally, goaded beyond endurance, exhausted, deep in alcoholic incoherence, McCarthy gave way under the strain. He believed he had an agreement with Welch. Welch was not to bring up the issue of homosexuality between Cohn and Schine—generally presumed to be the motive for Cohn's well-nigh obsessive efforts to spring Schine loose from basic training—if McCarthy did not bring up the issue of the membership of Welch's young associate Fred Fisher, in a Communist front, the National Lawyers Guild. McCarthy believed Welch had broken the agreement with the quip about the "pixie." McCarthy now accused Welch of harboring a Communist on his staff.

"Until this moment," Welch replied, "I think I never really gauged your cruelty or your recklessness. . . . Let us not assassinate this lad further, Senator. You have done enough. Have you no sense of decency, sir, at long last? Have you left no sense of deceny?" McCarthy's friends were "sickened" by the mortal thrust. Headlines across the country blared, "Have you no sense of decency?" Newsreels made the phrase the climax of the hearing, and a kind of epitaph for McCarthy. In full view of the television audience, Senator Stuart Symington told him, "The American people have had a look at you for six weeks. You are not fooling anyone."[80]

The hearings left McCarthy's Committee a shambles. McCarthy's colleagues were furious with Cohn, and they forced him to resign despite McCarthy's objections. A resolution of Senator Ralph Flanders to censure McCarthy was now supported by a bloc of anti-McCarthy senators made bolder by the Army hearings.

The committee to investigate the censure resolution, headed by Arthur V. Watkins of Utah, was made up of solid establishment conservatives from areas where McCarthy's support was weakest. But even though the Watkins Committee was stacked against McCarthy, if he had been willing he probably could have negotiated a minimal punishment, so reluctant was the Senate to discipline one of its own. While the committee deliberated, however, he became ever more defiant and alcoholic.

On September 27 the Watkins Committee recommended unanimously that McCarthy be censured for mistreating his colleagues and General Ralph Zwicker during the Fort Monmouth Hearings. The resolution came up for debate shortly after the 1954 election, whose returns revealed that the public had begun to turn against McCarthyism. His support had been whittled down to the Hearst press, the *Chicago Tribune*, and Catholic veterans groups. On December 2, 1954, the Senate voted 67 to 22 to condemn McCarthy. One of the last of the faithful, Senator William Jenner of Indiana, raged that McCarthy's censure had been "initiated by the Communist conspiracy."[81]

McCarthy's political power, and soon his career, was at end, and with them the force of American countersubversion. But McCarthyism lingered on for a short time in the original sense of reckless charges of disloyalty, and for the long term as a stereotype to discredit even responsible anticommunism.[82]

Between 1950 and 1954, Joseph McCarthy—abetted by his supporters and, in no small measure, by anticommunism's enemies—had turned himself into a symbol of anticommunism. When McCarthy went down, so, to a great extent, did anticommunism. Some anticommunists deserved their fate. Unable to pass up a ride to publicity and power, they had not been able to resist clutching McCarthy's coattails, and they could not let go as he plunged to disaster and disgrace.

Many—in the end most—anticommunists recognized McCarthy for what he was. They fought McCarthy and McCarthyism because they knew McCarthy was wrong and was dangerous, and because they saw that his lies would destroy the truth of what they had to say about communism. But to no avail. In the popular mind, anticommunism and McCarthyism were one and the same, and American anticommunism would never recover from the effects of that fatal embrace.

If anticommunism for a while in the late forties had succeeded in silencing the radical left, the backlash against McCarthyism had silenced anticommunism. After McCarthy, domestic Communists and their allies might be discussed gingerly, but only in general terms. No longer were names to be named.

After McCarthy, many liberals came to reject not just McCarthyism, but all conservative, popular forms of anticommunism as a threat to freedom. McCarthyism irrevocably split the anticommunist movement, left from right, elite from popular. It made liberal anticommunists fearful of grassroots anticommunism, afraid to involve the public in fundamental debates of great public issues. After McCarthy, President Eisenhower could still ritually call America's stand against communism a "great moral crusade," and could predict that communism could not prevail against the spiritual and military might of the United States, but he would also warn the public not to get involved itself, cautioning that there were at the most 25,000 members of the Communist Party, and "our great defense against those people is the FBI. The FBI has been doing for years in this line of work a magnificent job." He and other national leaders would discourage Americans from expressing their anticommunism, for fear of reawakening McCarthyism. With the President himself muting the urgency of the moral crusade against communism, the anticommunist movement was living on borrowed time. And deprived of the compass of a constantly reexamined and reinvigorated anticommunism, American foreign policy was at risk of losing its way in a world that was increasingly complex, in which communism's assault on freedom was still a fundamental fact of life around the globe.[83]

Chapter 10

DANGER ON THE RIGHT

The cadre of the John Birch Society seems to be formed primarily of wealthy business men, retired military officers and little old ladies in tennis shoes . . . bound together by an obsessive fear of "communism," a word which they define to include any ideas differing from their own.
—Report by the California Attorney General's Office, 1961[1]

Anticommunism survived McCarthyism—barely. But by 1954, the urgency of the controversy over communism had subsided, and for good reason. Stalin had died in 1953. The fighting was over in Korea. Eisenhower's hard-line federal loyalty program and his refusal to grant clemency to the Rosenbergs ended the public's worries about Communist infiltration and espionage.

Communism's few remaining shreds of moral respectability were demolished in the eyes of all but a few Party hacks in 1956, when at the Twentieth Congress of the Soviet Communist Party held in Moscow from February 14 to 25, 1956, Nikita Khrushchev informed the party hierarchy that Joseph Stalin, the former living god of the Communist world, had been a mass murderer on a grander scale than Hitler. The CIA obtained a copy of Khrushchev's secret speech, and in June the full text appeared around the world. Refusing to admit that the truth of what anticommunists had been saying since the twenties had been confirmed by Khrushchev himself, the American Party protested that "the facts disclosed about the errors of Stalin are, of course, new to us."[2]

That same year the Soviets' ruthless suppression of worker unrest in Eastern Europe drove the last few idealists out of the Party. The Polish Communist regime put down riots by their workers on June 28, 1956, at a cost of more than a hundred lives. Hungarian workers, encouraged by Poland, revolted on October 23. After a few days of indecision, Khrushchev sent in Soviet troops, crushed the uprising, and installed a hard-line regime to return Hungary to Soviet orthodoxy.

The American Communist Party endorsed the Soviet invasion, and rank and file members, still trying to absorb the revelations about Stalin, left the Party in numbers that recalled the exodus after the Hitler-Stalin Pact. After 1956, despite the alarms still regularly sounded by J. Edgar Hoover, the American Communist Party for all practical purposes ceased to exist.

The Hollywood blacklist survived until 1960, when Otto Preminger announced that blacklisted Dalton Trumbo's name would appear on *Exodus* as the writer, and Kirk Douglas gave Trumbo credit for *Spartacus*. The radio blacklist, hardly any longer in effect, was smashed when John Henry Faulk won his libel case against AWARE in 1962 and put it out of business.[3]

In academia McCarthyism was rolled back in 1956 when the American Association of University Professors voted that professors could not be fired for membership in the Communist Party or for taking the Fifth Amendment. Since the beginning of the academic purge, some one hundred professors had been forced from their positions.[4]

But if McCarthyism as a system of repression did not long survive McCarthy's political collapse in 1954 (and his death in 1957), McCarthyism as a stereotype for all anticommunism proved far more enduring. That image became even more deeply embedded in American culture in the late fifties and early sixties when hysteria over anticommunist "extremism," to a great extent manufactured and manipulated by self-styled "moderates" to suit their own political purposes, led to a general agreement that any further discussion of communism would only encourage undemocratic forces whose activities were a threat to the health of American society.

While the fifties were generally days of overall decline for the grass-roots anticommunist movement, there were still areas where it remained healthy, even showed signs of growth. Though McCarthy's fall was devastating to his Catholic anticommunist supporters, who often blamed all opposition to McCarthy on anti-Catholicism, his demise did not mean the end of American Catholic anticommunism. The fact was that anticommunism had become

> intimately intertwined with many elements of Catholic life. The *Brooklyn Tablet*, still edited by Patrick Scanlan, and Catholic papers like Indiana's *The Wanderer* continued to stoke the anticommunist fires. Missionary appeals featured dramatic descriptions of communist atrocities; American missionaries combined conversions with provision of food, clothing, and medical care, building democracy while building barriers against communism as well. Marian devotions flourished during the period, especially devotion to Our Lady of Fatima, and invariably these devotions were linked to the danger from Russia.[5]

Organizations like Christian Resistance and the Cardinal Mindszenty Foundation still thrived in Catholic America.

New York's Francis Cardinal Spellman, who had publicly endorsed McCarthy, still carried on his anticommunist activities. He continued to publicize the sufferings of Catholics behind the Iron Curtain, and during the Hungarian uprising he joined the Knights of Columbus in appealing to President Eisenhower to come to the aid of the revolt. The Knights managed to block Eisenhower's invitation to Tito to visit the United States in 1957. Catholics joined "Captive Nations" organizations, and helped pass a law in 1959 that designated the last week of each July as Captive Nations Week.[6]

In effect, Cardinal Spellman carried on his own very anticommunist foreign policy during the fifties and sixties. He called on America to support the French in Vietnam, and later urged Washington to shore up the South Vietnamese government to protect the Vietnamese Church against the Viet Cong. If America did not halt communism in Indochina, "we shall risk bartering our liberties for lunacies" he alliterated, "betraying the sacred trust of our forefathers, becoming serfs and slaves to the Red ruler's godless goons."[7] Spellman had first met South Vietnamese President Ngo Dinh Diem in 1950 when Diem was studying for the priesthood at the Maryknoll Seminary in Ossining, New York, and had urged Diem to return to Vietnam to enter politics. The Navy doctor Tom Dooley, whose books aroused American Catholics against Communist atrocities in Vietnam, was another friend of Spellman's. He also toured Latin America, and mobilized American support for the right-wing regimes that protected Church interests there against leftist insurgences.[8]

Devotion to the apparition of Mary at Fatima was also part of the struggle against communism for millions of Catholics. The last survivor of the three Portuguese girls who had reported the vision in 1917 had claimed in 1936 that if Catholics received Communion on the first Saturday of five consecutive months, Russia would return to God. In 1950 a New Jersey priest organized the Blue Army of Fatima, which soon had chapters in parishes across the country and which published a magazine with a circulation of 70,000 in 1951.[9]

In 1950 American Catholics got their own Marian cult when the Virgin appeared in Necedah, Wisconsin and promised world peace if enough Catholics prayed to Mary. The popularity of these cold war Marian cults among American Catholics suggests they saw the conflict with communism as a spiritual war "in which Christ and Mary had sided with the United States to fight Satan and his Communist allies. . . . [T]he thousands of Catholics who visited Necedah and the millions who believed in Our Lady of Fatima saw the Cold War on earth as a reflection of a war in heaven." Convinced that religious faith was America's strongest weapon against communism, Catholics were enthusiastic supporters of the campaign that persuaded Congress to include "under God" in the Pledge of Allegiance.[10]

The American Legion's Americanism Commission also continued its anticommunist activities despite the McCarthy debacle. It put out a reading list on communism which it distributed in cooperation with other civic and fraternal organizations. In 1954 its recommendations included exposés of the Soviet prison camp system, descriptions of Communist persecution of religion, and tales of Soviet espionage in the United States. Among them were George Orwell's *1984*, Gabriel Almond's *Appeals of Communism*, and Louis Budenz's *Techniques of Communism*, along with studies of Soviet communism by David Dalin, Igor Kravchenko's books on Soviet espionage, and Father Walsh's *Total Empire*. The list stressed works on Soviet communism, although there were also readings on the domestic Party and Soviet espionage.[11]

The Legion's "All American Conference to Combat Communism" sponsored a national Know Your America Week each year. Since 1949 it had been hosting national meetings to discuss the Communist issue. Among the many organizations that sent delegates were the Catholic

War Veterans, the Ukrainian Congress, the National Education Association, the National Association of Evangelicals, the American Medical Association, the Elks, the Disabled American Veterans, the Lions, the Knights of Pythias, the Junior Order of American Mechanics, and the American Jewish Committee. In 1955, the sixth annual meeting in Chicago heard Carlos Romulo speak on "Communism and Asia," George Meany on "Communist Propaganda," John Caldwell on "Education for a Chaotic World," Lyle G. Phillips on "Evaluation of the Menace of Communism in Hawaii," Jesuit Walter Jaskievicz, "Are the Russian People Moving Towards Freedom?," and Oleg Zabrodsky, "How May We Assist the People Caught in the U.S.S.R. Satellite Web?"[12]

The Legion's monthly pamphlet, *Freedom's Facts Against Communism*, provided knowledgeable analysis of Communist activities in America and abroad. In 1956, the Legion analysts reviewed *The American People Want Peace* by Communist Jessica Smith, and concluded that the goal of American Communists was still to persuade Americans not to resist Soviet foreign policy. The same year, the Legion analyzed Communist historian Herbert Aptheker's recommendation that the Party adopt the slogan an "end to McCarthyism"; the Legion argued that this was "the Reds' way of saying 'an end to anti-Communism.' "[13]

There was still strong support for educational programs in schools and universities, even after the McCarthy hysteria. Educators debated how students could best be exposed to the Communist issue in their course work, and there still seemed to be a consensus that high schools should make discussions of the Communist issue part of students' education. On a more sophisticated level, in 1961 Columbia founded the first major university institute devoted solely to the study of communism, its Research Institute on Communist Affairs.[14]

Responsible veteran anticommunist activists of the thirties like George Schuyler, Eugene Lyons, and Sidney Hook also worked to keep the issue of communism before the public. Schuyler's columns regularly argued that communism was still the great issue of the day. Hook and other stalwarts testified regularly before congressional committees, and their testimony was published by the committees and distributed to the press.[15]

Eugene Lyons was now a senior editor at the *Reader's Digest*, and its publisher, DeWitt Wallace, made analysis of Communist strategy Lyons's special responsibility. After the 1956 Hungarian uprising, his

Our Secret Allies (1954), which predicted Eastern European resistance to their Soviet-imposed regimes, won him new respect for his insights into the instability of the Soviet regime:

> The fears that obsess the tenants of the Kremlin are, of course, manifold. . . . Their authority has no sanction in tradition, no roots in convention. . . . Themselves masters of the insurrectionary technique, the *coup d'etat*, the stab in the back, they cannot for a moment escape the dread of such threats to their own survival. Better than anyone else they know that even a relatively small group of 'internal enemies,' given propitious conditions, can overturn a seemingly impregnable system. Have they not done it themselves?

In subsequent articles Lyons urged Western leaders to widen the gulf between Communist leaders and their subjects. He warned against putting too much hope in summit diplomacy with Soviet leaders, holding that it would take strong enforcement mechanisms to hold the Kremlin to its promises. Lyons kept warning that the Soviet Union had not changed its goals of permanent revolution and a worldwide Communist society. Despite hopes for peaceful coexistence, the free world had to keep up its military defenses and resist Soviet psychological pressure.[16]

The Pentagon also actively promoted efforts to ensure its troops understood the ideas and values involved in the cold war. In November 1955 Secretary of Defense Charles E. Wilson endorsed an educational program on communism drawn up by a consultant to the Joint Chiefs of Staff, John C. Broger, president of the Far East Broadcasting Company. Wilson recommended Broger's course of study, *Militant Liberty*, as providing "guiding precepts" for educational programs about communism within the Armed Forces. *Militant Liberty* adopted the liberal anticommunist perspective outlined in Arthur M. Schlesinger's *Vital Center*, emphasizing the positive values of the free society and the threat to it of totalitarianism. Broger's program was so careful to avoid any hint of McCarthyism that domestic communism was not mentioned at all. It insisted that the cold war was essentially a battle of ideas, and that Communists had been successful "in large measure because they know what they believe, why they believe it, and can explain it to people anywhere in understandable terms." Communist ideology, Broger wrote, "can only be defeated by a stronger *dynamic* ideology." Only if Americans understood the ideology of freedom could the country stand up to the Communist challenge, because "the real strength of the Free World lies in the *collective* will of its people to remain free."[17]

Responsible anticommunists tried to approach the Communist issue in a positive way that emphasized the clash of values between freedom and totalitarianism, rather than a negative focus on domestic red-hunting. Their efforts continued to be undercut, however, by the persistent activities of McCarthyites and other countersubversives. The popularity of anticommunist education persuaded countersubversives to repackage their enterprises as a combination religious revival and Chautauqua tent meeting. The anticommunist revivals sponsored by the likes of Billy James Hargis with his Christian Crusade reinforced the impression that any discussion of communism must be associated with paranoid red-hunting. Hargis's Christian Crusade, which he began in 1947, presented a lineup of extremely conservative, conspiracy-oriented speakers including J. Bracken Lee, governor of Utah and leader of the Mormon Church, McCarthyite Congressman John H. Rousselot, brainwashing "expert" Edgar Hunger, Captain Eddie Rickenbacker, Myers Lowman of the red-hunting Methodist Circuit Riders, and Ben Gitlow. They lectured on topics like "Red Stains on the Pages of American Textbooks" and "Red Front Associations of Clergymen," along with less hysterical presentations like Gitlow's "I Defied Stalin," and afterwards the audience could purchase films of the speeches along with copies of Hargis's monthly *Christian Crusade* magazine. In 1961 Hargis began offering "Anti-Communist Leadership Schools" with a faculty that included Bella Dodd, Ezra Taft Benson, General Bonner Fellers, Senator John Towers, General Albert C. Wedemeyer, and ex-FBI agent Dan Smoot, a conservative radio personality. There was also a Hargis-chaired Anti-Communist Congress at the 1962 Seattle World's Fair.[18]

But responsible anticommunists' efforts to distance their objective presentation of communism from the fulminations of the McCarthyites were largely unavailing. The two organizations most active during the fifties in trying to promote public awareness of communism, the House Un-American Activities Committee and the Federal Bureau of Investigation, were so closely associated with hard-line, aggressive countersubversion in the public mind that even when they tried to raise their sights and take the high road, they had the perverse effect of making even responsible discussions of communism seem somehow connected to the presumptively sinister activities of the two agencies.

For the most part, there was nothing exceptionable in HUAC's many publications about domestic or international communism. The Committee solicited the ideas of the best thinkers of the anticommunist movement on how to strengthen the popular base of opposition to communism, and it published many useful reports on all aspects of the Communist issue. The Committee could not refrain, however, from calling on irresponsible conspiracy theorists or proven smear artists like Louis Budenz and Clarence Manion to produce propandistic treatments of communism like *The Great Pretense* that argued, in HUAC chairman Francis Walter's words, that Khrushchev-era "anti-Stalinism is but a political artifice, fraudulent and more dangerous than any produced by the Kremlin thus far."[19] HUAC also continued to provide a forum for conspiratorial anticommunists like Myers G. Lowman of the Circuit Riders, who was dedicated to ridding the Methodist Church of left-wing clergy like Bishop G. Bromley Oxnam (a firm liberal anticommunist), and like Alfred Kohlberg who continued his one-man China lobby, sending off barrages of letters from his "American China Policy Association" and "Citizens China Policy Association."[20]

No one was more active in trying to strengthen anticommunist public opinion than J. Edgar Hoover, who effectively turned his FBI into the government's anticommunist propaganda center, but his generally sinister image in the liberal imagination tended to make even the Bureau's most scholarly efforts seem somehow part of what many assumed to be Hoover's real purpose, to eliminate all political dissent from the land. The Bureau published monographs on every aspect of foreign and domestic communism, and many of them were useful and valuable. There was a hard edge to them, however, so that even when the Bureau stayed close to the facts they seemed tendentious and repressive. One was a collection, drawn from the Bureau's vast library of radical publications, of excerpts from Communist documents that "openly attack, vilify, or attempt to vilify, any aspect of the United States, its officials or representatives; and which openly advocate revolt against the laws of the United States and directly, by implication or inference, endeavor to wield insolent sway over public opinion." The point was to show that the Party had "steadfastly tried to drive a wedge between the American people and the American way of life," and the Bureau decried the current tendency "to minimize the revolutionary intent of the Party and to ignore the viciously anti-American statements that are preserved in Communist archives."[21]

By far, the most widely read popular account of the Communist issue in American history was the Bureau's *Masters of Deceit* (1958), published under Hoover's name but actually written by a team of agents in the Bureau's Research Section of the Crime Records Division, its public relations department. Though written for a popular audience, *Masters* was filled with detailed historical background and theoretical analysis, as well as the expected adventure stories that dramatized Communist villainy and G-man heroism.

In the preface, Hoover recalled his own introduction to communism in 1919, when he read "party statements, resolutions, platforms, news accounts, manifestoes, the very first documents of American communism. I studied also the writings of Marx, Engels, and Lenin as well as the activities of the Third International." He then provided a survey of Communist history up to Khrushchev's speech at the Twentieth Party Congress on February 24, 1956, of which he said, "No single event in Party history so unnerved communists abroad—and inside Russia."

Evidently chastened by the McCarthy catastrophe, Hoover distinguished responsible anticommunism from red-smearing. He denounced the Jewish-Bolshevik stereotype: "one of the most malicious myths that has developed in the United States is that persons of the Jewish faith and Communists have something in common." In an oblique reference to McCarthy he observed, "Too often I have seen cases where loyal and patriotic but misguided Americans have thought they were 'fighting communism' by slapping the label of 'Red' or 'communist' on anybody who happened to be different from them [or] to have ideas with which they did not agree."

The real answer to communism, he said, was a rebirth of patriotism and a new commitment to American ideals. Hoover described Communists' failure to infiltrate the civil rights movement by exploiting racial injustice. Nevertheless, he wrote, "we need to counter communism by making the hopes and aspirations of the American ideal a reality for all to enjoy." This was an anticommunism that sounded more like Arthur Schlesinger's than McCarthy's: "We, as a people, have not been sufficiently articulate and forceful in expressing pride in our traditions and ideals. . . . If communists can be so inspired from error, falsehood and hate, just think what we could do with truth, justice, and love! I thrill to think of the even greater wonders America could fashion from its rich, glorious, and deep tradition. All we need is faith, *real faith*." As was so often the case throughout Hoover's career, his gang-busting, spy-chasing image defeated his not-infrequent attempts to talk sense about crime and communism. No matter *what* Hoover said, enlightened or not, it scared those who had long ago concluded that anything Hoover did had to be a threat to civil liberty.[22]

McCarthy's ruin released one of his ablest supporters, William F. Buckley, Jr., from the fruitless efforts to defend the senator that had been consuming his time and energy. The Buckleys (like the Kennedys) admired McCarthy and enjoyed his company. They had the same political friends as McCarthy, and hated the same enemies. Buckley's first national magazine article was a defense of McCarthy.[23] In 1953, Buckley and his brother-in-law Brent Bozell wrote *McCarthy and His Enemies*, which appeared just before the Army hearings. They tried to redeem the term "McCarthyism" by separating it from McCarthy's errors and redefining it as "a program of action against those in our land who help the enemy." "We cannot avoid the fact that the United States is at war against international Communism," Buckley and Bozell wrote, and the goal of McCarthyism was to promote an "orthodoxy still-in-the-making," using social sanctions to safeguard the American traditions of free enterprise and Christianity.[24]

Born in 1925, as a teenager in the thirties Buckley was already outspokenly anticommunist and conservative. He even named his first sailboat "Sweet Isolation." After the Army, Buckley entered Yale and crusaded against the "collectivism" and secularism that he found had replaced Yale's traditional commitment to God and country (and free enterprise). His *God and Man at Yale*, published in October 1951, was a best-seller, winning Buckley haughty anti-Catholic rebukes from Yale and Harvard administrators who complained that an heir of the Inquisition had no business lecturing Protestants about religious liberty.[25]

Two old-line anticommunist isolationist journals, *The Freeman* and *The American Mercury*, had tried to recruit Buckley, but after McCarthy's fall, *The Freeman* recast itself as an intellectual monthly and *American Mercury*, which Buckley had briefly worked for under its previous editor, William Bradford Huie, became a vehicle for anti-Semitism under a new owner, Russell Maguire, prompting an exodus of its old writers and editors. If Buckley wanted to edit an anticommunist magazine with any real political impact, he would have to start it himself.

Buckley's goal was to move conservative anticommunism in a responsible new direction, to "give the Right the kind of decent image it needs instead of the image that some people are giving it now." He was referring to old countersubversives like J. B. Matthews, who had gone into the business of selling smear information to customers like Southern segregationists out to red-bait the civil rights movement. Others had burrowed deeper into the depths of anti-Semitic conspiratorial extremism of the sort that had always discredited anticommunism. There were still others who were so angry and depressed over the McCarthy catastrophe that they "didn't really want to change anything. They wanted to lay a curse on the benighted."[26] But Buckley had no interest in moaning about the past. It was the future that interested him.

To get financing for his prospective magazine, Buckley first went to the Texas oilmen who had funded McCarthy and befriended J. Edgar Hoover, but found that they were more interested in settling scores with McCarthy's enemies than in winning the intellectual argument against the left. He discovered an alternative source of funds in Hollywood, where the prevailingly leftist political climate had produced a counterculture of anticommunist conservatives in the film industry who were more than willing to help Buckley out. Buckley's first Hollywood angel for the *National Review* was Morrie Ryskind. Later on, conservative actors like Charlton Heston and Tom Selleck would become reliable friends. Buckley also received contributions from fellow Yale alumni who liked the message of *God and Man*, and Buckley's father tossed something into the pot. To draw up the legal papers, Buckley called on the Wall Street lawyer—and future chairman of the Securities and Exchange Commission and Director of the Central Intelligence Agency— William F. Casey.

Buckley recruited Willi Schlamm, a Jewish antifascist and anticommunist refugee from Austria, to help run his new magazine. Schlamm had worked for the Socialist anticommunist *New Leader* before moving on to *Time*, where he was associated with Whittaker Chambers's anticommunist faction. Buckley made William A. Rusher, who had been special counsel of the Senate's Internal Security Subcommittee, the publisher of the magazine and filled the staff with former leftists whose anticommunism had finally carried them into the conservative camp: James Burnham, Willmoore Kendall, Max Eastman, Morrie Ryskind, Ralph de Toledano, Frank Meyer, Freda Utley, and Eugene Lyons (the last three former Communists).[27]

It was a new look for conservative anticommunism. None of the editors or contributors were ever part of the anti-Semitic right, and, in fact, many were Jewish. There were Southerners, and even the odd monarchist. All were fully committed to effective—not merely soul-satisfying—anticommunism, and that meant careful attention to the principles upon which a responsible opposition to communism must rest.

Buckley's first choice for chief editor was Whittaker Chambers, who had become a close friend, but Chambers was bothered by Buckley's association with McCarthy, whom Chambers despised, and by Buckley's dislike of Richard Nixon, whom Chambers adored. Chambers also objected to the "reactionary" slant of Buckley's conservatism, arguing that if conservatism were to compete effectively with radicalism, it must make the same accommodation to social democracy that had revived Disraeli's British Conservative Party during the nineteenth century.

The first issue of Buckley's *National Review* appeared in November 1955, and he staked a claim to a "responsible dissent from Liberal orthodoxy" that would clearly distinguish itself from the "irresponsible Right." His magazine, he wrote, would stand "athwart history, yelling Stop, at a time when no one is inclined to do so, or to have much patience with those who do."[28]

The *National Review* was predictably hard-line on communism, but it was willing to rethink anticommunism in light of historical developments. James Burnham thought, for example, that Khrushchev's revelations about Stalin's crimes really did signal a thaw—slight, but a thaw nonetheless—in Soviet totalitarianism. Burnham also insisted that anticommunists face the fact that the Hungarian revolt had proven that the United States would not, could not, and should not go to war to break up the Yalta empire. Instead of the empty rhetoric of liberation, anticommunists should work to neutralize Eastern Europe through negotiation and to reunify Germany in an independent "Eastern European federation." Though unwilling to go that far, Buckley did concede that the right's insistence on "liberation" instead of "containment" meant little more in practice than a condemnation of coexistence as "immoral, undesirable, and, in the long run, impossible."[29]

But if Buckley agreed that anticommunists had to adapt to changing international conditions, he insisted that America ground its foreign policy on moral opposition to communism. When President Eisenhower invited Khrushchev to visit the United States in September 1959, Buckley lashed out at the President as a man "undaunted by principle, unchained to any coherent ideas as to the nature of man and society, uncommitted to any estimate of the nature or potential of the enemy." Buckley helped organize a Committee Against Summit Entanglements that attracted 2,500 protesters (wearing black arm bands to mourn the victims of communism) to Carnegie Hall for speeches by McCarthy's widow and Eugene Lyons, among others.[30]

For Buckley, the goal was a conservative, anticommunist Republican party that would put a true conservative anticommunist in the White House. Liberalism meant a willingness to coexist permanently with communism, if communism abided by the rules of international law. Liberalism was bad enough when it was Democratic. Liberal Republicanism was totally unacceptable. In 1960 Buckley and the *National Review* refused to endorse Nixon because of his accommodations to Nelson Rockefeller's liberal Republicanism, although James Burnham argued that conservatives had to prefer Nixon, since "in support of Kennedy are virtually all the forces, groups, tendencies and individuals that *National Review* is not merely against, but recognizes as its primary targets."[31] Unpersuaded, Buckley invited the Youth for Goldwater organization to his Sharon, Connecticut, home on September 9, 1960, to found Young Americans for Freedom to begin to lay the groundwork for an uncompromisingly anticommunist Republican party.

But all enemies were not on the left. Buckley had to ride herd on the conservatives to make sure they stayed clear of the right-wing groups that had wrecked anticommunism in the past. He had Whittaker Chambers banish Ayn Rand and her "objectivism" from the conservative movement in a review of *Atlas Shrugged* titled "Big Sister is Watching You." Chambers charged that "Randian man, like Marxian man, is made the center of a Godless world," and that "Out of a lifetime of reading I can recall no other book in which a tone of overriding arrogance was so implacably sustained. . . . From almost any page of *Atlas Shrugged* a voice can be heard, from painful necessity, commanding: "To a gas chamber—go!" According to Buckley, Rand's "exclusion from the conservative movement" was necessary because of "her desiccated philosophy's conclusive incompatibility with the conservative's emphasis on transcendence, intellectual and moral." Buckley also fought to keep conservatism free of the anti-Semitism that had long infected the right. Responding to pleas from Morrie Ryskind and Alfred Kohlberg, in 1960 Buckley decreed that no *NR* editor could appear in Russell Maguire's *American Mercury*, which was now reprinting the *Protocols of the Elders of Zion*. "Conservatism," Buckley wrote, "must be wiped clean of the parasitic cant that defaces it."[32]

But all at once a new eruption of that "parasitic cant" routed Buckley's crusade to shape a new, respectable, and responsible conservative anticommunist movement, laying anticommunism open to the most devastating assaults it had suffered since the brown-smearing days of the early forties.

On March 20, 1961, North Dakota Senator Milton Young rose in the Senate to read thirteen pages of a book by a Massachusetts businessman. An astonished country learned that this Robert Welch, head of a hitherto unknown organization named the John Birch Society, had called Dwight David Eisenhower a Communist.[33]

In a different time Welch and his Birch Society would have been pitied as eccentrics whose bizarre views disqualified them from consideration by anyone save students of political pathology. But instead, Welch was seen as a danger to the Republic, and every public figure in America rushed to go on record as condemning the retired candy manufacturer who had had the nerve to call Ike a red.

Welch's bizarre effort to red-smear Eisenhower turned him into the nation's best-known example of what would be denounced as extremism, a fright word that would quickly become little more than a synonym for anticommunism, one that would link anticommunists in the popular mind with such violence-prone groups as George Lincoln Rockwell's American Nazis, the Ku Klux Klan, and the racist White Citizens' Councils.

Robert Welch was far from the devil he was painted, and the John Birch Society was not the Nazi-style menace it was made out to be.

Welch was not a hater, nor a Fascist, nor, as charged by the ADL, a covert anti-Semite. His ideas were bizarre and an offense to common sense, but no real threat to the commonwealth. Hardly the mysterious recluse of the scare stories, Welch was a successful businessman and civic leader who had served on the Belmont, Massachusetts, school committee and on the Cambridge Chamber of Commerce as one of its directors. Active in charities and business associations, he had also worked for the wartime Office of Price Administration and War Production Board, and then as Washington lobbyist for the confectionery trade association. From 1950 to 1957 he was on the national board of the National Association of Manufacturers.

There certainly *were* violent groups on the loose in the late fifties and early sixties, but the John Birch Society was not one of them. The JBS was nothing like the Klans, American Nazis, and Citizens Councils that *were* a threat to law and order. Some Birch chapters and members were involved in some rancorous political disputes, particularly in Texas, but southwestern politics has always been rather uninhibited. The Society's name-calling was not good manners, but good manners are not the norm in American political rhetoric. The John Birch Society, was, if truth be told, more in the nature of a study club devoted to the reading and discussion of Welch's literary productions than a threat to the country. And yet newspapers like the *New York Times* worried that there were not only "elements of the authoritarian state in Mr. Welch's program, but specific resemblances to the Nazi framework of Gauleiters and Fuhrer, of tight control and no questions, of shock tactics and emotional rantings."[34]

Welch's notoriety was largely bogus, concocted by enemies on the left and within the respectable elite. They knew from past experience that a weird figure like Welch, with his oddball turns of phrase, could be used to discredit the anticommunist right and the entire anticommunist movement. It had worked before with Hamilton Fish, Martin Dies, and Joseph McCarthy. In 1961 the liberal Democrats who had captured the presidency by frightening the public about missile gaps and Soviet threats may have needed a way to distance themselves from the scare tactics that had gotten them elected. They needed someone like Robert Welch.

If Robert Welch had deliberately decided to reduce everything valid anticommunists had ever said about communism to an absurdity, to turn himself into a demonstration of every ludicrous delusion that had discredited anticommunism in the past to make all anticommunists look like dangerous fools, he could not have done a better job.

In July 1951, Welch published *May God Forgive Us*, a conspiracy theorist attack on the Marshall-Acheson China policy. Readers complained to Welch about inaccuracies, so Welch asked his friend Senator William Knowland for access to the files of the Senate Internal Security Subcommittee on its investigations of Owen Lattimore.

While he was going over these files Welch came across a letter from John Birch, a young American missionary in China who was serving as a captain in the American army in that country. The letter to his parents was written in April 1945, four months before Birch was killed by Chinese Communist forces, a date that made Birch, according to Welch's estimate, the first American victim of the cold war. "In one blade of grass lies the key to all creation, could we only understand it," Welch wrote, "and in the forces that swirled around John Birch lay all the conflicts of philosophy, and of implementation, with which our whole world is now so imperatively concerned," and so he decided to write Birch's life story.[35]

Birch was executed by his erstwhile Red Chinese allies, Welch explained, to demonstrate to the Chinese that the Communists now ruled, not the Americans. Welch then shifted the scene to Washington, and to a cabal of powerful leftists working to sabotage Chiang and to promote the belief that a Communist victory was inevitable and desirable.

This gave Welch an excuse to outline the far right's old charges of treason in Washington: that Roosevelt, "acting under the influence of Lauchlin Currie, Harry Dexter White, Harry Hopkins, Alger Hiss, David Niles, his own vanity and an impulsive regard for his tragic 'hunches,' . . . gave Manchuria to the Communists, betrayed Poland into Soviet hands, and double-crossed fifty million European friends, who had fought with us faithfully against one tyranny, into the clutches of another one far worse."[36]

To explain Roosevelt's motives, Welch provided a short history of the left in America. He began with the Intercollegiate Socialist Society, which he said was founded by Upton Sinclair to promote the British Fabian notion that "socialism, instead of being willingly and consciously assumed by the masses as a desirable condition of life, was something to be imposed on a people from the top." Renamed the League for Industrial Democracy in 1921, it persuaded a generation of college students that there should be a new social order based on "production for use and not for profit."

This Fabian idea of socialism Welch traced back to the "fulminations" of Marx, Engels, John Stuart Mill, Jeremy Bentham, and Robert Owen, "that militant determination on the part of these self-appointed demigods, basking in the delightful glow of their own infallibility, to use any means to force governments and people into the mold designed and being built by themselves."

John Birch was killed, Welch said, because history had placed him at the "focal point of a physical and ideological struggle far greater and more important than has ever yet been generally realized." A battle line had been drawn "in a struggle from which either Communism or Christian-style civilization must emerge with one completely triumphant and the other completely destroyed."

In John Birch Welch had found the hero for his story of the epic battle between communism and freedom. He still needed a villain, and this was to be none other than Dwight David Eisenhower. Welch provided the evidence he thought proved Ike's treason in *The Politician*, his biography of the President. The book had its origins in a December 1954 conversation with three businessman friends about Eisenhower's failure to campaign (as promised) for conservative candidates in the recent congressional elections. His friends found Welch's theory that Eisenhower had intentionally sabotaged the conservatives so provocative that they asked him to set his argument down on paper. This he did in a letter of some nine thousand words that was circulated along the right-wing grapevine. By 1958 *The Politician* had grown to more than two hundred spiral-bound photo-offset pages, each numbered copy to be returned to Welch after reading.

Immediately after Stalin's death in 1953, Welch claimed, the Soviet empire faced its moment of truth. Led by HUAC and McCarthy, Americans had turned against containment and appeasement: "not since the siege of Stalingrad had the whole Communist tyranny been in so much danger of being wiped off the face of the earth." "Just one thing" pulled communism back from the brink: the election to the presidency of Dwight D. Eisenhower, "the most completely opportunistic and unprincipled politician America has ever raised to high office."[37]

Welch traced Eisenhower's rapid rise in the Army to the treasonous

George Marshall. "I defy *anybody*," Welch wrote, "who is not actually a Communist himself, to read all of the known facts about his career and not decide that since at least sometime in the 1930's George Catlett Marshall has been a conscious, deliberate agent of the Soviet conspiracy."[38]

According to Welch, Eisenhower's decisions as a military commander demonstrated that he too was a traitor: his eagerness for a premature second front in Europe, his refusal to advance into Prague and Berlin, his rejection of the Germans' overtures for an early surrender to the American forces, his failure to secure a land corridor for the West to Berlin. Once Eisenhower was President, he continued to do the Communists' bidding: destroying the Republican party, sabotaging British and French efforts to hold onto their colonies, forcing Radio Free Europe to put out "milk toast" propaganda instead of the real anticommunist McCoy. He suspected (correctly) that the Eisenhower White House had plotted against McCarthy. What it all meant, he concluded, was that Dwight David Eisenhower was a "dedicated, conscious agent of the Communist conspiracy."[39]

Welch claimed he never intended *The Politician* to be circulated outside his circle of friends. He said that Moscow saw how it could attack anticommunism through Welch, and in December 1960 it ordered the fellow-traveling press to go on the attack. (The real story is that liberal politicians, harassed by local Birchers, were looking for a way to strike back. Milton Young, who touched off the campaign against Welch, was being tormented by Birchers in his home state.)

It is likely that Welch's far-right friends were so hermetically sealed from the political mainstream that no one noticed anything amiss in his railings against Eisenhower. The far right had not really had access to public forums since 1954, when liberals had decided the ideas of the right were unworthy of serious notice. In 1949 William F. Buckley, Jr., could find no mainstream publisher to handle *God and Man at Yale*. Only three publishers were willing to handle right-wing projects: Caxton of Idaho, Devin-Adair in New York, and Chicago's Henry Regnery (*God and Man*'s publisher).[40] Countersubversives like Welch, therefore, no longer knew what it was like to appear before a skeptical mainstream audience. And the intended readers of *The Politician*, the members of his John Birch Society, came far from the mainstream, from the most alienated segment of the American right: the supporters of Robert Taft and Douglas MacArthur, seething with resentment over their heroes' defeat by Eisenhower's moderate Republicans, roused to new fury by the Eisenhower administration's complicity in McCarthy's demise.

Welch had founded the John Birch Society in 1958, at a seminar he conducted in Indianapolis for twelve well-off businessman friends. Welch's lectures there became *The Blue Book of the John Birch Society*, a plan for an anticommunist organization based on the front strategy of the Communist Party. The Birch Society would tie together its own network of right-wing groups, which would move the Republican party to the right as the Democratic party had been moved leftward by the ADA and the CIO's PACs.[41]

The "conspiracy" that Welch presented in his books was essentially the same red web theory, brought up to date, that had earlier been featured in Richard Whitney's *Reds in America*, Elizabeth Dilling's *Red Network* and *The Roosevelt Red Record and Its Background*, Martin Dies's *Trojan Horse in America*, and J. B. Matthews's *Odyssey of a Fellow Traveler*. But just before Welch's pronouncement about Eisenhower turned him into the public enemy *du jour*, he had added something new to the mix. Encouraged by one of the Society's founders, Dr. Revilo P. Oliver, he had begun to read Nesta Webster and other stalwarts of classical conspiracy theory, and was hooked. He now began to teach that communism was the latest incarnation of a conspiracy that had begun with the Bavarian Illuminati in 1776, and had survived and secretly prospered through the ages. The proper name for these almost eternal master conspirators was "Insiders," the internationalist establishment headed by the leading financiers of America and Europe.

What made Welch's rendition of classical conspiracy theory bearable and even attractive was his penchant for explaining otherwise inscrutable events as the clash of intellectual systems. John Birch Society members would get, then, along with their anticommunism, a course in the intellectual history of the West. He saw in the conflict between Communist-sympathizing liberal internationalists and anticommunist isolationists like himself a contest between the historical theories of Oswald Spengler and Arnold Toynbee. Welch explained that according to Spengler, civilizations passed through a life cycle of youth, maturity, and old age. European civilization, entering the stage of senility, had taken refuge in the security of collectivism. America, on the other hand, still enjoying the vigor of its youth, could preserve its health only by maintaining its distance from the disease and decay of Europe. But while Spengler warned America to steer clear of European infection, Toynbee, the darling of the internationalists, tempted America with the false notion that civilizations grew through contact, competition, and the exchange of ideas. Spengler, needless to say, got Welch's seal of approval.

Among American historians, Welch's favorite was Carroll Quigley of Georgetown University (also President Bill Clinton's when he was at Georgetown). What fascinated Welch in Quigley's 1,300-page *Tragedy and Hope* was that even though Quigley dismissed the conspiracy theory of the origins of World War II as a "radical Right fairy tale, which is now an accepted folk myth in many groups in America," he did concede that "this myth, like all fables, does in fact have a modicum of truth." Just as the conspiracy theorists argued, Quigley said, there really was a network of Anglophiles among the American elite who had once cooperated with British imperialists to protect the Empire, and still promoted an Anglo-American hegemony through institutions like the Rhodes Foundation and the Foreign Policy Association. Welch claimed that this was an endorsement of the theory of an "insider" conspiracy controlling world affairs, although Quigley went on to praise the benign and open influence of this "Eastern Establishment [which] has played a very significant role in the history of the United States in the last generation."[42]

Conservative anticommunists initially tried to laugh off Welch. Russell Kirk quipped, "Ike isn't a communist; he's a golfer." But what could not be laughed off was the massive onslaught Welch had touched off, not only against the paranoid right but against all ideologically grounded anticommunism, which was now labeled "extremism."[43]

Welch's pronouncements on Eisenhower were nutty enough to make the anticommunist right seem dangerous (the *New York Times* said that Welch reminded some of a "little Hitler") and comical (the attorney general of California said the Birch Society was made up of "wealthy business men, retired military officers and little old ladies in tennis shoes"). Lest those characterizations cancel one another out, the *Times* pointed out that "Hitler himself was generally considered a clown—at first."[44]

Ever since the beginning of McCarthyism in 1950, liberals had dealt with right-wing anticommunism by dismissing it as a psychological pathology rather than a legitimate political persuasion, a type of mental illness described by Seymour Martin Lipset in *The Politics of Unreason*.[45]

Welch's looniness encouraged the popular media to adopt that dismissive view of right-wing anticommunism, but now the attack was broadened so that "extremism" came to encompass not merely the undemocratic right and left castigated a decade before by Arthur M. Schlesinger, Jr., but all ideological anticommunism, the responsible as well as the manic variety exemplified by Welch.

The early sixties saw one blast after another in the direction of "extremism," and the entire conservative anticommunist movement was thoroughly peppered. There was Harry Allen Overstreet's *The Strange Tactics of Extremism*, which proposed a mental disease explanation for "extremist" activity. Murray Havens wrote *The Challenges to Democracy: Consensus and Extremism in American Politics*. Irwin Suall of the ADL wrote *The American Ultras: The Extreme Right and the Military Industrial Complex*. Brooks Walker published *The Christian Fright Peddlers*. Mark Sherwin wrote *The Extremists*. There was Donald Janson's *The Far Right*, Richard Dudman's *Men of the Far Right*, and Mike Newberry's *The Yahoos*.[46]

The Anti-Defamation League of B'nai B'rith took advantage of the Birch Society controversy to launch its own attack on the right, based on its belief—buttressed by a great deal of experience—that there was an almost inevitable progression in the steamy world of right-wing conspiracy theory towards anti-Semitism.

The ADL had been investigating right-wing organizations since the late thirties, and had supported Avedis Derounian (John Roy Carlson), whose best-selling *Undercover* and *The Plotters* were probably written (or at least edited) by ADL ghosts. The ADL had set up a national fact-gathering network to obtain information on anti-Semitism, primarily on the right. To do so, it had infiltrated nearly every active right-wing organization. In most instances its informants were sympathetic non-Jews worried by the spread of intolerance. The ADL disseminated this information in its newsletter, *Fact*, usually devoting each issue to a single anti-Semitic organization or individual.

In 1964 the ADL's general counsel, Arnold Forster, collaborated with its chief executive, Benjamin Epstein to produce a broadside attack on extremism. *Danger on the Right* argued that there was a radical right movement in the country that was in no wise "part of this nation's responsible political fabric" but was as dangerous and illegitimate as the "troublesome Communist conspiracy."[47] Drawing on materials from the ADL files, Forster and Epstein used the brown web technique to tie the John Birch Society to Fred Schwarz's Christian Anti-Communism Crusade, Billy James Hargis's Christian Crusade, George Benson's National Education Program, radio programs like Carl McIntire's 20th Century Reformation Hour, the Clarence Mannion Forum, and the Dan Smoot Report, Edgar Bundy's Church League of America, and Willis Stone's Liberty Amendment Committee of the USA. These constituted the radical right, consumed by conspiracy theories blaming the country's troubles on traitors in high places.

Then there were the extreme conservatives, the "frequent fellow travelers of today's radical right," perhaps less noxious, but almost "inextricably intertwined with the radical right."[48] The extreme conservatives included Admiral Ben Morell's Americans for Constitutional Action, James L. Wick's *Human Events* magazine, the Intercollegiate Society of Individualists, the Young Americans for Freedom, and *The National Review*.

Danger on the Right tied one organization to the next until it created an overall impression of an unbroken network of dangerous right-wingers ranging from anti-Semites, racists, and Birch Society paranoids to mainstream figures like Barry Goldwater and William F. Buckley, Jr. The authors demanded that William F. Buckley, Jr., whom they saw as the most significant force on the right, disavow the extremists. Buckley rightly resented the smear, complaining that he had no control over the John Birch Society, and had, in fact, taken the lead in criticizing the Society's imbecilities. He accurately charged that there had developed a "tendency among opponents of the American Right to fasten on the John Birch Society as a means of sandbagging conservative candidates."[49] The book's underlying argument was that extremism was a danger to America, and hence un-American; since extremists were often anti-Semites or associated with them, anti-Semitism was un-American too.

The ADL's strategy of using alarm over the John Birch Society to discredit other far right organizations with avowedly anti-Semitic agendas was undeniably effective, but it was hardly logical, since Welch had explicitly and repeatedly repudiated anti-Semitism. Furthermore, the effectiveness of the ADL's attack on the right had long-lasting consequences, as moderate political groups—liberal Democrats, moderate Republicans, Jewish defense organizations—all adopted that crude, blunt, but devastating tactic of imputing anti-Semitic guilt by association to their "extremist" opponents, and when the real offense of those "extremists" was to insist that the country had a moral obligation to keep faith with the victims of Communist regimes in Europe and Asia, and to prevent others from falling victim.

In 1962 Fred Schwarz's Christian Anti-Communist Crusade ran afoul of the ADL, and was confronted by a coalition of clergy, civic leaders, and local officials in Berkeley, California, who, responding to ADL charges that Schwarz was anti-Semitic, charged there were parallels between Nazi spectaculars in Nuremberg and Schwarz's teach-ins.[50] William F. Buckley challenged the ADL to produce evidence that the Crusade was anti-Semitic or "extremist." Eugene Lyons, a regular speaker at Schwarz's Crusades, supported Buckley and privately wrote to Arnold Forster to express his disagreement with the ADL over Schwarz. But there was the same dissension even on the right over Schwarz. George Sokolsky called Schwarz "a professional anticommunist who is in the game strictly for money purposes." Sokolsky's hostility may have been prompted by his discovery that "Dr. Schwarz was formerly a member of the Jewish faith but dishonored his faith and later became a Baptist," and so "he, Sokolsky, did not trust Schwarz."[51]

The Birch disaster grievously wounded the entire anticommunist movement. Through a predictable process of guilt by association, links could be found to tie the entire anticommunist right to anti-Semitic and antidemocratic groups that constituted an apparently dangerous extremist movement. Welch himself was so battered by the ADL's use of the Birch Society to attack anti-Semites, and anti-Semites to discredit the Birchers, that he put out a tape-recorded speech, "The Neutralizers," accusing the Communists of a plot to destroy the Birch Society by seeding its ranks with anti-Semites to be exposed to discredit honest anticommunists like himself.[52]

The respectable right tried to widen the distance between itself and the "extremists." Buckley risked offending many of his readers—and some of his wealthiest supporters—by excommunicating the Birch Society, holding that "there are bounds to the dictum, Anyone on the right is my ally." Welch's key error, he said, was an inability to make the "crucial moral and political distinction . . . between (1) an active pro-Communist and (2) an ineffectually anti-Communist liberal."[53] Once again, the disreputable right hand played into the hands of anticommunism's enemies, and the wounds were deep and perhaps fatal.

Outspoken anticommunism now identified an extremist in the public mind. Americans who had earlier proudly proclaimed their anticommunism—indeed had defined themselves by their anticommunism—now began to edge away from an ideology that might link them to groups, like Welch's, that were outside the pale of respectability.

American liberalism now seized on the extremism controversy to redefine itself just as it was about to lead the country into Vietnam. After World War II liberalism had differentiated itself from the progressive left by rejecting communism and defending freedom against totalitarianism, and it was liberals who had conceived the containment policies that had halted Communist expansion. During the fifties, liberals had taken an equally strong stand against McCarthyism, calling it "not only the abandonment of rationality and decency of means, but also the corruption of ends."[54] This stand had split the American Committee for Cultural Freedom. Some conservatives had withdrawn rather than attack an anticommunist, no matter how repellent, while some liberals refused to associate with anticommunists who supported the Wisconsin senator or who did not condemn him.

By the 1960s there were reasons for liberals to question the necessity and the wisdom of subordinating other goals, domestic and international, to anticommunism. Liberals had seldom based their anticommunism on the goals of the Communists—a planned economy, a social welfare net, and the like—because many of those goals were attractive to them as well. Conservative anticommunists argued that there was a necessary connection between the Communists' means and goals—political repression and economic collectivism—while liberals tended to direct their attention to the undemocratic means Communists employed to achieve goals that were not necessarily all that bad. Furthermore, some liberals held that if there was now no possibility of the Communists gaining power in the United States, then there was no reason to object to their participating in American politics or culture. It was only a short step, then, for some young liberals and radicals who had no experience in dealing with Communists in the thirties and forties to once again make common cause, if not with Communists, then with the progressive left in pursuit of the perennial dream of a united left.

The extremism controversy helped promote the reconciliation between liberals and the progressive left. Liberals had felt the sting of McCarthyism, so they also had that as a bond with their old leftist rivals. Now that the battle over extremism had removed communism as a topic of respectable political discourse, the last barrier between the two estranged wings of the left had fallen. There was nothing to stop liberal anticommunists from giving respectful consideration to the progressives' contention that improved relations with the Soviet Union and American disengagement from the cold war system of military alliances should be the goals of American foreign policy. Many anticommunist liberals, having decided that the Soviet Union was a diminished military threat, had come to agree with progressives that American alliances with anticommunist dictators were wrong—that the United States should instead align itself with the insurgences and national liberation movements, even though they were usually Marxist, that were exploding throughout the Third World. That stalwart spokesman for anticommunist liberalism, Arthur M. Schlesinger, Jr. himself, used a 1959 ADA forum to call for a new liberal anticommunism, since "a foreign policy designed for the age of Stalin is not necessarily perfect for the age of Khrushchev," now that there was less terror in the Soviet Union, more consumerism, and a breakdown of Communist bloc unity.[55]

The changing generational composition of American liberalism also weakened its commitment to anticommunism. Even in the ADA, young liberals were drawn to the new rising generation of young radicals in the New Left, some of them the red diaper offspring of Old Leftists the ADA had fought in the forties. In 1961 John Roche, president of the ADA, scolded his young colleagues for romanticizing the Communists of the thirties. There was a growing tendency, he warned, to sympathize with the Communist Party as a "pathetic, persecuted group," virtuous victims of American repression—that is, of anticommunism.[56]

At the height of the Birch Society uproar, the Kennedy administration made a policy decision to end official government programs to educate the public about communism.

Early in 1961, conservative anticommunists were outraged to learn that Arthur Sylvester, Defense Secretary Robert McNamara's public information officer, had heavily censored an anticommunist speech by Admiral Arleigh Burke. In April they learned that President Kennedy had removed Major General Edwin Walker, commander of the Twenty-Fourth Infantry Division in Germany, from his post for giving "political seminars" to his troops based on materials from the John Birch Society. Conservatives accused McNamara and the administration of "muzzling the military." Anticommunists were soon staggered to learn that the patriotic anticommunism that had become almost a civic religion was now being criticized as political opinion, and extremist politics at that, when Kennedy said, on August 10, 1961, that the armed forces must not engage in partisan politics. The administration now instituted a formal procedure to review anticommunist speeches by military officers. Why was the United States risking American lives to contain communism, if anticommunism was merely partisan "opinion," anticommunists asked.[57]

It was at this point that Senator J. William Fulbright of Arkansas joined the fray. He had recently learned that the army was holding a "strategy for survival" conference at Fort Smith in his home state of Arkansas, and that one of the speakers was the vice president of Harding College in Searcy, Arkansas, which Fulbright considered less an institution of higher learning than a think tank for the anticommunist lunatic fringe. Harding had produced a *Communism on the Map* film popular on the conservative anticommunist circuit. Fulbright was outraged that a speaker at the Fort Smith conference had accused Arkansas Congressman James W. Trimble of having an 89 percent pro-Communist voting record. He learned that there had been two other "strategy for survival" conferences in Arkansas, and that local army commanders had endorsed them. One of the speakers at all three conferences was the former counsel of the Senate Internal Security Subcommittee, Robert Morris. His speeches were "No Wonder We are Losing" and "We Are Losing From Within."[58]

Upon looking into the matter, Fulbright found out that President Eisenhower had given Admiral Arthur W. Radford, chairman of the Joint Chiefs of Staff, permission in May 1958 to conduct educational programs on international affairs for the public. Radford himself had appeared at a September 1960 seminar and had called for "total victory over the Communist system—not stalemate. . . . We are confused by fears, the fear of gaining some advantage, the fear of seeming imperialistic, the fear of being unpopular. The massive power providentially given us is frustrated by an abstract idealism that is apart from reality and does not recognize the basic conditions for the effective use of power." Radford had then ordered the implementation of military anticommunist indoctrination programs like "Militant Liberty," "Project Alert," and "Strategy for Survival."[59]

The conferences had become a nationwide phenomenon, and in Pittsburgh the Chamber of Commerce had joined local Army commanders as sponsors of a seminar where a retired admiral charged that the Kennedy administration employed advisors and officials like George Kennan and Adlai Stevenson who favored "a national sellout of freedom in order to buy peace." The Navy had cited that admiral at his retirement for "realistically expressed convictions concerning the Cold War and the Communist conspiracy." An active duty officer told the Pittsburgh group that the United States should commit itself to "an integrated national strategy based on military power to turn back Communism and extend the frontiers of freedom."[60]

Fulbright was able to gather more information from around the country about military-sponsored patriotic indoctrination programs. General Edwin Walker had urged his men in Germany to vote only for avowedly anticommunist candidates. Vice Admiral Robert Goldthwaite had told his sailors that they should "demand a more patriotic attitude" from political candidates, and should "join a citizens group dedicated to upholding American principles and resisting socialism-communism" and should "demand that the nation take the offensive in the cold war with the objective of victory over communism."[61]

At this point in his research, Fulbright was given an ADL report that linked retired military officers to far right organizations. He reached a conclusion as bizarre as any conspiracy theory spun by the radical right: There might well be a plot by right-wing military officers allied to the extremist right to stage a coup, perhaps to bring General Douglas MacArthur to power as an American De Gaulle.[62] (Harding College's president had been active in *Chicago Tribune* publisher Colonel Robert McCormick's anticommunist "For America" organization that had pushed General MacArthur for the Republican presidential nomination in 1952.)

Shaken and angry, Fulbright confronted Robert McNamara and demanded, "What in the hell are your generals up to?" McNamara asked the senator to sketch out his suspicions in a memo. This "Fulbright memorandum" of August 1961 entered anticommunist lore as the blueprint for the Kennedy administration's assault on anticommunists and anticommunism.[63]

The memorandum argued that "the American people have little, if any need to be alerted to the menace of the cold war. . . . The principal problem of leadership will be, if it is not already, to restrain the desire of the people to hit the communists with everything we've got, particularly if there are more Cubas and Laos. . . . Pride in victory, and frustration in restraint, during the Korean War, led to MacArthur's revolt and to McCarthyism."[64]

Fulbright rejected the very idea of "victory" over communism, which would require covert operations abroad, a cold war atmosphere in American schools and colleges, and restrictions on civil liberties. All this would stem from the original sin of "setting up a savage dichotomy between the Communist and Western world, and of making almost every issue a matter of irreconcilable competition."

There was a real possibility of a military coup if the military's anticommunist fervor were not brought under control.

> If the military is infected with the virus of right-wing radicalism, the danger is worthy of attention. If the military believes the public is, the danger is enhanced. If, by the process of the military 'educating' the public, the fervor of both groups is raised, the danger is great indeed. Perhaps it is farfetched to call forth the revolt of the French generals [in 1958] as an example of the ultimate danger. Nevertheless, military officers, French or American, have some common characteristics arising from the profession and there are numerous "fingers on the trigger" throughout the world.[65]

Fulbright ended by demanding that McNamara cancel Eisenhower's directive, that civilians be put in charge of military indoctrination programs, and that "a long range program dominated by a board of civilian educators [be] undertaken to expose officers to history, government and foreign policy."[66]

Soon after writing the memorandum to McNamara, Fulbright began to speak out publicly against anticommunism in the military. On August 21, 1961, he told the Naval War College that "radical extremism, whether right or left, is the true enemy of democratic society. They may form an unholy combine of 'disloyal opposition' which destroyed the Weimar Republic of Germany and plagued postwar Italy and France." In that same speech he defined "irresponsible extremists" as those "who cannot, or will not, accept the world as it is."[67]

It was not long before rumors of the memorandum reached conservative anticommunists. Senator Strom Thurmond violated Senate protocol by abruptly demanding that Fulbright give him a copy of the memorandum. Fulbright refused, but inserted it into the *Congressional Record*.[68] Later, on February 8, 1962, McNamara was grilled by Senator John Stennis and had to admit that anticommunist phrases were indeed being removed from military speeches. Some began to suspect leftist plots against anticommunists when they learned that the McNamara aide Adam Yarmolinsky, who sat on the review board charged with censoring anticommunist films, had attended two Young Communist League meetings in his student days.

The furor over Fulbright's memorandum attracted national attention to his campaign for reelection to the Senate in 1962, particularly when the radical right made him a symbol of "anti-anti-communism" and targeted him for defeat. The *Arkansas Statesman* editorialized that there was a "conservative grassroots rebellion spreading from shore to shore. The people of Arkansas can help save the United States by defeating a man who is a symbol of anti-anti-communism." Harding College's president wrote that "Fulbright has given comfort to the reds" and he said that "attempts to defend the Fulbright memorandum as an effort to keep civilian control over the military are just a lie."[69]

But Fulbright won easily. Once again it had been demonstrated that extremism was a danger only to any political movement that was tagged extremist. As of 1962, talking about communism was regarded as extremism.

Almost as notorious as the Fulbright memorandum in anticommunist circles was the so-called "Reuther memorandum." In the fall of 1961 Attorney General Robert Kennedy and the United Auto Workers' Reuther brothers, Victor and Walter, had a conversation about the radical right. Kennedy asked the brothers to summarize their ideas, which they did on December 19, 1961.[70]

The Reuther Memorandum was a proposal for a comprehensive attack by the administration on the "radical right," warning that "these radical right groups are probably stronger and are almost certainly better organized than at any time in recent history. More significant yet, they are growing in strength and there is no reason to expect a turning of the tide during the foreseeable Cold War period ahead. And, possibly most significant of all, their relationship to and infiltration of the Armed Services adds a new dimension to the seriousness with which they must be viewed." Like Fulbright, the Reuthers raised the specter of the French military's revolt against DeGaulle's Algerian policy, and called on Defense Secretary McNamara to remove "those generals and admirals who have lost confidence in democracy and who feel that the danger to our country is treason at home rather than the strength of the international Communist movement abroad." Purging the American military of ideologues "would go far to answer Soviet propaganda that American foreign policy is not in responsible hands and that there is a substantial 'preventive war' group in the Pentagon which may ultimately get the upper hand."

The Reuthers seemed to be especially concerned that the right—supposedly subliterate primitives barely able to think, according to liberal theory—were reading books and attending seminars. "Even such things as radical right book shops are beginning to spring up," they reported. They seemed to doubt that right-wingers had the mental equipment necessary to withstand the emotional stimulation of Fred Schwarz's anticommunist rallies and radio programs like "Life Line," which "traffic in fear." "Treason in high places is their slogan and slander is their weapon. They undermine loyal Americans' confidence in each other and in their Government."

The Reuthers recommended that the right be repressed and silenced. There should be "deliberate administration policies and programs to contain the radical right from further expansion and in the long run to reduce it to its historic role of the impotent lunatic fringe." The attorney general's list should be expanded to take in right-wing extremism, which would in itself frighten many out of activist organizations. The FBI should infiltrate these groups, the tax exempt status of foundations that funded the radical right should be ended, and the radio licenses of stations carrying radical right programs should be revoked. Militant groups like the Minute Men (who talked about guerrilla warfare after a Communist takeover) should be disbanded.

The Reuthers' key recommendation was that the Kennedy administration should launch a public information drive to deflate the public's illusions about the domestic Communist threat, which had been exaggerated by every administration since the beginning of the cold war. "There is no need for a further effort to dramatize the domestic Communist issue; the need now is to rein in those who have created the unreasoned fear of the domestic Communist movement in the minds of the American people and slowly to develop a more rational attitude toward the strength of this movement."

The gradual movement of liberals away from the anticommunist coalition in the early sixties was bad enough. Even more devastating was the erosion of American Catholics' enthusiasm for the anticommunist cause, since Catholics had always formed the hard core of American anticommunism.

Their anticommunism may have been a religious obligation for American Catholics, but it was also something of a status symbol, a mark of social respectability that demonstrated their superior patriotism in their competition with Jews and old-stock Protestants. By the sixties Catholics formed the largest single religious denomination in the United States, and they had made giant strides in power and social acceptance since the bitter days of Al Smith's presidential campaign in 1928. The extremism hysteria of the early sixties made anticommunism disreputable in a Catholic community proud of its respectability, however, and so the anticommunism that had once elevated Catholics' public image now associated them with the lunatic fringe of wild-eyed generals and little old ladies in tennis shoes.

That shift in Catholic attitudes could be seen in John Cronin's *Communism: Threat to Freedom*, which he published in 1962. Cronin now saw extremist anticommunism like the John Birch Society's, so attractive to Catholic conservatives, as more dangerous than communism itself. Communism, he insisted, was "primarily an external danger, that the threat required national unity, and that the best method of combating it was military strength combined with economic and military assistance to countries struggling to retain their freedom against subversion."[71]

Cronin's attack on extremism provoked some interesting responses. Leaders of the American Communist Party approached him in hopes of establishing a Catholic-Communist dialogue, perhaps even an alliance on social issues. Cronin was not interested. From the right, Westbrook Pegler complained that Cronin now seemed to be allying himself with persons who had "former Communist-front associations." These leftists now "live in fear lest mistakes in judgment (or even actual Communist associations long since repudiated) made years ago in a different climate of opinion, may be brought up today and used to cost them their jobs and their reputation." He asked Cronin to remember how anticommunists had been treated during the brown scare before concluding that the progressive left was no longer a problem. "Did they show us any chivalry? Did they forbear to get our jobs and smear our reputation when they were riding high? Have they ever publicly repudiated those 'associations' or did they just slink away?"[72] Cronin was also attacked by John Cross of Kenosha, Wisconsin, in his *What are the Facts Behind the Smearing of Anti-Communist Americans?*[73] In more measured terms, Frank Brophy's *Catholics, Communism and the Commonweal* also worried that Catholic liberals like Cronin were forgetting the realities of life in the Soviet bloc when they denied the continued necessity of vigorous anticommunism among Catholics.[74]

Kennedy's election reinforced the growing tendency of American Catholics to shun anything that threatened the social gains that had placed a Catholic in the White House. Catholic anticommunists saw that Kennedy's election had so bedazzled other Catholics that for the first time they were losing interest in the Communist issue. During the campaign, James Buckley, William F. Buckley, Jr.'s brother, drafted "An Open Letter to American Catholics." Kennedy's religion, he said, was the wrong "Catholic issue." The real "Catholic issue in the campaign was the Catholic opposition to Communism," and "Kennedy has chosen to identify himself with that segment of American society which is either unwilling or unable to regard Communism as more than a childish bugaboo."[75] But no matter how the issue was presented, if Catholics had to choose between Kennedy and anticommunism, they would have little difficulty making their choice.

As important as John Kennedy's election was in weakening American Catholics' anticommunism, Pope John XXIII's election was even more significant. That paragon of Catholic anticommunism, Pope Pius XII, died on October 9, 1958. As soon as John XXIII was installed two weeks later, he began to redefine the Church's relationship to the modern world. He started to withdraw the Church from Italian domestic politics, which meant that tensions between Italian Communists and

Catholics would no longer help determine the Church's policies toward international communism. And, in a shock to Catholics who regarded any contact at all with Marxists as unholy, he began to encourage a dialogue between Catholics and Communists.

The Pope's first major encyclical, *Mater et Magistra* of July 1961, dispensed with the standard papal denunciations of communism. It insisted that colonialism, not communism, was the cause of the third world's plight, and it was there in the third world that humanity faced its greatest challenges. Buckley's *National Review* was scandalized that at a time when "the most obtrusive social phenomena of the moment are surely the continuing and demonic successes of the Communists" the Pope had simply dispensed with the issue.[76] The magazine's attitude toward the Pope's apostasy was summed up in William F. Buckley's famous quip, "Mater si, Magistra no." But if forced to choose between anticommunism and the Pope, once again, Catholics would not find it difficult to choose.

Mater et Magistra signaled that anticommunism was no longer doctrine for Catholics. After Rome had spoken, anticommunism would become less and less important to American Catholics, and anticommunists would play an increasingly peripheral role in the American Catholic Church. Catholics like Buckley continued to believe that anticommunism was forced on Catholics by their religious faith, and that no other political conviction could take precedence over opposition to communism. Patrick Scanlan tried to keep *The Brooklyn Tablet* faithful to old-line anticommunism, but he faced a revolt on his own staff: Younger editors and reporters, caught up in the new spirit of Vatican II, were now "dedicated to the proposition that anti-Communism is a greater menace to America than Communism."[77] Another prominent Catholic anticommunist mournfully recalled how things suddenly changed. "Up until the end of 1960, to be anti-communist was accepted as natural, somewhat like being anti-sin and pro-mother. But by late spring of 1961, the climate was changed. By the spring of 1962, things were really rough for 'the right'—even in many Catholic circles."[78]

The Second Vatican Council Pope John XXIII convened in 1962 regarded anticommunism as an obstacle to the Church's influence in a world where Marxism seemed to be a permanent fixture in politics and culture. The American Catholic Church loyally followed Rome's lead, and so, to adapt an observation about Jews and the Communist Party, few Catholics would any longer be activist anticommunists after 1960, although many of the remaining activist anticommunists would still be Catholics.

The extremism controversy even affected an organization as steadfastly anticommunist as the American Legion. The Legion began to see itself as a moderate alternative to the radical right. "The radical left and the radical right," said the Legion, "argue from rigid ideological points of view." The "moderate middle," where the Legion located itself, "examines facts and makes decisions on both the principles involved and on the practical effect these decisions will have . . . believing that freedom comes from maintaining open positions and free discussions of issues."[79]

The furor over extremism made anticommunism too controversial for the schools, ending courses and programs to educate students about communism. By default, educators came to adopt the position long fostered by the progressive left, that any criticism of communism under official auspices smacked of inappropriate state indoctrination, if not McCarthyism. When the National Education Association denounced "inadequate and extremist" courses on communism in 1962, schools began to shy away from any discussion of the Communist issue, not knowing if their courses would be open to such attack. At the end of that year, the *New York Times* reported that there was a discernible national trend against courses on communism in the schools.[80]

The furor over extremism helped the radical left escape its political isolation by discrediting its anticommunist enemies. This rehabilitation had actually begun as early as 1956, when the Supreme Court, feeling that the emergency circumstances that had justified the Smith Act prosecutions of the Communist Party were now ended, began to overturn those convictions. The Party—at least that remnant that survived the debacle of Hungary and Khrushchev's speech on the crimes of Stalin, began to exploit the causes that were appealing to a generation of new young radicals: civil rights and the ban-the-bomb protests against nuclear weapons.

The battle against the House Un-American Activities Committee was the cause that did as much as anything to unite the Old with the emergent New Left. The Communist Party—employing as a front the Emergency Civil Liberties Committee—had launched "Operation

Abolition" in the mid-fifties. The primary target was HUAC. The ultimate goal was to dismantle the whole federal and local internal security apparatus: the Senate Internal Security Subcommittee, the Subversive Activities Control Board, the Internal Security Division of the Justice Department, the domestic security division of the FBI, state subversive activities committees, and local police and radical squads.

During the fifties HUAC made yearly visits to California, provoking some protest every time.[81] When it visited San Francisco in 1960, it encountered a well-organized activist movement already mobilized to protest the execution of convicted rapist Caryl Chessman. When HUAC began its hearings on May 8, 1960, there was pandemonium. Anti-Committee spectators who were denied admission to the hearings grew unruly and were dispersed with fire hoses. The next day five thousand protesters appeared and turned the hearings into a shambles.

To document its charges that Communists had planned the demonstration and had organized the campaign to abolish HUAC, the Committee produced a film, *Operation Abolition*. Often introduced by a HUAC staff member or professional witness, for years this was a featured attraction of anticommunist gatherings. In the long run, however, the film hurt the Committee more than it helped. HUAC was right about Communist involvement in the demonstrations and the abolition movement, but the majority of the demonstrators were independent of the Party. They objected to the Committee because by now it had come to be regarded as an unreformable blight on free speech and dissent. But what had the greatest impact on public opinion was the film's unflattering contrast between the youthful, idealistic demonstrators, and the anticommunists on the Committee: beefy, balding, bullying, lashing out against their enemies with wild, red-smearing invective, a crude and embarrassing relic of unreconstructed McCarthyism.[82]

Young radicals' infatuation with third world revolutionaries like Fidel Castro created a bond between the Old and New Left, subtly symbolized by the world's only monument to the Rosenbergs in Havana. The abortive Bay of Pigs invasion and the beginning of American involvement in Vietnam seemed to prove the validity of the Old Left's position that American opposition to Communist insurgences lacked any basis in morality.[83]

The sixties also saw a rebirth of the old united front refusal to exclude anyone on the left from the radical movement. In 1963 Dagmar Wilson of the Women's Strike for Peace opened her organization to Communists. The Fair Play for Cuba and the Berkeley Free Speech movements welcomed Communist participation, as did the black Students Non-Violent Coordinating Committee. The Students for a Democratic Society—which had broken away from its parent League for Industrial Democracy in 1960 over the League's opposition to communism—denounced "unreasoning anticommunism" at its 1962 organizational meeting at Port Huron. SDS went on to affirm that Communists were less dangerous to the country than their anticommunist persecutors.[84]

Once again, J. Edgar Hoover emerged as the symbol of the anticommunists' use of the Communism issue as a pretext to repress civil liberties and intellectual freedom. The FBI, an article in the *Nation* charged, was "a formidable deterrent to intellectual dissent on basic issues of our time." Hoover had manipulated the public's fear of communism to justify a permanent suspension of freedom of speech by creating a perpetual state of emergency. By constantly focusing the public's attention on Communist participation in "social reforms, peace, politics, veterans, women's and youth's problems," Hoover had made Americans think that "it is hardly safe to think about any of the issues in these all-embracing categories. For Communists may be thinking about them, too, and how is one to know whether one's thoughts are actually one's own, or the reflection of some subtle Communist thought-inoculation." In sum, decades of anticommunism had reduced Americans to a state of "sheepish conformity."[85]

Anticommunism had become so disreputable by the early sixties that President John F. Kennedy could define his new administration as a break with the past by crusading against it at home (calling it "extremism") and by rejecting it as a guide for foreign policy (calling it "moralism") even while pursuing a diplomacy that, in its readiness to confront all challenges to American power (which were inevitably Communist challenges), far exceeded in its militance anything proposed by avowed anticommunists.

During his congressional career Kennedy had paid the homage to anticommunism expected of any politician who represented a largely Catholic constituency. But as candidate and president, Kennedy's anticommunism was submerged within an expansive American nationalism that regarded foreign challenges as insults to American power, and which saw American power as the foundation of world order. During the 1960 campaign, Kennedy told a Catholic magazine that "Washington is the capital of the free world, [and] the president must be its leader. Our Constitution requires it, our history requires it, our survival requires it." His view of America's role in world affairs so far exceeded the Wilsonian norm of working within international law and through international organizations that it hardly could be described as liberal internationalism. Some would call it globalism; others, less kindly, imperialism.[86]

Kennedy's admirers praised him for basing his foreign policy decisions on the cool calculations of power politics, rather than on ideologies like anticommunism, which, depending on context, was regarded as dangerous extremism or hackneyed moralism. Arthur M. Schlesinger, Jr., said Kennedy approached the Soviet Union "without illusion about the character of Russian polity and purpose but also with considerable weariness over the rhetoric of the cold war." John Foster Dulles's "talk of the struggle between the God-anointed apostles of free enterprise and the regimented hordes of atheistic communism" simply bored Kennedy, Schlesinger wrote. The President, rather than mouthing "self-serving platitudes about the total virtue of one side and the total evil of the other" was inclined to view the superpower struggle in "national rather than ideological terms." For Kennedy the cold war was not "a final battle between democratic good and communist evil but an obscure and intricate drama, where men, institutions and ideals, all bedeviled by the sin of self-righteousness, threatened to rush humanity to the edge of destruction, and where salvation lay in man's liberation from myth, stereotype and fanaticism." Schlesinger's Kennedy was a rationalist who "was determined to take the hysteria out of the cold war and get down to the business at hand."[87]

As president, Kennedy's strident—even aggressive—view of America's role in the world ("pay any price . . . bear any burden") dispensed with Truman and Eisenhower's stress on the morality of the cold war clash between freedom and totalitarianism. For Kennedy, the fundamental issue was world leadership. It was, it seemed, competition for competition's sake. At times, Kennedy seemed to welcome the Soviet-American rivalry as good for the national health, the moral equivalent of a spirited fifty-mile hike or game of touch football.

Upon taking office, Kennedy was offered a choice between two competing groups of Democratic foreign policy advisors. One, represented by Dean Acheson and Paul Nitze, spoke for cold war anticommunism, and insisted that the goal of the Soviet Union remained unchanged: the domination of Europe. They believed that communism had to be contained everywhere, but that it was dangerous for the United States to become unduly distracted from the main arena by upheavals in the developing world.

The second group, which included Adlai Stevenson, Averell Harriman, J. William Fulbright, and George Kennan, held that the Yalta division of Europe was frozen into a stalemate. The real test of American resolve and enterprise was now in the developing nations of the third world, whose choice of the Soviet or American development model might well decide the cold war.

Kennedy associated Acheson-Nitze anticommunism with the static policies of the Eisenhower administration—and with the outmoded moralism of John Foster Dulles. Economic assistance to developing nations, combined with flexible and imaginative military assistance against Communist insurgences would be his response to the Soviet challenge to American world leadership. Khrushchev had recently boasted that "there is no longer any force in the world capable of barring the road to socialism." Kennedy would prove him wrong.[88]

The great questions of foreign policy could best be decided using objective information, objectively organized, not by referring to moral principles. Kennedy was seen and admired as representing "the new American breed, not ideological, and wary of those who were. . . . Kennedy was committed only to rationality and brains, nothing more." He had evolved beyond old pieties like anticommunism: "He symbolized that entire era—post-Depression, postwar, post-McCarthy America. Ideology seemed finished, humanism was on the decline as a political force; rationality and intelligence and analysis were the answers. There was no limit to what brilliant men, untrammeled by ideology and prejudice and partisanship, could do with their minds in solving the world's problems."[89]

The Cuban missile crisis was mythologized by New Frontiersmen as a model of crisis management—and as setting a standard for foreign policy: an objective assessment of the realities of power, then unflinching action based on a cold-blooded and rational evaluation of that calculus. Columnist Stewart Alsop told Americans that "the next time Khrushchev makes a wrong move" America's response would be guided by nerves-of-steel rationalists like Robert J. McNamara, the man with "the highest intelligence quotient of any leading public official in this century." Arthur Schlesinger, Jr. wrote that Kennedy's performance had been "a combination of toughness and restraint, of will, nerve, and wisdom, so brilliantly controlled, so matchlessly calibrated, that it dazzled the world."[90]

But there were others who worried that without a grasp of the moral issues involved, cold war, would become nothing but a dangerous test of strength in which every challenge to American power had to be met and defeated. Chester Bowles was concerned that the new administration

> lacks a genuine sense of conviction about what is right and what is wrong. . . . Anyone in public life who has strong convictions about the rights and wrongs of public morality, both domestic and international, has a very great advantage in times of strain, since his instincts on what to do are clear and immediate. Lacking such a framework of moral conviction or sense of what is right and what is wrong, he is forced to lean almost entirely upon his mental processes; he adds up the pluses and minuses of any question and comes up with a conclusion. Under normal conditions, when he is not tired or frustrated, this pragmatic approach should successfully bring him out on the right side of the question. What worries me are the conclusions that such an individual may reach when he is tired, angry, frustrated, or emotionally affected. The Cuban fiasco demonstrates how far astray a man as brilliant and well-intentioned as Kennedy can go who lacks a basic moral reference point.[91]

Without a basic moral reference point, without constant examination of first premises, American policy would go even further astray. Later students have marveled at "how casually" the decisions were made that led to intervention in Vietnam: "Partly, it seems, he [Kennedy] enlarged the American presence to impress Premier Khrushchev with his resolution, and partly because he didn't want to be charged with having 'lost' Vietnam."[92]

Kennedy's refusal to evaluate an objectively anticommunist action like Vietnam in terms of morality and ideology short-circuited debate about its wisdom, its relationship to overall strategy, and its dangers. In the forties and early fifties public debate over the cultural, political, and moral reasons for opposing communism had produced such a moral bond between the public and its leaders that President Eisenhower had been able to accept the political cost of not responding to Soviet provocations in Poland, Hungary, and Cuba, when he judged the risk to outrun the rewards. But the extremism hysteria of the early sixties made public discussion of communism seem too inflammatory to be tolerated, and analysis of moral issues seem a sign of weakness in an administration where only toughness and rationality were admired.

One of the greatest ironies in the history of American anticommunism is that the decisions to involve the United States in Vietnam were made with so little reference to the principles, values, or goals of anticommunism. It was ironic because objectively speaking, the Vietnam involvement was nothing if not anticommunist, and because the ensuing catastrophe would (quite logically) be blamed on anticommunism, turning anticommunism into the public scapegoat for a national disaster.

By 1964, anticommunists no longer seemed able to convince Americans that there were moral reasons to oppose communism. Conservative anticommunists in tune with political realities realized that "extremist" was now a term so stigmatized that it did no good to argue that its use was vague, inaccurate, or dishonest. Anticommunists had to join in denouncing extremists or else fall victim to the anti-extremist hysteria themselves. William F. Buckley, Jr., worked furiously to separate his conservative movement from irresponsible, conspiratorial, or simply silly anticommunists. He read Robert Welch and the John Birch Society out of the conservative movement in an editorial, "The Question of Robert Welch." [93]

When Birchers complained that Buckley was weakening anticommunist unity, he replied that if conservatives asked Americans to "join a movement whose leadership believes the drivel of Robert Welch, they will pass by crackpot alley, and will not pause until they feel the warm embrace of those way over on the other side, the Liberals." Eugene Lyons told Buckley he was right in insisting that responsible anticommunism divorce itself from conspiratorial paranoia. "The fact that much of the campaign against [extremism] is mendacious does not cancel out the truth that the anti-communism of the Extreme Right does contain elements of the exaggerated, the primitive, and above all, the irrelevant. . . . Integrity and good political sense alike demand that the struggle against communism be stripped of unrelated accretions. . . . [The extremists'] anti-communist emotions outstrip their understanding of the nature of communism." Their mistake was that they exaggerated the importance of domestic communism and did not pay enough attention to the current strategy of the Soviet high command.[94]

But other anticommunists like George Schuyler worried that Buckley was splitting the anticommunist movement by exiling Welch (whom Schuyler knew and liked). Schuyler told Buckley that it took people like Welch to get through to nonintellectuals. Another far-right counter-subversive, Archibald Roosevelt, told Schuyler that the war against extremism might be fatal to "Our Side." Roosevelt asked conservative New Hampshire newspaper publisher William Loeb, who had just denounced Welch, to keep quiet publicly, "in the interests of trying to save the republic"[95]

The countersubversive right even developed a new theory to absolve themselves of any guilt for having discredited the movement. Edgar Hunter, a self-styled expert on brainwashing, charged that Communists were engaged in a sophisticated and scientific public relations campaign to brainwash Americans into associating the term "anticommunist" with "extremist." The Senate Internal Security Subcommittee invited Hunter to testify that leftists had decided to use the term "Birchite" as a replacement for "McCarthyite" when they attacked anticommunists. The senators published Hunter's testimony as *The New Drive Against the Anti-Communist Programs* on July 11, 1961. No one was listening.

Two films of 1964 illustrate how deeply embedded had become the popular-culture image of the anticommunist as militarist, fascist, and extremist. In *Seven Days in May* John Frankenheimer had Burt Lancaster play an anticommunist Air Force general who mounts a coup to stop a liberal president from signing a nuclear arms treaty with the Soviet Union. The movie's semidocumentary authenticity depended on the audience's willingness to believe that the Pentagon housed a horde of fascists conspiring against democracy, and that the public was helpless against these out-of-control anticommunist maniacs in tanks, planes, and battleships.

The other film was Stanley Kubrick's black comedy, *Dr. Strangelove*. Here was another crazed anticommunist general, this time fighting communism by launching his own nuclear strike against Russia to force the United States into a preemptive attack on the Soviets to keep them from retaliating. *Dr. Strangelove's* satire, directed against Herman Kahn, Wernher von Braun, and other nuclear strategists, required the public to believe that "Better Dead than Red" anticommunists in the military were ready to push the button and blow up the world rather than accept peace with the Soviet Union. It was, by the way, a Soviet Union no worse than the United States, or, in Kubrick's Swiftian mode, no more contemptible.[96]

These films' image of American anticommunism was a grotesque caricature of the historical reality, but by the mid-sixties it had come to seem natural, normal, and uncontroversial to many Americans. Villainous anticommunists had become as much popular entertainment conventions as sinister Nazis and Ku Klux Klansmen.

When President Kennedy was murdered, the venerable Communist culture warrior Mike Gold, writing in the Party's newspaper, worried that the death of a president at the hands of a self-styled Communist might be "our Reichstag," leading to new anticommunist assaults on the Party. He need not have worried. Anyone who paid undue attention to Oswald's political convictions, or who called attention to the fact that he considered himself a Communist, would have been judged guilty of McCarthyism, Birchism, or extremism. Decisions were made in the White House and the Justice Department not to explore the links between the assassination and Oswald's Marxism out of fear that revelations about Oswald's pro-Castro sympathies might touch off such an anticommunist reaction that there might be another crisis with the Soviet Union. It was simply no longer acceptable to mention that a person was a Communist, not even if he were a presidential assassin.[97]

During the 1964 presidential campaign, anticommunism's disrepute enabled Barry Goldwater's enemies to portray him as a dangerous madman, and, by contrast, Lyndon Johnson as a man of peace and reason. The extremism controversy encouraged liberal anticommunists to redefine themselves as "moderates." Republicans had once gained a political advantage during debates over communism, since liberal Democrats had vestigial ties to the progressive left—Republicans did not. Democrats now recaptured the advantage when politics was recast as a struggle between moderates and extremists. Liberal Democrats had no party ties to right-wing extremists—Republicans did.

Goldwater was lifted toward the Republican nomination by the rising tide of conservatism among young Republicans, a development fondly nurtured by Buckley's *National Review*. Buckley's Young Americans for Freedom was hardly distinguishable from the Goldwater for President movement, and Buckley's brother-in-law L. Brent Bozell ghostwrote Goldwater's *Conscience of a Conservative*, which sold 3.5 million copies by 1964.[98]

In *Conscience of a Conservative* Goldwater had attacked both parties for not making "*victory* the goal of American policy," since "the central strategic fact of the Cold War is that the Communists are on the offensive and we are on the defensive."[99] In 1964 those words seemed to put Goldwater in step with the John Birch Society, and to label him one of those extremists that everyone was so worried about. Anyone who had seen *Seven Days in May* or *Dr. Strangelove* knew a Goldwater presidency meant nuclear war with the Soviets.

Nelson Rockefeller, Goldwater's rival for the Republican nomination, was the first to use the extremist label against the Arizona conservative. Rockefeller charged that Goldwater represented a "real danger" from "extremist elements" in the GOP who were engaged in a "ruthless" effort to take over the party. The radical right, he said, had been responsible for "threatening letters, smear and hate literature, strong-arm and goon tactics, bomb threats and bombings, infiltration and takeover of established political organizations by Communist and Nazi methods." Goldwater's supporters in the Young Americans for Freedom were using "tactics of totalitarianism" and Goldwater himself was a "dupe and a puppet of sinister right-wing forces." Just before the California primary, Rockefeller issued a pamphlet, "Who Do You Want in the Room with the H Bomb?"[100]

There were Dr. Strangelove-like parodies of the Goldwater slogan, "In Your Heart You Know He's Right": "In the Night You Know He Might," and even, "In Your Guts You Know He's Nuts." A tabloid publisher persuaded two thousand psychiatrists to complete a "psychological study" by mail that asked the question, "Do you think that Barry Goldwater is psychologically fit to serve as President of the United States?" Their answer, essentially, was that Goldwater was crazy. The *New York Times* was one of many newspapers that reported the survey and carried subscription ads for the tabloid that featured the survey.[101]

Just before the convention, Goldwater took a vacation in Germany.

Daniel Schorr of CBS News followed him there, and hysterically broadcast back to America that "Senator Goldwater, if nominated, will be starting his campaign here in Bavaria, center of Germany's right wing." When Schorr learned that Goldwater planned to visit the commander of the American Seventh Army in Germany, he also found out that the unit had a recreation area at Berchtesgaden. According to Schorr, Goldwater was making a spiritual pilgrimage to "Hitler's onetime stamping ground." "It is now clear," said Schorr,

> that Senator Goldwater's interview with *Der Spiegel*, with its hard line appealing to right-wing elements in Germany, was only the start of a move to link up with his opposite numbers in Germany, and this has added an element of confusion in German politics. . . . Thus there are signs that American and German right wings are joining up, and the election campaign is taking on a new dimension.

Goldwater's rivals at the Republican convention slipped a transcript of Schorr's report under every delegate's hotel room door.[102]

Soon Goldwater was being brown-smeared from all directions. Martin Luther King claimed he could see "dangerous signs of Hitlerism in the Goldwater campaign." California's Pat Brown said, "All we needed to hear [at the Republican convention] was 'Heil Hitler.' " The mayor of San Francisco said that "[the Republicans] had Mein Kampf as their political bible."[103]

Goldwater's anticommunism was all the media needed to make him out to be a dangerous extremist. CBS News ran a documentary on Goldwater titled "Thunder on the Right," and suggested Goldwater was the candidate of the "John Birch Society, the Minute Men and other extremists." William Scranton wrote Goldwater an open letter that told him, "You have too often allowed the radical extremists to use you. . . . Goldwaterism has come to stand for being afraid to condemn right-wing extremists."[104]

These relentless attacks on Goldwater's anticommunism set the stage for the most powerful political advertisements in American history. Ordered by Bill Moyers, then a top aide to Lyndon Johnson, from the Madison Avenue firm of Doyle Dane Bernbach, the most unforgettable ad had a little girl plucking petals from a daisy while an off-camera voice counted down to a final image of a nightmarish mushroom cloud. It closed with the words, "These are the stakes: To make a world in which all of God's children can live, or go into the dark. We must either love each other, or we must die. Vote for President Johnson on November third. The stakes are too high for you to stay home."

The follow-up was almost as striking. It had a girl licking an ice cream cone (milk was popularly associated at the time with fallout from nuclear tests), while a voice-over explained that children were being killed by fallout, until passage of the Nuclear Test Ban Treaty. And yet "a man—Barry Goldwater" had voted against the treaty. Accompanied by the clicks of a geiger counter, the voice urged, "Vote for President Johnson on November third. . . . The stakes are too high for you to stay home." Journalists seemed to use the ads as the leads for their reporting. C. L. Sulzberger of the *New York Times* wrote that if Goldwater should "enter the White House, there might not be a day after tomorrow." The ads could not have been any clearer, Goldwater recalled bitterly, if they had simply come out and said, "Barry Goldwater would blow up the world if he became President of the United States."[105]

During the campaign, Goldwater found that every time he tried to discuss communism, he reinforced the stereotype of himself as an extremist. Since there was no way for him to escape the label, he tried to redefine it in his speech accepting the nomination. Adapting a line from Cicero's speeches against Catiline, he argued that "extremism in the defense of liberty is no vice, and . . . moderation in the pursuit of justice is no virtue." But extremism now called up too many frightening associations for this to work. By simply mentioning the word, Goldwater confirmed the impression that he was too dangerous to be trusted.[106]

Goldwater's talk of victory against communism, his discussion of the moral issues involved in the cold war, and his frank discussion of military strategy made Lyndon Johnson seem the voice of reason by comparison. Women, who until then had tended to vote Republican, were particularly alarmed by Goldwater. For the first time a majority of them voted Democratic. Stigmatized as McCarthyism, Birchism, and now extremism, outspoken anticommunism had now been rejected at the polls as a danger to world peace. Lyndon Johnson could now justify almost anything he did in Southeast Asia by calling it moderation and pointing to the alternative—anticommunism.

America was now on the verge of a major land war in Asia, a disaster that would tear apart American society and destroy the age-old legacy of trust between the people and their government. It was a war in which the fundamental issue was communism: the Communist ideology of the North Vietnamese and the Viet Cong; the anticommunist alliances the United States had constructed in Asia and the rest of the world; America's commitment to a containment policy designed to stop the spread of communism.

But it was a war in which any thorough discussion of the fundamental issues of communism and anticommunism was avoided as being "boring," "embarrassing," "inflammatory," "extremist." If anticommunists thought Ike was a Communist, then anticommunists' thoughts were not worth thinking about. If anticommunism meant nuclear war, then anticommunism had to be kept out of power. The extremism debacle had ended in the rejection not only of "extremism" like Robert Welch's, but of the entire critique of communism built up by anticommunists over the past half century, the wisdom along with the wildness and the wackiness. No longer was national leadership making any effort to justify the sacrifices of the cold war in terms of the heritage of American values and Western civilization.

Anticommunists were appalled that America, a country forced by history and culture to be anticommunist, no longer knew that it was anticommunist, or why. It was fighting an anticommunist war without a memory of the moral foundations of anticommunism, and so without the ability to judge whether this was the right place or the right time or the right way to be fighting communism. The core of American anticommunism had always been its stubborn belief that resistance to communism was a moral obligation resting on moral judgments about the nature of communism. But now, by its own excesses, anticommunism had helped place in power leaders who made little use of moral principles in their foreign policy, and instead would measure success in terms of bomb tonnage and body counts.

Chapter 11

SHAME AND BLAME

The tables were now being turned. For twenty years anti-Communist liberalism had been riding high and fellow traveling liberalism had been lying low. Now fellow-traveling liberalism was once again in a position to make its bid, and it naturally proceeded to do so. This time, however, the issue was not the Soviet Union; it was the United States. . . . [Although they might admit having] been wrong about the Soviet Union. . . . they could and did still claim to have been right about the United States—right in having blamed it for starting the cold war, and right in believing that it was fundamentally an evil country. As they had been put on the defensive in the past because of the crimes of Stalin, they now sought to put the anti-Communist liberals on the defensive by focusing on the "crimes" of the United States.

—Norman Podhoretz, *Breaking Ranks*[1]

From 1965 until 1975, anticommunism would have to bear a growing burden of blame for the Vietnam disaster. A failed war against communism, many would conclude, must have been based on false premises. Anticommunism would come under attack not only as the cause of the catastrophe that was eating away at American society, but as a delusion that had led the country astray since the beginning of the cold war. There would even be those who would argue that American anticommunism had in fact been responsible for the cold war.

There is no reason to believe that the American people as a whole ever changed their ideas about communism or, indeed (judging by Nixon's victories in 1968 and 1972), ever turned en masse against the war. By the end of the American engagement in Vietnam, however, there would be a body of opinion, a minority opinion, perhaps, but that of a passionate and influential minority, that held anticommunism responsible for America's having developed a profoundly false view of the world that made it act disastrously and unjustly abroad; thus anticommunists would find themselves indicted as false prophets, guides who had led the country astray, morally as well as intellectually.

It was not long before criticism of the Vietnam war escalated to a critique of anticommunism. At the beginning, the opposition simply argued that the war was an ineffective and counterproductive way of fighting communism. Soon opponents began to raise doubts about whether the fight against communism was really necessary any longer, or even if it had ever been necessary.

Even before the Bay of Tonkin Resolution of August 7, 1965, Senator J. William Fulbright, already deeply suspicious of domestic anticommunism, was beginning to question its validity as a guide to foreign policy. On March 24, 1964, in his celebrated "Old Myths and New Realities" speech, Fulbright demanded that the United States adjust its foreign policies to the changes that had occurred since the death of Stalin. "The master myth of the cold war," he complained, "is that the Communist bloc is a monolith composed of governments which are not really governments at all but organized conspiracies, divided among themselves perhaps in certain matters of tactics, but all equally resolute and implacable in their determination to destroy the free world." Fulbright went on to reject not only the fiction of the Communist monolith, but the rest of the assumptions upon which American anticommunist foreign policy rested—that communism was so contrary to American values that the United States had an obligation to oppose it. "How the Soviet Union organizes its internal life," Fulbright said, "the gods and doctrines that it worships, are matters for the Soviet Union to determine."[2]

A few months later, Fulbright was beginning to question not just anticommunism, but the entire strategy of containment. "The Communism of Eastern Europe and the Soviet Union is slowly being humanized," he said in June 1965. "The terror of Stalin's time has largely disappeared. . . . As it becomes clear to each side that it is safe and profitable to do so, ideological barriers can be expected gradually to erode away. . . . Communists have unalterable bonds of humanity with all other men and these bonds of humanity can be the instrument of change."[3]

As he chipped away at containment, Fulbright redefined anticommunism to an absurdity: "A good many Americans are disposed to regard the Cold War as a struggle between two ways of life, one true and good the other unalterably evil. It would be ironic indeed were we to fall victim to the contagion of fanaticism that we find repugnant in Communism." To anticommunists it sounded as if he were saying that if communism were not completely evil and the democracies not completely virtuous, then the difference between them was not worth the quarrel. In a June 15, 1965 speech at Johns Hopkins, Fulbright made the practical suggestion that a Communist Vietnam might prove to be a valuable buffer against China. He went on to reject the very idea of basing diplomacy on moral values, demanding that the United States adopt "an approach that accepts the world as it is, with all its existing nations and ideologies, and with all its existing qualities and shortcomings." To many Americans, and not just anticommunists, that seemed to be asking America to stop being America, but as the Vietnam war spun out of control, the consequences of a foreign policy based on what anticommunists insisted were moral values seemed grim indeed.[4]

By the beginning of 1966, with almost 200,000 American troops in Vietnam, and massive American bombings of the North, elite support for Vietnam was beginning to crumble. In February 1966, Walter Lippmann went public with his opposition to Johnson's Vietnam policies, and that same month, Senator Fulbright organized a special series of hearings of his Foreign Relations Committee to debate the wisdom of American involvement in Vietnam. These hearings would have the revolutionary effect of rendering legitimate—even patriotic—what would have seemed almost treasonous just a few months before: raising fundamental questions about the entire policy of containing communism.

Fulbright's most sensational witness was George Kennan. Those who had been following Kennan's career knew that he had long ago abandoned the containment policy associated with his name, complaining that his original proposals had been misunderstood, misapplied, and militarized, and that conditions had fundamentally changed since the early days of the cold war. Containment, he now said, was "one of those semantic vulgarizations to which our mass media are prone when they lack the patience and inclination to look at things carefully."[5]

To the press and the general public, however, Kennan was still the architect of containment—and therefore a particularly authoritative expert on communism. For him to question not only Vietnam policies but the anticommunism that seemed to be the basic motivation for that war was stunning news indeed. Kennan's public criticism of anticommunism and containment at the Fulbright hearings created a sensation; the public would have been even more astounded to know that privately he was dismissing the idea that there was a meaningful moral difference between the American and Soviet systems. By now Kennan had developed a deep distaste for American culture and politics, and in many areas—restricting pornography and limiting environmental destruction were two examples—he preferred the manner in which the Soviets managed their affairs.[6]

Fulbright finished the hearings convinced that President Johnson was the captive of the anticommunist fanatics he had warned against in his memorandum against extremism in the military. He was convinced that the guiltiest of all was Dean Rusk, who was "locked in the religion of anti-Communism and the old Asia First strategy."[7] But since it was difficult to prove that the bland Secretary of State was an anticommunist zealot, or to locate evidence of anticommunist extremism in the policy papers of Robert McNamara's managerial technicians in the Defense Department, Fulbright began to look to history for the anticommunist roots of the Johnson administration's disastrous Asia policy. During seven days of hearings on China in March 1966, Fulbright and his witnesses argued that anticommunists were responsible for Vietnam because they—that is, McCarthy and his countersubversives—had driven the old China hands out of the State Department, thus drawing a "curtain" down over China that had kept American policymakers away from accurate information about China or the rest of Asia. According to this view, Kennedy, Johnson, and the American people were the ultimate victims of McCarthyism, since Service, Lattimore, and the other China hands would have been able to provide the advice that would have kept the country out of Vietnam. Opposition to the war was now expanding into an indictment of cold war anticommunism from its very inception.[8]

On April 21, 1966, Fulbright made his "Arrogance of Power" speech at Johns Hopkins. The root of America's difficulties, he argued, was its high-vaulting determination to impose order on a disorderly world and its belief that communism was the root of that disorder. But turmoil, though America refused to accept the fact, was the natural state of the world. This flawed view of the world, made worse by anticommunist obsessions, was leading America to war abroad and civil unrest at home.[9]

A few months later, Fulbright dismissed the idea that there was any significant moral difference between communist and noncommunist regimes: "We are told we are combating Communism. I don't understand this human obsession with abstractions. Communism is simply another way to organize society, and subject to the same abuses of any concentration of power. Stalin was a terrible ogre, but he would have been no matter what system he espoused. Communist Yugoslavia is a more open society today than the military regime in South Vietnam or military dictatorships in Latin America we support."[10]

Since most Americans persisted in seeing communism as dangerous, Fulbright called on psychiatrists to explain away these fears. The well-known Johns Hopkins psychiatrist Jerome D. Frank testified before Fulbright's committee on May 25, 1966, to suggest that fear of the outside world was irrational, and so the cold war might be considered a collective "sickness." The United States had become chained to the cold war with the Soviets, Frank argued, because of a "self-fulfilling prophecy": "We act toward an enemy in such a way that he is moved to react toward us in a way we predicted and dreaded. The threats and insults and bomb waving swapped by the United States and Russia from 1946 to 1963 forced both into an extravagant arms race, which may not have been either prudent or necessary."[11] Though the same argument could as easily explain away reasonable fears of real threats, Fulbright seemed on the verge of contending that the Soviet threat had from beginning to end been an illusion—a myth.

The media was also beginning to turn against the war, as the government's official optimism about "progress" was being contradicted by reports from the field by some of the country's best international correspondents. When they first began to report back to their editors that Washington's press releases did not gibe with the facts, the editors at first resolved the differences in the government's favor. By 1967 they were having second thoughts. The "credibility gap" was itself becoming a major story. That year the *New York Times*'s Harrison Salisbury reported from Hanoi that contrary to Washington's assurances, civilian sites were being bombed by American planes. *Life* magazine, still enormously influential, had sent publisher Hedley Donovan, Henry Luce's successor, to Vietnam in late 1965. He had reported that the war was well worth fighting. Eighteen months later, he changed his mind. The United States had gone to war for "honorable and sensible purposes," *Life* editorialized in October 1967, but the conflict had been "harder, longer, more complicated" than anyone had expected; now it was no longer "worth winning," and was not vital to American interests. Two years later, *Life* was so revolted by the war that it filled an issue with the portraits of the 250 American servicemen killed that week.

Liberal anticommunism was being devastated by the war, as more and more liberals shifted to the opposition, causing many of them to rethink the postulates of anticommunism. The founding fathers of liberal anticommunism like the ADA's Arthur M. Schlesinger, Jr. and John P. Roche had no difficulty continuing to support an anticommunist foreign policy even as they came to oppose a war against communism gone wrong, but they feared Vietnam was leading to "a new testing of the national faith in liberty." However, many of the liberals had entered liberal anticommunist organizations like the ADA as a way of "clearing" themselves of suspicion of fellow-traveling sympathies during the heyday of McCarthyism. All that kept them from rejecting anticommunism—which they had never fully embraced—was fear that the "loss" of Vietnam might lead to another wave of McCarthyism as the country searched for scapegoats. In 1967, giving voice to these fears, the ADA's John Kenneth Galbraith unhappily concluded that the United States could not withdraw from Vietnam, "for domestic reasons, if for no other," because it could not risk a resurgence of McCarthyism.[12]

The ADA's labor union faction, however, such as I. W. Abel of the Steelworkers and David Dubinsky of the International Ladies Garment Workers, was so adamantly anticommunist and so worried about weakening the anticommunist consensus, that it backed Johnson's Vietnam policy until the bitter end, despite internal dissension. When the ADA voted to require any candidate it endorsed in the 1968 election to pledge "restraint in the conduct of the war in Vietnam," almost all the union leaders on the executive committee threatened to bolt. When the ADA membership overwhelmingly supported the candidacy of Eugene McCarthy, the heads of the Steelworkers, the ILGWU, and the Communications Workers of America resigned in protest. Others stayed only to try to preserve what was left of the liberal anticommunist coalition.[13]

In 1969 the ADA finally voted to endorse complete withdrawal from Vietnam. That drove the few remaining labor unionists and many of the more conservative members out of the organization to join the neoconservative movement which was coming to be seen as the last refuge for anticommunist liberals and intellectuals. It would be some of these refugees from the ADA who would join *Commentary* editor Norman Podhoretz in organizing the Coalition for a Democratic Majority to fight to return the Democratic party to the anticommunist fold. After 1972, the ADA withered away as many liberals found it impossible to be both liberal and anticommunist. In the same manner, other liberal organizations nurtured on anticommunism split or perished because of their inability to reconcile their anticommunist convictions with their opposition to an anticommunist war.[14]

While opposition to the war was destroying liberal anticommunism, developments in Rome were continuing to weaken the American Catholic Church's hereditary anticommunism. During the sixties the American Catholic community was excited and for the most part gratified by Vatican II's renewal of the Church. The Council's *Pastoral Constitution on the Church in the Modern World* (*Gaudium et Spes*) called for an open attitude toward the non-Catholic world and led to official approval for an unprecedented "Christian-Marxist dialogue" that was institutionalized in a Secretariat for Non-Believers led by the Cardinal of Vienna, Franz Konig. An end had come to the reflexively hostile attitude toward communism popes had always required of Catholics.

For many American Catholics, there was another shock in the *Pastoral Constitution*'s denunciation of nuclear warfare as a "crime against God and Man." Vatican II went on to brand the nuclear arms race and the strategy of nuclear deterrence an "utterly treacherous trap for humanity," which threatened "lethal ruin." Cardinal Spellman and nine other American bishops dissented, saying that "the defense of a large part of the world against aggression (through possession of nuclear weapons) is not a crime, but a great service."[15]

It was clear the American Church was feeling pressure from the Vatican to end its automatic support for Washington's cold war policies. The change was slow, but, given the fundamental loyalty of Catholics to papal teaching, inevitable. In 1966 the bishops were still saying that, "in the light of the facts as they are known to us, it is reasonable to argue that our presence in Vietnam is justified." By 1968, the bishops had shifted enough to write in their pastoral letter, *Human Life in Our Day*, that "in assessing our country's involvement in Vietnam we must ask: Have we already reached, or passed, the point where the principle of proportionality becomes decisive? How much more of our resources in men and money should we commit to this struggle, assuming an acceptable cause or intention? Has the conflict in Vietnam provoked inhuman dimensions of suffering? Would not an untimely withdrawal be equally disastrous?"[16] Nevertheless, the bishops concluded, Catholics still must continue to support their government.

But finally, in November 1971, the bishops took the ultimate step of condemning the war. In their *Resolution on Southeast Asia* they again used the test of whether there was a "proportionality" between the war and its goals. They concluded that the war now failed this test and so had to be judged immoral. "At this point in history, it seems clear to us that whatever good we hope to achieve through continued involvement in this war is now outweighed by the destruction of human life and of moral values which it inflicts. It is our firm conviction, therefore, that the speedy ending of this war is a moral imperative of the highest priority. Hence, we feel a moral obligation to appeal to our nation's leaders and indeed to the leaders of all the nations involved in this tragic conflict to bring the war to an end with no further delay."[17]

Polls revealed that American Catholics had turned against the war even more strongly than the bishops. In 1969 the majority of American Catholics still supported Nixon's policy of gradually turning the war over to South Vietnam, but by 1970 a clear majority opposed the Cambodian invasion, and by January 1971, 80 percent supported immediate withdrawal. Liberal Catholics were even criticizing the bishops for being too moderate in their opposition to the war.[18]

Orthodox historians of the cold war, basing their analysis on State

Department and presidential papers and on the recollections of the officials who had shaped American policy in the forties, had long held that the cold war was America's defensive reaction against apparently aggressive Soviet violations of agreements on the future of Eastern Europe, particularly Poland.

During the sixties and seventies a brilliant group of "revisionist" historians associated with the so-called Wisconsin school led by William Appleman Williams, began to chip away at these comfortable assumptions.[19] Williams's own *Tragedy of American Diplomacy* (1959) had argued that American diplomacy had long been dominated by the search for commercial markets for American produce and products. Other revisionists followed Williams in discovering that motives far less lofty than altruistic Wilsonianism lay behind American policies at the beginning of the cold war. Denna Fleming's *The Cold War and Its Origins* (1961) argued that anticommunists in the Roosevelt and Truman administrations had sabotaged Roosevelt's plan for a postwar order that would have stressed friendly relations with the Soviet Union. Gabriel Kolko's *Politics of War: The World and United States Foreign Policy, 1943–1945* argued that America's anti-Soviet policies during World War II were largely responsible for the breakdown of the Soviet-American alliance and the beginning of the cold war. Lloyd C. Gardner's *Architects of Illusion: Men and Ideas in American Foreign Policy, 1941–1949* concluded that "responsibility for the way in which the Cold War developed, at least, belongs more to the United States." Gar Alperovitz's *Atomic Diplomacy: Hiroshima and Potsdam, the Use of the Atomic Bomb and the American Confrontation with Soviet Power* argued that the bomb had been dropped on Japan to warn Stalin against interfering with American plans for the postwar world.[20]

David Horowitz, whose *Free World Colossus: A Critique of American Foreign Policy in the Cold War* (1965), turned the revisionist thesis into a blistering anti-Vietnam polemic, later explained that his book had become a standard reading in college history courses by the end of the sixties because Vietnam had created a hunger for works that discredited the historical justifications for Vietnam. "Cold War revisionism," he said, "that is, accounts of post-war history significantly at variance with the State Department line, was still illegitimate [before 1965]: it had no status as serious scholarship inside or outside the university."[21] A seismic shift in academia was undermining the old cold war verities, deny-

ing the reality of the Soviet threat in questioning the motives behind
the containment doctrine.

Anticommunists mounted a furious attack on the revisionists, questioning their selection of sources, and their assumptions about Stalin's
intentions.[22] Nevertheless, in the end, the revisionist critique had taken
its place as an alternative and often accepted view of the cold war's origins. Anticommunists, by insisting that American policies at the end of
World War II were motivated by nothing except an idealistic defense
of freedom against aggressive totalitarianism, had made themselves vulnerable to anyone who could demonstrate, as the revisionists indubitably had, that there was a large measure of self-interest in American
cold war policies. "Neo-revisionists" would later make the obvious point
that self-interest is an inevitable motive in all human actions, and it
does not automatically discredit a nation to pursue objectives favorable
to its own interests.[23] But for the time being, anticommunists were demoralized to see what they had always held to be sacred truths scorned
and rejected by some of the brightest and most idealistic minds of the
rising generation.

Those disenchanted with the role of anticommunism in American politics had their choice of villains: J. Edgar Hoover, Richard Nixon, Joseph
McCarthy, to name just a few. The Vietnam era would give enemies of
America's anticommunist foreign policies one paramount villain: the
CIA. Now, in a most spectacular fashion, the CIA was revealed to have
been the hidden hand behind the most respectable and eminent of liberal anticommunist enterprises, the Congress for Cultural Freedom.

In April 1966 the *New York Times* began to run a series of articles on
the CIA. The third of these, appearing on April 27, 1966, contained the
statement that "the C.I.A. has supported . . . anti-Communist but also
liberal organizations of intellectuals such as the Congress for Cultural
Freedom and some of their newspapers and magazines." With the CIA
now being held liable for some of the most criticized American overseas
activities in the cold war, some of the CCF's best known members—
John Kenneth Galbraith, George Kennan, J. Robert Oppenheimer, and
Arthur Schlesinger, Jr.—wrote the *Times* to insist that whatever the facts
might be about the funding, they could "state categorically that we have
no questions regarding the independence of the CCF."[24]

The CCF was still able to rally most of New York anti-Stalinist intellectuals to its defense, and to obtain a subsidy from the Ford Foundation to replace its government funding. But the attacks continued, and, as opposition to the war among intellectuals spread, the reporting on the CCF became more vengeful. In March 1967 the muckraking San Francisco countercultural monthly *Ramparts* published a detailed exposé of the CIA's practice of using nonprofit foundations to funnel money to the supposedly independent (and anticommunist) groups like the National Students' Association.

What was emerging was the thesis that American anticommunism had never been anything except covert government manipulation and propaganda. This was the argument of Andrew Kopkind's article, "CIA: The Great Corrupter," in *The New Statesman.* In it he dubbed the anticommunist intellectuals of the CCF the spies "who came in for the gold."[25]

Finally, on May 20, 1967, in what could not have less adroit timing, the agency's project officer for financing the CCF, Thomas W. Braden, published a defense of the CIA in *The Saturday Evening Post* under the amazingly impolitic title, "I'm Glad the CIA is Immoral!" Braden wrote that when the decision was made to help the CCF in 1950, the Soviet Union was winning the cultural cold war through a network of fronts comparable to Willi Muenzenberg's propaganda empire of the 1930s. Braden boasted that he and Allen Dulles had created their own democratic front network, with the CIA's International Organization Division as its headquarters. They had funneled money specifically to the noncommunist left because they were "the only people who gave a damn about fighting Communism." Irving Brown, head of the AFL-CIO's European office, was one of the most effective of the anticommunists he had funded. The CIA had not only financed the CCF's magazine, *Encounter*, he bragged, but also the CIA had an "agent" in the CCF executive, and moreover another "agent" had worked as an *Encounter* editor.[26]

If Braden thought his candor would redeem the CCF with its critics, he was wildly mistaken. The Ugandan editor of the CCF's African magazine, *Transition*, was arrested, and the house of the CCF's Japanese editor was firebombed. In India an official investigation of the CCF was launched. The reaction in England was particularly vicious. Editors Stephen Spender and Frank Kermode resigned and only Melvin Lasky's personal prestige allowed him to stay on as editor after giving his word of honor that he had never been a CIA agent.

The Braden article let the old progressive left and its sympathizers, who had long been accused of corruption for accepting Communist support (and Moscow gold), use the same logic against their anticommunist tormentors. If the covert relationship between the Communist Party and the Popular Front had been bad, wrote Jason Epstein in the *New York Review of Books*, the CIA's secret ties with the CCF were even worse. The *Partisan Review* ran a manifesto against the secret subsidies signed by Hannah Arendt, Lillian Hellman, Dwight Macdonald, and Norman Mailer. Norman Mailer called the CCF liberals "cockroaches in a slum sink."[27]

Norman Podhoretz's *Commentary*, then self-consciously opening its pages to antiwar opinion, ran a symposium on the question of whether the subsidies proved that "liberal anti-communism has been a dupe of, or a slave to, the darker impulses of American foreign policy." Paul Goodman damned the CCF, the CIA, and American anticommunism as "diabolic" forces, while Dwight Macdonald saw them as responsible for the country's "genocidal crusade" in Vietnam. The guilt-by-association case against the CCF seemed so conclusive to many that it appeared beside the point to examine what the CCF had actually done or said, and whether it had in any way been led astray by its CIA support. Arthur Schlesinger, Jr. courageously pointed out that there had been a real world crisis during the early fifties, and that the CCF and the CIA had had to respond to an emergency under less than ideal circumstances. "During the last days of Stalinism," Schlesinger wrote,

> the non-Communist trade-union movements and the non-Communist intellectuals were under the most severe, unscrupulous, and unrelenting pressure. For the United States government to have stood self-righteously aside at this point would have seemed to me far more shameful than to do what, in fact, it did—which was through intermediaries to provide some of these groups subsidies to help them do better what they were doing anyway.[28]

It remained for Christopher Lasch, emerging as one of the nation's most brilliant cultural historians, to turn the CCF scandal into a sweeping attack on the moral underpinnings of the cold war. It was an argument that held liberal anticommunists wholly responsible for the cold war, the failure of social reform since the Second World War, and, of course, Vietnam, and it has survived as the most familiar and accepted analysis of the CCF funding scandal.

For Lasch, the Congress of Cultural Freedom's reliance on the CIA for funding proved that the anticommunists' argument against the progressive left in the forties and fifties could not have prevailed on its own merits. The liberal anticommunists had won the cultural cold war against the Soviet peace offensive under false pretenses, and their "victory" was tainted, bought and paid for by the CIA's gold. The CIA's covert support of the Congress proved that American "cultural freedom"—offered by liberal anticommunists as evidence of free society's superiority to communism—had been a fraud. The CCF could not have attracted its prestigious coalition of European socialists and liberals if the facts about the funding had been known. The funding scandal, Lasch argued, displayed the fraudulent means liberal anticommunists had employed to sabotage the radical critique of cold war policies, a critique—and here was the point—that could have prevented Vietnam.[29]

Lasch's reliance on guilt-by-association to demolish the CCF and liberal anticommunism may not have constituted a logical refutation of anticommunism, since he felt he could ignore the hard evidence anticommunists had piled up against communism in Russia and Eastern Europe once he had established that they had taken Washington's gold. Nevertheless, it was obviously embarrassing—even devastating—for liberal anticommunists to have been found taking funds from the same "war machine" (Lasch's phrase) responsible for Vietnam. In the politically feverish atmosphere of 1968, Lasch's logic seemed not only persuasive, but conclusive. The Congress had been mortally wounded although it survived until 1979 when, long having ceased to serve any useful purpose, it voted to disband.[30]

The progressive left, able to capitalize on the CCF–CIA funding scandal, on the new credibility of revisionist theories about the cold war, and on the growing tendency to hold anticommunism responsible for the Vietnam war, could now push the case against anticommunism to the extreme of branding it criminal. Where revisionist historians had charged that American cold war policy was based on a misunderstanding of Stalin's motives and was motivated by American business's drive toward economic hegemony, the far left denounced anticommunism as a criminal conspiracy to dominate the world in the interests of America's ruling elite. While these far left conspiracy theories had little if any influence outside the radical counterculture, they were now able to find mainstream publishers who could give them wider circulation than ever before.

Random House published Michael Parenti's *Anti-Communist Impulse* in 1969, which argued that "if America has an ideology, or a national purpose, it is anti-communism." Working backward from a description of Vietnam as a disaster for both America and Vietnam—which few of his readers would have disputed—Parenti gave a history of the cold war that argued that American anticommunism had always been a hypocritical cover America's elite used to dominate the world and eliminate threats to their power.[31]
America's Vietnam policies had their roots in a state of mind, anticommunism, completely divorced from reality. "A fear of this dimension tends to reify the feared object; communism becomes a political force divorced of the historical, national, ethnic, cultural, organizational, material, indeed, human, substances which give it form and identity."[32] Just as liberal anticommunists had diagnosed grass roots anticommunists and McCarthyites as "irrational," and Goldwater as "nuts," now Parenti patiently explained that anticommunists were dangerously deranged.

> "The anti-communist impulse possesses all the pernicious psychological advantages of reductionism, stereotyping, and self-fulfilling prophecy. It battens on the innate rigidity of fear and on that sense of boundless self-righteousness which is the expression of the collective ego. It offers itself as the last defense of Democracy, Capitalism, and the American Way of Life, and it enjoys the support of the multi-billion dollar military-industrial-scientific establishment it helped to create. It is the outgrowth of our loftiest messianic visions and our crudest materialistic drives and as such it tells us more about ourselves than about the world we inhabit."

Since anticommunists lived in a delusional world all their own, Parenti insisted, anything they said about communism could be dismissed out of hand. Had anticommunists charged Stalin with murdering millions? Laughable. "That Stalin could have maintained such popular devotion among the masses while so decimating their ranks is, to say the least, highly questionable." The Gulag was another fiction: "When the camps were abolished after Stalin's death, there was no sign of twenty million half-starved victims pouring back into Soviet life. Labor camp inmates numbered in the thousands." The idea that Russians could not change their jobs, or move about freely in their own country, Parenti derided as another anticommunist myth.[33]

The Old Left had been proposing conspiratorial explanations of anticommunism for years since 1917, and had been flatly denying commonly known facts about the Soviet Union. In that regard, Parenti's diatribe was nothing new. What was different was a moderate climate of opinion that also looked upon anticommunism as a fraud, and anticommunists as inveterately corrupt, so that Parenti's views, while probably persuasive to few outside Communist Party circles, could now be read as exaggerations, or at worst caricatures, of thoughts others were beginning to think.

The new case against anticommunism's responsibility for Vietnam, while cumulatively devastating, was still inferential and circumstantial: Anticommunists had lied about the Soviet Union, they had lied about the cold war, they had lied about the left, but they had not yet been proven to have willfully lied about Vietnam. What was lacking was proof that anticommunists had gotten the country into Vietnam in the same manner they were accused of having led the country into the cold war: secretly, deceptively, fraudulently.

That proof—what seemed to be that proof—was supplied by the Pentagon papers.

On June 17, 1967, Robert McNamara had ordered a "Vietnam History Task Force" to assemble a documentary history of the war in order to preserve those records from destruction or dispersal. To direct the study, McNamara brought Leslie Gelb, who had been Senator Jacob Javits's executive assistant, into the Pentagon's International Security Affairs think tank to direct the study. Among the researchers and writers who worked with Gelb, for a brief time, was Daniel Ellsberg. Gelb's team finished its work—all forty-seven volumes—on January 15, 1969. Only fifteen copies were printed. They were given a secret classification and their distribution was limited to the highest echelons of the defense establishment.

When Daniel Ellsberg eventually delivered a copy of the papers to the *New York Times*, which published them in a highly publicized series of articles beginning on June 13, 1971, they were decisive in convincing the media and the public that the government had been lying from the very start about the war. They revealed that at every stage in the history of American involvement, there was a wide discrepancy between the official rhetoric of confidence and optimism ("light at the end of the tunnel") and the real uncertainty within the government on the best course of action and the likelihood of success. They showed that the CIA and Pentagon had repeatedly warned the Kennedy and Johnson administrations that the war could not be won, but that those presidents had continued to assure the American people that victory was just around the corner. The papers revealed that Presidents Kennedy and Johnson had, presumably for political reasons, consistently implemented only parts of military plans despite being told that such half measures would be ineffective without being accompanied by the rest of the package. The papers also revealed gaps between the uncertainties and hesitations of policymakers behind the scenes and the confident front they projected for the public.

But why did this dismal record of dashed hopes and frustrated expectations have such devastating impact on the image of American anticommunism?

The answer lies less in the papers themselves than in the circumstances of their release, and the manner in which the *Times* framed the summaries and excerpts to the public.

Daniel Ellsberg had graduated from Harvard in 1952, where he wrote his senior thesis on the application of game theory to economics. He joined the Marines after Harvard, and extended his tour to go overseas with his battalion during the Middle East crisis of 1956.

After the Marines, Ellsberg returned to Harvard for graduate work, then moved to the Rand Corporation, where he contributed military policy papers to then Senator John F. Kennedy. While at Rand Ellsberg advised the Pentagon during the Cuban and Tonkin Bay crises, where he attracted notice for his zeal in advocating policies he was assigned to promote. In 1965 he personally lobbied on behalf of the administration in the offices of wavering senators, and visited campuses to defend the administration during Vietnam teach-ins.

In mid-1965 he left Washington for a tour of duty in Vietnam, and contributed an anonymous "Vietnam Diary" to the *Reporter* magazine, describing how Americans were "liberating" the country. He went on combat patrols, and saw action in fire fights, but by 1966 was becoming increasingly concerned about the discrepancy between the optimistic progress reports being sent to Washington and the deteriorating conditions he saw in the field. He tried to bypass channels in his own more pessimistic reports, though he still defended the war to journalists. In 1967, he wrote a message to his Harvard class reunion expressing his belief in the counterinsurgency theories of General Edward Lansdale, but complained that the military was not properly implementing Lansdale's ideas. Back in the States, Ellsberg told Paul Warnke that the goal of denying Vietnam to the Communists was still important, but he was troubled that the war was destroying the country it was trying to save.[34]

After Richard Nixon's election in 1968, Henry Kissinger had Ellsberg prepare policy options on Vietnam for the new administration. In early 1969, Rand assigned Ellsberg to a full-scale study of Vietnam policy, and it was then he was given access to Rand's complete set of the Pentagon papers.

By now Ellsberg had begun to redefine himself as an antiwar activist, having decided that the destruction was out of all proportion to any American interest in the country. The Pentagon papers completed his conversion, and he made an unauthorized copy for himself.

Ellsberg was now devoting himself to antiwar protest. He would appear at rallies and speak darkly about Nixon's plans to suspend the 1972 elections to continue the war. Rand let him go in the spring of 1970 because of his antiwar activities, and he moved on to MIT's Center for International Studies, where he had an office across from William P. Bundy's.[35]

Ellsberg had come to believe that if he released the Pentagon papers, their "explosive" impact on the public would end the war. By showing that the United States had begun its involvement to help the French hold their Vietnamese colonial empire, he felt the papers "stripped" American policy of "all the pretensions of legitimacy." Vietnam was "a case of aggression indeed. Our aggression entirely, our intervention." The papers proved the war was a crime, and he now accused himself of being a war criminal. Releasing the papers would atone for his guilt if it ended the war.[36]

At this point, Ellsberg begins to fit the pattern of earlier converts (or apostates) in the history of anticommunism who were convinced they could lay their hands on documentary evidence that would change the course of history by proving what had before been only suspected—a conspiracy against the republic. Whittaker Chambers went from government office to office trying to persuade officials to look at the papers he had copied from Alger Hiss. The Pumpkin Papers had turned Chambers into a cult figure, revered among anticommunists as the hero who had emerged from the heart of the Communist conspiracy to bear witness against it. Now Ellsberg and the Pentagon papers would figure in a ritual exposé of the anticommunist conspiracy.

Ellsberg began shopping the papers around Washington, hoping to avoid prosecution by having someone else release them. In February 1970 he showed portions of them to J. William Fulbright, but Fulbright did not see "of what use they actually were in stopping the war." Nonetheless, Fulbright tried in vain to get the papers released officially, fearing that making them public without authorization might divert attention from the contents to the violation of security regulations.

Ellsberg gave a copy of the papers to the leftist Institute for Policy Studies which was working on its own historical study of the war. He went to George McGovern and told him that the documents contained such a devastating exposure of Vietnam policy that they would "end the war." McGovern thought Ellsberg was "a hawk with a bad conscience" and wrote him off as fitting the profile of a dozen "professors and preachers and foreign service officers" who claimed they had memoranda that "would end the war if disclosed. . . . I didn't even know if he was rational."[37]

Then Ellsberg learned that *New York Times* reporter Neil Sheehan, whom he had known well in Vietnam, was writing an essay on thirty-three antiwar books for the *Sunday Times*. The title was going to be "Should We Have War Crime Trials?" Ellsberg was now simmering, and when he read Sheehan's review on March 28, 1971, he came to a boil. In that essay, Sheehan wrote, "If you credit as factual only a fraction of the information assembled here about what happened in Vietnam, and if you apply the laws of war to American conduct there, then the leaders of the United States for the past six years at least, including the incumbent President, Richard Milhous Nixon, may well be guilty of war crimes." The idea of a war crimes trial now became a fixation with Ellsberg. A few days later Ellsberg handed over the massive package of the Pentagon papers to Sheehan.[38]

Sheehan already seemed sold on the idea that the war was a crime. There had to be criminals somewhere. Now he had a massive collection of secret government documents that described the decisions that had led to that criminal war, and so, logically, these papers should be evidence of criminal behavior. At least that was how Ellsberg characterized them.[39]

Sheehan realized that Ellsberg had given him one of the great scoops in newspaper history. He and a team of writers were assigned to read the papers, pull out extracts, tie them together into a narrative, and furnish them with introductions, summaries, and conclusions. On Sunday, June 13, 1971, the *Times* started publishing the papers, starting off with a front-page story by Sheehan.

The government's reaction—rushing to court to enjoin publication—could not have been better calculated to make the Pentagon papers appear to be revelations of government criminality. Nixon's first impulse had been to let the *Times* publish and be damned. Since the most important decisions had been made during Johnson's watch, it would be the Democrats who would be most embarrassed. But Henry Kissinger persuaded Nixon that leaks on this scale, if uncontested, would persuade the Chinese—with whom the administration was then negotiating Nixon's historic visit to Peking—that Washington could not keep their discussions secret. When the Justice Department moved to stop the *Times* from publishing the papers, it made the papers seem more incriminating than they actually were—especially to the vast majority of the public, and even the majority of *Times* readers, who would not read the papers but only follow the controversy. And the controversy seemed to mean the government was seeking to cover up wrongdoing that had led to Vietnam.[40]

Neil Sheehan, a great reporter, was certainly no conspiracy theorist. Ellsberg was. Shortly before he handed the papers over to Sheehan, on March 7, 1971, he gave an interview to the *Boston Globe* in which he said that for six years he had been part of "a criminal conspiracy to wage aggressive war." And though the *Times* didn't use the word, they must have been subtly influenced by Ellsberg's view of the papers as evidence of conspiracy. In any case, Sheehan's introduction to the papers used rhetoric uncannily reminiscent of classic conspiracy literature.[41]

"To read the Pentagon Papers in their vast detail," Neil Sheehan wrote, "is to step through the looking glass into a new and different world. This world has a set of values, a dynamic, a language and a perspective quite distinct from the public world of the ordinary citizen and of the two other branches of the Republic—Congress and the judiciary."[42]

Sheehan described the war as something hatched by plotters in deepest secrecy. "The guarded world of the government insider and the public world are like two intersecting circles." Within these secret circles of power, the public and Congress are seen as "elements to be influenced" rather than as having a legitimate interest in knowing what the government is planning.

The war's planners, he said, lacked the human feelings that set moral bounds on actions. The papers revealed that Vietnam policymakers were incapable of feeling "emotional anguish or moral questioning of action." They were confident that "the conflict in Indochina" would "yield to the unfettered application of well-trained minds and of the bountiful resources in men, weapons and money that a great power can command." The Vietnam war had been the work of a secretive cabal of insiders. "The principal actors in this history, the leading decision-makers, emerge as confident men—confident of place, of education, and of accomplishment. They are problem-solvers, who seem rarely to doubt their ability to prevail." Sheehan's introduction had sarcastic references to Vietnam policymakers as "outstanding," "self-assured," "men accustomed to winning"—the words and phrases that seem to echo Mark Antony's view of Brutus as an "honorable man." Above all, Sheehan wrote, Vietnam policies had to be kept secret. "The papers also make clear the deep-felt need of the government insider for secrecy in order to keep the machinery of state functioning smoothly and to maintain maximum ability to affect the public world. The implication was that if the Vietnam decisions been made in full light of day, the public, the press, and Congress would have cried halt long before the final disaster.[43]

Senator Mike Gravel of Alaska, in his introduction to his own edition of the papers, amplified this theme of conspiracy: "The Pentagon papers tell of the purposeful withholding and distortion of facts. . . . The Pentagon papers show that we have created, in the last quarter-century, a new culture, a national security culture, protected from the influences of American life by the shield of secrecy. . . . The Pentagon papers reveal the inner workings of a government bureaucracy set up to defend this country, but now out of control, managing an international empire by garrisoning American troops around the world." They "show that our leaders never understood the human commitments which underlay the nationalist movement in Vietnam, or the degree to which the Vietnamese were willing to sacrifice." They "show that there was no concern in the decision-making process for the impact of our actions upon the Vietnamese people."[44]

The administration's response to the publication of the papers seemed to be a clumsy attempt to cover up a guilty conspiracy. On June 25 a warrant was issued for Ellsberg's arrest for illegally possessing and copying the Rand Corporation's copy of the papers. When he surrendered, he said, "Would you not go to prison to help end this war?"[45] The case against Ellsberg was finally dismissed when it was revealed that the White House "plumbers" had broken into Ellsberg's psychiatrist's office looking for incriminating information. The collapse of the case against Ellsberg seemed equivalent to a guilty verdict against the government.

It was hard to avoid the conclusion that anticommunism itself was the ultimate culprit exposed and indicted by the Pentagon papers, since anticommunism was presumably the motive driving the war-making elite to conspire against the public. And so concluded Mike Gravel, who wrote to Senator Alan Cranston that "the Pentagon papers that I have read convince me that the first and foremost reason that our nation is in a mess today and going toward bankruptcy is as a result of our paranoiac fear of communism."[46]

The Pentagon papers may not have ended the war, as Ellsberg hoped, but they did deepen anticommunism's disgrace in the dark days of Vietnam. Arthur M. Schlesinger, Jr. could protest against "Ellsberg's implications of evil intentions behind American policy," but for the time being, that argument was lost.[47] There was now an alienated and increasingly influential current of opinion in America making itself felt in education, culture, and politics that saw anticommunism as the American original sin.

That is not to say that there were no prominent Americans who still continued to insist that communism was still a menace. The labor union movement continued to be a bastion of anticommunism, and the venerable leader of the AFL-CIO, George Meany, spoke out on every occasion against underestimating the Communist threat. During discussions of the 1972 Nixon-Brezhnev agreement to limit strategic weapons (SALT), he asked if detente didn't expose Nixon as "an opportunist without deep beliefs or large ideals, cynically indifferent to the cause of human freedom? And, more frighteningly still, has he refashioned American foreign policy in his own image?"[48]

Meany sought out an appearance before J. William Fulbright's Senate Foreign Relations Committee on October 1, 1974, to challenge liberals to reject the idea "that liberalism is to be defined as a softer or friendlier attitude toward totalitarian powers, whereas conservatism means a harder or more hostile attitude toward totalitarian powers. . . . We live in strange times. We live in a time when a man whose whole political career was built on rabid anti-Communism [Richard Nixon] can become President and overnight be transformed into the chief advocate of unilateral concessions to the Soviet Union." He accused two members of the committee, Fulbright and Frank Church, of orchestrating a "vitriolic" attack on the "old-line cold warriors." Perhaps, he said, "we owe the cold warriors an apology."[49]

A year later, he attacked Henry Kissinger's ideas on detente: "I'm not blaming all of the world's troubles on Henry Kissinger, but I'm saying, in the final analysis, the cause of human rights in this world is dependent on the strength, the economic strength, the military strength, the moral strength of the United States of America. If we falter, freedom is shaken everywhere. . . . I believe, advisedly believe, sincerely believe, that Dr. Kissinger has presided over an era which has seen a decline of American strength—military, economic, and moral, of unprecedented proportions."[50]

Conservative Republicans were, of course, as adamantly anticommunist as ever, but even William F. Buckley had to admit that the times had left him discouraged. In 1975 he said that "the more I reflect on [our situation], the more convinced I am that the single greatest retreats were conducted under the aegis of Richard Nixon. For this reason alone: that under his tutelage, the entire anti-Communist constituency was virtually disarmed."[51]

During those bleakest winter days of American anticommunism, there was, however, the first faint stirring of new life, of rebirth, a sign of vigor at odds with the uncertainty and pessimism that pervaded the tired veterans of the old cause. One man summoned the will, the strength, and the imagination to commence the giant task of rebuilding the anticommunist coalition. This was Norman Podhoretz, editor of the American Jewish Committee's *Commentary*.

By 1965, with few exceptions, New York's anti-Stalinist intellectuals (Podhoretz included) had turned against the war. Many went on to repudiate anticommunism as well, perhaps giving in to that human penchant for turning the *opinion du jour* into a *weltanschauung* and then finally crafting it into a political theory.

Because of the New York intellectuals' polemical skills and their access to the journals that shaped intellectual opinion, this was a staggering blow to anticommunism. Podhoretz himself had opened the pages of *Commentary* to dissent against cold war orthodoxy as early as 1960. But by the end of the decade he had become convinced that the reaction against any opposition to communism had gone too far. "The opposition was winning," he said. "It had already triumphed in the intellectual world, where the general anti-Communist rationale . . . for years had been suffering a steady pounding at the hands of radical critics. Thus it was now very difficult to defend American policy by appealing to a consensus on the need to draw a line against the advance of Communism."[52]

When the Vietnam war discredited anticommunism, he realized that containment stood discredited as well. "The consequence was that those who had opposed [containment] from the beginning—unreconstructed Stalinists and their equally unreconstructed fellow travelers within the liberal community—could claim, with a plausibility they had never dreamed they would ever again be able to achieve in public debate, that their position was at least being vindicated."[53]

The revulsion against the Vietnam war—which he, too, had felt— had led

> to the idea that the entire policy of trying to check the spread of Communism was and always had been morally wrong as well. This was not an idea I could accept. I could not accept it in relation to the past, when that policy had saved Western Europe from the barbarism and misery which had become the lot of every country in the world with the misfortune to fall under Communist rule. And I could not accept it in relation to the future, when I believed that in the absence of active American resistance, this tide of barbarism and misery would almost certainly sweep over the entire world, and might even ultimately engulf the United States as well."[54]

What neither he nor other antiwar anticommunists had realized, he later explained, was

> how fragile the liberal anti-Communist consensus really was and conversely how deceptive was the apparent weakness of fellow-traveling liberalism, especially among intellectuals. Intimidated by McCarthyism and discredited by Stalinism, the fellow-traveling liberals had temporarily lost their nerve, but they had by no means been converted or given up. They were still there, waiting for just such a shift in the wind as the new *Commentary* at once represented and was helping to bring about.[55]

Alarmed that there was no place left where anticommunist intellectuals could gain a hearing for their views, Podhoretz decided to put himself and his magazine on the line. He invited anticommunists to use *Commentary* to defend themselves and their ideas against the opposition which, he felt, otherwise had the intellectual arena to themselves.

Podhoretz launched *Commentary's* offensive against the "Movement" in June 1970. The left and liberal writers who joined Podhoretz in his counterattack against the "Movement" had been "de-radicalized" (in Nathan Glazer's phrase) by the violence—physical and rhetorical—of the sixties' assault on American society and culture. They included Podhoretz's wife Midge Decter, Nathan Glazer, Dennis Wrong, Michael Novak, Jack Richardson, Walter Goodman, Joseph Epstein, Bayard Rustin, Dorothy Rabinowitz, Samuel McCracken, Edward Grossman, Carl Gershman, Penn Kemble, Elliott Abrams, Diane Ravitch, and Paul Goodman. There were others who had turned against radicalism much earlier, or who had never been radicals: Daniel Patrick Moynihan, Alexander M. Bickel, Irving Kristol, Hilton Kramer, Robert Alter, Seymour Martin Lipset, James Q. Wilson, Robert Nisbet, Leslie H. Farber, William Barrett, Joseph Adelson, Joseph W. Bishop, Jr., Paul Seabury, Charles Frankel, Jeane Kirkpatrick, Roger Starr, Daniel Bell, Paul Weaver, Suzanne Weaver, Edward Jay Epstein, Walter Laqueur, Theodore Draper, Robert W. Tucker, and Edward Luttwak.[56]

Achieving the goals Podhoretz had set for himself—returning anticommunism to its proper place in American foreign policy—looked to be difficult, if not impossible. The opposition had captured the commanding heights of culture. Vietnam had been as devastating to anticommunists in the sixties as the Hitler-Stalin Pact to fellow travelers in 1939. At home, history seemed to have rejected anticommunists and their beliefs.

And yet, events in the Communist world—the repression of Polish dissidents and workers and the Soviet invasion of Czechoslovakia in 1968, the suppression of the great anticommunist writings of Alexander Solzhenitsyn and his exile from the Soviet Union in 1974—made anticommunists believe that their critique of communism was as valid as ever, and that America was in danger unless they could convince Americans to once again pay heed to what anticommunism had to say.

Chapter 12

NATIONAL SCAPEGOAT

Being confident of our own future, we are now free of that inordinate fear of Communism which once led us to embrace any dictator who joined us in our fear. For too many years we have been willing to adopt the flawed principles and tactics of our adversaries, sometimes abandoning our values for theirs. We fought fire with fire, never thinking that fire is better fought with water. This approach failed, with Vietnam the best example of its intellectual and moral poverty. But through failure we have found our way back to our own principles and values, and we have regained our lost confidence.

—President Jimmy Carter, Notre Dame Commencement, May 22, 1977.[1]

During the last half of the seventies, anticommunists watched helplessly and resentfully as the legacy they had built over decades of principled opposition to communism was dissected, derided, and discarded. The worst misdeeds of countersubversive anticommunism were painstakingly exhumed from the most secret files of the FBI, and publicly arraigned as the real history of anticommunism. Anticommunism's enemies emerged as heroic victims of a disgraceful national inquisition, while the historical events that had led to the national reaction against domestic communism and the Soviet Union receded into the dim historical past. Anticommunists stood by watching anxiously as the Ford and Carter administrations appeared to cast aside anticommunism's hard-won and time-tested insights into the nature of communism and the reality of the Soviet threat, and to replace containment as the first principle of American foreign policy while searching for areas of agreement with a Soviet Union that some urged be treated as just another state, no worse than many with whom America had normal relations.

Worst of all, it seemed to anticommunists that the Soviet Union seemed to be responding to all this as a signal that the Brezhnev doctrine, which made all the world fair game for Soviet adventurism, need fear no response or retaliation from Washington. Anticommunists watched with rising fear and anger as Cuban troops began to be used as Soviet surrogates throughout Africa to support Marxist regimes against anticommunist insurgencies, and as Laos, Ethiopia, Mozambique, Afghanistan, and Cambodia fell to Soviet-supported revolutions.

While anticommunists outside the government looked for ways to convince Americans of the persistence of the Communist threat, congressional investigations tore into the murky secrets of the American security agencies, extracting a devastating record of FBI abuses of civil liberties under J. Edgar Hoover. This constituted the most convincing evidence ever assembled to support an indictment of anticommunism as nothing but a campaign of repression directed against dissenters who had vainly tried to warn Americans that the cold war was a tragic mistake.

Ever since the *Lawyers' Report* of 1920, anticommunism's enemies had argued that it was simply a plot against civil liberties and reform. Now the Vietnam and Watergate disasters gave them license to rifle through official records to buttress their arguments. And the post-Vietnam public was ready to believe the worst of the government that had led the country to disaster. Armed with the Freedom of Information Act and the power of subpoena, anticommunism's enemies were let loose on the files of the federal security agencies; their conclusion was that American anticommunism had been, from start to finish, a J. Edgar Hoover creation, a product of his own mad lusts, fantasies, and ambitions.[2] The charge that anticommunism was a plot by America's fascist ruling class would now be absorbed into the world view of some who moved in the highest circles of American politics and culture. Anticommunists now feared that the left's old view of anticommunism as America's original sin was now being absorbed into the country's conventional understanding of its past.[3]

Early in 1975 the House and Senate appointed select committees under Senator Frank Church and Congressman Otis Pike to investigate—in the words of the Senate resolution—"the conduct of domestic intelligence or counterintelligence operations against United States citizens" to see whether they threatened "the rights of Americans."[4]

Congress had been primed for an investigation of the FBI by the misdeeds of Acting FBI Director L. Patrick Gray during the Watergate crisis—he had destroyed the documents John Dean gave him detailing White House illegalities. The formidable J. Edgar Hoover had died in 1972 and could no longer scare off outside investigators. The CIA had become a subject of congressional interest in 1974 when the *New York Times* had printed exposés of CIA crimes based on the Agency's own investigations.

The Senate Committee's report, published in 1976, covered the FBI's covert domestic intelligence action programs, and its operations against Martin Luther King and the Black Panthers. It dug into the Bureau's use of informants, warrantless wiretapping, break-ins, and mail opening. There was also a review of the domestic intelligence activities of the CIA, the National Security Agency (NSA), the military, the Internal Revenue Service, and the Nixon administration's effort to coordinate all federal domestic intelligence programs (the Huston plan). The investigators wove together examples of illegal or at least unsavory actions by all these agencies, producing a narrative in which the historical context of the security agencies' misdeeds receded into the background, while the misdeeds seemed to take on a life of their own, self-justifying, self-motivated. The purpose of domestic anticommunism, it appeared, was simply to attack the rights of anyone who ran afoul of the government's power elite and their powerful sponsors.

The investigating committees managed to expose a vast amount of misbehavior by presidents and the Bureau that violated even the most elastic legal standard. What was omitted, deliberately or otherwise, was any inquiry into the historical context. The Pike and Church committees simply rejected as not worth considering the notion that there had ever been a domestic or international emergency involving communism. The domestic cold war was treated simply as a pattern of repression.

The Church Committee used the antiwar movement of the Vietnam era to represent all dissenting movements of the past. The "confusion and mistakes" of the FBI of the Vietnam years, argued the committee staff, "called into question some of the fundamental assumptions underlying the FBI intelligence programs of the previous three decades."[5]

The Committee used an April 1965 request to the FBI from McGeorge Bundy for "information concerning the Communist role in criticism of American policy in Vietnam" to argue that "the exaggeration of Communist participation, both by the FBI and White House Staff members, could only have had the effect of reinforcing President Johnson's original tendency to discount dissent against the Vietnam War as 'Communist inspired.' It is impossible to measure the larger impact on the fortunes of the nation from this distorted perception at the very highest policymaking level."[6]

Just as government repression had contributed to the Vietnam disaster, the Committee suggested, the repression of earlier dissent had probably contributed to the country's misguided cold war policies. In an offhand comment the Committee cast doubt on the key legal cases of the domestic cold war: "Nor does this report touch on many of the most controversial cases in the FBI's past, such as the Hiss and Rosenberg cases, which have recently been the subject of extensive historical reconsideration on the basis of materials made public under the Freedom of Information Act."[7]

Arguing backwards, the Committee held that if repression of Vietnam era dissent was unnecessary and wrong, so were the Bureau's earlier domestic intelligence campaigns, complaining that "from today's perspective it is harder to understand the nature of the domestic threats to security which, along with foreign espionage, were the reasons for establishing the FBI's intelligence program in the 1930s."[8]

The Committee began its history of the FBI's domestic intelligence operations with the Red Scare raids, again omitting any historical context. It stated the facts so baldly that it seemed Hoover and the Justice Department had simply decided to abrogate the Bill of Rights and abolish civil liberties for their own private reasons.

In outlining how FDR had established an internal security system to cope with the domestic Nazi movement, the Stalinist Comintern, and the Japanese espionage system, the Committee attached a quote from Madison, "Perhaps it is a universal truth that the loss of liberty at home is to be charged to provisions against danger real or pretended from abroad."[9]

Since the Bureau had not been able to provide unambiguous presidential directives or statutory authorizations for all its operations, the staff report questioned the FBI's authority to investigate subversive activities. Although Roosevelt had publicly ordered the Bureau to investigate plans by "foreign governments to try to sway American public opinion ... which would tend to be subversive," the Committee doubted that the Bureau ever had the authority to conduct general intelligence investigations of "subversive infiltration" or to engage in "preventative intelligence." To have admitted that the FBI had ever had authority to study radical and Nazi groups to learn about their "leading personnel, purposes, and aims, and the part they are likely to play at a time of national crisis" might have meant Hoover had the same authority to investigate the antiwar movement, and in 1975, this was unthinkable.[10]

Out of respect for the memory of FDR, the Committee tended to throw as much blame as possible on Hoover for what he had done in the thirties and forties. Describing Hoover's warnings to FDR about the possibility of Communist sabotage, the Senate Committee commented that "whether or not the FBI Director exaggerated the threat, no President could afford to ignore such dire warnings without some further investigation."[11]

The Committee exhibited memos from Hoover cautioning subordinates and superiors to keep domestic intelligence operations confidential to avoid stirring up "ill informed persons or individuals having some ulterior motive." In the post-Watergate era, which saw a "cover-up" as an admission of guilt, Hoover's efforts to keep his operations secret meant he knew what he was doing was wrong.[12]

The Committee devoted most of its energy to exposing the Bureau's counterintelligence programs (COINTELPROs), which ran from 1956 to 1971, and were aimed at disrupting, in chronological order, the Communist Party, the Socialist Workers Party, the Ku Klux Klan, black nationalist groups, particularly the Black Panthers, and the New Left antiwar movement. Dismissing all Bureau attempts to justify the programs, the Select Committee flatly stated that COINTELPRO was a "sophisticated vigilante program aimed squarely at preventing the exercise of First Amendment rights of speech and association, on the theory that preventing the growth of dangerous groups and the propagation of dangerous ideas would protect the national security and deter violence."[13]

Just as countersubversive anticommunists had always been most impressed by the revelations of disaffected ex-Communists, the Senate staff based its most negative conclusions on the testimony of disaffected agents and officials like ex-Assistant FBI Director William C. Sullivan, who had organized the worst of the COINTELPROs. The Committee managed to obtain statements from ex-agents that could have been ed-

itorials in the *Nation,* uttered in a strange bureaucratic marriage of
Greenwich Village Marxism with high school civics. A retired agent
testified that "the FBI now constitutes a degenerative dictatorship in
which the structure still remains but from which public support is rapidly
being withdrawn. I further submit that such a dictatorship is incompatible with the constitutional concepts upon which this Nation is
founded. I feel that this can be historically paralleled with the ascen-
sion of other dictatorships throughout the world."[14]

The Committee concluded that nearly everything the FBI had ever
done was discredited by its covert operations against the antiwar left
and the black power movement, and these were used to establish the
malignity of earlier cold war operations. After the outcome of the Vietnam war, the FBI's operations to maintain support for the LBJ-Nixon
Southeast Asia policy would find few defenders. The Committee treated
all earlier FBI efforts to influence public opinion as equally illegitimate.
Just as all liberal anticommunists had been discredited by revelations
that there had been a hidden underside to its activities, the Committee
used the Bureau's worst excesses against the antiwar movement and
against an American hero, Martin Luther King, Jr., to discredit all it had
ever done against communism.

The Committee concluded that throughout the cold war, the FBI's
domestic intelligence activities showed that the nation had been the
victim of an FBI plot. "The American people need to be reassured that
never again will an agency of the government be permitted to conduct
a secret war against those citizens it considers threats to the established
order."[15]

After the Church and Pike committee investigations, a context existed within which each new revelation of FBI domestic intelligence
could be taken as more proof that anticommunism had been a vicious
and dishonest conspiracy that had led the country into disastrous policies at home and abroad. And there were new revelations nearly every
day. Soon after Jimmy Carter was inaugurated as president in 1977, it
was learned that the CIA had given personal subsidies to Hussein of
Jordan, Syngman Rhee of Korea, Chiang Kai-shek of Nationalist
China, Ngo Dinh Diem of South Vietnam, and Sese Seko Mobuto of
the Congo. Another investigation revealed that the CIA and the FBI
used Nazi war criminals as sources of information about Communist

espionage. In vain would anticommunists protest that historical circumstances were being ignored when the government had to choose between competing evils in a time of crisis, when doing nothing would have been unthinkable.[16]

A certain lightheartedness toward communism became the fashion in media circles, as though it was hilarious to imagine that anyone could have ever feared or disliked something so innocuous. Kay Boyle ridiculed the materials she found in her FBI files. Poor spelling or bad grammar in an FBI file was triumphantly displayed as an example of the imbecility of the Bureau's anticommunists.[17]

As the public became accustomed to the legal notion that evidence illegally obtained could not be used in court, there was a related tendency to assume that political opinions or activities ought not to be held against anyone when the evidence had been acquired illegally. Those who had suffered at the hands of anticommunists now came in for rehabilitation, redeemed by the disgrace of their persecutors. McCarthy took on the role of national hobgoblin, the designated villain of the domestic cold war. The media celebrated its role in his fall to burnish its post-Watergate status as guardian of the national conscience. Heroes of the battle against McCarthy like Edward R. Murrow lent dignity to the view of anticommunism as an American disease—or an American crime. Nixon's Watergate disgrace meant that defenders of Alger Hiss could portray him as the victim of a certified national villain—an anticommunist villain.[18]

Anyone who had been attacked by anticommunists was assumed to have been wronged. The media joined with the progressive left and the liberal establishment to rehabilitate those attacked by the anticommunists over the years. Universities apologized for firing professors who refused to provide information on their Communist affiliations. In 1976, the ACLU rescinded its expulsion of Elizabeth Gurley Flynn. Jimmy Carter pardoned almost all draft evaders soon after taking office.[19]

The Hollywood blacklist took on mythic status as a roll call of cultural heroes—one historian said their "heroic" image moved after 1975 from the hidden precincts of the far left "through to the mainstream of the 'new' Hollywood." Obituaries of blacklisted writers and actors tended to describe them as martyrs for the cause of civil liberties, and made no mention of the political associations that had gotten them blacklisted, or the international situation that had made those associations a cause of concern.[20]

The media gave respectful accounts of the Rosenbergs' sons' battle to win posthumous reversal of their parents' verdict. On June 19, 1978, the twenty-fifth anniversary of the Rosenbergs' executions prompted a spate of media stories that took their side in the case. One was broadcast on PBS. Any new information that supported their innocence, such as a 1979 report, promptly denied, that Roy Cohn had doubted their guilt, was given wide publicity.[21]

Alger Hiss's unending campaign to clear his name gained respect from even those not willing to go so far as to think he had been framed. When historian Allen Weinstein published his exhaustive study, *Perjury*, that concluded Hiss had been guilty of perjury as charged, and that he had in fact been part of a Soviet espionage network, he was savaged by a radical left that insisted Hiss had been framed, and even if he had not been, he was redeemed by the despicable characters of his anticommunist persecutors, Nixon, Chambers, and Hoover. One of the country's most prestigious presses saw fit to pay Hiss the tribute of publishing a facsimile of his 1978 federal court petition to set aside his perjury conviction.[22]

Anticommunists began to worry that not only were the victims of McCarthyism being vindicated, but that, in some sense at least, the public would assume that their views on the Soviet Union and the cold war were being vindicated as well, views that anticommunists had felt had been decisively refuted by logic and by history. Norman Podhoretz thought that anticommunism was defenseless against these distortions of history because it had been rendered speechless, the vocabulary of anticommunism had been banned from respectable political debate. "Thanks to the legacy of McCarthyism," he said,

> the word "Communist" was no longer generally used even to describe self-proclaimed members of the Communist party. If they were black, like Angela Davis, they would be referred to in the press as "militants," and if they were white, like Dashiell Hammett, they would simply be called "radicals." And if the use of the word "Communist" to describe a Communist was interdicted as a species of McCarthyism, it was almost unthinkable to employ such subsidiary concepts as "fellow traveler" or "Stalinist" or Stalinoid to describe people who were not members of the Communist party but whose outlook had been largely shaped or influenced by its ideas and values.[23]

The cold war immigration restrictions that kept Communist aliens from entering the United States were denounced by the Carter administration, without any mention of the historical circumstances that had made them seem necessary to so many Americans. The new attitude seemed to be that any kind of ideological opposition to communism by the government was and always had been improper. Carter ended the ban on travel by Americans to Cuba, North Korea, and Cambodia, and if he intended these measures simply to show that the United States had finally shed its reflexive anticommunism, they seemed to anticommunists to represent repudiation of anticommunism altogether. Congress dismantled its own cold war internal security apparatus. On January 14, 1975 the House disbanded HUAC's successor committee; on April 1, 1977 the Senate abolished the Internal Security Subcommittee, and on May 2, 1977 a bill was introduced to repeal the Smith Act.[24]

While to Jimmy Carter and many liberals, dismantling cold war internal security measures and rehabilitating the victims of McCarthyism were simply good justice and good sense, to many anticommunists they seemed a rewriting of history that denied there ever had been a Soviet threat, and that assumed the Soviet Union was no more today than before a threat to America or to its own people. Both propositions seemed wrong and dangerous to anticommunists.

And indeed, it seemed to anticommunists that Carter was engaged in a dangerous experiment with American security to see if the Soviet challenge was indeed merely a defensive response to American militancy, and whether peaceful intentions would really produce peaceful responses on the Soviet side. Carter's major foreign policy appointments were drawn from that wing of the Democratic party that had, over the years, defined themselves in opposition to Vietnam and to containment. To anticommunists these views seemed hardly distinguishable from the progressive left's, in that they seemed to believe that America was as much to blame for world tensions as the Soviet Union. Their approach to international relations stressed relaxation of tensions with the Soviet Union, arms reductions, and American withdrawal from a world made more dangerous by America's far-flung anticommunist alliances.

Carter's choice for secretary of state was Cyrus Vance, whose view that it was "futile" to "oppose Soviet or Cuban involvement in Africa" infuriated anticommunists, who worried that Vance seemed resigned to America's reduced role in the world and to communism's growing influence. "The fact is," he said, "that we can no more stop change than Canute could still the waters."[25] Carter chose as his chief arms control negotiator a McNamara's protegé, Washington attorney Paul Warnke, who alarmed anticommunists with his statement that Americans were naturally "chauvinistic." In his famous 1975 "Apes on a Treadmill" essay in *Foreign Policy*, Warnke called for global downsizing of American power and an end to efforts to match Soviet armaments. Believing that the Soviet Union took its cue in foreign policy from the United States, his basic principle was that moderation breeds moderation, that voluntary actions by the United States to defuse tensions would produce equivalent concessions from the Soviets.[26]

When Carter proclaimed in 1977 that America had freed itself of its "inordinate fear of communism,"[27] his words shocked William F. Buckley, Jr., who asked, "What is an 'inordinate' fear of Communism?" and took Carter's reference to dictators "who joined us in our fear" to refer to Franco, whose fear of communism, he said, "was as genuine as anybody's would be whose direct experience of Communists was during a civil war in which a fair percentage of the population was slaughtered." Norman Podhoretz referred to Carter's speech as "notorious" and was appalled that Carter said that "historical trends have weakened the foundation" of the principles underlying containment: "a belief that Soviet expansion was almost inevitable and that it must be contained."[28]

In 1978 Buckley was given the opportunity to speak at the Notre Dame commencement, and he took advantage of the occasion to comment on the Carter speech of the year before. He sadly told the students that the national commitment to containing communism, itself a retreat from the moral obligation to rolling it back, had been so swamped in the "great seizure of self-disgust" over Vietnam that now an American president had drained even that weak policy of any moral basis by holding that it had been rooted in "inordinate" fears.[29]

Carter's public repudiation of anticommunism stirred the wrath of well-known anticommunists, but no longer was there a grassroots movement to be mobilized by their outrage. Veteran anticommunists like George Meany, William F. Buckley, Jr., Norman Podhoretz, and the cold war veterans who regularly wrote for magazines like *Encounter*, *National Review*, and *Commentary* could no longer assume they spoke for like-minded communities. The old guard like George Schuyler and Rabbi Schultz were passing on to their rewards, often sent on their way by hostile obituaries. When old countersubversives like the Senate Internal Security Subcommittee's former counsel Robert Morris mourned the end of the movement, they only reinforced the general belief that anticommunism had been a bad business, and good riddance to it.[30]

The American Catholic community continued the long goodbye to anticommunism that had started in the sixties. The Catholic hierarchy was by now fully enlisted in the drive to repudiate the cold war and the policy of nuclear deterrence that was the basis of containment. In their 1976 letter, "To Live in Jesus Christ," the American bishops told Catholics that, "with respect to nuclear weapons, at least those with massive destructive capability, the first imperative is to prevent their use. As possessors of a vast nuclear arsenal, we must also be aware that not only is it wrong to attack civilian populations, but it is also wrong to threaten to attack them as part of a strategy of deterrence." Archbishop John Krol of Philadelphia, testifying in 1979 in favor of SALT II, argued that "the primary moral imperative of the nuclear age is to prevent any use of strategic nuclear weapons . . . [and thus] the declared intent to use [strategic nuclear weapons] involved in our deterrence policy is wrong." Krol said the possession of such weapons could be defended as the lesser of two evils only while making progress toward arms control. If they could not be reduced by negotiation, they would have to be given up.[31]

The countersubversive radical right was by now so loony, so laughable, that it could hardly serve its historic function of discrediting responsible anticommunists, if there had been any appreciable number of those left to discredit. There was the Committee of Ten Million (by its own count) that listed as members such dubious letterhead groups as the American Militia, the Citizens Bar Association, the League of Lady Voters, the Starlight Survival School, the Pacific Northwest Patriots Leadership rally, the Minutemen, the American Pistol and Rifle Association, and the Freedom Fighters Family Funds. They tended to select their enemies from other groups on the extremist right or from respectable anticommunist organizations like Norman Podhoretz's Coalition for a Democratic Majority, which they suspected of being part of a Communist stratagem to absorb funds that might have otherwise gone to survivalists tracking down Communists in the Big Horn Mountains of Wyoming.[32]

The extreme radical right was melting down in the heat of insane power struggles. John Birch Society co-founder Revilo P. Oliver attacked Robert Welch ("Robert the Welcher," he called him) for being a covert ally of the Communist conspiracy, as well as for plotting against keeping Latin as the core of the liberal arts. (Oliver taught the classics at the University of Illinois.)[33]

The John Birch Society membership now consumed their energies attacking each other over real or fancied insults, and the rank and file demanded that their leaders stop worrying about the ADL and admit that the Insider conspiracy was directed by Jews. During the 1980 presidential campaign some Birch Society members attacked the Society for not seeing that Reagan was "an absolute fraud, created and promoted by the Conspiracy to be put into office to neutralize the Conservative, anti-Communist movement as a prelude to the final takeover." In 1983 and 1984 Birchers worked out a theory that "the Order," a conspiracy behind the Council on Foreign Relations and the Trilateral Commission, was really the Yale Skull and Bones Society, which they traced back to Adam Weishaupt's Bavarian Illuminati. One member wrote to the Birch Society's *American Opinion* magazine that he had been embarrassed to read there that the amount of control the Conspiracy had over the United States was 40 to 50 percent. In truth, he wrote, no patriot believed that it was less than 70 to 90 percent.[34]

Even wackier than the John Birch Society, and far more virulent, was the Liberty Lobby. Founded in August 1957 by Willis Carto as a typical nativist, anti-Semitic, conspiracy-theorist group, the Lobby reached its peak membership during the Carter years, when, by its own reckoning, its newspaper, *The Spotlight*, had a circulation of 300,000. The Liberty Lobby proposed a super conspiracy theory of a secret cabal that used all other conspiracies (communism, liberal internationalism, the British empire) as a front for its activities. This was not much different from John Birch Society doctrine, but the Lobby was willing to come out and say the secret conspirators were Jews, and that the conspiracy labored in pursuit of the goals of Zionism, hiding behind the Bilderberg bankers conference as a front, with "Soviet agent" Henry Kissinger as its executive officer.[35]

The Spotlight charged the John Birch Society and Robert Welch with being frauds and stooges of the Conspiracy, and Welch reciprocated in kind. In April 1980 the Birch Society chided *The Spotlight* for publishing articles that were "unreliable, in that they are not based upon sound scholarship." Meanwhile, Welch himself was running articles arguing that Jimmy Carter's election was part of a "determined long-range drive by Insiders of the Master Conspiracy, to reduce the dignity, prestige, and influence of the American Presidency to the lowest possible level." Welch had also decided that the *Maine* had been blown up by the Conspiracy "because the resulting [Spanish-American] war would . . . make an expansionist nation of the United States" and that while it could not be proven that the Conspiracy was responsible, "the whole episode was certainly in tune with the Conspiracy's methods." Welch had to defend himself against members like Russell W. Viering who charged that Welch was a fraud because "such anti-communist books as *The Protocols of the Learned Elders of Zion* and *Mein Kampf* do not appear on the American Opinion booklist. . . . *Mein Kampf* was written by a man who led the greatest attack against the Soviet Union that the world has ever seen. Shouldn't this book be of interest to any serious student of anticommunism?"[36]

Carter was supported in his repudiation of anticommunism and containment by many former liberal anticommunists who were repenting their Vietnam sins by repudiating their anticommunist pasts. Many made a careful distinction between anti-Stalinism, which they defended, and anticommunism, which they did not. Then, too, there were young liberals formed by the Vietnam era who often saw little to choose between the West and the totalitarian states.[37]

Anticommunists feared that Carter was institutionalizing this new post-anticommunist foreign policy in a way that could endure for years. Anticommunist historian Paul Johnson argued that an "arms-control lobby" had emerged "within the Washington bureaucracy, especially in the State Department, which secured the right to examine new weapons programmes at their research and development stage, and seek to veto them if they posed special problems of control which would upset the

SALT I arrangements." Similarly, Carter's human rights foreign policy created a "human rights lobby" in the State Department, which pointed out every violation of human rights by American allies, but cooperated with the arms control establishment by muting criticism of Soviet violations so as not to impede the arms control process.[38]

Carter's search for a foreign policy after anticommunism was supported by some of the old foreign policy elite who had been the fathers of cold war containment. Some had become alienated by Vietnam, others had been drifting away from cold war verities almost from the beginning. Of all of these apostates from the cold war creed, George Kennan continued to be the most upsetting to orthodox cold warriors. When anticommunists had to defend the anticommunist policy of containing the Soviet threat, they had to quote Kennan's Long Telegram of 1946 and his "Mr. X" article of 1947. It cut deeply when the father of containment himself testified that he had never intended that containment be as militarized as it was when implemented by Truman, and that after the death of Stalin, at the latest, it was no longer a productive policy.

Kennan seemed to be an anticommunist only when he was in a Communist country. Back in America, his distaste for Western society led him to decide that "the fuel of communism has always consisted of the deficiencies of the western example and western influence, and of the weaknesses and illnesses and follies of the West itself."[39] The worst of these follies seemed to be the refusal of the democratic masses to follow the privileged elite. Thus Kennan had sympathized with the besieged white segregationist leadership of the American South. He denounced democracies' mistreatment of the environment as opposed to the scientific elite's management of the environment in the Soviet bloc. About this, at least, he could not have been more mistaken.

Like many other students of international affairs, Kennan believed that the competition with communism would go to the system that offered the most attractive model for the third world to adopt. But by the mid-1970s, Kennan had come to the conclusion that the West had little to offer. America's "wasteful, self-indulgent and highly permissive social system" was useless as a guide for Asia and Africa. Democracy was irrelevant to the developing nations. He had abandoned containment because he had lost faith in America, and had finally come to believe that "we have nothing to teach the world" and we "have not got the answers to the problems of human society in the modern age."[40]

Kennan now called himself an isolationist, largely out of disgust with an American society that had nothing to offer the world—except corruption. "I sometimes wonder what use there is in trying to protect the Western world against fancied external threats when the signs of disintegration within are so striking. Wouldn't we be better advised if we put our main effort into making ourselves worth protecting?" America did not deserve world leadership "because the United States has nothing much to say to the outside world." Asked by an interviewer if there was no place for morality in foreign policy, Kennan replied, "If the idealistic component in American policy *has* ever been a force in its own right, it has been confused and really nullified by the crimes and mistakes of recent years: by Viet Nam, by the stupidities of the CIA, by the violation of the democratic process as witnessed by Watergate, and so forth. It would take a long period of withdrawal, a quiet time of minding our own business and rethinking our national purpose, to persuade the world that we had, *if* we had, anything worth while to say to it."[41]

Kennan now held that the United States had no right at all to act overseas unless it first reformed itself. "Show me first an America which has successfully coped with the problems of crime, drugs, deteriorating educational standards, urban decay, pornography, and decadence of one sort or another—show me an America that has pulled itself together and is what it ought to be, then I will tell you how we are going to defend ourselves from the Russians. But, as things are, I can see very little merit in organizing ourselves to defend from the Russians the pornoshops in central Washington. In fact, the Russians are much better in holding pornography at bay than we are."[42]

American anticommunism was now so weak and defeated that dissident voices within the Soviet empire itself were raised to berate Americans for having abandoned their moral resistance to the brutal tyranny that communism had imposed on Eastern Europe and Russia.

If anticommunism in America was almost silent, it was being reborn in the heart of the Soviet empire. In Russia, Andrei Sakharov and a band of brave colleagues had founded a Human Rights Committee in 1970. Coming to the aid of Soviet dissidents in December 1974, Senator Henry Jackson of Washington made freer emigration from the Soviet Union a precondition for any increases in Soviet-American trade, a principal Soviet foreign policy objective. This forced the State Department to establish contacts with Soviet Jews, and brought their plight to the attention of the American public. The Helsinki Final Act of 1975 internationalized human rights and gave dissidents in the Eastern bloc the protection of claiming they were "monitoring" abuses of the Helsinki accords.[43]

While Western revisionists were rejecting the term "totalitarianism," charging that it was an illusion fostered by cold war anti-Sovietism, dissidents in the Eastern bloc were resurrecting it to denounce communism in the very words once used by such anticommunist intellectuals as Arthur Koestler, George Orwell, Hannah Arendt, and Carl Friedrich.[44] Intellectuals in the Eastern bloc now referred to the free societies of the West as "normal societies," using the same images as Arthur Schlesinger, Jr. to describe the abnormality of totalitarian societies like the Soviet Union.

These dissidents warned Americans that they were seriously mistaken when they viewed Soviet leaders in the same light as the heads of free societies. In *My Country and the World* (1975), the Soviet physicist Andrei Sakharov wrote, "It is precisely the failure to understand what is hidden behind the Soviet facade, and the potential dangers of Soviet totalitarianism that explains the many illusions of the Western intelligentsia and, in the final analysis, the amazing miscalculations and defeats of Western foreign policy, which without a struggle is yielding one concession after another to its partner in detente.[45]

Sakharov was dismayed when New York Senator James Buckley visited Russia and told him about the collapse of American anticommunism. He denounced what he called "left-liberal faddishness" which he felt was dominant now in the West because of generational tensions and Soviet propaganda. "I am deeply convinced that the thoughtless, frivolous pursuit of leftist-liberal faddishness is fraught with great dangers. On the international level, one danger is the loss of Western unity and of a clear understanding of the ever constant global threat posed by the totalitarian nations. The West must not under any circumstances allow the weakening of its stand against totalitarianism."[46]

No one in the West could have been as blunt as Sakharov in charging that "leftist intellectuals are urging their governments toward unilateral disarmament," without being accused of McCarthyism. The views of the left had come to constitute, Sakharov charged, "a tremendous danger to mankind." Leftist intellectuals, he said, were supporting

"extremist and even terrorist groups in their own countries and throughout the world, if these groups are using a leftist mask," and then they attacked as "conservative and reactionary" any anticommunists who
"differed with their delusions."[47]

Sakharov warned the West that "the totalitarian challenge" was now
more subtle—but no less dangerous—than ever. The essential weapon
against communism, he insisted, was "the unity of the Western countries." Unity depends upon a leader, and "that leader, both by right and
by virtue of its great responsibilities, is the United States."[48]

The mightiest of the voices thundering from the East was Alexander
Solzhenitsyn. Expelled from the Soviet Union in February 1974, he
went first to Zurich and then to a small town in Vermont. There was no
American in the late seventies who dared voice sentiments as anti-
Soviet as Solzhenitsyn's. "On our crowded planet," he said, "there are
no longer any internal affairs. The Communists say, 'Don't interfere in
our internal affairs. Let us strangle our citizens in peace and quiet.' But
I tell you: Interfere more and more. Interfere as much as you can. We
beg you to come and interfere."[49]

But while almost all Americans had applauded Solzhenitsyn when
he spoke out against communism on Russian soil, in America his views
made uncomfortable many who had long since moved beyond what
sounded like the most unenlightened anticommunism. Solzhenitsyn's
hatred of communism was absolutely uncompromising, and his extreme
anticommunism was disturbing to American policymakers and opinion
molders who were dedicated to weaning America away from cold war
ideology.

Soon Solzhenitsyn was attacking detente and disarmament from such
prestigious forums as the *New York Times Magazine* (in December 1975)
and at Harvard, where he was the speaker at the commencement exercises of June 1978.[50]

Americans were not prepared for the vehemence of his Harvard address, "A World Split Apart." "The Western world," he charged, "has
lost its civic courage, both as a whole and separately, in each country,
in each government, in each political party, and of course, in the United
Nations. Such a decline in courage is particularly noticeable among the
ruling and intellectual elites, causing an impression of a loss of courage
by the entire society."

This Western cowardice he blamed on a pleasure-seeking humanistic culture that had detached morality from religion. His address was laced with denunciations of the flabbiness and degeneracy of Western society not all that different from George Kennan's, but he drew the opposite conclusions from Kennan, referring to him by name as a symbol of that cowardice, and mentioning with disgust Kennan's statement that "we cannot apply moral criteria to politics." Thus, Solzhenitsyn charged, "we mix good and evil, right and wrong, and make space for the absolute triumph of absolute evil in the world. Only moral criteria can help the West against communism's well-planned world strategy." He ridiculed American predictions that Angola would be the Soviet Union's Vietnam, or that friendly American overtures to Cuba would lead to the withdrawal of Cuban forces from Africa. "Kennan's advice to his own country—to begin unilateral disarmament—belongs to the same category. If you only knew how the youngest of the officials in Moscow's Old Square roar with laughter at your political wizards."[51]

He tore into America's failure in Vietnam. "Members of the U.S. antiwar movement became accomplices in the betrayal of Far Eastern nations, in the genocide and the suffering today imposed on thirty million people there. Do these convinced pacifists now hear the moans coming from there? Do they understand their responsibility today? Or do they prefer not to hear? The American intelligentsia lost its nerve and as a consequence the danger has come much closer to the United States." He reminded the West that it had not won a major war by itself in the twentieth century. It had needed its alliance with Stalin to defeat Hitler, and "raised up another enemy, one that would prove worse and more powerful, since Hitler had neither the resources nor the people, nor the ideas with broad appeal, nor such a large number of supporters in the West—a fifth column—as the Soviet Union possessed."

Now the West could imagine no greater good than preserving its peaceful enjoyment of a prosperous status quo, thus making concession after concession to the Soviet Union, ending with "the shameful Belgrade conference" at which "Western diplomats in their weakness surrendered the line of defense for which enslaved members of the Helsinki Watch Groups are sacrificing their lives."

Communism survived, he thundered, because Western intellectuals had stopped applying moral criteria to Communist regimes. "The Communist regime in the East could endure and grow due to the enthusiastic support from an enormous number of Western intellectuals who (feeling the kinship!) refused to see communism's crimes, and when they could no longer do so, they tried to justify these crimes. The problem persists: In our Eastern countries, communism has suffered a complete ideological defeat; it is zero and less than zero. And yet Western intellectuals still look at it with considerable interest and empathy, and this is precisely what makes it so immensely difficult for the West to withstand the East."

From the moral heights climbed during a lifetime of suffering under communism, a life dedicated to the memory of the victims of communism, Solzhenitsyn tried to reach the soul of America, pleading with Americans not to renounce their dedication to freedom in their haste to put Vietnam and the cold war behind them.

But not even a prophet like Solzhenitsyn would be honored if he violated the new taboo against denouncing communism. By condemning communism in such uncompromising terms, and by insisting that America and the West likewise use their best efforts to end its grip on Eastern Europe and the Soviet Union, Solzhenitsyn called down on himself the wrath of a cultural and foreign policy elite trying to put anticommunism and the cold war behind them. Not even Solzhenitsyn's moral stature exempted him from the penalties inflicted on anyone who publicly committed anticommunism in the seventies.

The *New York Times* worried that Solzhenitsyn's anti-Soviet words might endanger detente. He was an "enthusiast" who "believes himself to be in possession of The Truth and so sees error wherever he looks." That is, Solzhenitsyn, like all anticommunists, was an extremist, and so, like all extremists, a danger to democracy. "Life in a society run by zealots like Mr. Solzhenitsyn," said the *Times*, "is bound to be uncomfortable for those who do not share his vision or ascribe to his beliefs." Solzhenitsyn even fell victim to the usual psychiatric diagnosis of the anticommunist. James Reston of the *Times* referred to the Harvard speech as "the wanderings of a mind split apart."

For anyone, even Solzhenitsyn, to insist that a commitment to freedom implied taking a stand against communism meant that he was an anticommunist, and so in some quarters he would be regarded as a threat to a world peace that depended on Soviet-American accord. "As to this country's relations with the Communist states," the *Times* editorialized, we fear that Mr. Solzhenitsyn does the world no favor by calling up a holy war. The weapons are far too formidable, and the stakes in human life far too high. But there is something else as well. Much as we have been instructed and inspired by Mr. Solzhenitsyn, his willingness to set aside all other values in the crusade against communism bespeaks an obsession that we are happy to forgo in this nation's leaders. A certain amount of self-doubt is a valuable attribute for people who have charge of nuclear weapons.

The *Washington Post* joined the *Times* in denouncing Solzhenitsyn for trying to revive the "boundless cold war" that had, it was hoped, finally been consigned to the past.[52]

The reaction to Solzhenitsyn's Harvard address revealed that in 1978 there were Americans, many of them in places of influence, so viscerally opposed to anything that sounded like anticommunism that they would not give it a hearing even if it was given voice by a moral giant like Solzhenitsyn who had acquired his beliefs about communism in communism's gulags.

In America, the public debate about communism had largely been stilled by the late seventies. Not even a prophetic figure like Solzhenitsyn could gain a hearing for his grim revelations about communism's continuing abuse of human rights, and its undiminished threat to free societies. Americans had decided that there were objectives in life far more important than fighting communism. Anticommunism had become, in their minds, something outmoded, irrelevant, at best an embarrassment, at worst a danger to world peace—and a threat to human survival.

Anticommunism—after half a century of power, peril, and, ultimately, disgrace—seemed finally to have been consigned to the past. Marx, as is well known, claimed that everything in history occurs twice, first as tragedy, then as farce. But America, to say the least, is not a Marxist country, nor do Americans believe in tragedy. And as often as not, in America what first appears as tragedy, reappears in triumph. For anticommunism there was, despite all appearances, another chapter yet to be written.

Chapter 13

COMMON SENSE ABOUT THE
PRESENT DANGER

Socialism is the most dynamic and influential force in the world arena. On three continents, from the Republic of Cuba to the Democratic Republic of Vietnam, the new society of the peoples of Socialist states thrives and is being successfully constructed. The inexhaustible resources of these countries, imposing in their economic achievements, the power of their offensive might is placed at the service of peace and only peace.

— Andrei Gromyko, 1975.[1]

Too scattered to be called a movement any longer, American anticommunists during the Nixon, Ford, and Carter administrations continued to insist that the Soviet Union was still a threat to freedom, while many Americans, especially opinion leaders and policymakers, hoped that America's long national nightmare was finally over, not only the nightmare of Watergate and Vietnam, but the cold war as well.

At a time when the tide of opinion ran strongly against raising issues that might heighten tensions with the Soviet Union and endanger the more pressing issue of arms control, anticommunists pressed Washington not to break faith with the millions still denied fundamental rights under Communist regimes, and not to ignore what they saw as increasing Soviet adventurism around the world and close to the United States, or a growing Soviet strategic threat that posed a mounting risk to American security. During the mid-seventies, veterans of the scattered anticommunist movement began to regroup to deliver these warnings to the public, and from this emerged a reborn anticommunist movement, a movement that by the end of the decade had grown so formidable that it stood poised to elevate one of its own to the White House.

During the days of the deepest anticommunist demoralization over Vietnam, when Nixon and Kissinger were holding out the promise of detente to the Soviets, hoping that the Soviets would bring their influence to bear on the North Vietnamese, Senator Henry Jackson of Washington, powerful chairman of the Armed Services Committee, fought (at times it seemed almost singlehandedly) to keep the issues of the Soviet strategic threat and Communist violations of human rights before the public. In 1972 Jackson attached an amendment to the Strategic Arms Limitations Treaty (SALT I) that prohibited the President from allowing the United States to fall to "levels of intercontinental strategic forces inferior to the limits provided for the Soviet Union."[2] Jackson and other anticommunists meant this to call attention to their contention that SALT I actually permitted the Soviets to maintain a nuclear force superior in aggregate power to the American deterrent. Jackson also attached to the 1972 Soviet trade agreement the Jackson-Varnik Amendment that linked human rights and trade with the Soviet Union by making most favored nation trade status with the Soviets dependent on their granting their citizens the right to emigrate, this in response to the October 1972 crackdown on the emigration of Soviet Jews to the West. To indicate the importance of such measures to the human rights movement in the Soviet Union, dissident Andrei Sakharov sent a letter to Congress endorsing Jackson-Varnik.[3]

Jackson held hearings on these measures during which he extracted commitments from the Nixon, Ford, and Carter officials in charge of negotiating with the Soviets to preserve (at least) American military parity, and to tie improved relations with the Soviet Union to liberalization of the Soviet regime. The result of these efforts, in the view of anticommunists, was "a gradual change in public consciousness almost as profound as the sudden change produced by Churchill's Iron Curtain speech in 1946. It was a kind of legislative statesmanship rare in the history of democracies."[4]

Paul Nitze was another of the veteran anticommunist cold warriors who forcefully made known his doubts about detente. Nitze had begun his career as an arms analyst as vice chairman of the Army's Strategic

Bombing study after World War II. He helped draft the Marshall Plan, and headed the State Department's Policy Planning Staff when it drafted NSC-68. Later he served as assistant secretary of defense for International Security Affairs, which was the Pentagon's think tank. He was secretary of the navy under Kennedy and Johnson, and deputy defense secretary under secretaries of defense Robert McNamara and Clark Clifford.

Though hardly prone to the darker suspicions of the countersubversives, he shared some of their anxieties about Communist infiltration of the foreign policy establishment during the thirties and forties. He later made a point of recalling that he had car pooled with Alger Hiss and Laurence Duggan, and had come to suspect both of disloyalty. During Hiss's HUAC testimony, Charles Bohlen had told him that Hiss had lied about Yalta. "From then on I doubted the truthfulness of his testimony." Of Harry Dexter White he said, "It was never proven that he was a member of the Communist party. It was my view that he was such a dominating and objectionable character that the Communist party would have had doubts about admitting him to membership. But he certainly worked closely with the Communists."[5]

In 1969, just before joining the Nixon administration as a negotiator at the SALT talks, Nitze had become concerned about the number of influential voices being raised against the country's anti-ballistic missile program, which Nitze considered essential to the national security. "The more I looked into it," he said, "the more I believed that the basis of the anti-ABM campaign was to be found in the country's disenchantment with the Vietnam War, in the widespread alienation from the government of former supporters of the nuclear defense program, and in the desire of many to wish away the problems of national security."[6] And in fact some of the leaders of the anti-ABM coalition had been architects of the Vietnam war, now evidently determined to make amends for their misdeeds. Citizens Concerned About the ABM was founded by New Frontiersmen Roswell Gilpatric and Arthur J. Goldberg. Another anti-ABM group was led by Harper and Row editor Cass Canfield and Senator Edward Kennedy.

To counter this opposition to the ABM, Nitze recruited Dean Acheson and Rand Corporation defense analyst Albert Wohlstetter to form the Committee to Maintain a Prudent Defense Policy. He was able to raise money for the lobbying effort from future CIA director William F.

Casey, who had already organized his own group, Citizens Committee for Peace and Security, to lobby for the ABM, and had raised more money than he needed. To provide his Committee with expert analysis of these highly technical issues, Nitze put out calls to the graduate schools, and located young anticommunist defense analysts like Peter Wilson, Paul Wolfowitz, and Richard Perle, who would later be important defense policymakers during the Reagan administration.[7]

When the ABM program was rejected by Congress, Nitze was shocked by how the anticommunist consensus in the Democratic party "had largely broken down under the divisive effects of Vietnam and the unsettling political atmosphere generated by the Watergate affair."[8] Before long he had resigned from the SALT delegation because of disagreements over the Nixon-Kissinger policy of detente with the Soviet Union. He began to hold discussions with other defense experts worried that the Ford administration was placing too much trust in Soviet good intentions. In March 1976 he, Eugene Rostow, James Schlesinger, Henry Jackson, and David Packard set up an informal group to fight detente. They appointed Charles Tyroler II as its director. Tyroler had formed the Citizens Lobby for Peace with Freedom in Vietnam in 1967 to rally public support for the war, and he had long been lobbying within the Democratic party for stronger defense policies.

Nitze took part in another effort during the Ford administration to advance the argument against detente. In the spring of 1976, President Ford ordered CIA Director George Bush to organize an outside committee of defense experts to assess the reliability of the CIA's estimates of Soviet strength and goals, estimates that most conservatives—and the majority of President Ford's Foreign Intelligence Advisory Board—considered far too "soft" on the Soviets. This group, called "Team B," began its work in June 1976, chaired by Richard Pipes and including Nitze among its members. They put together a hard-line brief for the thesis that the Soviet Union's goal was still world supremacy, and that the Soviets, instead of adhering to the defensive nuclear strategy of mutual assured destruction, were striving for the sort of nuclear superiority that would put it in a position to threaten to fight and win a nuclear war. Team B's logic and evidence were so compelling that the CIA began to shift its own official estimate of Soviet capabilities toward a more hard-line analysis of Soviet intentions.[9]

The Team B report was leaked to the press soon after it was submitted on December 2, 1976, and was promptly disowned by the incoming Carter administration. Nevertheless, President-elect Carter had to develop his detente policies in the face of two estimates of Soviet intentions—Team B's and the CIA's—which contradicted Carter's view that the Soviets were as committed as he to the relaxation of superpower tensions through detente and arms control.[10]

Meanwhile, Nitze was meeting with other skeptics about detente to work out a campaign to convince the public that their leaders were indulging in dangerously wishful thinking about the Soviets. On November 11, 1976, these efforts finally bore fruit when he was able to announce the formation of the most consequential anticommunist organization of the late cold war, the Committee on the Present Danger (CPD).[11]

The CPD had been a working project for about two years before its November 1976 debut. With the encouragement of Gerald Ford's defense secretary, James Schlesinger, Nitze had been working with Johnson's under secretary of state Eugene V. Rostow, Nixon's deputy secretary of the treasury Charls E. Walker, Nixon's deputy assistant to the President for international economic affairs Richard V. Allen, Lane Kirkland, the secretary-treasurer of the AFL-CIO, Johnson's Secretary of the Treasury Henry H. Fowler, and former chief of naval operations Admiral Elmo R. Zumwalt to discuss what they could do about their concern that the Ford administration was grievously underestimating the Soviet threat. At a key organizational meeting at Washington's Metropolitan Club on March 12, 1976, the group was joined by James Schlesinger, attorney and arms negotiator Max Kampelman, Nixon's deputy secretary of defense David Packard, Charles Burton Marshall, a member of the State Department's policy planning staff under Truman, Fletcher School of Diplomacy Dean Edmund A. Gullion, and Charles Tyroler II, who had been director of manpower supply in the Defense Department under Truman, and served as director of the CPD.[12]

At that meeting the first draft of Rostow's "Common Sense and the Common Danger," the CPD's manifesto, was read, discussed, and edited. The group decided to open itself only to seasoned experts in foreign and defense policy. "What we were striving for was credibility—the essential ingredient in the process of persuasion."[13] The purpose, Kampelman later wrote, was "simple and straightforward—to alert American policy makers and opinion leaders and the public at large to the ominous Soviet military buildup and its implications, and to the unfavorable trends in the U.S.–Soviet military balance. We were all convinced that international stability and peace with freedom required a strong America—one that could and would deter Soviet adventurism and aggression."[14]

The organizers and members of the Committee were to a remarkable degree the veteran leaders of the groups that had made up the old and now disintegrated anticommunist movement of the early containment years. Their anticommunism forged in the thirties and forties, they had long ago lost any significant grassroots support in their organizations for anticommunist activism, since their younger members had no experience other than Vietnam for evaluating the reasons for and the consequences of anticommunist policies.

The anticommunist leadership of the labor union movement was particularly well represented. There were Sol Chaiken and Evelyn DuBrow of the ILGWU, William DuChessi of the Amalgamated, Rachelle Horowitz and Albert Shanker of the teachers union, Lane Kirkland and Jay Lovestone of the AFL-CIO, John H. Lyons of the Steelworkers, J. C. Turner of the engineers union, and Martin Ward of the plumbers union.

They were, of course, strongly supported by George Meany, an outspoken opponent of detente. Meany had burst out, "detente is a fraud" after hearing Secretary of State Henry Kissinger worry that it would strain relations with the Soviets to have President Ford receive Solzhenitsyn at the White House. Meany had kept the AFL-CIO a bulwark of American opposition to communism overseas, pulling his union out of the International Labor Organization (ILO) in 1977 when he decided that the United Nations agency had been turned into a political front for the Soviet bloc.[15]

Meany insisted that Americans ought to judge regimes by whether or not they allowed free labor unions. He kept his union active in support of the free workers movements in Eastern Europe, particularly Solidarity in Poland. He insisted that belief in freedom meant, "in my book, you have to be anti-Communist. You have to be anti-dictatorship. You have to be anti-Allende, you have to be anti-Franco, anti-Hitler, anti-Stalin, anti-South Africa. The people who consider themselves liberal become very selective. They can be very anti-South Africa—strongly against this apartheid policy—and shrug their shoulders about Czechoslovakia and Poland and the Soviet Union. We hold them all even."[16]

Albert Shanker also represented another group of anticommunists associated with the New York-based Social Democrats of America. The Social Democrats' memories went back to Communist persecution of Socialists in Europe, and to the Socialists' clashes with Communists in America during the thirties. Their magazine, *The New Leader*, was the most reliable source of information on communism in a decade when it was considered hawkish to pay undue attention to Communist violations of human rights.

Jeane Kirkpatrick, Ernest Lefever, Valerie Earle, William V. O'Brien, Estelle R. Ramey, and Peter Krogh represented another venerable stronghold of anticommunism, Georgetown University, whose Center for Strategic and International Studies, an affiliate of the American Enterprise Institute, was chaired by CPD member Ray Cline, former deputy director of Central Intelligence. Its journal, *Washington Quarterly*, tried to rebut the pro-detente views of the establishment's *Foreign Affairs* and *Foreign Policy*.[17]

Peter Grace of the Grace Corporation and William F. Casey, former SEC chairman and undersecretary of state, represented conservative Catholics alienated by the leftward movement of their church, though they could not speak for the majority of Catholics and did not claim to do so. Like William F. Buckley, they considered themselves faithful Catholics though they rejected Vatican II as interpreted by the American bishops.

There were many veteran anticommunists from the old foreign policy elite and young and old experts on Soviet affairs and defense, whose expertise had been discarded by the new detente-oriented arms control establishment. There was former Communist Bertram Wolfe, now of the Hoover Institution, Richard Pipes of Harvard, and authors Richard J. Whalen and James T. Farrell, along with Clare Boothe Luce, Dean Rusk, and generals Maxwell Taylor and Matthew Ridgway.

Particularly well represented on the CPD was the predominantly Jewish neoconservative movement, with Nobel Prize winner Saul Bellow, Nathan Glazer, Oscar Handlin, Seymour Martin Lipset, Norman Podhoretz, and his wife Midge Decter providing unsurpassed access to the intellectual media. No more than their Catholic colleagues, could these Jewish intellectuals not really claim to speak for their community, but because of their familiarity with the persecution of Jews in the Soviet Union and the importance of American military strength in protecting Israel, they were acutely aware of the dangers created by American decline in the face of surging Soviet power.[18]

One of the most distinctive features of the neoconservative movement of the seventies, in fact, was its preoccupation with communism at a time when the rest of the country had stopped worrying and learned to love coexistence. A critic called the movement "the final stage of the Old Left, the only element in American politics whose identity is principally derived from its view of Communism. . . . The conservatives believe that the Liberal Establishment has been running the country. Neoconservatives add to this general notion the belief that liberals are either a species of Stalinist fellow traveler or operate 'objectively,' whether they know it or not, in the broad interest of the Soviet Union. Conservatives would like to believe this too. But the neoconservatives, many with the benefit of the Trotskyist background, offer an unmatchable authenticity and intensity on the subject."[19]

Since real communism had all but disappeared from the American scene, the neoconservatives' darker suspicions about the fellow-traveling tendencies of the New Left and the new foreign policy elite had to be expressed in euphemisms that hid their origins. Nevertheless, sometimes echoes from the past slipped out, as when Norman Podhoretz called Cyrus Vance "Lillian Hellman in pinstripes." They specialized in analogies—often insightful—with the thirties: *Commentary* noted that the New Left "seems in a . . . short time to have traveled from a fresh rebellious idealism, sorely needed after the confusions and timidity of the fifties, to a fascination with populist totalitarianism that is scarcely distinguishable from that of the latter-day Communist apologists of the late thirties and early forties."[20]

The neoconservatives identified their enemy in the anti-anticommunism of the New Left. Podhoretz charged that the New Left was careful "to dissociate themselves from the Communists, [but] the blandness of their criticism of communism as compared with their heated denunciations of anti-Communism showed at the very least a lack of intellectual balance." In their refusal to stop speaking out about the immorality of communism, neoconservatives considered themselves a saving remnant keeping the truth alive in truth-denying times. Podhoretz recalled how lonely it was to be anticommunist: "to be pro-American in the sixties was like being anti-Soviet in the thirties, but just as radicalism then had been tied to support of the Soviet Union as the center of socialist hope, so radicalism now increasingly defined itself in opposition to the United States as the major obstacle to the birth of a better world. Here too, then, in dissenting from the anti-Americanism of the new radicals, I thought I was adapting the example of my elders who in the thirties had refused to accept the equation of radicalism with support of the Soviet Union."[21]

The executive committee of the CPD was chaired by Eugene W. Rostow, and its Policy Studies Committee by Nitze. Its co-chairs were Henry Fowler, Lane Kirkland, and David Packard. Charls Walker was treasurer, Max Kampelman general counsel. The executive committee included Richard Allen, Edmund Gullion, Rita Hauser (chair of the Foreign Affairs Committee of the American Jewish Committee), Richard Pipes, John P. Roche (former aide to LBJ), Dean Rusk, Richard Whalen, and Elmo Zumwalt. The group had decided against having a public membership arm, so it limited itself to a board of one hundred directors.

The CPD found that it did not need a large budget because there was so much high quality volunteer work available, and so its staff over its first eight years numbered only four full-time and two part-time employees. At its first public meeting, two days after the 1976 election, there were over a hundred media representatives. The manifesto, "Common Sense and the Common Danger," was read in turn by Henry H. Fowler, Lane Kirkland, and David Packard. In an echo of the classic call to arms of the French Revolution, it began: "Our country is in a period of danger, and the danger is increasing. Unless decisive steps are taken to alert the nation, and to change the course of its policy, our economic and military capacity will become inadequate to assure peace with security." Time was short, and "a conscious act of political will is needed to restore the strength and coherence of our foreign policy." Only then could the country "seek reliable conditions of peace with the Soviet Union, rather than an illusory peace."[22]

The CPD went on to warn that "the principal threat to our nation, to world peace, and to the cause of human freedom is the Soviet drive for dominance based upon an unparalleled military buildup. The Soviet Union has not altered its long-held goal of a world dominated from a single center—Moscow." The Soviet Union was exploiting every sign of American weakness, and "the scope and sophistication of the Soviet campaign have been increased in recent years."

America was reaching a point, they warned, where its military weakness would make it vulnerable to coercion, where it would be forced to concede interest after interest in the face of superior Soviet power. "If we continue to drift, we shall become second best to the Soviet Union in overall military strength; our alliances will weaken; our promising rapprochement with China could be reversed. Then we could find ourselves isolated in a hostile world. . . . Our national survival itself would be in peril, and we should face, one after another, bitter choices between war and acquiescence under pressure." The reason the country faced such peril was that "time, weariness, and the tragic experience of Vietnam have weakened the bipartisan consensus which sustained our foreign policy between 1940 and the mid-60s. We must build a fresh consensus."

Reading "Common Sense and the Common Danger" to the press took more than ninety minutes. Reporters listened politely, asked a few questions, but few stories resulted. It took two months for the *New York Times* to notice the organization. Conservative papers soon began to give the CPD favorable mention, however, and Moscow certainly paid attention, attacking it as "A Flock of Hawks," an event noted with pleasure by the CPD.

The CPD's second policy paper, "What is the Soviet Union Up To?" was released on April 4, 1977. It amounted to a restatement and rejustification of the fundamental principles of NSC-68 that had been the basis of containment since World War II. "The Soviet Union is radically different from our society," said the CPD, and its differences, which had their roots in Russian history and which were heightened by Communist ideology, resulted in a drive toward expansion and domination of other countries, near and far away. "No empire in history has expanded so persistently as the Russian."

It was an empire with many deep weaknesses, but its tightly organized dictatorship gave it key advantages in mobilizing its military strength and in pursuing its long-term strategic objective, which was "the worldwide triumph of communism." There was not necessarily a "timetable" or a "blueprint" for achieving that goal. There might also be conflict and disagreement within the Communist camp. But the Soviets had never stopped considering themselves the leaders of a movement at war with the rest of the world. That made the United States the principal enemy. "The attainment of the ultimate Soviet objective—a Communist world order—requires the reduction of the power, influence and prestige of the United States, the country which the Soviet leaders perceive as the central bastion of the 'capitalist' or enemy camp. . . . In that contest they see their task as isolating America and, despite temporary reverses for their side, reducing it to impotence."

In the CPD's analysis, the Soviets' short-term objectives involved gaining access to Western capital and technology to modernize the Soviet economy and military, binding Western Europe to the Soviet Union and loosening its ties to America, cutting the ties between the first and third worlds, and containing and isolating China. To attain these objectives, the Soviet Union had been engaged in an unprecedented and unmatched military buildup, which had already resulted in conventional military superiority, and within a few years would mean strategic superiority over the United States. "Soviet pressure, when supported by strategic and conventional military superiority, would be aimed at forcing our general withdrawal from a leading role in world affairs, and isolating us from other democratic societies, which could not then long survive." Neither SALT, detente, trade, nor human rights agreements have "weakened the Soviet drive," the CPD insisted. "Weakness invites aggression, strength deters it. Thus American strength holds the key to our quest for peace and to our survival as a free society in a world friendly to our hopes and ideals." The CPD concluded its analysis of Soviet actions with the stark statement that "the Soviet military buildup of all its armed forces over the past quarter century is, in part, reminiscent of Nazi Germany's rearmament in the 1930s."[23]

On August 4, 1977, Carter met with leaders of the CPD. He listened to their views, but claimed the public would not stand for increased defense spending.[24] But in fact the American public was, according to the polls, increasingly worried about the state of America's defenses. Between 1969 and 1976 the percentage of the public that felt too much was being spent on defense fell from 52 to 36, while those who favored increased spending rose from 8 to 22. In 1972 only 39 percent said the United States should strive to remain the world's dominant power; by 1976 56 percent believed in sacrificing to retain supremacy.[25] Pointing to these public concerns, the CPD's Eugene Rostow and Paul Nitze lobbied Congress to increase defense spending.

The CPD members had all formerly believed that foreign policy must be directed by an expert elite and that the public must be kept out of policy decisions. Now, faced with a radicalized elite's "explicit support of the Communist side and its undisguised wish for a defeat of the United States that would discredit the entire anti-Communist foreign policy of which Vietnam was a product," the CPD's cold warriors gained a new respect for "the general populace which preserved its sanity in the face of the peculiar hysteria of the highly educated." The Committee decided that after all they preferred the public to the experts, an opinion memorably expressed in William Buckley's preference for being governed by a random choice of names from the Boston phone book rather than the Harvard faculty. In the conviction that "the new isolationism is [not] as persuasive among the masses of Americans as it is among the elites," the CPD decided to heed Daniel Patrick Moynihan's call to arms. The anticommunists were "of the liberty party," he said, "and it might surprise us what energies might be released were we to unfurl those banners."[26]

The CPD sent Nitze, Rostow, Pipes, and Zumwalt to meet with editors and other opinion leaders across the country. Albert Shanker used his nationwide newspaper column to bring the Committee's message to a wide audience. So did John P. Roche in his nationally syndicated column. The committee could also call on "America's greatest living soldier," CPD founding member General Matthew Ridgway, to present its views to the public."[27]

The Committee's public papers—twenty in all between 1976 and 1984—were short, powerfully written, and filled with Paul Nitze's immense knowledge of the intricacies of strategic defense issues. They all drove home the same point: that the Soviet Union still was pursuing its original goal of a world-wide political and economic system dominated by Moscow, and that to accomplish this it was supporting foreign insurgences by anti-American regimes and building up its own forces. The United States, by contrast, had let its own forces deteriorate so badly that the Soviet Union would soon have a free hand in ordering the world to its liking.

The CPD submitted fifty-three names to the Carter administration to be considered for foreign policy appointments. Not one was chosen. Moreover, almost all the top arms negotiation positions went to experts with views diametrically opposed to the CPD's. Eugene Rostow's views of Carter's appointments were "unprintable." Nitze said, "Every soft liner I can think of is now part of the executive branch and the arms control administration."[28] The key position of policy planning in the State Department was given to Anthony Lake, who had resigned from Kissinger's staff over the Cambodia invasion and who had written with Leslie Gelb a series of articles proposing that containment be replaced by a new view of the world based on the north-south relationship between the industrialized and third world countries, expanded trade, and detente with the Soviet Union.

Nitze considered Carter's nomination of Paul Warnke for director of the SALT negotiations to be particularly unsuitable. His testimony on Warnke in the confirmation hearings was withering. He called Warnke's views "absolutely asinine" and "screwball, arbitrary and fictitious."

Henry Jackson also put Warnke through a grueling examination during his confirmation hearings. Jackson told Warnke:

You recommended:

1. Against the B-1.
2. Against the Trident submarine and the Trident II missile
3. Against the submarine launched cruise missile.
4. Against the AWACs programs
5. Against the development of a mobile ICBM, by the United States.
6. Against MIRV deployment
7. Against improvements to the U.S. ICBM force, including improved guidance and warhead design.
8. Against the development of the XM-1 tank and for reductions in the procurement of the M-60 tank.
9. For the reduction of U.S. tactical nuclear weapons in Europe from 7,000 to 1,000. I believe you just said a moment ago that you did not recommend a reduction in nuclear weapons in Europe.
10. For the withdrawal of some 30,000 troops from NATO without waiting for the conclusion of an MBRF [mutual and balanced force reduction] agreement.
11. For holding the army at 13 rather than 16 divisions, after improved efficiency made creation of three new divisions possible within existing manpower ceilings.

12. For a $14 billion cut in the defense budget in the fiscal year 1974 submission and a $11 billion cut in fiscal year 1975.
13. For a reduction in fiscal year 1975 of 3 percent per year in the defense budget with the result that, applied to the fiscal year 1978 budget, the total reduction would amount to some $26 billion from the Carter recommendation to Congress."

Warnke had to admit, "Yes, sir, Senator, that is absolutely correct."[29]

When Warnke was confirmed by a narrow 58–40 margin, it served notice on Carter that there was not enough support to get any new disarmament agreements through the Senate, since Jackson advertised before the vote that anything less than 60 votes for Warnke would mean that any treaty he negotiated would have no hope of gaining the two-thirds necessary for ratification.[30]

Carter soon began to realize that the CPD was succeeding in turning the strategic arms debate against him. After he signed the SALT II agreement on June 18, 1979, he found it necessary to replace Paul Warnke with American Security Council member George M. Seignious II in hopes of easing its way through the Senate. At the Senate hearings on the Treaty, Paul Nitze claimed that "with all its fallacies and implausibilities, [SALT II] can only incapacitate our minds and wills." The CPD managed to convince the Foreign Relations Committee to vote ten to zero (with seven abstentions) that SALT II was "not in the national security interests of the United States," just before the Soviet invasion of Afghanistan shelved it. During the SALT hearings CPD members appeared on seventeen different occasions before Senate committees. Nitze's papers were updated eleven times, once a month. In all the CPD participated in 479 public forums, and distributed 200,000 reports.[31]

The anti-Warnke campaign helped expand the new anticommunist coalition to the left and the right. Along with the CPD, there were both the liberal Committee for a Democratic Majority and conservative groups like the American Conservative Union, the National Conservative Political Action Committee and the Conservative Caucus. Other members of the steering Committee of the anti-Warnke Emergency Coalition included officials of the Young Americans for Freedom, the Young Republicans National Federation, and the National Security Council, along with groups associated with Richard Viguerie, mastermind of national conservative mass mail campaigns.[32]

During the Warnke hearings, it became apparent to all, but especially to the Carter administration, that a new and surprisingly potent anticommunist movement had reappeared on the American scene, its strength concentrated now within the beltway, with conservatives and liberals once again finding common cause in containing communism. Only the CPD itself, in fact, was more active than the American Security Council in fighting SALT II. The ASC had begun as a McCarthyite group and had evolved into a lobbying group for the defense industry. It organized the Coalition for Peace Through Strength in 1978, with 148 congressional members chaired by Robert Dole and Paul Laxalt, to oppose the efforts of a pro-detente coalition, Members of Congress for Peace Through Law. The ASC's Coalition had a rating system that publicized congressional support for defense appropriations. In an effective division of labor, the drive against SALT relied on the CPD for prestige and expertise, while the ASC applied the direct pressure on senators.[33]

The strongest anticommunist in the Carter administration was Carter's national security advisor, Zbigniew Brzezinski. He supported Carter and Secretary of State Cyrus Vance on detente, but felt it had been oversold to the public. While Vance and Carter saw the solution to the arms race as lying in greater cooperation with the Soviet Union, Brzezinski feared the Soviet military buildup. The USSR was using its strategic parity as a base for more daring adventures in the third world, using Cuban surrogates. This was a strategy Brzezinski felt "was paying off" for them and would lead to Soviet strategic and conventional superiority over the United States by 1985.[34]

Like the CPD, Brzezinski feared the Soviets had been made confident by their belief that the United States was debilitated by an "aggravated crisis of capitalism" and by its post-Vietnam trauma. In Brzezinski's analysis, the Soviets were using detente to transform the status quo. Where he differed from the CPD was in his conclusion. The danger—aside from the direct threat to the United States—he felt, was that the Soviets, because of their weak economy and "unappealing" ideology, would not be able to maintain international order. "This Soviet thrust toward global preeminence," Brzezinski said, "was less likely to lead to a Pax Sovietica than to international chaos."[35]

Frequently, in the days when anticommunism was riding high, blunders, misstatements, and exaggerations by anticommunists more confident about the rightness of their cause than careful with their facts had cast doubt on the competence of all anticommunists in the one area where above all they claimed expertise—that is, on the subject of communism.

Now, late in the cold war, the anticommunists would be able to lay hold of false or careless statements by opponents so confident that anticommunism was defeated, containment obsolete, and detente entrenched, that they seemed to exhibit a cavalier attitude regarding the one issue about which those who put themselves forward as national security experts were expected to demonstrate knowledge and precision— the state of the national defense against the Soviet Union.

The defense analysts of the Committee on the Present Danger could draw on an unsurpassed accumulation of theoretical knowledge and factual data to grind away at the best minds the Carter administration could throw at them. But besting nameless bureaucrats in eyeshades could not match the impact of a confrontation with an authority hailed by containment's opponents as uniquely qualified to evaluate the merits of policies toward the Soviet Union. This was the same George Kennan whose defection from containment had been so devastating to anticommunists during the Fulbright hearings, the same George Kennan who now took the position that the cold war should have been avoided by employing a less confrontational and ideological American diplomacy (that is, a less anticommunist diplomacy). Anticommunism's opponents had made signal use of Kennan's prestige to urge the rejection of containment and pursuit of detente; so, given the opportunity, the new anticommunists seized on statements by the venerable statesmen that exhibited either a lack of knowledge about defense matters, or an arrogant lack of seriousness in matters involving nothing less than national survival.

In 1976 an essay by Kennan appeared in *Die Zeit* of Hamburg in which he attacked containment in the most extreme terms. Anticommunists saw here a chance to open a debate over the Carter foreign policy on a terrain where they felt most comfortable—nuclear strategy.

In this essay, Kennan capped an analysis of the Soviet threat—really a nonthreat, in his eyes—with a blistering denunciation of any pretensions the West had to moral superiority over communism. It did not really matter whether or not the West was threatened by communism, he wrote, because the West had nothing left to defend as a society or as a culture:

Poor old West, succumbing day by day to its own decadence, sliding into debility on the slime of its own self-indulgent permissiveness; its drugs, its crime, its pornography, its pampering of the youth, its addiction to its bodily comforts, its rampant materialism and consumerism—and then trembling before the menace of the wicked Russians, all pictured as supermen, eight feet tall, their internal problems all essentially solved, and with nothing else now to think about except how to bring damage and destruction to Western Europe. This persistent externalization of the sense of danger—this persistent exaggeration of the threat from without and blindness to the threat from within: this is the symptom of some deep failure to come to terms with reality—and with one's self. If Western Europe could bring itself to think a little less about how defenseless it is in the face of the Russians, and a little more about what it is that it has to defend, I would feel more comfortable about its prospects for the future.[36]

Encounter, the anticommunist journal of the British Committee for Cultural Freedom, invited Kennan to sit for an interview with George Urban, who had written a book critical of detente. The result filled thirty-three pages of the September 1976 issue.

In the interview, Kennan availed himself of even more extravagant rhetoric, subjecting containment and America to a scorn that he must have imagined was withering, but which in print seemed appalling from someone whose views were so regularly employed by the administration in support of its policies.

How should Europe, Urban asked, or for that matter America, defend itself if the United States pulled back behind its shores waiting for moral reform to transform itself back to the godly nation of Kennan's childhood. The proper defense, Kennan said, was passive resistance, "the concept of making it impossible for a foreign occupier to run a conquered country." The national defense system should be scrapped in favor of plans for an underground guerilla movement after the country had been conquered. When he first breached this notion in Germany, Kennan complained, "everybody laughed at me."

Urban, hoping for more, refrained from laughing. Kennan obligingly drove his thoughts deeper into the intellectual rough. Peace, he said, required unilateral nuclear disarmament. But what if this lured the Soviets to try for a quick victory with a nuclear strike? He replied that "a nuclear strike would not be a rational action for any government." When Urban pointed out that governments are not always rational, all

Kennan could say was that if the Russians bombed the United States they would "destroy workers together with the bourgeoisie. What sense would that make?"[37]

For years advocates of detente had made good use of Kennan's defection from containment. Now the anticommunists, after having had Kennan's authority thrown at them since the days of the Fulbright hearings, could quote his caricature of the detente position as the work of its authoritative and representative spokesman.

Anticommunists assembled a collection of essays, *Decline of the West? George Kennan and his Critics* (1978), in which Eugene V. Rostow attacked Kennan (and, by implication, detente) as "exhausted, disillusioned and nearly without hope," a reflection of "a fashionable post-Vietnam mood about foreign affairs" that came "perilously close to preaching that we don't really need a foreign and defense policy at all."[38]

A year later, speaking before the Council on Foreign Relations, Kennan made an astonishing admission that gave anticommunists a chance to claim that he and the advocates of detente were no longer capable of handling the complexities of the most perilous issues in world affairs. "Like many of the rest of you," he said, "I have made my efforts to understand the arguments of these military enthusiasts. I have tried to follow them through the mazes of their intricate and sophisticated calculations of possible military advantage at various future points in time. . . . I come away from this exercise frustrated, and with two overpowering impressions. The first is that this entire science of long-range massive destruction—of calculated advantage or disadvantage in modern weaponry—has gotten seriously out of hand; that the variables, the complexities, the uncertainties it involves are rapidly growing beyond the power of either human mind or computer."[39]

If this meant anything at all, Kennan was pretending that the complexity of the strategic balance meant that it was incomprehensible, and hence meaningless. Indeed, it was a virtue not to be able to follow arguments about the strategic balance, as though anything he could not understand was not worth understanding.

But, of course, Kennan had no trouble understanding the complexities of the nuclear balance. He had been following the numbers and interpreting them since the dawn of the nuclear age. What had happened was that he realized that the numbers now showed that the Soviets were moving toward nuclear superiority. American stockpiles had peaked in 1965 and had since then steadily declined. The Soviets' arsenal had surpassed the Americans' in 1976. In fact, the Soviet stockpile would not peak until 1986.[40] It was in all likelihood because he realized that the numbers were against him that he was claiming that they didn't matter.

Kennan had given anticommunists a chance to inflict rhetorical mayhem on him and detente, and they did not hold back. Richard Pipes, Team B member and director of Harvard's Russian Research Center, wrote, "This statement renders me speechless," and warned Kennan and other spokesmen for the new foreign policy that if they were really serious about forging a new consensus in foreign policy, they had better stop ignoring facts brought up by those who were worried about the Soviet threat. Knowing that he had hold of a winning issue, Pipes pressed the attack. If the other side were serious in holding that the numbers, and hence Soviet superiority, did not matter, then anticommunists were quite willing to submit the question to the American people, and they were quite sure that the public would agree with them that the Soviet Union's military superiority over the United States did matter. And so Pipes ominously warned that "those who share Mr. Kennan's opinions will have to suffer through instruction about the strategic balance and the relationship between the Soviet military drive and Soviet intentions."[41]

Eugene V. Rostow also relished the notion of submitting detente and its consequences to the public. "Foreign policy," he said, "should be subject to democratic control. . . . No branch of policy, however technical, is beyond the reach of the informed good sense of the American people." The public's mistakes about foreign policy were due not to its instincts, which were sound, but to bad leadership, which Rostow proposed to remedy. "During the last decade, many who participated in the development of public opinion breached the basic rules of democratic ethics in failing to insist on the unpopular truth in their explanations of policy."[42] Like Pipes, Rostow was eager for a public debate that would pit the CPD's traditional anticommunist containment policies against what anticommunists were calling neoisolationism, and which they charged had been turned into dangerous policies by Carter's Secretary of State Cyrus Vance and his chief arms negotiator Paul Warnke.

What finally ended Jimmy Carter's experiment with a foreign policy free of the fear of communism, even more than the CPD's increasingly effective assault on detente, were the facts of international life, and facts are very stubborn things. During the late seventies, anticommunists warned persistently that the balance of international power was shifting dangerously against the United States, and that the Soviet Union was energetically exploiting its advantage. At the end of the decade events reached a climax that convinced even many of those who had been resisting the conclusion that the anticommunists were right.

Anticommunists watched apprehensively as, under Moscow's guidance, communism seemed to be evolving into a more flexible and attractive ideology, more capable of accommodating a diverse system in which power seemed to be shifting to the third world. In 1976 the Twenty-fifth Soviet Party Congress in Moscow affirmed the principle of Eurocommunism, recognizing the right of the national Communist parties to chart their own path to communism. That same year the Italian Communist Party won chairmanships of four parliamentary committees, and only by threatening to cut off loans were the United States, West Germany, Britain, and France able to keep Communists out of key security posts. In Sri Lanka, the fifth Colombo conference of unaligned nations met in August 1976 to denounce American "imperialism" in Korea, demand independence for Puerto Rico, and congratulate the Vietnamese for their triumph over the United States. Even the woebegone American Communists hoped to share in the increasing respectability of the international movement as Party chief Gus Hall traveled to Moscow to meet with Brezhnev in June 1977.

In the United Nations the center of balance had shifted to an increasingly anti-American third world. The United Nations had 144 members in 1975, with another 21 on the waiting list. Only 25 were not totalitarian or one-party regimes, and most were leftist. In the mid-seventies the UN went on a binge of blaming the West, particularly the United States, for world problems, an international vendetta that seemed to Americans to take on the character of a global "witch-hunt" that stigmatized America as a symbol of individualism, while the third world moved in the direction of Soviet-style command economies to accelerate development.[43]

The Soviets continued to insist that they would enforce the Brezhnev Doctrine, proclaimed after the Soviet invasion of Czechoslovakia in 1968. The Soviet Union would not "remain inactive," they warned, if faced with "anti-socialist degeneration" in the Soviet bloc. During the seventies Brezhnev expanded the doctrine to commit Soviet power to the maintenance of Marxist regimes anywhere in the Soviet sphere of influence, and to promise aid to Marxist insurgences.

The result was a marked increase in Soviet-backed insurgences. June 1978 saw a pro-Soviet coup in Yemen. In August of that same year the Sandinista Marxist rebels in Nicaragua seized the national palace in Managua and launched their final assault against the American-backed Somoza regime. The U.S. Senate sealed Somoza's doom by cutting off aid on September 22. In June 1980 Vietnamese Communist forces crossed the border into Thailand.

While anticommunists tried to raise the alarm, they watched as the Soviets reaped the strategic advantage of an enormous naval expansion program begun after the 1962 missile crisis. By 1976 the Soviets had outbuilt the United States 1,323 ships to 302, and they had 188 nuclear submarines, 46 with strategic missiles, as well as their first aircraft carriers. According to analysts trusted by anticommunists, the Soviet navy was dominant in the North Atlantic and the Pacific, equal in the Mediterranean, and was ready to move into the South Atlantic and Indian oceans.[44]

Even more worrisome was the Soviet use of Cubans as surrogates to extend the Soviet reach in Africa. The first Cubans arrived in Angola in December 1975. In 1976 they were in Ethiopia, and then Central and East Africa. By the late seventies the count of officially Marxist states in Africa had reached ten. In Central America, Nicaragua was a Soviet (or at least Cuban) satellite after 1979.[45]

Within the administration, Zbigniew Brzezinski tried to convince President Carter and Secretary of State Vance that the United States should respond to these Soviet advances, putting pressure on the Soviets by supporting dissidents in Eastern Europe, and he recommended that the United States project its armed forces into the Horn of Africa to counteract the Soviet-backed Cuban presence. His plans were blocked by the Defense and State departments, proving to Brzezinski that they had been "badly bitten by the Vietnam bug." In his view, American-Soviet relations began to "go wrong" in the mid-seventies when the United States failed to block Cuban intervention in Ethiopia, which tempted the Soviets to move recklessly in Afghanistan and elsewhere.[46]

Despite the 1975 Helsinki agreement there was no more freedom in the Soviet Union than before. Helsinki's "Basket III" accords on human rights were supposed to protect dissidents in the Eastern bloc but instead led to more repression when dissidents, encouraged by the treaties, made themselves more vulnerable by coming into the open. In December 1977, human rights activists in the groups set up to monitor the Helsinki accords were placed under house arrest. The next summer Anatoly Scharansky was jailed for spying for the United States and Aleksandr Ginzburg was sentenced to eight years of forced labor for his protests. The Soviets sent Andrei Sakharov into internal exile in January 1980 for protesting the Afghanistan invasion.[47]

Anticommunists were also worried by signs Soviet espionage in America was on the upswing. In one of the cases, Edwin G. Moore was convicted of spying for the Soviets in 1977, having done, according to the government, as much damage to the national security as any spy in history. In January 1980 the Canadians cracked a major ring operating out of their Soviet embassy. That October, David H. Barnett pleaded guilty to selling secrets to the Soviets. They were appalled when the Carter administration, instead of showing appropriate concern, congratulated itself for cutting back on counterespionage operations, slashing the number of cases from 4,868 in 1976 down to 214. When reporter Edward Jay Epstein argued that the KGB was winning the spy war because Congress and the press had made it impossible for the CIA to function professionally, liberals worried that putting too much emphasis on Soviet espionage might lead to anticommunist hysteria, witch-hunts, even war.[48]

International terrorists, while probably not constituting the full-blown international red web charged by some countersubversives, certainly were creating a system of mutual aid with Soviet support. Anticommunists noted that the leading terrorists were all Marxists, many graduates of the Soviets' terrorist school at Simteropol in the Crimea, which trained guerrillas for the Middle East, Latin America, and Africa.[49]

Throughout the seventies, anticommunists had been warning that the United States had so relaxed its defenses that it could no longer protect its interests, and that the Soviets were no longer being restrained by fear of American power or retaliation. The crises of 1979 seemed to prove to many, even in the Carter administration, that they had been right. On November 4, 1979, Iranian militants supported by the revolutionary Islamic government of Ayatollah Khomeini seized the American embassy in Teheran, taking sixty-five American embassy workers hostage. While America was writhing in impotent agony over this national humiliation, the Soviet Union, dissatisfied with the behavior of Afghanistan's Communist leadership, launched a full-scale invasion on Christmas Day, killed the head of state, and put its own man in charge.

Confessing that the Afghanistan invasion had completely changed his view of the Soviets, Carter recalled the American ambassador from Moscow, cut off grain sales and exports of technology to the Soviet Union, suspended fishing privileges, pulled the SALT II agreement from consideration by the Senate, and (on April 22) announced a boycott of the 1980 summer Olympics in Moscow. He sent a sharply larger defense budget request to Congress, along with plans to resume registration for the military draft.[50]

Once again, many Americans were coming around to the anticommunist view that to ignore the nature of communism and the Soviet Union was to ignore reality, and to ignore reality in foreign policy was a prescription for disaster. Containment of the Soviet Union again became the foundation of American foreign policy. On May 9, 1980, Carter delivered a foreign policy address that could be read as a retraction of his 1977 Notre Dame indictment of America's "inordinate fear of communism." Carter still insisted that foreign policy must "be based simultaneously on the primacy of certain basic moral principles—principles founded on the enhancement of human rights," but he now conceded that the United States must have military power second to none, and that "Americans must be mature enough to recognize that we need to be strong and we need to be accommodating at the same time."[51]

Even before Afghanistan, Carter had begun to worry about the state of American defenses. On December 12, 1979, he had proposed an increase in real defense spending by five percent a year, and had told the Business Council that "we must understand that not every instance of the firm application of power is a potential Vietnam."[52]

Carter's strong response to Afghanistan was attacked by many supporters of detente who worried that the invasion of Afghanistan and the spurt in Russian espionage could stimulate a resurgence of American anticommunism.[53] And during the last year of the Carter administration, American popular culture continued to reflect the view that, for the good of mankind, the best service Americans could render to mankind was to withdraw from contact with the outside world. Two powerful movies on Vietnam appeared that year: *The Deerhunter* and *Apocalypse Now;* both saw Vietnam as the fall of the American Eden, a descent into national corruption from which no redemption was possible.

George Kennan even made the astounding argument that any instability in Eastern Europe would justify Soviet repression. He called on Americans to understand the Soviets' need to maintain their empire, by force if necessary, and he chastised the Solidarity labor movement in Poland for rejecting socialism and for proposing that Poland leave the Warsaw pact. Demands for Polish freedom and independence were "inevitably self-defeating," and he even supported General Wojciech Jaruzelski's imposition of martial law as a positive step toward international stability.[54]

Appalled by this, Norman Podhoretz assembled his best arguments against detente and for an anticommunist foreign policy in a powerfully written popular polemic, *The Present Danger*, intended to help the anticommunist Ronald Reagan make his case against Carter in the 1980 election. *The Present Danger* offered a concise summary of all the arguments that the CPD had been making against detente for the past four years. Podhoretz began with a review of the original moral and strategic justifications for containment, and then marshaled the evidence that indicated containment was as necessary as ever despite, or even because of, the Vietnam debacle. Detente had been a delusion, he argued, and it had allowed Americans to ignore "the ominous consequences of a tilt in the balance of power from the United States to the Soviet Union." If detente were ever resurrected, he warned, "it would signify the final collapse of an American resolve to resist the forward surge of Soviet imperialism" leading to "the Finlandization of America, the political and economic subordination of the United States to superior power."[55]

The reason why America was now unable to understand the perilous reality of a world threatened by an expansive Soviet Union was that since Vietnam "a key term has quietly disappeared from the discussion of the Soviet-American conflict. It is the term 'communism.' " Communism remained the principal destabilizing force in the world, and yet, he charged, Carter never mentioned the word in his 1980 State of the

Union "Carter Doctrine" message when he announced that the United States would resist any effort by any outside force to gain control of the Persian Gulf area, when the most dangerous "outside power" Carter had in mind was the Soviet Union.

The fact was, Podhoretz insisted, the world could not be understood without using that missing term, because underlying all the tensions between the United States and the Soviet Union was the clash between communism and freedom. "The reason Soviet imperialism is a threat to us is not merely that the Soviet Union is a superpower bent on aggrandizing itself, but that it is a Communist state armed, as Sakharov says, to the teeth, and dedicated to the destruction of the free institutions which are our heritage and the political culture which is our glory." Wherever communism had gained power, it had been "a curse." It was a system built on terror, resting on genocide, that denied—even in the most liberal Communist regimes—the most elementary human rights.

The cold war, Podhoretz concluded, was the fight "for freedom and against Communism, for democracy and against totalitarianism." And yet, nowhere were American leaders expressing that truth, "with force and clarity." Only by once again affirming anticommunism as the moral imperative behind containment of the Soviet Union, he said, could America and the West again summon their strength to a struggle that would demand courage and patience. The policies needed to guard peace and security could be sustained only by the conviction that they were right—that is, only if they were anticommunist.[56]

On April 24, 1980, Carter launched Desert One, the attemped helicopter rescue of the Teheran hostages. Its failure, which cost eight soldiers their lives and wounded five others, was seen by anticommunists as "the lowest point of America's fortunes in this century."[57]

For anticommunists, the results of the attempt to banish anticommunism from American life were everywhere to be seen. A Soviet expeditionary force was fighting to reduce Afghanistan to the status of yet another satellite. Soviet surrogates from Cuba and East Germany were fighting to spread Communist power in Africa. A new Communist beachhead in Nicaragua had given communism a launching ground for interventions throughout Latin America. American weakness was encouraging terrorists to plan more outrages against American targets.

New Soviet espionage was being exposed almost every week. And, highlighting the spectacle of American retreat before Soviet power was the Brezhnev Doctrine, reserving to the Soviet Union the right to intervene anywhere to aid Marxist insurrections, the right to intervene anywhere to stamp out threats to Communist regimes. The Soviets could plausibly claim, in Andrei Gromyko's provocative words, that socialism was "the most dynamic and influential force in the world arena."

But now, only five years after anticommunism's disaster in Vietnam, there was a reborn and revitalized anticommunist movement in America, confident, experienced, and articulate. It could now accuse its opponents of being the architects of failure, and could insist, forcefully and persuasively, that it knew how to reverse that failure. And in a time of confusion, having the answers is often the prelude to being given the chance to lead.

Chapter 14

TO THE BERLIN WALL

I believe that communism is another sad, bizarre chapter in human history whose last pages even now are being written.
—Ronald Reagan, the "Evil Empire Speech," March 1983.[1]

Ronald Reagan's election in November 1980 was more than the victory of a genial and popular politician in the White House over a president regarded—perhaps unfairly—as a domestic and foreign policy failure. When he came to Washington, Reagan brought with him the ideas and values of American anticommunism—the men and the women of the self-confident anticommunist movement reborn in the last half of the seventies. His election was, in a real sense, the culmination of the long history of American anticommunism.

It was no secret that Reagan was an anticommunist, but few in 1980 realized how thoroughly he had absorbed the beliefs of American anticommunism, how important a role he had played in its history. The beliefs about communism—its moral squalor and political vulerability—that would fuel his foreign policy were the legacy of his career as an anticommunist. For him, communism had not changed since the early days of the cold war; indeed, it had not changed since 1917. Shortly after taking office, he said, "Every Soviet leader since Lenin up to and including the present one, Leonid Brezhnev, had said the goal of the Soviet Union was to Communize the world. Except for a brief time-out during World War II, the Russians had been our de facto enemies for almost sixty-five years; all this while, their policies had been consistently and religiously devoted to the single purpose of destroying democracy and imposing Communism."[2]

Reagan's views on communism contradicted the dominant consensus among Soviet experts, which was that the Communist system had

391

achieved a permanent and stable place in the world order, and that America would have to reconcile itself to that reality. Reagan's experience in the anticommunist movement, had left him with the belief that, "as an economic system, Communism was doomed" and that "the Soviet leadership . . . could not survive against the inherent drive of all men and women to be free." Reagan was determined to put that belief to the test.[3]

Reagan was known to be an ardent anticommunist before he began his run for the presidency, but the intensity of his commitment to the movement—as an anticommunist labor union leader, as a principal force behind the industry blacklist, and as a public spokesman for corporate anticommunism as a speaker for General Electric, were faint memories to most Americans. Reagan had developed friendships with right-wing anticommunists, speaking, for instance, at a 1961 rally of Fred Schwarz's Christian Anti-communist Crusade, and at a 1962 fund-raiser for Birch Society member Congressman John Rousselot. In 1964 he had been one of Barry Goldwater's most effective supporters. Goldwater's defeat, however, had impressed on Reagan how vulnerable anticommunists were to charges of extremism, so he softened his anticommunist rhetoric and emphasized that he was primarily concerned about the Soviet threat, and not domestic subversion.

During his 1980 campaign, the Committee on the Present Danger was perhaps Reagan's most important resource. He was drawn to the CPD by their compelling brief against détente and by their expert analysis of arms issues. He shared the Committee's belief that the Soviet arms buildup and the failure of the United States to keep pace had opened a window of vulnerability to Soviet expansion, even attack. Reagan's liaison with the CPD was Richard Allen, a founding member, and Reagan himself joined the Committee in January 1979, at which point the CPD effectively became a think tank for the Reagan campaign. Six of Reagan's campaign speeches on foreign policy were based on CPD founder Eugene V. Rostow's analysis of SALT II. Reagan used the CPD's technical data to attack Carter for having permitted the United States to lose its strategic superiority to the Soviet Union, which, he argued, was the underlying cause of America's problems in Iran and elsewhere in the world.[4]

Reagan came to Washington believing that the West had allowed the global balance of power to shift to the Soviet Union during the seventies. But he also believed that the Brezhnev Doctrine, committing the Soviets to defend clients in faraway corners of the world, had allowed a serious and potentially fatal imbalance to develop between their now nearly unlimited responsibilities and their overextended and diminishing resources. Reagan administration strategy aimed at turning the assets the Soviets had acquired during the seventies into liabilities.[5]

The perception that Carter's experiment with a foreign policy free of the "inordinate" fear of communism had failed gave Reagan and his advisors the chance to return to a thoroughly anticommunist foreign policy. The goal would be to press the confrontation with the Soviet Union to a decisive and victorious conclusion. In the face of opposition from the arms control establishment, the media, liberal Democrats, and the liberal internationalists in his own party, the Reagan Doctrine would aim at rolling back communism at the outermost reaches of the Soviet sphere, exploiting weaknesses in the heart of the Soviet empire, and engaging the Soviet Union in an arms race he was sure it could not win.[6]

To implement this radical change in foreign policy, Reagan brought no fewer than sixty members of the Committee on the Present Danger into the government.[7] He placed CPD founders Paul Nitze and Eugene Rostow into the most critical arms control positions. Jeane Kirkpatrick went to represent the United States at the United Nations. Her 1979 essay in Norman Podhoretz's *Commentary*, "Dictatorships and Double Standards," had given Reagan a rationale for distinguishing between "authoritarians" (right-wing Western-oriented dictators) and "totalitarians" (Marxist regimes).[8] Kirkpatrick's hard-line anti-Soviet rhetoric and votes against anti-Western measures sponsored by third world regimes grown fat on American aid showed a new readiness by the United States to reward its friends and punish its enemies.

The key foreign policy appointment of the Reagan administration was his choice for Director of Central Intelligence, another CPD member. This was William F. Casey, who would function as a shadow secretary of state. It would be Casey, more than anyone else, who would orchestrate and implement Reagan's covert war to destabilize the Soviet empire.

William F. Casey was, like Reagan, a lifelong anticommunist. Reared in an Irish Catholic neighborhood in Queens, he absorbed his anti-communism with his religion in Catholic parochial schools, at Fordham University at a time when the Jesuit college was an Irish enclave, and at St. John's University Law School. World War II introduced him to the world of espionage and covert operations when he served in the OSS under William Donovan, first as head of the OSS's London secretariat, finally as chief of Secret Intelligence for Europe. He was working with the Polish government in exile in London when the Yalta agreements handed power to Stalin's Communist puppets in Lublin. "I never forgot what caving in to the Russians did to those people," he recalled.[9]

After the war, Casey joined the conservative, Taft wing of New York's Republican Party. He was a McCarthy supporter because he thought it took a roughneck like McCarthy to "flush out" the Communists. Afterwards he stayed active in right-wing anticommunist circles in New York, "a very small club, maybe fifty members," William F. Buckley, Jr., used to joke, where "there was practically a secret handshake."[10] Casey sat on the board of directors of the conservative publishing house, Henry Regnery, kept the conservative magazine *Human Events* alive after its publisher's death, and drew up the financial plans for Buckley's *National Review*. As a member of the Veterans of the Office of Strategic Services (VOSS), he maintained connections with the OSS veterans' network in the CIA and the business world.[11]

Like other right-wing anticommunists, Casey was never reconciled to the containment doctrine, and was bitterly disappointed by the Eisenhower administration's failure to live up to its pledge to liberate Eastern Europe. He supported Nixon as a fellow anticommunist, and loathed Nelson Rockefeller for his assaults on anticommunist "extremism." He dreamed of winning the cold war: "I'm for throwing Castro out of Cuba and out of South America. I'm for encouraging Russia and China to feud with each other. I'm for putting on the pressure so we can open up Eastern Europe. I'm for pushing Russian and Chinese influence out of Africa. And I'm for winning in Southest Asia rather than neutralizing it." He denounced the Carter human rights policy, saying that "right now as we crusade for human rights in countries which do not threaten us, we conceal from public view the photos we take of slave labor camps in Siberia."[12]

Casey was an amateur historian with a special interest in the American Revolution. He loved to tour revolutionary war battle sites. He wrote a book for the Bicentennial: *Where and How the War Was Fought.* How did Washington's ragtag army beat the greatest military machine in the world? Casey asked. He thought he knew the answer: The rebels had been a native resistance, and native resistances always had the advantage over governments propped up by foreign allies. Casey was going to look for native resistances against Marxist regimes, and give them American support. "If the native resistance did not come banging on the door of the CIA . . . then maybe the CIA had to go out and discover it."[13]

On October 29, 1983, William Casey made a symbolic appearance at Fulton, Missouri's Westminster College, where Churchill had given his Iron Curtain speech in 1946. Quoting at length from that speech's litany of Soviet aggression after World War II, Casey extended Churchill's analysis to Communist gains since that earlier speech: Vietnam, Afghanistan, the Horn of Africa (Somalia and Ethiopia), southern Africa (Angola), and in the Caribbean (Cuba, Nicaragua, insurgencies in El Salvador). In Casey's view, the main Soviet target was the Middle East. The real purpose of its Central American adventures, he told his audience, was to redirect American forces away from the Middle Eastern cockpit.[14]

Casey believed the Soviet Union's successes in the seventies had lured it into overextending its resources. Reagan and Secretary of State Alexander Haig agreed. "Where can we get a rollback?" Haig asked, reviewing the list of recent Soviet gains. "I want to win one," Reagan would tell them.[15]

Reagan and Casey were able to build on the anticommunist policies of Carter's last year, when Carter abruptly lashed out against the Soviet invasion of Afghanistan. Carter's national security advisor, Zbigniew Brzezinski, had also believed that the Soviets had overextended themselves in Afghanistan and that it could be turned into their Vietnam. He had put together a coalition of Saudis, Egyptians, Pakistanis, and Chinese to support the Afghan resistance. Carter had also authorized covert aid to the Nicaraguan opposition almost as soon as the Sandinistas took over.[16]

Casey organized the scattered Carter-Brzezinski operations into an integrated program. His aim was to stretch Soviet resources to the breaking point by supporting anticommunist insurgencies all over the world.

The ultimate goal, almost unimaginable to anyone except Reagan and Casey, was the destruction of the Soviet empire. Liberation, and not just containment, had replaced détente as the basis of American foreign policy.[17, 18]

For Reagan's strategy to succeed, the United States had to maintain pressure wherever the Soviet Union was supporting regimes or movements far from its borders that were so weak, and had so little local support, that they would collapse if aid were withdrawn. Soon Casey was supporting sabotage operations against the Soviet-puppet regime in South Yemen. He helped install an anti-Qaddafi government in Chad. He obtained a presidential finding in the fall of 1982 authorizing nonlethal aid to the noncommunist opposition in Cambodia. Reagan sent aid to Jonas Savimbi, leader of the resistance against the Marxist regime of Angola. Casey and Reagan were going to "make the third world a more dangerous strategic frontier [for the Soviets]."[19]

Nowhere were the Soviets more overextended than in Nicaragua. "This is one you can win," Haig told Reagan. On December 1, 1981, Reagan authorized the CIA to begin furnishing arms and training to the contra rebels against the Marxist Sandinista government, ostensibly to prevent the Nicaraguans from subverting the El Salvadoran government. Casey also persuaded Reagan to funnel support to anti-Marxist elements in the El Salvadoran government. In 1983, with Congress denying him funds to overthrow the Communists in Nicaragua, Reagan signed a finding that the purpose of aid to the contras was to pressure the Sandinistas to democratize their government and to cease destabilizing El Salvador.[20]

Ironically, congressional opposition to Casey's operations in Nicaragua (a "bad war") may have garnered support for a "good war" in Afghanistan. Congressmen supporting aid to the Afghan rebels could validate their anti-Soviet credentials to balance against their criticism of Reagan's Central American policies. With the backing of Congress, therefore, Reagan could pour money and weapons into Afghanistan, bogging down the Soviet army in the same kind of endless and debilitating quagmire that had traumatized America in Vietnam.

Meanwhile, the Reagan Doctrine's second front, the drive to rebuild the military strength of the Western alliance, was stirring up a storm of opposition in Europe and America.

The first test was over the deployment in Europe of the so-called "Euromissiles," ground-launched cruise missiles and Pershing II intermediate range missiles. The issue had arisen in 1977 when the Soviets deployed the SS-20, a triple warhead mobile missile designed to meet the 1972 SALT I limits on missiles of greater than 5,000-kilometer range. The SS-20 threatened all of Europe and Asia and so Jimmy Carter, under pressure from the European allies, particularly Germany, agreed to send 108 Pershing IIs and 464 cruise missiles to Europe as a deterrent to the SS-20s.[21] At the same time he offered not to deploy the Euromissiles if the Soviets would agree to new limits on the SS-20s. This was Carter's "dual-track strategy."

The Euromissile plan gave rise to the largest, best-coordinated mass protests against containment since the peace offensive of the forties. This "nuclear freeze movement" demanded the West unilaterally halt new nuclear weapons development, testing, and deployment. The freeze movement in America was organized by Terry Provance and Randall Forsberg, who used popular entertainers like rocker Bruce Springsteen to draw enormous audiences to nuclear freeze concert rallies. *The New Yorker* magazine devoted its entire February 1982 issue to Jonathan Schell's *Fate of the Earth*. Schell's book was comparable to Norman Angell's *Great Illusion* (1910) in creating a militantly pacifist sentiment among intellectuals. Robert Sheer, in *With Enough Shovels*, accused the Reagan administration of cheerfully contemplating the possibility of surviving (and winning) a nuclear war, and his book was endorsed by MIT president Jerome Wiesner and Carter's Secretary of State Cyrus Vance. George F. Kennan's contribution to the freeze movement was *The Nuclear Delusion*. Robert McNamara and a group of "wise men"— himself, McGeorge Bundy, George F. Kennan, and SALT negotiator Gerard Smith—put forth a demand in *Foreign Affairs* in 1982 that the United States make a "no first use" pledge to the Soviets.[22]

The nuclear freeze movement was the greatest challenge to the West's ability to maintain a strategic balance against Soviet military power since the beginning of the cold war. Had the West backed down on Euromissile deployment, Reagan felt, the Soviet Union in the future would have been able to count on the peace movement's political pressure to keep the West from deploying any weapons permitted by arms control agreements and from retaliating against Soviet treaty violations, since the only credible Western retaliation would be to match Soviet deployments. Had the Euromissile protests succeeded in blocking deployment, Reagan worried, the Soviet Union could have kept and added to the nuclear superiority it had won in the seventies. While the Soviets and the left taunted Reagan for his "cowboy" foreign policy, he kept forging ahead with plans to deploy the Euromissiles. His experiences with Hollywood front groups may have taught him to be skeptical about the real strength of Soviet-backed peace offensives.

The nuclear freeze debate let the old left and the remnants of the Vietnam era New Left move further into the mainstream. A 1982 poll by the Potomac Associates found that "anticommunism as a national slogan or marching theme is increasingly on the wane, despite the Reagan Administration's attempts to emphasize it."[23] The far left now found that its historic position against the cold war helped it forge bonds with the media and the arms control establishment in a coalition against Reagan's policies. The scattered fragments of the old Communist Party were welcomed into a "Rainbow Coalition," and several black congressmen like John Conyers, Charles Hayes, Ron Dellums, and George Crockett welcomed Communist Party support, protected by "the now entrenched belief among custodians of American culture that any criticism of communism or Communists was a form of McCarthyism."[24]

On his side Reagan had the figures, the statistics on the relative strength of the two missile forces and on how the impact of arms limits on the mixes of weaponry in the two arsenals favored the Soviets. These comparisons were initially furnished by the CPD, but now were endorsed by the government's own analysts. The freeze movement, however, had the typewriters, the microphones, and the videocams. The media, the liberal wing of the Democratic party, and the arms control establishment all attacked Reagan for "gambling with history" (the title of a book by *Time* magazine's Strobe Talbott). Public opinion seemed to be against the President. In 1982, a poll found that 72 percent of those surveyed supported the concept of a nuclear freeze.[25]

Opposition mounted to Reagan's weapons programs. On March 23, 1982, Congress killed the mobile missile program Carter had designed to deter Russia's new ability to threaten America's land-based deterrent. Senators Edward Kennedy and Mark Hatfield introduced nuclear freeze legislation that was narrowly defeated in August 1982 only when Henry Jackson and John Warner introduced an alternative that called for a freeze at "sharply reduced levels," meaning that the Soviets would first have to reduce their arsenals. In October 1982, the Catholic bishops issued a pastoral letter denouncing the entire strategy of nuclear deterrence, and demanding the United States shift to a "no first strike" policy. Nuclear strategy, they said, could never be considered moral. The American bishops, once the most anticommunist in the world, were now more pacifist than the Pope.

Far from scaling back his arms buildup, in March 1983 Reagan unveiled the Strategic Defense Initiative, "Star Wars," his call for a massive American investment in a space-based antimissile system, thus shifting American strategy from Robert McNamara's Mutual Assured Destruction (MAD) deterrent strategy to one of building a defense against incoming missiles. Reagan's opponents promptly accused him of recklessly seeking to destabilize the balance of power.

As Reagan, with the firm support of the European allies, ignored the protests and proceeded with preparations for missile deployment, there were signs of alarm in the Kremlin. As the Soviets realized that the peace movement was not going to block Euromissile deployment they offered to reduce their intermediate range warheads to the combined number of Britain's and France's if the United States did not deploy the Euromissiles. Brushing this aside, Reagan and the allies pressed ahead. The Senate defeated a resolution for a unilateral freeze on nuclear weapons, 58 to 40. On October 31, 1983, Britain voted to deploy, and on November 22, West Germany authorized deployment. They were flown in the next day. The Soviets retaliated by walking out of the Strategic Arms Reduction Talks (START).

Reagan had won an enormous victory, diplomatic, military, and political. The Western peace movement, one of the Soviet Union's vital strategic assets, had been exposed as politically powerless. The pressure was now on the Soviets to return to the bargaining table and make concessions, since it was clear that in the absence of further arms control agreements, Reagan intended to arm the Western alliance at breakneck speed.

The Washington foreign policy establishment, however, interpreted Reagan's victory as a setback for peace, because it had halted the arms control process. Arms control, and not strategic superiority, should have continued to be the primary goal of American foreign policy. Reagan was accused of being a reckless gambler risking national survival for anticommunist ideological goals. In *The Russians and Reagan* (1984) *Time* magazine's Strobe Talbott claimed that superpower relations under Rea-

gan were "absolutely awful . . . the worst in more than two decades."
The Russians had concluded that Reagan intended to destroy Soviet
power, he wrote, and they felt backed into a corner "from which they
might yet lash out in some unpredictable way . . . and teach Reagan a
lesson."[26]

Strobe Talbott's *Deadly Gambits*, also of 1984, an insider's study of
arms negotiations under Reagan, charged that Reagan had deliberately
increased the risk of nuclear war through his anticommunist obsessions.
Talbott implied that only one thing could save the arms control process,
Reagan's defeat in 1984. Armed with books like Schell's and Talbott's,
the Democrats would campaign on a platform that accused Reagan of
having made the world more dangerous than it had been since the early
days of the cold war.[27]

While the Reagan Doctrine's support of anticommunist insurgencies
in the third world and the renewed arms race increased the pressure on
the Soviets, in the long run it was the third component of Reagan's strategy, support for anticommunist dissidents within the Soviet empire itself, that would have the most to do with the ultimate collapse of
communism.

Historians will long debate what brought the Soviet Union down,
and so far they have not been able to agree even on the nature of the
cause, economic, political, or moral. But certainly the *immediate* reason
the Soviet Union lost its empire was that in 1989 Poland demonstrated
to Eastern Europe, and ultimately to the Russian people, that they could
stand up to their Communist rulers without military retaliation from
Mikhail Gorbachev.

Reagan fully subscribed to the anticommunist axiom that the cold
war had begun with the abandonment of Poland at Yalta. Anticommunism's enemies called this a delusion, a conspiracy theory, "the Myth of
Yalta," and insisted that the irresistible forces of history and the position of troops at the end of the war had sealed the fate of Poland, not
the failure of Western leaders. But anticommunists like Reagan believed
that Poland had been sold out, and that the West owed Poland a moral
debt that could be satisfied only by redeeming Poland from captivity.

Poland was at the center of Ronald Reagan's determination to "re-
moralize" American foreign policy.[28] It was Reagan's background as an
anticommunist that made him realize what the defection of Poland

would mean to the Soviet empire, and that made him act with such determination to bring this about, even though it would so clearly upset the stability of the established order. When the Poles began their courageous but seemingly doomed revolt against their Communist rulers, it made a critical difference that America had an anticommunist in the White House and an anticommunist as director of Central Intelligence whose anticommunism made them think in terms of winning the cold war, not relaxing tensions by seeking compromise on issues like Poland. When Poland caught fire, Ronald Reagan and William F. Casey were prepared to fan the blaze, and not, as some Americans urged, to persuade the Poles to accommodate themselves to their fate to preserve a world order that depended upon accepting the permanence of the Communist regimes of post-Yalta Europe.[29]

Poland was on Reagan's mind when he entered the White House. "As seen from the Oval Office, the events in Poland were thrilling," he wrote. "One of man's most fundamental and implacable yearnings, the desire for freedom, was stirring to life beyond the Iron Curtain, the first break in the totalitarian dike of Communism. I wanted to be sure we did nothing to impede this process and everything we could to spur it along. This was what we had been waiting for since World War II. What was happening in Poland might spread like a contagion throughout Eastern Europe."[30] At his first press conference Reagan denounced detente as a one-way street, and at every meeting with the Soviets his representatives warned that "Poland must be spared."[31]

In December 1981, after the Polish authorities imposed martial law and outlawed Solidarity, Reagan told the National Security Council that "this may be the last chance in our lifetime to see a change in the Soviet Empire's colonial policy re Eastern Europe." He persuaded the NATO allies to make detente with the Soviets dependent on their behavior in Poland, and he told Brezhnev that Soviet intervention "could unleash a process which neither you nor we could fully control."[32]

In fact, a process had already begun which no one could control. The election of the Polish Karol Cardinal Wojtyla as Pope John Paul II on October 16, 1978, placed at the head of the Roman Catholic Church a man with much the same views on international affairs as Reagan and Casey. John Paul II also saw Yalta as a symbol of the moral catastrophe of modern times, calling Yalta "the (temporary) victory of violence over principle," and denouncing it as a moral abomination.[33]

As a Pole living under communism, the Pope's experience had

brought him to the same conclusion as Reagan and Casey, that "the communist system was in something approaching terminal condition."[34] And he, like them, had taken over from a predecessor, Pope Paul VI, who had given up any hope of overthrowing communism in the near future, if ever.

In the view of anticommunist students of the cold war papacy, Pope Paul VI had conceded that Marxism-Leninism had "historical staying power," that "the Yalta imperial system was a relatively permanent fact of the international scene" that would endure well into the next century (at least), and that the avoidance of nuclear war took precedence over all other diplomatic goals. Paul VI accepted the dominant view that if the cold war were to be resolved, it would be through the convergence of the two systems, with more political democracy in the East and more economic democracy in the West. Like Jimmy Carter, Paul VI moderated his criticism of Communist regimes in order to attain "negotiated gains." Under Paul the Church had criticized the West's involvement in Vietnam and the underdevelopment of the third world, much as Jimmy Carter had criticized America's repressive allies, while muting criticism of the Soviet Union so as not to disturb detente.[35]

As soon as he was elected, John Paul II abruptly reversed Paul VI's policies. He brought to the papacy his conviction that communism in Poland and throughout the Yalta empire was actually in a most precarious state, no matter how strong and stable it seemed. He knew that communism had no roots in the culture of Soviet bloc countries, was hated by the public, and maintained its power only through fear. If the Iron Curtain nations could overcome that fear, their Communist regimes must fall. Three times during his installation ceremony as Pope, John Paul II repeated the phrase—meaning it to be heard in Poland— "Be not afraid." And in Poland, John Paul II knew he could count on the remarkable legacy of the legendary Stefan Cardinal Wyszynski, primate from 1948 until his death in 1981. Under Wyszynski, Polish Catholicism had emerged as perhaps the most fervent Church in the world-wide Roman Catholic community and as the only authentic symbol of Polish nationalism.[36]

Ironically, the same Second Vatican Council that had shattered the staunch anticommunism of American Catholics was what gave John Paul II and the Polish Catholic Church the moral stature to challenge the European Communist regimes. The Vatican II encyclical *Pastoral*

Constitution on the Church in the Modern World (*Gaudium et Spes*) had encouraged American Catholics to abandon their adversarial relationship with the non-Catholic world, enter into a dialogue with the greater community and abandon their traditionally reflexive anticommunism.

In Eastern Europe, however, it was another Vatican II document, the *Declaration on Religious Liberty*, that liberated the Catholic Church to fight communism by committing the Church to the defense of individual liberty against the state or other social institutions, even churches, a revolutionary position for a church that had throughout history called on the state to repress religious dissent. The *Declaration on Religious Liberty* stated that

> the human person has a right to religious freedom. This freedom means that all men are to be immune from coercion on the part of individuals or of social groups and of any human power. . . . The right to religious freedom has its foundation in the very dignity of the human person, as this dignity is known through the revealed Word of God and by reason itself. This right of the human person to religious freedom is to be recognized in the constitutional law whereby society is governed. Thus it is to become a civil right.[37]

This *Declaration* allowed John Paul II and the Church to base their anticommunism on a commitment to individual freedom. John Paul could define history as the evolution of human rights, identify the Church with human progress, and brand as reactionary the Communist regimes that persecuted the Church.

Already by December 1970 the Polish Communist regime had mismanaged the economy to the point of food riots and strikes. There was another round of strikes in 1976, with further erosion of Party power as, for the first time, intellectuals formed an alliance with workers, founding the Committee for the Defense of Workers headed by Jacek Kuron, Bronislaw Geremek, and Adam Michnik. With the anticommunist resistance now well established, a year after his election John Paul II made a triumphant return to Poland in June 1979. He called for Poland to discard what was coming to be referred to as a "crust" on society: the Communist regime. "Come, Holy Spirit," he prayed, "renew the face . . . of *this* land!").[38]

A year later, in August 1980, an electrician named Lech Walesa took command of the striking workers at the Lenin shipyards in Gdansk, and founded the Solidarity labor movement. At the end of the month the strikers had forced the government to permit independent trade unions to represent the workers. Walesa fixed his signature to the agreement with a huge pen topped with a photo of John Paul II. In what may have been a response to the events in Poland, an attempt was made on the Pope's life in St. Peter's Square on May 13, 1981. It is unlikely that the assassin, Mehmet Ali Agca, an individual with ties to Bulgarian intelligence, acted on his own, though no conclusive proof of the involvement of the Warsaw Pact secret services has yet been discovered.

On December 12, 1981, with the authority of the Communist Party crumbling and Solidarity gaining strength, the Polish army seized control of the government, and installed a "Military Council of National Salvation" headed by General Wojciech Jaruzelski, declaring that the nation was in "a state of war." The leaders of Solidarity, Walesa included, were placed under arrest.

The Polish Communists and their Soviet sponsors had calculated that sheer force and terror once again would overawe their enemies and that the Polish Church would make peace with the government "over the corpse, so to speak, of Solidarity." They assumed that the West, as always, would ritually condemn the repression but do nothing to risk detente and its fruits of arms limitation treaties and increased trade.[39]

The difference this time was that the Soviets faced the opposition of three determined anticommunists who had no investment in detente, and who for their part doubted that the Communists had the stamina, support, or strength to endure a protracted war of nerves. Lech Walesa was not going to break; Pope John Paul II was not going to bend; and in Ronald Reagan the West had a leader who believed that the Yalta system was ready to fall if pushed, and that Poland was the right place to apply the pressure.

Poland created what reporter Carl Bernstein called a "Holy Alliance" between the Pope and the President to keep the Solidarity movement alive. In the spring of 1982, Reagan and the Pope met for the first time, and according to Bernstein, reaffirmed their refusal "to accept a fundamental fact of their lifetimes: the division of Europe as mandated at Yalta and the communist domination of Eastern Europe. A free, non-communist Poland, they were convinced, would be a dagger to the heart of the Soviet empire; and if Poland became democratic, other East European states would follow." Reagan said that he and the Pope "both felt that a great mistake had been made at Yalta and something should be done. Solidarity was the very weapon for bringing this about, because it was an organization of the laborers of Poland . . . contrary to anything the Soviets would want." Reagan assembled a coalition of Catholic anticommunists to mobilize American aid to Solidarity: William Casey, Richard Allen, William Clark, Alexander Haig, Vernon Walters, and the ambassador to the Vatican, William Wilson. John Cardinal Krol of Philadelphia (whose father was Polish-born) became the liaison between Casey and the American Catholic Church, which had also begun to help Solidarity. When some of Reagan's foreign policy advisors told him he was not being realistic about Solidarity's chances, Reagan lectured them about the evils of communism and the United States' duty to help.[40]

For the next several years, William Casey would meet with the Pope almost every time he went to Europe, while Vernon Walters maintained even more regular liaison. Casey became the "principal policy architect" for the administration's aid to Poland. The staunchly anti-Soviet Zbigniew Brzezinski, national security advisor under Carter, also assisted the effort.[41]

Reagan and his advisors were convinced that if Poland's Communist government fell, the rest of the Yalta empire would topple like a row of dominoes. Casey "was convinced that the system was falling and doomed to collapse one way or another—and Poland was the force that would lead to the dam breaking."[42] In May 1982 the destruction of the Soviet empire became official policy, when President Reagan issued National Security Decision Directive 32, authorizing a full range of efforts to "neutralize" the ability of the Soviet Union to hold onto its European satellites, with the immediate goal of the destabilization of the Polish government.[43]

To ensure that the Polish operations did not bog down in the usual bureaucratic morass, they were run outside the normal State Department channels through Casey or Clark. Casey drew on the CIA's experience of its postwar alliance with the European noncommunist left. He worked out arrangements with the Socialist International (the federation of European Socialists) to funnel aid to Solidarity, this to avoid the taint of a CIA connection that might be exploited by anti-American propagandists. Casey also made use of the CIA's contacts with another historic component of the anticommunist alliance, the AFL-CIO. The union's Lane Kirkland and Tom Kahn, who were deeply committed to Solidarity, worked with the National Security Council to make sure Solidarity got what it needed to survive. Casey found that the AFL-CIO's contacts with Solidarity were "so good that much of what the CIA needed could be financed and obtained through AFL-CIO channels." Soon Solidarity's headquarters in Brussels had become the "clearinghouse" for aid from the American National Endowment for Democracy, the AFL-CIO, the Vatican, the European Socialist parties, and the CIA. The Swedish Socialist government and unions played a particularly important role smuggling material into Poland, and the Scandinavian connection also may have been at work when Walesa was awarded the Nobel Peace Prize on October 5, 1983.[44]

All the far-flung operations of the Reagan Doctrine—the arms buildup, American support for anticommunist insurgencies, and the campaign to destabilize the Yalta empire—were knit together by Reagan's unrelentingly anticommunist rhetoric, rhetoric anticommunists firmly believe was pivotal in raising Western morale and demoralizing the leadership of the Communist bloc at a critical moment in the history of the cold war.

Reagan's public celebration of anticommunism flew in the face of the unrelentingly negative treatment of anticommunism that was by now almost a conditioned response in American culture. When Alger Hiss, the Rosenbergs, or American Communists were remembered, it was usually as the victims of anticommunism. When anticommunists reminded the public of the historical context of those episodes, they risked being accused of defending McCarthyism. Popular films on the domestic cold war rarely mentioned the relationship between the American Communists and Stalin. Sometimes it seemed that Americans had come to see the cold war as a purely American affair consisting of Hollywood blacklisting, academic witch-hunts, and J. Edgar Hoover's files on almost everyone. Having an FBI file now seemed to be a form of papal indulgence, conferring absolution for past or future political sins.

Increasingly, films, novels, and historical studies treated the American Communists not merely as victims of witch-hunts but as "moral exemplars."[45] A French TV documentary that exposed the "murder" of the Rosenbergs was shown on U.S. cable in November 1982. American television broadcast a study of American anticommunism in 1983 under the title, "The American Inquisition." Another 1983 television film, "The Day After," gave powerful and emotional support to the pro-freeze position. Even Reagan confessed he had been moved.[46]

The popular idea that the cold war was over survived despite a remarkable surge of Soviet espionage in the United States, with almost weekly arrests of Russian spies and their American agents. It was later learned that this reflected panic in the Kremlin over Reagan's intentions, and whether he was planning a preemptive war against the Soviets. The Soviets' search for Reagan's real agenda was given the code name RYAN by Soviet intelligence, after the Russian initials for Nuclear Missile Attack. But when anticommunists called for new internal security committees to investigate the surge in Soviet espionage, they were accused of trying to revive cold war hysteria and McCarthyism.[47]

While the Soviets and the left taunted Reagan for his "cowboy" foreign policy, he kept forging ahead, outmaneuvering the opposition with his remarkable communication skills, the strong support of Allied leaders, notably Margaret Thatcher, and the intellectual support of the neoconservative movement.[48]

Reagan's greatest resource was his ability to focus the attention of the world on the fundamental moral differences between free societies and the peoples' democracies, differences long dismissed by a West that had come to seem obsessed with its own faults. In his address to the British Parliament in June 1982, Reagan surprised his supporters, and infuriated his enemies, by returning to the liberal anticommunist doctrine that the cold war was a conflict between value systems.

> The struggle that's now going on in the world will not be bombs and rockets, but a test of wills and ideas, a trial of spiritual resolve, the values we hold, the beliefs we cherish, the ideals to which we are dedicated. . . . If history teaches us anything, it teaches self-delusion in the face of unpleasant facts is folly. We see around us today the marks of our terrible dilemma—predictions of doomsday, antinuclear demonstrations, an arms race in which the West must, for its own protection, be an unwilling participant. At the same time, we see totalitarian forces in the world who seek subversion and conflict around the globe to further their barbarous assault on the human spirit. What, then, is our course? Must civilization perish in a hail of fiery atoms? Must freedom wither in a quiet, deadening accommodation with totalitarian evil?

Reagan's answer was that in any competition with freedom, communism would lose. It was already near collapse, unable any longer to keep the human spirit in chains. It was dying, as he later put it, of "a terminal disease called tyranny," and its collapse was "imminent."

> In an ironic sense, Karl Marx was right. We are witnessing today a great revolutionary crisis. . . . But the crisis is happening not in the free, non-Marxist West, but in the home of Marxist Leninism, the Soviet Union. It is the Soviet Union that runs against the tide of history by denying human freedom and human dignity to its citizens. It also is in deep economic difficulty.

Soon, he predicted, Soviet communism would be relegated to the "ash-heap of history."[49]

In March 1983, while campaigning for Euromissile deployment, Reagan made the most celebrated (or notorious) speech of his career, regarded by anticommunists like William F. Buckley, Jr., as a major turning point of the cold war: his "Evil Empire" address to the National Association of Evangelicals in Florida. It may have been the single most powerful statement of the anticommunist creed in the history of the movement. He began by indicting the Soviet leadership for having

> openly and publicly declared that the only morality they recognize is that which will further their cause, which is world revolution. . . . I think the refusal of many influential people to accept this elementary fact of Soviet doctrine illustrates an historical reluctance to see totalitarian powers for what they are. We saw this phenomenon in the 1930s; we see it too often today. This does not mean we should isolate ourselves and refuse to seek an understanding with them. I intend to do everything I can to persuade them of our peaceful intent. . . . At the same time, however, they must be made to understand we will never compromise our principles and standards. We will never give away our freedom. We will never abandon our belief in God. . . .

In words headlined around the world, he continued:

> I urge you to beware the temptation of pride—the temptation blithely to declare yourselves above it all and label both sides equally at fault, to ignore the facts of history and the aggressive impulses of an evil empire.

Next Reagan turned to the moral dimension of anticommunism:

The real crisis we face today is a spiritual one; at root, it is a test of moral will and faith. Whittaker Chambers, the man whose own religious conversion made him a "witness" to one of the terrible traumas of our age, the Hiss-Chambers case, wrote that the crisis of the Western world exists to the degree to which the West is indifferent to God, the degree to which it collaborates in communism's attempt to make man stand alone without God. . . .

I believe that communism is another sad, bizarre chapter in human history whose last pages even now are being written. I believe this because the source of our strength in the quest for human freedom is not material but spiritual, and, because it knows no limitation, it must terrify and ultimately triumph over those who would enslave their fellow man.

Let us pray for the salvation of all those who live in totalitarian darkness, pray they will discover the joy of knowing God. But until they do, let us be aware that . . . they are the focus of evil in the modern world.[50]

It was a speech that launched a thousand quips in faculty common rooms, but among anticommunists it almost immediately acquired legendary status. William F. Buckley later said that Ronald Reagan

will emerge as the principal postwar figure of this century, and he will be cherished, in the nursery tales told in future generations to young children, as the American President who showed the same innocent audacity as the little boy who insisted that the Emperor wasn't wearing any clothes at all, when he said at a critical moment in Western history—about the Union of Soviet Socialist Republics—that it was an evil empire. It is my judgment that those words acted as a kind of harmonic resolution to the three frantic volumes of Solzhenitsyn. The *Gulag Archipelago* told us everything we needed to know about the pathology of Soviet Communism. We were missing only the galvanizing summation; and we got it, in the Mosaic code: and I think that the countdown for Communism began then.[51]

Reagan later explained that he had given the Evil Empire speech in part to free Americans from the taboo against using the vocabulary of anticommunism: "For too long our leaders were unable to describe the Soviet Union as it actually was. The keepers of our foreign-policy knowledge—in other words, most liberal foreign-affairs scholars, the State Department, and various columnists—found it illiberal and provocative to be so honest. I've always believed, however, that it's important to define differences, because there are choices and decisions to be made in life and history."[52]

It was time, he felt, that the truth be told, that a red be called a red. He had made the speech, he said, "with malice aforethought," since "the Soviet system over the years has purposely starved, murdered, and brutalized its own people. Millions were killed; it's all right there in the history books. It put other citizens it disagreed with into psychiatric hospitals, sometimes drugging them into oblivion. Is the system that allowed this not evil? Then why shouldn't we say so?" Moscow protested that the speech proved that Reagan could "think only in terms of confrontation and bellicose, lunatic anticommunism."[53] But anticommunists believed that "rarely have speeches [like Star Wars and the Evil Empire] had such impact on world events. . . . Mikhail Gorbachev's dramatically new approach to Soviet foreign policy beginning in 1985 could be seen, not entirely unfairly, as an attempt, first, to kill the Strategic Defense Initiative and, second, to prove to the world that the Soviet Union was not in fact an evil empire."[54]

During that same month, March 1983, Reagan backed up his anticommunist words with deeds. Taking advantage of a power struggle within the Cuban-supported Marxist government of Grenada, Reagan solicited an invitation from Grenada's neighbors to overthrow the Soviet-backed Marxist regime. The invasion was meant to warn Castro and his Soviet sponsors that in the future it would be expensive and dangerous to act as Moscow's surrogate in places like Angola, Mozambique, Ethiopia, and Nicaragua, where Cubans were also propping up Marxist governments. Anticommunists were elated. Grenada was the first instance of a Soviet-backed regime being ousted since Chile in 1973.[55]

At the end of Reagan's first term, he could be satisfied that he was making real progress. The Soviets were being beaten in Afghanistan. Jonas Savimbi had a 250,000-strong army fighting the Marxist regime in Angola. The CIA-sponsored resistance in Cambodia had the Vietnamese bogged down. The anticommunist resistance to the Marxist government in Ethiopia was growing. The contras were still fighting in Nicaragua, and Casey felt that if an election were ever held, the Sandinistas would lose. The El Salvadoran government was winning against its Cuban and Nicaraguan supported insurgents.[56]

Reagan coasted back into the White House in 1984 on the strength of a reviving economy and the perception that America's strategic position in the world was much improved. And just before the election he defused the charge that he had abandoned negotiations by meeting with the Russian foreign minister and making an arms control speech at the UN.[57]

During his first four years, Reagan had been remarkably successful in outmaneuvering all opposition to his anticommunist foreign policy, domestic and foreign. During his second term the Reagan Doctrine and his very survival as president would hang on the efforts by his enemies to prove that Reagan had funded the Nicaraguan contras during the period from April 1984 to December 1985 when it had been absolutely prohibited by Congress.[58]

The controversy had its origin in Congress's discovery in March 1982 that the CIA was involved in training anticommunist rebels in Nicaragua. Congress responded with the Boland amendment, which forbade funds "for the purpose of overthrowing the Government of Nicaragua." Since it was attached to a vital omnibus spending bill, Reagan reluctantly signed it into law on December 21, 1982. To keep the contras alive despite the injunction, Reagan and Casey invented the fiction that the goal of the contra funding was not to overthrow the Nicaraguan government, but to persuade it to hold democratic elections. The funding continued. In April 1984 Congress learned that Casey's CIA had mined Nicaragua's harbors, and so in December 1984 they strengthened the Boland amendment by prohibiting any support at all, "directly or indirectly," to the contras. His congressional foes had baited a trap to catch Reagan, and catch him they did.

Reagan told his foreign policy aides that despite Boland, "I don't want to pull out our support for the contras for any reason. This would be an unacceptable option."[59] The Boland amendment had prohibited American agencies "engaged in intelligence activities" from carrying out operations in Nicaragua, so the administration had its lawyers determine that the National Security Council, according to its legal charter, did not engage in intelligence activities, and so the administration shifted the contra campaign from the CIA to the National Security Council under John Poindexter and Oliver North. North then worked out a scheme to get funds to the contras by having the Israelis sell arms to Iran to obtain the release of Americans held hostage in Iran, funnel the money to contra paymasters, and then have the Israeli arms replaced by the United States.

For a year and a half Reagan, his National Security Advisor John Poindexter, and Poindexter's aide Oliver North ran a contra funding program in direct defiance of the will of Congress and the law. In December 1985 the administration persuaded Congress to permit "non-lethal" aid, training, and communications equipment for the contras. In October 1986 Reagan finally got the Boland ban lifted entirely, and $100 million in aid was earmarked for the contras. The contra phase of the Reagan Doctrine was legal again.[60]

But then, on November 25, 1986, Congress learned how the administration had diverted funds to the contras during the Boland amendment's absolute blackout period. It was a scandal unmatched since the days of Watergate. For the next six months Iran-contra dominated the news, with the media, the Democrats, and enemies of the Reagan foreign policy all straining to trace the contra funding back to Reagan.[61]

For a president to spend money in defiance of the express will of Congress was clearly an impeachable offense. There was no doubt that the administration had been sending money to the contras in violation of the law, nor that it had been done at the President's behest. Only proof that the President had given the orders was needed for the impeachment process to begin. Meanwhile, Reagan's ability to carry out foreign policy, particularly a foreign policy as controversial as the Reagan Doctrine, might come to an abrupt and humiliating halt.

The scandal brought down the President's national security advisor, John Poindexter, and Poindexter's aide Oliver North. Both admitted dealing with Iran in an arms-for-hostages deal, and diverting the money to the contras. Secretary of State George Shultz and Secretary of Defense Caspar Weinberger testified that they had been kept ignorant of the operation to keep them from stopping an operation they would have opposed. The trails all led to the President, who finally admitted in a televised address on August 12, 1987 that "I told the American people I did not trade arms for hostages. My heart and my best intentions still tell me that is true, but the facts and evidence tell me it is not." To the end he denied knowing about the diversion of funds to the contras, but it was impossible to escape the conclusion that he had known and probably authorized the illegal funding.

For any administration, a scandal like Iran-contra with possible impeachment in the offing would have been horrible enough, but for anticommunists it must have seemed particularly nightmarish. If their memories served them well enough, they would have had to concede ruefully that they too had long played the game they believed was being played against them: trying to turn foreign policy differences into crimes. Where countersubversive anticommunists had tried to criminalize containment, now their enemies harassed them by looking in the Pentagon's records, in the files of the FBI, and in the floppy disks of the NSC computers for proof that anticommunists in hot pursuit of their obsessions had conspired to overthrow the Constitution. Where anticommunists had used the Hiss case to claim that wartime pro-Soviet policies were the work of traitors, anticommunism's enemies had been charging since the sixties that anticommunists in the military and the CIA were plotting against democracy, that anticommunism itself was a conspiracy against freedom and democracy. And now, at a moment when anticommunists believed their policies had the Soviet Union staggering and ready to fall, they had given their enemies the proof they had so long sought—that to attain their goals anticommunists were ready to overthrow democracy itself.

It was hard for anticommunists inside and outside the administration not to believe that Reagan Doctrine was the underlying issue in the Iran-contra affair. They felt Reagan's opponents could not seriously challenge the authority of the President to conduct arms negotiations with the Soviet Union. His efforts on behalf of Poland and Eastern Europe were largely secret, and where they were not, they enjoyed broad popular and congressional support. But the CIA's secret wars to destabilize Marxist regimes in the third world were vulnerable because they raised fears of an America being dragged into a Vietnam-like quagmire. Worse, they recalled abuses of presidential authority by Johnson and Nixon, and they seemed to validate the fears expressed in the Fulbright and Reuther memoranda, and in films like *Seven Days in May*, that the military and the intelligence agencies were staffed by anticommunist fanatics ready to trample on the Constitution in their grim determination to keep on fighting the cold war no matter what the cost to humanity.

Anticommunists believed that Reagan's hold on the public's affections and his stature within the community of Western leaders had made the Reagan Doctrine invulnerable to frontal attacks, so the opposition had moved the struggle into the courtroom and the committee room,

where battles were decided on legal technicalities and not on the substance of the anticommunists' case against the Soviet Union. And so
for the last two years of his presidency, Reagan's enemies had him on
the run. And yet he survived.

Ironically, he may have been saved by the very gravity of his offense,
one of the most clearly impeachable presidential misdeeds in history,
as Seymour Hersh of the *New York Times* discovered a few years later
when he interviewed members of the House and Senate investigating
committees. Funding the contras had been legal before October of
1984 and legal after December 1985, which made it seem to the public more a legal squabble between contending branches of government
than a substantially criminal offense. And yet the only penalty that
could be imposed, if responsibility were traced to Reagan, was the impeachment and removal from office of an effective and popular president.[62]

Once the committees had begun their investigations they dreaded
pressing too far. Once past a point of no return they would have to recommend impeachment. Their nerve failed when they contemplated the
enormity of that act, particularly after Colonel Oliver North's spectac-
ularly effective appearance before the Senate investigating committee.
The overwhelmingly favorable response to North "shell-shocked" the
congressmen and their staff. "Thousands of pro-North telegrams began
flowing into Congressional offices, and the Iran-contra committees
found themselves in full political retreat." An advisor to the Senate investigating committee said that "North was the turning point. It was
the greatest battle of the investigation, and we lost it." The investigation, he said, turned into a "fiasco."[63]

Hersh found that the committees were also terrified that their investigation might be blamed for interfering with Reagan's negotiations for
the release of American hostages held by Palestinian terrorists in
Lebanon. And they were wary of looking too deeply into the arms-for-
hostages deal for fear of incensing defenders of Israel, if the investigation reflected badly on that key American ally.

Finally, Hersh learned that Reagan's rapport with Gorbachev may
have stayed some congressional knives. The striking progress Reagan
was making towards arms control and the possibility of a more friendly
relationship with the Soviet Union made the committees leery about
destroying the Reagan presidency just when he seemed to be shifting
from confrontation back to detente.

Anticommunists shuddered to think what might have happened had Iran-contra removed Reagan from office or crippled his power to pursue the objectives of the Reagan Doctrine. That might have returned to power the arms control establishment that had fought against Reagan's anticommunism since 1981. If the United States had canceled the plans for SDI, relaxed the pressure on Soviet regimes in the third world, ended aid to the Afghan insurgency, extended trade concessions to the Soviets to prop up the staggering Soviet economy, and, most of all, signaled to East Europe that in the interests of stability no Western support could be expected in any conflict between them and their Soviet masters, the Soviet Union might have staggered on. Perhaps Gorbachev's perestroika might have had a chance to succeed, given more time, less pressure, and if the citizens of the Soviet Union had not been able to contemplate the alternatives to communism that Poland, Hungary, Czechoslovakia, and Eastern Germany demonstrated when they began throwing out their Communist regimes in 1989. The possibility that communism might have been granted a reprieve was awful for anticommunists to contemplate.

But Iran-contra was not Reagan's only worry during his second term. The other was maintaining the momentum of his anti-Soviet policies in the face of Mikhail Gorbachev's vast international popularity, because after he solidified his control of the Soviet Union in March 1985, Gorbachev became the most admired figure in the history of communism—admired outside the borders of the Soviet Union, at least—and scarcely the sort of man who looked like the leader of an evil empire.

The Reagan-Gorbachev relationship—which deepened into mutual respect and friendship—was one of the most remarkable in history, between the man who strove harder than any American president to destroy communism, and the man who presided over its destruction.

In view of the role that Gorbachev's own policies played in communism's fall, it is interesting that Reagan himself may have helped Gorbachev move to the top of the Soviet hierarchy where he would confront and befriend his rival. In 1982 the shock of the Reagan Doctrine moved the Soviet leadership to commission a self-study, which was assigned to Gorbachev, and this was supposed to provide an agenda for an all-Soviet conference in 1985 that Gorbachev would chair. The month before the conference, however, Party leader Konstantin Chernenko died, and because of the reforms suggested by the self-study Gorbachev emerged as General Secretary to carry out the policies of perestroika and glasnost.[64]

At first, Reagan did not see any improvement in Soviet behavior after Gorbachev came to power. The fighting in Afghanistan escalated, the arms shipments to Nicaragua increased, Soviet spying continued, and Russian propaganda intensified. But soon there were indications of a new spirit in Soviet diplomacy, and Reagan was persuaded—first by Margaret Thatcher and then by his own experience—that Gorbachev was a man he could do business with. Soon, in fact, Reagan, the arch-anticommunist, came to trust Gorbachev, perhaps the last Communist true believer, though it was a trust always qualified by that phrase that sounded like a stuck needle to Gorbachev: "Trust, but verify."

Reagan's arms buildup, and SDI in particular, made the Soviets realize that they had fallen hopelessly behind in the technological race for strategic supremacy. They could clearly foresee that SDI—which they would have to try to match, whether or not it was feasible—would be only the first of a series of insurmountable technical challenges.[65]

At their first summit in Geneva in November 1985, Reagan told Gorbachev, "We can continue to disarm or we can continue the arms race. And I'll tell you now, you can't win the arms race. There is no way." From 1985 to 1989 Gorbachev became almost obsessed with derailing the SDI and reviving the arms control process. Reagan, on the other hand, refused to discuss arms control out of the context of regional conflicts and human rights. As he said again and again, Reagan believed in "linkage."[66]

While Gorbachev strained to meet Reagan's increasingly stringent conditions for further arms negotiations, Reagan's bargaining position became ever more demanding. Before Reagan, the arms control establishment had resisted publicizing or protesting Soviet violations, arguing that this needlessly angered the Soviets and might block further negotiations. Reagan not only called the Russians to account for violations, but scrapped the SALT II agreement in the spring of 1986 because of Soviet violations in building a prohibited ABM radar facility near Moscow. Once again the arms control establishment protested that dwelling on Soviet violations was counterproductive. Once again they charged that the "nuts" had "won" in Washington, that the Soviet Union would respond to Reagan by building more gigantic ICBMs. In fact, it was later revealed that the Russians had already reached the limit of their capacity to produce ICBMs: any further increase would have been out of the question.

Reagan's inflexibility extracted ever greater concessions from the Soviets as they desperately tried to do away with Star Wars and obtain most-favored-nation status in trade with the United States. Finally they were in such a weak bargaining position that they had to continually offer more concessions just to keep negotiations going.

With the American military and Reagan's conservative advisors resisting any new weapons treaties, Gorbachev desperately needed agreements with the West to buttress his position at home. He won the Nobel Prize by reaching an accord with the United States in April 1988 to withdraw from Afghanistan. By that time the Soviet forces had been battered by the Reagan-equipped rebels, and demoralized by their humiliating defeat. A malaise that could be called an "Afghan syndrome" may have rendered them unfit for use in putting down the revolts in Eastern Europe when those satellites began to defect from the Communist camp in 1989.

Reagan's personal popularity at home and abroad seems to have challenged Gorbachev to exhibit the same sort of leadership style as the American president and to try to demonstrate the openness and modernity of what was in reality a closed and backward society. Gorbachev's soaring popularity in the West made it difficult for him to abandon the appealing foreign and domestic policies that were the source of that popularity, but that were destroying his own and the Party's power at home. The populations of the European satellites, therefore, began to think they could defy Moscow and not suffer the traditional consequences. Gorbachev's relaxations of totalitarian controls demoralized the ruling elite in Moscow and in the Communist capitals. They could sense their power slipping away, and with it their ability to make a credible show of naked force, the ultimate, and, it turned out, the only real source of their authority.

Gorbachev mistakenly believed that by ending Soviet human rights abuses and the use of brute force he could reform communism and make it viable—which had long been the counsel of the left and other sympathetic Westerners. As a convinced Communist, he could scarcely be expected to believe what anticommunists like Reagan had always maintained: that the Soviet system depended on human rights abuses, that without them, the system was not viable. In the view of anticommunists, in order to maintain his relationship with Reagan, "Gorbachev made concessions that undermined the long-term power position, and ultimately the very existence, of the Soviet empire, a consequence that by all appearances he did not anticipate."[67] In his inability to understand the consequences of his actions, Gorbachev was, Henry Kissinger suggests, "like the somewhat abstract figures from the nineteenth century Russian novels—both cosmopolitan and provincial, intelligent and yet somehow unfocused; perceptive while missing his central dilemma."[68]

In Washington, Gorbachev had been permitted to move about at will, greeting American citizens. In May 1988, at the Moscow summit, he reciprocated by letting Reagan circulate through the city with the same freedom. But while Gorbachev's walks along the crowded Washington sidewalks, which set off frenzies of "Gorbymania," represented no real alteration of the normal state of American society, Reagan's trips around Moscow demonstrated a freedom unknown to foreigner or citizen since 1917. Reagan had given Soviet citizens a Western standard of normality against which to measure their regime, a standard the Soviet Communist Party could not meet without abandoning the repression that was the source of its power.

On that trip, Reagan told the students at Moscow State University what they already knew all too well: that communism had condemned them to live in a society ever more abnormal and bizarre, compared to the individual freedom characteristic of all non-Marxist western societies. "Freedom," he told them,

> doesn't begin or end with elections. Go to any American town, to take just an example, and you'll see dozens of churches, representing many different beliefs—in many places, synagogues and mosques—and you'll see families of every conceivable nationality worshiping together. . . . Go to any courtroom, and there will preside an independent judge, beholden to no government power. . . . Go to any university campus, and there you'll find an open, sometimes heated discussion of the problems of American society. . . . Go to any union hall, where the members know their right to strike is protected by law.[69]

But when Reagan left office, few others were so confident. The news media's retrospectives on his foreign policy concluded that it had been a failure. "History's overall verdict on the Reagan administration's foreign policy," wrote one analyst, "seemed destined to be largely negative. The administration's successes were incomplete and contained the seeds of their own undoing." A senior foreign affairs editor at the *Washington Post* even thought that the Soviet Union was on the road to regaining its power, strength, and savvy under the charismatic Gorbachev. "Soviet crisis management may prove more robust under Gorbachev. . . . The point is simply that the free ride of the early Reagan years is over. The next American president won't have the luxury of negotiating with a weak and slow-moving Soviet Union." That old anticommunist Barry Goldwater thought that the Soviet Union, though in trouble itself, would still be making trouble for the United States for years to come: "Communism is not retreating or withdrawing. It still rules by armed repression. . . . Despite the uncertainty of grappling with this policy and other problems, the Communists continue to foment troubles around the world. . . ." On the left, there was a collective sigh of relief that the Reagan nightmare of anticommunist hostility to the Soviet Union was finally over.[70]

Only Reagan, it seemed, was sure that communism was doomed, and that the end was in sight. At the Brandenburg Gate in June 1987 Reagan recalled Khrushchev's boast, "We will bury you," and he told his German audience that "in the West today, we see a free world that has achieved a level of prosperity and well-being unprecedented in all human history. In the Communist world, we see failure, technological backwardness, declining standards of health, even want of the most basic kind—too little food. . . . Freedom is the victor. And now the Soviets themselves, may, in a limited way, be coming to understand the importance of freedom."[71]

And so, in June 1987 Ronald Reagan would go to Berlin and shout, "Mr. Gorbachev, tear down this wall." Was it just the old actor responding to a theatrical backdrop, a good script, and one more chance to milk his great role? Or was it not seventy years of American anticommunism that stood with Reagan that day? Was it not the whole history of American anticommunism that stood in Berlin and dreamed that both the wall and what it symbolized must someday fall, solid as they seemed that day—though no one, not even Ronald Reagan, dared dream in 1987 the fall would come so soon.[72]

It would not be long before the Soviet empire and the Soviet Union both would be collapsing with a finality and a rapidity that still defy belief. And as communism crumbled, the debate would begin about how much eight years of Reagan, or seventy years of anticommunism had helped bring it down. Among American anticommunists, however, there was no doubt that the struggle had been worth the cost: they had fought the good fight, they had finished the course, they had kept the faith. And who among them would not agree with Ronald Reagan as he left the White House for the last time: "I am proud to say I am still an anti-communist."[73]

EPILOGUE

"We ought to admit the truth . . . that the West won the Cold War, even if it does go against the grain, against our political inclinations."

—Historian Christopher Lasch, June 1990.

When the end came, it came with dizzying speed. Poland's Communist rulers, reduced to desperation by the country's economic straits and told by Mikhail Gorbachev they could not count on any intervention by the Red Army, were forced to hold free elections. On June 4, 1989, Lech Walesa's anticommunist Solidarity coalition won an overwhelming victory. A Solidarity official, an ally of Walesa's, became prime minister on August 19, and Poland, cornerstone of Stalin's Yalta empire, was free at last.

In quick order, the remaining Eastern bloc Communist regimes fell from power. On October 7, 1989, Hungary abandoned communism. With hundreds of thousands of East Germans fleeing the country through Poland, the Communist authorities opened the borders to West Germany. Berliners celebrated by demolishing the Wall on November 11, 1989. A six-thousand-pound chunk went to Ronald Reagan for his Presidential Library in California. In the only violence in this remarkable anticommunist upheaval, on December 25, 1989, the Rumanians

421

captured and executed their Communist ruler. Four days later, Vaclav Havel, recently a guest in a Communist prison cell, was elected president of Czechoslovakia. In a not unrelated development, in February 1990, the Sandinista targets of Reagan and Casey's contra operations in Nicaragua unexpectedly lost the elections forced on them by the Bush administration. Communism had lost its Central American foothold. East and West Germany were formally reunited on October 3, 1990. To the alarm of some in the West worried about the stability of the post-communist European order, the Warsaw Pact formally dissolved itself in April 1991.

The end—the collapse of communism in the Russian homeland itself—still too incredible to be imagined by even the most optimistic anticommunist—was now at hand. In August 1991, hard-line Soviet Communists, alarmed by the Party's accelerating loss of power, took General Secretary Mikhail Gorbachev captive, seized control of the Parliament building and announced that they had taken power to preserve communism and national unity. Rallying the nation, Russian Federation President Boris Yeltsin ordered the army against the conspirators, released Gorbachev, outlawed the Communist Party, and ordered it dissolved.

Across the former Soviet Union, statues of Lenin and KGB founder Felix Dzerzhinsky were toppled to the ground. Citizens of Leningrad, birthplace of the Revolution, changed their city's name back to St. Petersburg. After seventy-four years, communism had been rejected in its first home. The epoch of world history that had begun in 1917—the age of communism and anticommunism— had come to a close. In 1919, it seemed that mankind would have to choose between Lenin and Wilson, between world revolution and a world order of liberal democracies. After three quarters of a century, mankind had chosen. The *New York Daily News* headlined a front page picture of a child playing on a fallen statue of Lenin, "Psst! Vladimir. You're history." Russians repeated an old and bitter joke, "What was communism? The longest and most costly path from capitalism to capitalism." How costly? Estimates ran as high as sixty million deaths from starvation or execution caused by the Communist regime.[1]

Communism still survived in Cuba, North Korea, North Vietnam, and China, but to paraphrase Lincoln Steffens, the future had not worked. As a force in world history, communism was dead.

And anticommunism? The history of anticommunism likewise had come to an end. Anticommunist journals and organizations wrapped up their operations: Midge Decter disbanded her Committee for the Free World, saying, "the play is over."[2] Anticommunists reassured themselves that their long struggle had played its part in the final result. "The Berlin Wall did not collapse of its own weight," conservative columnist George F. Will insisted. "It collapsed like a souffle under the weight of counter ideas. . . . But the ideas were in the air because someone put them there. They were put there by Margaret Thatcher, they were put there by Ronald Reagan. But before they could be put there, they had to be argued and preserved, perfected and burnished." But even anticommunists were saddened that it had taken so long. Bill Buckley's valedictory was bittersweet: "Whereas we can proudly say that Western will presented formidable obstacles to Soviet expansionism, we need to say this carefully." The last days of the cold war, he pointed out, had brought real victories to the Soviets. "And then, as some of us believers might put it, God cleared His throat. And lo, on March 11, 1990, the little state of Lithuania declared that it was independent of the Soviet Union." Was it "a triumph of Western policy?" he asked.

> Only if one chooses to believe that the mere survival of the West was itself triumphant. . . . But it was the agony of life under Communism that dictated the outcome. The West might have reason to bask in its diplomatic prowess if it had taken less than 45 years to liberate the swollen kingdom of the slave. . . . No history of the cold war will successfully assert that the demise of the Soviet Empire was a triumph of Western diplomacy. What we did, essentially, was to stand still. And, in the case of some, to pray for divine intervention.[3]

Outside their own ranks, anticommunists' role in the defeat of communism was minimized if not altogether denied. Americans seemed to watch the amazing events of 1989 through 1991 less concerned with understanding what was happening than with preserving their preconceptions about communism and anticommunism. While anticommunists folded their tents and declared their task complete, their critics strained their wits to explain how the collapse of communism in no way validated the reprehensible beliefs of anticommunists or justified the agony of the cold war. Jonathan Schell wrote that "Soviet totalitarianism has expired in its own lair" and he quoted an Albanian leader's verdict that "It committed suicide." Leftist historians, said a reporter at a forum on "Who Won the Cold War?" "were firm in their view that the revolutions in Eastern Europe had done nothing to vindicate the Cold War or invalidate . . . [revisionist] arguments against containment." "I don't think the U.S. won the Cold War," said a professor of history at New York University, "I think the Soviet Union stopped fighting, which is a different matter." When Christopher Lasch demanded that the left concede "that the West won the Cold war, even it it goes against the grain, against our political inclinations," he was attacked as justifying a "heroic view of America's world role."[4]

The cause of the collapse of communism will be debated for years, if not forever, and we are no more likely than Tolstoy to decide the relative importance of human will or impersonal forces in determining such historical events. There are already theories that deny responsibility for communism's defeat to any human agency. Harvard Professor Charles S. Maier argued that communism's failure was due to its inability to respond to structural changes in the world economy after 1968, changes the more flexible Western democracies learned to deal with by accepting a permanently high level of unemployment and transferring basic industry to the third world. According to this logic, the Soviets could be given credit for a noble failure in trying to resist the harsh consequences of postindustrialism.[5]

The collapse of communism had little impact on the stereotype of the anticommunist as American fascist. In Hollywood, while the Russians were shaking off the last remnants of Communist rule, director Oliver Stone was presenting the cold war as a vast conspiracy of high-level governmental security operatives, grassroots radical right-wingers, and anti-Castro nuts, all plotting to murder Kennedy to keep him from ending the struggle against communism. Stone based *JFK* on New Orleans District Attorney Jim Garrison's *On the Trail of the Assassins*, where Garrison claimed to have proven that "what happened at Dealey Plaza in Dallas on November 22, 1963, was a coup d'état. I believe that it was instigated and planned long in advance by fanatical anticommunists in the United States intelligence community . . . and that its purpose was to stop Kennedy from seeking detente with the Soviet Union and Cuba and ending the Cold War."[6] Since anticommunism was fascism, some now argued that the United States actually had become a fascist country during the cold war, or, as one oral history of the domestic cold war asserted, "It Did Happen Here." Historian Edward Pessen wrote (in *Losing Our Souls: The American Experience in the Cold War*) that "our cold war policy, for all its success, was so grievously flawed that the United States may never fully recover from its effects upon our values, our freedoms, our politics, our security, the conditions of our material life, the quality of our productive plant, and the very air we breathe."[7] History texts routinely held up Joseph McCarthy to symbolize the full meaning and meanness of all American anticommunism.[8] Some younger scholars thought that ridicule was the only appropriate response to anticommunism: Michael Barson's *Better Dead Than Red!: A Nostalgic Look at the Golden Years of Russiaphobia, Red-Baiting, and Other Commie Madness* laughed at the very idea that the cold war had ever rested on anything except the malevolent delusions of anticommunists.[9]

By the time the end came, real anticommunism had nearly faded from the American consciousness. It lived on only in the bitter memory of those wounded during the long struggle. In the country that organized the grand alliance against communism, anticommunists were hardly remembered except in the nightmares of civil libertarians. What the great majority of responsible anticommunists had really thought, what their role in American life really had been, all had been dropped from the historical record. And so when Ronald Reagan said as he left the presidency that he was still proud to be an anticommunist, few understood what he meant.[10] Real anticommunism—what it had been, what it was, how it had mattered—was long forgotten, a dim relic of an age gone by. Indeed, as communism itself faded into the past, so did the reasons why Americans once fought so savagely among themselves over how they should respond to it, or the reasons why Americans sacrificed so much for so long to confront, contain, and defeat it. What was recalled instead were the melodramatic excesses of anticommunism at its worst and most extreme, the stereotype of the anticommunist as McCarthyite, militarist, and bigot. Only the misdeeds of the anticommunists were remembered, not the beliefs distorted by the extremists. Lost was the memory of a movement as diverse as the nation itself, reflecting the con-

victions of nearly every group in America that their own peculiar experience, as well as their identity as Americans, demanded that they reject communism for themselves and come to the aid of those suffering
under it abroad.

The anticommunist movement had been something new in American history. It bore the marks of earlier American antiradical and nativist movements, but it was fundamentally different from anything seen
before, a reaction to a situation unprecedented in American history. Anticommunists carried the baggage of their earlier convictions and prejudices, but in the wake of the Communist Revolution in Russia in
November 1917 their attentions were dominated—even obsessed—by
the goals and activities of the Soviet Union and its defenders in America. Just as communism after 1917 was different from all previous radi-
calisms because it was part of a worldwide network with a secure base
in Moscow, American anticommunism was different from all previous
antiradical movements because its primary enemy was international and
foreign directed.

American anticommunism was a complex, pluralistic movement,
as pluralistic as the culture in which it was rooted. Memory's image of
anticommunism was painted by its enemies, a monolithic projection
of McCarthyism writ large. But the myth of monolithic anticommunism obscures the fundamental nature of American anticommunism:
that it was a diverse movement of Americans of very different beliefs
and goals who disagreed among themselves almost as much as they
disagreed with communism. It reflected the special concerns of Americans, not simply as members of the overall community, but as
Catholics, Protestants, Jews; blacks and whites; assimilated groups and
immigrants. There was no shared worldview among anticommunists,
no agreement as to methods, goals, or motives. There was no one thing
that was American anticommunism; there were many American an-
ticommunisms. All that anticommunists had in common was their hatred of communism, but each group of anticommunists hated it for
different reasons.

Anticommunism was made up of men and women who had come to
know a great deal about communism, and who believed that what they
were doing was urgent and important. For many of them, trying to tell
what they saw as the appalling truth about communism consumed their
lives. Some anticommunists built careers around fighting communism;

others sacrificed careers. As a consequence of their struggle to persuade the rest of the country to share their alarm about the danger of communism, they left behind books, magazine articles, petitions, and letters that constitute the record of America's collision with a political ideology and movement that at one time threatened to take the world by storm. That record is an essential part of the drama of twentieth-century American history, and without it, that history is incomplete.

American anticommunism was a protest movement. Though its enemies imagined that anticommunism controlled American institutions and culture, anticommunists saw themselves as a passionate minority pitted against a hostile power structure dominated by those willing to make concessions to communism and against a background of national indifference that ignored ideas at the expense of truth and principles.

To superimpose on this rich history the cartoon features of Joe McCarthy is to reject history for the easy comforts of moralism. McCarthy's ideas do scant justice to the anticommunists' case against communism. Far more representative were sober and realistic anticommunists like Louis Marshall, Abraham Cahan, George Schuyler, Sidney Hook, Isaac Don Levine, Eugene Lyons, William F. Buckley, Jr., Paul Nitze, and Norman Podhoretz, and overseas allies like Andre Malraux, Arthur Koestler, and Ignazio Silone. These were the anticommunists who were in truth the mainstream of American anticommunism.

The history of anticommunism is not the same as the story of anticommunist extremism, any more than the history of malpractice is the history of medicine. The victims of anticommunism were not persecuted simply because of their political views and associations, but because they defended (though sometimes unwittingly) a political movement and an ideology at war with human freedom, an ideology that persecuted, imprisoned, and killed tens of millions, and because in America Communists too often bent the ideals of justice and equality to suit the interests of the Soviet Union.

Anticommunism expressed the essential American determination to stand against attacks on human freedom and foster the growth of democracy throughout the world. Democracy's spread, not to say its very survival, throughout the world in the twentieth century is in no small part due to this persistent strain of idealism that burned so bright among American anticommunists. Anticommunists could count themselves among those Americans who have always believed, with Thomas Paine, that "the cause of America is in a great measure the cause of all mankind."[11]

In the twentieth century the United States has sacrificed hundreds of thousands of lives and incalculable amounts of treasure to defeat threats to democracy—Imperial Germany, the Japanese Empire, the Third Reich, and last of all, European and Asian communism. Without an understanding of the ideas and values that justified these sacrifices, Americans cannot take pride in what their country has done to build a better world for mankind. Blind to the moral issues in the struggle against communism, Americans find it hard to believe that it still makes sense to lead the world against new threats to democracy and human rights because, as Henry Kissinger has ruefully noted, Americans are unable to support a foreign policy that does not have a clear basis in morality.

While Americans have learned—perhaps all too well—about the seamy side of their history, they fail to take credit for the good they have done. Americans need to know the history of American anticommunism if they are to understand the great role they have played in ridding the world of the most murderous of the twentieth century totalitarianisms. They need to know that "anticommunism endured as a value precisely because there was more to it than just a diabolical enemy. Anticommunism envisioned a strong and positive purpose for America, a leadership role not just in containing Soviet communism but in expanding and perfecting democratic capitalism."[12]

It is only outside the country that American anticommunists have been given credit for having helped bring about the defeat of communism.[13] Czechoslovakia's Vaclav Havel told a joint session of the American Congress that the Soviet Union had "rightly" given "people nightmares because no one knew what would occur to its rulers next and what country they would decide to conquer." The United States, he said, had been the "defender of freedom" against the "sources of nightmares"; "the fact that we still exist" he credited to the security system America built after World War II.[14] Solzhenitsyn bluntly stated that "the Cold War was essentially won by Ronald Reagan when he embarked on the Star Wars program and the Soviet Union understood that it could not take this next step. Ending the Cold War had nothing to do with Gorbachev's generosity; he was compelled to end it. He had no choice but to disarm."[15] The heroes of the defeat of communism, Solzhenitsyn, Havel, Russians, Czechs, Poles—all have honored American anticommunists' stand against communism. Honored abroad, however, in their own country they are still without honor.

NOTES

Chapter 1. Lenin and Wilson

1. Hermann Kesser, in *Neue Zürcher Zeitung*, October 27, 1918, cited in the *Cambridge Magazine*, November 16, 1918, p. 143, quoted in Arno J. Mayer, *Political Origins of the New Diplomacy, 1917–1918* (New York: Howard Fertig, 1969), p. 393.

2. Mayer, *Political Origins of the New Diplomacy*, p. 262. See discussion of the decree in George F. Kennan, *Russia Leaves the War* (Princeton: Princeton University Press, 1956), p. 75.

3. Christopher Lasch, *The American Liberals and the Russian Revolution* (New York: Columbia University Press, 1962), p. 57.

4. The Fourteen Points speech was "primarily designed to counter the Soviet ideological assault on the bastions of civilization. . . . If a separate peace was made [by the Communists], Wilson could picture the Bolsheviks as men false to a sacred trust of the Russian people." Lloyd C. Gardner, *Safe for Democracy: The Anglo American Response to Revolution, 1913–1923* (New York: Oxford University Press, 1987), p. 161. The speech "was democracy's answer in its first full-dress debate with international communism. Lenin and Trotsky had appealed to the peace hunger of the world for the purpose of beginning a universal class war to destroy Western civilization in its democratic and Christian form. In contrast, Wilson had appealed for peace in the name of all that was high and holy in the democratic and Christian tradition for the purpose of saving Western civilization." Arthur S. Link, *Wilson the Diplomatist: A Look at His Major Foreign Policies* (Baltimore: Johns Hopkins University Press, 1957), p. 104.

5. Wilson's argument in the Fourteen Points was that only an Allied victory could protect Russia's integrity and sovereignty. Wilson proposed "the evacuation of all Russian territory and such a settlement of all questions affecting

431

Russia as will secure the best and freest cooperation of the other nations of the world in obtaining for her an unhampered and unembarrassed opportunity for the independent determination of her own political development and national policy and assure her of a sincere welcome into the society of free nations under institutions of her own choosing." If Russia rejoined the alliance, Wilson promised, she could expect "more than a welcome, assistance also of every kind that she may need and may herself desire. The treatment accorded Russia by her sister nations in the months to come will be the acid test of their good will, of their own comprehension of her needs as distinguished from their own interest, and of their intelligent and unselfish sympathy."

6. The Four Points speech of July 4, 1918.

7. Link, *Wilson the Diplomatist*, pp. 96–97.

8. For example, Wilson's closest advisor, Colonel Edward House, had made this vision the theme of a utopian novel of 1912 called *Philip Dru, Administrator*. This novel proposed making American participation in a world order ruled by international law the national purpose. It is now forgotten except on the far right, whose conspiracy-minded isolationists regard it as a blueprint for American foreign policy.

9. Link, *Wilson the Diplomatist*, pp. 131–32.

10. For an incisive study of the transformations of the American left from before World War I to the present, see John Patrick Diggins, *The Rise and Fall of the American Left* (New York: W. W. Norton, 1992).

11. Theodore Draper, *The Roots of American Communism* (1957; reprint, Chicago: Ivan R. Dee, 1985), p. 15.

12. The authors of this "St. Louis Declaration" were Hillquit, Ruthenberg (a future founder of the American Communist Party), and Algernon Lee (director of the Socialist Party's Rand School). Those who left the Socialist Party over the St. Louis declaration included John Spargo, William English Walling, A. M. Simmons, Charles Edward Russell, William J. Ghent, George D. Herron, Gustavus Myers, Winfield R. Gaylord, Robert Hunger, J. Stitt Wilson, Allan L. Benson, and Upton Sinclair. Draper, *Roots*, p. 93. Ray Ginger, *The Bending Cross* (New Brunswick, NJ: Rutgers University Press, 1949), p. 341.

13. Debs: *The Liberator*, May 1919, quoted in Draper, *Roots*, p. 110; Ginger, *Bending Cross*, p. 349. Haywood: Robert K. Murray, *Red Scare: A Study in National Hysteria, 1919–1920* (1964; reprint, Minneapolis: University of Minnesota Press, 1955), p. 30; Melvyn Dubofsky, *We Shall Be All: A History of the Industrial Workers of the World* (Chicago: Quadrangle Books, 1969), pp. 126, 133. Goldman: Candace Falk, *Love, Anarchy, and Emma Goldman* (New York: Holt, Rinehart and Winston, 1964), pp. 262, 287.

14. John Reed, *Ten Days that Shook the World* (1919; reprint, New York: International Publishers, 1967), with a foreword by V. I. Lenin, a preface by N. K.

Krupskaya, and a new introduction by John Howard Lawson. Robert A. Rosenstone, *Romantic Revolutionary: A Biography of John Reed* (1975; reprint, New York: Vintage, 1981), pp. 320, 346. Bertram D. Wolfe, *Strange Communists I Have Known* (1965; reprint New York: Stein and Day, 1982).

15. This was an umbrella organization that included leading religious figures like Episcopal Bishop Paul Jones, president of the Church Socialist League, the Unitarian John Haynes Holmes, later pastor of the progressive leftist Community Church in Manhattan, and Methodist Harry F. Ward, leading force in the Methodist Federation for Social Service; others included the Congregationalist A. J. Muste, Episcopalian John Nevin Sayre, and Presbyterian Norman Thomas. Allied to them were sympathetic rabbis like Judah L. Magnes and Stephen Wise. The influential Social Creed of the churches was written by Ward in 1907 and adopted by the National Council of Churches in 1908, and later by many other Christian and Jewish social action agencies, including the YM and YWCAs. During the war Ward agitated widely against Wilson's policies, and became a symbol of the socialist antiwar clergy. See Ralph Lord Roy, *Communism and the Churches* (New York: Harcourt Brace, 1960), pp. 15, 17, 47, 49, 64–65.

16. Throughout this book I will use the term "progressive left" to refer to that portion of the left that felt and often proclaimed its solidarity with the American Communist Party, the international Communist movement and the Soviet Union, and was united in its opposition to anticommunism and the program of the liberal internationalists. At times they referred to themselves as progressives or as the Popular Front, but they often used the term I have adopted—the progressive left—although anticommunists would refer to them pejoratively as the "fellow-traveling" or "Popular Front."

17. John Higham, *Strangers in the Land: Patterns of American Nativism, 1860–1925* (1963; reprint, New York: Atheneum, 1973), p. 200.

18. There were many of these groups, more than anyone has been able to document (including the Anti-Yellow Dog League, which claimed to have a thousand branches, and a membership restricted to boys over ten). The APL was founded by a Chicago advertiser, A. M. Briggs. For a history of the APL, see Joan M. Jensen, *The Price of Vigilance* (Chicago: Rand McNally, 1968), and Higham, *Strangers in the Land*, pp. 211–12.

19. The National Security League was founded in 1914 by S. Stanwood Menken, the ADS in 1915, and led during the war by Elon H. Hooker. Higham, *Strangers in the Land*, p. 209. Among the officials of the NCF were V. Everit Macy, August Belmont, Elbert H. Gary, as well as Samuel Gompers. The NSL had T. Coleman DuPont, Henry C. Frick, J. P. Morgan, and John D. Rockefeller. Murray thinks that there were about twenty-five thousand members in these groups. Murray, *Red Scare*, p. 85.

20. There were other antiunion organizations—like the Loyal Woodsmen in the timber industry—specifically formed to fight the Wobblies.
21. At this time the IWW had sixty thousand members, the AFL four million. Murray, *Red Scare*, p. 106. M. J. Heale, *American Anticommunism: Combating the Enemy Within, 1830–1970* (Baltimore: Johns Hopkins University Press, 1990), p. 57.
22. Both quotes are from Heale, *American Anticommunism*, p. 51.
23. Gardner, *Safe for Democracy*, p. 244.
24. George F. Kennan, "American Troops in Russia," *Atlantic Monthly*, January 1959, pp. 36–42, quoted in Betty Miller Unterberger (ed.), *American Intervention in the Russian Civil War* (Lexington, MA: D. C. Heath, 1969), p. 54. Betty Miller Unterberger shares this view: "President Wilson and the Decision to Send American Troops to Siberia," *Pacific Historical Review* 24 (February 1955): 63–74, quoted in Unterberger, *American Intervention*, p. 63.
25. George F. Kennan, "American Troops in Russia," p. 60. Griswold argues that Wilson had an additional motive in keeping the troops in Siberia so long. He was worried that the British and French would encourage the Japanese to launch an anti-Bolshevik campaign in Siberia to be rewarded by annexations of Russian territory. By April, the collapse of White Russian strength in Siberia had made such an operation impossible. Japan did not evacuate until November 1922. A. Whitney Griswold, *The Far Eastern Policy of the United States* (New York: Harcourt, Brace, 1938), pp. 223–39, quoted in Unterberger, *American Intervention*, p. 26.
26. He was guided here by one of his favorite books, Edmund Burke's *Reflections on the Revolution in France*. N. Gordon Levin, *Woodrow Wilson and World Politics: America's Response to War and Revolution* (New York: Oxford University Press, 1968), p. 163. Quote from Kennan, "American Troops in Russia," p. 54.
27. Gardner, *Safe for Democracy*, p. 195. See George F. Kennan, "The Sisson Documents," *Journal of Modern History* 28 (June 1956): 130–54.

Chapter 2. Red Years and Red Scares

1. William Henry Chamberlain, *The Russian Revolution* (1935; reprint, New York: Grosset and Dunlap, 1965), Vol. II, p. 378.
2. "The eventual German revolution, coupled with his expectancy of assuming control over it and whatever it might lead to, is the real key to Lenin's attitude in the period of the Brest negotiations. It was upon this belief in his own destiny that he staked the national existence of Russia and the destinies of a hundred million people." Stanley W. Page, *Lenin and World Revolution* (New York: New York University Press, 1959), p. 109.

3. Theodore Draper, *The Roots of American Communism* (1957; reprint, Chicago: Ivan R. Dee, 1985), pp. 133–34.

4. "Letter to the Workers of Europe and America," in Page, *Lenin and World Revolution*, p. 121.

5. Some four million American workers went out on 3,600 strikes in 1919.

6. Robert K. Murray, *Red Scare: A Study in National Hysteria, 1919–1920* (New York: McGraw-Hill, 1964), pp. 63, 65.

7. On February 5 Gregory proposed that Congress authorize him to deport interned enemy aliens who seemed dangerous to him. It was because of O'Brian's concern that the wartime deportation regulations might be misused for political purposes that he delayed leaving the Justice Department until May 1. Stanley Coben, *A. Mitchell Palmer: Politician* (New York: Columbia University Press, 1963), p. 199; Joan M. Jensen, *The Price of Vigilance* (Chicago: Rand McNally, 1968), p. 267.

8. When the "Special" arrived at Ellis Island, Secretary of Labor Wilson (an immigrant himself from Scotland) stepped in to review the Wobblies' deportation orders, releasing twelve on March 14, and two more a few days later. Five voluntarily accepted deportation, and of the remaining nineteen, only six had their orders confirmed by the court. The rest had their cases dismissed. By the time the Immigration Bureau had concluded its drive against the IWW, 150 had been arrested, but it was able to deport only 27. William Preston, *Aliens and Dissenters* (Cambridge, MA: Harvard University Press, 1963), p. 206.

9. Page, *Lenin and World Revolution*, p. 124.

10. Murray, *Red Scare*, p. 94. Max Lowenthal, *The Federal Bureau of Investigation* (New York: William Sloane Associates, 1950), p. 36.

11. U.S. House, Committee on Rules, *Attorney General A. Mitchell Palmer on Charges Made Against Department of Justice by Louis F. Post and Others*, 65th Cong., 2nd sess., June 1, 1920, p. 386.

12. Chamberlain, *Russian Revolution*, p. 378.

13. William K. Klingaman, *1919: The Year Our World Began* (New York: St. Martin's Press, 1987), p. 331.

14. Ibid., pp. 207–208, 294.

15. Winston Churchill was now British Secretary of State for War. As he surveyed the shambles in Europe in 1919, he wrote, "With Russia on our hands in a state of utter ruin, with a greater part of Europe on the brink of famine, with bankruptcy, anarchy, and revolution threatening the victorious as well as the vanquished, I do not think . . . the structure of the civilized world is strong enough to stand the strain." As an imperialist and a traditional balance of power theorist, he was frightened at the prospect of a hostile Russia that might make common cause with a Germany abused by the Allies. Churchill begged

Lloyd George to support the White Russian opposition to the Bolsheviks. When Lloyd George refused, Churchill, like Oliver North years later, orchestrated a secret campaign to supply the anticommunist resistance. The press in Britain called the conflict in Russia "Churchill's private war." April 11, 1919, in Sir Winston Churchill, *Winston Churchill: His Complete Speeches, 1897–1963* (New York: Chelsea, 1974), III, pp. 2772–73. *Washington Post*, July 9, 1919. Cited in Klingaman, *1919*, pp. 217, 447.

16. Clemenceau of France was wounded by a "Bolshevik agent" on February 20, 1919. Julian F. Jaffe, *Crusade Against Radicalism*, (Port Washington, NY: Kennikat, 1972), p. 171. As commissioner of baseball Landis would banish Shoeless Joe Jackson from the game for life for his part in fixing the 1919 World Series, although Jackson had been acquitted by a jury. Murray, *Red Scare*, p. 71.

17. Paul Avrich, *Sacco and Vanzetti: The Anarchist Background* (Princeton: Princeton University Press, 1991), pp. 156–57.

18. Coben, A. *Mitchell Palmer*, pp. 206, 207, 211; Murray, *Red Scare*, p. 80. *New York Times*, June 4, 1919; *Washington Post*, June 19, 1919. Hoover's General Intelligence Division later published a detailed account of its investigation of this bombing, which concluded it was the work of a Brooklyn-based group of Italian anarchists. See U.S. House, Committee on Rules, *Attorney General A. Mitchell Palmer on Charges*, pp. 157–65.

19. U. S. Senate, *Investigation Activities of the Department of Justice*, 66th Cong., 1st sess., November 15, 1919, pp. 48, 57.

20. U. S. House, Committee on Rules, *Attorney General A. Mitchell Palmer on Charges*, p. 452. Harold Lasswell later put forward an analysis of international conflict as a struggle between the ideologies of "nationalism" and "proletarianism." See Harold D. Lasswell, *World Politics and Personal Insecurity* (New York: The Free Press, 1965).

21. A card file of the publications read by Hoover's division exists in the National Archives, while a sample of the publications themselves can be found in a collection in the Library of Congress. *Investigation Activities of the Department of Justice*, p. 10. *Annual Report of the Attorney General, 1920* (Washington, DC: U.S. Government Printing Office, 1921), p. 179.

22. Hoover's deportation campaign was a stopgap measure until legislation might be passed to "punish the citizen for the offenses" for which aliens could be deported. *Attorney General A. Mitchell Palmer on Charges*, p. 14. Preston, *Aliens and Dissenters*, p. 194. *Attorney General A. Mitchell Palmer on Charges*, p. 29.

23. *Attorney General A. Mitchell Palmer on Charges*, p. 364; Don Whitehead, *The F.B.I. Story* (New York: Random House, 1956), p. 44. Draper, *Roots of American Communism*, p. 158. For a concise history American communism from

the beginning to the end, see Guenter Lewy, *The Cause that Failed: Communism in American Political Life* (New York: Oxford University Press, 1990).

24. Hemingway's story "The Revolutionist" is a tribute to the martyred Communists of Hungary.

25. Lloyd C. Gardner, *Safe for Democracy: The Anglo American Response to Revolution, 1913–1923* (New York: Oxford University Press, 1987), pp. 256; 261.

26. Klingaman, *1919*, p. 512.

27. The so-called "Poindexter" resolution.

28. Coben, A. *Mitchell Palmer*, pp. 220, 221. Coben cites the *New York Times* and *New York World* for November 8, 1919.

29. This was Wesley Everest. See Tom Copeland, "Wesley Everest, IWW Martyr," *Pacific Northwest Quarterly*, October 1986.

30. See Sowers to Palmer, November 14, 1919, DJ File 203557-8, RG 60, National Archives (hereafter abbreviated NA). *Investigation Activities of the Department of Justice*. Shorr to Palmer, November 13, 1919, cited in Coben, A. *Mitchell Palmer*, p. 221.

31. *New York Tribune*, December 22, 1919, Hoover Memorabilia Collection, RG 65, NA. The *Tribune* credited Hoover with being in charge of the operation, saying that "he, with Immigration Commissioner Anthony Caminetti and Chief William A. Flynn of the secret service, supervised the large job of getting the 249 anarchists to Ellis Island from various parts of the country in which they had been apprehended and in putting them aboard the transport Buford, which sailed at 6 a.m. yesterday from Sandy Hook for some point in bolsheviki Russia."

32. The memorandum brief on the Communist Party is printed in its entirety in James D. Bales (ed.), *J. Edgar Hoover Speaks Concerning Communism* (Washington, DC: Capitol Hill Press, 1970), pp. 266–88. It is also in the files of the Research Unit, External Affairs Division, FBI.

33. Hoover to Caminetti, December 24, 1919, DJ File 205492-9, December 22, 1919, DJ File 205492-6, December 24, 1919, DJ File 205492-10, all RG 60, NA.

34. Murray, *Red Scare*, p. 213. Hoover to Caminetti, December 27, 1919, DJ File 205492-14, December 31, 1919, DJ File 205492 following 14, RG 60, NA. Coben, A. *Mitchell Palmer*, p. 226.

35. Hoover to Wilson (initialed JEH), January 2, 1920, DJ File 205492-243, RG 60, NA. Baker to Powers, April 11, 1985, Table of FBI Personnel Levels. Jensen, *The Price of Vigilance*, p. 283.

36. Murray, *Red Scare*, p. 218.

37. Hoover to Stone, January 17, 1920, DJ File 205492-226, RG 60, NA.

38. Hoover to Bowen, December 24, 1919, DJ File 205492-8; Hoover to [George F.] Lamb, February 6, 1920 DJ File 205492-21, both RG 60, NA. There is noth-

ing to suggest he ever got this list of "silk-stockinged men and women," or that such a list ever existed.

39. *New York Times*, January 4, 1920, *Scrapbook*, Hoover Memorabilia Collection, RG 65, NA.

40. Originally titled the *Bulletin of Radical Activities*, first published biweekly and then, after June, on a weekly basis. It lasted until around October 1921. These are on Reels 16-18 of *U.S. Military Intelligence Reports: Surveillance of Radicals in the United States, 1917–1941* (Frederick, MD: University Publications, ca. 1984).

41. Keeping the Legion at bay was a concern of Hoover's throughout his career; his worries about its capacity for vigilantism may have been as much caused by the example of the *Freikorps* as by the Centralia lynching.

42. Also see Palmer to Abbott, January 27, 1920, DJ File 205492-338 1/2, RG 60, NA, which is also reprinted in National Popular Government League, R. G. Brown, Zechariah Chafee, Jr. et al., *Report Upon the Illegal Practices of the United States Department of Justice* (1920; reprint, New York: Arno Press, 1969), pp. 64–65, referred to below as *Lawyers' Report*. Among the publications included with the letter were Louis Fraina's description of the program and platform of the Communist Party, the manifesto of the Third International, the Manifesto of the Communist Party of America, and an example of "Russian Bolshevik propaganda among our soldiers in Siberia." The Justice Department helpfully noted that "striking passages in these exhibits are marked for convenience."

43. "The impracticability of Communist reconstruction on the merely national scale."

44. *Attorney General A. Mitchell Palmer on Charges*, p. 244.

45. Hoover to Burke, February 21, 1920, DJ File 186701-14, RG 60, NA.

46. Louis Post, seventy-one years old, had served as assistant secretary of labor for the past seven years. Post himself came out of the prewar progressive movement that viewed radicals—like the Communists—as a valuable and honored part of the reform community. Before joining the Wilson administration he had edited the liberal weekly *Public* and had befriended many radicals. He and his wife had entertained Emma Goldman in their home and had defended her and other radicals during the wartime free speech battles. With his wild hair, unkempt moustache and Vandyke beard, Post looked like the popular stereotype of the radical.

47. Louis F. Post, *The Deportations Delirium of Nineteen-Twenty: A Personal Narrative of an Historic Official Experience* (1923; reprint, New York: Da Capo, 1970), p. 152.

48. *General Intelligence Bulletin*, February 21–27, 1920, p. 39.

49. Quoted in Coben, *A. Mitchell Palmer*, p. 233. Preston, *Aliens and Dissenters*, p. 225.

50. Murray, *Red Scare*, p. 249.
51. Coben, *A. Mitchell Palmer*, p. 235.
52. For Frankfurter's role in defending the victims of the Red Scare, see Michael E. Parrish, *Felix Frankfurter and His Times: The Reform Years* (New York: The Free Press, 1982).
53. Coben, *A. Mitchell Palmer*, p. 238.
54. *Lawyers' Report*, p. 8.
55. Ibid., pp. 3, 8.
56. William A. Donahue, *The Politics of the American Civil Liberties Union* (New Brunswick, NJ: Transaction Publishers, 1985), p. 28.
57. Ibid., pp. 30, 31.
58. Ibid., pp. 32, 35.
59. "The Russian Question," *Social Service Bulletin*, January–February 1919, quoted in Eugene P. Link, *Labor-Religion Prophet: The Times and Life of Harry F. Ward* (Boulder, CO: Westview Press, 1984), p. 136.
60. Ibid., pp. 136, 137.
61. Ibid., p. 138.
62. Ibid., p. 93.
63. Chamberlain, *Russian Revolution*, pp. 164, 173–203.
64. Ibid., p. 249.
65. Ibid., p. 301.
66. Eugene Lyons, *Assignment in Utopia* (1937; rpt. New Brunswick: Transaction, 1991), p. 25.
67. Albert S. Lindemann, *The 'Red Years'* (Berkeley: University of California Press, 1974), p. 132.
68. Hoover to Caminetti, June 5, 1920, DJ File 209264, RG 60, NA.
69. *Scrapbook*, Hoover Memorabilia Collection, RG 65, NA.
70. James Weinstein, *The Decline of Socialism in America: 1912–1925* (New Brunswick, NJ: Rutgers University Press, 1984), p. 232. Weinstein gives these further figures: January 1921, 24,661 socialists; 1926, 8,477 (ibid., p. 239). Irving Howe and Lewis Coser (*The American Communist Party* [New York: Praeger, 1962], pp. 91, 92.) point out that it is difficult to establish exactly how many Communists there actually were when the radical factions of the Socialist Party were at their strongest. Estimates of the combined membership of the two parties at their formation in August and September 1919 range from 60,000 to 88,000, but many of these members, possibly the majority, were members of the various language federations of the Socialist Party and were "automatically" transferred to the rolls of the Communist parties once they were organized. According to the parties' own statistics, the membership had dropped to 38,623 by December 1919. The left wing, in the course of formally organizing itself into Communist parties, had lost three fifths of its member-

ship even before the Palmer raids. Hoover's raids were directed against a Communist movement that was already losing its mass base.

71. Howe and Coser, *The American Communist Party*, p. 60, 92.

72. Murray, *Red Scare*, p. 257.

73. "The Radical Division of the Department of Justice," in *Attorney General A. Mitchell Palmer on Charges*, p. 177.

Chapter 3. A New Breed

1. Martin Malia, *The Soviet Tragedy: A History of Socialism in Russia, 1917–1991* (New York: The Free Press, 1994), p. 115. For the fictionalized experience of one who lived through those days, see Ayn Rand, *We the Living* (1936; reprint, New York: Signet, 1983).

2. Irving Howe, *World of Our Fathers* (1983; rpt. New York: Schocken, 1989), p. 292.

3. Ibid., p. 287.

4. The leader delivering that warning was Louis Marshall. Ibid., pp. 317; 319.

5. Ibid., p. 327.

6. Ibid., p. 328.

7. Arthur Liebman, *Jews and the Left* (New York: John Wiley, 1979), p. 387.

8. He was the father of a radical socialist, Bob Marshall, founder of the Wilderness Society, one of the great figures of American conservation.

9. The Bureau was organized and run by Arkady Joseph Sack, a Russian Jew. Sack published a newsletter and a magazine, *Struggling Russia*. Zosa Szajkowski, *Jews, Wars, and Communism, Vol. II, The Impact of the 1919–1920 Red Scare on American Jewish Life* (New York: Ktav Publishing House, 1974), p. 194, 199.

10. Naomi W. Cohen, *Not Free to Desist: The American Jewish Committee, 1906–1966* (Philadelphia: Jewish Publication Society of America, 1972), p. 126.

11. The Levine pamphlet was sent out on April 17, 1920. Szajkowski, *Jews, Wars, and Communism, Vol. II*, p. 193.

12. Albert Lee, *Henry Ford and the Jews* (New York: Stein and Day, 1980), p. 27.

13. Cohen, *Not Free to Desist*, p. 129.

14. Lee, *Henry Ford and the Jews*, p. 14.

15. See Marshall's letter to Ford, June 3, 1920, in *Louis Marshall, Champion of Liberty, Vol. II* (Philadelphia: Jewish Publication Society of America, 1957).

16. Lee, *Henry Ford and the Jews*, p. 41.

17. Jerome C. Rosenthal, "Dealing with the Devil: Louis Marshall and the Partnership Between the Joint Distribution Committee and Soviet Russia," *American Jewish Archives* XXXIX (April 1987), pp. 6, 7, 9.

18. Howe, *World of Our Fathers*, p. 541.

19. Ibid.

20. Ibid., p. 542.
21. Jules Chametzky, "Abraham Cahan," *Encyclopedia of the American Left* (Urbana: University of Illinois Press), p. 118.
22. Easley to Gompers, April 20, 1923, NCF Papers, New York Public Library (hereafter abbreviated NYPL).
23. David J. O'Brien, *American Catholics and Social Reform: The New Deal Years* (New York: Oxford University Press, 1968), pp. 81–82.
24. Patrick Scanlan, "From the Managing Editor's Desk," *The Brooklyn Tablet*, December 1, 1917, p. 2.
25. William F. Buckley, "What's Wrong in Mexico," *Columbia* 3 (March 1923): 10, in Christopher J. Kauffman, *Faith and Fraternalism: The History of the Knights of Columbus* (New York: Harper and Row, 1982), p. 290.
26. Senator William Borah, powerful chairman of the Senate Foreign Relations Committee, was a supporter of recognition. See Gompers to King, Ladd, and Frear, July 10, 1923, NCF Papers, NYPL.
27. Joseph J. Mereto, *The Socialist Conspiracy Against Religion* (Chicago: Iconoclast, 1919), p. 30.
28. Peter W. Collins, *Socialist Opportunism and the Bolshevik Mind* (New Haven: Knights of Columbus, 1920), p. 15.
29. Peter W. Collins, *The Red Glow of Bolshevism in America* (New Haven: Knights of Columbus, 1920), p. 7.
30. See, for example, Scanlan on Ireland, *Brooklyn Tablet*, January 10, 1920, p. 1.
31. "From the Managing Editor's Desk," *Brooklyn Tablet*, January 5, 1918.
32. "From the Managing Editor's Desk," *Brooklyn Tablet*, April 24, 1920.
33. "From the Managing Editor's Desk," *Brooklyn Tablet*, May 15, 1920.
34. "From the Managing Editor's Desk," "The Curse of Secularism," *Brooklyn Tablet*, January 3, 1920. "From the Managing Editor's Desk," *Brooklyn Tablet*, February 9, 1918.
35. "From the Managing Editor's Desk," *Brooklyn Tablet*, October 13, 1917, p. 4.
36. David O'Brien, *Public Catholicism* (New York: Macmillan, 1989), pp. 150–51.
37. Scanlan's editorial for January 21, 1920 praises Gompers and the bishops for condemning the Sterling peacetime sedition law.
38. Wilson Record, *Race and Radicalism: The NAACP and the Communist Party in Conflict* (Ithaca: Cornell University Press, 1964), p. 25. Theodore Draper, *The Roots of American Communism* (1957; reprint, Chicago: Ivan R. Dee, 1989), p. 192. See also Harold Cruse, *The Crisis of the Negro Intellectual from Its Origins to the Present* (New York: William Morrow, 1967).
39. Lovett Fort-Whiteman was one prominent black Socialist who joined the Communist Party in 1920. Decades later, towards the end of his long life Socialist intellectual W. E. B. DuBois became a Communist. Cruse, *The Crisis of the Negro Intellectual*, p. 118.
40. Draper, *Roots of American Communism*, p. 387.

41. George Schuyler, *Black and Conservative* (New Rochelle, NY: Arlington House, 1964), p. 145.
42. Record, *Race and Radicalism*, p. 38.
43. Schuyler, *Black and Conservative*, p. 146.
44. Ibid., pp. 148, 152.
45. This summary is in James Weinstein, *The Decline of Socialism in America, 1912–1925* (1967; reprinted New Brunswick, NJ: Rutgers University Press, 1984), p. 292.
46. Morris Hillquit, quoted in Weinstein, *Decline of Socialism*, pp. 244–45.
47. Franz Borkenau, *World Communist: A History of the Communist International* (New York: W. W. Norton, 1939), pp. 193–95, 197–99. W. Knorin, *Communist Party of the Soviet Union: A Short History* (Moscow: Cooperative Publishing Society, 1935), p. 508.
48. Weinstein, *Decline of Socialism*, pp. 247, 248, 253.
49. Quoted in ibid., p. 277.
50. Sources of membership figures: 1919: Communist Party, report to the 8th Convention, 1934; 1920: claim of the United Communist Party. See Guenter Lewy, *The Cause that Failed* (New York: Oxford University Press, 1990), p. 307.
51. Foster, leader of the nation-wide steel strike in 1919, had become a Communist in 1920.
52. Weinstein, *Decline of Socialism*, p. 285.
53. Ibid., p. 288.
54. Ibid., p. 303.
55. Ibid., pp. 310–312.
56. Ibid., pp. 313, 314.
57. Ibid., p. 322.
58. Ibid., p. 323.

Chapter 4. Tangled in Red Webs

1. Blair Coan, *The Red Web* (1925; reprint, Belmont, MA: Americanist Classics, 1969), pp. viii, ix.
2. Max Lowenthal, *The Federal Bureau of Investigation* (New York: William Sloan Associates, 1950), p. 272.
3. "The Conspiracy Against Labor," *American Federationist* 29 (October 1992): 721, 723, 739; quoted in David Brion Davis, *The Fear of Conspiracy: Images of Un-American Subversion from the Revolution to the Present* (Ithaca: Cornell University Press, 1971), pp. 247–49.
4. For the prevalent view of the ACLU's role in ending federal surveillance of radicals, see the speech of December 15, 1926 by Matthew Woll of the AFL and the NCF, "Subversive Forces in Our Country," before the New York Chamber of Commerce, NCF Papers, NYPL. On January 27, 1925 the *Pitts-*

burgh Press reported favorably that the newly appointed head of the Bureau of Investigation, J. Edgar Hoover, "is not possessed of the notion that the 'reds' are about to eat us and that it's up to him to spoil their dinner." The story quotes Hoover as giving assurances that he will not investigate radicals or campaign against them.

5. Francis Russell, *The Shadow of Blooming Grove: Warren G. Harding in His Times* (New York: McGraw-Hill, 1968), p. 620.

6. Coan, *The Red Web*, pp. 9–10. See also Samuel Hopkins Adams, *Incredible Era* (1939; reprint, New York: Capricorn, 1964), p. 320.

7. Coan, *The Red Web*, p. 15.

8. Ibid., p. 24.

9. "Concerning the Next Tasks of the Communist Party in America." Coan, *The Red Web*, pp. 47, 67.

10. Ibid., pp. 178, 180.

11. Ibid., p. 117.

12. Theodore Draper, *American Communism and Soviet Russia* (1960; reprint, New York: Vintage, 1986), p. 185.

13. Anthony Cave Brown and Charles B. MacDonald, *On a Field of Red: The Communist International and the Coming of World War II* (New York: G. P. Putnam's Sons, 1981), pp. 464–67.

14. Julian F. Jaffe, *Crusade Against Radicalism* (Port Washington, NY: Kennikat, 1972), p. 230.

15. Hoover provided Ruch with information on Communist infiltation of the unions after Ruch went to work for U. S. Steel. Ruch named his son "John Edgar," and John Edgar Ruch got one of Hoover's two signet rings after Hoover's death. The other went to "John Edgar Nichols," son of Hoover's long-time public relations director, Louis Nichols. Interviews with Ruch and Nichols.

16. R. M. Whitney, *Reds in America* (1924; reprint, Boston: Western Islands, 1970), pp. 121, 225.

17. It can hardly be coincidental that so many conspiracy-minded countersubversives are also interested in the occult, often combining the two strains of delusion. Anticommunist writer Taylor Caldwell was a notorious example, obsessed with finding a simpler than natural explanation of reality. For Webster's biography, see Richard Gilman, *Behind World Revolution: The Strange Career of Nesta Webster* (Ann Arbor: Insights, 1982).

18. She is one of the sources playfully cited in Umberto Eco's *Foucault's Pendulum*.

19. American Coalition, Wilcox Collection, Kansas. See list of original invitees to join the Coalition. Lowman Papers, Box 62, Hoover Institution.

20. See Karl Baarslag, "What Has Really Happened to the American Legion," p. 3, n.d., Baarslag Papers, Box 3, Hoover Institution on War, Revolution and Peace, Stanford, CA. The notorious Elizabeth Dilling (of *Red Network* fame) also made use of the Steele files.

21. William Pencak, *For God and Country: The American Legion, 1919–1941* (Boston: Northeastern University Press, 1989), pp. 164, 165. William Gellerman, *The American Legion as Educator* (New York: Columbia University Teachers College Press, 1938).

22. Pencak, *For God and Country*, p. 163. The *National Legionnaire* originated in 1928 as the *Huddle*.

23. Pencak, *For God and Country*, pp. 167, 168.

24. Ibid., p. 169.

25. See Conde Pallen's draft of the principles for the subversive department, February 9, 1920, Box 104, NCF Papers, NYPL. Marguerite Green, *The National Civic Federation and the American Labor Movement* (Washington, DC: Catholic University Press, 1956), p. 398.

26. Green, *National Civic Federation*, p. 398.

27. Robins and Thompson had been on the Red Cross Commission President Wilson sent to Russia in July 1917. There they lost faith in the provisional government and came to admire the Bolsheviks.

28. Isolationists like senators Johnson and Borah regarded nonrecognition of the Soviets as a violation of the traditional prohibition against American involvement in European disputes.

29. Box 384, NCF Papers, NYPL.

30. In a memo to the House Appropriations Committee, December 16, 1924, Hoover describes his January 24, 1924 memo to the secretary of state on Communist activities in the United States emanating from the Third International. Hoover to House Appropriations Committee, Justice Department Appropriations for fiscal 1926, December 1924, p. 74.

31. Easley to Gompers, February 22, 1919, April 22, 1919, April 23, 1919, October 3, 1919, Box 46; October 20, 1919, Box 99; April 22, 1919, Box 46. NCF Papers, NYPL.

32. See Welsh to Coolidge, January 13, 1927, in which another anticommunist charges that Borah was a Communist (Coolidge Papers). *New York Times*, January 1, 1919.

33. U.S. Senate, *Investigation of Alleged Payments by the Mexican Government to United States Senators*, 70th Cong. 2nd sess., Part 5.

34. H. R. Knickerbocker, *New York Evening Post*, March 2, 1929. See also *New York Times*, August 23, 1929, on the Berlin trial of the forgers.

35. Gaston B. Means, *The Strange Death of President Harding*, from *The Diaries of Gaston B. Means, as told to May Dixon Thacker* (New York: Guild, 1930).

36. Besides the March 13, 1929 interview, there was another on March 31, 1929, at 402 Fairfax Road, Bethesda. Box 124, NCF Papers, NYPL.

37. RME to A. L. Bulwinkle, Manville-Jenckes, Loray Mill, Gastonia NC, September 19, 1929, NCF Papers, NYPL.

38. Lucien C. Wheeler to Easley, October 12, 1929, NCF Papers, NYPL.

39. Easley to Wheeler, October 23, 1929, NCF Papers, NYPL.

40. Easley, to Bulwinkle, December 14, 1929, NCF Papers, NYPL.

41. See Fish, "Religious Persecution in Russia, Irrepressible Conflict Between Communism and Belief in God," February 28, 1930. Steele Papers, Hoover Institution.

42. He claimed a Fish had been the second youngest American general in the Revolutionary War, edged out only by Alexander Hamilton—a friend of the Revolutionary Fish. Fish was educated in public elementary schools near Garrison, New York, then in boarding school in Switzerland and finally at St. Mark's, which then sent most of its graduates to Harvard. Fish, too, went to Harvard (to the consternation of his family, which had always attended Columbia). During his senior year at Harvard (1908–9) he worked in Washington for his father, Theodore Roosevelt's assistant secretary of the treasury. After graduation he ran for the New York State Assembly on the Bull Moose ticket, commanded a black regiment during the War, and then served in Congress from 1920 to 1945 (he was the famous, or notorious, Fish of the legendary jingle "Martin Barton and Fish" that FDR used so well in his campaign. Interview with RGP. See also Anthony Troncone, "Hamilton Fish, Sr., and the Politics of American Nationalism, 1912–1945," Ph.D. dissertation, Rutgers University, 1993.

43. Interview with RGP.

44. Interview with RGP.

45. *Daily Worker*, November 21, 1930.

46. *New York Times*, January 10, 1931. See also the souvenir booklet for the meeting, Steele Papers, Hoover Institution. The Committee was chaired by Martin W. Littleton, and met at the Waldorf in New York, January 17, 1932. See George Djamgaroff, announcement, January 6, 1932, Steele papers, Hoover Institution.

47. See Donald J. Lisio, *The President and Protest: Hoover, Conspiracy, and the Bonus Riot* (Columbia: University of Missouri Press, 1974).

Chapter 5. A School for Anticommunists

1. For an overview, see Martin Malia, *The Soviet Tragedy: A History of Socialism in Russia, 1917–1991* (New York: The Free Press, 1994), pp. 177–226.

2. For a brilliant study of the careers of ex-Communist anticommunists, see John P. Diggins, *Up From Communism: Conservative Odysseys in American Intellectual History* (New York: Harper and Row, 1975). Diggins focuses on Max Eastman, John Dos Passos, Will Herberg, and James Burnham.

3. Francis Russell, *Sacco and Vanzetti: The Case Resolved* (New York: Harper and Row, 1986), p. 118.

4. Ibid., pp. 117, 118.

5. Ibid., p. 132. Stephen Koch suggests that Communist manipulation moved from the Party through Gardner Jackson through Frankfurter's wife Marion,

who was emotionally unbalanced and was fanatically devoted to the Sacco-Vanzetti campaign. Stephen Koch, *Double Lives: Spies and Writers in the Secret Soviet War of Ideas Against the West* (New York: The Free Press, 1994), p. 36.

6. Russell, *Sacco and Vanzetti*, pp. 111–17; 118. Russell cites Johannes Zelt's *Proletarian Internationalism in the Battle for Sacco and Vanzetti* (Berlin: Dietz Verlag, 1958), an examination of the Moscow archives on the case, which boasts that the international agitation over the case was Communist directed.

7. Russell, *Sacco and Vanzetti*.

8. In 1977 she wrote her memoir of the case, *The Never Ending Wrong*.

9. Townsend Luddington, *John Dos Passos: A Twentieth Century Odyssey* (New York: E. P. Dutton, 1980), p. 262.

10. Russell, *Sacco and Vanzetti*, p. 214.

11. The Gastonia strike's leader, Fred Beal, fled to Russia after the strike collapsed. He would emerge a few years later as a hard-line countersubversive anticommunist. Harvey Klehr, *The Heyday of American Communism: The Depression Decade* (New York: Basic Books, 1984), p. 31.

12. For a full discussion of Communist activities in Harlan Country, see ibid., pp. 45–47.

13. Ibid., pp. 335, 338; Wilson Record, *Race and Radicalism: The NAACP and the Communist Party in Conflict* (Ithaca: Cornell University Press, 1964), p. 61.

14. Klehr, *Heyday of American Communism*, p. 338.

15. He was not freed until 1937, when the insurrection law was struck down by the courts. Ibid., p. 333.

16. Ibid., p. 35.

17. Bertram Wolfe, *A Life in Two Centuries: An Autobiography* (New York: Stein and Day, 1981), p. 416.

18. Russell, *Sacco and Vanzetti*, p. 139. For Levine material, author's interview with Ruth (Mrs. Isaac Don) Levine. Levine Papers in the Possession of Mrs. Levine, Washington, DC. Levine FBI file 4040-45153. Levine ADL file, ADL Library, New York City. For Lyons, see Eugene Lyons Papers, University of Oregon Library, Eugene, OR. Lyons ADL File, ADL Library, New York City. Lyons FBI file 62-95331.

19. Russell, *Sacco and Vanzetti*, p. 137.

20. Klehr, *Heyday of American Communism*, p. 339. When the Party line changed in 1935 to one favoring a popular front of cooperation between the Party and other progressive forces, the Communists ceded control of the case to a joint defense committee representing the NAACP, the ACLU, the League for Industrial Democracy, and the Methodist Federation for Social Service.

21. George S. Schuyler, *Black and Conservative* (New Rochelle, NY: Arlington House, 1966), p. 187. See the George S. Schuyler Papers, Schomburg Center, New York Public Library, and the Schuyler Collection, Syracuse Uni-

versity. Schuyler ADL file, ADL Library, New York City. Schuyler FBI file 100-7660.

22. Schuyler, *Black and Conservative*, pp. 188, 189.
23. Ibid., p. 191.
24. The attack on Jones was dated April 15, 1931. Schuyler, *Black and Conservative*, pp. 191–93.
25. Ibid., pp. 193, 195.
26. Ibid., p. 197–98. This was December 1932.
27. Ibid., pp. 205, 206.
28. Ibid., pp. 152, 153.
29. Mark Naison, *Communists in Harlem During the Depression* (Urbana: University of Illinois Press, 1983), p. 39.
30. Klehr, *Heyday of American Communism*, p. 84. Foster got only 48,000 votes, Socialist Norman Thomas 884,000; Roosevelt got 22.8 million, Hoover 15.7 million.
31. J. B. Matthews, *Odyssey of a Fellow Traveler* (New York: Mt. Vernon Publishers, 1938), p. 96. Author's interview with Ruth (Mrs. J. B.) Matthews. Matthews's extensive collection of personal papers and research materials is in the Perkins Library, Duke University, Durham, NC. Matthews ADL file, ADL Library, New York City. Matthews FBI file 100-5821.
32. Jay Lovestone was the Party secretary and one of the founders of the American Party; Ben Gitlow was another founder and a former Party vice presidential candidate; Bertram Wolfe was the American delegate to the Comintern's Executive Committee. These were men who had proven their Communist loyalties during the raids and repression of the twenties—Gitlow had served three years in Sing Sing.
33. Wolfe, *Life in Two Centuries*, pp. 512, 522.
34. Klehr, *Heyday of American Communism*, pp. 49, 54. After these splits, there were perhaps 10,000 still in the Party in 1930.
35. Irving Howe, *World of Our Fathers* (1983; reprint, New York: Schocken, 1989), pp. 333, 334.
36. Ibid., pp. 337, 338.
37. For Hillman, see Steven Fraser, *Labor Will Rule: Sidney Hillman and the Rise of American Labor* (New York: The Free Press, 1991).
38. Judah J. Shapiro, *The Friendly Society: A History of the Workmen's Circle* (New York: Doron, 1970), p. 85.
39. Howe, *World of Our Fathers*, pp. 342, 343.
40. Klehr, *Heyday of American Communism*, pp. 45–46.
41. Louis J. Gallagher, S.J., *Edmund A. Walsh, S.J.* (New York: Benziger, 1962), p. 84. Walsh's papers are in the Georgetown University Library Special Collections.

42. "Barriers Raised by Evil Soviet Theories Prevent Recognition of Russia by U.S." *Washington Star*, May 24, 1925. "Soviet Assailed at DAR Congress," *New York Times*, April 18, 1929. *Washington Star*, ca. January 31, 1924.

43. Christopher J. Kauffmann, *Faith and Fraternalism: The History of the Knights of Columbus, 1882–1982* (New York: Harper and Row, 1982), p. 296; Chapter 11. "Report on Radical Activities," December 1926, Hart Papers, Knights of Columbus Archives, Hartford, CT, makes it clear that the Knights subscribed to a private research service on radical activities, with particular reference to the situation in Mexico.

44. David O'Brien, *Public Catholicism* (New York: Macmillan, 1989), p. 163.

45. Bishop's letter, March 13, 1930, Walsh Papers, Georgetown University.

46. *Washington Star*, October 19, 1931; *New York Herald Tribune*, October 19, 1931.

47. This was the International Committee for Political Prisoners, *Letters from Russian Prisons* (New York: Boni, 1925).

48. Walsh papers, Georgetown.

49. Gallagher, *Edmund A. Walsh, S.J.*, p. 89.

50. For an example of Protestants throwing Catholics' appeals for religious liberty back in their face, see Box 103, NCF Papers, NYPL, in which an NCF investigation of Methodist Bishop Blake quoted from his speech of July 12, 1923: "There is undoubtedly a larger measure of religious tolerance in Russia than in any country of Europe and America that is dominated by the Roman Catholic Church. This will doubtless be strange reading to those who have accepted as trustworthy the propaganda that has filled the American press since the execution of the Roman Catholic priest Butchkevitch. . . . One does not need to be an expert in secret service to discover the hand of the Jesuit in the present propaganda. . . . It is not alone the Soviets who have been misrepresented. Others and particularly the Methodists, have received their full share of misrepresentation. We have been accused again and again by the Catholic controlled press of being in league with the Soviets and supporting their effort to destroy religion and the church in Russia."

51. O'Brien, *Public Catholicism*, p. 180, cites Peter Filene, "American Attitudes Toward Soviet Russia, 1917–1933," Vol. 1, Ph.D. dissertation, Harvard University, pp. 492–518, for Catholic attitudes toward recognition.

52. William Bullit, "For the President," FDR Library, PSF 115, cited in Ted Morgan, *FDR: A Biography* (New York: Simon and Schuster, 1985), p. 397.

Chapter 6. The Red Decade

1. Eugene Lyons, *The Red Decade: The Stalinist Penetration of America* (Indianapolis: Bobbs, Merrill, 1941), p. 11.

2. See Anthony Cave Brown and Charles B. MacDonald, *On a Field of Red* (New

York: Putnam's 1981), p. 473. See also Babette Gross, *Willi Munzenberg: A Political Biography* (East Lansing: MSU Press, 1974). *The Brown Book* was the model, at the end of the decade, for the final report of John Dewey's inquiry into the charges against Trotsky, *Not Guilty: Report of the Commission of Inquiry into Charges Made Against Leon Trotsky and Leon Sedoff in the Moscow Trials* (New York and London: Harper, 1938), which argued that Stalin, not Trotsky, had betrayed the ideals of the left. See Sidney Hook, *Out of Step* (New York: Harper and Row, 1987), pp. 218–47, and E. H. Carr, *Twilight of the Comintern, 1930–1935* (New York: Pantheon, 1982).

3. Stephen Koch, *Double Lives: Spies and Writers in the Secret Soviet War of Ideas Against the West* (New York: The Free Press, 1994), p. 105.

4. For an analysis of American foreign policy in the face of isolationist pressure, see Selig Adler, *The Uncertain Giant: American Foreign Policy Between the Wars, 1921–1941* (1965; reprint, New York: Collier, 1969).

5. Herbert Lottman, *The Left Bank: Writers in Paris from Popular Front to Cold War* (London: Heinemann, 1982), pp. 51–53. Eugene Lyons, *The Red Decade*, pp. 150–51. J. B. Matthews, *Odyssey of a Fellow-Traveler* (New York: Mt. Vernon Publishers, 1938), Chapter 8. See also William L. O'Neill, *A Better World. The Great Schism: Stalinism and the American Intellectuals* (New York: Simon and Schuster, 1982); Alan M. Wald, *The New York Intellectuals: The Rise and Decline of the Anti-Stalinist Left from the 1930s to the 1980s* (Chapel Hill: University of North Carolina Press, 1987); and Alexander Bloom, *Prodigal Sons: The New York Intellectuals and Their World* (New York: Oxford University Press, 1986).

6. Walter Goodman, *The Committee: The Extraordinary Career of the House Committee on Un-American Activities* (New York: Farrar, Straus and Giroux, 1968), p. 78.

7. See David Caute, *The Fellow Travelers: A Postscript to the Enlightenment* (New York: Macmillan, 1973).

8. Harvey Klehr, *The Heyday of American Communism: The Depression Decade* (New York: Basic Books, 1984), p. 225.

9. Ibid., p. 238.

10. Ibid., p. 251.

11. Ibid., p. 247.

12. Steve Rosswurm, "The Catholic Church and the Left-Led Unions: Labor Priests, Labor Schools, and the ACTU," in Steve Rosswurm (ed.), *The CIO's Left-Led Unions* (New Brunswick, NJ.: Rutgers University Press, 1992), p. 122. See also Douglas Seaton, *Catholics and Radicals: The Association of Catholic Trade Unionists and the American Labor Movement from the Depression to Cold War* (Lewisburg, PA: Bucknell University Press, 1981).

13. There were two liberals on the committee, John J. Dempsey of New Mexico and Arthur D. Healey of Massachusetts. The other Democrats were Joe Starnes

of Alabama and Harold Mosier of Ohio. The Republicans were Noah M. Mason of Illinois and J. Parnall Thomas of New Jersey. Goodman, *The Committee,* pp. 24, 35.

14. Matthews, *Odyssey of a Fellow Traveler,* pp. 268–69.

15. Ibid., p. 115.

16. Ibid., p. 216.

17. Goodman, *The Committee,* pp. 43; 54.

18. Ibid., pp. 49, 50.

19. Ibid., pp. 75–77.

20. Klehr, *Heyday of American Communism,* pp. 317–23. Goodman, *The Committee,* p. 80.

21. Goodman, *The Committee,* p. 86.

22. Matthews, *Odyssey of a Fellow Traveler,* p. 226.

23. "Who is Elizabeth Dilling?" Lowman Papers, Hoover Institution. Milton S. Mayer, "Mrs. Dilling: Lady of the Red Network," *America Mercury,* July 1939, pp. 292–99. Dilling file, Wilcox Collection, University of Kansas.

24. Elizabeth Dilling, *The Red Network* (Kenilworth, IL: published by the author, 1934), p. 89.

25. Elizabeth Dilling, *The Roosevelt Red Record and Its Background* (Chicago: published by the author, 1936), p. 104.

26. Dilling, *The Red Network,* p. 52.

27. Dilling, *The Roosevelt Red Record,* p. 148.

28. Alan Brinkley, *Voices of Protest: Huey Long, Father Coughlin and the Great Depression* (1982; reprint, New York: Vintage, 1983), p. 119.

29. John Cooney, *The American Pope: The Life and Times of Francis Cardinal Spellman* (New York: Times Books, 1984), p. 41. See a NCWC News Service cable, May 12, 1936, in the Cronin folder, U. S. Catholic Conference.

30. See unidentified clipping, April 10, 1933, Steele Collection, Hoover Institution. *New York Times,* November 4, 1936, p. 27. The Nazi newspaper *Angriff* complained that Pacelli's visit to the United States was intended to deprive "National Socialism of the historic credit of having started the anti-Bolshevist campaign."

31. *Non Abbiamo Bisogno.*

32. Cooney, *American Pope,* p. 48.

33. *New York Times,* July 12, 1935, p. 17; September 18, 1935, p. 11. The catechism is in the Steele Collection, Hoover Institution.

34. David J. O'Brien, *American Catholics and Social Reform: The New Deal Years* (New York: Oxford University Press, 1968), p. 86. Donald F. Crosby, "Boston's Catholics and the Spanish Civil War: 1936–1939," *New England Quarterly* 44 (March 1971): 82–100. Alden V. Brown, *The Tablet: The First Seventy-Five Years* (Brooklyn: Tablet, 1983), p. 33.

35. *New York Times*, December 14, 1936, p. 11; December 20, 1936, IV, p. 4; December 25, 1936, p. 1. O'Brien, *American Catholics and Social Reform*, p. 82.

36. September 10, 1937, January 1, 1938, March 18, 1937, Knights of Columbus Papers. *Boston Post*, May 26, 1937, cited in Crosby, "Boston's Catholics," p. 100. Walsh to Talbot, September 23, 1938, Walsh Papers, Georgetown. O'Brien, *American Catholics and Social Reform*, p. 83.

37. February 22, 1937, Knights of Columbus Papers.

38. Brinkley, *Voices of Protest*, p. 135.

39. Charles J. Tull, "Father Coughlin, the New Deal, and the Election of 1936," Ph.D. dissertation, Notre Dame, 1962, p. 187, cited in George Q. Flynn, *American Catholics and the Roosevelt Presidency, 1932–1936* (Lexington: University of Kentucky Press, 1968), p. 204. Arthur M. Schlesinger, Jr., *The Age of Roosevelt: The Politics of Upheaval* (Boston: Houghton Mifflin, 1960), p. 620, cited in Flynn, *American Catholics*, p. 205.

40. Brinkley, *Voices of Protest*, p. 125.

41. Ryan to Roosevelt, September 25, 1936, Reel 3, Sel. Mat., Franklin D. Roosevelt Library, Hyde Park, NY, cited in Flynn, *American Catholics*, pp. 213, 227. Brinkley, *Voices of Protest*, p. 260.

42. Brinkley, *Voices of Protest*, p. 266; Flynn, *American Catholics*, p. 181.

43. See report of speech by *Catholic Worker* editor William M. Callahan, *New York Post*, February 9, 1939. Gretta Palmer, "The Jews Fight the Reds," *Commentator*, February 1939, pp. 8–13. *American Jewish Federation News*, November 17, 1938. *New York Daily News*, December 20, 1938. *New York World Telegram*, December 20, 1938.

44. *New York Herald Tribune*, December 20, 1938. Milton R. Jacobs, *Can You Shut Your Eyes to These Facts?* (Brooklyn, NY: Brooklyn Division of the American Jewish Federation to Combat Communism and Fascism, 1939).

45. *American Jewish Federation News*, November 17, 1938.

46. Sidney Hook, *Out of Step: An Unquiet Life in the Twentieth Century* (New York: Harper and Row, 1987), p. 420.

47. One of the principal conduits of information about the trials was Walter Duranty of the *New York Times*, whose willingness to shade his reports to conform to the Kremlin's propaganda line has become notorious. See S. J. Taylor, *Stalin's Apologist: Walter Duranty, the New York Times's Man in Moscow* (New York: Oxford University Press, 1990).

48. Robert Conquest, *The Great Terror, a Reassessment* (New York: Oxford University Press, 1990), pp. 484–89.

49. Ibid., pp. 48, 103.

50. Ibid., pp. 148, 162.

51. Ibid., p. 342.

52. The proceedings were published in two volumes: *The Case of Leon Trotsky*

(1937), the verbatim text of the hearings in Mexico City, and *Not Guilty: The Final Report of the Commission of Inquiry into Charges Made Against Leon Trotsky and Leon Sedoff in the Moscow Trials* (1938).

53. Hook, *Out of Step*, p. 225.

54. *New Republic*, February 3, 1937, September 2, 1936, cited in Hook, *Out of Step*, pp. 230, 231, 234.

55. Hook, *Out of Step*, p. 238.

56. Hook, *Out of Step*, pp. 240–41, makes the point that everything that was revealed or known in 1956 about Stalin's terror could have been read in the two volumes of the Dewey Commission and in the three volumes of trial testimony published by the Soviet Union: *The Trotskyite-Zinovievite Terrorist Center* (Moscow, 1936), *The Anti-Soviet Trotskyist Center* (Moscow, 1937), and *The Anti-Soviet Bloc of Rights and Trotskyists* (Moscow, 1938).

57. Hook, *Out of Step*, p. 259.

58. The remainder of the text follows: "The tide of totalitarianism is rising throughout the world. It is washing away cultural and creative freedom along with other expressions of independent human reason. Never before in modern times has the integrity of the writer, the artist, the scientist and the scholar been threatened so seriously. The existence of this danger and the urgent need for common defensive action inspire the undersigned in issuing this statement.

"Under varying labels and colors, but with an unvarying hatred for the free mind, the totalitarian idea is already enthroned in Germany, Italy, Russia, Japan, and Spain. There, intellectual and creative independence is suppressed and punished as a form of treason. Art, science and education—all have been forcibly turned into lackeys for a supreme state, a deified leader and an official pseudo-philosophy.

"The Nazis have proclaimed: 'There can no longer be a single artist who creates otherwise than nationally and with a national purpose. Every writer who withdraws from this preoccupation must be hunted as an enemy of the nation until he gives up his intolerable resistance.'

"The words and acts of all other totalitarian regimes conform to this view. They apply it to the educator, the scientist and the historian no less than to the artist. The results have been artistic sterility, an enslaved intellectual life, a tragic caricature of culture. Literally thousands of German, Italian, Russian and other victims of cultural dictatorships have been silenced, imprisoned, tortured or hounded into exile.

"Triumphant in a large sector of the civilized world, the totalitarian idea is winning too dangerous an influence in many other countries. It threatens to overwhelm nations where the democratic way of life, with its cultural liberty, is still dominant. Even in the United States, its beginnings are all too evident—in the emergence of local political dictators, the violation of civil rights, the alarming spread of phobias of hatred directed against racial, religious and political minorities. Ominous shadows of war are gathering in our own land. Behind them lurk dangers not only to a free labor movement but to a free culture.

"Through subsidized propaganda, through energetic agents, through political pressure, the totalitarian states succeed in infecting other countries with their false doctrines, in intimidating independent artists and scholars, and in spreading panic among intellectuals. Already many of those who would be crippled or destroyed by totalitarianism are themselves yielding to panic. In fear or despair they hasten to exalt one brand of intellectual servitude over another; to make fine distinctions between various methods of humiliating the human spirit and outlawing intellectual integrity. Many of them have already declared a moratorium on reason and creative freedom. Instead of resisting and denouncing all attempts to straitjacket the human mind, they glorify, under deceptive slogans and names, the color or the cut of one straitjacket rather than another.

"These are immediate and pervasive realities. Unless totalitarianism is combated wherever and in whatever form it manifests itself, it will spread in America. We, as writers, artists and scholars, are deeply conscious of our responsibilities to our vocations. The circumstance that free culture, persecuted and proscribed in vast areas of Europe and Asia, seeks a refuge in America, raises these responsibilities to the plane of pressing moral duty.

"We therefore call for the formation of a COMMITTEE FOR CULTURAL FREEDOM, an organization independent of control, whether open or secret, by any political group, pledged to expose repression of intellectual freedom under whatever pretext, to defend individuals and groups victimized by totalitarian practices anywhere, to propagate courageously the ideal of untrammeled intellectual activity. This commits us as a group to no particular social philosophy—but only to one of the fundamental criteria for evaluating all social philosophies today, viz:

Whether it permits the thinker and the artist to function independently of political, religious, or racial dogmas. We have come together, and call upon others to join us, on the basis of the least common denominator of a civilized culture—the defense of creative and intellectual freedom." Hook, *Out of Step*, p. 259.

59. The CCF manifesto's signers:
Louis Adamic, author
Frederick L. Allen, Associate Editor, *Harper's Magazine*
Van Meter Ames, Professor of Philosophy, University of Cincinnati
Howard R. Anderson, Assistant Professor of Education, Cornell University
Sherwood Anderson, author

W. A. Anderson, Professor of Rural Social Organization, Cornell University
Cyrus Leroy Baldridge, author
Robert O. Ballou, publisher
Ernest Sutherland Bates, author
W. H. Baumgardner, educator, Allen University
Carl Becker, Professor of History and Political Science, Cornell University
Arthur F. Bentley
Thomas H. Benton, artist
David Bernstein, writer
Knight Biggerstaff, educator, Cornell University
George Boas, Professor of Philosophy, Johns Hopkins University
Boyd H. Bode, Professor of Education, Ohio State University
S. L. Boothroyd, Professor of Astronomy and Geodesy, Cornell University
Paul F. Brissenden, Assistant Professor of Economics, Columbia University
Dorothy Dunbar Bromley, columnist
Robert C. Brooks, Professor Economics and Political Science, Swarthmore
    College
Edmund DeS. Brunner, Professor of Sociology, Columbia University
Struthers Burt, author
E. A. Burtt, Professor of Philosophy, Cornell University
Witter Bynner, author
V. F. Calverton, writer
Henry S. Canby, editor
W. B. Cannon, Professor of Physiology, Harvard University
Rudolf Carnap, Professor of Philosophy, University of Chicago
John Chamberlain, writer
John L. Childs, Professor of Education, Columbia University
Albert Sprague Coolidge, Professor of Chemistry, Harvard University
L. S. Cottrell, Professor of Sociology and Anthropology, Cornell University
George S. Counts, Professor of Education, Columbia University
Philip W. L. Cox, Professor of Secondary Education, New York University
Countee Cullen, author
G. Watts Cunningham, Professor of Philosophy, Cornell University
Merle Curti, Professor of History, Columbia University
Robert E. Cushman, Professor of Government, Cornell University
Wendell P. Dabney, editor
Walter Damrosch, musician
Elmer Davis, writer
Ned H. Dearborn, Professor of Education and Dean of New York University
Leon Dennen, writer
Babette Deutsch, writer

John Dewey, philosopher and educator

Arnold Dresden, Professor of Mathematics, Swarthmore College

Mary Eva Duthie, Assistant Professor of Rural Social Organization, Cornell University

Max Eastman, author

Irwin Edman, Professor of Philosophy, Columbia University

Edwin R. Embree, President, Julius Rosenwald Fund

Abraham Epstein, Executive Director, American Association for Social Security

Morris L. Ernst, lawyer

Edna Ferber, author

Herbert F. Fraser, Professor of Economics, Swarthmore College

Paul W. Gates, Assistant Professor of History, Cornell University

Harry Glicksman, Professor and Assistant Dean of the University of Wisconsin

Abram Harris, Professor of Economics, Howard University

Herbert E. Harris, educator

George W. Hartmann, Associate Professor of Education, Columbia University

Henry Hazlitt, editor and author

Milton P. Herrmann

Philip M. Hicks, Professor of English, Swarthmore College

Jesse H. Holmes, Emeritus Professor of Philosophy, Swarthmore College

Rev. John Haynes Holmes, Community Church, New York

Sidney Hook, Professor of Philosophy, New York University

Sidney Howard, playwright

B. W. Huebsch, publisher

Inez Haynes Irwin, author

James W. Ivy, Instructor in English, Hampton Institute

Horace M. Kallen, Professor of Philosophy, New School for Social Research

Edwin C. Kemble, Professor of Physics, Harvard University

William H. Kilpatrick, Emeritus Professor of Education, Columbia University

Suzanne LaFollette, writer

George W. Lee

S. M. Levitas, editor

Newman Levy, author

Ludwig Lore, columnist

Arthur O. Lovejoy, Professor of Philosophy, Johns Hopkins University

Robert H. Lowie, Professor of Anthropology, University of California

Ferdinand Lundberg, author

Eugene Lyons, editor

F. C. Marchan, Professor of English History, Cornell University

Benjamin C. Marsh, writer

Milton S. Mayer, writer

Claude McKay, writer

Nelson P. Mean, Professor of History and Acting President of the College of the City of New York

Felix Robert Mendelssohn, Professor of Music, School of Education, New York University

Ernest L. Meyer, columnist

Wesley C. Mitchell, Professor of Economics, Columbia University and Director of Research for the National Bureau of Economic Research

Marston Morse, Professor of Mathematics, Princeton University

Philip E. Mosely, Professor of History, Cornell University

Gorham Munson, writer

David S. Muzzey, Professor of American History, Columbia University

Henry Newmann, Leader, Ethical Culture Society

Jesse H. Newlon, Professor of Education, Columbia University

Bryce Oliver, radio commentator

James O'Neal, editor

H. A. Overstreet, Professor, Head of the Philosophy Department, College of the City of New York

Walter Pach, artist

Saul K. Padover, historian

R. A. Palson, Professor, Cornell University

John Dos Passos, writer

Ralph Baron Perry, Professor of Philosophy, Harvard University

Lorine Pruette, writer

Winifred Raushenbush, writer

Victor Reisel, writer

Frederick W. Roe, Professor of English, University of Wisconsin

James Rorty, writer

Leonard Q. Ross, writer

Charles Edward Russell, journalist and author

Morrie Ryskind, writer

George H. Sabine, Professor of Philosophy, Cornell University

Dwight Sanderson, Professor of Rural Social Organization, Cornell University

J. Salwyn Schapiro, Professor of History, College of the City of New York

Willi Schlamm, editor

Arthur M. Schlesinger, Professor of History, Harvard University

George S. Schuyler, journalist
Evelyn Scott, author
Gerhart Seger, editor
Max A. Shepard, Professor of Government, Cornell University
Caroline Singer, writer
John Sloan, artist
Joseph Hilton Smyth, publisher
Carl Stephenson, Professor of History, Cornell University
Clara G. Stillman, writer
Benjamin Stolberg, author
W. T. Thayer, educator, Ethical Culture School
Norman Thomas, writer
Dorothy Thompson, journalist
Frank N. Trager, writer
Carlo Tresca, editor
Howard M. Trueblood
Frederic F. Van de Water, author
Oswald Garrison Villard, journalist
M. R. Werner, author
William Carlos Williams, author
Louis Wirth, Associate Professor of Sociology, University of Chicago
Helen Woodward, author

60. Hook, *Out of Step*, p. 263.
61. Never a Party member, he was a most reliable fellow traveler. See Ellen Frankel Paul's "Introduction" to *Assignment in Utopia* (1937; reprint, New Brunswick: Transaction Publishers, 1991), p. xiii.
62. Lyons, *Assignment in Utopia*, p. 621.
63. Ibid., p. 624.
64. Ibid., pp. 631; 635.
65. Ibid., p. 646.
66. Ibid., p. 647.
67. Holmes to Lyons, October 29, 1937; Cahan to Lyons, March 11, 1938; Chamberlain to Lyons, March 12, 1938, Box 2, Lyons Papers, University of Oregon.
68. Goldman to Lyons, August 2, 1938, Box 2, Lyons Papers, University of Oregon.
69. Kirchwey to Lyons, September 15, 1938, Box 2, Lyons Papers, University of Oregon.
70. William J. Hood, "Preface" to Walter Krivitsky, *In Stalin's Secret Service* (1939; reprint, Frederick, MD: University Publications of America, 1985), p. vii.
71. Krivitsky, *In Stalin's Secret Service*, p. xxxiii.
72. Ibid., pp. xxxix, 3.

73. Ibid., p. xii.
74. Jan Valtin, "Communist Agent," *American Mercury*, XLVIII (November 1939): 264–71. (Eugene Lyons was his editor.)
75. Jan Valtin, *Out of the Night* (New York: Alliance, 1941, p. 722.
76. Ibid., p. 745.

Chapter 7. Dancing with the Devil: The Alliance with Stalin

1. Quoted by George Sirgiovanni, *An Undercurrent of Suspicion*, (New Brunswick, NJ: Transaction Publishers, 1990), p. 107.
2. Harvey Klehr and John Earl Haynes, *The American Communist Movement: Storming Heaven Itself* (New York: Twayne Publishers, 1992), p. 101.
3. Eugene Lyons, *The Red Decade* (Indianapolis: Bobbs-Merrill, 1941), p. 356.
4. Mark Naison, *Communists in Harlem During the Depression* (Urbana: University of Illinois Press, 1983), pp. 173, 176.
5. Schuyler, *Pittsburgh Courier* columns, December 31, 1938; April 2, 1938; June 1, 1939. "Revolution and the Afra-american," *Pittsburgh Courier*, ca. January 1, 1935.
6. Naison, *Communists in Harlem*, pp. 180–81, 265. See also Harold Cruse, *The Crisis of the Negro Intellectual from Its Origins to the Present* (New York: William Morrow, 1967), pp. 147–70.
7. Naison, *Communists in Harlem*, p. 289.
8. Sidney Hook, *Out of Step: An Unquiet Life in the Twentieth Century* (New York: Harper and Row, 1987), pp. 264–65. The executive committee included Lamont, Dashiell Hammett, Dorothy Brewster, Vincent Sheean, Walter Rautenstraugh, Donald Ogden Stewart, Rebecca Janny Timbres, and Mary Van Kleek.
9. Lyons, *The Red Decade*, p. 351.
10. Hook, *Out of Step*, pp. 269, 270.
11. Quoted in Walter Goodman, *The Committee: The Extraordinary Career of the House Committee on Un-American Activities* (New York: Farrar, Straus and Giroux, 1968), p. 57.
12. *The Daily Worker*, September 19, 1941, quoted in Harvey Klehr, *The Heyday of American Communism: The Depression Decade* (New York: Basic Books, 1984), p. 395.
13. Leo P. Ribuffo, *The Old Christian Right: The Protestant Far Right from the Great Depression to the Cold War* (Philadelphia: Temple University Press, 1983), p. 219.
14. The law involved was Sec. 22 Title 18 U.S.C., cited in Don Whitehead, *The F.B.I. Story* (New York: Random House, 1956), p. 340. The arrests of the Abraham Lincoln Brigade veterans were part of a general crackdown on foreign-oriented extremist groups. Between December and March the De-

partment charged several Russian agents with failing to register, and in January 1940 arrested seventeen members of the Christian Front on charges of conspiring to overthrow the government. Robert J. Goldstein, *Political Repression in Modern America* (Cambridge, MA: Two Continents, 1978), p. 249.

15. Whitehead, *The F.B.I. Story*, p. 176. Peter N. Carroll, *The Odyssey of the Abraham Lincoln Brigade: Americans in the Spanish Civil War* (Stanford: Stanford University Press, 1994).

16. "Our Lawless G-Men," *Nation*, March 2, 1940, pp. 296–97.

17. Goodman, *The Committee*, p. 98.

18. Ibid., p. 75.

19. The lobbyist was an aide to Gardner Jackson, a former New Dealer, then with the League. Ibid., p. 92.

20. The phrase was coined by Leo P. Ribuffo in *The Old Christian Right*.

21. Justus D. Doenecke, "The America First Committee, Origins and Outcome," *Chronicles*, December 1991, pp. 17, 18.

22. Ribuffo, *The Old Christian Right*, p. 192.

23. Institute for Propaganda Analysis, *Propaganda Analysis: A Bulletin to Help the Intelligent Citizen Detect and Analyze Propaganda*, November 1937, p. 5.

24. Ibid., May 1938, p. 78.

25. Ibid., January 20, 1940, p. 1.

26. Harold Lavine, *Fifth Column in America* (New York: Doubleday, 1940); George Seldes, *Witch Hunt: The Technique and Profits of Red-Baiting* (New York: Modern Age, 1940). See also Ribuffo, *The Old Christian Right*, pp. 178–224.

27. *Propaganda Analysis*, June 10, 1940, p. 6.

28. Hoover told the White House that Franz Boas, who had protested the Lincoln Brigade arrests, was not a Communist, but belonged to suspect organizations like the New School for Social Research and the World Association for the Advancement of Atheism. (Hoover to Watson, April 13, 1940, Official File 10-B, FBI Numbered Report 55, FDR Library). On December 6, 1940, he told the President that the Communist Party had begun a peace campaign, which he called "a typical Communist stratagem." (Hoover to Watson, Dec. 6, 1940, Official File 10-B, FBI Numbered Report 520, FDR Library.) The Lindbergh anecdote is in Ted Morgan, *FDR: A Biography* (New York: Simon and Schuster, 1985), p. 523. There are many accounts of FDR's press banquet endorsement of Hoover. See Whitehead, *The FBI Story*, p. 180.

29. Ribuffo, *The Old Christian Right*, pp. 179, 186.

30. "Looking for chinks in the armor of their respectable noninterventionist adversaries, the Chief Executive, members of the administration, and other ardent friends of European democracy had discovered a weakness. The fight to extend aid to Britain and France might indeed be won on the battlefield of patriotism; and here, as the extremists had learned already, antisubversive

activity sanctioned by the liberal establishment (and three centuries of accumulated history), could be far more effective than their own countersubversion, directed, as it were, from the bottom up." Geoffrey S. Smith, *To Save a Nation: American 'Extremism,' the New Deal, and the Coming of World War II* (1973; reprint, Chicago: Ivan R. Dee, 1992), p. 157. Ribuffo, *The Old Christian Right*, p. 185.

31. Smith, *To Save a Nation*, p. 173.
32. Alan Brinkley, *Voices of Protest: Huey Long, Father Coughlin and the Great Depression* (1983; reprint, New York: Vintage, 1983), p. 267.
33. John Roy Carlson [pseudonym for Avedis Derounian], *Undercover: My Four Years in the Nazi Underground in America* (New York: E. P. Dutton, 1943), p. 226.
34. Henry Hoke, *Blackmail* (New York: Readers Book Service, 1944), pp. 56–58.
35. Daniel Yergin, *Shattered Peace: The Origins of the Cold War and the National Security State* (Boston: Houghton Mifflin, 1977), p. 51.
36. Joseph E. Davies, *Mission to Moscow* (New York: Simon and Schuster, 1941), p. 511.
37. Ralph de Toledano and Victor Lasky, *Seeds of Treason: The True Story of the Hiss-Chambers Tragedy* (New York: Funk and Wagnalls, 1950), p. 106.
38. Connelly to Hoover, September 17, 1941, FBI 94-4-5168 refiled 62-95331; Foxworth to Hoover, September 25, 1941, 94-4-5168-3. Refiled 62-95331-X7.
39. Smith, *To Save a Nation*, pp. 170, 172.
40. Ibid., pp. 176, 178, 180.
41. Vladimir Tchernavin's *I Speak for the Silent Prisoners of the Soviets* (Boston: Hale, Cushman and Flint, 1935). Tatiana Tchernavin, *Escape From the Soviets* (New York: E. P. Dutton, 1934). See de Toledano and Lasky, *Seeds of Treason*, p. 68.
42. Whittaker Chambers, *Witness* (1952; reprint, Chicago: Regnery Gateway, n.d.), p. 463. Jordan A. Schwarz, *Liberal: Adolf A. Berle and the Vision of an American Era* (New York: The Free Press, 1987), pp. 298–300.
43. Chambers, *Witness*, p. 470.
44. Ibid., p. 473.
45. Will Brownell and Richard N. Billings, *So Close to Greatness: A Biography of William C. Bullitt* (New York: Macmillan, 1987).
46. November 11, 1942, Pegler ADL File; George Sirgiovanni, *An Undercurrent of Suspicion: Anti-Communism in America During World War II* (New Brunswick, NJ: Transaction Publishers, 1990), p. 138; *New York Times*, February 11, 1943, p. 3.
47. Cited in Sirgiovanni, *An Undercurrent of Suspicion*, p. 149.
48. Ibid., pp. 148, 160, 161, 162.
49. Ibid., p. 161.

50. Ibid., p. 151.
51. Ibid., p. 152.
52. Ibid., pp. 147, 154–55.
53. Ibid., p. 158.
54. Ibid., pp. 157, 158, 163.
55. Ibid., p. 148.
56. Ibid., p. 95.
57. Ibid., p. 97.
58. Ibid., pp. 101, 102, 103.
59. Ibid., pp. 104, 106.
60. Ibid., p. 99.
61. Ibid., pp. 106, 107.
62. Ibid., p. 108.
63. Ibid., pp. 112, 114.
64. Ibid., p. 113.
65. This discussion follows Ronald Radosh, *American Labor and United States Foreign Policy* (New York: Random House, 1969), pp. 307–310. Philip Taft, quoted in Radosh, p. 306.
66. Hook, *Out of Step*, p. 314; Sirgiovanni, *An Undercurrent of Suspicion*, pp. 180–81.
67. Cited in Sirgiovanni, *An Undercurrent of Suspicion*, p. 75.
68. Ibid., p. 78.
69. Ibid., pp. 81, 88.
70. Ibid., pp. 89, 90, 135, 136, 138.
71. Ibid., pp. 138–39.
72. Ibid., p. 139.
73. Ribuffo, *The Old Christian Right*, p. 188.
74. Carlson, *Undercover*, p. 519.
75. Ibid., p. 191.
76. Ribuffo, *The Old Christian Right*, pp. 192–93.
77. Cited in Sirgiovanni, *An Undercurrent of Suspicion*, p. 168.
78. Lawrence Dennis and Maximilian St. George, *A Trial on Trial: The Great Sedition Trial of 1944* (New York: National Civil Rights Committee, 1945), pp. 359, 361.
79. Ibid., pp. 53, 459.
80. Ribuffo, *The Old Christian Right*, p. 201.
81. Sirgiovanni, *An Undercurrent of Suspicion*, p. 90.
82. Klehr and Haynes, *The American Communist Movement*, p. 97.
83. Ibid., pp. 99, 101.
84. *PM*, March 22, 1945, in Steele Collection, Box 379, Hoover Institution. A "Town Meeting of the Air" discussion on "How Can Russia and America Live

in Peace?" for August 2, 1945, was typical of the atmosphere of the day. The participants were William L. White, Louis Fischer, Walter Duranty, and Vera Micheles Dean.

85. Ribuffo, *The Old Christian Right*, p. 193.

Chapter 8. Cold War Anticommunism

1. For a comprehensive history of the origins and course of the cold war, see Walter LeFeber, *America, Russia and the Cold War, 1945–1992* (New York: McGraw-Hill, 1991); Stephen E. Ambrose, *Rise to Globalism: American Foreign Policy Since 1938* (London: Penguin, 1971); and Hugh Thomas, *Armed Truce: The Beginnings of the Cold War* (New York: Atheneum, 1987). See also Dean Acheson, *Present at the Creation: My Years in the State Department* (New York: W. W. Norton, 1969).

2. *Catholic Herald Citizen*, August 26, 1944, quoted in George Sirgiovanni, *An Undercurrent of Suspicion: Anti-Communism in America During World War II* (New Brunswick, NJ: Transaction Publishers, 1990), p. 158.

3. Donald F. Crosby, S.J., *God, Church, and Flag: Senator Joseph R. McCarthy and the Catholic Church, 1950–1957* (Chapel Hill: University of North Carolina Press, 1978), p. 10.

4. Daniel Yergin, *Shattered Peace* (Boston: Houghton Mifflin, 1977), pp. 122–32.

5. Irving Howe and Lewis Coser, *The American Communist Party* (New York: Praeger, 1962), pp. 437–49. Joseph R. Starobin, *American Communism in Crisis, 1943–1957* (1972; reprint, Berkeley: University of California Press, 1975).

6. Hoover to Vaughan, Jan. 4, 1946, Subject File FBI P, President's Secretary's File, Harry S. Truman Library, Independence, MO. For the Easter crisis memo, see Hoover to Attorney General, Subject File Communist, President's Secretary's File, HST Library. For the uprisings in France, see Hoover to Vaughan, Feb. 15, 1946, Subject File FBI H, President's Secretary's File, HST Library. For more war warnings, see Hoover to Attorney General, Oct. 12, 1946, Subject File FBI S, President's Secretary's File, HST Library; Hoover to Vaughan, March 25, 1946, PSF 60, Hoover to Attorney General, June 20, 1946, Hoover to Vaughan, July 30, 1946, Hoover to Allen, September 10, 1946, Subject File FBI Communist, HST Library.

7. Crosby, *God, Church, and Flag*, p. 30. Two years later Sheen pleaded for Eastern European Catholicism in *Communism and the Conscience of the West* (Indianapolis: Bobbs-Merrill, 1948).

8. Crosby, *God, Church, and Flag*, pp. 16–18.

9. In 1950 there were two inquiries into sensational charges that the Justice Department had fixed the case: one by a Senate panel under Millard Tydings, and another by a New York grand jury. Those suspicions have recently been

proven to have been correct. For a balanced and detailed treatment of the case, see Earl Latham, *The Communist Controversy in Washington* (Cambridge, MA: Harvard University Press, 1966), pp. 203–16. Also see the *Nation*, June 17, 1950. Harvey Klehr and Ronald Radosh, "Anatomy of a Fix," *New Republic*, April 21, 1986, trace the methods used by the influential Washington lawyer Tommy Corcoran to have charges against John Stewart Service dropped; they surmise the motive for the Justice Department's reluctance to prosecute the case was to avoid providing opponents of Chaing Kai-shek a forum for publicizing the failures of the administration's China policy. For an earlier narrative of the case and its background, see Ralph de Toledano, *Spies, Dupes, and Diplomats* (New York: Duell, Sloan and Pearce, 1952). For Hoover's resentment of Clark and the Justice Department, see Nichols to Hoover, February 24, 1955, FBI File 94-3-4-317-366, in which Nichols says it not would be "in good taste to express our real feelings on Tom Clark," and Hoover to Tolson et al., May 31, 1950, "Jaffe II," Nichols Official and Confidential File, FBI. While Radosh thinks that Hoover acquiesced in the cover-up to avoid revealing the wiretaps he was maintaining on Tommy Corcoran at Truman's request, Louis Nichols informed Peyton Ford on May 29, 1950 that while the Bureau did not want to admit the wiretapping, it was prepared to do so "and point out we were ordered to do this." Given Hoover's dislike for Truman and Clark, he probably would not have minded revealing that he had been tapping one of Truman's enemies on orders from the White House. Nichols to file, May 29, 1950, "Jaffe I," Nichols O & C, FBI. See also Anthony Cave Brown, *Wild Bill Donovan: The Last Hero* (New York: Times Books, 1982) and Mark Riebling, *Wedge: The Secret War Between the FBI and CIA* (New York: Knopf, 1994) for details on FBI suspicions about Communist infiltration of the OSS and CIA.

10. See "Underground Soviet Espionage Organization (NKVD) in Agencies of the United States Government," October 21, 1946, Justice Department, White House Central Files, HST Library. Allen Weinstein, *Perjury* (New York: Knopf, 1978), pp. 347, 356. Ralph de Toledano, *J. Edgar Hoover, The Man in His Time* (New Rochelle, NY: Arlington House, 1973), p. 249. On November 8, 1945, the day after Bentley's interview, Hoover sent his first report on White to Truman (through Harry Vaughan), stating that Harry Dexter White was a member of a Communist espionage ring. On December 4 he buttressed this with a seventy-one-page memo (dated November 27) on all of Bentley's revelations, specifically her charges against White. Still another memo, dated February 1, was delivered to the White House on February 4. On October 21, 1946, Hoover sent the White House another complete summary of Bentley's testimony. Hoover to Vaughan, November 8, 1945, Subject File FBI S, Hoover to Vaughan, February 1, 1946, Subject File FBI W, President's

Secretary's File, HST Library. See also Elizabeth Bentley, *Out of Bondage* (1951; reprint, New York: Ivy Books, 1988). This edition has a remarkable "Afterword" by Hayden B. Peake that indicates the historical accuracy of most of Bentley's allegations.

11. The Truman administration obviously thought Hoover's reports were as inconsequential as those of Martin Dies, whose "lists" of security risks were notoriously partisan and inaccurate. For example, on May 29, 1946, Hoover sent the White House an extraordinary example of the sort of unevaluated reports he often submitted to his superiors. He said that a "source believed to be reliable" said there was an enormous Soviet espionage ring in Washington that was trying to obtain information about atomic energy. Those involved were "noted for their pro-Soviet leanings": Dean Acheson, Herbert Marks, John J. McCloy, Howard C. Peterson, Henry A. Wallace, Paul Appleby, George Schwartzwalder, Edward U. Condon, Alger Hiss, Abe Feller, James R. Newman. He called special attention to Alger Hiss, Paul Appleby, Edward Condon, Schwartzwalder, and McCloy. Condon, Hoover reported, was "nothing more or less than an espionage agent in disguise." The Bureau had learned "through various sources" of the "pro-Russian" political views of Acheson, Peterson, and Henry Wallace, so "it is not beyond the realm of conjecture that they would fit into a scheme as set out above." He reminded the White House that Hiss "has been reported to this Bureau as a former member of the Communist underground organization." Hoover to Allen, May 29, 1946, Subject File FBI Atomic Bomb, President's Secretary's Files, HST Library. Walter Goodman, *The Committee: The Extraordinary Career of the House Committee on Un-American Activities* (New York: Farrar, Straus, 1968), pp. 125, 126, 131, 135, 141. George Seldes, *Witch Hunt* (New York: Modern Age, 1940), pp. 153–160. Weinstein, *Perjury,* p. 341, comments on the "general ineptitude" of the Bureau in investigating Soviet espionage during the war.

12. By 1945 there were almost one hundred "labor schools" throughout the United States, training seven thousand Catholic trade unionists annually. The nerve center of this movement was the Association of Catholic Trade Unionists (founded in 1937), with its two newspapers *The Labor Leader* and *The Wage Earner.* Crosby, *God, Church, and Flag,* pp. 21–22.

13. Later Cronin became Assistant Secretary of the Social Action Department of the National Catholic Welfare Council, was a liaison between Nixon and the FBI during the Hiss case, and was the chief speech writer for Vice President Nixon in the fifties. Joshua B. Freeman and Steve Rosswurm, "The Education of an Anti-Communist: Father John F. Cronin and the Baltimore Labor Movement," *Labor History* 33 (Spring 1992): 218.

14. John F. Cronin, S.S., *The Problem of American Communism in 1945: Facts and Recommendations* (Baltimore: St. Mary's Seminary, 1945), p. 61.

15. Ibid., p. 62.

16. Ibid., p. 81.

17. David Caute, *The Great Fear: The Anti-Communist Purge Under Truman and Eisenhower* (New York: Simon and Schuster, 1978), p. 26. Robert J. Goldstein, *Political Repression in America* (Cambridge, MA: Schenckman/Two Continents, 1978), p. 295. Peter H. Irons, "American Business and the Origins of McCarthyism: The Cold War Crusade of the United States Chamber of Commerce," in Robert Griffith and Athan Theoharis, *The Specter: Original Essays on the Cold War and the Origins of McCarthyism* (New York: New Viewpoints, 1974), p. 78.

18. David Caute, *The Great Fear: The Anti-Communist Purge Under Truman and Eisenhower* (New York: Simon and Schuster, 1978) is a detailed examination of the Loyalty Programs and their aftermath.

19. It took several years for the finality of this transfer to sink into the minds of some important members of the Anglo-American establishment. Walter Lippmann, for example, never lost his inbred conviction that the United States could always rely on Great Britain to backstop it in any crisis. Indeed, a similar conviction helps explain Franklin D. Roosevelt's outlook on world affairs.

20. Walter L. Hixson, *George F. Kennan: Cold War Iconoclast* (New York: Columbia University Press, 1989), p. 21. For a group biography of Kennan and other major architects of cold war foreign policy (Dean Acheson, Averill Harriman, Charles Bohlen, Robert Lovett, and John McCloy), see Walter Isaacson and Evan Thomas, *The Wise Men* (New York: Simon and Schuster, 1986).

21. Hixson, *George F. Kennan*, p. 42.

22. John L. Spivack, *Pattern for American Fascism* (New York: New Century Publishers, 1947); Michael Sayers and Albert E. Kahn, *The Great Conspiracy: The Secret War Against Soviet Russia* (Boston: Little, Brown, 1946); Avedis Derounian tried to repeat the success of *Undercover* with *The Plotters* (New York: E. P. Dutton, 1946).

23. Harvey Klehr and John Earl Haynes, *The American Communist Movement: Storming Heaven Itself* (New York: Twayne Publishers, 1992), p. 111.

24. Norman Markowitz, "A View from the Left: From the Popular Front to Cold War Liberalism," in Robert Griffith and Athan Theoharis (eds.), *The Specter: Original Essays on the Cold War and the Origins of McCarthyism* (New York: New Viewpoints, 1974), p. 109.

25. Markowitz, "A View from the Left," p. 112.

26. Arthur M. Schlesinger, Jr., *The Vital Center: The Politics of Freedom* (Boston: Houghton Mifflin, 1949), p. 166.

27. Quote is by James Wechsler, liberal editor of the *New York Post*. Steven M. Gillon, *Politics and Vision: The ADA and American Liberalism, 1947–1985* (New York: Oxford University Press, 1987), p. 55. For critical discussions of the liberal attack on the Wallace campaign, see Norman D. Markowitz, *The*

Rise and Fall of the People's Century: Henry A. Wallace and American Liberalism, 1941–1948 (New York: The Free Press, 1973), and Curtis D. MacDougall, *Gideon's Army* (New York: Marzani and Munsell, 1965).

28. Klehr and Haynes, *The American Communist Movement*, p. 116.
29. Ibid., p. 120.
30. Ibid., p. 122.
31. Ibid., p. 125.
32. On the strategy of rebuilding Europe, see Charles L. Mee, *The Marshall Plan: The Launching of the Pax Americana* (New York: Simon and Schuster, 1984); Gregory A. Fossedal, *Our Finest Hour: Will Clayton, the Marshall Plan, and the Triumph of Democracy* (Stamford: Hoover Institution Press, 1993); Sallie Pisani, *The CIA and the Marshall Plan* (Lawrence: University of Kansas Press, 1991); Peter Duignan and L. H. Gann, *The Rebirth of the West* (Cambridge, MA: Blackwell, 1992).
33. Schlesinger, *Vital Center*, pp. 97; 224; 239.
34. Ibid., pp. 101, 102, 128.
35. Ibid., pp. 204, 210.
36. Ibid., p. 253.
37. Ibid., p. x. George F. Kennan's "Mr. X" article in *Foreign Affairs* also predicted that the Soviet threat would stir Americans to moral reform and a new faith in freedom. In the same vein, *Time* magazine predicted that the challenge of the cold war would inaugurate an "American century," as the nation rose to greatness in response to the challenge of Communist aggression. To support this idea, *Time* embraced Arnold Toynbee's theory that the creativity of a people was stimulated by challenges from rival civilizations.
38. James Burnham, *The Struggle for the World* (New York: John Day, 1945), p. 4. For a thorough treatment of Burnham's career, see Kevin J. Smant, *How Great the Triumph: James Burnham, Anticommunism, and the Conservative Movement* (Lanham, MD: University Press of America, 1992).
39. Kevin J. Smant, "James Burnham and American Anti-Communism," unpublished paper in possession of the author, p. 3.
40. Schlesinger, *Vital Center*, pp. 168, 169.
41. Sidney Hook, *Out of Step: An Unquiet Life in the 20th Century* (New York: Harper and Row, 1987), p. 389.
42. George Orwell and William Barrett, quoted in Peter Coleman, *The Liberal Conspiracy: The Congress for Cultural Freedom and the Struggle for the Mind of Postwar Europe* (New York: The Free Press, 1989), p. 2.
43. Hook, *Out of Step*, p. 389.
44. Coleman, *The Liberal Conspiracy*, p. 7.
45. Ibid., p. 15.
46. Ibid., p. 19.

47. Ibid., pp. 31, 39. Raymond Aron, *Memoirs: Fifty Years of Political Reflections* (New York: Holmes and Meier, 1990), especially p. 174.

48. Iain Hamilton, *Koestler, A Life* (New York: Macmillan, 1982), p. 199.

49. Coleman, *The Liberal Conspiracy*, pp. 29, 33.

50. Ibid., p. 37.

51. Ibid., p. 41.

53. Ibid., p. 48. See Rhodri Jeffreys-Jones, *The CIA and American Democracy* (New Haven: Yale University Press, 1989), p. 69.

53. There was a library of anticommunist novels that would grow over the next few years, including such works as John Dos Passos, *Adventures of a Young Man* (New York: Harcourt Brace, 1939); Ralph Ellison, *Invisible Man* (New York: Random House, 1952); Lionel Trilling, *The Middle of the Journey* (New York: Viking, 1947); Richard Wright, *The Outsider* (New York: Harpers, 1953).

54. This discussion follows Ernest R. May, "Introduction," *American Cold War Strategy: Interpreting NSC 68* (New York: Bedford, 1993), which includes the text of the document. The events are also covered in Strobe Talbott, *The Master of the Game: Paul Nitze and the Nuclear Age* (New York: Knopf, 1988), pp. 54–59. Also Paul H. Nitze, *From Hiroshima to Glasnost: At the Center of Decision, a Memoir* (New York: Grove-Weidenfeld, 1989), pp. 82–100.

55. NSC-68, in May, *American Cold War Strategy*, pp. 26–27.

56. Ibid., p. 35.

57. Ibid., p. 52.

58. Ibid., pp. 27–28.

59. Ibid., pp. 27–28, 43.

60. Hoover's cold war custodial detention programs originated in a June 1940 discussion between Hoover, Attorney General Jackson, and Secretary of War Stimson over emergency plans for dealing with alien enemies. Jackson had the Justice Department, not the Bureau, assume this responsibility, and they stayed within the Department until 1943, when Biddle ordered the program terminated. Hoover, however, disobeyed and ordered that the program be continued under the new name of the Security Index. Senate Select Committee, *Final Report*, Book III, pp. 418, 420–21.

61. Ladd to Hoover, February 27, 1946, in Senate Select Committee, *Final Report*, Book III, p. 430.

62. For an exhaustive description of the development of this effort to influence public opinion through the media, see Kenneth O'Reilly, *Hoover and the Un-Americans* (Philadelphia: Temple University Press, 1983), pp. 75–100 and passim.

63. The Security Index, Hoover told Clark, included "known members of the Communist Party, USA; strongly suspected members of the Communist Party; and persons who have given evidence through their activities, utterances and

affiliations of their adherence to the aims and objectives of the party and the Soviet Union." (Ladd to Hoover, February 27, 1946, Hoover to Attorney General, March 8, 1946, Hoover to Attorney General, Sept. 5, 1946, cited in Senate Select Committee, *Final Report*, Book III, p. 430, 8.

64. Roosevelt had always been able to limit the damage caused by HUAC's forerunner, the Dies Committee, but Truman did not have FDR's ability to overawe congressmen, and, more importantly, the Dies Committee had been a Democratic committee. In 1947 HUAC was under the control of Republicans who smelled Presidential blood on the water in November 1947 and were going into a feeding frenzy in anticipation of 1948. The new chairman was Republican J. Parnall Thomas of New Jersey, but the brains and energy were supplied by that rising star in the anticommunist firmament, Richard M. Nixon, the young congressman from California.

65. Earl Latham, *The Communist Controversy in Washington* (Cambridge, MA: Harvard University Press, 1966), pp. 373–93. All quotes are from Hoover's testimony before HUAC, reprinted in the *Congressional Record, Appendix*, March 28, 1947, p. A1409-A1412.

66. When *Newsweek* ran a feature on "Communism and Its Influence in America" it turned to Hoover, "the one responsible Federal official most directly concerned with Communism and Communists." *Newsweek*, June 9, 1947, p. 30.

67. Peter H. Irons, "American Business and the Origins of McCarthyism," in Griffith and Theoharis, *The Specter*, p. 83.

68. John Cogley, *Report on Blacklisting, I—Movies* (n.c.: Fund for the Republic, 1956), p. 22.

69. Ibid., p. 55.

70. Ibid., pp. 63, 64.

71. Garry Wills, *Reagan's America: Innocents at Home* (Garden City, NY: Doubleday, 1987), pp. 220–21, 234, 254.

72. Ronald Reagan, *An American Life* (New York: Pocket Books, 1990), p. 113.

73. Wills, *Reagan's America*, pp. 248, 250.

74. Ibid., p. 255.

75. Reagan, *An American Life*, pp. 115, 121; Wills, *Reagan's America*, p. 253.

76. Reagan, *An American Life*, p. 115.

77. Allen Weinstein, *Perjury: The Hiss-Chambers Case* (New York: Knopf, 1978), pp. 340–41, 349, 351. Chambers first talked to Adolf Berle in the State Department in 1939, and had incorrectly assumed that Berle had passed the information along to the FBI. Actually the FBI did not get Berle's memo until 1943.

78. Weinstein, *Perjury*, pp. 357, 359, 365–67. There is a resemblance between the Hoover-Truman arrangement regarding Hiss, and Truman's erroneous recol-

lections of another deal he thought had worked out to handle the Harry Dexter White case. Truman, speaking carelessly, may have confused the cases.

79. Ibid., p. 6.

80. Ibid., p. 15.

81. Nixon gives his own version of the Hiss-Chambers affair in his *RN: The Memoirs of Richard Nixon* (New York: Grosset and Dunlap, 1978), pp. 47–71, and in *Six Crises* (Garden City, NY: Doubleday, 1962). HUAC's chief investigator, Robert E. Stripling, presented a melodramatic version of the case embedded in a red web theory in his *The Red Plot Against America* (edited by Bob Considine) (Drexel Hill, PA: Bell Publishing, 1949). The case is also analyzed in Stephen E. Ambrose, *Nixon: Volume 1—The Education of a Politician, 1913–1962* (New York: Simon and Schuster, 1987), pp. 166–96, and Herbert S. Parmet, *Richard Nixon and His America* (Boston: Little, Brown, 1990), pp. 161–81.

82. Weinstein, *Perjury*, p. 273.

83. "The body of available evidence proves that he did in fact perjure himself when describing his secret dealings with Chambers, so that the jurors in the second trial made no mistake in finding Alger Hiss guilty as charged." Weinstein, *Perjury*, p. 565. FBI informant and former Soviet espionage agent Hede Massing testified at the trial, and wrote *This Deception* (1951; reprint, New York: Ivy Books, 1987).

84. Richard Nixon, January 26, 1950, *Congressional Record*, 81st. Cong., 2nd sess., pp. 999–1000, reprinted in Athan G. Theoharis, *The Truman Presidency: The Origins of the Imperial Presidency and the National Security State* (Stanfordville, NY: Earl M. Coleman Enterprises, 1979), p. 355.

85. Ladd to Hoover, January 22, 1948; Hoover told the attorney general that in his opinion Congress would "readily" pass this legislation. Hoover to AG, January 27, 1948, both in Senate Select Committee, *Final Report*, Book III, p. 439.

86. Gil Green, *Cold War Fugitive* (New York: International Publishers, 1984), p. 26.

87. In later trials Philbrick and Calomiris would be joined as government witnesses by John Lautner, who had set up much of the Party's underground in the United States. Lautner defected to the FBI when he was falsely accused of being a double agent and expelled from the Party in January 1950.

88. Budenz had already published the story of his life in the Party, and his break with communism in *This Is My Story* (New York: McGraw-Hill, 1947). Another of the government's witnesses, Angela Calomiris, told her story in *Red Masquerade: Undercover for the FBI* (Philadelphia: Lippincott, 1950).

89. Michael R. Belknap, *Cold War Political Justice: The Smith Act, the Communist Party and American Civil Liberties* (Westport, CT: Greenwood, 1977), p. 156.

90. Hoover also found the well-publicized and highly popular Smith Act cases an

effective way of extracting increases in appropriations and manpower from Congress. Belknap, *Cold War Political Justice*, pp. 174, 175.

91. Donald F. Crosby, S.J., "The Politics of Religion: American Catholics and the Anti-Communist Impulse," in Griffith and Theoharis, *The Specter*, p. 27.

92. James F. Kearney, S. J., "The American Failure in China," *Columbia* (the Knights of Columbus magazine), December 1948. Anticommunists particularly faulted best-selling books like Edgar Snow's *Red Star Over China* (1938; reprint, New York: Bantam, 1978) and Theodore H. White and Annalee Jacoby's *Thunder Out of China* (1946; reprint, New York: William Sloane Associates, 1961) for romanticizing Chinese communism and demonizing Chiang.

93. Other anticommunists in the ACPA were Edna Lonigan, Clare Booth Luce, and Irene Corbally Kuhn. Joseph Keeley, *The China Lobby Man: The Story of Alfred Kohlberg* (New Rochelle, NY: Arlington House, 1969), p. 235. The Kohlberg ADL file, February 24, 1950, has the story of Kohlberg's founding of the American China Policy Association to fight the Institute of Pacific Relations. That file, May 25, 1950, also has Kohlberg addressing a Pro-America group in East Orange, New Jersey, claiming American China policy was influenced by Communist agents. For defenses of the IPR, see Frederick Vanderbilt Field, *From Right to Left: An Autobiography* (Westport, CT: Lawrence Hill, 1983), and Ross Y. Koen, *The China Lobby in American Politics* (New York: Macmillan, 1960), which makes many of the most extreme charges against the Lobby.

94. See Frederick Woltman, *Exposing the Red Threat to Free Enterprise and Individual Liberty* (New York: World Telegram, 1947).

95. *New York Times*, 3/15/48, p. 7.

96. Matthews Collection, Duke, Box 39, Folder 2, November 17, 1947; Box 2, February 5, 1949; *New York Times*, January 27, 1950, p. 14. See Victor Lasky (ed.), *The American Legion Reader* (New York: Hawthorn, 1953), for examples of Legion articles on communism. Ben Gitlow's *The Whole of Their Lives: Communism in America, A Personal History and Intimate Portrayal of Its Leaders* (New York: Charles Scribners's, 1948) was one of the more useful works produced by these anticommunists.

97. For a sympathetic view of the former isolationists as perceptive critics of the dangers of American globalism, see Ronald Radosh, *Prophets on the Right: Profiles of Conservative Critics of American Globalism, Charles A. Beard, John T. Flynn, Oswald Garrison Villard, Senator Robert A. Taft, Lawrence Dennis* (New York: Simon and Schuster, 1975).

98. John T. Flynn, *The Secret About Pearl Harbor* (New York: Published by the author, 1944). Flynn's *The Smear Terror* (New York: Published by the author, 1947) attacked Friends of Democracy for smearing its political enemies with pro-fascist and anti-Semitic libels. See John T. Flynn ADL file, September 7,

1946–December 25, 1947. As early as 1945 Flynn was attending meetings with anti-Semites and Roosevelt haters like Elizabeth Dilling. Flynn ADL file, January 14, 1945. Joining with Flynn were William Regnery, Maurice Frank, Harry Jung, Charles Vincent, Norman Vincent Peale, Samuel Pettingill, Merwin K. Hart, Λ. Dwight Nims, and Howard Emmet Rogers. Flynn ADL File, August 6, 1945; September 4, 1945; September 29, 1945. Hamilton Fish spent the rest of his life on the same conspiratorial delusion, eventually paying to have his *FDR: The Other Side of the Coin: How We Were Tricked into World War II* (New York: Vantage, 1976) printed.

99. John Roy Carlson, *The Plotters* (New York: E. P. Dutton, 1946), p. 82, has Edward Lodge Curran speaking at a Save America Rally in defense of Tyler Kent, in November 1945. *PM*, April 1, 1946, p. 9, reports that Hamilton Fish, Jr. was in Queens, trying to start a new anticommunist party. Supporters included Gen. Emmett O'Donnell, Robert M. Harriss, Vincent C. Rottkamp, Judge Nicholas M. Pette, and Judge Frank F. Adel. The ADL's *Facts* for May 1946 reported a revival of the American Defense Society with the participation of Laura Ingalls. *Facts*, January 1947 has a story about a riot at a Chicago Gerald L. K. Smith meeting August 4, 1946; Albert K. Dilling, Elizabeth, and son Kirkpatrick were in attendance.

100. See the Matthews files at Duke University. RGP interview with Ruth Matthews, July 30, 1988.

101. George Sokolsky ADL file, July 24, 1946; September 21, 1946; December 27, 1948.

102. Sokolsky, syndicated column, December 9, 1949.

103. Sokolsky, syndicated column, April 17, 1950 and September 19, 1950.

104. Keeley, *The China Lobby Man*, 196, 197; Kenneth O'Reilly, *Hoover and the Un-Americans* (Philadelphia: Temple University Press, 1983), p. 90. The most important articles from Levine's magazine appear in *Plain Talk: An Anthology from the Leading Anti-Communist Magazine of the 40s*, Isaac Don Levine (ed.) (New Rochelle, NY: Arlington House, 1976).

105. Isaac Don Levine ADL File, May 16, 1950; April 21, 1950; J. B. Matthews ADL File, May 24, 1950.

Chapter 9. McCarthyism

1. Thomas C. Reeves, *The Life and Times of Joe McCarthy: A Biography* (New York: Stein and Day, 1982), p. 224.

2. For the Rosenberg case, see Ronald Radosh and Joyce Milton, *The Rosenberg File: A Search for the Truth* (New York: Holt, Rinehart and Winston, 1983) and Robert Chadwell Williams, *Klaus Fuchs, Atom Spy* (Cambridge, MA: Harvard University Press, 1987).

3. See Robert Griffith, *The Politics of Fear* (1970; reprint, Amherst: University of Massachusetts Press, 1987).

4. The speech was to the Young Republicans in Eau Claire in April 1946. Reeves, *Life and Times of Joe McCarthy*, pp. 72, 84, 102.

5. Ibid., pp. 127, 128, 129.

6. He may have been encouraged to become an anticommunist activist at a famous—though perhaps apocryphal—meeting at Washington's Colony restaurant with Father Walsh, Kraus, and Drew Pearson's lawyer, William A. Roberts, when Walsh supposedly urged McCarthy to ride the Communists-in-government issue in his 1952 reelection campaign. Reeves, *Life and Times of Joe McCarthy*, pp. 203–4.

7. Reeves, *Life and Times of Joe McCarthy*, pp. 198–9.

8. Hurley to Truman, November 1945, in Reeves, *Life and Times of Joe McCarthy*, p. 218.

9. Ibid., p. 221.

10. Ibid., p. 224.

11. Ibid., p. 229.

12. Ibid., p. 288.

13. David M. Oshinsky, *A Conspiracy So Immense: The World of Joe McCarthy* (New York: The Free Press, 1983), p. 118.

14. Reeves, *Life and Times of Joe McCarthy*, p. 253.

15. Ibid., p. 263. For Lattimore's account of the case, see *Ordeal by Slander* (Boston: Little, Brown, 1950).

16. Reeves, *Life and Times of Joe McCarthy*, pp. 266–7.

17. Ibid., p. 268; Oshinsky, *A Conspiracy So Immense*, p. 122.

18. Reeves, *Life and Times of Joe McCarthy*, p. 273.

19. Freda Kirchwey, "The McCarthy Blight," *Nation*, June 24, 1950.

20. Joseph R. McCarthy, *America's Retreat from Victory: The Story of George Catlett Marshall* (1951; reprint, Milwaukee: Joseph R. McCarthy Educational Foundation, 1979), pp. 169, 171, 172.

21. *New York Times*, February 12, 1954, p. 8.

22. Ellen Schrecker, *The Age of McCarthyism: A Brief History with Documents* (New York: Bedford, 1994), p. 84. For a full account, see her *No Ivory Towers: McCarthyism and the Universities* (New York: Oxford University Press, 1986). See also Sigmund Diamond, *Compromised Campus: The Collaboration of Universities with the Intelligence Community, 1945–1955* (New York: Oxford University Press, 1992).

23. See Stefan Kanfer, *A Journal of the Plague Years* (New York: Atheneum, 1973).

24. John Cogley, *Report on Blacklisting, Vol I: The Movies* (New York: Fund for the Republic, 1956), pp. 155, 157.

25. Cogley, *Report on Blacklisting, Vol I: The Movies*, pp. 22, 110. See also Victor S. Navasky, *Naming Names* (1980; reprint, New York: Penguin, 1981).

26. Cogley, *Report on Blacklisting, Vol I: The Movies*, pp. 119, 125.

27. Ibid., pp. 134–35.

28. Ibid., pp. 1–3.

29. Ibid., pp. 26; 94. John Henry Faulk, *Fear on Trial* (1964; reprint, Austin: University of Texas Press, 1983), p. 81.

30. Cogley, *Report on Blacklisting, Vol I: The Movies*, p. 107.

31. During the forties *Firing Line* was known as *Summary of Trends and Developments Exposing the Communist Conspiracy*. Cogley, *Report on Blacklisting, Vol I: The Movies*, p. 10.

32. *Program* in Sokolsky Papers, Columbia.

33. *New York Times*, January 27, 1950, p. 14; January 28, 1950; January 29, 1950, p. 19. See, for example, President Eisenhower's message to the 1953 Conference, chaired by Daniel A. Poling, editor of the *Christian Herald*. *New York Times*, May 20, 1953, p. 39.

34. *New York Times*, April 9, 1952, p. 25. The National Council for Social Studies held that the study of communism was essential to preserve democracy (*New York Times*, November 25, 1951, p. 64); the National Education Association called for teaching about communism and all forms of totalitarianism, including the record of the Communist Party in the United States (*New York Times*, July 5, 1952, p. 17.). J. Edgar Hoover, "The Communists Are After Our Minds," *The American Magazine*, October 1, 1954. Sokolsky, syndicated column, May 28, 1952.

35. Alvin Illig, CSP, "The Church Has Turned to America," *Columbia* (Knights of Columbus magazine), March 1, 1953. *New York Times*, March 18, 1951, p. 70; June 13, 1953, p. 102.

36. *New York Times*, May 21, 1951, p. 9.

37. *Houston Chronicle*, March 6, 1953. *Our Sunday Messenger*, March 29, 1953. Walsh promptly denied that he had said any such thing: *New York Times*, June 15, 1953, p. 26; June 17, 1953, p. 26. "The Strange Case of O'Clavichord," *Columbia*, June 1, 1953.

38. Speeches by Senators Taft and Lehman. *New York Times*, March 1, 1953, p. 30. Terry Miller, *Southern Jewish Outlook*, November 19, 1954.

39. The show had the same producer as TV's "I Led Three Lives."

40. Sokolsky, syndicated column, April 29, 1952.

41. Hoover's *Reader's Digest* article was actually written by Special Agent Fern Stukenbroeker of the Crime Records Division. For an overview of anticommunist films, see Nora Sayre, "Cold War Cinema," *The Nation* (February 24, 1979; March 3, 1979), and her *Running Time: Films of the Cold War* (New York: Dial Press, 1982). Other anticommunist films include *Walk a Crooked Mile* (1948), which held that "a communist is a Benedict Arnold," *The Red Menace* (1949), *Pick Up on South Street*, and *The Atomic City*.

42. J. Fred MacDonald, *Television and the Red Menace* (New York: Praeger, 1985),

pp. 103–5. For Philbrick's story, see *I Led Three Lives* (New York: McGraw-Hill, 1952).

43. *New York Times*, May 1, 1950, p. 1; May 2, 1950, p. 6.

44. Compare this to Ignazio's Silone's famous prediction that "the final conflict will be between the Communists and the ex-Communists" in Allen Weinstein, *Perjury: The Hiss-Chambers Case* (New York: Knopf, 1978), p. 520. J. Edgar Hoover, "Secularism, Breeder of Crime," Conference of Methodist Ministers, Evanston, Illinois, November 26, 1947, Office of Congressional and Public Affairs, FBI.

45. See Sidney Hook, *Heresy Yes, Conspiracy No!* (New York: American Committee for Cultural Freedom, n.d.), originally published in the *New York Times Magazine*, July 9, 1950 and September 30, 1951, the latter section under the title "The Dangers of Cultural Vigilantism." See also Ernest Van Den Haag, "Academic Freedom and Its Defense," in *Strengthening Education at All Levels: A Report of the Eighteenth Educational Conference*, 1953.

46. *New York Times*, September 19, 1954, p. VI-4; November 21, 1950, p. 36. The group was the Christophers, founded by the Rev. James Keller: *New York Times*, May 2, 1950, p. 4.

47. *New York Times*, December 26, 1954, p. VI-25.

48. Harry S. Truman, *Memoirs*, Vol. II (Garden City, NY: Doubleday, 1956), pp. 272–73. See "Witch Hunting and Hysteria," Internal Security File Vol. III, Spingarn Papers, Harry S Truman Library, Independence, MO.

49. Ken Hechler, *Working with Truman: A Personal Memoir of the White House Years* (New York: Putnam's, 1982), p. 185–88. Truman was reassured to learn that after each of these periods, "the common sense of the American people soon began to tire of the alarms of the extremists" as they had "more serious things to think about." Truman, *Memoirs*, Vol. II, pp. 272–73.

50. Richard Hofstadter, "The Pseudo-Conservative Revolt," in Daniel Bell (ed.), *The Radical Right* (Garden City, NY: Anchor, 1964), p. 84. For a critique of this approach to McCarthyism, see Michael Rogin, *The Intellectuals and McCarthy: The Radical Specter* (Cambridge, MA: MIT Press, 1967).

51. Daniel Bell, "Preface," in Bell, *The Radical Right*, pp. 47–48, 57. See also Daniel Bell, *The End of Ideology: The Exhaustion of Political Ideas in the Fifties* (1960; reprint, New York: Collier Books, 1961).

52. Steven M. Gillon, *Politics and Vision: The ADA and American Liberalism, 1947–1985* (New York: Oxford University Press, 1987), pp. 77–78.

53. Gillon, *Politics and Vision*, pp. 79, 106. The debate was on American Forum of the Air, November 1953.

54. Peter Coleman, *The Liberal Conspiracy: The Congress for Cultural Freedom and the Struggle for the Mind of Postwar Europe* (New York: The Free Press, 1989),

p. 53. Burnham tried to substantiate the general thrust of McCarthy's investigations in *The Web of Subversion: Underground Networks in the U.S. Government* (New York: John Day, 1954).

55. Coleman, *The Liberal Conspiracy*, p. 54.

56. Ibid., p. 65.

57. Ibid., pp. 62, 63.

58. Ibid., p. 67; the Fiedler essay was reprinted in Leslie Fiedler, *An End to Innocence: Essays on Culture and Politics* (1952; reprint, Boston: Beacon Press, 1955), along with "Hiss, Chambers, and the Age of Innocence" and "McCarthy and the Intellectuals."

59. Coleman, *The Liberal Conspiracy*, pp. 54–55.

60. Ibid., p. 71.

61. January 15, 1952, Westbrook Pegler file, ADL; April 21, 1950, Isaac Don Levine file, ADL. Schultz, "A Letter to the Members from the National Chairman." February 1, 1951, Schultz file, AJC. April 24, 1952, Lyons file, ADL; April 13, 1952, Levine file, ADL. Arnold Forster, *Square One* (New York: Donald I. Fine, 1988), p. 120.

62. Reeves, *Life and Times of Joe McCarthy*, p. 474.

63. For a dramatic narrative of the Eisenhower administration's behind-the-scenes strategy to destroy McCarthy, see William Bragg Ewald, Jr., *Who Killed Joe McCarthy* (New York: Simon and Schuster, 1984).

64. Reeves, *Life and Times of Joe McCarthy*, p. 484.

65. Ibid., p. 480.

66. The trip was urged on McCarthy by Freda Utley and by Karl Baarslag of the American Legion. Ibid., p. 489.

67. Herbert S. Parmet, *Eisenhower and the American Crusades* (New York: Macmillan, 1972), p. 197.

68. Ibid., p. 201.

69. A "former senior FBI official" said that Kaufman "was historically pro-Hoover. . . . Why, Hoover was like Jesus Christ to him." (Maybe some irony there!) Kaufman had had personal contact with Hoover when Kaufman worked in the Justice Department as special assistant to the attorney general. Ronald Radosh and Joyce Milton, *The Rosenberg File: A Search for the Truth* (New York: Holt, Rinehart and Winston, 1983), p. 288. See Transcript of Record, *United States of America v. Julius Rosenberg, Ethel Rosenberg, Anatoli A. Yakovlev, David Greenglass and Morton Sobell*, U.S. District Court, Southern District of New York, C. 134–245, March 6–April 6, 1951, pp. 1613–14, quoted in Don Whitehead, *The F.B.I. Story* (New York: Random House, 1956), p. 317, and Radosh, *The Rosenberg File*, pp. 283–84.

70. "The primary consideration was that going through with the executions would

send a message to the Communists that from now on American nationals recruited into Soviet espionage networks would be treated with utmost sever-
ity." Radosh, *The Rosenberg File*, p. 380. Parmet, *Eisenhower*, p. 259. For a
slightly different account see H. Montgomery Hyde, *The Atom Bomb Spies*
(London: Hamish Hamilton, 1980), p. 210.

71. Reeves, *Life and Times of Joe McCarthy*, p. 499.
72. Ibid., pp. 503–4.
73. Ibid., pp. 506, 519.
74. Oshinsky, *A Conspiracy So Immense*, pp. 363, 388.
75. Ibid., p. 397.
76. Ibid., p. 399.
77. Reeves, *Life and Times of Joe McCarthy*, p. 590.
78. Ibid., pp. 591, 494.
79. Ibid., pp. 597, 604, 605.
80. Ibid., p. 635.
81. Ibid., p. 660.
82. The *Christian Science Monitor* (August 24, 25, 26, 27, 1954) ran a devastat-
    ing indictment of McCarthy's failure to discover any spies or to secure any
    indictments. James Rorty and Moshe Dechter, *McCarthy and the Communists*
    (Boston: Beacon Press, 1954), written for the Congress for Cultural
    Freedom, made the same point. Reeves, *Life and Times of Joe McCarthy*,
    p. 647.
83. *New York Times*, July 26, 1954, p. 1; April 6, 1954, p. 1.

Chapter 10. Danger on the Right

1. *New York Times Sunday Magazine*, August 20, 1961, p. 12.
2. Harvey Klehr and John Earl Haynes, *The American Communist Movement:
   Storming Heaven Itself* (New York: Twayne Publishers, 1992), p. 143. See statement by Peggy Dennis, ibid., p. 144.
3. Larry Ceplair and Steven Englund, *The Inquisition in Hollywood: Politics in the
   Film Community, 1930–1960* (Berkeley: University of California Press, 1979),
   p. 419. John Henry Faulk, *Fear on Trial* (1963; reprint, Austin: University of
   Texas Press, 1983), p. 272.
4. See Ellen W. Schrecker, *No Ivory Towers* (New York: Oxford University Press,
   1986), pp. 331–37.
5. David O'Brien, *Public Catholicism* (New York: Macmillan, 1989), p. 221.
6. John Cooney, *American Pope: The Life and Times of Francis Cardinal Spellman*
   (New York: Times Books, 1984), p. 207. Captive Nations Week was ordered
   in Public Law 86–90: Christopher J. Kauffman, *Faith and Fraternalism: The
   History of the Knights of Columbus, 1882–1982* (New York: Harper and Row,
   1982), p. 386.

7. Cooney, *American Pope*, pp. 239, 240.

8. Ibid, p. 243. The books were *Deliver Us From Evil: The Story of Viet Nam's Flight to Freedom* (1956), *The Edge of Tomorrow* (1958), *The Night They Burned the Mountain* (1960), and *Doctor Tom Dooley, My Story* (1960).

9. *University of Notre Dame Religious Bulletin*, October 6, 1951, quoted in Thomas A. Kselman and Steven Avella, "Marian Piety and the Cold War in the United States," *The Catholic Historical Review* 72 (July 1986): 412–13.

10. Kselman and Avella, "Marian Piety and the Cold War," p. 419. Kauffman, *Faith and Fraternalism*, p. 385.

11. Others included Bouscaren's *America Faces World Communism*, Nolan's *Communism Versus the Negro*, Spolansky's *Communist Trail in America*, Burnham's *Containment or Liberation*, Budenz's *The Cry Is Peace*, Mares's *Know Your Enemy*, Flynn's *The Lattimore Story*, Budenz's *Men Without Faces*, Bentley's *Out of Bondage*, Calomiris's *Red Masquerade*, Fineberg's *The Rosenberg Case, Fact and Fiction*, Evans's *The Secret War for the A-Bomb*, DeToledano's *Spies, Dupes, and Diplomats*, Flynn's *While You Slept*, and Gitlow's *The Whole of Their Lives*. There were even novels on the list: Orwell's *Animal Farm*, Serge's *The Case of Comrade Tulayev*, Pearce's *The Darby Trial*, Koestler's *Darkness at Noon*, Caldwell's *The Devil's Advocate*, Gouzenko's *The Fall of a Titan*, Hazlitt's *The Great Idea*, Helen MacInnes's *Neither Five Nor Three*, and Soloviev's *When the Gods Are Silent*. See the Order of the Knights of Pythias in Cooperation with the All-American Conference to Combat Communism, *Suggested Reading List on Communism and How to Combat It*, September 1954, Matthews Papers, Duke University Library, Durham, NC.

12. American Legion File, Matthews Papers.

13. *Freedom's Facts*, March 1956, p. 2; January 1957, p. 2

14. Lowell (Massachusetts) High School's Lectures on Communism were described in the *New York Times*, May 4, 1958, IV-9. Pennsylvania started a two-week course for high school seniors and juniors: *New York Times*, December 10, 1956, p. 19. The ABA endorsed the Florida Bar Association program for high schools: *New York Times*, February 11, 1957, p. 10; February 19, 1957, p. 14. Cardinal Cushing urged that high schools have courses in communism: *New York Times*, June 22, 1959, p. 16. The Legion's Americanism Committee endorsed a call by Allen Dulles for high school courses: *New York Times*, August 24, 1960, p. 7. Dulles's call was endorsed again the next year by the ABA: *New York Times*, February 17, 1961, p. 25. Massachusetts had a TV course on communism for the high schools in 1961: *New York Times*, October 8, 1961, p. 13. Ambassador Boland urged a course in communism be required for graduation from Catholic schools, in a speech at New York City's St. John's University: *New York Times*, June 11, 1962, p. 15. In 1963, educational panels in New York (*New York Times*, May 5, 1963, p. 64) and Illinois (*New York Times*, September 22, 1963, p. 68) called

on high schools to teach about the Communist issue, as did Conant of Harvard: *New York Times*, July 16, 1957, p. 9. Columbia: *New York Times*, October 24, 1961, p. 30.

15. Eugene Lyons testified on "The Crimes of Stalin," on September 4, 1959. See Box 7, Martin Dies Collection, Sam Houston Regional Library and Research Center, Liberty, TX.

16. Wallace to Hoover, November 3, 1959, Lyons file. Hearst Magazines to Hoover, November 14, 1956, Lyons ADL file. Eugene Lyons, "The Coming Revolution," *Human Events*, June 15, 1957, cited in Lyons ADL file. Eugene Lyons, "Negotiating with the Kremlin," *Reader's Digest*, April 1958, pp. 1–11. Eugene Lyons, "Seeing Through the Reds," speech to the Chicago Executives Club, May 8, 1959.

17. *Militant Liberty: A Program of Evaluation and Assessment of Freedom* (Washington, DC: U.S. Government Printing Office, 1955).

18. Arnold Forster and Benjamin R. Epstein, *Danger on the Right: The Attitudes, Personnel and Influence of the Radical Right and Extreme Conservatives* (New York: Random House, 1964), pp. 68–86.

19. J. Edgar Hoover provided the book's "summary." Walter Goodman, *The Committee: The Extraordinary Career of the House Committee on Un-American Activities* (New York: Farrar, Straus and Giroux, 1968), p. 397.

20. See Lowman to Walter, November 22, 1954, Circuit Riders File, Matthews Papers, Duke. Lowman emphasizes to Walter that the source for his report on Bishop Oxnam was J. B. Matthews. In another letter from Matthews to Lowman, April 29, 1955, Matthews offers a complete file on the Methodist clergy for $2,000. For Kohlberg, see the file in Box 308, Matthews Papers, Duke. One of the Committee's more notable witnesses was a black FBI informant, Julia Brown, who told her story in *I Testify: My Years as an FBI Undercover Agent* (Boston: Western Islands, 1966).

21. Hoover to Jackson, September 18, 1956, enclosing "Communist Press, USA, Statements Directed Against American Society," September–December 1919, Dwight D. Eisenhower Library, Abilene, KS.

22. J. Edgar Hoover, *Masters of Deceit* (New York: Henry Holt, 1958), pp. v, 50, 253, 255, 312, 337.

23. In *The Freeman*, May 1951.

24. John B. Judis, *William F. Buckley, Jr.: Patron Saint of the Conservatives* (New York: Simon and Schuster), pp. 105, 106. William F. Buckley, Jr., and L. Brent Bozell, *McCarthy and His Enemies* (Chicago: Henry Regnery, 1954).

25. Judis, *William F. Buckley, Jr.*, pp. 18, 93–94. RGP interview with William F. Buckley, Jr., May 13, 1991.

26. Judis, *William F. Buckley, Jr.*, pp. 119, 120.

27. Ibid., p. 130.

28. The issue was dated November 19. Ibid., p. 135.

29. Ibid., pp. 150, 153.

30. Ibid., pp. 136; 176.

31. Ibid., p. 178.

32. Chambers's piece was in *National Review* 4 (December 28, 1957), p. 35. Judis, *William F. Buckley, Jr.*, pp. 161, 173.

33. Right-wing anticommunist circles firmly believed that the drive against extremism was launched by Moscow, supposedly on December 5, 1960, with a call for action against "anti-Communism, that poisoned weapon which the bourgeois uses to fence off the masses from Socialism." See *New York Times*, December 7, 1960, pp. 16–17.

34. George Barrett, "Close-Up of the Birchers 'Founder,' " *New York Times Magazine* (May 14, 1961), p. 89.

35. G. Edward Griffin, *The Life and Words of Robert Welch, Founder of the John Birch Society* (Thousand Oaks, CA: American Media, 1975), p. 190.

36. Robert Welch, *The Life of John Birch* (1954; reprint, Boston: Western Islands, 1960), p. 77.

37. Robert Welch, *The Politician* (1963; reprint, Belmont, MA: Belmont Publishing Company, 1964), p. 5.

38. Ibid., p. 15.

39. Ibid., p. 25; the famous phrase appeared only in the unpublished edition of *The Politician*. In the published editions, Welch omitted that statement and explained in a note "At this point in the original manuscript there was one paragraph in which I expressed my own personal belief as to the most likely explanation of the events and actions which this document had tried to bring into focus," p. 278 n.

40. Judis, *William F. Buckley, Jr.*, p. 88.

41. Robert Welch, *The Blue Book of the John Birch Society* (Belmont, MA: Western Islands, 1959). The book was also filled with blasts against anti-anticommunists Leon Birkhead, John Roy Carlson, and Gordon Hall (the last a veteran of the fight against America First who had transferred his attentions to the Birch Society).

42. Carroll Quigley, *Tragedy and Hope* (New York: Macmillan, 1966), p. 950.

43. Quoted in Judis, *William F. Buckley, Jr.*, p. 198.

44. Barrett, "Close-Up of the Birchers' Founder," p. 89; Stanley Mosk and Howard H. Jewel, "The Birch Phenomenon Analyzed," *New York Times Magazine* (August 20, 1961); Thomas M. Storke, "How Some Birchers Were Birched," *New York Times Magazine*, (December 10, 1961), p. 102.

45. Hofstadter's essay "The Paranoid Style in American Politics" first appeared in *Harper's* magazine in November 1964, and is reprinted together with other studies on the American right in Richard Hofstadter, *The Paranoid Style in*

American Politics and Other Essays (1964; reprint, Chicago: University of Chicago Press, 1979). For differing views on this issue see David Brion Davis, *The Fear of Conspiracy: Images of Un-American Subversion from the Revolution to the Present* (Ithaca: Cornell University Press, 1971); Seymour Martin Lipset and Earl Raab, *The Politics of Unreason: Right-Wing Extremism in America, 1790–1970* (New York: Harper and Row, 1970).

46. Harry Allen Overstreet, *The Strange Tactics of Extremism* (New York: W. W. Norton, 1964). Murray Clark Havens, *The Challenges to Democracy: Consensus and Extremism in American Politics* (Austin: University of Texas Press, 1965). Irwin Suall, *The American Ultras: The Extreme Right and the Military-Industrial Complex* (New York: New America, 1962). Brooks R. Walker, *The Christian Fright Peddlers* (Garden City, NY: Doubleday, 1964). Mark Sherwin, *The Extremists* (New York: St. Martin's Press, 1963). Donald Janson, *The Far Right* (New York: McGraw-Hill, 1963). Richard Dudman, *Men of the Far Right* (New York: Pyramid Books, 1962). Mike Newberry, *The Yahoos* (New York: Marzani and Musell, 1964). See also John H. Bunzel, *Anti-Politics in America* (1967; New York: Vintage, 1970). Welch and the Birch Society were particularly stung by the Overstreets' success in portraying the radical right as a psychological pathology, and retaliated with Edward Janisch, *What We Must Know About the Overstreets* (Belmont, MA: American Opinion, 1959).

47. Arnold Forster and Benjamin R. Epstein, *Danger on the Right: The Attitudes, Personnel and Influence of the Radical Right and Extreme Conservatives* (New York: Random House, 1964), p. xvi. See also their *The Radical Right: Report on the John Birch Society and Its Allies* (New York: Vintage, 1967), which was commissioned by the ADL. For Forster's background, see his *Square One: The Memoirs of a True Freedom Fighter's Life-Long Struggle Against Anti-Semitism, Domestic and Foreign* (New York: Donald I. Fine, 1988). RGP's interviews with Arnold Forster and Irwin Suall.

48. Forster and Epstein, *Danger on the Right*, pp. 181–82.

49. Ibid., p. 252.

50. William L. O'Neill, *Coming Apart: An Informal History of America in the 1960's* (Chicago: Quadrangle Books, 1971), p. 48.

51. 1962, Lyons ADL file; March 14, 1962, Sokolsky FBI file.

52. Robert Welch, "The Neutralizers," tape in the Laird Wilcox Collection, University of Kansas Library, Lawrence, KS.

53. Judis, *William F. Buckley, Jr.*, p. 199.

54. Steven M. Gillon, *Politics and Vision: The ADA and American Liberalism, 1947–1985* (New York: Oxford University Press, 1987), p. 110.

55. Ibid., p. 127.

56. Ibid., p. 146.

57. O'Neill, *Coming Apart*, p. 47; Tristram Coffin, *Senator Fulbright: Portrait of a Public Philosopher* (New York: E. P. Dutton, 1966), p. 159.
58. Coffin, *Senator Fulbright*, p. 152.
59. Ibid., p. 157; O'Neill, *Coming Apart*, p. 47.
60. The title of the conference was "Fourth-Dimensional [psychological] Warfare." Coffin, *Senator Fulbright*, pp. 153–54.
61. Ibid., p. 155.
62. Ibid., p. 156.
63. Ibid., p. 157.
64. *Human Events*, August 11, 1961, p. 510, in John A. Stormer, *None Dare Call It Treason* (Florissant, MO: Liberty Bell Press, 1964), p. 77.
65. Coffin, *Senator Fulbright*, pp. 157–58.
66. Ibid., p. 158. Lee Riley Powell, J. *William Fulbright and America's Lost Crusade: Fulbright's Opposition to the Vietnam War* (Little Rock: Rose Publishing, 1984), p. 75.
67. Coffin, *Senator Fulbright*, p. 158.
68. Ibid., p. 160, 162.
69. George Benson, quoted in ibid., p. 165.
70. Victor Reuther, "The Radical Right," December 19, 1961, in William Mallett, *Reuther Memorandum* (Washington, D.C.: Liberty Lobby, 1963).
71. David O'Brien, *Public Catholicism* (New York: Macmillan, 1989), p. 222.
72. Westbrook Pegler, "Calls Cronin Book Attack on Anti-Reds," syndicated column, April 23, 1962.
73. John Cross, *What Are the Facts Behind the Smearing of Anti-Communist Americans?* (Kenosha, WI: Cross Publications, ca. 1964).
74. Frank Brophy, *Catholics, Communism and the Commonweal* (n.p.: n.d.). Brophy was one of the founders of the liberal Catholic magazine.
75. Cooney, *The American Pope*, p. 267.
76. Judis, *William F. Buckley, Jr.*, p. 186.
77. In a column on the Fund for the Republic's report on blacklisting by Marie Williams in *The Tablet*, November 24, 1962.
78. Cross, *What Are the Facts*, p. 16.
79. All-American Conference to Combat Communism, "Know Your America Week" pamphlet, November 24–30, 1963, Matthews Papers, Box 7, Duke University.
80. See a debate between James Rorty and his son Richard Rorty in the *Columbia Teachers College Record*, *New York Times*, April 22, 1962, p. 49. *New York Times*, July 3, 1962, p. 2 and July 4, 1962, p. 5. New York State's Department of Education issued a report opposing propaganda in the schools: *New York Times*, November 15, 1962. Fred Hechinger, *New York Times*, December 19, 1962, p. 6.

81. O'Neill, *Coming Apart*, p. 276.

82. For HUAC's usefulness as a *reductio ad absurdum* of anticommunism, see Charlotte Pomerantz (ed.), *A Quarter Century of Un-Americana, A Tragico-Comical Memorabilia of HUAC* (New York: Marzani and Munsell, 1963), and Eric Bentley (ed.), *Thirty Years of Treason: Excerpt from Hearings Before the House Committee on Un-American Activities, 1938–1968* (New York: Viking, 1971).

83. Klehr and Haynes, *The American Communist Movement*, p. 150.

84. Ibid., p. 152.

85. Fred J. Cook, "The Virus of Our Time," *The Nation*, May 24, 1958, pp. 478–80. The same author wrote one of the first exposés of Hoover's FBI, *The FBI Nobody Knows* (New York: Macmillan, 1965).

86. *Catholic World*, quoted in Deborah Shapley, *Promise and Power: The Life and Times of Robert McNamara* (Boston: Little, Brown, 1993), p. 88. See John Taft, *American Power: The Rise and Decline of U.S. Globalism* (New York: Harper and Row, 1989), and William Taubman (ed.), *Globalism and Its Critics: The American Foreign Policy Debate of the 1960s* (Lexington, MA: D. C. Heath, 1973).

87. Arthur M. Schlesinger, Jr., *A Thousand Days: John F. Kennedy in the White House* (Boston: Houghton Mifflin, 1965), pp. 298–99.

88. Ibid., p. 303.

89. Hence his efforts to rehabilitate the purged China hands. Kennedy believed that they had been banished for being objective about Chinese communism: They actually had been as infatuated with Mao as a revolutionary hero as the China Lobby had been enthralled by Generalissimo and Madame Chiang's anticommunism. David Halberstam, *The Best and the Brightest* (1972; reprint, New York: Penguin, 1983), 120–21, 125.

90. Shapley, *Promise and Power*, p. 187; O'Neill, *Coming Apart*, p. 71.

91. Halberstam, *The Best and the Brightest*, p. 88.

92. O'Neill, *Coming Apart*, p. 79.

93. Judis, *William F. Buckley, Jr.*, p. 199.

94. Ibid., p. 200. "Anti-Communism and the 'Radical Right'," *New Guard*, n.d. (ca. 1963).

95. Schuyler to Buckley, February 7, 1962; Archibald Roosevelt to Schuyler, February 9, 1962; Archibald Roosevelt to William Loeb, March 5, 1962, Schuyler collection, New York Public Library.

96. Herman Kahn, *Thinking About the Unthinkable* (New York: Horizon, 1962). See Charles Maland, "*Dr. Strangelove* (1964): Nightmare Comedy and the Ideology of Liberal Consensus," *American Quarterly* (Winter 1979): 697–717.

97. Gold is quoted in *Facts*, March 1964, p. 285 (published by the ADL). Richard Gid Powers, *Secrecy and Power* (New York: The Free Press, 1987), p. 384.

98. George H. Nash, *The Conservative Intellectual Movement in America Since 1945* (New York: Basic Books, 1976), p. 291.
99. Herbert S. Parmet, *Eisenhower and the American Crusades* (New York: Macmillan, 1972), p. 566.
100. Barry M. Goldwater with Jack Casserly, *Goldwater* (New York: Doubleday, 1988), pp. 143, 144, 171.
101. Ibid., p. 205.
102. Ibid., p. 176.
103. Nash, *The Conservative Intellectual Movement in America*, pp. 291–92.
104. Goldwater and Casserly, *Goldwater*, pp. 176, 181.
105. Ibid., pp. 198, 199, 204. In his memoirs Goldwater wrote, "Moyers and the New York firm will long be remembered for helping to launch this ugly development in our political history." Every time he sees Moyers on television lecturing the public on morality, Goldwater said, "I get sick to my stomach and want to throw up" (p. 199).
106. Called to his attention by conservative intellectual Henry Jaffa of Claremont College.

Chapter 11. Shame and Blame

1. Norman Podhoretz, *Breaking Ranks: A Political Memoir* (New York: Harper and Row, 1979), p. 254.
2. Tristram Coffin, *Senator Fulbright: Portrait of a Public Philosopher* (New York: E. P. Dutton, 1966), p. 321.
3. Ibid., p. 251.
4. Ibid., pp. 251, 252.
5. Walter L. Hixson, *George F. Kennan: Cold War Iconoclast* (New York: Columbia University Press, 1989), p. 231.
6. Hixson, *George F. Kennan*, pp. 239–40.
7. Coffin, *Senator Fulbright*, p. 301.
8. Ibid., p. 293. A version of this theory can also be found in David Halberstam, *The Best and the Brightest* (1972; reprint, New York: Penguin, 1983), p. 462.
9. William L. O'Neill, *Coming Apart: An Informal History of America in the 1960's* (Chicago: Quadrangle Books, 1971), p. 324.
10. Coffin, *Senator Fulbright*, p. 317.
11. Ibid., pp. 28, 29.
12. Arthur M. Schlesinger, Jr., *The Bitter Heritage: Vietnam and American Democracy, 1941–1966* (Boston: Houghton Mifflin, 1967), p. 51. See also Arthur M. Schlesinger, Jr., "Origins of the Cold War," *Foreign Affairs* 46 (October 1967):22–52. Steven M. Gillon, *Politics and Vision: The ADA and American Liberalism, 1947–1985* (New York: Oxford University Press, 1987), p. 194.

13. Gillon, *Politics and Vision*, pp. 193, 221.

14. Ibid., p. 214.

15. Timothy A. Byrnes, *Catholic Bishops in American Politics* (Princeton: Princeton University Press, 1991), pp. 42, 43.

16. Ibid., p. 95.

17. Ibid., p. 96.

18. Ibid.

19. William Appleman Williams, *The Tragedy of American Diplomacy* (Cleveland: World, 1959); David Horowitz, *The Free World Colossus* (1965; rev. ed., New York: Hill and Wang, 1971); D. F. Fleming, *The Cold War and Its Origins* (New York: Doubleday, 1961); Gar Alperovitz, *Atomic Diplomacy: Hiroshima and Potsdam, the Use of the Atomic Bomb and the American Confrontation with Soviet Power* (New York: Simon and Schuster, 1965); Gabriel Kolko, *The Politics of War: The World and United States Foreign Policy, 1943–1945* (New York: Random House, 1968); Lloyd C. Gardner, *Architects of Illusion: Men and Ideas in American Foreign Policy, 1941–1949* (Chicago: Quadrangle Books, 1970).

20. Gardner, *Architects of Illusion*, p. 317.

21. Horowitz, *Free World Colossus*, pp. 4–6.

22. Robert J. Maddox, *The New Left and the Origins of the Cold War* (Princeton: Princeton University Press, 1972).

23. Melvyn P. Leffler, *A Preponderance of Power: National Security, the Truman Administration and the Cold War* (Stanford: Stanford University Press, 1992), and, earlier, John L. Gaddis, *The United States and the Origins of the Cold War, 1941–1947* (New York: Columbia University Press, 1972).

24. Peter Coleman, *The Liberal Conspiracy: The Congress for Cultural Freedom and the Struggle for the Mind of Postwar Europe* (New York: The Free Press, 1989), pp. 222, 223. For Raymond Aron's reflections on the CIA connection, see his *Memoirs: Fifty Years of Political Reflections* (New York: Holmes and Meier, 1990), p. 174.

25. Coleman, *The Liberal Conspiracy*, p. 226.

26. May 20, 1967. Braden had been the first head of the CIA's International Organization Division.

27. Coleman, *The Liberal Conspiracy*, p. 230; Norman Podhoretz, *Breaking Ranks: A Political Memoir* (New York: Harper and Row, 1979), pp. 254–55.

28. Coleman, *The Liberal Conspiracy*, p. 231.

29. Hugh Trevor-Roper, quoted in Christopher Lasch, *The Agony of the American Left* (New York: Vintage, 1969), p. 63.

30. Coleman, *The Liberal Conspiracy*, p. 240.

31. Michael Parenti, *The Anticommunist Impulse* (New York: Random House, 1969), p. 4. The jacket subtitle of the book is noteworthy: "An examination

of how our obsession with anticommunism has warped our national commitments to freedom and prosperity, immobilized us in our efforts to remedy national ills, and caused the pursuit of a foreign policy that has led to the death and maiming of hundreds of thousands of young Americans."

32. Ibid., pp. 32, 301.
33. Ibid., p. 48.
34. Sanford J. Ungar, *The Papers and The Papers: An Account of the Legal and Political Battle over The Pentagon Papers* (1972; reprint, New York: Columbia University American, 1989), p. 55. See also Peter Schrag, *Test of Loyalty: Daniel Ellsberg and the Rituals of Secret Government* (New York: Touchstone, 1974).
35. Ungar, *The Papers and The Papers*, p. 61
36. Ibid., pp. 65, 66.
37. Ibid., p. 82.
38. Ibid., p. 83.
39. Preparing for his trial, Ellsberg said that a jury would have to decide, "Was I right in my thinking that the papers deal with high crimes by officials of our government?" Ibid., p. 274.
40. Ibid., p. 193.
41. Ibid., p. 84.
42. Neil Sheehan, "Introduction," Neil Sheehan, Hedrick Smith, E. W. Kenworthy, and Fox Butterfield [of the *New York Times*] (eds.), *The Pentagon Papers* (New York: Bantam, 1971), p. xii.
43. Sheehan, "Introduction," *The Pentagon Papers*, pp. xiii, xv.
44. Ungar, *The Papers and The Papers*, p. 37.
45. Ibid., p. 241. The Plumbers of the June 17, 1972, Watergate burglary were created to investigate the Ellsberg leak of the Pentagon Papers after J. Edgar Hoover declined to press a full-scale investigation. Howard Hunt and G. Gordon Liddy burglarized the offices of Ellsberg's psychiatrist on September 3, 1971. This was revealed April 26, 1972, and led to dismissal of charges against Ellsberg on May 11, 1973.
46. Ibid., p. 258.
47. Ibid., p. 278.
48. Archie Robinson, *George Meany and His Times: A Biography* (New York: Simon & Schuster, 1981), pp. 396–97.
49. Ibid., p. 399.
50. Ibid., p. 399.
51. John B. Judis, *William F. Buckley, Jr.: Patron Saint of the Conservatives* (New York: Simon & Schuster, 1988), p. 388.
52. Podhoretz, *Breaking Ranks*, p. 250.
53. Ibid., pp. 251, 252.
54. Ibid., p. 338.

55. Ibid., p. 173.
56. Ibid., p. 308.

Chapter 12. National Scapegoat

1. "The President's Address at Commencement Exercises at the University of Notre Dame, May 22, 1977," *Presidential Documents: Jimmy Carter*, 1977, vol. 13. no. 22:774. See also *New York Times*, May 23, 1977, p. 12.

2. See some of the bitter exposés of FBI domestic intelligence, such as Frank J. Donner, *The Age of Surveillance: The Aims and Methods of America's Political Intelligence System* (New York: Knopf, 1980); Pat Watters and Stephen Gillers (eds.), *Investigating the FBI* (Garden City, NY: Doubleday, 1973);. Cathy Perkus (ed.), *COINTELPRO: The FBI's Secret War on Political Freedom* (New York: Monad, 1975). Later, but in the same vein, Athan G. Theoharis and John Stuart Cox, *The Boss: J. Edgar Hoover and the Great American Inquisition* (Philadelphia: Temple University Press, 1988); William W. Keller, *The Liberals and J. Edgar Hoover* (Princeton: Princeton University Press, 1989).

3. Their success may be judged from the appearance of such works as Robert Ludlum, *The Chancellor Manuscript* (New York: Dial, 1977) and Irving Wallace, *The R Document* (New York: Simon and Schuster, 1976), novels which make use of J. Edgar Hoover as a demonic figure at the center of a government conspiracy against the country. See also Richard Gid Powers, *G-men: Hoover's FBI in American Popular Culture* (Carbondale: Southern Illinois University Press, 1983).

4. Senate Resolution 21, 94th Congress, 1975. U. S. Senate, Select Committee to Study Governmental Operations with Respect to Intelligence Activites, *Final Report*, Intelligence Activities and the Rights of Americans, Book II. 94th Cong., 2nd sess., Report No. 94-755, p. 1.

5. U. S. Senate, Select Committee to Study Governmental Operations with Respect to Intelligence Activites, *Final Report*, Supplementary Detailed Staff Reports on Intelligence Activities and the Rights of Americans, Book III. 94th Cong., 2nd sess., Report 94-755, Serial 13133–5, p. 377.

6. Ibid., pp. 483, 489.

7. Ibid., p. 375.

8. Ibid., p. 376.

9. Ibid., p. 391.

10. Ibid., pp. 405, 413.

11. Ibid., p. 394.

12. Ibid., pp. 398, 399.

13. Senate Select Committee to Study Governmental Operations with Respect to Intelligence Activities, 94th Cong. 2nd sess., *Final Report* (94-755), Book III, p. 3.

14. Testimony of Retired Special Agent Arthur Murtagh, U.S. House, Select Committee on Intelligence, *Hearings*, U S. Intelligence Agencies and Activities: Domestic Intelligence Programs, Part 3, 94th Cong., 1st sess., p. 1048.

15. Senate, Select Committee, Supplementary Detailed Staff Reports, Book III, p. 77.

16. *New York Times*, February 18, 1977; May 17, 1978, p. 19. Renegade CIA agent Philip Agee made a career out of CIA exposés. See Philip Agee and Louis Wolf, *Dirty Work: The CIA in Western Europe* (New York: Dorset Press, 1978); John Stockwell, *In Search of Enemies: A CIA Story* (New York: W. W. Norton, 1978).

17. See Richard Appignanesi, *Marx for Beginners* and *Lenin for Beginners*, *New York Times*, May 13, 1978, p. VII-14. *New York Times*, June 1, 1979, p. III-24. Dr. James K. Lyon of the University of California condemned the FBI for having kept files on Bertolt Brecht: *New York Times*, March 31, 1979, p. 12. Also see *New York Times*, April 3, 1979, p. 18; November 11, 1980, p. 23. Senate, Select Committee, Supplementary Detailed Staff Reports, Book III, p. 447.

18. Murrow: *New York Times*, March 4, 1979, p. IV-31. McCarthy: *New York Times*, April 24, 1979, p. III-19. *New York Times*, May 12, 1979, p. 11. "Review" of *Robert Oppenheimer, Letters and Recollections*, by Alice Kimball Smith and Charles Weiner, *New York Times*, May 11, 1980, p. VII-9. Hiss: *New York Times*, June 22, 1979, p. III-26; March 9, 1980, p. 46.

19. *New York Times*, March 26, 1980, p. II-1. Eugene P. Link, *Labor-Religion Prophet: The Times and Life of Harry F. Ward* (Boulder, CO: Westview Press, 1984), p. 104. *New York Times*, January 21, 1977.

20. Larry Ceplair and Steven Englund, *The Inquisition in Hollywood: Politics in the Film Community, 1930–1960* (Berkeley: University of California Press, 1979), p. 421. See *New York Times*, August 14, 1977, p. 46, for an obituary of John Howard Lawson; see related editorial on August 16 and a letter from Ring Lardner Jr., August 26. Blacklisting of Vonne Dogfrey, *New York Times*, January 19, 1980, p. 23. Obituary for Gene Weltfish, *New York Times*, August 5, 1980, p. II-10.

21. *New York Times*, May 24, 1978, p. III-22. Muriel Rukeyser on the executions, *New York Times*, June 19, 1978, p. 19. *New York Times*, July 16, 1979, p. 16; January 27, 1980, p. IV-18; January 27, 1980.

22. *New York Times*, March 20, 1977, p. IV-16; February 2, 1978, p. 16. *Time Magazine* ran an abridgement of Weinstein's book, which Hiss called "another inaccurate harassment." *New York Times*, April 25, 1978, p. 36. *Times* columnist Walter Goodman commented that only a conspiracy mentality could explain those who still held to a belief in Hiss's innocence, despite the fact that Weinstein's book presents seemingly irrefutable evidence of his guilt. *New York Times*, January 26, 1979, p. III-20.

23. Podhoretz, *Breaking Ranks*, p. 253.

24. *New York Times*, February 24, 1977, p. 34; March 26, 1977; April 4, 1977, p. 8; May 2, 1977, p. 1. For anguish over this by an old anticommunist, see Robert Morris, *Self-Destruct: Dismantling America's Internal Security* (New Rochelle, NY: Arlington House, 1979).

25. Paul Johnson, *Modern Times: The World from the Twenties to the Eighties* (1983; reprint New York: Harper and Row, 1985), p. 674.,

26. Patrick Glynn, *Closing Pandora's Box: Arms Races, Arms Control, and the History of the Cold War* (New York: Basic Books, 1992), pp. 277, 278.

27. *Presidential Documents: Jimmy Carter*, 1977, vol. 13, no. 22:774. *New York Times*, May 23, 1977, p. 12.

28. John B. Judis, *William F. Buckley, Jr.: Patron Saint of the Conservatives* (New York: Simon and Schuster, 1988), pp. 395–96. Norman Podhoretz, *The Present Danger* (New York: Simon & Schuster, 1980), pp. 46–47. *New York Times*, May 14, 1978, p. IV-19; July 14, 1978; July 24, 1978.

29. Judis, *William F. Buckley, Jr.*, p. 402.

30. Schuyler: *New York Times*, September 7, 1977; Schultz: ibid., April 25, 1978. Robert Morris, *Dismantling America's Internal Security* (New Rochelle, NY: Arlington House, 1979).

31. Timothy A. Byrnes, *Catholic Bishops in American Politics* (Princeton: Princeton University Press, 1991), pp. 97, 98.

32. Committee of Ten Million, *Newsletter*, October 20, 1979; August 15, 1980, Laird Wilcox Collection, University of Kansas Library, Lawrence, KA. For a look at the lunatic right in its later manifestations, see Alan Crawford, *Thunder on the Right: The "New Right" and the Politics of Resentment* (New York: Pantheon, 1980); ADL, *Extremism on the Right* (New York: ADL, 1988); James Aho, *The Politics of Righteousness: Idaho Christian Patriotism* (Seattle: University of Washington Press, 1990); Phillip Finch, *God, Guts, and Guns: A Close Look at the Radical Right* (New York: Putnam, 1983).

33. Revilo P. Oliver to Curtis Dall, n.d. (ca. July 1970), Wilcox Collection, University of Kansas.

34. David Macko to Clifford Barker, November 28, 1985; December 1, 1985. Wilcox Collection, University of Kansas.

35. Frank P. Mintz, *The Liberty Lobby and the American Right* (Westport, CT: Greenwood, 1985), p. 85.

36. Memorandum on the *Spotlight*, April 2, 1980; *John Birch Society Bulletin*, June 1977; Russell W. Viering, "What's Wrong with the John Birch Society?" *The Liberty Bell* (July 1976), p. 11, Birch file, Wilcox Collection, University of Kansas.

37. Arthur Schlesinger, Jr., letter to the *American Historical Review* (1973): 190; David Halberstam, *The Best and the Brightest* (1972; reprint, New York: Pen-

guin, 1983), p. 799. The ADA criticized the Soviets for invading Afghanistan, for example, but called Carter's response provocative. Steven P. Gillon, *Politics and Vision: The ADA and American Liberalism, 1947–1985* (New York: Oxford University Press, 1987), p. 234.

38. Johnson, *Modern Times*, p. 673.
39. Walter L. Hixson, *George F. Kennan: Cold War Iconoclast* (New York: Columbia University Press, 1989), p. 253.
40. Ibid., pp. 254, 256.
41. Kennan, interviewed in Martin F. Herz (ed.), *Decline of the West? George Kennan and His Critics* (Washington, DC: Ethics and Public Policy Center, 1978), pp. 14, 19, 20.
42. Ibid., p. 33.
43. See Michael Scammell, "The Prophet and the Wilderness: How the Idea of Human Rights Crippled Communism," *The New Republic*, February 25, 1991.
44. Martin Malia, "A Fatal Logic," in *National Interest* (Spring 1993), p. 83. The works mentioned were *Darkness At Noon, 1984, Origins of Totalitarianism*, and *Totalitarian Dictatorship and Autocracy*.
45. Andrei D. Sakharov, *My Country and the World* (New York: Vintage, 1975), p. 6.
46. Ibid., p. 89.
47. Ibid., pp. 94, 95.
48. Ibid., p. 104.
49. Alexander Solzhenitsyn, 1975, quoted by Stephen Sestanovich, "Did the West Undo the East?" *National Interest* (Spring 1993), p. 26.
50. Judis, *William F. Buckley, Jr.*, p. 388
51. Aleksandr I. Solzhenitsyn, "A World Split Apart," quoted in Ronald Berman (ed.), *Solzhenitsyn at Harvard* (Washington, DC: Ethics and Public Policy Center, 1980), pp. 13–14.
52. James Reston, in Berman, *Solzhenitsyn at Harvard*, p. 37. Even some anticommunists had a hard time digesting the violence of Solzhenitsyn's attack on American society. Buckley's *National Review* applauded the Russian's insistence that only religious values would defeat communism, but thought that the writer was wildly off the mark in claiming that Russians were more spiritual than Americans. The Russians, to Buckley's eye, seemed far more materialistic. And those two doughty liberal anticommunists, Arthur M. Schlesinger, Jr. and Sidney Hook, both took exception to Solzhenitsyn's belief that the Western failure of nerve against communism was caused by the West's idolization of individual freedom. They insisted that in fact it had been the Western idea of freedom, and not religion, that had made the West reject and defy communism. Hook predicted that if the West once again summoned up the courage to fight communism, it would be on the basis of its commit-

ment to freedom, and not by rejecting modern society for the religiously based nationalism championed by Solzhenitsyn.

Chapter 13. *Common Sense About the Present Danger*

1. Gromyko, quoted in Patrick Glynn, *Closing Pandora's Box: Arms Races, Arms Control, and the History of the Cold War* (New York: Basic Books, 1992), p. 272.
2. Ibid., p. 265.
3. Ibid., p. 266.
4. Ibid., p. 264.
5. Paul H. Nitze, *From Hiroshima to Glasnost: At the Center of Decision—A Memoir* (New York: Grove Weidenfeld, 1989), pp. 20, 56–57.
6. Ibid., p. 294.
7. Ibid., pp. 294–95.
8. Ibid., p. 346.
9. Other members were General Daniel O. Graham, former director of the Defense Intelligence Agency, Professor William Van Cleave, an armament expert from the University of Southern California, Paul Wolfowitz of the Arms Control and Disarmament Agency, Thomas Wolfe, an Air Force Soviet expert then at Rand, Seymour Weiss, former director of the State Department's Bureau of Politico-Military Affairs, and General John M. Vogt, Jr., retired commander of the Air Force in Europe. Nitze, *From Hiroshima to Glasnost,* pp. 351, 352.
10. Ibid., pp. 352–53.
11. A name also used by an organization of the early fifties also formed to lobby for increased defense appropriations.
12. Charles Tyroler II (ed.), *Alerting America: The Papers of the Committee on the Present Danger* (Washington: Pergamon-Brassey's, 1984), p. xv.
13. Ibid., p. xvi.
14. Ibid., p. iv–xvi.
15. Archie Robinson, *George Meany and His Times* (New York: Simon & Schuster, 1981), pp. 393; 401.
16. Ibid., p. 123.
17. Jerry W. Sanders, *Peddlers of Crisis: The Committee on the Present Danger and the Politics of Containment* (Boston: South End Press, 1983), p. 221.
18. For an insightful discussion of the movement by one of its more significant figures, see Irving Kristol, *Reflections of a Neoconservative: Looking Back, Looking Ahead* (New York: Basic Books, 1983). The following is largely based on RGP interview with Norman Podhoretz, February 27, 1991.
19. Sidney Blumenthal, *The Rise of the Counter-Establishment: From Conservative Ideology to Political Power* (1986; reprint, New York: Harper and Row, 1988), p. 130.
20. Ibid., p. 131; Dennis Wrong, *Commentary,* February 1962, quoted in Norman

Podhoretz, *Breaking Ranks: A Political Memoir* (New York: Harper and Row, 1979), p. 195.

21. Ibid., pp. 196; 219. The new conservatives could also count on the scorn of their former friends in radical and liberal circles, as in Lewis A. Coser and Irving Howe, *The New Conservatives: A Critique from the Left* (New York: New American Library, 1977). Bob Woodward writes that "Casey and Buckley were members of the anti-Communist, anti-liberal fraternity in New York City. It was a very small club, maybe fifty members. There was practically a secret handshake, Buckley used to joke." Bob Woodward, *Veil: The Secret Wars of the CIA, 1981–1987* (New York: Simon & Schuster, 1987), p. 37.

22. Tyroler, *Alerting America*, p. xvi.

23. Ibid., p. 13.

24. Sanders, *Peddlers of Crisis*, pp. 247–48.

25. Sanders, *Peddlers of Crisis*, p. 194.

26. Sanders, *Peddlers of Crisis*, p. 195. Podhoretz, *Breaking Ranks*, p. 324; Moynihan quoted on p. 346; Blumenthal, *The Rise of the Counter-Establishment*, p. 124.

27. Tyroler, *Alerting America*, p. xxi.

28. Sanders, *Peddlers of Crisis*, p. 191.

29. Glynn, *Closing Pandora's Box*, pp. 279–80.

30. Sanders, *Peddlers of Crisis*, p. 210.

31. Glynn, *Closing Pandora's Box*, p. 304; Sanders, *Peddlers of Crisis*, pp. 259–60; 264.

32. Nitze, *From Hiroshima to Glasnost*, p. 355; Sanders, *Peddlers of Crisis*, pp. 207; 209.

33. Sanders, *Peddlers of Crisis*, pp. 223, 227.

34. Zbigniew Brzezinski, *Power and Principle: Memoirs of the National Security Advisor, 1977–1981* (1983; reprint, New York: Farrar, Straus and Giroux, 1985), p. 146.

35. Ibid., p. 148.

36. Kennan, quoted in Martin F. Herz (ed.), *Decline of the West? George Kennan and His Critics* (Washington, DC: Ethics and Public Policy Center, 1978), pp. 8–9.

37. Kennan, quoted in Herz, *Decline of the West*, pp. 36–37.

38. Walter L. Hixson, *George F. Kennan: Cold War Iconoclast* (New York: Columbia University Press, 1989), p. 276.

39. George Kennan, "Soviet Doves and American Hawks," speech before the Council on Foreign Affairs, November 22, 1977, quoted in Herz, *Decline of the West*, p. 54.

40. These facts were afterwards verified using the Soviets' own figures: *New York Times*, September 26, 1993, p. 1.

41. Richard Pipes, in Herz, *Decline of the West*, p. 69.

42. Eugene Rostow, in ibid., p. 121.
43. Paul Johnson, *Modern Times: The World from the Twenties to the Eighties* (1983; reprint, New York: Harper Colophon, 1985), pp. 689, 691.
44. Ibid., pp. 683–84.
45. Ibid., p. 685.
46. Brzezinski, *Power and Principle*, p. 183.
47. Johnson, *Modern Times*, p. 680
48. *New York Times*, May 6, 1977, p. 14; June 7, 1977, p. 27; January 22, 1980, p. 6; October 30, 1980, p. 1; September 28, 1980, VI, 34; October 7, 1980, p. 19.
49. Johnson, *Modern Times*, pp. 687–88.
50. Glynn, *Closing Pandora's Box*, p. 305. *New York Times*, January 1, 1980, p. A4. See also Jimmy Carter, *Keeping Faith: Memoirs of a President* (New York: Bantam, 1982), pp. 471–81.
51. Brzezinski, *Power and Principle*, p. 460.
52. Sanders, *Peddlers of Crisis*, p. 236.
53. See *New York Times*, October 7, 1980, p. 19. See also a warning by the New York Civil Liberties Union denouncing efforts to revive a House Committee for investigating internal security. *New York Times*, November 23, 1980, p. 21.
54. Hixson, *George F. Kennan*, pp. 275–76.
55. Norman Podhoretz, *The Present Danger* (New York: Simon & Schuster, 1980), p. 12.
56. Podhoretz, *Present Danger*, pp. 90–101.
57. Johnson, *Modern Times*, p. 674.

Chapter 14. To the Berlin Wall

1. Ronald Reagan, *Speaking My Mind* (New York: Simon & Schuster, 1989), p. 179.
2. Ronald Reagan, *An American Life* (New York: Pocket Books, 1990), p. 265.
3. Ibid., pp. 237–38.
4. Robert Sheer, *With Enough Shovels: Reagan, Bush and Nuclear War* (New York: Random House, 1982), pp. 41, 48. Cited in Garry Wills, *Reagan's America: Innocents at Home* (Garden City, NY: Doubleday, 1987), p. 442 n. The broadcasts were called Rostow I–VI (Ibid., p. 337).
5. This was precisely the criticism Lippmann had made of the Truman Doctrine in 1947.
6. For definitions and analysis of the Reagan Doctrine, see Christopher Layne, "Requiem for the Reagan Doctrine," in David Boaz (ed.), *Assessing the Reagan Years* (Washington, DC: Cato, 1988), p. 98. Layne points out that the term "Reagan Doctrine" did not become current until columnist Charles Krauthammer applied it to some sentences in Reagan's 1985 State of the Union address.

7. These included:

Kenneth Adelman, Director, Arms Control and Disarmament Agency

Richard V. Allen, Assistant to the President for National Security Affairs

Martin Anderson, Assistant to the President for Policy Development; Member, President's Foreign Intelligence Advisory Board

James L. Buckley, Under Secretary of State for Security Assistance, Science and Technology; Counselor, Department of State; President Radio Free Europe/Radio Liberty

W. Glenn Campbell, Chairman, President's Intelligence Oversight Board; Member, President's Foreign Intelligence Advisory Board

William J. Casey, Director of Central Intelligence

William P. Clements, Jr., Member, President's Commission on Strategic Forces

John B. Connally, Member, President's Foreign Intelligence Advisory Board

Midge Decter, Member, Task Force on Food Assistance

John S. Foster, Jr., Member, President's Foreign Intelligence Advisory Board

William R. Graham, Chairman, General Advisory Committee on Arms Control and Disarmament

Colin S. Gray, Member, General Advisory Committee on Arms Control and Disarmament

Amoretta M. Hoeber, Member, General Advisory Committee on Arms Control and Disarmament

Fred Charles Ikle, Under Secretary of Defense for Policy

Eli S. Jacobs, Member, General Advisory Committee on Arms Control and Disarmament

David C. Jordan, Ambassador to Peru

Max M. Kampelman, Chairman, U.S. Delegation to Conference on Security and Cooperation in Europe

Geoffrey Kemp, Director for Near East and South Asian Affairs, NSC; Special Assistant to the President, NSC

Lane Kirkland, Member, National Bipartisan Commission on Central America

Jeane J. Kirkpatrick, U.S. Representative to the United Nations

John F. Lehman, Secretary of the Navy

Clare Boothe Luce, Member, President's Foreign Intelligence Advisory Board

John H. Lyons, Member, President's Commission on Strategic Forces

Charles Burton Marshall, Member, General Advisory Committee on Arms Control and Disarmament

Paul W. McCracken, Member, President's Economic Policy Advisory Board

Paul H. Nitze, Chief Negotiator to Intermediate Range Nuclear Forces Talk; Special Representative for Arms Control and Disarmament Negotiations

Michael Novak, U.S. Representative to the United Nations Commission on Human Rights

Jaime Oaxaca, Member, General Advisory Committee on Arms Control and Disarmament

Peter O'Donnell, Jr., Member, President's Foreign Intelligence Advisory Board

David Packard, Member, White House Science Council

Richard N. Perle, Assistant Secretary of Defense for International Security Policy

Richard Pipes, Director of Soviet Affairs, National Security Council

John P. Roche, Member, General Advisory Committee on Arms Control and Disarmament

Eugene V. Rostow, Director, Arms Control and Disarmament Agency

Donald H. Rumsfeld, Member, General Advisory Committee on Arms Control and Disarmament

Richard M. Scaife, Member, U.S. Advisory Commission on Public Diplomacy

Richard Schifter, U.S. Representative to the United Nations

Paul Seabury, Member, President's Foreign Intelligence Advisory Board

Frank Shakespeare, Chairman, Board for International Broadcasting

George P. Shultz, Secretary of State

John R. Silber, Member, National Bipartisan Commission on Central America

Laurence H. Silberman, Member, General Advisory Committee on Arms Control and Disarmament

Herbert Stein, Member, President's Economic Policy Advisory Board

R. G. Stilwell, Deputy Under Secretary of Defense for Policy

Richard B. Stone, Member, President's Commission on Broadcasting to Cuba

Robert Strausz-Hupe, Ambassador to Turkey

W. Scott Thompson, Associate Director, Bureau of Programs, US Information Agency

Charles Tyroler II, Member, President's Intelligence Oversight Board

Joe. D. Waggonner, Commissioner, National Commission on Social Security Reform

Charls E. Walker, Member, President's Economic Policy Advisory Board

W. Allen Wallis, Under Secretary of State for Economic Affairs

Seymour Weiss, member, President's Foreign Intelligence Advisory Board

Edward Bennett Williams, Member, President's Foreign Intelligence Advisory Board

See Charles Tyroler II (ed.), *Alerting America: The Papers of the Committee on the Present Danger* (Washington, DC: Pergamon-Brassey's, 1984), pp. 5–9.

8. Garry Wills thinks the distinction between authoritarian and totalitarian originated with Ernest Lefever a year earlier. In a speech Alexander Haig delivered to the Trilateral Commission after the 1981 inauguration he made the same distinction. Wills, *Reagan's America*, pp. 348–49.

9. Joseph Persico, *Casey: From the OSS to the CIA* (New York: Viking, 1990), p. 79.

10. Bob Woodward, *Veil: The Secret Wars of the CIA 1981–1987* (New York: Simon & Schuster, 1987), p. 37.

11. Persico, *Casey*, pp. 93, 114.

12. Ibid., 123; Woodward, *Veil*, p. 53.

13. Woodward, *Veil*, p. 137.

14. William J. Casey, *Scouting the Future: The Public Speeches of William J. Casey* (Herbert E. Meyer, ed.) (Washington, DC: Regnery Gateway, 1989), pp. 141–43.

15. Woodward, *Veil*, p. 135–36.

16. Ibid., pp. 79, 113.

17. Ibid., p. 373, Christopher Layne, "Requiem for the Reagan Doctrine," in David Boaz, (ed), *Assessing the Reagan Years* (Washington, DC: Cato, 1988), p. 98: "The Reagan Doctrine has never been authoritatively defined, but its content can be inferred from various statements made by President Reagan and Secretary of State George Shultz and the writings of such neoconservative foreign policy theorists as Charles Krauthammer, Irving Kristol and Norman Podhoretz. As commonly understood, the Reagan Doctrine committed the United States to resisting Soviet and Soviet-supported aggression wherever it arose, to building U.S.-style democracies in Third World countries, and to rolling back communism by aiding anticommunist insurgencies. The Reagan Doctrine sought to create an ideologically congenial world and assumed that U.S. security required nothing less. In some quarters, moreover, the doctrine's objectives were framed more expansively to include bringing about the Soviet empire's breakup and, ultimately, the collapse of the Soviet state itself by inflicting a series of what Kristol called "small defeats" on Moscow in the Third World (presumably undermining the Soviet regime's domestic legitimacy), engaging the Kremlin in a high-tech arms race, and pressuring the Soviet Union economically."

18. Layne, "Reagan Doctrine," p. 98: "Another novel aspect of the Reagan foreign policy is a penchant for rolling back Soviet power, particularly in the Third World. This is a tendency that has not reached the surface of U.S. foreign policy since the early Eisenhower-Dulles era, although rollback was then soon submerged after our failure to intervene in uprisings in Eastern Europe, particularly in Hungary in 1956 to prevent the Soviets from snuffing out Hungary's brief rebellion and independence from the Warsaw Pact. The policy of

rollback was implicit in the orientation of the Reagan administration from its inception, though the title 'Reagan Doctrine' awaited the columnist Charles Krauthammer's exegesis of a few sentences tucked away in Reagan's January 1985 state-of-the-union address."

19. This had been prohibited in 1976 by the Clark amendment, which Casey and Reagan got repealed in 1985. Woodward, *Veil*, p. 216. William G. Hyland, *The Cold War Is Over* (New York: Random House, 1990), p. 185.

20. Woodward, *Veil*, p. 117.

21. Glynn, *Closing Pandora's Box*, p. 313.

22. Ibid., p. 319; Mark P. Lagon, review of Deborah Shapley's *Promise and Power: The Life and Times of Robert S. McNamara*, in *National Interest*, Summer 1993, p. 100. George F. Kennan, *The Nuclear Delusion: Soviet-American Relations in the Atomic Age* (1982; rev. ed. New York: Pantheon, 1983).

23. The survey was done by Daniel Yankelovich, "New Rules in American Life: Searching for Self-fulfillment in a World Turned Upside Down," *Psychology Today*, April 1981, pp. 35–91, cited in Layne, "Reagan Doctrine," p. 103.

24. Harvey Klehr and John Earl Haynes, *The American Communist Movement: Storming Heaven Itself* (New York: Twayne Publishers, 1992), p. 174.

25. The monolithic opposition among intellectuals to any revival of anticommunism can be seen in the abuse heaped on Susan Sontag for her notorious speech on behalf of Solidarity in February 1982 which was published in the *Los Angeles Times* for February 14, 1982, and then in *The Nation*. In that speech Sontag pointed out that subscribers to the *Reader's Digest* got a clearer picture of the reality of communism and life in the Soviet bloc than readers of the *Nation*, and she stated her belief that "Communism is Fascism." See reactions in *Soho News*, February 24–March 2, 1982, pp. 10–13, 42–43.

26. Strobe Talbott, *The Russians and Reagan* (New York: Vintage, 1984), pp. 3, 7. Attacking Reagan from a different direction was Sanford J. Ungar (ed.), *Estrangement: America and the World* (New York: Oxford University Press, 1985) that claimed Reagan's policies had isolated the United States from the rest of the world. Richard J. Barnet, *Real Security: Restoring American Power in a Dangerous Decade* (New York: Simon and Schuster, 1981) and *The Alliance: America-Europe-Japan, Makers of the Postwar World* (New York: Simon and Schuster, 1983) also made the argument that the Reagan foreign policy constituted a dangerous new variety of isolationism in that it conferred on the United States the right to act against the Soviets without the approval or consent of the world community.

27. Strobe Talbott, *Deadly Gambits: The Reagan Administration and the Stalemate in Nuclear Arms Control* (New York: Knopf, 1984).

28. The phrase has been attributed to George Will.

29. For a perhaps overly uncritical analysis of the Reagan administration's foreign

policy's anticommunist goals, see Peter Schweizer, *Victory: The Reagan Administration's Secret Strategy that Hastened the Collapse of the Soviet Union* (New York: Atlantic Monthly Press, 1994).

30. Reagan, *Life*, p. 301.
31. Patrick Glynn, *Closing Pandora's Box: Arms Races, Arms Controls and the History of the Cold War* (New York: Basic Books, 1992), p. 310.
32. Reagan, *Life*, p. 303; Glynn, p. 311.
33. George Weigel, *The Final Revolution: The Resistance Church and the Collapse of Communism* (New York: Oxford University Press, 1992), p. 97.
34. Ibid., p. 97.
35. Ibid., pp. 76, 87.
36. Ibid., p. 121.
37. Ibid., pp. 71–72.
38. Ibid., p. 136.
39. Ibid., p. 146.
40. Carl Bernstein, "The Holy Alliance," *Time*, February 24, 1992, pp. 29, 30.
41. Ibid., p. 31.
42. Ibid., p. 33.
43. NSDD-32 is discussed in Schweizer, *Victory*, pp. 76–77. Schweizer also discussed the NSDD-56 and NSDD-75 that escalated "neutralization" to "bankrupting" and "rolling back" Soviet power.
44. Bernstein, "The Holy Alliance," pp. 33–34. For a hostile, but well-informed survey of labor's cooperation with Reagan, see Beth Sims, *Workers of the World Undermined: American Labor's Role in U.S. Foreign Policy* (Boston: South End, 1992). For background, Ronald Radosh, *American Labor and United States Foreign Policy* (New York: Random House, 1969).
45. The phrase is Victor Navasky's, editor of the *Nation*. "Unsurprisingly, then, the Reagan Doctrine's militant anticommunism had little resonance with public opinion. Indeed, in 1982—when the mood of assertive America supposedly was at its peak—a Potomac Associates survey found that 'anticommunism as a national slogan or marching theme is increasingly on the wane, despite the Reagan Administration's attempts to emphasize it.' " Layne, "Reagan Doctrine," p. 103. See Barbara Caress and Stephen Leberstein on the history of the City College of New York's efforts to identify and dismiss Communist faculty members, *New York Times*, June 2, 1981, p. 15; William Styron on Sacco and Vanzetti, *New York Times*, June 7, 1981, p. IV-21. See Anthony Lewis, *New York Times*, November 28, 1983, p. I-23, on Penn Kimball's book on his FBI file. Senator Weicker argued that the government owed Kimball an apology, *New York Times*, December 15, 1985, p. 47. Klehr and Haynes, *The American Communist Movement*, p. 174. See Herbert Mitgang, *Dangerous Dossiers: Exposing the Secret War Against America's Greatest Authors* (New York: Don-

ald I. Fine, 1988), Natalie Robins, *Alien Ink: The FBI's War on Freedom of Expression* (New York: William Morrow, 1992), and Penn Kimball, *The File* (1983; reprint New York: Avon, 1985).

46. *New York Times*, Hiss, July 18, 1982, p. 35. The appeal was rejected the next year by the Supreme Court, October 12, 1983, p. I-21; Chambers: May 25, 1986, p. 24; August 5, 1986, p. II-5. Rosenbergs: November 6, 1982, p. 48. Inquisition: June 23, 1983, p. III-24. Morning After: November 20, 1983.

47. Glynn, *Pandora's Box*, p. 330; *New York Times*, February 19, 1981, p. 31; April 25, 1981, p. 10; May 5, 1981, p. 23. Melvin Beck, *Secret Contenders: The Myth of Cold War Counterintelligence* (New York: Sheridan Square, 1984) ridiculed counterintelligence as a hoax.

48. For example, Norman Podhoretz produced *Why We Were in Vietnam*. See Geoffrey Smith, *Reagan and Thatcher* (New York: W. W. Norton, 1991).

49. *Weekly Compilation of Presidential Documents*, June 14, 1982, pp. 764–69.

50. *Weekly Compilation of Presidential Documents*, March 14, 1983, p. 369. Reagan, *Speaking My Mind*, pp. 179–80.

51. Mockery of Reagan for speeches like this, treating him as an unsophisticated buffoon inhabiting a mental universe indistinguishable from a B-movie, became habitual in academic circles. For an example, see Michael Rogin, *Ronald Reagan, The Movie and Other Episodes in Political Demonology* (Berkeley: University of California Press, 1987). William F. Buckley, Jr., "Remarks at the *National Review* 35th Anniversary Dinner," *National Review*, November 5, 1990, p. 117.

52. Reagan, *Speaking My Mind*, pp. 179–180.

53. Ibid.

54. Glynn, *Closing Pandora's Box*, p. 329. See also Donald R. Baucom, *The Origins of SDI, 1944–1983* (Lawrence: University of Kansas Press, 1992).

55. Woodward, *Veil*, p. 293.

56. Ibid., p. 385.

57. Glynn, *Closing Pandora's Box*, p. 338.

58. The authoritative study of the affair is Theodore Draper, *A Very Thin Line: The Iran Contra Affairs* (New York: Touchstone, 1991). An insider's view is Donald T. Regan, *For the Record: From Wall Street to Washington* (New York: Harcourt Brace Jovanovich, 1988).

59. Persico, *Casey*, pp. 410–11.

60. Summarized in Woodward, *Veil*, pp. 508–9. See also Frances Fitzgerald, "Annals of Justice: Iran-Contra," *The New Yorker*, October 16, 1989, pp. 51–84.

61. *New York Times*, November 26, 1987.

62. Seymour M. Hersh, "The Iran-Contra Committees: Did They Protect Reagan?" *New York Times Magazine*, May 6, 1990, pp. 47, 61–78.

63. Ibid., p. 67.

64. Glynn, *Closing Pandora's Box*, p. 332.
65. Henry Kissinger, *Diplomacy* (New York: Simon and Schuster, 1994), p. 775.
66. Martin Anderson, *Revolution*, cited in *Wall Street Journal*, "Who Won Eastern Europe?" February 22, 1990.
67. Glynn, *Closing Pandora's Box*, p. 340.
68. Kissinger, *Diplomacy*, p. 786.
69. Glynn, *Closing Pandora's Box*, p. 358.
70. Layne, "Requiem for the Reagan Doctrine," p. 108. David Ignatius, "Reagan's Foreign Policy and the Rejection of Diplomacy" in Sidney Blumenthal and Thomas Byrne Edsall (eds.), *The Reagan Legacy* (New York: Pantheon, 1988), pp. 209, 211. Barry Goldwater with Jack Casserly, *Goldwater* (New York: Doubleday, 1988), pp. 399–400. The progressive left felt encouraged enough by events to hold a conference at Harvard in November 1988 to pronounce a post-mortem on anticommunism and its doleful impact on America and the world: see David Evanier and Harvey Klehr, "Among the Intellectualoids/ Anticommunism and Mental Health," *The American Spectator*, February 1989, pp. 28–30. For the composition of the new radical left, see Harvery Klehr, *Far Left of Center: The American Radical Left Today* (New Brunswick, NJ: Transaction Publishers, 1991). Moreover, there seemed to be a revival of the old brown-smearing technique of trying to link Reagan's (and Bush's) anticommunism with domestic or foreign neo-Nazi movements. See Russ Bellant, *Old Nazis, The New Right and the Reagan Administration: The Role of Domestic Fascist Networks in the Republican Party and Their Effect on U.S. Cold War Politics* (Cambridge, MA: Political Research Associates, 1988); Scott Anderson and Jon Lee Anderson, *Inside the League: The Shocking Expose of How Terrorists, Nazis, and Latin American Death Squads Have Infiltrated the World Anti-Communist League* (New York: Dodd, Mead, 1986); and John S. Saloma III, *Ominous Politics: The New Conservative Labyrinth* (New York: Hill and Wang, 1984). But there was a counterattack against these ideas by a new generation of young anticommunists who had had—in their own words—"second thoughts" about the "adversary culture" of the new academic left. See Peter Collier and David Horowitz, *Destructive Generation: Second Thoughts About the '60s* (New York: Summit, 1990), and John H. Bunzel (ed.), *Political Passages: Journeys of Change Through Two Decades, 1968–1988* (New York: The Free Press, 1988). See also Paul Hollander, *The Survival of the Adversary Culture* (New Brunswick, NJ: Transaction Publishers, 1988).
71. Reagan, *An American Life*, p. 682. A few years later he could say, "I could not in good conscience today call the Soviet Union an evil empire. As I write this, the Soviets have just conducted the most democratic elections since their revolution. Remarkable things are happening under Mikhail Gorbachev." Reagan, *Speaking My Mind*, pp. 168–69.

72. Reagan, *An American Life*, p. 683.

73. Lou Cannon, "Ron's Dread of Reds Gives Way to Trust," *Newsday*, December 13, 1988.

Epilogue

1. R. J. Rummel, *Lethal Politics, Soviet Genocide and Mass Murder Since 1917* (New Brunswick, NJ: Transaction Publishers, 1990).

2. Ralph Z. Hallow, *Washington Post*, November 6, 1990.

3. William F. Buckley, Jr., "On the Right, A History of the Cold War?" *National Review*, April 16, 1990, p. 62.

4. Jonathan Schell, "How We Demonized the Red Devil," *Newsday*, October 3, 1991, p. 100. E. J. Dionne, Jr., "Who Won the Cold War? New Left Historians Debate the Demise of Socialism," *Washington Post*, June 12, 1990.

5. David Warsh, "External Economics and the End of the Cold War," *Washington Post*, February 26, 1992.

6. Jim Garrison, *On the Trail of the Assassins* (New York: Warner, 1988), p. 324.

7. Edward Pessen, *Losing Our Souls: The American Experience in the Cold War* (Chicago: Ivan R. Dee, 1993), p. 11. Bud Schultz and Ruth Schultz, *It Did Happen Here: Recollections of Political Repression in America* (Berkeley: University of California Press, 1989).

8. This can be seen in otherwise valuable works such as Richard M. Fried, *Nightmare in Red: The McCarthy Era in Perspective* (New York: Oxford University Press, 1990), and Ellen Schrecker, *The Age of McCarthyism: A Brief History with Documents* (New York: St. Martin's Press, 1994), as well as the wholly irresponsible Joel Koval, *Red Hunting in the Promised Land: Anticommunism and the Making of America* (New York: Basic Books, 1994). See also Arch Puddington, "The Anti-Cold War Brigade," *Commentary*, August 1990, pp. 30–38. "Why Johnny's Not Anti-Communist," *National Review*, February 5, 1990, p. 44.

9. Michael Barson, *Better Dead Than Red!: A Nostalgic Look at the Golden Years of Russiaphobia, Red-Baiting, and Other Commie Madness* (New York: Hyperion, 1992).

10. Lou Cannon, "Ron's Dread of Reds Gives Way to Trust," *Newsday*, December 13, 1988.

11. For the early period, see Frederick Merk, *Manifest Destiny and Mission in American History* (1963; reprint, New York: Vintage, 1966). For the twentieth century, see Tony Smith, *America's Mission: The United States and the Worldwide Struggle for Democracy in the Twentieth Century* (Princeton: Princeton University Press, 1994).

12. Norman J. Ornstein and Mark Schmitt, "Dateline Campaign '92: Post Cold War Politics," *Foreign Policy* 79 (Summer 1990).

13. William G. Hyland writes that the end of communism brought to Russia a "new openness in discussing the history of Soviet foreign policy. For the first time it was admitted, albeit grudgingly, that the Soviet Union had to bear a considerable responsibility for the cold war. One historian even went so far as to assert that the West was justified in regarding the Soviet Union as a dangerous adversary that wanted to eliminate its opponents by military means. Another Soviet writer claimed that 'unquestionably' the 'severe exacerbation of tensions' in Soviet-Western relations in the late 1970s and early 1980s could have been avoided because the tensions were caused by the miscalculations and incompetence of the Brezhnev regime." William G. Hyland, *The Cold War Is Over New York* (New York: Random House, 1990), pp. 185–86.

14. Vaclav Havel, February 21, 1990, quoted in the *New York Times*, February 22, 1990. See also Vaclav Havel, *Living in Truth* (Jan Vladislav, ed.) (New York: Faber and Faber, 1990).

15. David Remnick, "The Exile Returns," *The New Yorker*, February 14, 1994, p. 77.

BIBLIOGRAPHY

Writing this book radically altered my view of American anticommunism. I began with the idea that anticommunism displayed America at its worst, but I came to see in anticommunism America at its best. That shift also changed the focus of my research. I started by searching the archives for the sensational activities of countersubversive anticommunists obsessed with uncovering plots that were, for the most part, figments of their imaginations. I learned that extremists, far from being representative of the American anticommunist movement, were for the most part digressions and distractions. The real story of American anticommunism was out in the open, and could be read in the words of responsible Americans with an anticommunism rooted in a realistic and principled view of the world.

For the most part, the archives at universities, religious and ethnic organizations, and government agencies concern the activities of anticommunist conspiracy theorists, who posed a danger to other anticommunists or even to the entire society. The record of responsible anticommunists based on a realistic assessment of communism was writ large in the popular press and in their own writings.

Archival research should start with John Earl Haynes's *Communism and Anti-Communism in the United States: An Annotated Guide to Historical Writings* (New York: Garland, 1987). Other important guides are the quarterly *Newsletter* of the Historians of American Communism, and Ellen Schrecker's "Archival Sources for the Study of McCarthyism" (*Journal of American History* 75 [June 1988]: 197–208).

The files of the FBI contain important information on both extremist and mainstream anticommunists, among them Isaac Don Levine, Eugene Lyons, George S. Schuyler, J. B. Matthews, and Ralph Easley. Since the 1930s the Anti-Defamation League of B'nai B'rith has maintained clipping files and an informant network reporting on political activity involving communism or anticommunism. These files can be viewed on microfilm at the ADL's New York headquarters, and those on Isaac Don Levine, Eugene Lyons, Robert Welch, George S. Schuyler, J. B. Matthews, John T. Flynn, George Sokolsky, and Westbrook Pegler were especially useful. The American Jewish Committee has files on Communist and anticommunist activities involving Jews, and contains important holdings on Jewish groups especially formed to combat communism such as Benjamin Schultz's American Jewish League Against Communism and the earlier American Jewish Federation to Combat Communism and Fascism.

Libraries with special strengths in the area of anticommunist extremism include the Laird Wilcox Collection at the University of Kansas (with special strengths in the area of post-World War II right-wing extremists, with large holdings relating to the John Birch Society, the Liberty Lobby and its *Spotlight*, and Elizabeth Dilling and Gerald L. K. Smith) and Brown University's Gordon Hall Collection (excellent on right-wing extremism from the forties through the seventies.) The Perkins Library at Duke University has J. B. Matthews's extensive files, as well as those of Ben Mandel. Martin Dies's papers are at the Sam Houston Regional Library and Research Center, Liberty, Texas.

The archives of Georgetown University hold the papers of Father Edmund Walsh. The archives of the U.S. Catholic Conference have the papers of Father John Ryan, as well as some relating to John F. Cronin. The archives at the Knights of Columbus headquarters in New Haven are essential for understanding Catholic anticommunism.

The Hoover Institution on War, Revolution and Peace has the George Sokolsky Papers, the Jay Lovestone Papers, and the Sidney Hook Papers, not yet open to scholars during research for this book, but the open files were exceedingly rich on Bertram D. Wolfe, Benjamin Gitlow, Theodore Draper, Paul Crouch, the *National Republic*, Karl Baarslag, Walter B. Steele, and Myers G. Lowman. A far larger collection of Theodore Draper papers is held by Emory University.

Columbia University has George Sokolsky's scrapbooks, which are very valuable because of his role in the movement, and because he so often discussed anticommunist activities in his columns. Columbia also has the papers of Lewis Corey, Carleton J. H. Hayes, Hubert Knickerbocker, Benjamin Stolberg, and Spruille Braden. George S. Schuyler's papers are in the Schomberg Collection of the New York Public Library and at Syracuse University. The manuscript division of the New York Public Library has the papers of Ralph M. Easley in its National Civic Federation Collection. The University of Oregon Library has extensive collections on conservative intellectuals, among them Eugene Lyons and John T. Flynn.

I conducted interviews with John Edgar Ruch, Louis B. Nichols, Ruth (Mrs. Isaac Don) Levine (who also maintains custody of her husband's papers), Ruth (Mrs. J. B.) Matthews, William F. Buckley, Jr., Arnold Forster and Irwin Suall of the ADL, Norman Podhoretz and Midge Decter, Hamilton Fish, Corliss Lamont, Alden V. Brown, and Don Zirkel (on Patrick Scanlan, whose papers have been lost).

Among the publications that chronicled various aspects of anticommunism were the ADL publication *Facts*, along with *American Magazine*, *American Mercury*, *The Brooklyn Tablet*, *Commentary*, *Encounter*, *Human Events*, *National Review*, and *Plain Talk*.

Acheson, Dean. *Present at the Creation: My Years in the State Department*. New York: Norton, 1969.

Adams, Samuel Hopkins. *Incredible Era*. 1939; reprint, New York: Capricorn, 1964.

Adler, Les K. *The Red Image: American Attitudes Toward Communism in the Cold War Era*. New York: Garland, 1991.

Adler, Selig. *The Uncertain Giant: American Foreign Policy Between the Wars, 1921–1941*. 1965; reprint, New York: Collier, 1969.

Agee, Philip and Louis Wolf. *Dirty Work: The CIA in Western Europe*. New York: Dorset Press, 1978.

Aho, James. *The Politics of Righteousness: Idaho Christian Patriotism*. Seattle: University of Washington Press, 1990.

Alperovitz, Gar. *Atomic Diplomacy: Hiroshima and Potsdam, the Use of the Atomic Bomb and the American Confrontation with Soviet Power*. New York: Simon & Schuster, 1965.

Ambrose, Stephen E. *Rise to Globalism: American Foreign Policy Since 1938*. London: Penguin, 1971.

———. *Nixon: Volume 1—The Education of a Politician, 1913–1962*. New York: Simon & Schuster, 1987.

Anderson, Martin. *Revolution*. San Diego: Harcourt Brace Jovanovich, 1988.

Anderson, Scott, and Jon Lee Anderson. *Inside the League: The Shocking Exposé of How Terrorists, Nazis, and Latin American Death Squads Have Infiltrated the World Anti-Communist League*. New York: Dodd, Mead, 1986.

Anti-Defamation League. *Extremism on the Right*. New York: ADL, 1988.

Aron, Raymond. *Memoirs: Fifty Years of Political Reflections*. New York: Holmes and Meier, 1990.

Avrich, Paul. *Sacco and Vanzetti: The Anarchist Background*. Princeton: Princeton University Press, 1991.

Bales, James D. (ed.). *J. Edgar Hoover Speaks Concerning Communism*. Washington, DC: Capitol Hill Press, 1970.

Barrett, George. "Close-Up of the Birchers 'Founder.' " *New York Times Magazine*, May 14, 1961.

Barson, Michael. *"Better Dead Than Red!:* A Nostalgic Look at the Golden Years of Russiaphobia, Red-Baiting, and Other Commie Madness. New York: Hyperion, 1992.

Bassow, Whitman. *The Moscow Correspondents: Reporting on Russia from the Revolution to Glasnost.* New York: Morrow, 1988.

Baucom, Donald R. *The Origins of SDI, 1944–1983.* Lawrence: University of Kansas, 1992.

Beck, Melvin. *Secret Contenders: The Myth of Cold War Counterintelligence.* New York: Sheridan Square, 1984.

Beichman, Arnold. *Anti-American Myths: Their Causes and Consequences.* New Brunswick, NJ: Transaction, 1992.

Belknap, Michal R. *Cold War Political Justice: The Smith Act, The Communist Party and American Civil Liberties.* Westport, CT: Greenwood. 1977.

Bell, Daniel (ed.) *The Radical Right.* Garden City, NY: Anchor, 1964.

———. *The End of Ideology: The Exhaustion of Political Ideas in the Fifties.* 1960; reprint, New York: Collier Books, 1961.

Bellant, Russ. *Old Nazis, The New Right and the Reagan Administration: The Role of Domestic Fascist Networks in the Republican Party and their Effect on U. S. Cold War Politics.* Cambridge, MA: Political Research Associates, 1988.

Bentley, Elizabeth. *Out of Bondage.* 1951; reprint, New York: Ivy Books, 1988.

Bentley, Eric (ed.). *Thirty Years of Treason: Excerpt from Hearings before the House Committee on Un-American Activities, 1938–1968.* New York: Viking, 1971.

Berman, Ronald (ed.). *Solzhenitsyn at Harvard.* Washington, DC: Ethics and Public Policy Center, 1980.

Bernstein, Carl. *Loyalties: A Son's Memoir.* New York: Simon & Schuster, 1989.

———. "The Holy Alliance." *Time,* February 24, 1992.

Blumenthal, Sidney. *The Rise of the Counter-Establishment: From Conservative Ideology to Political Power.* 1986; reprint, New York: Harper & Row, 1988.

Blumenthal, Sidney, and Thomas Byrne Edsall. *The Reagan Legacy.* New York: Pantheon, 1988.

Boaz, David (ed.). *Assessing the Reagan Years.* Washington, DC: Cato, 1988.

Borkenau, Franz. *World Communism: A History of the Communist International.* New York: Norton, 1939.

Bouscaren, Anthony. *A Guide to Anti-communist Action.* Chicago: Regnery, 1958.

———. *America Faces World Communism.* New York: Vantage, 1953.

Brinkley, Alan. *Voices of Protest: Huey Long, Father Coughlin and the Great Depression.* 1982; reprint, New York: Vintage, 1983.

Brown, Alden V. *The Tablet: The First Seventy-Five Years.* Brooklyn, NY: Tablet, 1983.

Brown, Anthony Cave. *Wild Bill Donovan: The Last Hero.* New York: Times Books, 1982.

Brown, Anthony Cave, and Charles B. MacDonald. *On a Field of Red: The Communist International and the Coming of World War II*. New York: Putnam's, 1981.

Brown, Julia. *I Testify: My Years as an FBI Undercover Agent*. Boston: Western Islands, 1966.

Brownell, Will, and Richard N. Billings. *So Close to Greatness: A Biography of William C. Bullitt*. New York: Macmillan, 1987.

Brzezinski, Zbigniew. *Power and Principle: Memoirs of the National Security Advisor, 1977–1981*. 1983; reprint, New York: Farrar, Straus & Giroux, 1985.

Buckingham, Peter H. *America Sees Red: A Review of Issues and References*. Claremont, CA: Regina, 1988.

Buckley, William F., Jr. *Keeping the Tablets: Modern American Conservative Thought*. New York: Harper & Row, 1988.

———. "Remarks at the *National Review* 35th Anniversary Dinner." *National Review*, November 5, 1990.

Buckley, William F., Jr., and L. Brent Bozell. *McCarthy and His Enemies*. Chicago: Regnery, 1954.

Budenz, Louis. *The Bolshevik Invasion of the West*. Linden, NJ: Bookmailer, 1966.

———. *Men Without Faces: The Communist Conspiracy in the USA*. New York: Harper, 1950.

———. *The Cry Is Peace*. Linden, NJ: Bookmailer, 1966.

———. *This Is My Story*. New York: McGraw-Hill, 1947.

Bunzel, John H. *Anti-Politics in America*. 1967; reprint, New York: Vintage, 1970.

———. (ed.). *Political Passages: Journeys of Change Through Two Decades, 1968–1988*. New York: Free Press, 1988.

Burnham, James. *The Coming Defeat of Communism*. New York: J. Day, 1950.

———. *Containment or Liberation*. New York: J. Day, 1953.

———. *The Struggle for the World*. New York: J. Day, 1945.

———. *The Web of Subversion: Underground Networks in the U.S. Government*. New York: J. Day, 1954.

Byrnes, Timothy A. *Catholic Bishops in American Politics*. Princeton: Princeton University Press, 1991.

Calomiris, Angela. *Red Masquerade: Undercover for the FBI*. Philadelphia: Lippincott, 1950.

Carlton, Don E. *Red Scare! Right-Wing Hysteria, Fifties Fanaticism, and Their Legacy in Texas*. Austin: Texas Monthly Press, 1985.

Carlson, John Roy [pseudonym for Avedis Derounian]. *Undercover: My Four Years in the Nazi Underground in America*. New York: Dutton, 1943.

———. *The Plotters*. New York: Dutton, 1946.

Carr, E. H. *Twilight of the Comintern, 1930–1935*. New York: Pantheon, 1982.

Carroll, Peter N. *The Odyssey of the Abraham Lincoln Brigade: Americans in the Spanish Civil War*. Stanford: Stanford University Press, 1994.

Carter, Jimmy. *Keeping Faith: Memoirs of a President*. New York: Bantam, 1982.

Casey, William J. *Scouting the Future: The Public Speeches of William J. Casey* (Herbert E. Meyer, ed.). Washington, DC: Regnery Gateway, 1989.

Caute, David. *The Fellow Travelers: A Postscript to the Enlightenment*. New York: Macmillan, 1973.

———. *The Great Fear: the Anti-Communist Purge Under Truman and Eisenhower*. New York: Simon & Schuster, 1978.

Ceplair, Larry, and Steven Englund. *The Inquisition in Hollywood: Politics in the Film Community, 1930–1960*. Berkeley: University of California Press, 1979.

Chafe, William H. *The Unfinished Journey: America Since World War II*. New York: Oxford University Press, 1986.

Chamberlin, William Henry. *The Russian Revolution*. 1935; reprint, New York: Grosset & Dunlap, 1965.

Chambers, Whittaker. *Odyssey of a Friend: Letters to William F. Buckley, Jr., 1954–1961*. New York: National Review, 1969.

———. *Witness*. 1952; reprint, Chicago: Regnery Gateway, 1980.

Coan, Blair. *The Red Web*. 1925; reprint, Belmont, MA: Americanist Classics, 1969.

Coben, Stanley. *A. Mitchell Palmer: Politician*. New York: Columbia University Press, 1963.

Coffin, Tristram. *Senator Fulbright: Portrait of a Public Philosopher*. New York: Dutton, 1966.

Cogley, John. *Report on Blacklisting*. New York: Fund for the Republic, 1956.

Cohen, Naomi W. *Not Free to Desist: The American Jewish Committee, 1906–1966*. Philadelphia: Jewish Publication Society of America, 1972.

Coleman, Peter. "The Brief Life of Liberal Anti-Communism." *National Review*, September 15, 1989.

Coleman, Peter. *The Liberal Conspiracy: The Congress for Cultural Freedom and the Struggle for the Mind of Postwar Europe*. New York: Free Press, 1989.

Collier, Peter, and David Horowitz. "McCarthyism: The Last Refuge of the Left." *Commentary*, 85 (January 1988).

———. *Destructive Generation: Second Thoughts About the '60s*. New York: Summit, 1990.

Collins, Peter W. *Socialist Opportunism and the Bolshevik Mind*. New Haven: Knights of Columbus, 1920.

Collins, Peter W. *The Red Glow of Bolshevism in America*. New Haven: Knights of Columbus, 1920.

Congdon, Lee. "Anti-Anti-Communism." *Academic Questions*, 1 (Summer 1988).

Conquest, Robert. *The Great Terror, a Reassessment*. New York: Oxford University Press, 1990.

Cook, Fred J. *The FBI Nobody Knows*. New York: Macmillan, 1965.

Cooney, John. *The American Pope: The Life and Times of Francis Cardinal Spellman*. New York: Times Books, 1984.

Crawford, Alan. *Thunder on the Right: The "New Right" and the Politics of Resentment*. New York: Pantheon, 1980.

Cronin, John F., S. S. *The Problem of American Communism in 1945: Facts and Recommendations*. Baltimore: St. Mary's Seminary, 1945.

Crosby, Donald F. "Boston's Catholics and the Spanish Civil War: 1936–1939." *New England Quarterly*, 44 (March 1971).

———, S. J. "The Politics of Religion: American Catholics and the Anti-Communist Impulse." In Robert Griffith and Athan Theoharis, *The Specter: Original Essays on the Cold War and the Origins of McCarthyism*. New York: New Viewpoints, 1974.

———. *God, Church, and Flag: Senator Joseph R. McCarthy and the Catholic Church, 1950–1957*. Chapel Hill: University of North Carolina Press, 1978.

Cross, John. *What Are the Facts Behind the Smearing of Anti-Communist Americans?* Kenosha: Cross Publications, ca. 1964.

Cruse, Harold. *The Crisis of the Negro Intellectual from Its Origins to the Present*. New York: Morrow, 1967.

Davies, Joseph E. *Mission to Moscow*. New York: Simon & Schuster, 1941.

Davis, David Brion. *The Fear of Conspiracy: Images of Un-American Subversion from the Revolution to the Present*. Ithaca: Cornell University Press, 1971.

Dawson, Nelson L. "From Fellow Traveler to Anticommunist: The Odyssey of J. B. Matthews." *The Register of the Kentucky Historical Society*. 84 (Summer 1986).

Dennis, Lawrence, and Maximilian St. George. *A Trial on Trial: The Great Sedition Trial of 1944*. New York: National Civil Rights Committee, 1945.

DeToledano, Ralph. *Spies, Dupes, and Diplomats*. New York: Duell, Sloan and Pearce, 1952.

———. *J. Edgar Hoover: The Man in His Time*. New Rochelle, NY: Arlington House, 1973.

DeToledano, Ralph, and Victor Lasky. *Seeds of Treason: The True Story of the Hiss-Chambers Tragedy*. New York: Funk and Wagnalls, 1950.

Diamond, Sigmund. *Compromised Campus: The Collaboration of Universities with the Intelligence Community, 1945–1955*. New York: Oxford University Press, 1992.

Diggins, John Patrick. *Up from Communism: Conservative Odysseys in American Intellectual History*. New York: Harper & Row, 1975.

Diggins, John Patrick. *The Rise and Fall of the American Left*. New York: Norton, 1992.

Dilling, Elizabeth. *The Red Network*. Kenilworth, IL: published by the author, 1934.

————. *The Roosevelt Red Record and Its Background*. Chicago: Published by the Author, 1936.

Dionne, E. J., Jr. "Who Won the Cold War? New Left Historians Debate the Demise of Socialism." *Washington Post*, June 12, 1990.

Doenecke, Justus D. "The America First Committee, Origins and Outcome." *Chronicles*, December 1991.

Donahue, William A. *The Politics of the American Civil Liberties Union*. New Brunswick, NJ: Transaction, 1985.

Donner, Frank J. *The Age of Surveillance: The Aims and Methods of America's Political Intelligence System*. New York: Knopf, 1980.

Dos Passos, John. *Adventures of a Young Man*. New York: Harcourt Brace, 1939.

Draper, Theodore. *The Roots of American Communism*. 1957; reprint, Chicago: Ivan R. Dee, 1985.

————. *American Communism and Soviet Russia*. 1960; reprint, New York: Vintage, 1986.

————. *A Very Thin Line: The Iran Contra Affair*. New York: Touchstone, 1991.

————. "The Life of the Party." *New York Review of Books*, January 13, 1994.

Dubofsky, Melvyn. *We Shall Be All: A History of the Industrial Workers of the World*. Chicago: Quadrangle, 1969.

Dudman, Richard. *Men of the Far Right*. New York: Pyramid Books, 1962.

Duignan, Peter, and L. H. Gann. *The Rebirth of the West: The Americanization of the Democratic World*. Cambridge, MA: Blackwell, 1992.

Dyson, Lowell K. *Red Harvest: The Communist Party and American Farmers*. Lincoln: University of Nebraska Press, 1982.

Ellison, Ralph. *Invisible Man*. New York: Random House, 1952.

Evanier, David, and Harvey Klehr. "Among the Intellectualoids/Anticommunism and Mental Health." *The American Spectator*, February 1989.

Evans, Medford. *The Secret War for the A-Bomb*. Chicago: Regnery, 1953.

Ewald, William Bragg, Jr., *Who Killed Joe McCarthy?* New York: Simon & Schuster, 1984.

Falk, Candace. *Love, Anarchy, and Emma Goldman*. New York: Holt, Rinehart & Winston, 1964.

Farah, Joseph. "The Real Blacklist." *National Review*, October 7, 1989.

Faulk, John Henry. *Fear on Trial*. 1964; reprint, Austin: University of Texas Press, 1983.

Fiedler, Leslie. *An End to Innocence: Essays on Culture and Politics*. 1952; reprint, Boston: Beacon Press, 1955.

Field, Frederick Vanderbilt. *From Right to Left: An Autobiography*. Westport, CT: Lawrence Hill, 1983.

Filene, Peter. *Americans and the Soviet Experiment, 1917–1933*. Cambridge: Harvard University Press, 1967.

Finch, Phillip. *God, Guts, and Guns: A Close Look at the Radical Right*. New York: Putnam, 1983.

Fineberg, Solomon. *The Rosenberg Case, Fact and Fiction*. New York: Oceana, 1953.

Fish, Hamilton. *FDR: The Other Side of the Coin: How We Were Tricked into World War II*. New York: Vantage, 1976.

Fitzgerald, Frances. "Annals of Justice: Iran-Contra." *The New Yorker*, October 16, 1989.

Fleming, D. F. *The Cold War and Its Origins* (New York: Doubleday, 1961.

Flynn, George Q. *American Catholics and the Roosevelt Presidency, 1932–1936*. Lexington: University of Kentucky Press, 1968.

Flynn, John T. *The Secret About Pearl Harbor*. New York: Published by the author, 1944.

———. *The Smear Terror*. New York: Published by the author, 1947.

———. *The Lattimore Story*. New York: Devin-Adair, 1953.

Forster, Arnold. *Square One: The Memoirs of a True Freedom Fighter's Life-Long Struggle Against Anti-Semitism, Domestic and Foreign*. New York: Donald I. Fine, 1988.

Forster, Arnold, and Benjamin R. Epstein. *Danger on the Right: The Attitudes, Personnel and Influence of the Radical Right and Extreme Conservatives*. New York: Random House, 1964.

———. *The Radical Right: Report on the John Birch Society and Its Allies*. New York: Vintage, 1967.

Fossedal, Gregory A. *Our Finest Hour: Will Clayton, the Marshall Plan, and the Triumph of Democracy*. Stanford: Hoover Institution Press, 1993.

Fox, Richard W. *Reinhold Niebuhr: A Biography*. New York: Pantheon, 1985.

Frank, Robert L. "Prelude to Cold War: American Catholics and Communism." *Journal of Church and State*, 34 (Winter 1992).

Fraser, Steven. *Labor Will Rule, Sidney Hillman and the Rise of American Labor*. New York: Free Press, 1991.

Freeman, Joshua B., and Steve Rosswurm. "The Education of an Anti-Communist: Father John F. Cronin and the Baltimore Labor Movement." *Labor History*, 33 (Spring 1992).

Fried, Richard M. *Nightmare in Red: The McCarthy Era in Perspective*. New York: Oxford University Press, 1990.

Gaddis, John L. *The United States and the Origins of the Cold War, 1941–1947*. New York: Columbia University Press, 1972.

Gaddis, John Lewis. *The United States and the End of the Cold War*. New York: Oxford University Press, 1992.

Gallagher, Louis J., S.J. *Edmund A. Walsh, S.J.* New York: Benziger, 1962.

Gardner, Lloyd C. *Architects of Illusion: Men and Ideas in American Foreign Policy, 1941–1949*. Chicago: Quadrangle, 1970.

———. *Safe for Democracy: The Anglo American Response to Revolution, 1913–1923*. New York: Oxford University Press, 1987.

Garrison, Jim. *On the Trail of the Assassins*. New York: Warner, 1988.

Garrow, David J. *The FBI and Martin Luther King, Jr.: From "Solo" to Memphis*. New York: Norton, 1981.

Gellerman, William. *The American Legion as Educator*. New York: Columbia University Teachers College Press, 1938.

George, John, and Laird Wilcox. *Nazis, Communists, Klansmen, and Others on the Fringe*. Buffalo: Prometheus, 1992.

Gillon, Steven M. *Politics and Vision: The ADA and American Liberalism, 1947–1985*. New York: Oxford University Press, 1987.

Ginger, Ray. *The Bending Cross*. New Brunswick, NJ: Rutgers University Press, 1949.

Gitlow, Ben. *The Whole of Their Lives: Communism in America, A Personal History and Intimate Portrayal of Its Leaders*. New York: Charles Scribners's, 1948.

Glazer, Nathan. "Did We Go Too Far?" *The National Interest*, 31 (Spring 1993).

Glynn, Patrick. *Closing Pandora's Box: Arms Races, Arms Control, and the History of the Cold War*. New York: Basic Books, 1992.

Goldstein, Robert J. *Political Repression in Modern America*. (Cambridge, MA: Schenckman/Two Continents, 1978.

Goldwater, Barry M., with Jack Casserly. *Goldwater*. New York: Doubleday, 1988.

Goodman, Walter. *The Committee: The Extraordinary Career of the House Committee on Un-American Activities*. New York: Farrar, Straus & Giroux, 1968.

Gouzenko, Igor. *The Fall of a Titan*. New York: Norton, 1954.

Green, Gil. *Cold War Fugitive*. New York: International Publishers, 1984.

Green, Marguerite. *The National Civic Federation and the American Labor Movement*. Washington, DC: Catholic University Press, 1956.

Griffin, G. Edward. *The Life and Words of Robert Welch, Founder of the John Birch Society*. Thousand Oaks, CA: American Media, 1975.

Griffith, Robert. *The Politics of Fear*. 1970; reprint, Amherst: University of Massachusetts Press, 1987.

Griffith, Robert, and Athan Theoharis. *The Specter: Original Essays on the Cold War and the Origins of McCarthyism*. New York: New Viewpoints, 1974.

Griswold, A. Whitney. *The Far Eastern Policy of the United States*. New York: Harcourt Brace, 1938.

Gross, Babette. *Willi Munzenberg: A Political Biography*. East Lansing: Michigan State University Press, 1974.

Halberstam, David. *The Best and the Brightest*. 1972; reprint, New York: Penguin, 1983.

Hamilton, Ian. *Koestler, A Life*. New York: Macmillan, 1982.

Havel, Vaclav. *Living in Truth* (Jan Vladislav, ed.). New York: Faber and Faber, 1990.

Havens, Murray Clark. *The Challenges to Democracy: Consensus and Extremism in American Politics*. Austin: University of Texas Press, 1965.

Haynes, John Earl. *Communism and Anti-Communism in the United States: An Annotated Guide to Historical Writings*. New York: Garland, 1987.

Hazlitt, Henry. *The Great Idea*. New York: Appleton-Century-Crofts, 1951.

Heale, M. J. *American Anticommunism: Combating the Enemy Within, 1830–1970*. Baltimore: Johns Hopkins University Press, 1990.

Hechler, Ken. *Working With Truman: A Personal Memoir of the White House Years*. New York: Putnam's, 1982.

Hersh, Seymour M. "The Iran-Contra Committees: Did They Protect Reagan?" *New York Times Magazine*, May 6, 1990.

Herz, Martin F. (ed.). *Decline of the West? George Kennan and His Critics*. Washington, DC: Ethics and Public Policy Center, 1978.

———. *How the Cold War Is Taught*. Washington, DC: Ethics and Public Policy Center, 1978.

Hessen, Robert (ed.). *Breaking with Communism: The Intellectual Odyssey of Bertram D. Wolfe*. Stanford: Hoover Institution Press, 1990.

Higham, John. *Strangers in the Land: Patterns of American Nativism, 1860–1925*. 1963; reprint, New York: Atheneum, 1973.

Himmelstein, Jerome L. *To the Right: The Transformation of American Conservatism*. Berkeley: University of California Press, 1990.

Hixson, Walter L. *George F. Kennan: Cold War Iconoclast*. New York: Columbia University Press, 1989.

Hofstadter, Richard. "The Pseudo-Conservative Revolt." In Daniel Bell (ed.), *The Radical Right*. Garden City, NY: Anchor, 1964.

———. *The Paranoid Style in American Politics and Other Essays*. 1964; reprint, Chicago: University of Chicago Press, 1979.

Hoke, Henry. *Blackmail*. New York: Readers Book Service, 1944.

Hollander, Paul. *The Survival of the Adversary Culture*. New Brunswick, NJ: Transaction, 1988.

Hood, William J. "Preface" to Walter Krivitsky, *In Stalin's Secret Service*. 1939; reprint, Frederick, MD: University Publications of America, 1985.

Hook, Sidney. *Out of Step*. New York: Harper & Row, 1987.

———. *Heresy Yes, Conspiracy No!* New York: American Committee for Cultural Freedom, n.d. (Originally published in the *New York Times Magazine*, July 9, 1950 and September 30, 1951.)

Hoover, J. Edgar. *Masters of Deceit*. New York: Henry Holt, 1958.

Horner, Charles. "Why Whittaker Chambers was Wrong." *Commentary*, April 1990.

Horowitz, David. *The Free World Colossus*. 1965; revised edition, New York: Hill and Wang, 1971.

House, Colonel Edward. *Philip Dru, Administrator*. New York: B. W. Huebsch, 1912.

Howe, Irving. *The New Conservatives: A Critique from the Left.* New York: New American Library, 1977.

———. *World of Our Fathers.* 1983; reprint, New York: Schocken, 1989.

Howe, Irving, and Lewis Coser. *The American Communist Party.* New York: Praeger, 1962.

Hyde, H. Montgomery. *The Atom Bomb Spies.* London: Hamish Hamilton, 1980.

Hyland, William G. *The Cold War Is Over.* New York: Random House, 1990.

Illig, Alvin, CSP. "The Church Has Turned to America." *Columbia,* March 1953.

International Committee for Political Prisoners. *Letters from Russian Prisons.* New York: Boni, 1925.

Irons, Peter H. "American Business and the Origins of McCarthyism: The Cold War Crusade of the United States Chamber of Commerce." In Robert Griffith and Athan Theoharis, *The Specter: Original Essays on the Cold War and the Origins of McCarthyism.* New York: New Viewpoints, 1974.

Isaacson, Walter, and Evan Thomas. *The Wise Men.* New York: Simon & Schuster, 1986.

Jacobs, Milton R. *Can You Shut Your Eyes to These Facts?* Brooklyn, NY: Brooklyn Division of the American Jewish Federation to Combat Communism and Fascism, 1939.

Jaffe, Julian F. *Crusade Against Radicalism.* Port Washington, NY: Kennikat, 1972.

Janisch, Edward. *What We Must Know About the Overstreets.* Belmont, MA: American Opinion, 1959.

Janson, Donald. *The Far Right.* New York: McGraw-Hill, 1963.

Jeansonne, Glen. *Gerald L. K. Smith: Minister of Hate.* New Haven: Yale University Press, 1988.

———. "Women Anti-Communists in the Age of FDR." Convention Paper, Organization of American Historians, 1990.

Jeffreys-Jones, Rhodri. *The CIA and American Democracy.* New Haven: Yale University Press, 1989.

Jensen, Joan M. *The Price of Vigilance.* Chicago: Rand McNally, 1968.

Johnson, Paul. *Modern Times: The World from the Twenties to the Eighties.* 1983; reprint, New York: Harper & Row, 1985.

Judis, John B. *William F. Buckley, Jr.: Patron Saint of the Conservatives.* New York: Simon & Schuster, 1988.

Kanfer, Stefan. *A Journal of the Plague Years.* New York: Atheneum, 1973.

Kauffman, Christopher J. *Faith and Fraternalism: The History of the Knights of Columbus.* New York: Harper & Row, 1982.

Kearney, James F., S.J. "The American Failure in China." *Columbia,* December 1948.

Keeley, Joseph. *The China Lobby Man: The Story of Alfred Kohlberg.* New Rochelle, NY: Arlington House, 1969.

Keller, William W. *The Liberals and J. Edgar Hoover*. Princeton: Princeton University Press, 1989.

Kennan, George F. *Russia Leaves the War*. Princeton: Princeton University Press, 1956.

———. "The Sisson Documents." *Journal of Modern History*, 28 (June 1956).

———. "American Troops in Russia." *Atlantic Monthly*, 203 (January 1959).

———. *The Nuclear Delusion: Soviet-American Relations in the Atomic Age*. 1982; revised edition, New York: Pantheon, 1983.

Kimball, Penn. *The File*. 1983; reprint, New York: Avon, 1985.

Kirkpatrick, Jeane. "Dictatorships and Double Standards." *Commentary*, November 1979.

Kissinger, Henry. *Diplomacy*. New York: Simon & Schuster, 1994.

Klehr, Harvey. *The Heyday of American Communism: The Depression Decade*. New York: Basic Books, 1984.

———. *Far Left of Center: The American Radical Left Today*. New Brunswick, NJ: Transaction, 1991.

Klehr, Harvey, and John Earl Haynes. *The American Communist Movement: Storming Heaven Itself*. New York: Twayne Publishers, 1992.

Klehr, Harvey, and Ronald Radosh. "Anatomy of a Fix." *New Republic*, April 21, 1986.

Klingaman, William K. *1919: The Year Our World Began*. New York: St. Martin's Press, 1987.

Klotz, Daniel J. "Freda Utley: From Communist to Anti-Communist." Ph.D. dissertation, Yale University, 1987.

Koch, Stephen. *Double Lives: Spies and Writers in the Secret Soviet War of Ideas Against the West*. New York: Free Press, 1994.

Koen, Ross Y. *The China Lobby in American Politics*. New York: Macmillan, 1960.

Koestler, Arthur. *Darkness at Noon*. New York: Macmillan, 1941.

Kolko, Gabriel. *The Politics of War: The World and United States Foreign Policy, 1943–1945*. New York: Random House, 1968.

Koval, Joel. *Red Hunting in the Promised Land: Anticommunism and the Making of America*. New York: Basic Books, 1994.

Kramer, Hilton. "Anti-communism and the Sontag Circles." *The New Criterion*, September 1986.

———. "The Importance of Sidney Hook." *Commentary*, 84 (August 1987).

———. "Thinking About *Witness*." *The New Criterion*, March 1988.

Kristol, Irving. *Reflections of a Neoconservative: Looking Back, Looking Ahead*. New York: Basic Books, 1983.

———. "My Cold War." *The National Interest*, 31 (Spring 1993).

Krivitsky, Walter. *In Stalin's Secret Service*. 1939; reprint, Frederick, MD: University Publications of America, 1985.

Kselman, Thomas A., and Steven Avella. "Marian Piety and the Cold War in the United States." *The Catholic Historical Review*. 72 (July 1986).

Lasch, Christopher. *The American Liberals and the Russian Revolution*. New York: Columbia University Press, 1962.

————. *The Agony of the American Left*. New York: Vintage, 1969.

Lasky, Victor (ed.). *The American Legion Reader*. New York: Hawthorn, 1953.

Lasswell, Harold D. *World Politics and Personal Insecurity*. New York: Free Press, 1965.

Latham, Earl. *The Communist Controversy in Washington*. Cambridge, MA: Harvard University Press, 1966.

Lattimore, Owen. *Ordeal by Slander*. Boston: Little, Brown, 1950.

Lavine, Harold. *Fifth Column in America*. New York: Doubleday, 1940.

Layne, Christopher. "Requiem for the Reagan Doctrine." In David Boaz (ed.), *Assessing the Reagan Years*. Washington, DC: Cato, 1988.

Leab, Daniel J. "Anti-communism, the FBI, and Matt Cvetic: The Ups and Downs of a Professional Informer." *Pennsylvania Magazine of History and Biography* 115 (October 1991).

Lee, Albert. *Henry Ford and the Jews*. New York: Stein and Day, 1980.

LeFeber, Walter. *America, Russia and the Cold War, 1945–1992*. New York: McGraw-Hill, 1991.

Leffler, Melvyn P. *A Preponderance of Power: National Security, The Truman Administration and the Cold War*. Stanford: Stanford University Press, 1992.

Levenstein, Harvey A. *Communism, Anticommunism, and the CIO*. Westport, CT: Greenwood, 1981.

Levin, N. Gordon. *Woodrow Wilson and World Politics: America's Response to War and Revolution*. New York: Oxford University Press, 1968.

Levine, Isaac Don (ed.). *Plain Talk: An Anthology from the Leading Anti-Communist Magazine of the 40s*. New Rochelle, NY: Arlington House, 1976.

Lewy, Guenter. *The Cause That Failed: Communism in American Political Life*. New York: Oxford University Press, 1990.

Liebman, Arthur. *Jews and the Left*. New York: John Wiley, 1979.

Lindemann, Albert S. *The 'Red Years'*. Berkeley: University of California Press, 1974.

Link, Arthur S. *Wilson the Diplomatist: A Look at His Major Foreign Policies*. Baltimore: Johns Hopkins University Press, 1957.

Link, Eugene P. *Labor-Religion Prophet: The Times and Life of Harry F. Ward*. Boulder, CO: Westview Press, 1984.

Lipset, Seymour Martin, and Earl Raab. *The Politics of Unreason: Right-Wing Extremism in America, 1790–1970*. New York: Harper & Row, 1970.

Lisio, Donald J. *The President and Protest: Hoover, Conspiracy, and the Bonus Riot*. Columbia: University of Missouri Press, 1974.

Lottman, Herbert. *The Left Bank: Writers in Paris from Popular Front to Cold War*. London: Heinemann, 1982.

Lowenthal, Max. *The Federal Bureau of Investigation*. New York: William Sloane Associates, 1950.

Luddington, Townsend. *John Dos Passos: A Twentieth Century Odyssey*. New York: Dutton, 1980.

Ludlum, Robert. *The Chancellor Manuscript*. New York: Dial, 1977.

Lyons, Eugene. *The Red Decade: The Stalinist Penetration of America*. Indianapolis: Bobbs-Merrill, 1941.

———. "The Coming Revolution." *Human Events*, June 15, 1957.

———. "Negotiating with the Kremlin." *Reader's Digest*, April 1958.

———. *Assignment in Utopia*. 1937; reprint, New Brunswick, NJ: Transaction, 1991.

MacDonald, J. Fred. *Television and the Red Menace*. New York: Praeger, 1985.

MacDougall, Curtis D. *Gideon's Army*. New York: Marzani and Munsell, 1965.

Maddox, Robert J. *The New Left and the Origins of the Cold War*. Princeton: Princeton University Press, 1972.

Maier, Charles. S. *Why Did Communism Collapse in 1989?* Cambridge: Harvard Program on Central and Eastern Europe Working Paper Series, 1991.

Maland, Charles. "*Dr. Strangelove* (1964): Nightmare Comedy and the Ideology of Liberal Consensus." *American Quarterly*, Winter 1979.

Malia, Martin. "A Fatal Logic." *National Interest*, Spring 1993.

———. *The Soviet Tragedy: A History of Socialism in Russia, 1917–1991*. New York: Free Press, 1994.

Markowitz, Norman D. *The Rise and Fall of the People's Century: Henry A. Wallace and American Liberalism, 1941–1948*. New York: Free Press, 1973.

———. "A View From the Left: From the Popular Front to Cold War Liberalism." In Robert Griffith and Athan Theoharis (eds.), *The Specter: Original Essays on the Cold War and the Origins of McCarthyism*. New York: New Viewpoints, 1974.

Marshall, Louis. *Louis Marshall, Champion of Liberty*. Philadelphia: Jewish Publication Society of America, 1957.

Massing, Hede. *This Deception*. 1951; reprint, New York: Ivy Books, 1987.

Mathews, Jane De Hart. "Art and Politics in Cold War America." *American Historical Review*, 81 (October 1976).

Matthews, J. B. *Odyssey of a Fellow Traveler*. New York: Mt. Vernon Publishers, 1938.

May, Ernest R. "Introduction" to *American Cold War Strategy: Interpreting NSC 68*. New York: Bedford, 1993.

May, Gary. *Un-American Activities: The Trials of William Remington*. New York: Oxford University Press, 1994.

Mayer, Arno J. *Political Origins of the New Diplomacy, 1917–1918*. New York: Howard Fertig, 1969.

Mayer, Milton S. "Mrs. Dilling: Lady of the Red Network." *American Mercury*, July 1939.

McCarthy, Joseph R. *America's Retreat from Victory: The Story of George Catlett Marshall*. 1951; reprint, Milwaukee: Joseph R. McCarthy Educational Foundation, 1979.

McDaniel, Dennis K. "Martin Dies of Un-American Activities: His Life and Times." Ph.D. dissertation, University of Houston, 1988.

Meany, George. "The Conspiracy Against Labor." *American Federationist*, 29 (October 1922).

Mee, Charles L. *The Marshall Plan: The Launching of the Pax Americana*. New York: Simon & Schuster, 1984.

Mereto, Joseph J. *The Socialist Conspiracy Against Religion*. Chicago: Iconoclast, 1919.

Merk, Frederick. *Manifest Destiny and Mission in American History*. 1963; reprint, New York: Vintage, 1966.

Militant Liberty: A Program of Evaluation and Assessment of Freedom. Washington: U.S. Government Printing Office, 1955.

Mintz, Frank P. *The Liberty Lobby and the American Right*. Westport, CT: Greenwood, 1985.

Mitgang, Herbert. *Dangerous Dossiers: Exposing the Secret War Against America's Greatest Authors*. New York: Donald I. Fine, 1988.

Morgan, Ted. *FDR: A Biography*. New York: Simon & Schuster, 1985.

Morris, Robert. *Self-Destruct: Dismantling America's Internal Security*. New Rochelle, NY: Arlington House, 1979.

Mosk, Stanley, and Howard H. Jewel. "The Birch Phenomenon Analyzed." *New York Times Magazine*, August 20, 1961.

Muravchik, Joshua. "How the Cold War Really Ended." *Commentary*, 98 (November 1994).

Murray, Robert K. *Red Scare: A Study in National Hysteria, 1919–1920*. 1955; reprint, Minneapolis: University of Minnesota Press, 1964.

Naison, Mark. *Communists in Harlem During the Depression*. Urbana: University of Illinois Press, 1983.

Nash, George H. *The Conservative Intellectual Movement in America Since 1945*. New York: Basic Books, 1976.

National Popular Government League, R. G. Brown, Zechariah Chafee, Jr., et al. *Report Upon the Illegal Practices of the United States Department of Justice*. 1920; reprint, New York: Arno Press, 1969.

Navasky, Victor S. *Naming Names*. 1980; reprint, New York: Penguin, 1981.

Newberry, Mike. *The Yahoos*. New York: Marzani and Munsell, 1964.

Nitze, Paul H. *From Hiroshima to Glasnost: At the Center of Decision—A Memoir*. New York: Grove Weidenfeld, 1988.

Nixon, Richard M. *Six Crises*. Garden City, NY: Doubleday, 1962.

———. *RN: The Memoirs of Richard Nixon*. New York: Grosset & Dunlap, 1978.

Nolan, William Anthony. *Communism Versus the Negro*. Chicago: Regnery, 1951.

Not Guilty: The Final Report of the Commission of Inquiry into Charges Made Against Leon Trotsky and Leon Sedoff in the Moscow Trials. New York: Harbor, 1938.

O'Brien, David J. *American Catholics and Social Reform: The New Deal Years.* New York: Oxford University Press, 1968.

———. *Public Catholicism.* New York: Macmillan, 1989.

O'Neill, William L. *Coming Apart: An Informal History of America in the 1960's.* Chicago: Quadrangle, 1971.

———. *A Better World. The Great Schism: Stalinism and the American Intellectuals.* New York: Simon & Schuster, 1982.

O'Reilly, Kenneth. *Hoover and the Un-Americans.* Philadelphia: Temple University Press, 1983.

Order of the Knights of Pythias in Cooperation with the All-American Conference to Combat Communism. *Suggested Reading List on Communism and How to Combat It.* September 1954.

Orme, Alexandra. *Comes the Comrade!* New York: Morrow, 1950.

Ornstein, Norman J., and Mark Schmitt. "Dateline Campaign '92: Post Cold War Politics." *Foreign Policy,* 79 (Summer 1990).

Orwell, George. *Animal Farm.* New York: Harcourt, Brace, 1946.

Oshinsky, David M. *A Conspiracy So Immense: The World of Joe McCarthy.* New York: Free Press, 1983.

Overstreet, Harry Allen. *The Strange Tactics of Extremism.* New York: Norton, 1964.

Page, Stanley W. *Lenin and World Revolution.* New York: New York University Press, 1959.

Palmer, Gretta. "The Jews Fight the Reds." *Commentator,* February 1939.

Parenti, Michael. *The Anticommunist Impulse.* New York: Random House, 1969.

Parmet, Herbert S. *Eisenhower and the American Crusades.* New York: Macmillan, 1972.

———. *Richard Nixon and His America.* Boston: Little, Brown, 1990.

Parrish, Michael E. *Felix Frankfurter and His Times: The Reform Years.* New York: Free Press, 1982.

Paul, Ellen Frankel. "Introduction" to Eugene Lyons. *Assignment in Utopia.* 1937; reprint, New Brunswick, NJ: Transaction, 1991.

Peake, Hayden B. "Afterword" to Elizabeth Bentley, *Out of Bondage.* 1951; reprint, New York: Ivy Books, 1988.

Pencak, William. *For God and Country: The American Legion, 1919–1941.* Boston: Northeastern University Press, 1989.

Perkus, Cathy (ed.). *COINTELPRO: The FBI's Secret War on Political Freedom.* New York: Monad, 1975.

Persico, Joseph. *Casey: From the OSS to the CIA.* New York: Viking, 1990.

Pessen, Edward. *Losing Our Souls: The American Experience in the Cold War.* Chicago: Ivan R. Dee, 1993.

Philbrick, Herbert. *I Led Three Lives.* New York: McGraw-Hill, 1952.

Pisani, Sallie. *The CIA and the Marshall Plan*. Lawrence: University of Kansas Press, 1991.

Podhoretz, Norman. *Breaking Ranks: A Political Memoir*. New York: Harper & Row, 1979.

———. *The Present Danger*. New York: Simon & Schuster, 1980.

———. *Why We Were in Vietnam*. New York: Simon & Schuster, 1982.

Pomerantz, Charlotte (ed.). *A Quarter Century of Un-Americana, A Tragico-Comical Memorabilia of HUAC*. New York: Marzani and Munsell, 1963.

Porter, Katherine Ann. *The Never Ending Wrong*. Boston: Little, Brown, 1977.

Post, Louis F. *The Deportations Delirium of Nineteen-Twenty: A Personal Narrative of an Historic Official Experience*. 1923; reprint, New York: Da Capo, 1970.

Powell, Lee Riley. J. *William Fulbright and America's Lost Crusade: Fulbright's Opposition to the Vietnam War*. Little Rock: Rose Publishing, 1984.

Powers, Richard Gid. "The Cold War in the Rockies." *Art Journal*, 33 (September 1974).

———. *G-Men: Hoover's FBI in American Popular Culture*. Carbondale: Southern Illinois University Press, 1983.

———. *Secrecy and Power*. New York: Free Press, 1987.

———. "Anticommunist Lives." *American Quarterly*, 41 (December 1989).

Preston, William. *Aliens and Dissenters*. Cambridge, MA: Harvard University Press, 1963.

Propaganda Analysis: A Bulletin to Help the Intelligent Citizen Detect and Analyze Propaganda. New York: Institute for Propaganda Analysis, 1938–1942.

Prychodko, Nicholas. *One of the Fifteen Million: The True Story of One Man's Experience in a Soviet Slave Labor Camp*. Boston: Little, Brown, 1952.

Puddington, Arch. "Why Johnny's Not Anti-Communist." *National Review*, February 5, 1990.

———. "The Anti-Cold War Brigade." *Commentary*, August 1990.

Quigley, Carroll. *Tragedy and Hope*. New York: Macmillan, 1966.

Radosh, Ronald. *American Labor and United States Foreign Policy*. New York: Random House, 1969.

———. *Prophets on the Right: Profiles of Conservative Critics of American Globalism, Charles A. Beard, John T. Flynn, Oswald Garrison Villard, Senator Robert A. Taft, Lawrence Dennis*. New York: Simon & Schuster, 1975.

Radosh, Ronald, and Joyce Milton. *The Rosenberg File: A Search for the Truth*. New York: Holt, Rinehart & Winston, 1983.

Rand, Ayn. *We the Living*. 1936; reprint, New York: Signet, 1983.

Reagan, Ronald. *Speaking My Mind*. New York: Simon & Schuster, 1989.

———. *An American Life*. New York: Pocket Books, 1990.

Record, Wilson. *Race and Radicalism: The NAACP and the Communist Party in Conflict*. Ithaca: Cornell University Press, 1964.

Reed, John. *Ten Days That Shook the World*. 1919; reprint, New York: International Publishers, 1967. With a foreword by V. I. Lenin, a preface by N. K. Kruskaya, and a new introduction by John Howard Lawson.

Reeves, Thomas C. *The Life and Times of Joe McCarthy: A Biography*. New York: Stein and Day, 1982.

Regan, Donald T. *For the Record: From Wall Street to Washington*. New York: Harcourt Brace Jovanovich, 1988.

Remnick, David. "The Exile Returns." *The New Yorker*, February 14, 1994.

Ribuffo, Leo P. *The Old Christian Right: The Protestant Far Right from the Great Depression to the Cold War*. Philadelphia: Temple University Press, 1983.

Rice, Monsignor Charles Owen. "Confessions of an Anti-communist." *Labor History*, 30 (Summer 1989).

Riebling, Mark. *Wedge: The Secret War Between the FBI and CIA*. New York: Knopf, 1994.

Robins, Natalie. *Alien Ink: The FBI's War on Freedom of Expression*. New York: Morrow, 1992.

Robinson, Archie. *George Meany and His Times: A Biography*. New York: Simon & Schuster, 1981.

Roche, John P. "Was Everyone Terrified? The Mythology of 'McCarthyism.' " *Academic Questions*, 2 (Spring 1989).

Rogin, Michael. *The Intellectuals and McCarthy: The Radical Specter*. Cambridge: Massachusetts Institute of Technology Press, 1967.

———. *Ronald Reagan, The Movie and Other Episodes in Political Demonology*. Berkeley: University of California Press, 1987.

Rorty, James, and Moshe Dechter. *McCarthy and the Communists*. Boston: Beacon Press, 1954.

Rose, Gideon. "The New Cold War Debate." *The National Interest*, Winter 1994–1995.

Rosenstone, Robert A. *Romantic Revolutionary: A Biography of John Reed*. 1975; reprint, New York: Vintage, 1981.

Rosenthal, Jerome C. "Dealing with the Devil: Louis Marshall and the Partnership Between the Joint Distributing Committee and Soviet Russia." *American Jewish Archives*, 39 (April 1987).

Rosswurm, Steve. "The Catholic Church and the Left-Led Unions: Labor Priests, Labor Schools, and the ACTU." In Steve Rosswurm (ed.), *The CIO's Left-Led Unions*. New Brunswick, NJ: Rutgers University Press, 1992.

Roy, Ralph Lord. *Communism and the Churches*. New York: Harcourt Brace, 1960.

Rummel, R. J. *Lethal Politics, Soviet Genocide and Mass Murder Since 1917*. New Brunswick, NJ: Transaction, 1990.

Russell, Francis. *The Shadow of Blooming Grove: Warren G. Harding in His Times*. New York: McGraw-Hill, 1968.

————. *Sacco and Vanzetti: The Case Resolved.* New York: Harper & Row, 1986.

Sakharov, Andrei D. *My Country and the World.* New York: Vintage, 1975.

Saloma, John S., III. *Ominous Politics: The New Conservative Labyrinth.* New York: Hill and Wang, 1984.

Sanders, Jerry W. *Peddlers of Crisis: The Committee on the Present Danger and the Politics of Containment.* Boston: South End Press, 1983.

Sayers, Michael, and Albert E. Kahn. *The Great Conspiracy: The Secret War Against Soviet Russia.* Boston: Little, Brown, 1946.

Sayre, Nora. "Cold War Cinema." *The Nation,* February 24, 1979; March 3, 1979.

————. *Running Time: Films of the Cold War.* New York: Dial Press, 1982.

Scammell, Michael. "The Prophet and the Wilderness: How the Idea of Human Rights Crippled Communism." *The New Republic,* February 25, 1991.

Schell, Jonathan. "How We Demonized the Red Devil." *Newsday,* October 3, 1991.

Schlesinger, Arthur M., Jr., *The Vital Center: The Politics of Freedom.* Boston: Houghton Mifflin, 1949.

————. *The Age of Roosevelt: The Politics of Upheaval.* Boston: Houghton Mifflin, 1960.

————. *A Thousand Days: John F. Kennedy in the White House.* Boston: Houghton Mifflin, 1965.

————. *The Bitter Heritage: Vietnam and American Democracy, 1941–1966.* Boston: Houghton Mifflin, 1967.

————. "Origins of the Cold War." *Foreign Affairs,* 46 (October 1967).

Schrag, Peter. *Test of Loyalty: Daniel Ellsberg and the Rituals of Secret Government.* New York: Touchstone, 1974.

Schrecker, Ellen. *No Ivory Towers: McCarthyism and the Universities.* New York: Oxford University Press, 1986.

————. *The Age of McCarthyism: A Brief History with Documents.* New York: Bedford Books, 1994.

Schultz, Bud, and Ruth Schultz. *It Did Happen Here: Recollections of Political Repression in America.* Berkeley: University of California Press, 1989.

Schuyler, George S. *Black and Conservative.* New Rochelle, NY: Arlington House, 1966.

Schwarz, Jordan A. *Liberal: Adolf A. Berle and the Vision of an American Era.* New York: Free Press, 1987.

Schweizer, Peter. *Victory: The Reagan Administration's Secret Strategy That Hastened the Collapse of the Soviet Union.* New York: Atlantic Monthly Press, 1994.

Seaton, Douglas. *Catholics and Radicals: The Association of Catholic Trade Unionists and the American Labor Movement from the Depression to the Cold War.* Lewisburg, PA: Bucknell University Press, 1981.

Selcraig, James Truett. *The Red Scare in the Midwest, 1945–1955: A State and Local Study.* Ann Arbor, MI: UMI Research Press, 1982.

Seldes, George. *Witch Hunt: The Technique and Profits of Red-Baiting*. New York: Modern Age, 1940.

Serge, Victor. *The Case of Comrade Tulayev*. Garden City, N.Y.: Doubleday, 1950.

Sestanovich, Stephen. "Did the West Undo the East?" *National Interest*, Spring 1993.

Shadegg, Stephen. *Clare Boothe Luce*. New York: Simon & Schuster, 1970.

Shapiro, Judah J. *The Friendly Society: A History of the Workmen's Circle*. New York: Doron, 1970.

Shapley, Deborah. *Promise and Power: The Life and Times of Robert McNamara*. Boston: Little, Brown, 1993.

Sheehan, Neil. "Introduction" to Neil Sheehan, Hedrick Smith, E. W. Kenworthy, and Fox Butterfield [of the *New York Times*], *The Pentagon Papers*. New York: Bantam, 1971.

Sheen, Fulton J. *Communism and the Conscience of the West*. Indianapolis: Bobbs-Merrill, 1948.

Sheer, Robert. *With Enough Shovels: Reagan, Bush and Nuclear War*. Random House, 1982.

Sherwin, Mark. *The Extremists*. New York: St. Martin's Press, 1963.

Sims, Beth. *Workers of the World Undermined: American Labor's Role in U.S. Foreign Policy*. Boston: South End, 1992.

Sirgiovanni, George. *An Undercurrent of Suspicion*. New Brunswick, NJ: Transaction, 1990.

Smant, Kevin J. "Whither Conservatism? James Burnham and *National Review* 1955–1964." *Continuity*, 15 (Fall-Winter 1991).

———. *How Great the Triumph: James Burnham, Anticommunism, and the Conservative Movement*. Lanham, MD: University Press of America, 1992.

Smith, Geoffrey. *Reagan and Thatcher*. New York: Norton, 1991.

———. *To Save a Nation: American 'Extremism,' the New Deal, and the Coming of World War II*. 1973; reprint, Chicago: Ivan R. Dee, 1992.

Smith, Tony. *America's Mission: The United States and the Worldwide Struggle for Democracy in the Twentieth Century*. Princeton: Princeton University Press, 1994.

Snow, Edgar. *Red Star Over China*. 1938; reprint, New York: Bantam, 1978.

Soloviev, Mikhail. *When the Gods Are Silent*. New York: D. McKay, 1952.

"Special Issue on the Strange Death of Soviet Communism." *The National Interest*, Spring 1993.

Spivak, John L. *Pattern for American Fascism*. New York: New Century Publishers, 1947.

Spolansky, Jacob. *Communist Trail in America*. New York: Macmillan, 1951.

Spritzer, Alan. B. "John Dewey, The 'Trial' of Leon Trotsky and the Search for Historical Truth." *History and Theory*. 29 (1990).

Starobin, Joseph R. *American Communism in Crisis, 1943–1957*. 1972; reprint, Berkeley: University of California Press, 1975.

Steinberg, Peter L. *The Great "Red Menace": United States Prosecution of American Communists, 1947–1952*. Westport, CT: Greenwood, 1984.

Stockwell, John. *In Search of Enemies: A CIA Story*. New York: Norton, 1978.

Storke, Thomas M. "How Some Birchers Were Birched." *New York Times Magazine*, December 10, 1961.

Stormer, John A. *None Dare Call It Treason*. Florissant, MO: Liberty Bell Press, 1964.

Stripling, E. Robert. *The Red Plot Against America* (Bob Considine, ed.). Drexel Hill, PA.: Bell Publishing, 1949.

Suall, Irwin. *The American Ultras: The Extreme Right and the Military-Industrial Complex*. New York: New America, 1962.

Sundquist, Eric J. " 'Witness' Recalled." *Commentary*, December 1988.

"Symposium: An Inquest on the Death of Communism." *Encounter*, July-August 1990; September 1990.

"Symposium on the American 80s—Disaster or Triumph." *Commentary*, September 1990.

"Symposium on Liberal Anti-Communism Revisited." *Commentary*, September 1967.

Szajkowski, Zosa. *Jews, Wars, and Communism*. New York: Ktav Publishing House, 1974.

Taft, John. *American Power: The Rise and Decline of U.S. Globalism*. New York: Harper & Row, 1989.

Talbott, Strobe. *Deadly Gambits: The Reagan Administration and the Stalemate in Nuclear Arms Control*. New York: Knopf, 1984.

———. *The Russians and Reagan*. New York: Vintage, 1984.

———. *The Master of the Game: Paul Nitze and the Nuclear Age*. New York: Knopf, 1988.

Taubman, William (ed.). *Globalism and Its Critics: The American Foreign Policy Debate of the 1960s*. Lexington, MA: D. C. Heath, 1973.

Taylor, S. J. *Stalin's Apologist: Walter Duranty, the New York Times's Man in Moscow*. New York: Oxford University Press, 1990.

Tchernavin, Tatiana. *Escape From the Soviets*. New York: Dutton, 1934.

Tchernavin, Vladimir. *I Speak for the Silent Prisoners of the Soviets*. Boston: Hale, Cushman & Flint, 1935.

Theoharis, Athan G. *The Truman Presidency: The Origins of the Imperial Presidency and the National Security State*. Stanfordville, NY: Earl M. Coleman, 1979.

Theoharis, Athan G., and John Stuart Cox. *The Boss: J. Edgar Hoover and the Great American Inquisition*. Philadelphia: Temple University Press, 1988.

Thomas, Hugh. *Armed Truce: The Beginnings of the Cold War*. New York: Atheneum, 1987.

Trilling, Diana. "How McCarthy Gave Anti-communism a Bad Name." *Newsweek*, January 11, 1993.

Trilling, Lionel. *The Middle of the Journey*. New York: Viking, 1947.

Troncone, Anthony. "Hamilton Fish, Sr., and the Politics of American Nationalism, 1912–1945." Ph.D. dissertation, Rutgers University, 1993.

Truman, Harry S. *Memoirs*. Garden City, NY: Doubleday, 1956.

Tull, Charles J. "Father Coughlin, the New Deal, and the Election of 1936." Ph.D. dissertation, Notre Dame, 1962.

Tyroler, Charles, II (ed.). *Alerting America: The Papers of the Committee on the Present Danger*. Washington, DC: Pergamon-Brassey's, 1984.

U.S. House, Committee on Rules. *Attorney General A. Mitchell Palmer on Charges Made Against Department of Justice by Louis F. Post and Others*. 65th Congress, 2nd session, June 1, 1920.

U.S. House, Select Committee on Intelligence. *Hearings. U. S. Intelligence Agencies and Activities: Domestic Intelligence Programs, Part 3*. 94th Congress, 1st session, 1976.

U.S. Military Intelligence Reports: Surveillance of Radicals in the United States, 1917–1941. Frederick, MD: University Publications, 1984.

U.S. Senate. *Investigation Activities of the Department of Justice*. 66th Congress, 1st session, November 15, 1919.

U.S. Senate. *Investigation of Alleged Payments by the Mexican Government to United States Senators*. 70th Congress, 2nd session, 1928

U.S. Senate, Select Committee to Study Governmental Operations with Respect to Intelligence Activities. *Final Report, Intelligence Activities and the Rights of Americans*. 94th Congress, 2nd session, 1976.

Ungar, Sanford J. (ed). *Estrangement: America and the World*. New York: Oxford University Press, 1985.

Ungar, Sanford J. *The Papers and The Papers: An Account of the Legal and Political Battle over The Pentagon Papers*. 1972; reprint, New York: Columbia University Press, 1989.

Unterberger, Betty Miller. "President Wilson and the Decision to Send American Troops to Siberia." *Pacific Historical Review*, 24 (February 1955).

———— (ed.). *American Intervention in the Russian Civil War*. Lexington MA: D. C. Heath, 1969.

Valtin, Jan. "Communist Agent." *American Mercury*, November 1939.

————. *Out of the Night*. New York: Alliance, 1941.

Van Den Haag, Ernest. "Academic Freedom and Its Defense." In *Strengthening Education at All Levels*. A Report of the Eighteenth Educational Conference, 1953.

Wald, Alan M. *The New York Intellectuals: The Rise and Decline of the Anti-Stalinist Left from the 1930s to the 1980s*. Chapel Hill: University of North Carolina Press, 1987.

Walker, Brooks R. *The Christian Fright Peddlers*. Garden City, NY: Doubleday, 1964.

Wallace, Irving. *The R Document*. New York: Simon & Schuster, 1976.

Warsh, David. "External Economics and the End of the Cold War." *Washington Post*, February 26, 1992.

Watters, Pat, and Stephen Gillers (eds.). *Investigating the FBI*. Garden City, NY: Doubleday, 1973.

Weigel, George. *The Final Revolution: The Resistance Church and the Collapse of Communism*. New York: Oxford University Press, 1992.

Weinstein, Allen. *Perjury: The Hiss-Chambers Case*. New York: Knopf, 1978.

Weinstein, James. *The Decline of Socialism in America, 1912–1925*. 1967; reprint, New Brunswick, NJ: Rutgers University Press, 1984.

Welch, Robert. *The Blue Book of the John Birch Society*. Belmont, MA: Western Islands, 1959.

———. *The Life of John Birch*. 1954; reprint, Boston: Western Islands, 1960.

———. *The Politician*. 1963; reprint, Belmont, MA: Belmont Publishing, 1964.

———. "The Neutralizers." Tape in the Wilcox Collection, University of Kansas, 1963.

Whitehead, Don. *The F.B.I. Story*. New York: Random House, 1956.

Whitney, Richard M. *Reds in America*. 1924; reprint, Boston: Western Islands, 1970.

Williams, Robert Chadwell. *Klaus Fuchs, Atom Spy*. Cambridge, MA: Harvard University Press, 1987.

Williams, William Appleman. *The Tragedy of American Diplomacy*. Cleveland: World, 1959.

Wills, Garry. *Reagan's America: Innocents at Home*. Garden City, NY: Doubleday, 1987.

Wolfe, Bertram D. *A Life in Two Centuries: An Autobiography*. New York: Stein and Day, 1981.

———. *Strange Communists I Have Known*. 1965; reprint, New York: Stein and Day, 1982.

Woltman, Frederick. *Exposing the Red Threat to Free Enterprise and Individual Liberty*. New York: World Telegram, 1947.

Woodward, Bob. *Veil: The Secret Wars of the CIA 1981–1987*. New York: Simon & Schuster, 1987.

Wright, Richard. *The Outsider*. New York: Harpers, 1953.

Yankelovich, Daniel. "New Rules in American Life: Searching for Self-fulfillment in a World Turned Upside Down." *Psychology Today*, April 1981.

Yergin, Daniel. *Shattered Peace: The Origins of the Cold War and the National Security State*. Boston: Houghton Mifflin, 1977.

Zelt, Johannes. *Proletarian Internationalism in the Battle for Sacco and Vanzetti*. Berlin: Dietz Verlag, 1958.

ACKNOWLEDGMENTS

This book would not have been begun, nor finished, without the inspiration, confidence, and encouragement of the late Erwin Glikes, President of The Free Press, and my editor there, Joyce Seltzer. After they left the Press, I was also given the finest assistance and treatment by their successors, Adam Bellow and Peter Dougherty. I was given superb scholarly criticism at a time when I needed it most by Leo P. Ribuffo, and editorial assistance by Fred Binder. David Garrow, Steve Rosswurm, Kenneth O'Reilly, Ellen Schrecker, Ronald Radosh, Harvey Klehr, Herbert Parmet, Kevin Smant, Sue Rosenfeld, Dennis McDaniel, and David Evanier shared with me the results of their pioneering research into America's struggle with communism. J. Fred MacDonald at J. Fred MacDonald Associates' archives provided me with open access to his amazing media collection, the benefit of his encyclopedic knowledge of radio, television, and film, and, not least, a place to stay in Chicago. Laird Wilcox, founder of the Wilcox Collection of Contemporary Political Movements at the University of Kansas, was untiringly, unselfishly, and imaginatively helpful. I was provided with homes away from home while working in Washington by Roy and Cora Hoopes, Jan and Bill Cohn, and Steve and Judy Hopkins. I am grateful for the friendship and contributions, some even helpful, of Louis Phillips, Gerry O'Connor, and Bart St. Armand. Appropriate sentiments also to my father, Richard M. Powers, to my Goldwater Girl, Eileen, and to Sarah and Evelyn, who gave communism all the attention it deserved.

527

INDEX